48th Annual Meeting of the Association for Computational Linguistics 2010 (ACL 2010)

Short Papers

Uppsala, Sweden
11-16 July 2010

ISBN: 978-1-61738-825-5

Printed from e-media with permission by:

Curran Associates, Inc.
57 Morehouse Lane
Red Hook, NY 12571

Some format issues inherent in the e-media version may also appear in this print version.

Printed by Curran Associates, Inc. (2010)

For permission requests, please contact the Association for Computational Linguistics
at the address below.

Association for Computational Linguistics
209 N. Eighth Street
Stroudsburg, Pennsylvania 18360

Phone: 1-570-476-8006
Fax: 1-570-476-0860

acl@aclweb.org

Additional copies of this publication are available from:

Curran Associates, Inc.
57 Morehouse Lane
Red Hook, NY 12571 USA
Phone: 845-758-0400
Fax: 845-758-2634
Email: curran@proceedings.com
Web: www.proceedings.com

Table of Contents

Paraphrase Lattice for Statistical Machine Translation

Takashi Onishi and **Masao Utiyama** and **Eiichiro Sumita**
Language Translation Group, MASTAR Project
National Institute of Information and Communications Technology
3-5 Hikaridai, Keihanna Science City, Kyoto, 619-0289, JAPAN
{takashi.onishi,mutiyama,eiichiro.sumita}@nict.go.jp

Abstract

Lattice decoding in statistical machine translation (SMT) is useful in speech translation and in the translation of German because it can handle input ambiguities such as speech recognition ambiguities and German word segmentation ambiguities. We show that lattice decoding is also useful for handling input variations. Given an input sentence, we build a lattice which represents paraphrases of the input sentence. We call this a paraphrase lattice. Then, we give the paraphrase lattice as an input to the lattice decoder. The decoder selects the best path for decoding. Using these paraphrase lattices as inputs, we obtained significant gains in BLEU scores for IWSLT and Europarl datasets.

1 Introduction

Lattice decoding in SMT is useful in speech translation and in the translation of German (Bertoldi et al., 2007; Dyer, 2009). In speech translation, by using lattices that represent not only 1-best result but also other possibilities of speech recognition, we can take into account the ambiguities of speech recognition. Thus, the translation quality for lattice inputs is better than the quality for 1-best inputs.

In this paper, we show that lattice decoding is also useful for handling input variations. "Input variations" refers to the differences of input texts with the same meaning. For example, *"Is there a beauty salon?"* and *"Is there a beauty parlor?"* have the same meaning with variations in *"beauty salon"* and *"beauty parlor"*. Since these variations are frequently found in natural language texts, a mismatch of the expressions in source sentences and the expressions in training corpus leads to a decrease in translation quality. Therefore, we propose a novel method that can handle input variations using paraphrases and lattice decoding. In the proposed method, we regard a given source sentence as one of many variations (1-best). Given an input sentence, we build a paraphrase lattice which represents paraphrases of the input sentence. Then, we give the paraphrase lattice as an input to the Moses decoder (Koehn et al., 2007). Moses selects the best path for decoding. By using paraphrases of source sentences, we can translate expressions which are not found in a training corpus on the condition that paraphrases of them are found in the training corpus. Moreover, by using lattice decoding, we can employ the source-side language model as a decoding feature. Since this feature is affected by the source-side context, the decoder can choose a proper paraphrase and translate correctly.

This paper is organized as follows: Related works on lattice decoding and paraphrasing are presented in Section 2. The proposed method is described in Section 3. Experimental results for IWSLT and Europarl dataset are presented in Section 4. Finally, the paper is concluded with a summary and a few directions for future work in Section 5.

2 Related Work

Lattice decoding has been used to handle ambiguities of preprocessing. Bertoldi et al. (2007) employed a confusion network, which is a kind of lattice and represents speech recognition hypotheses in speech translation. Dyer (2009) also employed a segmentation lattice, which represents ambiguities of compound word segmentation in German, Hungarian and Turkish translation. However, to the best of our knowledge, there is no work which employed a lattice representing paraphrases of an input sentence.

On the other hand, paraphrasing has been used to enrich the SMT model. Callison-Burch et

Proceedings of the ACL 2010 Conference Short Papers, pages 1–5,
Uppsala, Sweden, 11-16 July 2010.

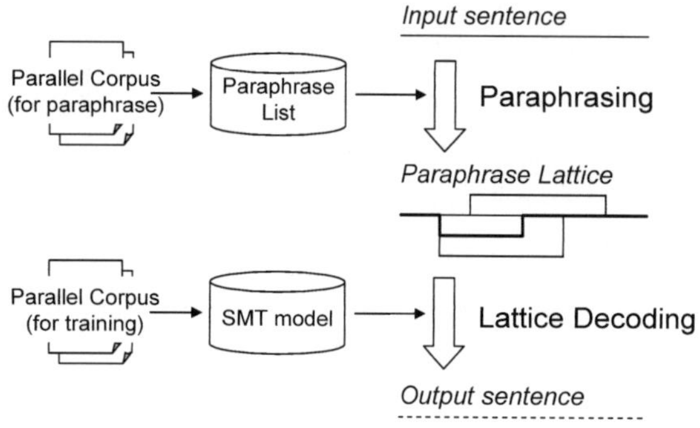

Figure 1: Overview of the proposed method.

al. (2006) and Marton et al. (2009) augmented the translation phrase table with paraphrases to translate unknown phrases. Bond et al. (2008) and Nakov (2008) augmented the training data by paraphrasing. However, there is no work which augments input sentences by paraphrasing and represents them in lattices.

3 Paraphrase Lattice for SMT

Overview of the proposed method is shown in Figure 1. In advance, we automatically acquire a paraphrase list from a parallel corpus. In order to acquire paraphrases of unknown phrases, this parallel corpus is different from the parallel corpus for training.

Given an input sentence, we build a lattice which represents paraphrases of the input sentence using the paraphrase list. We call this lattice a paraphrase lattice. Then, we give the paraphrase lattice to the lattice decoder.

3.1 Acquiring the paraphrase list

We acquire a paraphrase list using Bannard and Callison-Burch (2005)'s method. Their idea is, if two different phrases e_1, e_2 in one language are aligned to the same phrase c in another language, they are hypothesized to be paraphrases of each other. Our paraphrase list is acquired in the same way.

The procedure is as follows:

1. Build a phrase table.

   Build a phrase table from parallel corpus using standard SMT techniques.

2. Filter the phrase table by the sigtest-filter.

   The phrase table built in 1 has many inappropriate phrase pairs. Therefore, we filter the phrase table and keep only appropriate phrase pairs using the sigtest-filter (Johnson et al., 2007).

3. Calculate the paraphrase probability.

   Calculate the paraphrase probability $p(e_2|e_1)$ if e_2 is hypothesized to be a paraphrase of e_1.

$$p(e_2|e_1) = \sum_c P(c|e_1)P(e_2|c)$$

   where $P(\cdot|\cdot)$ is phrase translation probability.

4. Acquire a paraphrase pair.

   Acquire (e_1, e_2) as a paraphrase pair if $p(e_2|e_1) > p(e_1|e_1)$. The purpose of this threshold is to keep highly-accurate paraphrase pairs. In experiments, more than 80% of paraphrase pairs were eliminated by this threshold.

3.2 Building paraphrase lattice

An input sentence is paraphrased using the paraphrase list and transformed into a paraphrase lattice. The paraphrase lattice is a lattice which represents paraphrases of the input sentence. An example of a paraphrase lattice is shown in Figure 2. In this example, an input sentence is *"is there a beauty salon ?"*. This paraphrase lattice contains two paraphrase pairs *"beauty salon"* = *"beauty parlor"* and *"beauty salon"* = *"salon"*, and represents following three sentences.

- *is there a beauty salon ?*
- *is there a beauty parlor ?*
- *is there a salon ?*

In the paraphrase lattice, each node consists of a token, the distance to the next node and features for lattice decoding. We use following four features for lattice decoding.

- Paraphrase probability (p)

  A paraphrase probability $p(e_2|e_1)$ calculated when acquiring the paraphrase.

  $h_p = p(e_2|e_1)$

- Language model score (l)

  A ratio between the language model probability of the paraphrased sentence (para) and that of the original sentence (orig).

  $h_l = \frac{lm(para)}{lm(orig)}$

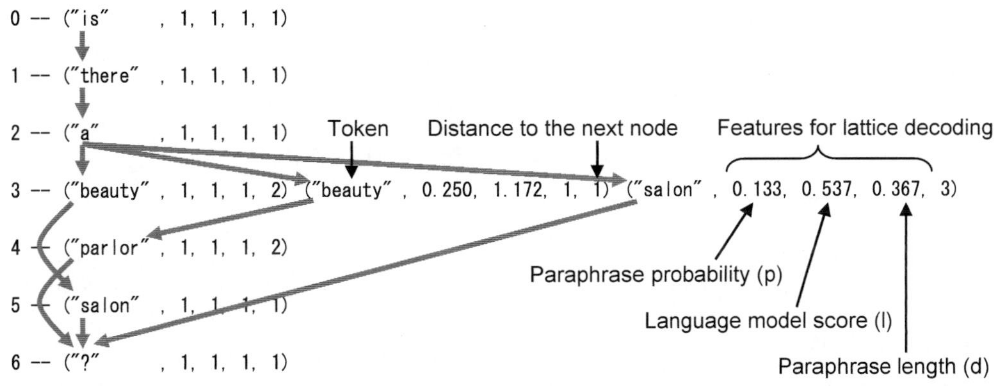

Figure 2: An example of a paraphrase lattice, which contains three features of (p, l, d).

- Normalized language model score (L)

  A language model score where the language model probability is normalized by the sentence length. The sentence length is calculated as the number of tokens.

  $h_L = \frac{LM(para)}{LM(orig)}$,

  where $LM(sent) = lm(sent)^{\frac{1}{length(sent)}}$

- Paraphrase length (d)

  The difference between the original sentence length and the paraphrased sentence length.

  $h_d = \exp(length(para) - length(orig))$

The values of these features are calculated only if the node is the first node of the paraphrase, for example the second *"beauty"* and *"salon"* in line 3 of Figure 2. In other nodes, for example *"parlor"* in line 4 and original nodes, we use 1 as the values of features.

The features related to the language model, such as (l) and (L), are affected by the context of source sentences even if the same paraphrase pair is applied. As these features can penalize paraphrases which are not appropriate to the context, appropriate paraphrases are chosen and appropriate translations are output in lattice decoding. The features related to the sentence length, such as (L) and (d), are added to penalize the language model score in case the paraphrased sentence length is shorter than the original sentence length and the language model score is unreasonably low.

In experiments, we use four combinations of these features, (p), (p, l), (p, L) and (p, l, d).

3.3 Lattice decoding

We use Moses (Koehn et al., 2007) as a decoder for lattice decoding. Moses is an open source SMT system which allows lattice decoding. In lattice decoding, Moses selects the best path and the best translation according to features added in each node and other SMT features. These weights are optimized using Minimum Error Rate Training (MERT) (Och, 2003).

4 Experiments

In order to evaluate the proposed method, we conducted English-to-Japanese and English-to-Chinese translation experiments using IWSLT 2007 (Fordyce, 2007) dataset. This dataset contains EJ and EC parallel corpus for the travel domain and consists of 40k sentences for training and about 500 sentences sets (dev1, dev2 and dev3) for development and testing. We used the dev1 set for parameter tuning, the dev2 set for choosing the setting of the proposed method, which is described below, and the dev3 set for testing.

The English-English paraphrase list was acquired from the EC corpus for EJ translation and 53K pairs were acquired. Similarly, 47K pairs were acquired from the EJ corpus for EC translation.

4.1 Baseline

As baselines, we used Moses and Callison-Burch et al. (2006)'s method (hereafter CCB). In Moses, we used default settings without paraphrases. In CCB, we paraphrased the phrase table using the automatically acquired paraphrase list. Then, we augmented the phrase table with paraphrased phrases which were not found in the original phrase table. Moreover, we used an additional feature whose value was the paraphrase probability (p) if the entry was generated by paraphrasing and

	Moses (w/o Paraphrases)	CCB	Proposed Method
EJ	38.98	39.24 (+0.26)	**40.34** (+1.36)
EC	25.11	26.14 (+1.03)	**27.06** (+1.95)

Table 1: Experimental results for IWSLT (%BLEU).

1 if otherwise. Weights of the feature and other features in SMT were optimized using MERT.

4.2 Proposed method

In the proposed method, we conducted experiments with various settings for paraphrasing and lattice decoding. Then, we chose the best setting according to the result of the dev2 set.

4.2.1 Limitation of paraphrasing

As the paraphrase list was automatically acquired, there were many erroneous paraphrase pairs. Building paraphrase lattices with all erroneous paraphrase pairs and decoding these paraphrase lattices caused high computational complexity. Therefore, we limited the number of paraphrasing per phrase and per sentence. The number of paraphrasing per phrase was limited to three and the number of paraphrasing per sentence was limited to twice the size of the sentence length.

As a criterion for limiting the number of paraphrasing, we use three features (p), (l) and (L), which are same as the features described in Subsection 3.2. When building paraphrase lattices, we apply paraphrases in descending order of the value of the criterion.

4.2.2 Finding optimal settings

As previously mentioned, we have three choices for the criterion for building paraphrase lattices and four combinations of features for lattice decoding. Thus, there are $3 \times 4 = 12$ combinations of these settings. We conducted parameter tuning with the dev1 set for each setting and used as best the setting which got the highest BLEU score for the dev2 set.

4.3 Results

The experimental results are shown in Table 1. We used the case-insensitive BLEU metric for evaluation. In EJ translation, the proposed method obtained the highest score of 40.34%, which achieved an absolute improvement of 1.36 BLEU points over Moses and 1.10 BLEU points over CCB. In EC translation, the proposed method also obtained the highest score of 27.06% and achieved an absolute improvement of 1.95 BLEU points over Moses and 0.92 BLEU points over CCB. As the relation of three systems is Moses $<$ CCB $<$ Proposed Method, paraphrasing is useful for SMT and using paraphrase lattices and lattice decoding is especially more useful than augmenting the phrase table. In Proposed Method, the criterion for building paraphrase lattices and the combination of features for lattice decoding were (p) and (p, L) in EJ translation and (L) and (p, l) in EC translation. Since features related to the source-side language model were chosen in each direction, using the source-side language model is useful for decoding paraphrase lattices.

We also tried a combination of Proposed Method and CCB, which is a method of decoding paraphrase lattices with an augmented phrase table. However, the result showed no significant improvements. This is because the proposed method includes the effect of augmenting the phrase table.

Moreover, we conducted German-English translation using the Europarl corpus (Koehn, 2005). We used the WMT08 dataset[1], which consists of 1M sentences for training and 2K sentences for development and testing. We acquired 5.3M pairs of German-German paraphrases from a 1M German-Spanish parallel corpus. We conducted experiments with various sizes of training corpus, using 10K, 20K, 40K, 80K, 160K and 1M. Figure 3 shows the proposed method consistently get higher score than Moses and CCB.

5 Conclusion

This paper has proposed a novel method for transforming a source sentence into a paraphrase lattice and applying lattice decoding. Since our method can employ source-side language models as a decoding feature, the decoder can choose proper paraphrases and translate properly. The experimental results showed significant gains for the IWSLT and Europarl dataset. In IWSLT dataset, we obtained 1.36 BLEU points over Moses in EJ translation and 1.95 BLEU points over Moses in

[1]http://www.statmt.org/wmt08/

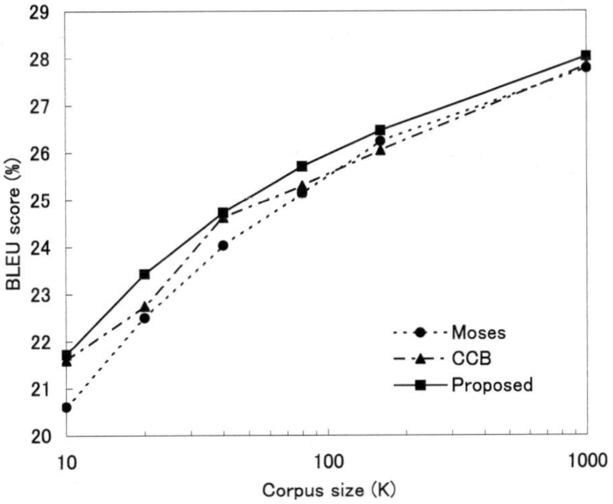

Figure 3: Effect of training corpus size.

EC translation. In Europarl dataset, the proposed method consistently get higher score than baselines.

In future work, we plan to apply this method with paraphrases derived from a massive corpus such as the Web corpus and apply this method to a hierarchical phrase based SMT.

References

Colin Bannard and Chris Callison-Burch. 2005. Paraphrasing with Bilingual Parallel Corpora. In *Proceedings of the 43rd Annual Meeting of the Association for Computational Linguistics (ACL)*, pages 597–604.

Nicola Bertoldi, Richard Zens, and Marcello Federico. 2007. Speech translation by confusion network decoding. In *Proceedings of the International Conference on Acoustics, Speech, and Signal Processing (ICASSP)*, pages 1297–1300.

Francis Bond, Eric Nichols, Darren Scott Appling, and Michael Paul. 2008. Improving Statistical Machine Translation by Paraphrasing the Training Data. In *Proceedings of the International Workshop on Spoken Language Translation (IWSLT)*, pages 150–157.

Chris Callison-Burch, Philipp Koehn, and Miles Osborne. 2006. Improved Statistical Machine Translation Using Paraphrases. In *Proceedings of the Human Language Technology conference - North American chapter of the Association for Computational Linguistics (HLT-NAACL)*, pages 17–24.

Chris Dyer. 2009. Using a maximum entropy model to build segmentation lattices for MT. In *Proceedings of the Human Language Technology conference - North American chapter of the Association for Computational Linguistics (HLT-NAACL)*, pages 406–414.

Cameron S. Fordyce. 2007. Overview of the IWSLT 2007 Evaluation Campaign. In *Proceedings of the International Workshop on Spoken Language Translation (IWSLT)*, pages 1–12.

J Howard Johnson, Joel Martin, George Foster, and Roland Kuhn. 2007. Improving Translation Quality by Discarding Most of the Phrasetable. In *Proceedings of the 2007 Joint Conference on Empirical Methods in Natural Language Processing and Computational Natural Language Learning (EMNLP-CoNLL)*, pages 967–975.

Philipp Koehn, Hieu Hoang, Alexandra Birch, Chris Callison-Burch, Marcello Federico, Nicola Bertoldi, Brooke Cowan, Wade Shen, Christine Moran, Richard Zens, Chris Dyer, Ondrej Bojar, Alexandra Constantin, and Evan Herbst. 2007. Moses: Open Source Toolkit for Statistical Machine Translation. In *Proceedings of the 45th Annual Meeting of the Association for Computational Linguistics (ACL)*, pages 177–180.

Philipp Koehn. 2005. Europarl: A Parallel Corpus for Statistical Machine Translation. In *Proceedings of the 10th Machine Translation Summit (MT Summit)*, pages 79–86.

Yuval Marton, Chris Callison-Burch, and Philip Resnik. 2009. Improved Statistical Machine Translation Using Monolingually-Derived Paraphrases. In *Proceedings of the Conference on Empirical Methods in Natural Language Processing (EMNLP)*, pages 381–390.

Preslav Nakov. 2008. Improved Statistical Machine Translation Using Monolingual Paraphrases. In *Proceedings of the European Conference on Artificial Intelligence (ECAI)*, pages 338–342.

Franz Josef Och. 2003. Minimum Error Rate Training in Statistical Machine Translation. In *Proceedings of the 41st Annual Meeting of the Association for Computational Linguistics (ACL)*, pages 160–167.

A Joint Rule Selection Model for Hierarchical Phrase-based Translation*

Lei Cui[†], **Dongdong Zhang**[‡], **Mu Li**[‡], **Ming Zhou**[‡], and **Tiejun Zhao**[†]

[†]School of Computer Science and Technology
Harbin Institute of Technology, Harbin, China
{cuilei,tjzhao}@mtlab.hit.edu.cn
[‡]Microsoft Research Asia, Beijing, China
{dozhang,muli,mingzhou}@microsoft.com

Abstract

In hierarchical phrase-based SMT systems, statistical models are integrated to guide the hierarchical rule selection for better translation performance. Previous work mainly focused on the selection of either the source side of a hierarchical rule or the target side of a hierarchical rule rather than considering both of them simultaneously. This paper presents a joint model to predict the selection of hierarchical rules. The proposed model is estimated based on four sub-models where the rich context knowledge from both source and target sides is leveraged. Our method can be easily incorporated into the practical SMT systems with the log-linear model framework. The experimental results show that our method can yield significant improvements in performance.

1 Introduction

Hierarchical phrase-based model has strong expression capabilities of translation knowledge. It can not only maintain the strength of phrase translation in traditional phrase-based models (Koehn et al., 2003; Xiong et al., 2006), but also characterize the complicated long distance reordering similar to syntactic based statistical machine translation (SMT) models (Yamada and Knight, 2001; Quirk et al., 2005; Galley et al., 2006; Liu et al., 2006; Marcu et al., 2006; Mi et al., 2008; Shen et al., 2008).

In hierarchical phrase-based SMT systems, due to the flexibility of rule matching, a huge number of hierarchical rules could be automatically learnt from bilingual training corpus (Chiang, 2005). SMT decoders are forced to face the challenge of proper rule selection for hypothesis generation, including both source-side rule selection and target-side rule selection where the source-side rule determines what part of source words to be translated and the target-side rule provides one of the candidate translations of the source-side rule. Improper rule selections may result in poor translations.

There is some related work about the hierarchical rule selection. In the original work (Chiang, 2005), the target-side rule selection is analogous to the model in traditional phrase-based SMT system such as Pharaoh (Koehn et al., 2003). Extending this work, (He et al., 2008; Liu et al., 2008) integrate rich context information of non-terminals to predict the target-side rule selection. Different from the above work where the probability distribution of source-side rule selection is uniform, (Setiawan et al., 2009) proposes to select source-side rules based on the captured function words which often play an important role in word reordering. There is also some work considering to involve more rich contexts to guide the source-side rule selection. (Marton and Resnik, 2008; Xiong et al., 2009) explore the source syntactic information to reward exact matching structure rules or punish crossing structure rules.

All the previous work mainly focused on either source-side rule selection task or target-side rule selection task rather than both of them together. The separation of these two tasks, however, weakens the high interrelation between them. In this paper, we propose to integrate both source-side and target-side rule selection in a unified model. The intuition is that the joint selection of source-side and target-side rules is more reliable as it conducts the search in a larger space than the single selection task does. It is expected that these two kinds of selection can help and affect each other, which may potentially lead to better hierarchical rule selections with a relative global optimum instead of a local optimum that might be reached in the pre-

*This work was finished while the first author visited Microsoft Research Asia as an intern.

Proceedings of the ACL 2010 Conference Short Papers, pages 6–11,
Uppsala, Sweden, 11-16 July 2010.

vious methods. Our proposed joint probability model is factored into four sub-models that can be further classified into source-side and target-side rule selection models or context-based and context-free selection models. The context-based models explore rich context features from both source and target sides, including function words, part-of-speech (POS) tags, syntactic structure information and so on. Our model can be easily incorporated as an independent feature into the practical hierarchical phrase-based systems with the log-linear model framework. The experimental results indicate our method can improve the system performance significantly.

2 Hierarchical Rule Selection Model

Following (Chiang, 2005), $\langle \alpha, \gamma \rangle$ is used to represent a synchronous context free grammar (SCFG) rule extracted from the training corpus, where α and γ are the source-side and target-side rule respectively. Let C be the context of $\langle \alpha, \gamma \rangle$. Formally, our joint probability model of hierarchical rule selection is described as follows:

$$P(\alpha, \gamma | C) = P(\alpha | C) P(\gamma | \alpha, C) \quad (1)$$

We decompose the joint probability model into two sub-models based on the Bayes formulation, where the first sub-model is *source-side rule selection model* and the second one is the *target-side rule selection model*.

For the source-side rule selection model, we further compute it by the interpolation of two sub-models:

$$\theta P_s(\alpha) + (1 - \theta) P_s(\alpha | C) \quad (2)$$

where $P_s(\alpha)$ is the *context-free source model* (CFSM) and $P_s(\alpha|C)$ is the *context-based source model* (CBSM), θ is the interpolation weight that can be optimized over the development data.

CFSM is the probability of source-side rule selection that can be estimated based on maximum likelihood estimation (MLE) method:

$$P_s(\alpha) = \frac{\sum_{\gamma} Count(\langle \alpha, \gamma \rangle)}{Count(\alpha)} \quad (3)$$

where the numerator is the total count of bilingual rule pairs with the same source-side rule that are extracted based on the extraction algorithm in (Chiang, 2005), and the denominator is the total amount of source-side rule patterns contained in the monolingual source side of the training corpus. CFSM is used to capture how likely the source-side rule is linguistically motivated or has the corresponding target-side counterpart.

For CBSM, it can be naturally viewed as a classification problem where each distinct source-side rule is a single class. However, considering the huge number of classes may cause serious data sparseness problem and thereby degrade the classification accuracy, we approximate CBSM by a binary classification problem which can be solved by the maximum entropy (ME) approach (Berger et al., 1996) as follows:

$$\begin{aligned} P_s(\alpha|C) &\approx P_s(\upsilon|\alpha, C) \\ &= \frac{exp[\sum_i \lambda_i h_i(\upsilon, \alpha, C)]}{\sum_{\upsilon'} exp[\sum_i \lambda_i h_i(\upsilon', \alpha, C)]} \end{aligned} \quad (4)$$

where $\upsilon \in \{0, 1\}$ is the indicator whether the source-side rule is applied during decoding, $\upsilon = 1$ when the source-side rule is applied, otherwise $\upsilon = 0$; h_i is a feature function, λ_i is the weight of h_i. CBSM estimates the probability of the source-side rule being selected according to the rich context information coming from the surface strings and sub-phrases that will be reduced to non-terminals during decoding.

Analogously, we decompose the target-side rule selection model by the interpolation approach as well:

$$\varphi P_t(\gamma) + (1 - \varphi) P_t(\gamma | \alpha, C) \quad (5)$$

where $P_t(\gamma)$ is the *context-free target model* (CFTM) and $P_t(\gamma|\alpha, C)$ is the *context-based target model* (CBTM), φ is the interpolation weight that can be optimized over the development data.

In the similar way, we compute CFTM by the MLE approach and estimate CBTM by the ME approach. CFTM computes how likely the target-side rule is linguistically motivated, while CBTM predicts how likely the target-side rule is applied according to the clues from the rich context information.

3 Model Training of CBSM and CBTM

3.1 The acquisition of training instances

CBSM and CBTM are trained by ME approach for the binary classification, where a training instance consists of a label and the context related to SCFG rules. The context is divided into source context

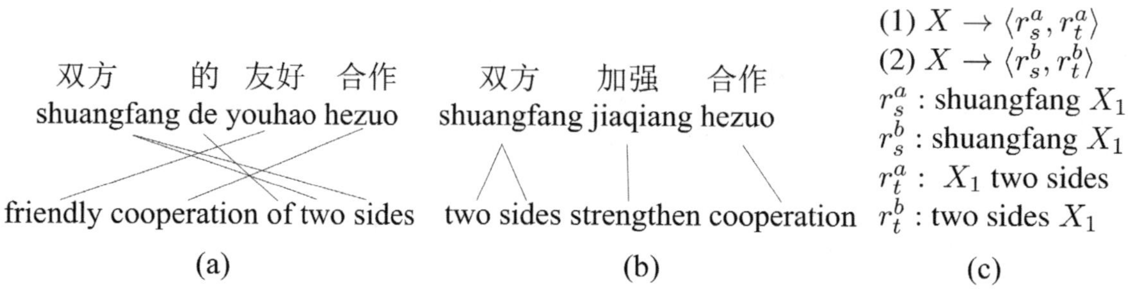

Figure 1: Example of training instances in CBSM and CBTM.

and target context. CBSM is trained only based on the source context while CBTM is trained over both the source and the target context. All the training instances are automatically constructed from the bilingual training corpus, which have labels of either positive (i.e., $\upsilon = 1$) or negative (i.e., $\upsilon = 0$). This section explains how the training instances are constructed for the training of CBSM and CBTM.

Let s and t be the source sentence and target sentence, W be the word alignment between them, r_s be a source-side rule that pattern-matches a sub-phrase of s, r_t be the target-side rule pattern-matching a sub-phrase of t and being aligned to r_s based on W, and $C(r)$ be the context features related to the rule r which will be explained in the following section.

For the training of CBSM, if the SCFG rule $\langle r_s, r_t \rangle$ can be extracted based on the rule extraction algorithm in (Chiang, 2005), $\langle \upsilon = 1, C(r_s) \rangle$ is constructed as a positive instance, otherwise $\langle \upsilon = 0, C(r_s) \rangle$ is constructed as a negative instance. For example in Figure 1(a), the context of source-side rule "X_1 hezuo" that pattern-matches the phrase "youhao hezuo" produces a positive instance, while the context of "X_1 youhao" that pattern-matches the source phrase "de youhao" or "shuangfang de youhao" will produce a negative instance as there are no corresponding plausible target-side rules that can be extracted legally[1].

For the training of CBTM, given r_s, suppose there is a SCFG rule set $\{\langle r_s, r_t^k \rangle | 1 \leq k \leq n\}$ extracted from multiple distinct sentence pairs in the bilingual training corpus, among which we assume $\langle r_s, r_t^i \rangle$ is extracted from the sentence pair $\langle s, t \rangle$. Then, we construct $\langle \upsilon = 1, C(r_s), C(r_t^i) \rangle$ as a positive instance, while the elements in $\{\langle \upsilon = 0, C(r_s), C(r_t^j) \rangle | j \neq i \wedge 1 \leq j \leq n\}$ are viewed as negative instances since they fail to be applied to the translation from s to t. For example in Figure 1(c), Rule (1) and Rule (2) are two different SCFG rules extracted from Figure 1(a) and Figure 1(b) respectively, where their source-side rules are the same. As Rule (1) cannot be applied to Figure 1(b) for the translation and Rule (2) cannot be applied to Figure 1(a) for the translation either, $\langle \upsilon = 1, C(r_s^a), C(r_t^a) \rangle$ and $\langle \upsilon = 1, C(r_s^b), C(r_t^b) \rangle$ are constructed as positive instances while $\langle \upsilon = 0, C(r_s^a), C(r_t^b) \rangle$ and $\langle \upsilon = 0, C(r_s^b), C(r_t^a) \rangle$ are viewed as negative instances. It is noticed that this instance construction method may lead to a large quantity of negative instances and choke the training procedure. In practice, to limit the size of the training set, the negative instances constructed based on low-frequency target-side rules are pruned.

3.2 Context-based features for ME training

ME approach has the merit of easily combining different features to predict the probability of each class. We incorporate into the ME based model the following informative context-based features to train CBSM and CBTM. These features are carefully designed to reduce the data sparseness problem and some of them are inspired by previous work (He et al., 2008; Gimpel and Smith, 2008; Marton and Resnik, 2008; Chiang et al., 2009; Setiawan et al., 2009; Shen et al., 2009; Xiong et al., 2009):

1. **Function word features**, which indicate whether the hierarchical source-side/target-side rule strings and sub-phrases covered by non-terminals contain function words that are often important clues of predicting syntactic structures.

[1]Because the aligned target words are not contiguous and "cooperation" is aligned to the word outside the source-side rule.

2. **POS features**, which are POS tags of the boundary source words covered by non-terminals.

3. **Syntactic features**, which are the constituent constraints of hierarchical source-side rules exactly matching or crossing syntactic subtrees.

4. **Rule format features**, which are non-terminal positions and orders in source-side/target-side rules. This feature interacts between source and target components since it shows whether the translation ordering is affected.

5. **Length features**, which are the length of sub-phrases covered by source non-terminals.

4 Experiments

4.1 Experiment setting

We implement a hierarchical phrase-based system similar to the Hiero (Chiang, 2005) and evaluate our method on the Chinese-to-English translation task. Our bilingual training data comes from FBIS corpus, which consists of around 160K sentence pairs where the source data is parsed by the Berkeley parser (Petrov and Klein, 2007). The ME training toolkit, developed by (Zhang, 2006), is used to train our CBSM and CBTM. The training size of constructed positive instances for both CBSM and CBTM is 4.68M, while the training size of constructed negative instances is 3.74M and 3.03M respectively. Following (Setiawan et al., 2009), we identify function words as the 128 most frequent words in the corpus. The interpolation weights are set to $\theta = 0.75$ and $\varphi = 0.70$. The 5-gram language model is trained over the English portion of FBIS corpus plus Xinhua portion of the Gigaword corpus. The development data is from NIST 2005 evaluation data and the test data is from NIST 2006 and NIST 2008 evaluation data. The evaluation metric is the case-insensitive BLEU4 (Papineni et al., 2002). Statistical significance in BLEU score differences is tested by paired bootstrap re-sampling (Koehn, 2004).

4.2 Comparison with related work

Our baseline is the implemented Hiero-like SMT system where only the standard features are employed and the performance is state-of-the-art. We compare our method with the baseline and some typical approaches listed in Table 1 where XP+ denotes the approach in (Marton and Resnik, 2008) and TOFW (topological ordering of function words) stands for the method in (Setiawan et al., 2009). As (Xiong et al., 2009)'s work is based on phrasal SMT system with bracketing transduction grammar rules (Wu, 1997) and (Shen et al., 2009)'s work is based on the string-to-dependency SMT model, we do not implement these two related work due to their different models from ours. We also do not compare with (He et al., 2008)'s work due to its less practicability of integrating numerous sub-models.

Methods	NIST 2006	NIST 2008
Baseline	0.3025	0.2200
XP+	0.3061	0.2254
TOFW	0.3089	0.2253
Our method	0.3141	0.2318

Table 1: Comparison results, our method is significantly better than the baseline, as well as the other two approaches ($p < 0.01$)

As shown in Table 1, all the methods outperform the baseline because they have extra models to guide the hierarchical rule selection in some ways which might lead to better translation. Apparently, our method also performs better than the other two approaches, indicating that our method is more effective in the hierarchical rule selection as both source-side and target-side rules are selected together.

4.3 Effect of sub-models

Due to the space limitation, we analyze the effect of sub-models upon the system performance, rather than that of ME features, part of which have been investigated in previous related work.

Settings	NIST 2006	NIST 2008
Baseline	0.3025	0.2200
Baseline+CFSM	0.3092*	0.2266*
Baseline+CBSM	0.3077*	0.2247*
Baseline+CFTM	0.3076*	0.2286*
Baseline+CBTM	0.3060	0.2255*
Baseline+CFSM+CFTM	0.3109*	0.2289*
Baseline+CFSM+CBSM	0.3104*	0.2282*
Baseline+CFTM+CBTM	0.3099*	0.2299*
Baseline+all sub-models	0.3141*	0.2318*

Table 2: Sub-model effect upon the performance, *: significantly better than baseline ($p < 0.01$)

As shown in Table 2, when sub-models are integrated as independent features, the performance is improved compared to the baseline, which shows that each of the sub-models can improve the hierarchical rule selection. It is noticeable that the performance of the source-side rule selection model is comparable with that of the target-side rule selection model. Although CFSM and CFTM perform only slightly better than the others among the individual sub-models, the best performance is achieved when all the sub-models are integrated.

5 Conclusion

Hierarchical rule selection is an important and complicated task for hierarchical phrase-based SMT system. We propose a joint probability model for the hierarchical rule selection and the experimental results prove the effectiveness of our approach.

In the future work, we will explore more useful features and test our method over the large scale training corpus. A challenge might exist when running the ME training toolkit over a big size of training instances from the large scale training data.

Acknowledgments

We are especially grateful to the anonymous reviewers for their insightful comments. We also thank Hendra Setiawan, Yuval Marton, Chi-Ho Li, Shujie Liu and Nan Duan for helpful discussions.

References

Adam L. Berger, Vincent J. Della Pietra, and Stephen A. Della Pietra. 1996. *A Maximum Entropy Approach to Natural Language Processing. Computational Linguistics*, 22(1): pages 39-72.

David Chiang. 2005. *A Hierarchical Phrase-Based Model for Statistical Machine Translation.* In *Proc. ACL*, pages 263-270.

David Chiang, Kevin Knight, and Wei Wang. 2009. *11,001 New Features for Statistical Machine Translation.* In *Proc. HLT-NAACL*, pages 218-226.

Michel Galley, Jonathan Graehl, Kevin Knight, Daniel Marcu, Steve DeNeefe, Wei Wang, and Ignacio Thayer. 2006. *Scalable Inference and Training of Context-Rich Syntactic Translation Models.* In *Proc. ACL-Coling*, pages 961-968.

Kevin Gimpel and Noah A. Smith. 2008. *Rich Source-Side Context for Statistical Machine Translation.* In *Proc. the Third Workshop on Statistical Machine Translation*, pages 9-17.

Zhongjun He, Qun Liu, and Shouxun Lin. 2008. *Improving Statistical Machine Translation using Lexicalized Rule Selection.* In *Proc. Coling*, pages 321-328.

Philipp Koehn. 2004. *Statistical Significance Tests for Machine Translation Evaluation.* In *Proc. EMNLP*.

Philipp Koehn, Franz J. Och, and Daniel Marcu. 2003. *Statistical Phrase-Based Translation.* In *Proc. HLT-NAACL*, pages 127-133.

Qun Liu, Zhongjun He, Yang Liu, and Shouxun Lin. 2008. *Maximum Entropy based Rule Selection Model for Syntax-based Statistical Machine Translation.* In *Proc. EMNLP*, pages 89-97.

Yang Liu, Yun Huang, Qun Liu, and Shouxun Lin. 2007. *Forest-to-String Statistical Translation Rules.* In *Proc. ACL*, pages 704-711.

Yang Liu, Qun Liu, and Shouxun Lin. 2006. *Tree-to-String Alignment Template for Statistical Machine Translation.* In *Proc. ACL-Coling*, pages 609-616.

Daniel Marcu, Wei Wang, Abdessamad Echihabi, and Kevin Knight. 2006. *SPMT: Statistical Machine Translation with Syntactified Target Language Phrases.* In *Proc. EMNLP*, pages 44-52.

Yuval Marton and Philip Resnik. 2008. *Soft Syntactic Constraints for Hierarchical Phrased-Based Translation.* In *Proc. ACL*, pages 1003-1011.

Haitao Mi, Liang Huang, and Qun Liu. 2008. *Forest-Based Translation.* In *Proc. ACL*, pages 192-199.

Kishore Papineni, Salim Roukos, Todd Ward, and Wei-Jing Zhu. 2002. *Bleu: a Method for Automatic Evaluation of Machine Translation.* In *Proc. ACL*, pages 311-318.

Slav Petrov and Dan Klein. 2007. *Improved Inference for Unlexicalized Parsing.* In *Proc. HLT-NAACL*, pages 404-411.

Chris Quirk, Arul Menezes, and Colin Cherry. 2005. *Dependency Treelet Translation: Syntactically Informed Phrasal SMT.* In *Proc. ACL*, pages 271-279.

Libin Shen, Jinxi Xu, and Ralph Weischedel. 2008. *A New String-to-Dependency Machine Translation Algorithm with a Target Dependency Language Model.* In *Proc. ACL*, pages 577-585.

Libin Shen, Jinxi Xu, Bing Zhang, Spyros Matsoukas, and Ralph Weischedel. 2009. *Effective Use of Linguistic and Contextual Information for Statistical Machine Translation.* In *Proc. EMNLP*, pages 72-80.

Hendra Setiawan, Min Yen Kan, Haizhou Li, and Philip Resnik. 2009. *Topological Ordering of Function Words in Hierarchical Phrase-based Translation.* In *Proc. ACL*, pages 324-332.

Dekai Wu. 1997. *Stochastic Inversion Transduction Grammars and Bilingual Parsing of Parallel Corpora. Computational Linguistics*, 23(3): pages 377-403.

Deyi Xiong, Qun Liu, and Shouxun Lin. 2006. *Maximum Entropy Based Phrase Reordering Model for Statistical Machine Translation.* In *Proc. ACL-Coling*, pages 521-528.

Deyi Xiong, Min Zhang, Aiti Aw, and Haizhou Li. 2009. *A Syntax-Driven Bracketing Model for Phrase-Based Translation.* In *Proc. ACL*, pages 315-323.

Kenji Yamada and Kevin Knight. 2001. *A Syntax-based Statistical Translation Model.* In *Proc. ACL*, pages 523-530.

Le Zhang. 2006. *Maximum entropy modeling toolkit for python and c++.* available at http://homepages.inf.ed.ac.uk/lzhang10/maxent_toolkit.html.

Learning Lexicalized Reordering Models from Reordering Graphs

Jinsong Su, Yang Liu, Yajuan Lü, Haitao Mi, Qun Liu
Key Laboratory of Intelligent Information Processing
Institute of Computing Technology
Chinese Academy of Sciences
P.O. Box 2704, Beijing 100190, China
{sujinsong,yliu,lvyajuan,htmi,liuqun}@ict.ac.cn

Abstract

Lexicalized reordering models play a crucial role in phrase-based translation systems. They are usually learned from the word-aligned bilingual corpus by examining the reordering relations of adjacent phrases. Instead of just checking whether there is one phrase adjacent to a given phrase, we argue that it is important to take the number of adjacent phrases into account for better estimations of reordering models. We propose to use a structure named *reordering graph*, which represents all phrase segmentations of a sentence pair, to learn lexicalized reordering models efficiently. Experimental results on the NIST Chinese-English test sets show that our approach significantly outperforms the baseline method.

1 Introduction

Phrase-based translation systems (Koehn et al., 2003; Och and Ney, 2004) prove to be the state-of-the-art as they have delivered translation performance in recent machine translation evaluations. While excelling at memorizing local translation and reordering, phrase-based systems have difficulties in modeling permutations among phrases. As a result, it is important to develop effective reordering models to capture such non-local reordering.

The early phrase-based paradigm (Koehn et al., 2003) applies a simple distance-based distortion penalty to model the phrase movements. More recently, many researchers have presented lexicalized reordering models that take advantage of lexical information to predict reordering (Tillmann, 2004; Xiong et al., 2006; Zens and Ney, 2006; Koehn et al., 2007; Galley and Manning, 2008). These models are learned from a word-aligned corpus to predict three orientations of a phrase pair with respect to the previous bilingual phrase: monotone (M), swap (S), and discontinuous (D). Take the bilingual phrase bp in Figure 1(a) for example. The word-based reordering model (Koehn et al., 2007) analyzes the word alignments at positions $(s-1, u-1)$ and $(s-1, v+1)$. The orientation of bp is set to D because the position $(s-1, v+1)$ contains no word alignment. The phrase-based reordering model (Tillmann, 2004) determines the presence of the adjacent bilingual phrase located in position $(s-1, v+1)$ and then treats the orientation of bp as S. Given no constraint on maximum phrase length, the hierarchical phrase reordering model (Galley and Manning, 2008) also analyzes the adjacent bilingual phrases for bp and identifies its orientation as S.

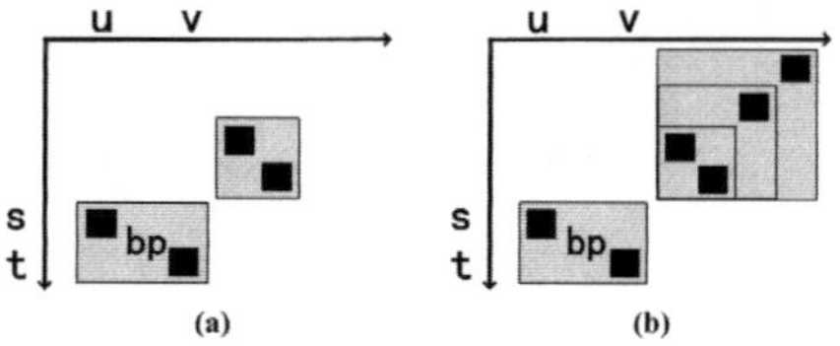

Figure 1: Occurrence of a swap with different numbers of adjacent bilingual phrases: only one phrase in (a) and three phrases in (b). Black squares denote word alignments and gray rectangles denote bilingual phrases. [s,t] indicates the target-side span of bilingual phrase *bp* and [u,v] represents the source-side span of bilingual phrase *bp*.

However, given a bilingual phrase, the above-mentioned models just consider the presence of an adjacent bilingual phrase rather than the number of adjacent bilingual phrases. See the examples in Fig-

Proceedings of the ACL 2010 Conference Short Papers, pages 12–16,
Uppsala, Sweden, 11-16 July 2010.

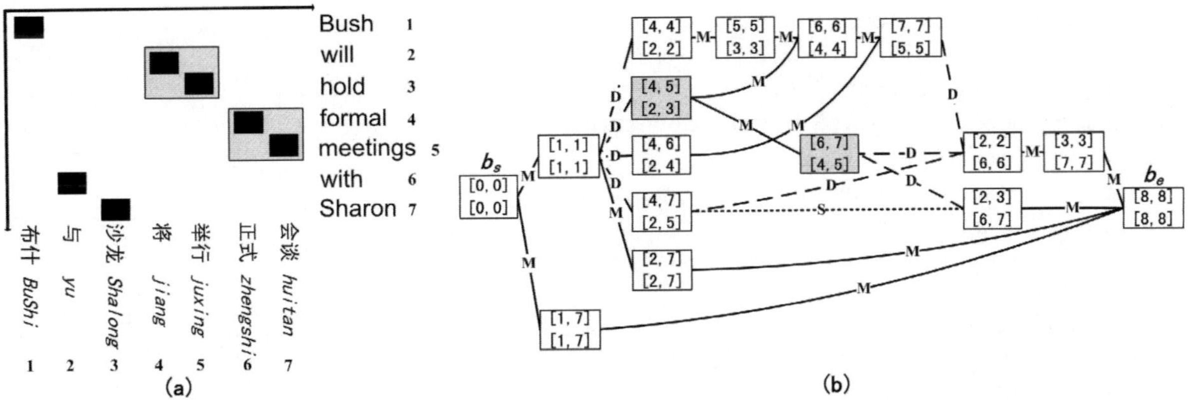

Figure 2: (a) A parallel Chinese-English sentence pair and (b) its corresponding reordering graph. In (b), we denote each bilingual phrase with a rectangle, where the upper and bottom numbers in the brackets represent the source and target spans of this bilingual phrase respectively. M = monotone (solid lines), S = swap (dotted line), and D = discontinuous (segmented lines). The bilingual phrases marked in the gray constitute a reordering example.

ure 1 for illustration. In Figure 1(a), *bp* is in a swap order with only one bilingual phrase. In Figure 1(b), *bp* swaps with three bilingual phrases. Lexicalized reordering models do not distinguish different numbers of adjacent phrase pairs, and just give *bp* the same count in the swap orientation.

In this paper, we propose a novel method to better estimate the reordering probabilities with the consideration of varying numbers of adjacent bilingual phrases. Our method uses reordering graphs to represent all phrase segmentations of parallel sentence pairs, and then gets the fractional counts of bilingual phrases for orientations from reordering graphs in an inside-outside fashion. Experimental results indicate that our method achieves significant improvements over the traditional lexicalized reordering model (Koehn et al., 2007).

This paper is organized as follows: in Section 2, we first give a brief introduction to the traditional lexicalized reordering model. Then we introduce our method to estimate the reordering probabilities from reordering graphs. The experimental results are reported in Section 3. Finally, we end with a conclusion and future work in Section 4.

2 Estimation of Reordering Probabilities Based on Reordering Graph

In this section, we first describe the traditional lexicalized reordering model, and then illustrate how to construct reordering graphs to estimate the reordering probabilities.

2.1 Lexicalized Reordering Model

Given a phrase pair $bp = (\overline{e}_i, \overline{f}_{a_i})$, where a_i defines that the source phrase $\overline{f}_{a_i}$ is aligned to the target phrase $\overline{e}_i$, the traditional lexicalized reordering model computes the reordering count of *bp* in the orientation o based on the word alignments of boundary words. Specifically, the model collects bilingual phrases and distinguishes their orientations with respect to the previous bilingual phrase into three categories:

$$o = \begin{cases} M & a_i - a_{i-1} = 1 \\ S & a_i - a_{i-1} = -1 \\ D & |a_i - a_{i-1}| \neq 1 \end{cases} \tag{1}$$

Using the relative-frequency approach, the reordering probability regarding *bp* is

$$p(o|bp) = \frac{Count(o, bp)}{\sum_{o'} Count(o', bp)} \tag{2}$$

2.2 Reordering Graph

For a parallel sentence pair, its reordering graph indicates all possible translation derivations consisting of the extracted bilingual phrases. To construct a reordering graph, we first extract bilingual phrases using the way of (Och, 2003). Then, the adjacent bilingual phrases are linked according to the target-side order. Some bilingual phrases, which have no adjacent bilingual phrases because of maximum length limitation, are linked to the nearest bilingual phrases in the target-side order.

Shown in Figure 2(b), the reordering graph for the parallel sentence pair (Figure 2(a)) can be represented as an undirected graph, where each rectangle corresponds to a phrase pair, each link is the orientation relationship between adjacent bilingual phrases, and two distinguished rectangles b_s and b_e indicate the beginning and ending of the parallel sentence pair, respectively. With the reordering graph, we can obtain all reordering examples containing the given bilingual phrase. For example, the bilingual phrase ⟨*zhengshi huitan*, formal meetings⟩ (see Figure 2(a)), corresponding to the rectangle labeled with the source span [6,7] and the target span [4,5], is in a monotone order with one previous phrase and in a discontinuous order with two subsequent phrases (see Figure 2(b)).

2.3 Estimation of Reordering Probabilities

We estimate the reordering probabilities from reordering graphs. Given a parallel sentence pair, there are many translation derivations corresponding to different paths in its reordering graph. Assuming all derivations have a uniform probability, the fractional counts of bilingual phrases for orientations can be calculated by utilizing an algorithm in the inside-outside fashion.

Given a phrase pair *bp* in the reordering graph, we denote the number of paths from b_s to *bp* with $\alpha(bp)$. It can be computed in an iterative way $\alpha(bp) = \sum_{bp'} \alpha(bp')$, where bp' is one of the previous bilingual phrases of *bp* and $\alpha(b_s)$=1. In a similar way, the number of paths from b_e to *bp*, notated as $\beta(bp)$, is simply $\beta(bp) = \sum_{bp''} \beta(bp'')$, where bp'' is one of the subsequent bilingual phrases of *bp* and $\beta(b_e)$=1. Here, we show the α and β values of all bilingual phrases of Figure 2 in Table 1. Especially, for the reordering example consisting of the bilingual phrases bp_1=⟨*jiang juxing*, will hold⟩ and bp_2=⟨*zhengshi huitan*, formal meetings⟩, marked in the gray color in Figure 2, the α and β values can be calculated: $\alpha(bp_1)$ = 1, $\beta(bp_2)$ = 1+1 = 2, $\beta(b_s)$ = 8+1 = 9.

Inspired by the parsing literature on pruning (Charniak and Johnson, 2005; Huang, 2008), the fractional count of (o, bp', bp) is

$$Count(o, bp', bp) = \frac{\alpha(bp') \cdot \beta(bp)}{\beta(b_s)} \quad (3)$$

where the numerator indicates the number of paths containing the reordering example (o, bp', bp) and the denominator is the total number of paths in the reordering graph. Continuing with the reordering example described above, we obtain its fractional count using the formula (3): $Count(M, bp_1, bp_2) = (1 \times 2)/9 = 2/9$.

Then, the fractional count of *bp* in the orientation *o* is calculated as described below:

$$Count(o, bp) = \sum_{bp'} Count(o, bp', bp) \quad (4)$$

For example, we compute the fractional count of bp_2 in the monotone orientation by the formula (4): $Count(M, bp_2) = 2/9$.

As described in the lexicalized reordering model (Section 2.1), we apply the formula (2) to calculate the final reordering probabilities.

src span	*trg span*	α	β
[0, 0]	[0, 0]	1	9
[1, 1]	[1, 1]	1	8
[1, 7]	[1, 7]	1	1
[4, 4]	[2, 2]	1	1
[4, 5]	[2, 3]	1	3
[4, 6]	[2, 4]	1	1
[4, 7]	[2, 5]	1	2
[2, 7]	[2, 7]	1	1
[5, 5]	[3, 3]	1	1
[6, 6]	[4, 4]	2	1
[6, 7]	[4, 5]	1	2
[7, 7]	[5, 5]	3	1
[2, 2]	[6, 6]	5	1
[2, 3]	[6, 7]	2	1
[3, 3]	[7, 7]	5	1
[8, 8]	[8, 8]	9	1

Table 1: The α and β values of the bilingual phrases shown in Figure 2.

3 Experiments

We conduct experiments to investigate the effectiveness of our method on the **msd-fe** reordering model and the **msd-bidirectional-fe** reordering model. These two models are widely applied in phrase-based system (Koehn et al., 2007). The msd-fe reordering model has three features, which represent the probabilities of bilingual phrases in three orientations: monotone, swap, or discontinuous. If a msd-bidirectional-fe model is used, then the number of features doubles: one for each direction.

3.1 Experiment Setup

Two different sizes of training corpora are used in our experiments: one is a small-scale corpus that comes from FBIS corpus consisting of 239K bilingual sentence pairs, the other is a large-scale corpus that includes 1.55M bilingual sentence pairs from LDC. The 2002 NIST MT evaluation test data is used as the development set and the 2003, 2004, 2005 NIST MT test data are the test sets. We choose the MOSES[1] (Koehn et al., 2007) as the experimental decoder. GIZA++ (Och and Ney, 2003) and the heuristics "grow-diag-final-and" are used to generate a word-aligned corpus, where we extract bilingual phrases with maximum length 7. We use SRILM Toolkits (Stolcke, 2002) to train a 4-gram language model on the Xinhua portion of Gigaword corpus.

In exception to the reordering probabilities, we use the same features in the comparative experiments. During decoding, we set ttable-limit = 20, stack = 100, and perform minimum-error-rate training (Och, 2003) to tune various feature weights. The translation quality is evaluated by case-insensitive BLEU-4 metric (Papineni et al., 2002). Finally, we conduct paired bootstrap sampling (Koehn, 2004) to test the significance in BLEU scores differences.

3.2 Experimental Results

Table 2 shows the results of experiments with the small training corpus. For the msd-fe model, the BLEU scores by our method are 30.51 32.78 and 29.50, achieving absolute improvements of **0.89, 0.66** and **0.62** on the three test sets, respectively. For the msd-bidirectional-fe model, our method obtains BLEU scores of 30.49 32.73 and 29.24, with absolute improvements of **1.11, 0.73** and **0.60** over the baseline method.

[1]The phrase-based lexical reordering model (Tillmann, 2004) is also closely related to our model. However, due to the limit of time and space, we only use Moses-style reordering model (Koehn et al., 2007) as our baseline.

model	method	MT-03	MT-04	MT-05
m-f	baseline	29.62	32.12	28.88
	RG	30.51**	32.78**	29.50*
m-b-f	baseline	29.38	32.00	28.64
	RG	30.49**	32.73**	29.24*

Table 2: Experimental results with the **small-scale** corpus. m-f: msd-fe reordering model. m-b-f: msd-bidirectional-fe reordering model. RG: probabilities estimation based on Reordering Graph. * or **: significantly better than baseline ($p < 0.05$ or $p < 0.01$).

model	method	MT-03	MT-04	MT-05
m-f	baseline	31.58	32.39	31.49
	RG	32.44**	33.24**	31.64
m-b-f	baseline	32.43	33.07	31.69
	RG	33.29**	34.49**	32.79**

Table 3: Experimental results with the **large-scale** corpus.

Table 3 shows the results of experiments with the large training corpus. In the experiments of the msd-fe model, in exception to the MT-05 test set, our method is superior to the baseline method. The BLEU scores by our method are 32.44, 33.24 and 31.64, which obtain **0.86, 0.85** and **0.15** gains on three test set, respectively. For the msd-bidirectional-fe model, the BLEU scores produced by our approach are 33.29, 34.49 and 32.79 on the three test sets, with **0.86, 1.42** and **1.1** points higher than the baseline method, respectively.

4 Conclusion and Future Work

In this paper, we propose a method to improve the reordering model by considering the effect of the number of adjacent bilingual phrases on the reordering probabilities estimation. Experimental results on NIST Chinese-to-English tasks demonstrate the effectiveness of our method.

Our method is also general to other lexicalized reordering models. We plan to apply our method to the complex lexicalized reordering models, for example, the hierarchical reordering model (Galley and Manning, 2008) and the MEBTG reordering model (Xiong et al., 2006). In addition, how to further improve the reordering model by distinguishing the derivations with different probabilities will become another study emphasis in further research.

Acknowledgement

The authors were supported by National Natural Science Foundation of China, Contracts 60873167 and 60903138. We thank the anonymous reviewers for their insightful comments. We are also grateful to Hongmei Zhao and Shu Cai for their helpful feedback.

References

Eugene Charniak and Mark Johnson. 2005. Coarse-to-fine n-best parsing and maxent discriminative reranking. In *Proc. of ACL 2005*, pages 173–180.

Michel Galley and Christopher D. Manning. 2008. A simple and effective hierarchical phrase reordering model. In *Proc. of EMNLP 2008*, pages 848–856.

Liang Huang. 2008. Forest reranking: Discriminative parsing with non-local features. In *Proc. of ACL 2008*, pages 586–594.

Philipp Koehn, Franz Josef Och, and Daniel Marcu. 2003. Statistical phrase-based translation. In *Proc. of HLT-NAACL 2003*, pages 127–133.

Philipp Koehn, Hieu Hoang, Alexandra Birch, Chris Callison-Burch, Marcello Federico, Nicola Bertoldi, Brooke Cowan, Wade Shen, Christine Moran, Richard Zens, Chris Dyer, Ondrej Bojar, Alexandra Constantin, and Evan Herbst. 2007. Moses: Open source toolkit for statistical machine translation. In *Proc. of ACL 2007, Demonstration Session*, pages 177–180.

Philipp Koehn. 2004. Statistical significance tests for machine translation evaluation. In *Proc. of EMNLP 2004*, pages 388–395.

Franz Josef Och and Hermann Ney. 2003. A systematic comparison of various statistical alignment models. *Computational Linguistics*, 29(1):19–51.

Franz Joseph Och and Hermann Ney. 2004. The alignment template approach to statistical machine translation. *Computational Linguistics*, pages 417–449.

Franz Josef Och. 2003. Minimum error rate training in statistical machine translation. In *Proc. of ACL 2003*, pages 160–167.

Kishore Papineni, Salim Roukos, Todd Ward, and Wei-Jing Zhu. 2002. Bleu: a method for automatic evaluation of machine translation. In *Proc. of ACL 2002*, pages 311–318.

Andreas Stolcke. 2002. Srilm - an extensible language modeling toolkit. In *Proc. of ICSLP 2002*, pages 901–904.

Christoph Tillmann. 2004. A unigram orientation model for statistical machine translation. In *Proc. of HLT-ACL 2004, Short Papers*, pages 101–104.

Deyi Xiong, Qun Liu, and Shouxun Lin. 2006. Maximum entropy based phrase reordering model for statistical machine translation. In *Proc. of ACL 2006*, pages 521–528.

Richard Zens and Hermann Ney. 2006. Discriminvative reordering models for statistical machine translation. In *Proc. of Workshop on Statistical Machine Translation 2006*, pages 521–528.

Filtering Syntactic Constraints for Statistical Machine Translation

Hailong Cao and **Eiichiro Sumita**
Language Translation Group, MASTAR Project
National Institute of Information and Communications Technology
3-5 Hikari-dai, Seika-cho, Soraku-gun, Kyoto, Japan, 619-0289
{hlcao, eiichiro.sumita }@nict.go.jp

Abstract

Source language parse trees offer very useful but imperfect reordering constraints for statistical machine translation. A lot of effort has been made for soft applications of syntactic constraints. We alternatively propose the selective use of syntactic constraints. A classifier is built automatically to decide whether a node in the parse trees should be used as a reordering constraint or not. Using this information yields a 0.8 BLEU point improvement over a full constraint-based system.

1 Introduction

In statistical machine translation (SMT), the search problem is NP-hard if arbitrary reordering is allowed (Knight, 1999). Therefore, we need to restrict the possible reordering in an appropriate way for both efficiency and translation quality. The most widely used reordering constraints are IBM constraints (Berger et al., 1996), ITG constraints (Wu, 1995) and syntactic constraints (Yamada et al., 2000; Galley et al., 2004; Liu et al., 2006; Marcu et al., 2006; Zollmann and Venugopal 2006; and numerous others). Syntactic constraints can be imposed from the source side or target side. This work will focus on syntactic constraints from source parse trees.

Linguistic parse trees can provide very useful reordering constraints for SMT. However, they are far from perfect because of both parsing errors and the crossing of the constituents and formal phrases extracted from parallel training data. The key challenge is how to take advantage of the prior knowledge in the linguistic parse trees without affecting the strengths of formal phrases. Recent efforts attack this problem by using the constraints softly (Cherry, 2008; Marton and Resnik, 2008). In their methods, a candidate translation gets an extra credit if it respects the parse tree but may incur a cost if it violates a constituent boundary.

In this paper, we address this challenge from a less explored direction. Rather than use all constraints offered by the parse trees, we propose using them selectively. Based on parallel training data, a classifier is built automatically to decide whether a node in the parse trees should be used as a reordering constraint or not. As a result, we obtain a 0.8 BLEU point improvement over a full constraint-based system.

2 Reordering Constraints from Source Parse Trees

In this section we briefly review a constraint-based system named IST-ITG (Imposing Source Tree on Inversion Transduction Grammar, Yamamoto et al., 2008) upon which this work builds.

When using ITG constraints during decoding, the source-side parse tree structure is not considered. The reordering process can be more tightly constrained if constraints from the source parse tree are integrated with the ITG constraints. IST-ITG constraints directly apply source sentence tree structure to generate the target with the following constraint: the target sentence is obtained by rotating any node of the source sentence tree structure.

After parsing the source sentence, a bracketed sentence is obtained by removing the node syntactic labels; this bracketed sentence can then be directly expressed as a tree structure. For example[1], the parse tree "(S1 (S (NP (DT This)) (VP (AUX is) (NP (DT a) (NN pen)))))" is obtained from the source sentence "This is a pen", which consists of four words. By removing

[1] We use English examples for the sake of readability.

Proceedings of the ACL 2010 Conference Short Papers, pages 17–21,
Uppsala, Sweden, 11-16 July 2010.

the node syntactic labels, the bracketed sentence "((This) ((is) ((a) (pen))))" is obtained. Such a bracketed sentence can be used to produce constraints.

For example, for the source-side bracketed tree "((f1 f2) (f3 f4)) ", eight target sequences [e1, e2, e3, e4], [e2, e1, e3, e4], [e1, e2, e4, e3], [e2, e1, e4, e3], [e3, e4, e1, e2], [e3, e4, e2, e1], [e4, e3, e1, e2], and [e4, e3, e2, e1] are possible. For the source-side bracketed tree "(((f1f2) f3) f4)," eight sequences [e1, e2, e3, e4], [e2, e1, e3, e4], [e3, e1, e2, e4], [e3, e2, e1, e4], [e4, e1, e2, e3], [e4, e2, e1, e3], [e4, e3, e1, e2], and [e4, e3, e2, e1] are possible. When the source sentence tree structure is a binary tree, the number of word orderings is reduced to 2^{N-1} where N is the length of the source sentence.

The parsing results sometimes do not produce binary trees. In this case, some subtrees have more than two child nodes. For a non-binary subtree, any reordering of child nodes is allowed. For example, if a subtree has three child nodes, six reorderings of the nodes are possible.

3 Learning to Classify Parse Tree Nodes

In IST-ITG and many other methods which use syntactic constraints, all of the nodes in the parse trees are utilized. Though many nodes in the parse trees are useful, we would argue that some nodes are not trustworthy. For example, if we constrain the translation of "f1 f2 f3 f4" with node N2 illustrated in Figure 1, then word "e1" will never be put in the middle the other three words. If we want to obtain the translation "e2 e1 e4 e3", node N3 can offer a good constraint while node N2 should be filtered out. In real corpora, cases such as node N2 are frequent enough to be noticeable (see Fox (2002) or section 4.1 in this paper).

Therefore, we use the definitions in Galley et al. (2004) to classify the nodes in parse trees into two types: frontier nodes and interior nodes. Though the definitions were originally made for target language parse trees, they can be straightforwardly applied to the source side. A node which satisfies both of the following two conditions is referred as a frontier node:

- All the words covered by the node can be translated separately. That is to say, these words do not share a translation with any word outside the coverage of the node.
- All the words covered by the node remain contiguous after translation.

Otherwise the node is an interior node.

For example, in Figure 1, both node N1 and node N3 are frontier nodes. Node N2 is an interior node because the source words f2, f3 and f4 are translated into e2, e3 and e4, which are not contiguous in the target side.

Clearly, only frontier nodes should be used as reordering constraints while interior nodes are not suitable for this. However, little work has been done on how to explicitly distinguish these two kinds of nodes in the source parse trees. In this section, we will explore building a classifier which can label the nodes in the parse trees as frontier nodes or interior nodes.

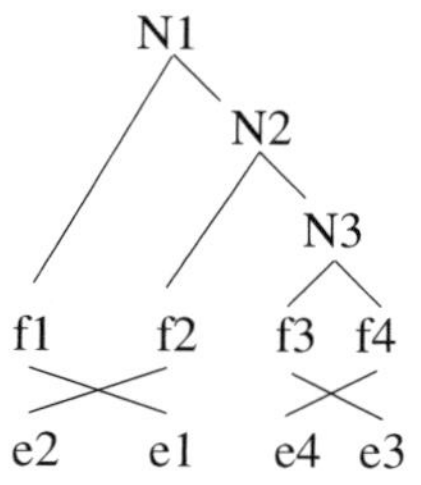

Figure 1: An example parse tree and alignments

3.1 Training

Ideally, we would have a human-annotated corpus in which each sentence is parsed and each node in the parse trees is labeled as a frontier node or an interior node. But such a target language specific corpus is hard to come by, and never in the quantity we would like.

Instead, we generate such a corpus automatically. We begin with a parallel corpus which will be used to train our SMT model. In our case, it is the FBIS Chinese-English corpus.

Firstly, the Chinese sentences are segmented, POS tagged and parsed by the tools described in Kruengkrai et al. (2009) and Cao et al. (2007), both of which are trained on the Penn Chinese Treebank 6.0.

Secondly, we use GIZA++ to align the sentences in both the Chinese-English and English-Chinese directions. We combine the alignments using the "grow-diag-final-and" procedure provided with MOSES (Koehn, 2007). Because there are many errors in the alignment, we remove the links if the alignment count is less than three for the source or the target word. Additionally, we also remove notoriously bad links in {de, le} × {the, a, an} following Fossum and Knight (2008).

Thirdly, given the parse trees and the alignment information, we label each node as a frontier node or an interior node according to the definition introduced in this section. Using the labeled nodes as training data, we can build a classifier. In theory, a broad class of machine learning tools can be used; however, due to the scale of the task (see section 4), we utilize the Pegasos [2] which is a very fast *SVM* solver (Shalev-Shwartz et al, 2007).

3.2 Features

For each node in the parse trees, we use the following feature templates:

- A context-free grammar rule which rewrites the current node (In this and all the following grammar based features, a mark is used to indicate which non terminal is the current node.)
- A context-free grammar rule which rewrites the current node's father
- The combination of the above two rules
- A lexicalized context-free grammar rule which rewrites the current node
- A lexicalized context-free grammar rule which rewrites the current node's father
- Syntactic label, head word, and head POS tag of the current node
- Syntactic label, head word, and head POS tag of the current node's left child
- Syntactic label, head word, and head POS tag of the current node's right child
- Syntactic label, head word, and head POS tag of the current node's left brother
- Syntactic label, head word, and head POS tag of the current node's right brother
- Syntactic label, head word, and head POS tag of the current node's father
- The leftmost word covered by the current node and the word before it
- The rightmost word covered by the current node and the word after it

4 Experiments

Our SMT system is based on a fairly typical phrase-based model (Finch and Sumita, 2008). For the training of our SMT model, we use a modified training toolkit adapted from the MOSES decoder. Our decoder can operate on the same principles as the MOSES decoder. Minimum error rate training (MERT) with respect to BLEU score is used to tune the decoder's parameters, and it is performed using the standard technique of Och (2003). A lexical reordering model was used in our experiments.

The translation model was created from the FBIS corpus. We used a 5-gram language model trained with modified Knesser-Ney smoothing. The language model was trained on the target side of FBIS corpus and the Xinhua news in GIGAWORD corpus. The development and test sets are from NIST MT08 evaluation campaign. Table 1 shows the statistics of the corpora used in our experiments.

Data	Sentences	Chinese words	English words
Training set	243,698	7,933,133	10,343,140
Development set	1664	38,779	46,387
Test set	1357	32377	42,444
GIGAWORD	19,049,757	-	306,221,306

Table 1: Corpora statistics

4.1 Experiments on Nodes Classification

We extracted about 3.9 million example nodes from the training data, i.e. the FBIS corpus. There were 2.37 million frontier nodes and 1.59 million interior nodes in these examples, give rise to about 4.4 million features. To test the performance of our classifier, we simply use the last ten thousand examples as a test set, and the rest being used as Pegasos training data. All the parameters in Pegasos were set as default values. In this way, the accuracy of the classifier was 71.59%.

Then we retrained our classifier by using all of the examples. The nodes in the automatically parsed NIST MT08 test set were labeled by the classifier. As a result, 17,240 nodes were labeled as frontier nodes and 5,736 nodes were labeled as interior nodes.

4.2 Experiments on Chinese-English SMT

In order to confirm that it is advantageous to distinguish between frontier nodes and interior nodes, we performed four translation experiments.

The first one was a typical beam search decoding without any syntactic constraints.

All the other three experiments were based on the IST-ITG method which makes use of syntac-

[2] http://www.cs.huji.ac.il/~shais/code/index.html

tic constraints. The difference between these three experiments lies in what constraints are used. In detail, the second one used all nodes recognized by the parser; the third one only used frontier nodes labeled by the classifier; the fourth one only used interior nodes labeled by the classifier.

With the exception of the above differences, all the other settings were the same in the four experiments. Table 2 summarizes the SMT performance.

Syntactic Constraints	BLEU
none	17.26
all nodes	16.83
frontier nodes	17.63
interior nodes	16.59

Table 2: Comparison of different constraints by SMT quality

Clearly, we obtain the best performance if we constrain the search with only frontier nodes. Using just frontier yields a 0.8 BLEU point improvement over the baseline constraint-based system which uses all the constraints.

On the other hand, constraints from interior nodes result in the worst performance. This comparison shows it is necessary to explicitly distinguish nodes in the source parse trees when they are used as reordering constraints.

The improvement over the system without constraints is only modest. It may be too coarse to use pare trees as hard constraints. We believe a greater improvement can be expected if we apply our idea to finer-grained approaches that use constraints softly (Marton and Resnik (2008) and Cherry (2008)).

5 Conclusion and Future Work

We propose a selectively approach to syntactic constraints during decoding. A classifier is built automatically to decide whether a node in the parse trees should be used as a reordering constraint or not. Preliminary results show that it is not only advantageous but necessary to explicitly distinguish between frontier nodes and interior nodes.

The idea of selecting syntactic constraints is compatible with the idea of using constraints softly; we plan to combine the two ideas and obtain further improvements in future work.

Acknowledgments

We would like to thank Taro Watanabe and Andrew Finch for insightful discussions. We also would like to thank the anonymous reviewers for their constructive comments.

Reference

A.L. Berger, P.F. Brown, S.A.D. Pietra, V.J.D. Pietra, J.R. Gillett, A.S. Kehler, and R.L. Mercer. 1996. Language translation apparatus and method of using context-based translation models. United States patent, patent number 5510981, April.

Hailong Cao, Yujie Zhang and Hitoshi Isahara. Empirical study on parsing Chinese based on Collins' model. 2007. In *PACLING*.

Colin Cherry. 2008. Cohesive phrase-Based decoding for statistical machine translation. In *ACL- HLT*.

Andrew Finch and Eiichiro Sumita. 2008. Dynamic model interpolation for statistical machine translation. In *SMT Workshop*.

Victoria Fossum and Kevin Knight. 2008. Using bilingual Chinese-English word alignments to resolve PP attachment ambiguity in English. In *AMTA Student Workshop*.

Heidi J. Fox. 2002. Phrasal cohesion and statistical machine translation. In *EMNLP*.

Michel Galley, Mark Hopkins, Kevin Knight, and Daniel Marcu. 2004. What's in a translation rule? In *HLT-NAACL*.

Kevin Knight. 1999. Decoding complexity in word replacement translation models. *Computational Linguistics*, 25(4):607–615.

Philipp Koehn, Hieu Hoang, Alexandra Birch, Chris Callison-Burch, Marcello Federico, Nicola Bertoldi, Brooke Cowan, Wade Shen, Christine Moran, Richard Zens, Chris Dyer, Ondrej Bojar, Alexandra Constantin, Evan Herbst. 2007. Moses: Open Source Toolkit for Statistical Machine Translation. In *ACL demo and poster sessions*.

Canasai Kruengkrai, Kiyotaka Uchimoto, Jun'ichi Kazama, Yiou Wang, Kentaro Torisawa and Hitoshi Isahara. 2009. An error-driven word-character hybrid model for joint Chinese word segmentation and POS tagging. In *ACL-IJCNLP*.

Yang Liu, Qun Liu, Shouxun Lin. 2006. Tree-to-string alignment template for statistical machine translation. In *ACL-COLING*.

Daniel Marcu, Wei Wang, Abdessamad Echihabi, and Kevin Knight. 2006. SPMT: Statistical machine translation with syntactified target language phrases. In *EMNLP*.

Yuval Marton and Philip Resnik. 2008. Soft syntactic constraints for hierarchical phrased-based translation. In *ACL-HLT*.

Franz Och. 2003. Minimum error rate training in statistical machine translation. In *ACL*.

Shai Shalev-Shwartz, Yoram Singer and Nathan Srebro. 2007. Pegasos: Primal estimated sub-gradient solver for SVM. In *ICML*.

Dekai Wu. 1995. Stochastic inversion transduction grammars with application to segmentation, bracketing, and alignment of parallel corpora. In *IJCAI*.

Kenji Yamada and Kevin Knight. 2000. A syntax-based statistical translation model. In *ACL*.

Hirofumi Yamamoto, Hideo Okuma and Eiichiro Sumita. 2008. Imposing constraints from the source tree on ITG constraints for SMT. In *Workshop on syntax and structure in statistical translation*.

Andreas Zollmann and Ashish Venugopal. 2006. Syntax augmented machine translation via chart parsing. In *SMT Workshop, HLT-NAACL*.

Diversify and Combine: Improving Word Alignment for Machine Translation on Low-Resource Languages

Bing Xiang, Yonggang Deng, and Bowen Zhou
IBM T. J. Watson Research Center
Yorktown Heights, NY 10598
{bxiang,ydeng,zhou}@us.ibm.com

Abstract

We present a novel method to improve word alignment quality and eventually the translation performance by producing and combining complementary word alignments for low-resource languages. Instead of focusing on the improvement of a single set of word alignments, we generate multiple sets of diversified alignments based on different motivations, such as linguistic knowledge, morphology and heuristics. We demonstrate this approach on an English-to-Pashto translation task by combining the alignments obtained from syntactic reordering, stemming, and partial words. The combined alignment outperforms the baseline alignment, with significantly higher F-scores and better translation performance.

1 Introduction

Word alignment usually serves as the starting point and foundation for a statistical machine translation (SMT) system. It has received a significant amount of research over the years, notably in (Brown et al., 1993; Ittycheriah and Roukos, 2005; Fraser and Marcu, 2007; Hermjakob, 2009). They all focused on the improvement of word alignment models. In this work, we leverage existing aligners and generate multiple sets of word alignments based on complementary information, then combine them to get the final alignment for phrase training. The resource required for this approach is little, compared to what is needed to build a reasonable discriminative alignment model, for example. This makes the approach especially appealing for SMT on low-resource languages.

Most of the research on alignment combination in the past has focused on how to combine the alignments from two different directions, source-to-target and target-to-source. Usually people start from the intersection of two sets of alignments, and gradually add links in the union based on certain heuristics, as in (Koehn et al., 2003), to achieve a better balance compared to using either intersection (high precision) or union (high recall). In (Ayan and Dorr, 2006) a maximum entropy approach was proposed to combine multiple alignments based on a set of linguistic and alignment features. A different approach was presented in (Deng and Zhou, 2009), which again concentrated on the combination of two sets of alignments, but with a different criterion. It tries to maximize the number of phrases that can be extracted in the combined alignments. A greedy search method was utilized and it achieved higher translation performance than the baseline.

More recently, an alignment selection approach was proposed in (Huang, 2009), which computes confidence scores for each link and prunes the links from multiple sets of alignments using a hand-picked threshold. The alignments used in that work were generated from different aligners (HMM, block model, and maximum entropy model). In this work, we use soft voting with weighted confidence scores, where the weights can be tuned with a specific objective function. There is no need for a pre-determined threshold as used in (Huang, 2009). Also, we utilize various knowledge sources to enrich the alignments instead of using different aligners. Our strategy is to diversify and then combine in order to catch any complementary information captured in the word alignments for low-resource languages.

The rest of the paper is organized as follows.

Proceedings of the ACL 2010 Conference Short Papers, pages 22–26,
Uppsala, Sweden, 11-16 July 2010.

We present three different sets of alignments in Section 2 for an English-to-Pashto MT task. In Section 3, we propose the alignment combination algorithm. The experimental results are reported in Section 4. We conclude the paper in Section 5.

2 Diversified Word Alignments

We take an English-to-Pashto MT task as an example and create three sets of additional alignments on top of the baseline alignment.

2.1 Syntactic Reordering

Pashto is a subject-object-verb (SOV) language, which puts verbs after objects. People have proposed different syntactic rules to pre-reorder SOV languages, either based on a constituent parse tree (Drábek and Yarowsky, 2004; Wang et al., 2007) or dependency parse tree (Xu et al., 2009). In this work, we apply syntactic reordering for verb phrases (VP) based on the English constituent parse. The VP-based reordering rule we apply in the work is:

- $VP(VB*, *) \to VP(*, VB*)$

where $VB*$ represents VB, VBD, VBG, VBN, VBP and VBZ.

In Figure 1, we show the reference alignment between an English sentence and the corresponding Pashto translation, where E is the original English sentence, P is the Pashto sentence (in romanized text), and E' is the English sentence after reordering. As we can see, after the VP-based reordering, the alignment between the two sentences becomes monotone, which makes it easier for the aligner to get the alignment correct. During the reordering of English sentences, we store the index changes for the English words. After getting the alignment trained on the reordered English and original Pashto sentence pairs, we map the English words back to the original order, along with the learned alignment links. In this way, the alignment is ready to be combined with the baseline alignment and any other alternatives.

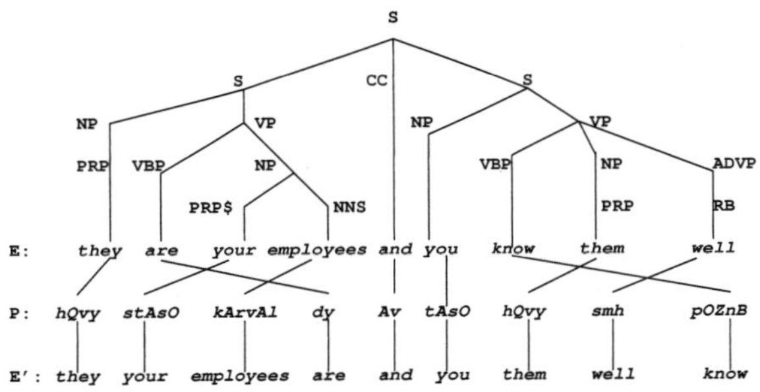

Figure 1: Alignment before/after VP-based reordering.

2.2 Stemming

Pashto is one of the morphologically rich languages. In addition to the linguistic knowledge applied in the syntactic reordering described above, we also utilize morphological analysis by applying stemming on both the English and Pashto sides. For English, we use Porter stemming (Porter, 1980), a widely applied algorithm to remove the common morphological and inflexional endings from words in English. For Pashto, we utilize a morphological decompostion algorithm that has been shown to be effective for Arabic speech recognition (Xiang et al., 2006). We start from a fixed set of affixes with 8 prefixes and 21 suffixes. The prefixes and suffixes are stripped off from the Pashto words under the two constraints:(1) Longest matched affixes first; (2) Remaining stem must be at least two characters long.

2.3 Partial Word

For low-resource languages, we usually suffer from the data sparsity issue. Recently, a simple method was presented in (Chiang et al., 2009), which keeps partial English and Urdu words in the training data for alignment training. This is similar to the stemming method, but is more heuristics-based, and does not rely on a set of available affixes. With the same motivation, we keep the first 4 characters of each English and Pashto word to generate one more alternative for the word alignment.

3 Confidence-Based Alignment Combination

Now we describe the algorithm to combine multiple sets of word alignments based on weighted confidence scores. Suppose a_{ijk} is an alignment link in the i-th set of alignments between the j-th source word and k-th target word in sentence pair (S,T). Similar to (Huang, 2009), we define the confidence of a_{ijk} as

$$c(a_{ijk}|S,T) = \sqrt{q_{s2t}(a_{ijk}|S,T)q_{t2s}(a_{ijk}|T,S)}, \quad (1)$$

where the source-to-target link posterior probability

$$q_{s2t}(a_{ijk}|S,T) = \frac{p_i(t_k|s_j)}{\sum_{k'=1}^{K} p_i(t_{k'}|s_j)}, \quad (2)$$

and the target-to-source link posterior probability $q_{t2s}(a_{ijk}|T,S)$ is defined similarly. $p_i(t_k|s_j)$ is the lexical translation probability between source word s_j and target word t_k in the i-th set of alignments.

Our alignment combination algorithm is as follows.

1. Each candidate link a_{jk} gets soft votes from N sets of alignments via weighted confidence scores:

$$v(a_{jk}|S,T) = \sum_{i=1}^{N} w_i * c(a_{ijk}|S,T), \quad (3)$$

   where the weight w_i for each set of alignment can be optimized under various criteria. In this work, we tune it on a hand-aligned development set to maximize the alignment F-score.

2. All candidates are sorted by soft votes in descending order and evaluated sequentially. A candidate link a_{jk} is included if one of the following is true:
   - Neither s_j nor t_k is aligned so far;
   - s_j is not aligned and its left or right neighboring word is aligned to t_k so far;
   - t_k is not aligned and its left or right neighboring word is aligned to s_j so far.

3. Repeat scanning all candidate links until no more links can be added.

In this way, those alignment links with higher confidence scores have higher priority to be included in the combined alignment.

4 Experiments

4.1 Baseline

Our training data contains around 70K English-Pashto sentence pairs released under the DARPA TRANSTAC project, with about 900K words on the English side. The baseline is a phrase-based MT system similar to (Koehn et al., 2003). We use GIZA++ (Och and Ney, 2000) to generate the baseline alignment for each direction and then apply grow-diagonal-final (*gdf*). The decoding weights are optimized with minimum error rate training (MERT) (Och, 2003) to maximize BLEU scores (Papineni et al., 2002). There are 2028 sentences in the tuning set and 1019 sentences in the test set, both with one reference. We use another 150 sentence pairs as a heldout hand-aligned set to measure the word alignment quality. The three sets of alignments described in Section 2 are generated on the same training data separately with GIZA++ and enhanced by *gdf* as for the baseline alignment. The English parse tree used for the syntactic reordering was produced by a maximum entropy based parser (Ratnaparkhi, 1997).

4.2 Improvement in Word Alignment

In Table 1 we show the precision, recall and F-score of each set of word alignments for the 150-sentence set. Using partial word provides the highest F-score among all individual alignments. The F-score is 5% higher than for the baseline alignment. The VP-based reordering itself does not improve the F-score, which could be due to the parse errors on the conversational training data. We experiment with three options (c_0, c_1, c_2) when combining the baseline and reordering-based alignments. In c_0, the weights w_i and confidence scores $c(a_{ijk}|S,T)$ in Eq. (3) are all set to 1. In c_1, we set confidence scores to 1, while tuning the weights with hill climbing to maximize the F-score on a hand-aligned tuning set. In c_2, we compute the confidence scores as in Eq. (1) and tune the weights as in c_1. The numbers in Table 1 show the effectiveness of having both weights and confidence scores during the combination.

Similarly, we combine the baseline with each of the other sets of alignments using c_2. They all result in significantly higher F-scores. We also generate alignments on VP-reordered partial words (X in Table 1) and compared $B + X$ and $B + V + P$. The better results with $B + V + P$ show the benefit of keeping the alignments as diversified as possible before the combination. Finally, we compare the proposed alignment combination c_2 with the heuristics-based method (*gdf*), where the latter starts from the intersection of all 4 sets of alignments and then applies grow-diagonal-final (Koehn et al., 2003) based on the links in the union. The proposed combination approach on $B + V + S + P$ results in close to 7% higher F-scores than the baseline and also 2% higher than *gdf*. We also notice that its higher F-score is mainly due to the higher precision, which should result from the consideration of confidence scores.

Alignment	Comb	P	R	F
Baseline		0.6923	0.6414	0.6659
V		0.6934	0.6388	0.6650
S		0.7376	0.6495	0.6907
P		0.7665	0.6643	0.7118
X		0.7615	0.6641	0.7095
B+V	c_0	0.7639	0.6312	0.6913
B+V	c_1	0.7645	0.6373	0.6951
B+V	c_2	0.7895	0.6505	0.7133
B+S	c_2	0.7942	0.6553	0.7181
B+P	c_2	0.8006	0.6612	0.7242
B+X	c_2	0.7827	0.6670	0.7202
B+V+P	c_2	0.7912	0.6755	0.7288
B+V+S+P	*gdf*	0.7238	0.7042	0.7138
B+V+S+P	c_2	0.7906	0.6852	**0.7342**

Table 1: Alignment precision, recall and F-score (B: baseline; V: VP-based reordering; S: stemming; P: partial word; X: VP-reordered partial word).

4.3 Improvement in MT Performance

In Table 2, we show the corresponding BLEU scores on the test set for the systems built on each set of word alignment in Table 1. Similar to the observation from Table 1, c_2 outperforms c_0 and c_1, and $B + V + S + P$ with c_2 outperforms $B + V + S + P$ with *gdf*. We also ran one experiment in which we concatenated all 4 sets of alignments into one big set (shown as *cat*). Overall, the BLEU score with confidence-based combination was increased by 1 point compared to the baseline, 0.6 compared to *gdf*, and 0.7 compared to *cat*. All results are statistically significant with $p < 0.05$ using the sign-test described in (Collins et al., 2005).

Alignment	Comb	Links	Phrase	BLEU
Baseline		963K	565K	12.67
V		965K	624K	12.82
S		915K	692K	13.04
P		906K	716K	13.30
X		911K	689K	13.00
B+V	c_0	870K	890K	13.20
B+V	c_1	865K	899K	13.32
B+V	c_2	874K	879K	13.60
B+S	c_2	864K	948K	13.41
B+P	c_2	863K	942K	13.40
B+X	c_2	871K	905K	13.37
B+V+P	c_2	880K	914K	13.60
B+V+S+P	*cat*	3749K	1258K	13.01
B+V+S+P	*gdf*	1021K	653K	13.14
B+V+S+P	c_2	907K	771K	**13.73**

Table 2: Improvement in BLEU scores (B: baseline; V: VP-based reordering; S: stemming; P: partial word; X: VP-reordered partial word).

5 Conclusions

In this work, we have presented a word alignment combination method that improves both the alignment quality and the translation performance. We generated multiple sets of diversified alignments based on linguistics, morphology, and heuristics, and demonstrated the effectiveness of combination on the English-to-Pashto translation task. We showed that the combined alignment significantly outperforms the baseline alignment with both higher F-score and higher BLEU score. The combination approach itself is not limited to any specific alignment. It provides a general framework that can take advantage of as many alignments as possible, which could differ in preprocessing, alignment modeling, or any other aspect.

Acknowledgments

This work was supported by the DARPA TRANSTAC program. We would like to thank Upendra Chaudhari, Sameer Maskey and Xiaoqiang Luo for providing useful resources and the anonymous reviewers for their constructive comments.

References

Necip Fazil Ayan and Bonnie J. Dorr. 2006. A maximum entropy approach to combining word alignments. In *Proc. HLT/NAACL*, June.

Peter Brown, Vincent Della Pietra, Stephen Della Pietra, and Robert Mercer. 1993. The mathematics of statistical machine translation: parameter estimation. *Computational Linguistics*, 19(2):263–311.

David Chiang, Kevin Knight, Samad Echihabi, et al. 2009. Isi/language weaver nist 2009 systems. In *Presentation at NIST MT 2009 Workshop*, August.

Michael Collins, Philipp Koehn, and Ivona Kučerová. 2005. Clause restructuring for statistical machine translation. In *Proc. of ACL*, pages 531–540.

Yonggang Deng and Bowen Zhou. 2009. Optimizing word alignment combination for phrase table training. In *Proc. ACL*, pages 229–232, August.

Elliott Franco Drábek and David Yarowsky. 2004. Improving bitext word alignments via syntax-based reordering of english. In *Proc. ACL*.

Alexander Fraser and Daniel Marcu. 2007. Getting the structure right for word alignment: Leaf. In *Proc. of EMNLP*, pages 51–60, June.

Ulf Hermjakob. 2009. Improved word alignment with statistics and linguistic heuristics. In *Proc. EMNLP*, pages 229–237, August.

Fei Huang. 2009. Confidence measure for word alignment. In *Proc. ACL*, pages 932–940, August.

Abraham Ittycheriah and Salim Roukos. 2005. A maximum entropy word aligner for arabic-english machine translation. In *Proc. of HLT/EMNLP*, pages 89–96, October.

Philipp Koehn, Franz Och, and Daniel Marcu. 2003. Statistical phrase-based translation. In *Proc. NAACL/HLT*.

Franz Josef Och and Hermann Ney. 2000. Improved statistical alignment models. In *Proc. of ACL*, pages 440–447, Hong Kong, China, October.

Franz Josef Och. 2003. Minimum error rate training in statistical machine translation. In *Proc. of ACL*, pages 160–167.

Kishore Papineni, Salim Roukos, Todd Ward, and Weijing Zhu. 2002. Bleu: a method for automatic evaluation of machine translation. In *Proc. of ACL*, pages 311–318.

Martin Porter. 1980. An algorithm for suffix stripping. In *Program*, volume 14, pages 130–137.

Adwait Ratnaparkhi. 1997. A linear observed time statistical parser based on maximum entropy models. In *Proc. of EMNLP*, pages 1–10.

Chao Wang, Michael Collins, and Philipp Koehn. 2007. Chinese syntactic reordering for statistical machine translation. In *Proc. EMNLP*, pages 737–745.

Bing Xiang, Kham Nguyen, Long Nguyen, Richard Schwartz, and John Makhoul. 2006. Morphological decomposition for arabic broadcast news transcription. In *Proc. ICASSP*.

Peng Xu, Jaeho Kang, Michael Ringgaard, and Franz Och. 2009. Using a dependency parser to improve smt for subject-object-verb languages. In *Proc. NAACL/HLT*, pages 245–253, June.

Efficient Path Counting Transducers for Minimum Bayes-Risk Decoding of Statistical Machine Translation Lattices

Graeme Blackwood, Adrià de Gispert, William Byrne
Machine Intelligence Laboratory
Cambridge University Engineering Department
Trumpington Street, CB2 1PZ, U.K.
{gwb24|ad465|wjb31}@cam.ac.uk

Abstract

This paper presents an efficient implementation of linearised lattice minimum Bayes-risk decoding using weighted finite state transducers. We introduce transducers to efficiently count lattice paths containing n-grams and use these to gather the required statistics. We show that these procedures can be implemented exactly through simple transformations of word sequences to sequences of n-grams. This yields a novel implementation of lattice minimum Bayes-risk decoding which is fast and exact even for very large lattices.

1 Introduction

This paper focuses on an exact implementation of the linearised form of lattice minimum Bayes-risk (LMBR) decoding using general purpose weighted finite state transducer (WFST) operations[1]. The LMBR decision rule in Tromble et al. (2008) has the form

$$\hat{E} = \underset{E' \in \mathcal{E}}{\text{argmax}} \left\{ \theta_0 |E'| + \sum_{u \in \mathcal{N}} \theta_u \#_u(E') p(u|\mathcal{E}) \right\} \quad (1)$$

where $\mathcal{E}$ is a lattice of translation hypotheses, $\mathcal{N}$ is the set of all n-grams in the lattice (typically, $n = 1 \ldots 4$), and the parameters θ are constants estimated on held-out data. The quantity $p(u|\mathcal{E})$ we refer to as the path posterior probability of the n-gram u. This particular posterior is defined as

$$p(u|\mathcal{E}) = p(\mathcal{E}_u|\mathcal{E}) = \sum_{E \in \mathcal{E}_u} P(E|F), \quad (2)$$

where $\mathcal{E}_u = \{E \in \mathcal{E} : \#_u(E) > 0\}$ is the subset of lattice paths containing the n-gram u at least once. It is the efficient computation of these path posterior n-gram probabilities that is the primary focus of this paper. We will show how general purpose WFST algorithms can be employed to efficiently compute $p(u|\mathcal{E})$ for all $u \in \mathcal{N}$.

Tromble et al. (2008) use Equation (1) as an approximation to the general form of statistical machine translation MBR decoder (Kumar and Byrne, 2004):

$$\hat{E} = \underset{E' \in \mathcal{E}}{\text{argmin}} \sum_{E \in \mathcal{E}} L(E, E') P(E|F) \quad (3)$$

The approximation replaces the sum over all paths in the lattice by a sum over lattice n-grams. Even though a lattice may have many n-grams, it is possible to extract and enumerate them exactly whereas this is often impossible for individual paths. Therefore, while the Tromble et al. (2008) linearisation of the gain function in the decision rule is an approximation, Equation (1) can be computed exactly even over very large lattices. The challenge is to do so efficiently.

If the quantity $p(u|\mathcal{E})$ had the form of a conditional expected count

$$c(u|\mathcal{E}) = \sum_{E \in \mathcal{E}} \#_u(E) P(E|F), \quad (4)$$

it could be computed efficiently using counting transducers (Allauzen et al., 2003). The statistic $c(u|\mathcal{E})$ counts the number of times an n-gram occurs on each path, accumulating the weighted count over all paths. By contrast, what is needed by the approximation in Equation (1) is to identify all paths containing an n-gram and accumulate their probabilities. The accumulation of probabilities at the path level, rather than the n-gram level, makes the exact computation of $p(u|\mathcal{E})$ hard.

Tromble et al. (2008) approach this problem by building a separate word sequence acceptor for each n-gram in $\mathcal{N}$ and intersecting this acceptor

[1]We omit an introduction to WFSTs for space reasons. See Mohri et al. (2008) for details of the general purpose WFST operations used in this paper.

Proceedings of the ACL 2010 Conference Short Papers, pages 27–32,
Uppsala, Sweden, 11-16 July 2010.

with the lattice to discard all paths that do not contain the n-gram; they then sum the probabilities of all paths in the filtered lattice. We refer to this as the *sequential method*, since $p(u|\mathcal{E})$ is calculated separately for each u in sequence.

Allauzen et al. (2010) introduce a transducer for simultaneous calculation of $p(u|\mathcal{E})$ for all unigrams $u \in \mathcal{N}_1$ in a lattice. This transducer is effective for finding path posterior probabilities of unigrams because there are relatively few unique unigrams in the lattice. As we will show, however, it is less efficient for higher-order n-grams.

Allauzen et al. (2010) use exact statistics for the unigram path posterior probabilities in Equation (1), but use the conditional expected counts of Equation (4) for higher-order n-grams. Their hybrid MBR decoder has the form

$$\begin{aligned}\hat{E} &= \underset{E' \in \mathcal{E}}{\operatorname{argmax}} \Big\{ \theta_0 |E'| \\ &+ \sum_{u \in \mathcal{N}: 1 \le |u| \le k} \theta_u \#_u(E') p(u|\mathcal{E}) \\ &+ \sum_{u \in \mathcal{N}: k < |u| \le 4} \theta_u \#_u(E') c(u|\mathcal{E}) \Big\}, \quad (5)\end{aligned}$$

where k determines the range of n-gram orders at which the path posterior probabilities $p(u|\mathcal{E})$ of Equation (2) and conditional expected counts $c(u|\mathcal{E})$ of Equation (4) are used to compute the expected gain. For $k < 4$, Equation (5) is thus an approximation to the approximation. In many cases it will be perfectly fine, depending on how closely $p(u|\mathcal{E})$ and $c(u|\mathcal{E})$ agree for higher-order n-grams. Experimentally, Allauzen et al. (2010) find this approximation works well at $k = 1$ for MBR decoding of statistical machine translation lattices. However, there may be scenarios in which $p(u|\mathcal{E})$ and $c(u|\mathcal{E})$ differ so that Equation (5) is no longer useful in place of the original Tromble et al. (2008) approximation.

In the following sections, we present an efficient method for simultaneous calculation of $p(u|\mathcal{E})$ for n-grams of a fixed order. While other fast MBR approximations are possible (Kumar et al., 2009), we show how the exact path posterior probabilities can be calculated and applied in the implementation of Equation (1) for efficient MBR decoding over lattices.

2 N-gram Mapping Transducer

We make use of a trick to count higher-order n-grams. We build transducer Φ_n to map word sequences to n-gram sequences of order n. Φ_n has a similar form to the WFST implementation of an n-gram language model (Allauzen et al., 2003). Φ_n includes for each n-gram $u = w_1^n$ arcs of the form:

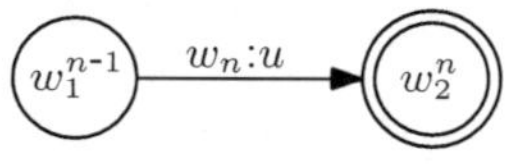

The n-gram lattice of order n is called $\mathcal{E}_n$ and is found by composing $\mathcal{E} \circ \Phi_n$, projecting on the output, removing ϵ-arcs, determinizing, and minimising. The construction of $\mathcal{E}_n$ is fast even for large lattices and is memory efficient. $\mathcal{E}_n$ itself may have more states than $\mathcal{E}$ due to the association of distinct n-gram histories with states. However, the counting transducer for unigrams is simpler than the corresponding counting transducer for higher-order n-grams. As a result, counting unigrams in $\mathcal{E}_n$ is easier than counting n-grams in $\mathcal{E}$.

3 Efficient Path Counting

Associated with each $\mathcal{E}_n$ we have a transducer Ψ_n which can be used to calculate the path posterior probabilities $p(u|\mathcal{E})$ for all $u \in \mathcal{N}_n$. In Figures 1 and 2 we give two possible forms[2] of Ψ_n that can be used to compute path posterior probabilities over n-grams $u_{1,2} \in \mathcal{N}_n$ for some n. No modification to the ρ-arc matching mechanism is required even in counting higher-order n-grams since all n-grams are represented as individual symbols after application of the mapping transducer Φ_n.

Transducer Ψ_n^L is used by Allauzen et al. (2010) to compute the exact unigram contribution to the conditional expected gain in Equation (5). For example, in counting paths that contain u_1, Ψ_n^L retains the *first* occurrence of u_1 and maps every other symbol to ϵ. This ensures that in any path containing a given u, only the first u is counted, avoiding multiple counting of paths.

We introduce an alternative path counting transducer Ψ_n^R that effectively deletes all symbols except the *last* occurrence of u on any path by ensuring that any paths in composition which count earlier instances of u do not end in a final state. Multiple counting is avoided by counting only the last occurrence of each symbol u on a path.

We note that initial ϵ:ϵ arcs in Ψ_n^L effectively create $|\mathcal{N}_n|$ copies of $\mathcal{E}_n$ in composition while searching for the first occurrence of each u. Com-

[2]The special composition symbol σ matches any arc; ρ matches any arc other than those with an explicit transition. See the OpenFst documentation: http://openfst.org

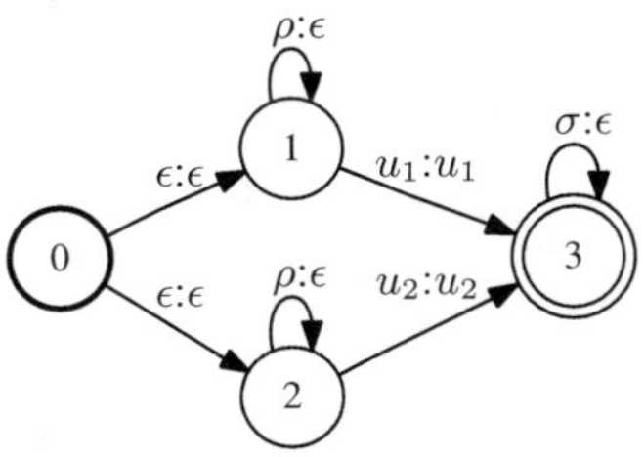

Figure 1: Path counting transducer Ψ_n^L matching first (left-most) occurrence of each $u \in \mathcal{N}_n$.

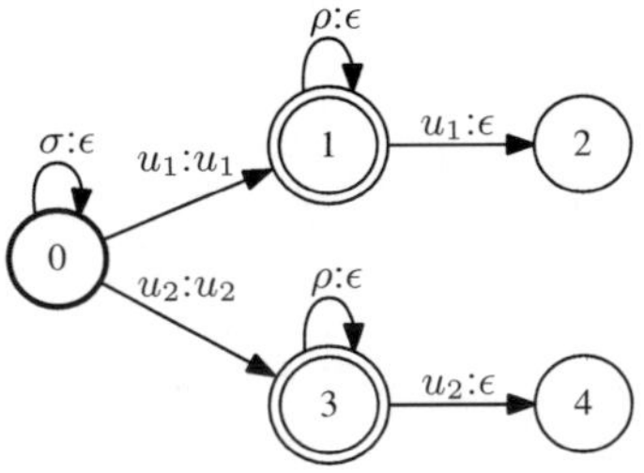

Figure 2: Path counting transducer Ψ_n^R matching last (right-most) occurrence of each $u \in \mathcal{N}_n$.

posing with Ψ_n^R creates a single copy of $\mathcal{E}_n$ while searching for the last occurrence of u; we find this to be much more efficient for large $\mathcal{N}_n$.

Path posterior probabilities are calculated over each $\mathcal{E}_n$ by composing with Ψ_n in the log semiring, projecting on the output, removing ϵ-arcs, determinizing, minimising, and pushing weights to the initial state (Allauzen et al., 2010). Using either Ψ_n^L or Ψ_n^R, the resulting counts acceptor is $\mathcal{X}_n$. It has a compact form with one arc from the start state for each $u_i \in \mathcal{N}_n$:

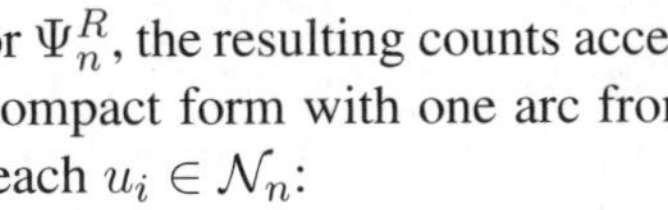

3.1 Efficient Path Posterior Calculation

Although $\mathcal{X}_n$ has a convenient and elegant form, it can be difficult to build for large $\mathcal{N}_n$ because the composition $\mathcal{E}_n \circ \Psi_n$ results in millions of states and arcs. The log semiring ϵ-removal and determinization required to sum the probabilities of paths labelled with each u can be slow.

However, if we use the proposed Ψ_n^R, then each path in $\mathcal{E}_n \circ \Psi_n^R$ has only one non-ϵ output label u and all paths leading to a given final state share the same u. A modified forward algorithm can be used to calculate $p(u|\mathcal{E})$ without the costly ϵ-removal and determinization. The modification simply requires keeping track of which symbol u is encountered along each path to a final state. More than one final state may gather probabilities for the same u; to compute $p(u|\mathcal{E})$ these probabilities are added. The forward algorithm requires that $\mathcal{E}_n \circ \Psi_n^R$ be topologically sorted; although sorting can be slow, it is still quicker than log semiring ϵ-removal and determinization.

The statistics gathered by the forward algorithm could also be gathered under the expectation semiring (Eisner, 2002) with suitably defined features. We take the view that the full complexity of that approach is not needed here, since only one symbol is introduced per path and per exit state.

Unlike $\mathcal{E}_n \circ \Psi_n^R$, the composition $\mathcal{E}_n \circ \Psi_n^L$ does not segregate paths by u such that there is a direct association between final states and symbols. The forward algorithm does not readily yield the per-symbol probabilities, although an arc weight vector indexed by symbols could be used to correctly aggregate the required statistics (Riley et al., 2009). For large $\mathcal{N}_n$ this would be memory intensive. The association between final states and symbols could also be found by label pushing, but we find this slow for large $\mathcal{E}_n \circ \Psi_n$.

4 Efficient Decoder Implementation

In contrast to Equation (5), we use the exact values of $p(u|\mathcal{E})$ for all $u \in \mathcal{N}_n$ at orders $n = 1 \ldots 4$ to compute

$$\hat{E} = \underset{E' \in \mathcal{E}}{\operatorname{argmin}} \left\{ \theta_0 |E'| + \sum_{n=1}^{4} g_n(E, E') \right\}, \quad (6)$$

where $g_n(E, E') = \sum_{u \in \mathcal{N}_n} \theta_u \#_u(E') p(u|\mathcal{E})$ using the exact path posterior probabilities at each order. We make acceptors Ω_n such that $\mathcal{E} \circ \Omega_n$ assigns order n partial gain $g_n(E, E')$ to all paths $E \in \mathcal{E}$. Ω_n is derived from Φ_n directly by assigning arc weight $\theta_u \times p(u|\mathcal{E})$ to arcs with output label u and then projecting on the input labels. For each n-gram $u = w_1^n$ in $\mathcal{N}_n$ arcs of Ω_n have the form:

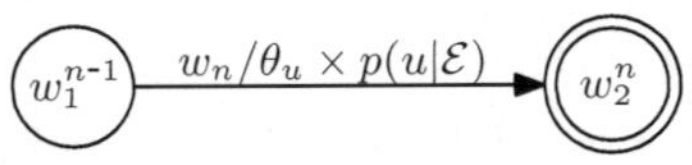

To apply θ_0 we make a copy of $\mathcal{E}$, called $\mathcal{E}_0$, with fixed weight θ_0 on all arcs. The decoder is formed as the composition $\mathcal{E}_0 \circ \Omega_1 \circ \Omega_2 \circ \Omega_3 \circ \Omega_4$ and $\hat{E}$ is extracted as the maximum cost string.

5 Lattice Generation for LMBR

Lattice MBR decoding performance and efficiency is evaluated in the context of the NIST

		mt0205tune	mt0205test	mt08nw	mt08ng
ML		54.2	53.8	51.4	36.3
k	0	52.6	52.3	49.8	34.5
	1	54.8	54.4	52.2	36.6
	2	54.9	54.5	52.4	36.8
	3	54.9	54.5	52.4	36.8
LMBR		55.0	54.6	52.4	36.8

Table 1: BLEU scores for Arabic→English maximum likelihood translation (ML), MBR decoding using the hybrid decision rule of Equation (5) at $0 \leq k \leq 3$, and regular linearised lattice MBR (LMBR).

		mt0205tune	mt0205test	mt08nw	mt08ng
Posteriors	sequential	3160	3306	2090	3791
	Ψ_n^L	6880	7387	4201	8796
	Ψ_n^R	1746	1789	1182	2787
Decoding	sequential	4340	4530	2225	4104
	Ψ_n	284	319	118	197
Total	sequential	7711	8065	4437	8085
	Ψ_n^L	7458	8075	4495	9199
	Ψ_n^R	2321	2348	1468	3149

Table 2: Time in seconds required for path posterior n-gram probability calculation and LMBR decoding using sequential method and left-most (Ψ_n^L) or right-most (Ψ_n^R) counting transducer implementations.

Arabic→English machine translation task[3]. The development set mt0205tune is formed from the odd numbered sentences of the NIST MT02–MT05 testsets; the even numbered sentences form the validation set mt0205test. Performance on NIST MT08 newswire (mt08nw) and newsgroup (mt08ng) data is also reported.

First-pass translation is performed using HiFST (Iglesias et al., 2009), a hierarchical phrase-based decoder. Word alignments are generated using MTTK (Deng and Byrne, 2008) over 150M words of parallel text for the constrained NIST MT08 Arabic→English track. In decoding, a Shallow-1 grammar with a single level of rule nesting is used and no pruning is performed in generating first-pass lattices (Iglesias et al., 2009).

The first-pass language model is a modified Kneser-Ney (Kneser and Ney, 1995) 4-gram estimated over the English parallel text and an 881M word subset of the GigaWord Third Edition (Graff et al., 2007). Prior to LMBR, the lattices are rescored with large stupid-backoff 5-gram language models (Brants et al., 2007) estimated over more than 6 billion words of English text.

The n-gram factors $\theta_0, \ldots, \theta_4$ are set according to Tromble et al. (2008) using unigram precision $p = 0.85$ and average recall ratio $r = 0.74$. Our translation decoder and MBR procedures are implemented using OpenFst (Allauzen et al., 2007).

[3]http://www.itl.nist.gov/iad/mig/tests/mt

6 LMBR Speed and Performance

Lattice MBR decoding performance is shown in Table 1. Compared to the maximum likelihood translation hypotheses (row ML), LMBR gives gains of +0.8 to +1.0 BLEU for newswire data and +0.5 BLEU for newsgroup data (row LMBR).

The other rows of Table 1 show the performance of LMBR decoding using the hybrid decision rule of Equation (5) for $0 \leq k \leq 3$. When the conditional expected counts $c(u|\mathcal{E})$ are used at all orders (i.e. $k = 0$), the hybrid decoder BLEU scores are considerably lower than even the ML scores. This poor performance is because there are many unigrams u for which $c(u|\mathcal{E})$ is much greater than $p(u|\mathcal{E})$. The consensus translation maximising the conditional expected gain is then dominated by unigram matches, significantly degrading LMBR decoding performance. Table 1 shows that for these lattices the hybrid decision rule is an accurate approximation to Equation (1) only when $k \geq 2$ and the exact contribution to the gain function is computed using the path posterior probabilities at orders $n = 1$ and $n = 2$.

We now analyse the efficiency of lattice MBR decoding using the exact path posterior probabilities of Equation (2) at all orders. We note that the sequential method and both simultaneous implementations using path counting transducers Ψ_n^L and Ψ_n^R yield the same hypotheses (allowing for numerical accuracy); they differ only in speed and memory usage.

Posteriors Efficiency Computation times for the steps in LMBR are given in Table 2. In calculating path posterior n-gram probabilities $p(u|\mathcal{E})$, we find that the use of Ψ_n^L is more than twice as slow as the sequential method. This is due to the difficulty of counting higher-order n-grams in large lattices. Ψ_n^L is effective for counting unigrams, however, since there are far fewer of them. Using Ψ_n^R is almost twice as fast as the sequential method. This speed difference is due to the simple forward algorithm. We also observe that for higher-order n, the composition $\mathcal{E}_n \circ \Psi_n^R$ requires less memory and produces a smaller machine than $\mathcal{E}_n \circ \Psi_n^L$. It is easier to count paths by the final occurrence of a symbol than by the first.

Decoding Efficiency Decoding times are significantly faster using Ω_n than the sequential method; average decoding time is around 0.1 seconds per sentence. The total time required for lattice MBR is dominated by the calculation of the path posterior n-gram probabilities, and this is a function of the number of n-grams in the lattice $|\mathcal{N}|$. For each sentence in mt0205tune, Figure 3 plots the total LMBR time for the sequential method (marked 'o') and for probabilities computed using Ψ_n^R (marked '+'). This compares the two techniques on a sentence-by-sentence basis. As $|\mathcal{N}|$ grows, the simultaneous path counting transducer is found to be much more efficient.

7 Conclusion

We have described an efficient and exact implementation of the linear approximation to LMBR using general WFST operations. A simple transducer was used to map words to sequences of n-grams in order to simplify the extraction of higher-order statistics. We presented a counting transducer Ψ_n^R that extracts the statistics required for all n-grams of order n in a single composition and allows path posterior probabilities to be computed efficiently using a modified forward procedure.

We take the view that even approximate search

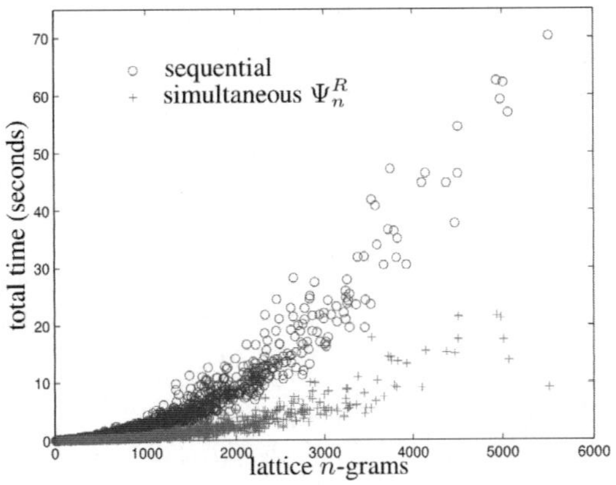

Figure 3: Total time in seconds versus $|\mathcal{N}|$.

criteria should be implemented exactly where possible, so that it is clear exactly what the system is doing. For machine translation lattices, conflating the values of $p(u|\mathcal{E})$ and $c(u|\mathcal{E})$ for higher-order n-grams might not be a serious problem, but in other scenarios – especially where symbol sequences are repeated multiple times on the same path – it may be a poor approximation.

We note that since much of the time in calculation is spent dealing with ϵ-arcs that are ultimately removed, an optimised composition algorithm that skips over such redundant structure may lead to further improvements in time efficiency.

Acknowledgments

This work was supported in part under the GALE program of the Defense Advanced Research Projects Agency, Contract No. HR0011-06-C-0022.

References

Cyril Allauzen, Mehryar Mohri, and Brian Roark. 2003. Generalized algorithms for constructing statistical language models. In *Proceedings of the 41st Meeting of the Association for Computational Linguistics*, pages 557–564.

Cyril Allauzen, Michael Riley, Johan Schalkwyk, Wojciech Skut, and Mehryar Mohri. 2007. OpenFst: a general and efficient weighted finite-state transducer library. In *Proceedings of the 9th International Conference on Implementation and Application of Automata*, pages 11–23. Springer.

Cyril Allauzen, Shankar Kumar, Wolfgang Macherey, Mehryar Mohri, and Michael Riley. 2010. Expected sequence similarity maximization. In *Human Language Technologies 2010: The 11th Annual Conference of the North American Chapter of the Association for Computational Linguistics*, Los Angeles, California, June.

Thorsten Brants, Ashok C. Popat, Peng Xu, Franz J. Och, and Jeffrey Dean. 2007. Large language models in machine translation. In *Proceedings of the 2007 Joint Conference on Empirical Methods in Natural Language Processing and Computational Natural Language Learning*, pages 858–867.

Yonggang Deng and William Byrne. 2008. HMM word and phrase alignment for statistical machine translation. *IEEE Transactions on Audio, Speech, and Language Processing*, 16(3):494–507.

Jason Eisner. 2002. Parameter estimation for probabilistic finite-state transducers. In *Proceedings of the 40th Annual Meeting of the Association for Computational Linguistics (ACL)*, pages 1–8, Philadelphia, July.

David Graff, Junbo Kong, Ke Chen, and Kazuaki Maeda. 2007. English Gigaword Third Edition.

Gonzalo Iglesias, Adrià de Gispert, Eduardo R. Banga, and William Byrne. 2009. Hierarchical phrase-based translation with weighted finite state transducers. In *Proceedings of Human Language Technologies: The 2009 Annual Conference of the North American Chapter of the Association for Computational Linguistics*, pages 433–441, Boulder, Colorado, June. Association for Computational Linguistics.

R. Kneser and H. Ney. 1995. Improved backing-off for m-gram language modeling. In *Acoustics, Speech, and Signal Processing*, pages 181–184.

Shankar Kumar and William Byrne. 2004. Minimum Bayes-risk decoding for statistical machine translation. In *Proceedings of Human Language Technologies: The 2004 Annual Conference of the North American Chapter of the Association for Computational Linguistics*, pages 169–176.

Shankar Kumar, Wolfgang Macherey, Chris Dyer, and Franz Och. 2009. Efficient minimum error rate training and minimum bayes-risk decoding for translation hypergraphs and lattices. In *Proceedings of the Joint Conference of the 47th Annual Meeting of the Association for Computational Linguistics and the 4th International Joint Conference on Natural Language Processing of the AFNLP*, pages 163–171, Suntec, Singapore, August. Association for Computational Linguistics.

M. Mohri, F.C.N. Pereira, and M. Riley. 2008. Speech recognition with weighted finite-state transducers. *Handbook on Speech Processing and Speech Communication*.

Michael Riley, Cyril Allauzen, and Martin Jansche. 2009. OpenFst: An Open-Source, Weighted Finite-State Transducer Library and its Applications to Speech and Language. In *Proceedings of Human Language Technologies: The 2009 Annual Conference of the North American Chapter of the Association for Computational Linguistics, Companion Volume: Tutorial Abstracts*, pages 9–10, Boulder, Colorado, May. Association for Computational Linguistics.

Roy Tromble, Shankar Kumar, Franz Och, and Wolfgang Macherey. 2008. Lattice Minimum Bayes-Risk decoding for statistical machine translation. In *Proceedings of the 2008 Conference on Empirical Methods in Natural Language Processing*, pages 620–629, Honolulu, Hawaii, October. Association for Computational Linguistics.

The Same-head Heuristic for Coreference

Micha Elsner and Eugene Charniak
Brown Laboratory for Linguistic Information Processing (BLLIP)
Brown University
Providence, RI 02912
{melsner,ec}@cs.brown.edu

Abstract

We investigate coreference relationships between NPs with the same head noun. It is relatively common in unsupervised work to assume that such pairs are coreferent– but this is not always true, especially if realistic mention detection is used. We describe the distribution of non-coreferent same-head pairs in news text, and present an unsupervised generative model which learns not to link some same-head NPs using syntactic features, improving precision.

1 Introduction

Full NP coreference, the task of discovering which non-pronominal NPs in a discourse refer to the same entity, is widely known to be challenging. In practice, however, most work focuses on the subtask of linking NPs with different head words. Decisions involving NPs with the same head word have not attracted nearly as much attention, and many systems, especially unsupervised ones, operate under the assumption that all same-head pairs corefer. This is by no means always the case– there are several systematic exceptions to the rule. In this paper, we show that these exceptions are fairly common, and describe an unsupervised system which learns to distinguish them from coreferent same-head pairs.

There are several reasons why relatively little attention has been paid to same-head pairs. Primarily, this is because they are a comparatively easy subtask in a notoriously difficult area; Stoyanov et al. (2009) shows that, among NPs headed by common nouns, those which have an exact match earlier in the document are the easiest to resolve (variant MUC score .82 on MUC-6) and while those with partial matches are quite a bit harder (.53), by far the worst performance is on those without any match at all (.27). This effect is magnified by most popular metrics for coreference, which reward finding links within large clusters more than they punish proposing spurious links, making it hard to improve performance by linking conservatively. Systems that use gold mention boundaries (the locations of NPs marked by annotators)[1] have even less need to worry about same-head relationships, since most NPs which disobey the conventional assumption are not marked as mentions.

In this paper, we count how often same-head pairs fail to corefer in the MUC-6 corpus, showing that gold mention detection hides most such pairs, but more realistic detection finds large numbers. We also present an unsupervised generative model which learns to make certain same-head pairs non-coreferent. The model is based on the idea that pronoun referents are likely to be salient noun phrases in the discourse, so we can learn about NP antecedents using pronominal antecedents as a starting point. Pronoun anaphora, in turn, is learnable from raw data (Cherry and Bergsma, 2005; Charniak and Elsner, 2009). Since our model links fewer NPs than the baseline, it improves precision but decreases recall. This tradeoff is favorable for CEAF, but not for b^3.

2 Related work

Unsupervised systems specify the assumption of same-head coreference in several ways: by as-

[1]Gold mention detection means something slightly different in the ACE corpus, where the system input contains every NP annotated with an entity type.

Proceedings of the ACL 2010 Conference Short Papers, pages 33–37,
Uppsala, Sweden, 11-16 July 2010. ©2010 Association for Computational Linguistics

sumption (Haghighi and Klein, 2009), using a head-prediction clause (Poon and Domingos, 2008), and using a sparse Dirichlet prior on word emissions (Haghighi and Klein, 2007). (These three systems, perhaps not coincidentally, use gold mentions.) An exception is Ng (2008), who points out that head identity is not an entirely reliable cue and instead uses exact string match (minus determiners) for common NPs and an alias detection system for proper NPs. This work uses mentions extracted with an NP chunker. No specific results are reported for same-head NPs. However, while using exact string match raises precision, many non-matching phrases are still coreferent, so this approach cannot be considered a full solution to the problem.

Supervised systems do better on the task, but not perfectly. Recent work (Stoyanov et al., 2009) attempts to determine the contributions of various categories of NP to coreference scores, and shows (as stated above) that common NPs which partially match an earlier mention are not well resolved by the state-of-the-art RECONCILE system, which uses pairwise classification. They also show that using gold mention boundaries makes the coreference task substantially easier, and argue that this experimental setting is "rather unrealistic".

3 Descriptive study: MUC-6

We begin by examining how often non-same-head pairs appear in the MUC-6 coreference dataset. To do so, we compare two artificial coreference systems: the **link-all** strategy links all, and only, full (non-pronominal) NP pairs with the same head which occur within 10 sentences of one another. The **oracle** strategy links NP pairs with the same head which occur within 10 sentences, but only if they are actually coreferent (according to the gold annotation)[2] The link-all system, in other words, does what most existing unsupervised systems do on the same-head subset of NPs, while the oracle system performs perfectly.

We compare our results to the gold standard using two metrics. b^3(Bagga and Baldwin, 1998) is a standard metric which calculates a precision and recall for each mention. The mention CEAF (Luo, 2005) constructs a maximum-weight bipartite matching between gold and proposed clusters, then gives the percentage of entities whose gold label and proposed label match. b^3 gives more weight to errors involving larger clusters (since these lower scores for several mentions at once); for mention CEAF, all mentions are weighted equally.

We annotate the data with the self-trained Charniak parser (McClosky et al., 2006), then extract mentions using three different methods. The **gold mentions** method takes only mentions marked by annotators. The **nps** method takes all base noun phrases detected by the parser. Finally, the **nouns** method takes all nouns, even those that do not head NPs; this method maximizes recall, since it does not exclude prenominals in phrases like "a **Bush** spokesman". (High-precision models of the internal structure of flat Penn Treebank-style NPs were investigated by Vadas and Curran (2007).) For each experimental setting, we show the number of **mentions** detected, and how many of them are **linked** to some antecedent by the system.

The data is shown in Table 1. b^3 shows a large drop in precision when all same-head pairs are linked; in fact, in the *nps* and *nouns* settings, only about half the same-headed NPs are actually coreferent (864 real links, 1592 pairs for *nps*). This demonstrates that non-coreferent same-head pairs not only occur, but are actually rather common in the dataset. The drop in precision is much less obvious in the *gold mentions* setting, however; most unlinked same-head pairs are not annotated as mentions in the gold data, which is one reason why systems run in this experimental setting can afford to ignore them.

Improperly linking same-head pairs causes a loss in precision, but scores are dominated by recall[3]. Thus, reporting b^3 helps to mask the impact of these pairs when examining the final f-score.

We roughly characterize what sort of same-headed NPs are non-coreferent by hand-examining 100 randomly selected pairs. 39 pairs denoted different entities ("recent employees" vs "employees who have worked for longer") disambiguated by modifiers or sometimes by discourse position. The next largest group (24) consists of time and measure phrases like "ten miles". 12 pairs refer to parts or quantities

[2]The choice of 10 sentences as the window size captures most, but not all, of the available recall. Using *nouns* mention detection, it misses 117 possible same-head links, or about 10%. However, precision drops further as the window size increases.

[3]This bias is exaggerated for systems which only link same-head pairs, but continues to apply to real systems; for instance (Haghighi and Klein, 2009) has a b^3 precision of 84 and recall of 67.

	Mentions	Linked	b^3 pr	rec	F	mention CEAF
Gold mentions						
Oracle	1929	**1164**	100	32.3	**48.8**	**54.4**
Link all	1929	**1182**	80.6	31.7	**45.5**	**53.8**
Alignment	1929	495	93.7	22.1	35.8	40.5
NPs						
Oracle	3993	**864**	100	30.6	**46.9**	**73.4**
Link all	3993	**1592**	67.2	29.5	**41.0**	**62.2**
Alignment	3993	518	87.2	24.7	38.5	67.0
Nouns						
Oracle	5435	**1127**	100	41.5	**58.6**	**83.5**
Link all	5435	**2541**	56.6	40.9	**45.7**	**67.0**
Alignment	5435	935	83.0	32.8	47.1	74.4

Table 1: Oracle, system and baseline scores on MUC-6 test data. **Gold mentions leave little room for improvement** between baseline and oracle; **detecting more mentions widens the gap between them**. With realistic mention detection, precision and CEAF scores improve over baselines, while recall and f-scores drop.

("members of..."), and 12 contained a generic ("In a corporate campaign, a union tries..."). 9 contained an annotator error. The remaining 4 were mistakes involving proper noun phrases headed by *Inc.* and other abbreviations; this case is easy to handle, but apparently not the primary cause of errors.

4 System

Our system is a version of the popular IBM model 2 for machine translation. To define our generative model, we assume that the parse trees for the entire document D are given, *except* for the subtrees with root nonterminal NP, denoted n_i, which our system will generate. These subtrees are related by a hidden set of alignments, a_i, which link each NP to another NP (which we call a *generator*) appearing somewhere before it in the document, or to a null antecedent. The set of potential generators G (which plays the same role as the source-language text in MT) is taken to be all the NPs occurring within 10 sentences of the target, plus a special null antecedent which plays the same role as the null word in machine translation– it serves as a dummy generator for NPs which are unrelated to any real NP in G.

The generative process fills in all the NP nodes in order, from left to right. This process ensures that, when generating node n_i, we have already filled in all the NPs in the set G (since these all precede n_i). When deciding on a generator for NP n_i, we can extract features characterizing its relationship to a potential generator g_j. These features, which we denote $f(n_i, g_j, D)$, may depend on their relative position in the document D, and on any features of g_j, since we have already generated its tree. However, we cannot extract features from the subtree under n_i, since we have yet to generate it!

As usual for IBM models, we learn using EM, and we need to start our alignment function off with a good initial set of parameters. Since antecedents of NPs and pronouns (both salient NPs) often occur in similar syntactic environments, we use an alignment function for pronoun coreference as a starting point. This alignment can be learned from raw data, making our approach unsupervised.

We take the pronoun model of Charniak and Elsner (2009)[4] as our starting point. We re-express it in the IBM framework, using a log-linear model for our alignment. Then our alignment (parameterized by feature weights w) is:

$$p(a_i = j|G, D) \propto exp(f(n_i, g_j, D) \bullet w)$$

The weights w are learned by gradient descent on the log-likelihood. To use this model within EM, we alternate an E-step where we calculate the expected alignments $E[a_i = j]$, then an M-step where we run gradient descent. (We have also had some success with stepwise EM as in (Liang and Klein, 2009), but this requires some tuning to work properly.)

[4]Downloaded from http://bllip.cs.brown.edu.

As features, we take the same features as Charniak and Elsner (2009): sentence and word-count distance between n_i and g_j, sentence position of each, syntactic role of each, and head type of g_j (proper, common or pronoun). We add binary features for the nonterminal directly over g_j (NP, VP, PP, any S type, or other), the type of phrases modifying g_j (proper nouns, phrasals (except QP and PP), QP, PP-of, PP-other, other modifiers, or nothing), and the type of determiner of g_j (possessive, definite, indefinite, deictic, other, or nothing). We designed this feature set to distinguish prominent NPs in the discourse, and also to be able to detect abstract or partitive phrases by examining modifiers and determiners.

To produce full NPs and learn same-head coreference, we focus on learning a good alignment using the pronoun model as a starting point. For translation, we use a trivial model, $p(n_i|g_{a_i}) = 1$ if the two have the same head, and 0 otherwise, except for the null antecedent, which draws heads from a multinomial distribution over words.

While we could learn an alignment and then treat all generators as antecedents, so that only NPs aligned to the null antecedent were not labeled coreferent, in practice this model would align nearly all the same-head pairs. This is true because many words are "bursty"; the probability of a second occurrence given the first is higher than the a priori probability of occurrence (Church, 2000). Therefore, our model is actually a mixture of two IBM models, p_C and p_N, where p_C produces NPs with antecedents and p_N produces pairs that share a head, but are not coreferent. To break the symmetry, we allow p_C to use any parameters w, while p_N uses a uniform alignment, $w \equiv \vec{0}$. We interpolate between these two models with a constant λ, the single manually set parameter of our system, which we fixed at .9.

The full model, therefore, is:

$$
\begin{aligned}
p(n_i|G,D) =& \lambda p_T(n_i|G,D) \\
&+ (1-\lambda)p_N(n_i|G,D) \\
p_T(n_i|G,D) =& \frac{1}{Z}\sum_{j \in G} exp(f(n_i, g_j, D) \bullet w) \\
&\times \mathbb{I}\{head(n_i) = head(j)\} \\
p_T(n_i|G,D) =& \sum_{j \in G} \frac{1}{|G|}\mathbb{I}\{head(n_i) = head(g_j)\}
\end{aligned}
$$

NPs for which the maximum-likelihood generator (the largest term in either of the sums) is from p_T and is not the null antecedent are marked as coreferent to the generator. Other NPs are marked not coreferent.

5 Results

Our results on the MUC-6 formal test set are shown in Table 1. In all experimental settings, the model improves precision over the baseline while decreasing recall– that is, it misses some legitimate coreferent pairs while correctly excluding many of the spurious ones. Because of the precision-recall tradeoff at which the systems operate, this results in reduced b^3 and link F. However, for the *nps* and *nouns* settings, where the parser is responsible for finding mentions, the tradeoff is positive for the CEAF metrics. For instance, in the *nps* setting, it improves over baseline by 57%.

As expected, the model does poorly in the gold mentions setting, doing worse than baseline on both metrics. Although it is possible to get very high precision in this setting, the model is far too conservative, linking less than half of the available mentions to anything, when in fact about 60% of them are coreferent. As we explain above, this experimental setting makes it mostly unnecessary to worry about non-coreferent same-head pairs because the MUC-6 annotators don't often mark them.

6 Conclusions

While same-head pairs are easier to resolve than same-other pairs, they are still non-trivial and deserve further attention in coreference research. To effectively measure their effect on performance, researchers should report multiple metrics, since under b^3 the link-all heuristic is extremely difficult to beat. It is also important to report results using a realistic mention detector as well as gold mentions.

Acknowledgements

We thank Jean Carletta for the SWITCHBOARD annotations, and Dan Jurafsky and eight anonymous reviewers for their comments and suggestions. This work was funded by a Google graduate fellowship.

References

Amit Bagga and Breck Baldwin. 1998. Algorithms for scoring coreference chains. In *LREC Workshop on Linguistics Coreference*, pages 563–566.

Eugene Charniak and Micha Elsner. 2009. EM works for pronoun anaphora resolution. In *Proceedings of EACL*, Athens, Greece.

Colin Cherry and Shane Bergsma. 2005. An Expectation Maximization approach to pronoun resolution. In *Proceedings of CoNLL*, pages 88–95, Ann Arbor, Michigan.

Kenneth W. Church. 2000. Empirical estimates of adaptation: the chance of two Noriegas is closer to p/2 than p^2. In *Proceedings of ACL*, pages 180–186.

Aria Haghighi and Dan Klein. 2007. Unsupervised coreference resolution in a nonparametric Bayesian model. In *Proceedings of ACL*, pages 848–855.

Aria Haghighi and Dan Klein. 2009. Simple coreference resolution with rich syntactic and semantic features. In *Proceedings of EMNLP*, pages 1152–1161.

Percy Liang and Dan Klein. 2009. Online EM for unsupervised models. In *HLT-NAACL*.

Xiaoqiang Luo. 2005. On coreference resolution performance metrics. In *Proceedings of HLT-EMNLP*, pages 25–32, Morristown, NJ, USA. Association for Computational Linguistics.

David McClosky, Eugene Charniak, and Mark Johnson. 2006. Effective self-training for parsing. In *Proceedings of HLT-NAACL*, pages 152–159.

Vincent Ng. 2008. Unsupervised models for coreference resolution. In *Proceedings of EMNLP*, pages 640–649, Honolulu, Hawaii. Association for Computational Linguistics.

Hoifung Poon and Pedro Domingos. 2008. Joint unsupervised coreference resolution with Markov Logic. In *Proceedings of EMNLP*, pages 650–659, Honolulu, Hawaii, October. Association for Computational Linguistics.

Veselin Stoyanov, Nathan Gilbert, Claire Cardie, and Ellen Riloff. 2009. Conundrums in noun phrase coreference resolution: Making sense of the state-of-the-art. In *Proceedings of ACL-IJCNLP*, pages 656–664, Suntec, Singapore, August. Association for Computational Linguistics.

David Vadas and James Curran. 2007. Adding noun phrase structure to the penn treebank. In *Proceedings of ACL*, pages 240–247, Prague, Czech Republic, June. Association for Computational Linguistics.

Authorship Attribution Using Probabilistic Context-Free Grammars

Sindhu Raghavan Adriana Kovashka Raymond Mooney
Department of Computer Science
The University of Texas at Austin
1 University Station C0500
Austin, TX 78712-0233, USA
{sindhu,adriana,mooney}@cs.utexas.edu

Abstract

In this paper, we present a novel approach for authorship attribution, the task of identifying the author of a document, using probabilistic context-free grammars. Our approach involves building a probabilistic context-free grammar for each author and using this grammar as a language model for classification. We evaluate the performance of our method on a wide range of datasets to demonstrate its efficacy.

1 Introduction

Natural language processing allows us to build language models, and these models can be used to distinguish between languages. In the context of written text, such as newspaper articles or short stories, the author's style could be considered a distinct "language." Authorship attribution, also referred to as authorship identification or prediction, studies strategies for discriminating between the styles of different authors. These strategies have numerous applications, including settling disputes regarding the authorship of old and historically important documents (Mosteller and Wallace, 1984), automatic plagiarism detection, determination of document authenticity in court (Juola and Sofko, 2004), cyber crime investigation (Zheng et al., 2009), and forensics (Luyckx and Daelemans, 2008).

The general approach to authorship attribution is to extract a number of style markers from the text and use these style markers as features to train a classifier (Burrows, 1987; Binongo and Smith, 1999; Diederich et al., 2000; Holmes and Forsyth, 1995; Joachims, 1998; Mosteller and Wallace, 1984). These style markers could include the frequencies of certain characters, function words, phrases or sentences. Peng et al. (2003) build a character-level n-gram model for each author. Stamatatos et al. (1999) and Luyckx and Daelemans (2008) use a combination of word-level statistics and part-of-speech counts or n-grams. Baayen et al. (1996) demonstrate that the use of syntactic features from parse trees can improve the accuracy of authorship attribution. While there have been several approaches proposed for authorship attribution, it is not clear if the performance of one is better than the other. Further, it is difficult to compare the performance of these algorithms because they were primarily evaluated on different datasets. For more information on the current state of the art for authorship attribution, we refer the reader to a detailed survey by Stamatatos (2009).

We further investigate the use of syntactic information by building complete models of each author's syntax to distinguish between authors. Our approach involves building a probabilistic context-free grammar (PCFG) for each author and using this grammar as a language model for classification. Experiments on a variety of corpora including poetry and newspaper articles on a number of topics demonstrate that our PCFG approach performs fairly well, but it only outperforms a bigram language model on a couple of datasets (e.g. poetry). However, combining our approach with other methods results in an ensemble that performs the best on most datasets.

2 Authorship Attribution using PCFG

We now describe our approach to authorship attribution. Given a training set of documents from different authors, we build a PCFG for each author based on the documents they have written. Given a test document, we parse it using each author's grammar and assign it to the author whose PCFG produced the highest likelihood for the document.

In order to build a PCFG, a standard statistical parser takes a corpus of parse trees of sentences as training input. Since we do not have access to authors' documents annotated with parse trees, we use a statistical parser trained on a generic

Proceedings of the ACL 2010 Conference Short Papers, pages 38–42,
Uppsala, Sweden, 11-16 July 2010.

corpus like the Wall Street Journal (WSJ) or Brown corpus from the Penn Treebank (http://www.cis.upenn.edu/~treebank/) to automatically annotate (i.e. treebank) the training documents for each author. In our experiments, we used the Stanford Parser (Klein and Manning, 2003b; Klein and Manning, 2003a) and the OpenNLP sentence segmenter (http://opennlp.sourceforge.net/). Our approach is summarized below:

Input – A training set of documents labeled with author names and a test set of documents with unknown authors.

1. Train a statistical parser on a generic corpus like the WSJ or Brown corpus.

2. Treebank each training document using the parser trained in Step 1.

3. Train a PCFG G_i for each author A_i using the treebanked documents for that author.

4. For each test document, compute its likelihood for each grammar G_i by multiplying the probability of the top PCFG parse for each sentence.

5. For each test document, find the author A_i whose grammar G_i results in the highest likelihood score.

Output – A label (author name) for each document in the test set.

3 Experimental Comparison

This section describes experiments evaluating our approach on several real-world datasets.

3.1 Data

We collected a variety of documents with known authors including news articles on a wide range of topics and literary works like poetry. We downloaded all texts from the Internet and manually removed extraneous information as well as titles, author names, and chapter headings. We collected several news articles from the New York Times online journal (http://global.nytimes.com/) on topics related to business, travel, and football. We also collected news articles on cricket from the ESPN cricinfo website (http://www.cricinfo.com). In addition, we collected poems from the Project Gutenberg website (http://www.gutenberg.org/wiki/Main_Page). We attempted to collect sets of documents on a shared topic written by multiple authors. This was done to ensure that the datasets truly tested authorship attribution as opposed to topic identification. However, since it is very difficult to find authors that write literary works on the same topic, the Poetry dataset exhibits higher topic variability than our news datasets. We had 5 different datasets in total – Football, Business, Travel, Cricket, and Poetry. The number of authors in our datasets ranged from 3 to 6.

For each dataset, we split the documents into training and test sets. Previous studies (Stamatatos et al., 1999) have observed that having unequal number of words per author in the training set leads to poor performance for the authors with fewer words. Therefore, we ensured that, in the training set, the total number of words per author was roughly the same. We would like to note that we could have also selected the training set such that the total number of sentences per author was roughly the same. However, since we would like to compare the performance of the PCFG-based approach with a bag-of-words baseline, we decided to normalize the training set based on the number of words, rather than sentences. For testing, we used 15 documents per author for datasets with news articles and 5 or 10 documents per author for the Poetry dataset. More details about the datasets can be found in Table 1.

Dataset	# authors	# words/auth	# docs/auth	# sent/auth
Football	3	14374.67	17.3	786.3
Business	6	11215.5	14.16	543.6
Travel	4	23765.75	28	1086
Cricket	4	23357.25	24.5	1189.5
Poetry	6	7261.83	24.16	329

Table 1: Statistics for the training datasets used in our experiments. The numbers in columns 3, 4 and 5 are averages.

3.2 Methodology

We evaluated our approach to authorship prediction on the five datasets described above. For news articles, we used the first 10 sections of the WSJ corpus, which consists of annotated news articles on finance, to build the initial statistical parser in

Step 1. For Poetry, we used 7 sections of the Brown corpus which consists of annotated documents from different areas of literature.

In the basic approach, we trained a PCFG model for each author based solely on the documents written by that author. However, since the number of documents per author is relatively low, this leads to very sparse training data. Therefore, we also augmented the training data by adding one, two or three sections of the WSJ or Brown corpus to each training set, and up-sampling (replicating) the data from the original author. We refer to this model as "PCFG-I", where I stands for *interpolation* since this effectively exploits linear interpolation with the base corpus to smooth parameters. Based on our preliminary experiments, we replicated the original data three or four times.

We compared the performance of our approach to bag-of-words classification and n-gram language models. When using bag-of-words, one generally removes commonly occurring "stop words." However, for the task of authorship prediction, we hypothesized that the frequency of specific stop words could provide useful information about the author's writing style. Preliminary experiments verified that eliminating stop words degraded performance; therefore, we did not remove them. We used the Maximum Entropy (MaxEnt) and Naive Bayes classifiers in the MALLET software package (McCallum, 2002) as initial baselines. We surmised that a discriminative classifier like MaxEnt might perform better than a generative classifier like Naive Bayes. However, when sufficient training data is not available, generative models are known to perform better than discriminative models (Ng and Jordan, 2001). Hence, we chose to compare our method to both Naive Bayes and MaxEnt.

We also compared the performance of the PCFG approach against n-gram language models. Specifically, we tried unigram, bigram and trigram models. We used the same background corpus mixing method used for the PCFG-I model to effectively smooth the n-gram models. Since a generative model like Naive Bayes that uses n-gram frequencies is equivalent to an n-gram language model, we also used the Naive Bayes classifier in MALLET to implement the n-gram models. Note that a Naive-Bayes bag-of-words model is equivalent to a unigram language model.

While the PCFG model captures the author's writing style at the syntactic level, it may not accurately capture lexical information. Since both syntactic and lexical information is presumably useful in capturing the author's overall writing style, we also developed an ensemble using a PCFG model, the bag-of-words MaxEnt classifier, and an n-gram language model. We linearly combined the confidence scores assigned by each model to each author, and used the combined score for the final classification. We refer to this model as "PCFG-E", where E stands for *ensemble*. We also developed another ensemble based on MaxEnt and n-gram language models to demonstrate the contribution of the PCFG model to the overall performance of PCFG-E. For each dataset, we report *accuracy*, the fraction of the test documents whose authors were correctly identified.

3.3 Results and Discussion

Table 2 shows the accuracy of authorship prediction on different datasets. For the n-gram models, we only report the results for the bigram model with smoothing (Bigram-I) as it was the best performing model for most datasets (except for Cricket and Poetry). For the Cricket dataset, the trigram-I model was the best performing n-gram model with an accuracy of 98.34%. Generally, a higher order n-gram model (n = 3 or higher) performs poorly as it requires a fair amount of smoothing due to the exponential increase in all possible n-gram combinations. Hence, the superior performance of the trigram-I model on the Cricket dataset was a surprising result. For the Poetry dataset, the unigram-I model performed best among the smoothed n-gram models at 81.8% accuracy. This is unsurprising because as mentioned above, topic information is strongest in the Poetry dataset, and it is captured well in the unigram model. For bag-of-words methods, we find that the generatively trained Naive Bayes model (unigram language model) performs better than or equal to the discriminatively trained MaxEnt model on most datasets (except for Business). This result is not suprising since our datasets are limited in size, and generative models tend to perform better than discriminative methods when there is very little training data available. Amongst the different baseline models (MaxEnt, Naive Bayes, Bigram-I), we find Bigram-I to be the best performing model (except for Cricket and Poetry). For both Cricket and Poetry, Naive Bayes

Dataset	MaxEnt	Naive Bayes	Bigram-I	PCFG	PCFG-I	PCFG-E	MaxEnt+Bigram-I
Football	84.45	86.67	86.67	**93.34**	80	91.11	86.67
Business	83.34	77.78	90.00	77.78	85.56	91.11	**92.22**
Travel	83.34	83.34	**91.67**	81.67	86.67	**91.67**	90.00
Cricket	91.67	**95.00**	91.67	86.67	91.67	**95.00**	93.34
Poetry	56.36	78.18	70.90	78.18	83.63	**87.27**	76.36

Table 2: Accuracy in % for authorship prediction on different datasets. Bigram-I refers to the bigram language model with smoothing. PCFG-E refers to the ensemble based on MaxEnt, Bigram-I, and PCFG-I. MaxEnt+Bigram-I refers to the ensemble based on MaxEnt and Bigram-I.

is the best performing baseline model. While discussing the performance of the PCFG model and its variants, we consider the best performing baseline model.

We observe that the basic PCFG model and the PCFG-I model do not usually outperform the best baseline method (except for Football and Poetry, as discussed below). For Football, the basic PCFG model outperforms the best baseline, while for Poetry, the PCFG-I model outperforms the best baseline. Further, the performance of the basic PCFG model is inferior to that of PCFG-I for most datasets, likely due to the insufficient training data used in the basic model. Ideally one would use more training documents, but in many domains it is impossible to obtain a large corpus of documents written by a single author. For example, as Luyckx and Daelemans (2008) argue, in forensics one would like to identify the authorship of documents based on a limited number of documents written by the author. Hence, we investigated smoothing techniques to improve the performance of the basic PCFG model. We found that the interpolation approach resulted in a substantial improvement in the performance of the PCFG model for all but the Football dataset (discussed below). However, for some datasets, even this improvement was not sufficient to outperform the best baseline.

The results for PCFG and PCFG-I demonstrate that syntactic information alone is generally a bit less accurate than using n-grams. In order to utilize *both* syntactic and lexical information, we developed PCFG-E as described above. We combined the best n-gram model (Bigram-I) and PCFG model (PCFG-I) with MaxEnt to build PCFG-E. For the Travel dataset, we find that the performance of the PCFG-E model is equal to that of the best constituent model (Bigram-I). For the remaining datasets, the performance of PCFG-E is better than the best constituent model. Furthermore, for the Football, Cricket and Poetry datasets this improvement is quite substantial. We now find that the performance of some variant of PCFG is always better than or equal to that of the best baseline. While the basic PCFG model outperforms the baseline for the Football dataset, PCFG-E outperforms the best baseline for the Poetry and Business datasets. For the Cricket and Travel datasets, the performance of the PCFG-E model equals that of the best baseline. In order to assess the statistical significance of any performance difference between the best PCFG model and the best baseline, we performed the McNemar's test, a non-parametric test for binomial variables (Rosner, 2005). We found that the difference in the performance of the two methods was not statistically significant at .05 significance level for any of the datasets, probably due to the small number of test samples.

The performance of PCFG and PCFG-I is particularly impressive on the Football and Poetry datasets. For the Football dataset, the basic PCFG model is the best performing PCFG model and it performs much better than other methods. It is surprising that smoothing using PCFG-I actually results in a drop in performance on this dataset. We hypothesize that the authors in the Football dataset may have very different syntactic writing styles that are effectively captured by the basic PCFG model. Smoothing the data apparently weakens this signal, hence causing a drop in performance. For Poetry, PCFG-I achieves much higher accuracy than the baselines. This is impressive given the much looser syntactic structure of poetry compared to news articles, and it indicates the value of syntactic information for distinguishing between literary authors.

Finally, we consider the specific contribution of the PCFG-I model towards the performance of the PCFG-E ensemble. Based on comparing the results for PCFG-E and MaxEnt+Bigram-I, we find that there is a drop in performance for most datasets when removing PCFG-I from the ensemble. This drop is quite substantial for the Football and Poetry datasets. This indicates that PCFG-I is contributing substantially to the performance of PCFG-E. Thus, it further illustrates the importance of broader syntactic information for the task of authorship attribution.

4 Future Work and Conclusions

In this paper, we have presented our ongoing work on authorship attribution, describing a novel approach that uses probabilistic context-free grammars. We have demonstrated that both syntactic and lexical information are useful in effectively capturing authors' overall writing style. To this end, we have developed an ensemble approach that performs better than the baseline models on several datasets. An interesting extension of our current approach is to consider discriminative training of PCFGs for each author. Finally, we would like to compare the performance of our method to other state-of-the-art approaches to authorship prediction.

Acknowledgments

Experiments were run on the Mastodon Cluster, provided by NSF Grant EIA-0303609.

References

H. Baayen, H. van Halteren, and F. Tweedie. 1996. Outside the cave of shadows: using syntactic annotation to enhance authorship attribution. *Literary and Linguistic Computing*, 11(3):121–132, September.

Binongo and Smith. 1999. A Study of Oscar Wilde's Writings. *Journal of Applied Statistics*, 26:781.

J Burrows. 1987. Word-patterns and Story-shapes: The Statistical Analysis of Narrative Style.

Joachim Diederich, Jörg Kindermann, Edda Leopold, and Gerhard Paass. 2000. Authorship Attribution with Support Vector Machines. *Applied Intelligence*, 19:2003.

D. I. Holmes and R. S. Forsyth. 1995. The Federalist Revisited: New Directions in Authorship Attribution. *Literary and Linguistic Computing*, 10:111–127.

Thorsten Joachims. 1998. Text categorization with Support Vector Machines: Learning with many relevant features. In *Proceedings of the 10th European Conference on Machine Learning (ECML)*, pages 137–142, Berlin, Heidelberg. Springer-Verlag.

Patrick Juola and John Sofko. 2004. Proving and Improving Authorship Attribution Technologies. In *Proceedings of Canadian Symposium for Text Analysis (CaSTA)*.

Dan Klein and Christopher D. Manning. 2003a. Accurate unlexicalized parsing. In *Proceedings of the 41st Annual Meeting on Association for Computational Linguistics (ACL)*, pages 423–430, Morristown, NJ, USA. Association for Computational Linguistics.

Dan Klein and Christopher D. Manning. 2003b. Fast Exact Inference with a Factored Model for Natural Language Parsing. In *Advances in Neural Information Processing Systems 15 (NIPS)*, pages 3–10. MIT Press.

Kim Luyckx and Walter Daelemans. 2008. Authorship Attribution and Verification with Many Authors and Limited Data. In *Proceedings of the 22nd International Conference on Computational Linguistics (COLING)*, pages 513–520, August.

Andrew Kachites McCallum. 2002. MALLET: A Machine Learning for Language Toolkit. http://mallet.cs.umass.edu.

Frederick Mosteller and David L. Wallace. 1984. *Applied Bayesian and Classical Inference: The Case of the Federalist Papers*. Springer-Verlag.

Andrew Y. Ng and Michael I. Jordan. 2001. On Discriminative vs. Generative classifiers: A comparison of logistic regression and naive Bayes. In *Advances in Neural Information Processing Systems 14 (NIPS)*, pages 841–848.

Fuchun Peng, Dale Schuurmans, Viado Keselj, and Shaojun Wang. 2003. Language Independent Authorship Attribution using Character Level Language Models. In *Proceedings of the 10th Conference of the European Chapter of the Association for Computational Linguistics (EACL)*.

Bernard Rosner. 2005. *Fundamentals of Biostatistics*. Duxbury Press.

E. Stamatatos, N. Fakotakis, and G. Kokkinakis. 1999. Automatic Authorship Attribution. In *Proceedings of the 9th Conference of the European Chapter of the Association for Computational Linguistics (EACL)*, pages 158–164, Morristown, NJ, USA. Association for Computational Linguistics.

E. Stamatatos. 2009. A Survey of Modern Authorship Attribution Methods. *Journal of the American Society for Information Science and Technology*, 60(3):538–556.

Rong Zheng, Yi Qin, Zan Huang, and Hsinchun Chen. 2009. Authorship Analysis in Cybercrime Investigation. *Lecture Notes in Computer Science*, 2665/2009:959.

The impact of interpretation problems on tutorial dialogue

Myroslava O. Dzikovska and **Johanna D. Moore**
School of Informatics, University of Edinburgh, Edinburgh, United Kingdom
{m.dzikovska,j.moore}@ed.ac.uk

Natalie Steinhauser and **Gwendolyn Campbell**
Naval Air Warfare Center Training Systems Division, Orlando, FL, USA
{natalie.steihauser,gwendolyn.campbell}@navy.mil

Abstract

Supporting natural language input may improve learning in intelligent tutoring systems. However, interpretation errors are unavoidable and require an effective recovery policy. We describe an evaluation of an error recovery policy in the BEETLE II tutorial dialogue system and discuss how different types of interpretation problems affect learning gain and user satisfaction. In particular, the problems arising from student use of non-standard terminology appear to have negative consequences. We argue that existing strategies for dealing with terminology problems are insufficient and that improving such strategies is important in future ITS research.

1 Introduction

There is a mounting body of evidence that student self-explanation and contentful talk in human-human tutorial dialogue are correlated with increased learning gain (Chi et al., 1994; Purandare and Litman, 2008; Litman et al., 2009). Thus, computer tutors that understand student explanations have the potential to improve student learning (Graesser et al., 1999; Jordan et al., 2006; Aleven et al., 2001; Dzikovska et al., 2008). However, understanding and correctly assessing the student's contributions is a difficult problem due to the wide range of variation observed in student input, and especially due to students' sometimes vague and incorrect use of domain terminology.

Many tutorial dialogue systems limit the range of student input by asking short-answer questions. This provides a measure of robustness, and previous evaluations of ASR in spoken tutorial dialogue systems indicate that neither word error rate nor concept error rate in such systems affect learning gain (Litman and Forbes-Riley, 2005; Pon-Barry et al., 2004). However, limiting the range of possible input limits the contentful talk that the students are expected to produce, and therefore may limit the overall effectiveness of the system.

Most of the existing tutoring systems that accept unrestricted language input use classifiers based on statistical text similarity measures to match student answers to open-ended questions with pre-authored anticipated answers (Graesser et al., 1999; Jordan et al., 2004; McCarthy et al., 2008). While such systems are robust to unexpected terminology, they provide only a very coarse-grained assessment of student answers. Recent research aims to develop methods that produce detailed analyses of student input, including correct, incorrect and missing parts (Nielsen et al., 2008; Dzikovska et al., 2008), because the more detailed assessments can help tailor tutoring to the needs of individual students.

While the detailed assessments of answers to open-ended questions are intended to improve potential learning, they also increase the probability of misunderstandings, which negatively impact tutoring and therefore negatively impact student learning (Jordan et al., 2009). Thus, appropriate error recovery strategies are crucially important for tutorial dialogue applications. We describe an evaluation of an implemented tutorial dialogue system which aims to accept unrestricted student input and limit misunderstandings by rejecting low confidence interpretations and employing a range of error recovery strategies depending on the cause of interpretation failure.

By comparing two different system policies, we demonstrate that with less restricted language input the rate of non-understanding errors impacts both learning gain and user satisfaction, and that problems arising from incorrect use of terminology have a particularly negative impact. A more detailed analysis of the results indicates that, even though we based our policy on an approach ef-

Proceedings of the ACL 2010 Conference Short Papers, pages 43–48,
Uppsala, Sweden, 11-16 July 2010. ©2010 Association for Computational Linguistics

fective in task-oriented dialogue (Hockey et al., 2003), many of our strategies were not successful in improving learning gain. At the same time, students appear to be aware that the system does not fully understand them even if it accepts their input without indicating that it is having interpretation problems, and this is reflected in decreased user satisfaction. We argue that this indicates that we need better strategies for dealing with terminology problems, and that accepting non-standard terminology without explicitly addressing the difference in acceptable phrasing may not be sufficient for effective tutoring.

In Section 2 we describe our tutoring system, and the two tutoring policies implemented for the experiment. In Section 3 we present experimental results and an analysis of correlations between different types of interpretation problems, learning gain and user satisfaction. Finally, in Section 4 we discuss the implications of our results for error recovery policies in tutorial dialogue systems.

2 Tutorial Dialogue System and Error Recovery Policies

This work is based on evaluation of BEETLE II (Dzikovska et al., 2010), a tutorial dialogue system which provides tutoring in basic electricity and electronics. Students read pre-authored materials, experiment with a circuit simulator, and then are asked to explain their observations. BEETLE II uses a deep parser together with a domain-specific diagnoser to process student input, and a deep generator to produce tutorial feedback automatically depending on the current tutorial policy. It also implements an error recovery policy to deal with interpretation problems.

Students currently communicate with the system via a typed chat interface. While typing removes the uncertainty and errors involved in speech recognition, expected student answers are considerably more complex and varied than in a typical spoken dialogue system. Therefore, a significant number of interpretation errors arise, primarily during the semantic interpretation process. These errors can lead to *non-understandings*, when the system cannot produce a syntactic parse (or a reasonable fragmentary parse), or when it does not know how to interpret an out-of-domain word; and *misunderstandings*, where a system arrives at an incorrect interpretation, due to either an incorrect attachment in the parse, an incorrect word sense assigned to an ambiguous word, or an incorrectly resolved referential expression.

Our approach to selecting an error recovery policy is to prefer non-understandings to misunderstandings. There is a known trade-off in spoken dialogue systems between allowing misunderstandings, i.e., cases in which a system accepts and acts on an incorrect interpretation of an utterance, and non-understandings, i.e., cases in which a system rejects an utterance as uninterpretable (Bohus and Rudnicky, 2005). Since misunderstandings on the part of a computer tutor are known to negatively impact student learning, and since in human-human tutorial dialogue the majority of student responses using unexpected terminology are classified as incorrect (Jordan et al., 2009), it would be a reasonable approach for a tutorial dialogue system to deal with potential interpretation problems by treating low-confidence interpretations as non-understandings and focusing on an effective non-understanding recovery policy.[1]

We implemented two different policies for comparison. Our baseline policy does not attempt any remediation or error recovery. All student utterances are passed through the standard interpretation pipeline, so that the results can be analyzed later. However, the system does not attempt to address the student content. Instead, regardless of the answer analysis, the system always uses a neutral acceptance and bottom out strategy, giving the student the correct answer every time, e.g., "OK. One way to phrase the correct answer is: the open switch creates a gap in the circuit". Thus, the students are never given any indication of whether they have been understood or not.

The full policy acts differently depending on the analysis of the student answer. For correct answers, it acknowledges the answer as correct and optionally restates it (see (Dzikovska et al., 2008) for details). For incorrect answers, it restates the correct portion of the answer (if any) and provides a hint to guide the student towards the completely correct answer. If the student's utterance cannot be interpreted, the system responds with a help message indicating the cause of the problem together with a hint. In both cases, after 3 unsuccessful attempts to address the problem the system uses the bottom out strategy and gives away the answer.

[1]While there is no confidence score from a speech recognizer, our system uses a combination of a parse quality score assigned by the parser and a set of consistency checks to determine whether an interpretation is sufficiently reliable.

The content of the bottom out is the same as in the baseline, except that the full system indicates clearly that the answer was incorrect or was not understood, e.g., "Not quite. Here is the answer: the open switch creates a gap in the circuit".

The help messages are based on the Targeted-Help approach successfully used in spoken dialogue (Hockey et al., 2003), together with the error classification we developed for tutorial dialogue (Dzikovska et al., 2009). There are 9 different error types, each associated with a different targeted help message. The goal of the help messages is to give the student as much information as possible as to why the system failed to understand them but without giving away the answer.

In comparing the two policies, we would expect that the students in both conditions would learn something, but that the learning gain and user satisfaction would be affected by the difference in policies. We hypothesized that students who receive feedback on their errors in the full condition would learn more compared to those in the baseline condition.

3 Evaluation

We collected data from 76 subjects interacting with the system. The subjects were randomly assigned to either the baseline (BASE) or the full (FULL) policy condition. Each subject took a pre-test, then worked through a lesson with the system, and then took a post-test and filled in a user satisfaction survey. Each session lasted approximately 4 hours, with 232 student language turns in FULL ($SD = 25.6$) and 156 in BASE ($SD = 2.02$). Additional time was taken by reading and interacting with the simulation environment. The students had little prior knowledge of the domain. The survey consisted of 63 questions on the 5-point Likert scale covering the lesson content, the graphical user interface, and tutor's understanding and feedback. For purposes of this study, we are using an averaged tutor score.

The average learning gain was 0.57 ($SD = 0.23$) in FULL, and 0.63 ($SD = 0.26$) in BASE. There was no significant difference in learning gain between conditions. Students liked BASE better: the average tutor evaluation score for FULL was 2.56 out of 5 ($SD = 0.65$), compared to 3.32 ($SD = 0.65$) in BASE. These results are significantly different (t-test, $p < 0.05$). In informal comments after the session many students said that they were frustrated when the system said that it did not understand them. However, some students in BASE also mentioned that they sometimes were not sure if the system's answer was correcting a problem with their answer, or simply phrasing it in a different way.

We used mean frequency of non-interpretable utterances (out of all student utterances in each session) to evaluate the effectiveness of the two different policies. On average, 14% of utterances in both conditions resulted in non-understandings.[2] The frequency of non-understandings was negatively correlated with learning gain in FULL: $r = -0.47, p < 0.005$, but not significantly correlated with learning gain in BASE: $r = -0.09, p = 0.59$. However, in both conditions the frequency of non-understandings was negatively correlated with user satisfaction: FULL $r = -0.36, p = 0.03$, BASE $r = -0.4, p = 0.01$. Thus, even though in BASE the system did not indicate non-understanding, students were negatively affected. That is, they were not satisfied with the policy that did not directly address the interpretation problems. We discuss possible reasons for this below.

We investigated the effect of different types of interpretation errors using two criteria. First, we checked whether the mean frequency of errors was reduced between BASE and FULL for each individual strategy. The reduced frequency means that the recovery strategy for this particular error type is effective in reducing the error frequency. Second, we looked for the cases where the frequency of a given error type is negatively correlated with either learning gain or user satisfaction. This is provides evidence that such errors are negatively impacting the learning process, and therefore improving recovery strategies for those error types is likely to improve overall system effectiveness,

The results, shown in Table 1, indicate that the majority of interpretation problems are not significantly correlated with learning gain. However, several types of problems appear to be particularly significant, and are all related to improper use of domain terminology. These were *irrelevant_answer*, *no_appr_terms*, *selectional_restriction_failure* and *program_error*.

An *irrelevant_answer* error occurs when the student makes a statement that uses domain termi-

[2] We do not know the percentage of misunderstandings or concept error rate as yet. We are currently annotating the data with the goal to evaluate interpretation correctness.

	full			baseline		
error type	mean freq. (std. dev)	satisfaction r	gain r	mean freq (std. dev)	satisfaction r	gain r
irrelevant_answer	0.008 (0.01)	-0.08	-0.19	0.012 (0.01)	-0.07	-0.47**
no_appr_ terms	0.005 (0.01)	-0.57**	-0.42**	0.003 (0.01)	-0.38**	-0.01
selectional_restr_failure	0.032 (0.02)	-0.12	-0.55**	0.040 (0.03)	0.13	0.26*
program_error	0.002 (0.003)	0.02	0.26	0.003 (0.003)	0	-0.35**
unknown_word	0.023 (0.01)	0.05	-0.21	0.024 (0.02)	-0.15	-0.09
disambiguation_failure	0.013 (0.01)	-0.04	0.02	0.007 (0.01)	-0.18	0.19
no_parse	0.019 (0.01)	-0.14	-0.08	0.022(0.02)	-0.3*	0.01
partial_interpretation	0.004 (0.004)	-0.11	-0.01	0.004 (0.005)	-0.19	0.22
reference_failure	0.012 (0.02)	-0.31*	-0.09	0.017 (0.01)	-0.15	-0.23
Overall	0.134 (0.05)	-0.36**	-0.47**	0.139 (0.04)	-0.4**	-0.09

Table 1: Correlations between frequency of different error types and student learning gain and satisfaction. ** - correlation is significant with $p < 0.05$, * - with $p <= 0.1$.

nology but does not appear to answer the system's question directly. For example, the expected answer to "In circuit 1, which components are in a closed path?" is "the bulb". Some students misread the question and say "Circuit 1 is closed." If that happens, in FULL the system says "Sorry, this isn't the form of answer that I expected. I am looking for a component", pointing out to the student the kind of information it is looking for. The BASE system for this error, and for all other errors discussed below, gives away the correct answer without indicating that there was a problem with interpreting the student's utterance, e.g., "OK, the correct answer is the bulb."

The *no_appr_terms* error happens when the student is using terminology inappropriate for the lesson in general. Students are expected to learn to explain everything in terms of connections and terminal states. For example, the expected answer to "What is voltage?" is "the difference in states between two terminals". If instead the student says "Voltage is electricity", FULL responds with "I am sorry, I am having trouble understanding. I see no domain concepts in your answer. Here's a hint: your answer should mention a terminal." The motivation behind this strategy is that in general, it is very difficult to reason about vaguely used domain terminology. We had hoped that by telling the student that the content of their utterance is outside the domain as understood by the system, and hinting at the correct terms to use, the system would guide students towards a better answer.

Selectional_restr_failure errors are typically due to incorrect terminology, when the students phrased answers in a way that contradicted the system's domain knowledge. For example, the system can reason about damaged bulbs and batteries, and open and closed paths. So if the student says "The path is damaged", the FULL system would respond with "I am sorry, I am having trouble understanding. Paths cannot be damaged. Only bulbs and batteries can be damaged."

Program_error were caused by faults in the underlying network software, but usually occurred when the student was using extremely long and complicated utterances.

Out of the four important error types described above, only the strategy for *irrelevant_answer* was effective: the frequency of *irrelevant_answer* errors is significantly higher in BASE (t-test, $p < 0.05$), and it is negatively correlated with learning gain in BASE. The frequencies of other error types did not significantly differ between conditions.

However, one other finding is particularly interesting: the frequency of *no_appr_terms* errors is negatively correlated with user satisfaction in BASE. This indicates that simply accepting the student's answer when they are using incorrect terminology and exposing them to the correct answer is not the best strategy, possibly because the students are noticing the unexplained lack of alignment between their utterance and the system's answer.

4 Discussion and Future Work

As discussed in Section 1, previous studies of short-answer tutorial dialogue systems produced a counter-intuitive result: measures of interpretation accuracy were not correlated with learning gain. With less restricted language, misunderstandings negatively affected learning. Our study provides further evidence that interpretation quality significantly affects learning gain in tutorial dialogue. Moreover, while it has long been known that user satisfaction is negatively correlated with interpretation error rates in spoken dialogue, this is the first attempt to evaluate the impact of different types of interpretation errors on task success and usability of a tutoring system.

Our results demonstrate that different types of errors may matter to a different degree. In our system, all of the error types negatively correlated with learning gain stem from the same underlying problem: the use of incorrect or vague terminology by the student. With the exception of the *irrelevant_answer* strategy, the targeted help strategies we implemented were not effective in reducing error frequency or improving learning gain. Additional research is needed to understand why. One possibility is that *irrelevant_answer* was easier to remediate compared to other error types. It usually happened in situations where there was a clear expectation of the answer type (e.g., a list of component names, a yes/no answer). Therefore, it was easier to design an effective prompt. Help messages for other error types were more frequent when the expected answer was a complex sentence, and multiple possible ways of phrasing the correct answer were acceptable. Therefore, it was more difficult to formulate a prompt that would clearly describe the problem in all contexts.

One way to improve the help messages may be to have the system indicate more clearly when user terminology is a problem. Our system apologized each time there was a non-understanding, leading students to believe that they may be answering correctly but the answer is not being understood. A different approach would be to say something like "I am sorry, you are not using the correct terminology in your answer. Here's a hint: your answer should mention a terminal". Together with an appropriate mechanism to detect paraphrases of correct answers (as opposed to vague answers whose correctness is difficult to determine), this approach could be more beneficial in helping students learn. We are considering implementing and evaluating this as part of our future work.

Some of the errors, in particular instances of *no_appr_terms* and *selectional_restr_failure*, also stemmed from unrecognized paraphrases with non-standard terminology. Those answers could conceivably be accepted by a system using semantic similarity as a metric (e.g., using LSA with preauthored answers). However, our results also indicate that simply accepting the incorrect terminology may not be the best strategy. Users appear to be sensitive when the system's language does not align with their terminology, as reflected in the decreased satisfaction ratings associated with higher rates of incorrect terminology problems in BASE. Moreover, prior analysis of human-human data indicates that tutors use different restate strategies depending on the "quality" of the student answers, even if they are accepting them as correct (Dzikovska et al., 2008). Together, these point at an important unaddressed issue: existing systems are often built on the assumption that only incorrect and missing parts of the student answer should be remediated, and a wide range of terminology should be accepted (Graesser et al., 1999; Jordan et al., 2006). While it is obviously important for the system to accept a range of different phrasings, our analysis indicates that this may not be sufficient by itself, and students could potentially benefit from addressing the terminology issues with a specifically devised strategy.

Finally, it could also be possible that some differences between strategy effectiveness were caused by incorrect error type classification. Manual examination of several dialogues suggests that most of the errors are assigned to the appropriate type, though in some cases incorrect syntactic parses resulted in unexpected interpretation errors, causing the system to give a confusing help message. These misclassifications appear to be evenly split between different error types, though a more formal evaluation is planned in the future. However from our initial examination, we believe that the differences in strategy effectiveness that we observed are due to the actual differences in the help messages. Therefore, designing better prompts would be the key factor in improving learning and user satisfaction.

Acknowledgments

This work has been supported in part by US Office of Naval Research grants N000140810043 and N0001410WX20278. We thank Katherine Harrison, Leanne Taylor, Charles Callaway, and Elaine Farrow for help with setting up the system and running the evaluation. We would like to thank anonymous reviewers for their detailed feedback.

References

V. Aleven, O. Popescu, and K. R. Koedinger. 2001. Towards tutorial dialog to support self-explanation: Adding natural language understanding to a cognitive tutor. In *Proceedings of the 10th International Conference on Artificial Intelligence in Education (AIED '01)"*.

Dan Bohus and Alexander Rudnicky. 2005. Sorry, I didn't catch that! - An investigation of non-understanding errors and recovery strategies. In *Proceedings of SIGdial-2005*, Lisbon, Portugal.

Michelene T. H. Chi, Nicholas de Leeuw, Mei-Hung Chiu, and Christian LaVancher. 1994. Eliciting self-explanations improves understanding. *Cognitive Science*, 18(3):439–477.

Myroslava O. Dzikovska, Gwendolyn E. Campbell, Charles B. Callaway, Natalie B. Steinhauser, Elaine Farrow, Johanna D. Moore, Leslie A. Butler, and Colin Matheson. 2008. Diagnosing natural language answers to support adaptive tutoring. In *Proceedings 21st International FLAIRS Conference*, Coconut Grove, Florida, May.

Myroslava O. Dzikovska, Charles B. Callaway, Elaine Farrow, Johanna D. Moore, Natalie B. Steinhauser, and Gwendolyn C. Campbell. 2009. Dealing with interpretation errors in tutorial dialogue. In *Proceedings of SIGDIAL-09*, London, UK, Sep.

Myroslava O. Dzikovska, Johanna D. Moore, Natalie Steinhauser, Gwendolyn Campbell, Elaine Farrow, and Charles B. Callaway. 2010. Beetle II: a system for tutoring and computational linguistics experimentation. In *Proceedings of ACL-2010 demo session*.

A. C. Graesser, P. Wiemer-Hastings, P. Wiemer-Hastings, and R. Kreuz. 1999. Autotutor: A simulation of a human tutor. *Cognitive Systems Research*, 1:35–51.

Beth Ann Hockey, Oliver Lemon, Ellen Campana, Laura Hiatt, Gregory Aist, James Hieronymus, Alexander Gruenstein, and John Dowding. 2003. Targeted help for spoken dialogue systems: intelligent feedback improves naive users' performance. In *Proceedings of the tenth conference on European chapter of the Association for Computational Linguistics*, pages 147–154, Morristown, NJ, USA.

Pamela W. Jordan, Maxim Makatchev, and Kurt VanLehn. 2004. Combining competing language understanding approaches in an intelligent tutoring system. In James C. Lester, Rosa Maria Vicari, and Fábio Paraguaçu, editors, *Intelligent Tutoring Systems*, volume 3220 of *Lecture Notes in Computer Science*, pages 346–357. Springer.

Pamela Jordan, Maxim Makatchev, Umarani Pappuswamy, Kurt VanLehn, and Patricia Albacete. 2006. A natural language tutorial dialogue system for physics. In *Proceedings of the 19th International FLAIRS conference*.

Pamela Jordan, Diane Litman, Michael Lipschultz, and Joanna Drummond. 2009. Evidence of misunderstandings in tutorial dialogue and their impact on learning. In *Proceedings of the 14th International Conference on Artificial Intelligence in Education (AIED)*, Brighton, UK, July.

Diane Litman and Kate Forbes-Riley. 2005. Speech recognition performance and learning in spoken dialogue tutoring. In *Proceedings of EUROSPEECH-2005*, page 1427.

Diane Litman, Johanna Moore, Myroslava Dzikovska, and Elaine Farrow. 2009. Generalizing tutorial dialogue results. In *Proceedings of 14th International Conference on Artificial Intelligence in Education (AIED)*, Brighton, UK, July.

Philip M. McCarthy, Vasile Rus, Scott Crossley, Arthur C. Graesser, and Danielle S. McNamara. 2008. Assessing forward-, reverse-, and average-entailment indeces on natural language input from the intelligent tutoring system, iSTART. In *Proceedings of the 21st International FLAIRS conference*, pages 165–170.

Rodney D. Nielsen, Wayne Ward, and James H. Martin. 2008. Learning to assess low-level conceptual understanding. In *Proceedings 21st International FLAIRS Conference*, Coconut Grove, Florida, May.

Heather Pon-Barry, Brady Clark, Elizabeth Owen Bratt, Karl Schultz, and Stanley Peters. 2004. Evaluating the effectiveness of SCoT: A spoken conversational tutor. In J. Mostow and P. Tedesco, editors, *Proceedings of the ITS 2004 Workshop on Dialog-based Intelligent Tutoring Systems*, pages 23–32.

Amruta Purandare and Diane Litman. 2008. Content-learning correlations in spoken tutoring dialogs at word, turn and discourse levels. In *Proceedings 21st International FLAIRS Conference*, Coconut Grove, Florida, May.

The Prevalence of Descriptive Referring Expressions in News and Narrative

Raquel Hervás
Departamento de Ingenieria
del Software e Inteligencía Artificial
Universidad Complutense de Madrid
Madrid, 28040 Spain
raquelhb@fdi.ucm.es

Mark Alan Finlayson
Computer Science and
Artificial Intelligence Laboratory
Massachusetts Institute of Technology
Cambridge, MA, 02139 USA
markaf@mit.edu

Abstract

Generating referring expressions is a key step in Natural Language Generation. Researchers have focused almost exclusively on generating *distinctive* referring expressions, that is, referring expressions that uniquely identify their intended referent. While undoubtedly one of their most important functions, referring expressions can be more than distinctive. In particular, *descriptive* referring expressions – those that provide additional information not required for distinction – are critical to fluent, efficient, well-written text. We present a corpus analysis in which approximately one-fifth of 7,207 referring expressions in 24,422 words of news and narrative are descriptive. These data show that if we are ever to fully master natural language generation, especially for the genres of news and narrative, researchers will need to devote more attention to understanding how to generate descriptive, and not just distinctive, referring expressions.

1 A Distinctive Focus

Generating referring expressions is a key step in Natural Language Generation (NLG). From early treatments in seminal papers by Appelt (1985) and Reiter and Dale (1992) to the recent set of Referring Expression Generation (REG) Challenges (Gatt et al., 2009) through different corpora available for the community (Eugenio et al., 1998; van Deemter et al., 2006; Viethen and Dale, 2008), generating referring expressions has become one of the most studied areas of NLG.

Researchers studying this area have, almost without exception, focused exclusively on how to generate *distinctive* referring expressions, that is, referring expressions that unambiguously identify their intended referent. Referring expressions, however, may be more than distinctive. It is widely acknowledged that they can be used to achieve multiple goals, above and beyond distinction. Here we focus on *descriptive* referring expressions, that is, referring expressions that are not only distinctive, but provide additional information not required for identifying their intended referent. Consider the following text, in which some of the referring expressions have been underlined:

> *Once upon a time there was a man, who had three daughters. They lived in a house and their dresses were made of fabric.*

While a bit strange, the text is perfectly well-formed. All the referring expressions are distinctive, in that we can properly identify the referents of each expression. But the real text, the opening lines to the folktale *The Beauty and the Beast*, is actually much more lyrical:

> *Once upon a time there was a **rich merchant**, who had three daughters. They lived in a **very fine** house and their **gowns** were made of **the richest** fabric **sewn with jewels**.*

All the boldfaced portions – namely, the choice of head nouns, the addition of adjectives, the use of appositive phrases – serve to perform a descriptive function, and, importantly, are all unnecessary for distinction! In all of these cases, the author is using the referring expressions as a vehicle for communicating information about the referents. This descriptive information is sometimes new, sometimes necessary for understanding the text, and sometimes just for added flavor. But when the expression is *descriptive*, as opposed to *distinctive*, this additional information is not required for identifying the referent of the expression, and it is these sorts of referring expressions that we will be concerned with here.

Proceedings of the ACL 2010 Conference Short Papers, pages 49–54,
Uppsala, Sweden, 11-16 July 2010.

Although these sorts of referring expression have been mostly ignored by researchers in this area[1], we show in this corpus study that descriptive expressions are in fact quite prevalent: nearly one-fifth of referring expressions in news and narrative are descriptive. In particular, our data, the trained judgments of native English speakers, show that 18% of all distinctive referring expressions in news and 17% of those in narrative folktales are descriptive. With this as motivation, we argue that descriptive referring expressions must be studied more carefully, especially as the field progresses from referring in a physical, immediate context (like that in the REG Challenges) to generating more literary forms of text.

2 Corpus Annotation

This is a corpus study; our procedure was therefore to define our annotation guidelines (Section 2.1), select texts to annotate (2.2), create an annotation tool for our annotators (2.3), and, finally, train annotators, have them annotate referring expressions' constituents and function, and then adjudicate the double-annotated texts into a gold standard (2.4).

2.1 Definitions

We wrote an annotation guide explaining the difference between distinctive and descriptive referring expressions. We used the guide when training annotators, and it was available to them while annotating. With limited space here we can only give an outline of what is contained in the guide; for full details see (Finlayson and Hervás, 2010a).

Referring Expressions We defined referring expressions as referential noun phrases and their coreferential expressions, e.g., "John kissed Mary. She blushed.". This included referring expressions to generics (e.g., "Lions are fierce"), dates, times, and numbers, as well as events if they were referred to using a noun phrase. We included in each referring expression all the determiners, quantifiers, adjectives, appositives, and prepositional phrases that syntactically attached to that expression. When referring expressions were nested, all the nested referring expressions were also marked separately.

Nuclei vs. Modifiers In the only previous corpus study of descriptive referring expressions, on museum labels, Cheng et al. (2001) noted that descriptive information is often integrated into referring expressions using modifiers to the head noun. To study this, and to allow our results to be more closely compared with Cheng's, we had our annotators split referring expressions into their constituents, portions called either *nuclei* or *modifiers*. The nuclei were the portions of the referring expression that performed the 'core' referring function; the modifiers were those portions that could be varied, syntactically speaking, independently of the nuclei. Annotators then assigned a distinctive or descriptive function to each constituent, rather than the referring expression as a whole.

Normally, the nuclei corresponded to the head of the noun phrase. In (1), the nucleus is the token *king*, which we have here surrounded with square brackets. The modifiers, surrounded by parentheses, are *The* and *old*.

(1) *(The) (old) [king] was wise.*

Phrasal modifiers were marked as single modifiers, for example, in (2).

(2) *(The) [roof] (of the house) collapsed.*

It is significant that we had our annotators mark and tag the nuclei of referring expressions. Cheng and colleagues only mentioned the possibility that additional information could be introduced in the modifiers. However, O'Donnell et al. (1998) observed that often the choice of head noun can also influence the function of a referring expression. Consider (3), in which the word *villain* is used to refer to the King.

(3) *The King assumed the throne today.*
I don't trust (that) [villain] one bit.

The speaker could have merely used *him* to refer to the King–the choice of that particular head noun *villain* gives us additional information about the disposition of the speaker. Thus *villain* is descriptive.

Function: Distinctive vs. Descriptive As already noted, instead of tagging the whole referring expression, annotators tagged each constituent (nuclei and modifiers) as distinctive or descriptive.

The two main tests for determining descriptiveness were (a) if presence of the constituent was unnecessary for identifying the referent, or (b) if

[1] With the exception of a small amount of work, discussed in Section 4.

the constituent was expressed using unusual or ostentatious word choice. If either was true, the constituent was considered descriptive; otherwise, it was tagged as distinctive. In cases where the constituent was completely irrelevant to identifying the referent, it was tagged as descriptive. For example, in the folktale *The Princess and the Pea*, from which (1) was extracted, there is only one king in the entire story. Thus, in that story, *the king* is sufficient for identification, and therefore the modifier *old* is descriptive. This points out the importance of context in determining distinctiveness or descriptiveness; if there had been a roomful of kings, the tags on those modifiers would have been reversed.

There is some question as to whether copular predicates, such as *the plumber* in (4), are actually referring expressions.

(4) *John is the plumber*

Our annotators marked and tagged these constructions as normal referring expressions, but they added an additional flag to identify them as copular predicates. We then excluded these constructions from our final analysis. Note that copular predicates were treated differently from appositives: in appositives the predicate was included in the referring expression, and in most cases (again, depending on context) was marked descriptive (e.g., John, the plumber, slept.).

2.2 Text Selection

Our corpus comprised 62 texts, all originally written in English, from two different genres, news and folktales. We began with 30 folktales of different sizes, totaling 12,050 words. These texts were used in a previous work on the influence of dialogues on anaphora resolution algorithms (Aggarwal et al., 2009); they were assembled with an eye toward including different styles, different authors, and different time periods. Following this, we matched, approximately, the number of words in the folktales by selecting 32 texts from Wall Street Journal section of the Penn Treebank (Marcus et al., 1993). These texts were selected at random from the first 200 texts in the corpus.

2.3 The Story Workbench

We used the Story Workbench application (Finlayson, 2008) to actually perform the annotation. The Story Workbench is a semantic annotation program that, among other things, includes the ability to annotate referring expressions and coreferential relationships. We added the ability to annotate nuclei, modifiers, and their functions by writing a workbench "plugin" in Java that could be installed in the application.

The Story Workbench is not yet available to the public at large, being in a limited distribution beta testing phase. The developers plan to release it as free software within the next year. At that time, we also plan to release our plugin as free, downloadable software.

2.4 Annotation & Adjudication

The main task of the study was the annotation of the constituents of each referring expression, as well as the function (distinctive or descriptive) of each constituent. The system generated a first pass of constituent analysis, but did not mark functions. We hired two native English annotators, neither of whom had any linguistics background, who corrected these automatically-generated constituent analyses, and tagged each constituent as descriptive or distinctive. Every text was annotated by both annotators. Adjudication of the differences was conducted by discussion between the two annotators; the second author moderated these discussions and settled irreconcilable disagreements. We followed a "train-as-you-go" paradigm, where there was no distinct training period, but rather adjudication proceeded in step with annotation, and annotators received feedback during those sessions.

We calculated two measures of inter-annotator agreement: a kappa statistic and an f-measure, shown in Table 1. All of our f-measures indicated that annotators agreed almost perfectly on the location of referring expressions and their breakdown into constituents. These agreement calculations were performed on the annotators' original corrected texts.

All the kappa statistics were calculated for two tags (nuclei vs. modifier for the constituents, and distinctive vs. descriptive for the functions) over both each token assigned to a nucleus or modifier and each referring expression pair. Our kappas indicate moderate to good agreement, especially for the folktales. These results are expected because of the inherent subjectivity of language. During the adjudication sessions it became clear that different people do not consider the same information as obvious or descriptive for the same concepts, and even the contexts deduced by each annotators from the texts were sometimes substantially different.

	Tales	Articles	Total
Ref. Exp. (F_1)	1.00	0.99	0.99
Constituents (F_1)	0.99	0.98	0.98
Nuc./Mod. (κ)	0.97	0.95	0.96
Const. Func. (κ)	0.61	0.48	0.54
Ref. Exp. Func. (κ)	0.65	0.54	**0.59**

Table 1: Inter-annotator agreement measures

	Tales	Articles	Total
Nuclei	3,666	3,502	7,168
Max. Nuc/Ref	1	1	1
Dist. Nuc.	95%	97%	96%
Desc. Nuc.	5%	3%	**4%**
Modifiers	2,277	3,627	5,904
Avg. Mod/Ref	0.6	1.0	0.8
Max. Mod/Ref	4	6	6
Dist. Mod.	78%	81%	80%
Desc. Mod.	22%	19%	**20%**

Table 3: Breakdown of Constituent Tags

3 Results

Table 2 lists the primary results of the study. We considered a referring expression descriptive if any of its constituents were descriptive. Thus, 18% of the referring expressions in the corpus added additional information beyond what was required to unambiguously identify their referent. The results were similar in both genres.

	Tales	Articles	Total
Texts	30	32	62
Words	12,050	12,372	24,422
Sentences	904	571	1,475
Ref. Exp.	3,681	3,526	7,207
Dist. Ref. Exp.	3,057	2,830	5,887
Desc. Ref. Exp.	609	672	1,281
% Dist. Ref.	83%	81%	82%
% Desc. Ref.	17%	19%	**18%**

Table 2: Primary results.

Table 3 contains the percentages of descriptive and distinctive tags broken down by constituent. Like Cheng's results, our analysis shows that descriptive referring expressions make up a significant fraction of all referring expressions. Although Cheng did not examine nuclei, our results show that the use of descriptive nuclei is small but not negligible.

4 Relation to the Field

Researchers working on generating referring expressions typically acknowledge that referring expressions can perform functions other than distinction. Despite this widespread acknowledgment, researchers have, for the most part, explicitly ignored these functions. Exceptions to this trend are three. First is the general study of *aggregation* in the process of referring expression generation. Second and third are corpus studies by Cheng et al. (2001) and Jordan (2000a) that bear on the prevalence of descriptive referring expressions.

The NLG subtask of aggregation can be used to imbue referring expressions with a descriptive function (Reiter and Dale, 2000, §5.3). There is a specific kind of aggregation called *embedding* that moves information from one clause to another inside the structure of a separate noun phrase. This type of aggregation can be used to transform two sentences such as *"The princess lived in a castle. She was pretty"* into *"The pretty princess lived in a castle"*. The adjective *pretty*, previously a copular predicate, becomes a descriptive modifier of the reference to the princess, making the second text more natural and fluent. This kind of aggregation is widely used by humans for making the discourse more compact and efficient. In order to create NLG systems with this ability, we must take into account the caveat, noted by Cheng (1998), that any non-distinctive information in a referring expression must not lead to confusion about the distinctive function of the referring expression. This is by no means a trivial problem – this sort of aggregation interferes with referring and coherence planning at both a local and global level (Cheng and Mellish, 2000; Cheng et al., 2001). It is clear, from the current state of the art of NLG, that we have not yet obtained a deep enough understanding of aggregation to enable us to handle these interactions. More research on the topic is needed.

Two previous corpus studies have looked at the use of descriptive referring expressions. The first showed explicitly that people craft descriptive referring expressions to accomplish different goals. Jordan and colleagues (Jordan, 2000b; Jordan, 2000a) examined the use of referring expressions using the COCONUT corpus (Eugenio et al., 1998). They tested how domain and discourse goals can influence the content of non-pronominal referring expressions in a dialogue context, checking whether or not a subject's goals led them to include non-referring information in a referring expression. Their results are intriguing because they point toward heretofore unexamined constraints, utilities and expectations (possibly genre- or style-dependent) that may underlie the use of descriptive information to perform different functions, and are not yet captured by aggregation modules in particular or NLG systems in general.

In the other corpus study, which partially inspired this work, Cheng and colleagues analyzed a set of museum descriptions, the GNOME corpus (Poesio, 2004), for the pragmatic functions of referring expressions. They had three functions in their study, in contrast to our two. Their first function (marked by their `uniq` tag) was equivalent to our distinctive function. The other two were specializations of our descriptive tag, where they differentiated between additional information that helped to understand the text (`int`), or additional information not necessary for understanding (`attr`). Despite their annotators seeming to have trouble distinguishing between the latter two tags, they did achieve good overall inter-annotator agreement. They identified 1,863 modifiers to referring expressions in their corpus, of which 47.3% fulfilled a descriptive (`attr` or `int`) function. This is supportive of our main assertion, namely, that descriptive referring expressions, not only crucial for efficient and fluent text, are actually a significant phenomenon. It is interesting, though, that Cheng's fraction of descriptive referring expression was so much higher than ours (47.3% versus our 18%). We attribute this substantial difference to genre, in that Cheng studied museum labels, in which the writer is space-constrained, having to pack a lot of information into a small label. The issue bears further study, and perhaps will lead to insights into differences in writing style that may be attributed to author or genre.

5 Contributions

We make two contributions in this paper.

First, we assembled, double-annotated, and adjudicated into a gold-standard a corpus of 24,422 words. We marked all referring expressions, coreferential relations, and referring expression constituents, and tagged each constituent as having a descriptive or distinctive function. We wrote an annotation guide and created software that allows the annotation of this information in free text. The corpus and the guide are available on-line in a permanent digital archive (Finlayson and Hervás, 2010a; Finlayson and Hervás, 2010b). The software will also be released in the same archive when the Story Workbench annotation application is released to the public. This corpus will be useful for the automatic generation and analysis of both descriptive and distinctive referring expressions. Any kind of system intended to generate text as humans do must take into account that identification is not the only function of referring expressions. Many analysis applications would benefit from the automatic recognition of descriptive referring expressions.

Second, we demonstrated that descriptive referring expressions comprise a substantial fraction (18%) of the referring expressions in news and narrative. Along with museum descriptions, studied by Cheng, it seems that news and narrative are genres where authors naturally use a large number of descriptive referring expressions. Given that so little work has been done on descriptive referring expressions, this indicates that the field would be well served by focusing more attention on this phenomenon.

Acknowledgments

This work was supported in part by the Air Force Office of Scientific Research under grant number A9550-05-1-0321, as well as by the Office of Naval Research under award number N00014091059. Any opinions, findings, and conclusions or recommendations expressed in this paper are those of the authors and do not necessarily reflect the views of the Office of Naval Research. This research is also partially funded the Spanish Ministry of Education and Science (TIN2009-14659-C03-01) and Universidad Complutense de Madrid (GR58/08). We also thank Whitman Richards, Ozlem Uzuner, Peter Szolovits, Patrick Winston, Pablo Gervás, and Mark Seifter for their helpful comments and discussion, and thank our annotators Saam Batmanghelidj and Geneva Trotter.

References

Alaukik Aggarwal, Pablo Gervás, and Raquel Hervás. 2009. Measuring the influence of errors induced by the presence of dialogues in reference clustering of narrative text. In *Proceedings of ICON-2009: 7th International Conference on Natural Language Processing*, India. Macmillan Publishers.

Douglas E. Appelt. 1985. Planning English referring expressions. *Artificial Intelligence*, 26:1–33.

Hua Cheng and Chris Mellish. 2000. Capturing the interaction between aggregation and text planning in two generation systems. In *INLG '00: First international conference on Natural Language Generation 2000*, pages 186–193, Morristown, NJ, USA. Association for Computational Linguistics.

Hua Cheng, Massimo Poesio, Renate Henschel, and Chris Mellish. 2001. Corpus-based np modifier generation. In *NAACL '01: Second meeting of the North American Chapter of the Association for Computational Linguistics on Language technologies 2001*, pages 1–8, Morristown, NJ, USA. Association for Computational Linguistics.

Hua Cheng. 1998. Embedding new information into referring expressions. In *ACL-36: Proceedings of the 36th Annual Meeting of the Association for Computational Linguistics and 17th International Conference on Computational Linguistics*, pages 1478–1480, Morristown, NJ, USA. Association for Computational Linguistics.

Barbara Di Eugenio, Johanna D. Moore, Pamela W. Jordan, and Richmond H. Thomason. 1998. An empirical investigation of proposals in collaborative dialogues. In *Proceedings of the 17th international conference on Computational linguistics*, pages 325–329, Morristown, NJ, USA. Association for Computational Linguistics.

Mark A. Finlayson and Raquel Hervás. 2010a. Annotation guide for the UCM/MIT indications, referring expressions, and coreference corpus (UMIREC corpus). Technical Report MIT-CSAIL-TR-2010-025, MIT Computer Science and Artificial Intelligence Laboratory. http://hdl.handle.net/1721.1/54765.

Mark A. Finlayson and Raquel Hervás. 2010b. UCM/MIT indications, referring expressions, and coreference corpus (UMIREC corpus). Work product, MIT Computer Science and Artificial Intelligence Laboratory. http://hdl.handle.net/1721.1/54766.

Mark A. Finlayson. 2008. Collecting semantics in the wild: The Story Workbench. In *Proceedings of the AAAI Fall Symposium on Naturally-Inspired Artificial Intelligence*, pages 46–53, Menlo Park, CA, USA. AAAI Press.

Albert Gatt, Anja Belz, and Eric Kow. 2009. The TUNA-REG challenge 2009: overview and evaluation results. In *ENLG '09: Proceedings of the 12th European Workshop on Natural Language Generation*, pages 174–182, Morristown, NJ, USA. Association for Computational Linguistics.

Pamela W. Jordan. 2000a. Can nominal expressions achieve multiple goals?: an empirical study. In *ACL '00: Proceedings of the 38th Annual Meeting on Association for Computational Linguistics*, pages 142–149, Morristown, NJ, USA. Association for Computational Linguistics.

Pamela W. Jordan. 2000b. Influences on attribute selection in redescriptions: A corpus study. In *Proceedings of CogSci2000*, pages 250–255.

Mitchell P. Marcus, Mary Ann Marcinkiewicz, and Beatrice Santorini. 1993. Building a large annotated corpus of english: the penn treebank. *Computational Linguistics*, 19(2):313–330.

Michael O'Donnell, Hua Cheng, and Janet Hitzeman. 1998. Integrating referring and informing in NP planning. In *Proceedings of COLING-ACL'98 Workshop on the Computational Treatment of Nominals*, pages 46–56.

Massimo Poesio. 2004. Discourse annotation and semantic annotation in the GNOME corpus. In *DiscAnnotation '04: Proceedings of the 2004 ACL Workshop on Discourse Annotation*, pages 72–79, Morristown, NJ, USA. Association for Computational Linguistics.

Ehud Reiter and Robert Dale. 1992. A fast algorithm for the generation of referring expressions. In *Proceedings of the 14th conference on Computational linguistics*, Nantes, France.

Ehud Reiter and Robert Dale. 2000. *Building Natural Language Generation Systems*. Cambridge University Press.

Kees van Deemter, Ielka van der Sluis, and Albert Gatt. 2006. Building a semantically transparent corpus for the generation of referring expressions. In *Proceedings of the 4th International Conference on Natural Language Generation (Special Session on Data Sharing and Evaluation), INLG-06*.

Jette Viethen and Robert Dale. 2008. The use of spatial relations in referring expressions. In *Proceedings of the 5th International Conference on Natural Language Generation*.

Preferences versus Adaptation during Referring Expression Generation

Martijn Goudbeek
University of Tilburg
Tilburg, The Netherlands
m.b.goudbeek@uvt.nl

Emiel Krahmer
University of Tilburg
Tilburg, The Netherlands
e.j.krahmer@uvt.nl

Abstract

Current Referring Expression Generation algorithms rely on domain dependent preferences for both content selection and linguistic realization. We present two experiments showing that human speakers may opt for dispreferred properties and dispreferred modifier orderings when these were salient in a preceding interaction (without speakers being consciously aware of this). We discuss the impact of these findings for current generation algorithms.

1 Introduction

The generation of referring expressions is a core ingredient of most Natural Language Generation (NLG) systems (Reiter and Dale, 2000; Mellish et al., 2006). These systems usually approach Referring Expression Generation (REG) as a two-step procedure, where first it is decided which properties to include (content selection), after which the selected properties are turned into a natural language referring expression (linguistic realization). The basic problem in both stages is one of choice; there are many ways in which one could refer to a target object and there are multiple ways in which these could be realized in natural language. Typically, these choice problems are tackled by giving preference to some solutions over others. For example, the Incremental Algorithm (Dale and Reiter, 1995), one of the most widely used REG algorithms, assumes that certain attributes are preferred over others, partly based on evidence provided by Pechmann (1989); a chair would first be described in terms of its color, and only if this does not result in a unique characterization, other, less preferred attributes such as orientation are tried. The Incremental Algorithm is arguably unique in assuming a complete preference order of attributes, but other REG algorithms rely on similar distinctions. The Graph-based algorithm (Krahmer et al., 2003), for example, searches for the cheapest description for a target, and distinguishes cheap attributes (such as color) from more expensive ones (orientation). Realization of referring expressions has received less attention, yet recent studies on the ordering of modifiers (Shaw and Hatzivassiloglou, 1999; Malouf, 2000; Mitchell, 2009) also work from the assumption that some orderings (*large red*) are preferred over others (*red large*).

We argue that such preferences are less stable when referring expressions are generated in interactive settings, as would be required for applications such as spoken dialogue systems or interactive virtual characters. In these cases, we hypothesize that, besides domain preferences, also the referring expressions that were produced earlier in the interaction are important. It has been shown that if one dialogue participant refers to a couch as a *sofa*, the next speaker is more likely to use the word *sofa* as well (Branigan et al., in press). This kind of micro-planning or "lexical entrainment" (Brennan and Clark, 1996) can be seen as a specific form of "alignment" (Pickering and Garrod, 2004) between speaker and addressee. Pickering and Garrod argue that alignment may take place on all levels of interaction, and indeed it has been shown that participants also align their intonation patterns and syntactic structures. However, as far as we know, experimental evidence for alignment on the level of content planning has never been given, and neither have alignment effects in modifier orderings during realization been shown. With a few notable exceptions, such as Buschmeier et al. (2009) who study alignment in micro-planning, and Janarthanam and Lemon (2009) who study alignment in expertise levels, alignment has received little attention in NLG so far.

This paper is organized as follows. Experiment I studies the trade-off between adaptation

Proceedings of the ACL 2010 Conference Short Papers, pages 55–59,
Uppsala, Sweden, 11-16 July 2010. ©2010 Association for Computational Linguistics

and preferences during content selection while Experiment II looks at this trade-off for modifier orderings during realization. Both studies use a novel interactive reference production paradigm, applied to two domains – the Furniture and People domains of the TUNA data-set (Gatt et al., 2007; Koolen et al., 2009) – to see whether adaptation may be domain dependent. Finally, we contrast our findings with the performance of state-of-the-art REG algorithms, discussing how they could be adapted so as to account for the new data, effectively adding plasticity to the generation process.

2 Experiment I

Experiment I studies what speakers do when referring to a target that can be distinguished in a preferred (*the blue fan*) or a dispreferred way (*the left-facing fan*), when in the prior context either the first or the second variant was made salient.

Method

Participants 26 students (2 male, mean age = 20 years, 11 months), all native speakers of Dutch without hearing or speech problems, participated for course credits.

Materials Target pictures were taken from the TUNA corpus (Gatt et al., 2007) that has been extensively used for REG evaluation. This corpus consists of two domains: one containing pictures of people (famous mathematicians), the other containing furniture items in different colors depicted from different orientations. From previous studies (Gatt et al., 2007; Koolen et al., 2009) it is known that participants show a preference for certain attributes: color in the Furniture domain and glasses in the People domain, and disprefer other attributes (orientation of a furniture piece and wearing a tie, respectively).

Procedure Trials consisted of four turns in an interactive reference understanding and production experiment: a prime, two fillers and the experimental description (see Figure 1). First, participants listened to a pre-recorded female voice referring to one of three objects and had to indicate which one was being referenced. In this subtask, references either used a preferred or a dispreferred attribute; both were distinguishing. Second, participants themselves described a filler picture, after which, third, they had to indicate which filler picture was being described. The two filler turns always concerned stimuli from the alternative domain and were intended to prevent a too direct connection between the prime and the target. Fourth, participants described the target object, which could always be distinguished from its distractors in a preferred (*The blue fan*) or a dispreferred (*The left facing fan*) way. Note that *at-*

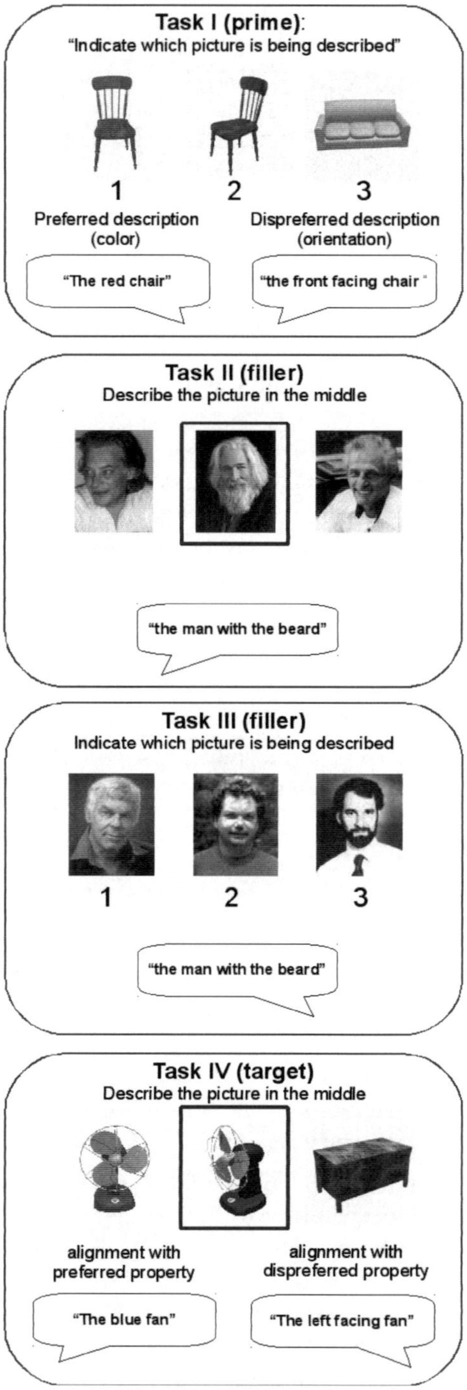

Figure 1: The 4 tasks per trial. A furniture trial is shown; people trials have an identical structure.

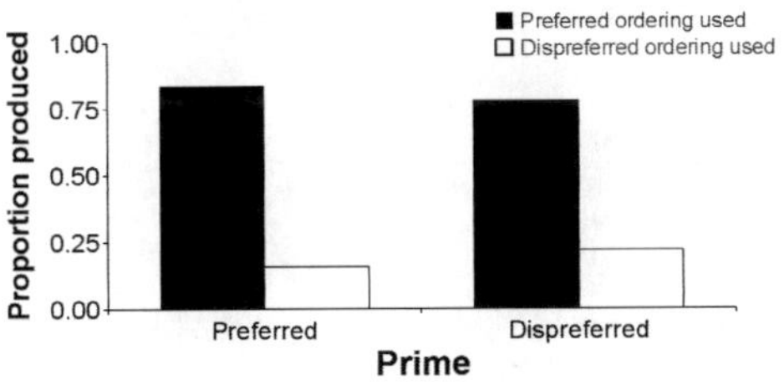

Figure 2: Proportions of preferred and dispreferred attributes in the Furniture domain.

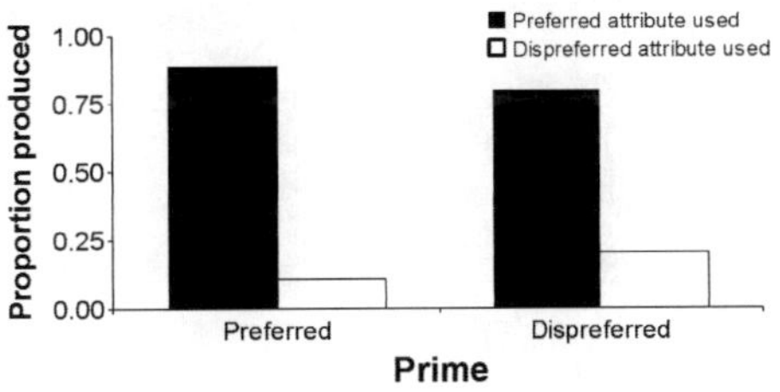

Figure 3: Proportions of preferred and dispreferred attributes in the People domain.

tributes are primed, not values; a participant may have heard *front facing* in the prime turn, while the target has a different value for this attribute (cf. Fig. 1).

For the two domains, there were 20 preferred and 20 dispreferred trials, giving rise to 2 x (20 + 20) = 80 critical trials. These were presented in counter-balanced blocks, and within blocks each participant received a different random order. In addition, there were 80 filler trials (each following the same structure as outlined in Figure 1). During debriefing, none of the participants indicated they had been aware of the experiment's purpose.

Results

We use the proportion of attribute alignment as our dependent measure. Alignment occurs when a participant uses the same attribute in the target as occurred in the prime. This includes overspecified descriptions (Engelhardt et al., 2006; Arnold, 2008), where both the preferred and dispreferred attributes were mentioned by participants. Overspecification occurred in 13% of the critical trials (and these were evenly distributed over the experimental conditions).

The use of the preferred and dispreferred attribute as a function of prime and domain is shown in Figure 2 and Figure 3. In both domains, the preferred attribute is used much more frequently than the dispreferred attribute with the preferred primes, which serves as a manipulation check. As a test of our hypothesis that adaptation processes play an important role in attribute selection for referring expressions, we need to look at participants' expressions with the *dispreferred* primes (with the preferred primes, effects of adaptation and of preferences cannot be teased apart). Current REG algorithms such as the Incremental Algorithm and the Graph-based algorithm predict that participants will always opt for the preferred attribute, and hence will not use the dispreferred attribute. This is not what we observe: our participants used the dispreferred attribute at a rate significantly larger than zero when they had been exposed to it three turns earlier ($t_{furniture}$ [25] = 6.64, $p < 0.01$; t_{people} [25] = 4.78 $p < 0.01$). Additionally, they used the dispreferred attribute significantly *more* when they had previously heard the dispreferred attribute rather than the preferred attribute. This difference is especially marked and significant in the Furniture domain ($t_{furniture}$ [25] = 2.63, $p < 0.01$, t_{people} [25] = 0.98, $p < 0.34$), where participants opt for the dispreferred attribute in 54% of the trials, more frequently than they do for the preferred attribute (Fig. 2).

3 Experiment II

Experiment II uses the same paradigm used for Experiment I to study whether speaker's preferences for modifier orderings can be changed by exposing them to dispreferred orderings.

Method

Participants 28 Students (ten males, mean age = 23 years and two months) participated for course credits. All were native speakers of Dutch, without hearing and speech problems. None participated in Experiment I.

Materials The materials were identical to those used in Experiment I, except for their arrangement in the critical trials. In these trials, the participants could only identify the target picture using two attributes. In the Furniture domain these were color and size, in the People domain these were having a beard and wearing glasses. In the prime turn (Task I, Fig. 1), these attributes were realized in a preferred way ("size first": e.g., *the big red sofa*, or "glasses first": *the bespectacled and bearded man*) or in a dispreferred way ("color first": *the red big sofa* or "beard first" *the bespectacled and bearded*

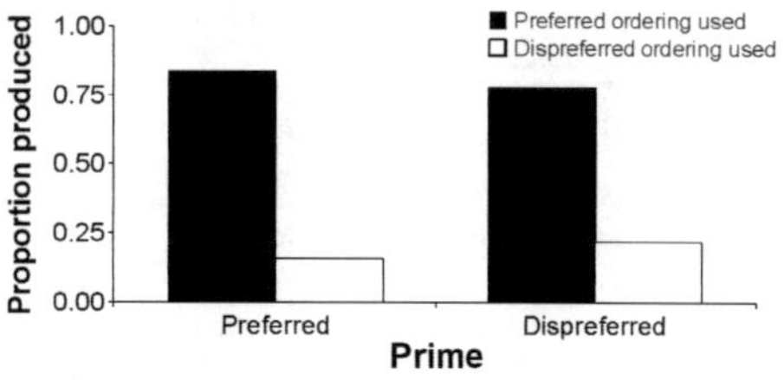

Figure 4: Proportions of preferred and dispreferred modifier orderings in the Furniture domain.

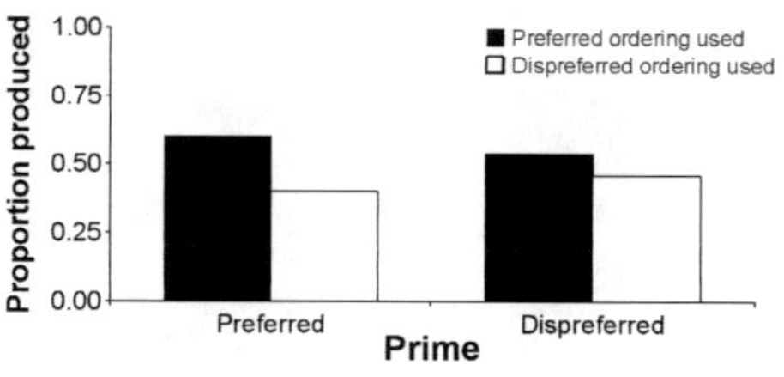

Figure 5: Proportions of preferred and dispreferred modifier orderings in the People domain.

man). Google counts for the original Dutch modifier orderings reveal that the ratio of preferred to dispreferred is in the order of 40:1 in the Furniture domain and 3:1 in the People domain.
Procedure As above.

Results

We use the proportion of modifier ordering alignments as our dependent measure, where alignment occurs when the participant's ordering coincides with the primed ordering. Figure 4 and 5 show the use of the preferred and dispreferred modifier ordering per prime and domain. It can be seen that in the preferred prime conditions, participants produce the expected orderings, more or less in accordance with the Google counts.

State-of-the-art realizers would always opt for the most frequent ordering of a given pair of modifiers and hence would never predict the dispreferred orderings to occur. Still, the use of the dispreferred modifier ordering occurred significantly more often than one would expect given this prediction, $t_{furniture}$ [27] = 6.56, $p < 0.01$ and t_{people} [27] = 9.55, $p < 0.01$. To test our hypotheses concerning adaptation, we looked at the dispreferred realizations when speakers were exposed to dispreferred primes (compared to preferred primes). In both domains this resulted in an increase of the anount of dispreferred realizations, which was significant in the People domain (t_{people} [27] = 1.99, $p < 0.05$, $t_{furniture}$ [25] = 2.63, $p < 0.01$).

4 Discussion

Current state-of-the-art REG algorithms often rest upon the assumption that some attributes and some realizations are preferred over others. The two experiments described in this paper show that this assumption is incorrect, when references are produced in an interactive setting. In both experiments, speakers were more likely to select a dispreferred attribute or produce a dispreferred modifier ordering when they had previously been exposed to these attributes or orderings, without being aware of this. These findings fit in well with the adaptation and alignment models proposed by psycholinguists, but ours, as far as we know, is the first experimental evidence of alignment in attribute selection and in modifier ordering. Interestingly, we found that effect sizes differ for the different domains, indicating that the trade-off between preferences and adaptions is a gradual one, also influenced by the *a priori* differences in preference (it is more difficult to make people say something truly dispreferred than something more marginally dispreferred).

To account for these findings, GRE algorithms that function in an interactive setting should be made sensitive to the production of dialogue partners. For the Incremental Algorithm (Dale and Reiter, 1995), this could be achieved by augmenting the list of preferred attributes with a list of "previously mentioned" attributes. The relative weighting of these two lists will be corpus dependent, and can be estimated in a data-driven way. Alternatively, in the Graph-based algorithm (Krahmer et al., 2003), costs of properties could be based on two components: a relatively fixed domain component (preferred is cheaper) and a flexible interactive component (recently used is cheaper). Which approach would work best is an open, empirical question, but either way this would constitute an important step towards interactive REG.

Acknowledgments

The research reported in this paper forms part of the VICI project "Bridging the gap between psycholinguistics and Computational linguistics: the case of referring expressions", funded by the Netherlands Organization for Scientific Research (NWO grant 277-70-007).

References

Jennifer Arnold. 2008. Reference production: Production-internal and addressee-oriented processes. *Language and Cognitive Processes*, 23(4):495–527.

Holly P. Branigan, Martin J. Pickering, Jamie Pearson, and Janet F. McLean. in press. Linguistic alignment between people and computers. *Journal of Pragmatics*, 23:1–2.

Susan E. Brennan and Herbert H. Clark. 1996. Conceptual pacts and lexical choice in conversation. *Journal of Experimental Psychology: Learning, Memory, and Cognition*, 22:1482–1493.

Hendrik Buschmeier, Kirsten Bergmann, and Stefan Kopp. 2009. An alignment-capable microplanner for Natural Language Generation. In *Proceedings of the 12th European Workshop on Natural Language Generation (ENLG 2009)*, pages 82–89, Athens, Greece, March. Association for Computational Linguistics.

Robert Dale and Ehud Reiter. 1995. Computational interpretations of the gricean maxims in the generation of referring expressions. *Cognitive Science*, 19(2):233–263.

Paul E. Engelhardt, Karl G. Bailey, and Fernanda Ferreira. 2006. Do speakers and listeners observe the gricean maxim of quantity? *Journal of Memory and Language*, 54(4):554–573.

Albert Gatt, Ielka van der Sluis, and Kees van Deemter. 2007. Evaluating algorithms for the generation of referring expressions using a balanced corpus. In *Proceedings of the 11th European Workshop on Natural Language Generation.*

Srinivasan Janarthanam and Oliver Lemon. 2009. Learning lexical alignment policies for generating referring expressions for spoken dialogue systems. In *Proceedings of the 12th European Workshop on Natural Language Generation (ENLG 2009)*, pages 74–81, Athens, Greece, March. Association for Computational Linguistics.

Ruud Koolen, Albert Gatt, Martijn Goudbeek, and Emiel Krahmer. 2009. Need I say more? on factors causing referential overspecification. In *Proceedings of the PRE-CogSci 2009 Workshop on the Production of Referring Expressions: Bridging the Gap Between Computational and Empirical Approaches to Reference.*

Emiel Krahmer, Sebastiaan van Erk, and André Verleg. 2003. Graph-based generation of referring expressions. *Computational Linguistics*, 29(1):53–72.

Robert Malouf. 2000. The order of prenominal adjectives in natural language generation. In *Proceedings of the 38th Annual Meeting of the Association for Computational Linguistics*, pages 85–92.

Chris Mellish, Donia Scott, Lynn Cahill, Daniel Paiva, Roger Evans, and Mike Reape. 2006. A reference architecture for natural language generation systems. *Natural Language Engineering*, 12:1–34.

Margaret Mitchell. 2009. Class-based ordering of prenominal modifiers. In *ENLG '09: Proceedings of the 12th European Workshop on Natural Language Generation*, pages 50–57, Morristown, NJ, USA. Association for Computational Linguistics.

Thomas Pechmann. 1989. Incremental speech production and referential overspecification. *Linguistics*, 27:89–110.

Martin Pickering and Simon Garrod. 2004. Towards a mechanistic psychology of dialogue. *Behavioural and Brain Sciences*, 27:169–226.

Ehud Reiter and Robert Dale. 2000. *Building Natural Language Generation Systems*. Cambridge University Press.

James Shaw and Vasileios Hatzivassiloglou. 1999. Ordering among premodifiers. In *Proceedings of the 37th annual meeting of the Association for Computational Linguistics on Computational Linguistics*, pages 135–143.

Cognitively Plausible Models of Human Language Processing

Frank Keller
School of Informatics, University of Edinburgh
10 Crichton Street, Edinburgh EH8 9AB, UK
keller@inf.ed.ac.uk

Abstract

We pose the development of cognitively plausible models of human language processing as a challenge for computational linguistics. Existing models can only deal with isolated phenomena (e.g., garden paths) on small, specifically selected data sets. The challenge is to build models that integrate multiple aspects of human language processing at the syntactic, semantic, and discourse level. Like human language processing, these models should be incremental, predictive, broad coverage, and robust to noise. This challenge can only be met if standardized data sets and evaluation measures are developed.

1 Introduction

In many respects, human language processing is the ultimate goldstandard for computational linguistics. Humans understand and generate language with amazing speed and accuracy, they are able to deal with ambiguity and noise effortlessly and can adapt to new speakers, domains, and registers. Most surprisingly, they achieve this competency on the basis of limited training data (Hart and Risley, 1995), using learning algorithms that are largely unsupervised.

Given the impressive performance of humans as language processors, it seems natural to turn to psycholinguistics, the discipline that studies human language processing, as a source of information about the design of efficient language processing systems. Indeed, psycholinguists have uncovered an impressive array of relevant facts (reviewed in Section 2), but computational linguists are often not aware of this literature, and results about human language processing rarely inform the design, implementation, or evaluation of artificial language processing systems.

At the same time, research in psycholinguistics is often oblivious of work in computational linguistics (CL). To test their theories, psycholinguists construct computational models of human language processing, but these models often fall short of the engineering standards that are generally accepted in the CL community (e.g., broad coverage, robustness, efficiency): typical psycholinguistic models only deal with isolated phenomena and fail to scale to realistic data sets. A particular issue is evaluation, which is typically anecdotal, performed on a small set of handcrafted examples (see Sections 3).

In this paper, we propose a challenge that requires the combination of research efforts in computational linguistics and psycholinguistics: the development of cognitively plausible models of human language processing. This task can be decomposed into a modeling challenge (building models that instantiate known properties of human language processing) and a data and evaluation challenge (accounting for experimental findings and evaluating against standardized data sets), which we will discuss in turn.

2 Modeling Challenge

2.1 Key Properties

The first part of the challenge is to develop a model that instantiates key properties of human language processing, as established by psycholinguistic experimentation (see Table 1 for an overview and representative references).[1] A striking property of the human language processor is its *efficiency and robustness*. For the vast majority of sentences, it will effortlessly and rapidly deliver the correct analysis, even in the face of noise and ungrammaticalities. There is considerable experimental evi-

[1]Here an in the following, we will focus on sentence processing, which is often regarded as a central aspect of human language processing. A more comprehensive answer to our modeling challenge should also include phonological and morphological processing, semantic inference, discourse processing, and other non-syntactic aspects of language processing. Furthermore, established results regarding the interface between language processing and non-linguistic cognition (e.g., the sensorimotor system) should ultimately be accounted for in a fully comprehensive model.

Proceedings of the ACL 2010 Conference Short Papers, pages 60–67,
Uppsala, Sweden, 11-16 July 2010.

Property	Evidence	Model Rank	Surp	Pred	Stack
Efficiency and robustness	Ferreira et al. (2001); Sanford and Sturt (2002)	−	−	−	+
Broad coverage	Crocker and Brants (2000)	+	+	−	+
Incrementality and connectedness	Tanenhaus et al. (1995); Sturt and Lombardo (2005)	+	+	+	+
Prediction	Kamide et al. (2003); Staub and Clifton (2006)	−	±	+	−
Memory cost	Gibson (1998); Vasishth and Lewis (2006)	−	−	+	+

Table 1: Key properties of human language processing and their instantiation in various models of sentence processing (see Section 2 for details)

dence that shallow processing strategies are used to achieve this. The processor also achieves *broad coverage:* it can deal with a wide variety of syntactic constructions, and is not restricted by the domain, register, or modality of the input.

Human language processing is also word-by-word *incremental.* There is strong evidence that a new word is integrated as soon as it is available into the representation of the sentence thus far. Readers and listeners experience differential processing difficulty during this integration process, depending on the properties of the new word and its relationship to the preceding context. There is evidence that the processor instantiates a strict form of incrementality by building only fully connected trees. Furthermore, the processor is able to make *predictions* about upcoming material on the basis of sentence prefixes. For instance, listeners can predict an upcoming post-verbal element based on the semantics of the preceding verb. Or they can make syntactic predictions, e.g., if they encounter the word *either*, they predict an upcoming *or* and the type of complement that follows it.

Another key property of human language processing is the fact that it operates with limited memory, and that structures in memory are subject to decay and interference. In particular, the processor is known to incur a distance-based *memory cost:* combining the head of a phrase with its syntactic dependents is more difficult the more dependents have to be integrated and the further away they are. This integration process is also subject to interference from similar items that have to be held in memory at the same time.

2.2 Current Models

The challenge is to develop a computational model that captures the key properties of human language processing outlined in the previous section. A number of relevant models have been developed, mostly based on probabilistic parsing techniques, but none of them instantiates all the key properties discussed above (Table 1 gives an overview of model properties).[2]

The earliest approaches were *ranking-based models* (Rank), which make psycholinguistic predictions based on the ranking of the syntactic analyses produced by a probabilistic parser. Jurafsky (1996) assumes that processing difficulty is triggered if the correct analysis falls below a certain probability threshold (i.e., is pruned by the parser). Similarly, Crocker and Brants (2000) assume that processing difficulty ensures if the highest-ranked analysis changes from one word to the next. Both approaches have been shown to successfully model garden path effects. Being based on probabilistic parsing techniques, ranking-based models generally achieve a broad coverage, but their efficiency and robustness has not been evaluated. Also, they are not designed to capture syntactic prediction or memory effects (other than search with a narrow beam in Brants and Crocker 2000).

The ranking-based approach has been generalized by *surprisal models* (Surp), which predict processing difficulty based on the change in the probability distribution over possible analyses from one word to the next (Hale, 2001; Levy, 2008; Demberg and Keller, 2008a; Ferrara Boston et al., 2008; Roark et al., 2009). These models have been successful in accounting for a range of experimental data, and they achieve broad coverage. They also instantiate a limited form of prediction, viz., they build up expectations about the next word in the input. On the other hand, the efficiency and robustness of these models has largely not been evaluated, and memory costs are not modeled (again except for restrictions in beam size).

The *prediction model* (Pred) explicitly predicts syntactic structure for upcoming words (Demberg and Keller, 2008b, 2009), thus accounting for experimental results on predictive language processing. It also implements a strict form of incre-

[2]We will not distinguish between model and linking theory, i.e., the set of assumptions that links model quantities to behavioral data (e.g., more probably structures are easier to process). It is conceivable, for instance, that a stack-based model is combined with a linking theory based on surprisal.

Factor	Evidence
Word senses	Roland and Jurafsky (2002)
Selectional restrictions	Garnsey et al. (1997); Pickering and Traxler (1998)
Thematic roles	McRae et al. (1998); Pickering et al. (2000)
Discourse reference	Altmann and Steedman (1988); Grodner and Gibson (2005)
Discourse coherence	Stewart et al. (2000); Kehler et al. (2008)

Table 2: Semantic factors in human language processing

mentality by building fully connected trees. Memory costs are modeled directly as a distance-based penalty that is incurred when a prediction has to be verified later in the sentence. However, the current implementation of the prediction model is neither robust and efficient nor offers broad coverage.

Recently, a *stack-based model* (Stack) has been proposed that imposes explicit, cognitively motivated memory constraints on the parser, in effect limiting the stack size available to the parser (Schuler et al., 2010). This delivers robustness, efficiency, and broad coverage, but does not model syntactic prediction. Unlike the other models discussed here, no psycholinguistic evaluation has been conducted on the stack-based model, so its cognitive plausibility is preliminary.

2.3 Beyond Parsing

There is strong evidence that human language processing is driven by an interaction of syntactic, semantic, and discourse processes (see Table 2 for an overview and references). Considerable experimental work has focused on the semantic properties of the verb of the sentence, and verb sense, selectional restrictions, and thematic roles have all been shown to interact with syntactic ambiguity resolution. Another large body of research has elucidated the interaction of discourse processing and syntactic processing. The most-well known effect is probably that of referential context: syntactic ambiguities can be resolved if a discourse context is provided that makes one of the syntactic alternatives more plausible. For instance, in a context that provides two possible antecedents for a noun phrase, the processor will prefer attaching a PP or a relative clause such that it disambiguates between the two antecedents; garden paths are reduced or disappear. Other results point to the importance of discourse coherence for sentence processing, an example being implicit causality.

The challenge facing researchers in computational and psycholinguistics therefore includes the development of language processing models that combine syntactic processing with semantic and discourse processing. So far, this challenge is largely unmet: there are some examples of models that integrate semantic processes such as thematic role assignment into a parsing model (Narayanan and Jurafsky, 2002; Padó et al., 2009). However, other semantic factors are not accounted for by these models, and incorporating non-lexical aspects of semantics into models of sentence processing is a challenge for ongoing research. Recently, Dubey (2010) has proposed an approach that combines a probabilistic parser with a model of co-reference and discourse inference based on probabilistic logic. An alternative approach has been taken by Pynte et al. (2008) and Mitchell et al. (2010), who combine a vector-space model of semantics (Landauer and Dumais, 1997) with a syntactic parser and show that this results in predictions of processing difficulty that can be validated against an eye-tracking corpus.

2.4 Acquisition and Crosslinguistics

All models of human language processing discussed so far rely on supervised training data. This raises another aspect of the modeling challenge: the human language processor is the product of an acquisition process that is largely unsupervised and has access to only limited training data: children aged 12–36 months are exposed to between 10 and 35 million words of input (Hart and Risley, 1995). The challenge therefore is to develop a model of language acquisition that works with such small training sets, while also giving rise to a language processor that meets the key criteria in Table 1. The CL community is in a good position to rise to this challenge, given the significant progress in unsupervised parsing in recent years (starting from Klein and Manning 2002). However, none of the existing unsupervised models has been evaluated against psycholinguistic data sets, and they are not designed to meet even basic psycholinguistic criteria such as incrementality.

A related modeling challenge is the development of processing models for languages other than English. There is a growing body of experimental research investigating human language processing in other languages, but virtually all existing psycholinguistic models only work for English (the only exceptions we are aware of are Dubey et al.'s (2008) and Ferrara Boston et al.'s

(2008) parsing models for German). Again, the CL community has made significant progress in crosslinguistic parsing, especially using dependency grammar (Hajič, 2009), and psycholinguistic modeling could benefit from this in order to meet the challenge of developing crosslinguistically valid models of human language processing.

3 Data and Evaluation Challenge

3.1 Test Sets

The second key challenge that needs to be addressed in order to develop cognitively plausible models of human language processing concerns test data and model evaluation. Here, the state of the art in psycholinguistic modeling lags significantly behind standards in the CL community. Most of the models discussed in Section 2 have not been evaluated rigorously. The authors typically describe their performance on a small set of hand-picked examples; no attempts are made to test on a range of items from the experimental literature and determine model fit directly against behavioral measures (e.g., reading times). This makes it very hard to obtain a realistic estimate of how well the models achieve their aim of capturing human language processing behavior.

We therefore suggest the development of standard test sets for psycholinguistic modeling, similar to what is commonplace for tasks in computational linguistics: parsers are evaluated against the Penn Treebank, word sense disambiguation systems against the SemEval data sets, co-reference systems against the Tipster or ACE corpora, etc. Two types of test data are required for psycholinguistic modeling. The first type of test data consists of a collection of representative experimental results. This collection should contain the actual experimental materials (sentences or discourse fragments) used in the experiments, together with the behavioral measurements obtained (reading times, eye-movement records, rating judgments, etc.). The experiments included in this test set would be chosen to cover a wide range of experimental phenomena, e.g., garden paths, syntactic complexity, memory effects, semantic and discourse factors. Such a test set will enable the standardized evaluation of psycholinguistic models by comparing the model predictions (rankings, surprisal values, memory costs, etc.) against behavioral measures on a large set of items. This way both the coverage of a model (how many phenomena can it account for) and its accuracy (how well does it fit the behavioral data) can be assessed.

Experimental test sets should be complemented by test sets based on corpus data. In order to assess the efficiency, robustness, and broad coverage of a model, a corpus of unrestricted, naturally occurring text is required. The use of contextualized language data makes it possible to assess not only syntactic models, but also models that capture discourse effects. These corpora need to be annotated with behavioral measures, e.g., eye-tracking or reading time data. Some relevant corpora have already been constructed, see the overview in Table 3, and various authors have used them for model evaluation (Demberg and Keller, 2008a; Pynte et al., 2008; Frank, 2009; Ferrara Boston et al., 2008; Patil et al., 2009; Roark et al., 2009; Mitchell et al., 2010).

However, the usefulness of the psycholinguistic corpora in Table 3 is restricted by the absence of gold-standard linguistic annotation (though the French part of the Dundee corpus, which is syntactically annotated). This makes it difficult to test the accuracy of the linguistic structures computed by a model, and restricts evaluation to behavioral predictions. The challenge is therefore to collect a standardized test set of naturally occurring text or speech enriched not only with behavioral variables, but also with syntactic and semantic annotation. Such a data set could for example be constructed by eye-tracking section 23 of the Penn Treebank (which is also part of Propbank, and thus has both syntactic and thematic role annotation).

In computational linguistics, the development of new data sets is often stimulated by competitions in which systems are compared on a standardized task, using a data set specifically designed for the competition. Examples include the CoNLL shared task, SemEval, or TREC in computational syntax, semantics, and discourse, respectively. A similar competition could be developed for computational psycholinguistics – maybe along the lines of the model comparison challenges that held at the International Conference on Cognitive Modeling. These challenges provide standardized task descriptions and data sets; participants can enter their cognitive models, which were then compared using a pre-defined evaluation metric.[3]

[3]The ICCM 2009 challenge was the Dynamic Stock and Flows Task, for more information see http://www.hss.cmu.edu/departments/sds/ddmlab/modeldsf/.

Corpus	Language	Words	Participants	Method	Reference
Dundee Corpus	English, French	50,000	10	Eye-tracking	Kennedy and Pynte (2005)
Potsdam Corpus	German	1,138	222	Eye-tracking	Kliegl et al. (2006)
MIT Corpus	English	3,534	23	Self-paced reading	Bachrach (2008)

Table 3: Test corpora that have been used for psycholinguistic modeling of sentence processing; note that the Potsdam Corpus consists of isolated sentences, rather than of continuous text

3.2 Behavioral and Neural Data

As outlined in the previous section, a number of authors have evaluated psycholinguistic models against eye-tracking or reading time corpora. Part of the data and evaluation challenge is to extend this evaluation to neural data as provided by event-related potential (ERP) or brain imaging studies (e.g., using functional magnetic resonance imaging, fMRI). Neural data sets are considerably more complex than behavioral ones, and modeling them is an important new task that the community is only beginning to address. Some recent work has evaluated models of word semantics against ERP (Murphy et al., 2009) or fMRI data (Mitchell et al., 2008).[4] This is a very promising direction, and the challenge is to extend this approach to the sentence and discourse level (see Bachrach 2008). Again, it will again be necessary to develop standardized test sets of both experimental data and corpus data.

3.3 Evaluation Measures

We also anticipate that the availability of new test data sets will facilitate the development of new evaluation measures that specifically test the validity of psycholinguistic models. Established CL evaluation measures such as Parseval are of limited use, as they can only test the linguistic, but not the behavioral or neural predictions of a model.

So far, many authors have relied on qualitative evaluation: if a model predicts a difference in (for instance) reading time between two types of sentences where such a difference was also found experimentally, then that counts as a successful test. In most cases, no quantitative evaluation is performed, as this would require modeling the reading times for individual item and individual participants. Suitable procedures for performing such tests do not currently exist; linear mixed effects models (Baayen et al., 2008) provide a way of dealing with item and participant variation, but crucially do not enable direct comparisons between models in terms of goodness of fit.

[4]These data sets were released as part of the NAACL-2010 Workshop on Computational Neurolinguistics.

Further issues arise from the fact that we often want to compare model fit for multiple experiments (ideally without reparametrizing the models), and that various mutually dependent measures are used for evaluation, e.g., processing effort at the sentence, word, and character level. An important open challenge is there to develop evaluation measures and associated statistical procedures that can deal with these problems.

4 Conclusions

In this paper, we discussed the modeling and data/evaluation challenges involved in developing cognitively plausible models of human language processing. Developing computational models is of scientific importance in so far as models are implemented theories: models of language processing allow us to test scientific hypothesis about the cognitive processes that underpin language processing. This type of precise, formalized hypothesis testing is only possible if standardized data sets and uniform evaluation procedures are available, as outlined in the present paper. Ultimately, this approach enables qualitative and quantitative comparisons between theories, and thus enhances our understanding of a key aspect of human cognition, language processing.

There is also an applied side to the proposed challenge. Once computational models of human language processing are available, they can be used to predict the difficulty that humans experience when processing text or speech. This is useful for a number applications: for instance, natural language generation would benefit from being able to assess whether machine-generated text or speech is easy to process. For text simplification (e.g., for children or impaired readers), such a model is even more essential. It could also be used to assess the readability of text, which is of interest in educational applications (e.g., essay scoring). In machine translation, evaluating the fluency of system output is crucial, and a model that predicts processing difficulty could be used for this, or to guide the choice between alternative translations, and maybe even to inform human post-editing.

References

Altmann, Gerry T. M. and Mark J. Steedman. 1988. Interaction with context during human sentence processing. *Cognition* 30(3):191–238.

Baayen, R. H., D. J. Davidson, and D. M. Bates. 2008. Mixed-effects modeling with crossed random effects for subjects and items. *Journal of Memory and Language* to appear.

Bachrach, Asaf. 2008. *Imaging Neural Correlates of Syntactic Complexity in a Naturalistic Context*. Ph.D. thesis, Massachusetts Institute of Technology, Cambridge, MA.

Brants, Thorsten and Matthew W. Crocker. 2000. Probabilistic parsing and psychological plausibility. In *Proceedings of the 18th International Conference on Computational Linguistics*. Saarbrücken/Luxembourg/Nancy, pages 111–117.

Crocker, Matthew W. and Thorsten Brants. 2000. Wide-coverage probabilistic sentence processing. *Journal of Psycholinguistic Research* 29(6):647–669.

Demberg, Vera and Frank Keller. 2008a. Data from eye-tracking corpora as evidence for theories of syntactic processing complexity. *Cognition* 101(2):193–210.

Demberg, Vera and Frank Keller. 2008b. A psycholinguistically motivated version of TAG. In *Proceedings of the 9th International Workshop on Tree Adjoining Grammars and Related Formalisms*. Tübingen, pages 25–32.

Demberg, Vera and Frank Keller. 2009. A computational model of prediction in human parsing: Unifying locality and surprisal effects. In Niels Taatgen and Hedderik van Rijn, editors, *Proceedings of the 31st Annual Conference of the Cognitive Science Society*. Cognitive Science Society, Amsterdam, pages 1888–1893.

Dubey, Amit. 2010. The influence of discourse on syntax: A psycholinguistic model of sentence processing. In *Proceedings of the 48th Annual Meeting of the Association for Computational Linguistics*. Uppsala.

Dubey, Amit, Frank Keller, and Patrick Sturt. 2008. A probabilistic corpus-based model of syntactic parallelism. *Cognition* 109(3):326–344.

Ferrara Boston, Marisa, John Hale, Reinhold Kliegl, Umesh Patil, and Shravan Vasishth. 2008. Parsing costs as predictors of reading difficulty: An evaluation using the Potsdam Sentence Corpus. *Journal of Eye Movement Research* 2(1):1–12.

Ferreira, Fernanda, Kiel Christianson, and Andrew Hollingworth. 2001. Misinterpretations of garden-path sentences: Implications for models of sentence processing and reanalysis. *Journal of Psycholinguistic Research* 30(1):3–20.

Frank, Stefan L. 2009. Surprisal-based comparison between a symbolic and a connectionist model of sentence processing. In Niels Taatgen and Hedderik van Rijn, editors, *Proceedings of the 31st Annual Conference of the Cognitive Science Society*. Cognitive Science Society, Amsterdam, pages 1139–1144.

Garnsey, Susan M., Neal J. Pearlmutter, Elisabeth M. Myers, and Melanie A. Lotocky. 1997. The contributions of verb bias and plausibility to the comprehension of temporarily ambiguous sentences. *Journal of Memory and Language* 37(1):58–93.

Gibson, Edward. 1998. Linguistic complexity: locality of syntactic dependencies. *Cognition* 68:1–76.

Grodner, Dan and Edward Gibson. 2005. Consequences of the serial nature of linguistic input. *Cognitive Science* 29:261–291.

Hajič, Jan, editor. 2009. *Proceedings of the 13th Conference on Computational Natural Language Learning: Shared Task*. Association for Computational Linguistics, Boulder, CO.

Hale, John. 2001. A probabilistic Earley parser as a psycholinguistic model. In *Proceedings of the 2nd Conference of the North American Chapter of the Association for Computational Linguistics*. Association for Computational Linguistics, Pittsburgh, PA, volume 2, pages 159–166.

Hart, Betty and Todd R. Risley. 1995. *Meaningful Differences in the Everyday Experience of Young American Children*. Paul H. Brookes, Baltimore, MD.

Jurafsky, Daniel. 1996. A probabilistic model of lexical and syntactic access and disambiguation. *Cognitive Science* 20(2):137–194.

Kamide, Yuki, Gerry T. M. Altmann, and Sarah L. Haywood. 2003. The time-course of prediction in incremental sentence processing: Evidence from anticipatory eye movements. *Journal of Memory and Language* 49:133–156.

Kehler, Andrew, Laura Kertz, Hannah Rohde, and Jeffrey L. Elman. 2008. Coherence and coreference revisited. *Journal of Semantics* 25(1):1–44.

Kennedy, Alan and Joel Pynte. 2005. Parafoveal-on-foveal effects in normal reading. *Vision Research* 45:153–168.

Klein, Dan and Christopher Manning. 2002. A generative constituent-context model for improved grammar induction. In *Proceedings of the 40th Annual Meeting of the Association for Computational Linguistics*. Philadelphia, pages 128–135.

Kliegl, Reinhold, Antje Nuthmann, and Ralf Engbert. 2006. Tracking the mind during reading: The influence of past, present, and future words on fixation durations. *Journal of Experimental Psychology: General* 135(1):12–35.

Landauer, Thomas K. and Susan T. Dumais. 1997. A solution to Plato's problem: The latent semantic analysis theory of acquisition, induction and representation of knowledge. *Psychological Review* 104(2):211–240.

Levy, Roger. 2008. Expectation-based syntactic comprehension. *Cognition* 106(3):1126–1177.

McRae, Ken, Michael J. Spivey-Knowlton, and Michael K. Tanenhaus. 1998. Modeling the influence of thematic fit (and other constraints) in on-line sentence comprehension. *Journal of Memory and Language* 38(3):283–312.

Mitchell, Jeff, Mirella Lapata, Vera Demberg, and Frank Keller. 2010. Syntactic and semantic factors in processing difficulty: An integrated measure. In *Proceedings of the 48th Annual Meeting of the Association for Computational Linguistics*. Uppsala.

Mitchell, Tom M., Svetlana V. Shinkareva, Andrew Carlson, Kai-Min Chang, Vicente L. Malave, Robert A. Mason, and Marcel Adam Just3. 2008. Predicting human brain activity associated with the meanings of nouns. *Science* 320(5880):1191–1195.

Murphy, Brian, Marco Baroni, and Massimo Poesio. 2009. EEG responds to conceptual stimuli and corpus semantics. In *Proceedings of the Conference on Empirical Methods in Natural Language Processing*. Singapore, pages 619–627.

Narayanan, Srini and Daniel Jurafsky. 2002. A Bayesian model predicts human parse preference and reading time in sentence processing. In Thomas G. Dietterich, Sue Becker, and Zoubin Ghahramani, editors, *Advances in Neural Information Processing Systems 14*. MIT Press, Cambridge, MA, pages 59–65.

Padó, Ulrike, Matthew W. Crocker, and Frank Keller. 2009. A probabilistic model of semantic plausibility in sentence processing. *Cognitive Science* 33(5):794–838.

Patil, Umesh, Shravan Vasishth, and Reinhold Kliegl. 2009. Compound effect of probabilistic disambiguation and memory retrievals on sentence processing: Evidence from an eye-tracking corpus. In A. Howes, D. Peebles, and R. Cooper, editors, *Proceedings of 9th International Conference on Cognitive Modeling*. Manchester.

Pickering, Martin J. and Martin J. Traxler. 1998. Plausibility and recovery from garden paths: An eye-tracking study. *Journal of Experimental Psychology: Learning Memory and Cognition* 24(4):940–961.

Pickering, Martin J., Matthew J. Traxler, and Matthew W. Crocker. 2000. Ambiguity resolution in sentence processing: Evidence against frequency-based accounts. *Journal of Memory and Language* 43(3):447–475.

Pynte, Joel, Boris New, and Alan Kennedy. 2008. On-line contextual influences during reading normal text: A multiple-regression analysis. *Vision Research* 48(21):2172–2183.

Roark, Brian, Asaf Bachrach, Carlos Cardenas, and Christophe Pallier. 2009. Deriving lexical and syntactic expectation-based measures for psycholinguistic modeling via incremental top-down parsing. In *Proceedings of the Conference on Empirical Methods in Natural Language Processing*. Singapore, pages 324–333.

Roland, Douglas and Daniel Jurafsky. 2002. Verb sense and verb subcategorization probabilities. In Paola Merlo and Suzanne Stevenson, editors, *The Lexical Basis of Sentence Processing: Formal, Computational, and Experimental Issues*, John Bejamins, Amsterdam, pages 325–346.

Sanford, Anthony J. and Patrick Sturt. 2002.

Depth of processing in language comprehension: Not noticing the evidence. *Trends in Cognitive Sciences* 6:382–386.

Schuler, William, Samir AbdelRahman, Tim Miller, and Lane Schwartz. 2010. Broad-coverage parsing using human-like memory constraints. *Computational Linguistics* 26(1):1–30.

Staub, Adrian and Charles Clifton. 2006. Syntactic prediction in language comprehension: Evidence from either ... or. *Journal of Experimental Psychology: Learning, Memory, and Cognition* 32:425–436.

Stewart, Andrew J., Martin J. Pickering, and Anthony J. Sanford. 2000. The time course of the influence of implicit causality information: Focusing versus integration accounts. *Journal of Memory and Language* 42(3):423–443.

Sturt, Patrick and Vincenzo Lombardo. 2005. Processing coordinated structures: Incrementality and connectedness. *Cognitive Science* 29(2):291–305.

Tanenhaus, Michael K., Michael J. Spivey-Knowlton, Kathleen M. Eberhard, and Julie C. Sedivy. 1995. Integration of visual and linguistic information in spoken language comprehension. *Science* 268:1632–1634.

Vasishth, Shravan and Richard L. Lewis. 2006. Argument-head distance and processing complexity: Explaining both locality and antilocality effects. *Language* 82(4):767–794.

The Manually Annotated Sub-Corpus: A Community Resource For and By the People

Nancy Ide
Department of Computer Science
Vassar College
Poughkeepsie, NY, USA
ide@cs.vassar.edu

Collin Baker
International Computer Science Institute
Berkeley, California USA
collinb@icsi.berkeley.edu

Christiane Fellbaum
Princeton University
Princeton, New Jersey USA
fellbaum@princeton.edu

Rebecca Passonneau
Columbia University
New York, New York USA
becky@cs.columbia.edu

Abstract

The Manually Annotated Sub-Corpus (MASC) project provides data and annotations to serve as the base for a community-wide annotation effort of a subset of the American National Corpus. The MASC infrastructure enables the incorporation of contributed annotations into a single, usable format that can then be analyzed as it is or ported to any of a variety of other formats. MASC includes data from a much wider variety of genres than existing multiply-annotated corpora of English, and the project is committed to a fully open model of distribution, without restriction, for all data and annotations produced or contributed. As such, MASC is the first large-scale, open, community-based effort to create much needed language resources for NLP. This paper describes the MASC project, its corpus and annotations, and serves as a call for contributions of data and annotations from the language processing community.

1 Introduction

The need for corpora annotated for multiple phenomena across a variety of linguistic layers is keenly recognized in the computational linguistics community. Several multiply-annotated corpora exist, especially for Western European languages and for spoken data, but, interestingly, broad-based English language corpora with robust annotation for diverse linguistic phenomena are relatively rare. The most widely-used corpus of English, the British National Corpus, contains only part-of-speech annotation; and although it contains a wider range of annotation types, the fifteen million word Open American National Corpus annotations are largely unvalidated. The most well-known multiply-annotated and validated corpus of English is the one million word *Wall Street Journal* corpus known as the Penn Treebank (Marcus et al., 1993), which over the years has been fully or partially annotated for several phenomena over and above the original part-of-speech tagging and phrase structure annotation. The usability of these annotations is limited, however, by the fact that many of them were produced by independent projects using their own tools and formats, making it difficult to combine them in order to study their inter-relations. More recently, the OntoNotes project (Pradhan et al., 2007) released a one million word English corpus of newswire, broadcast news, and broadcast conversation that is annotated for Penn Treebank syntax, PropBank predicate argument structures, coreference, and named entities. OntoNotes comes closest to providing a corpus with multiple layers of annotation that can be analyzed as a unit via its representation of the annotations in a "normal form". However, like the *Wall Street Journal* corpus, OntoNotes is limited in the range of genres it includes. It is also limited to only those annotations that may be produced by members of the OntoNotes project. In addition, use of the data and annotations with software other than the OntoNotes database API is not necessarily straightforward.

The sparseness of reliable multiply-annotated corpora can be attributed to several factors. The greatest obstacle is the high cost of manual production and validation of linguistic annotations. Furthermore, the production and annotation of corpora, even when they involve significant scientific research, often do not, *per se*, lead to publishable research results. It is therefore understand-

Proceedings of the ACL 2010 Conference Short Papers, pages 68–73,
Uppsala, Sweden, 11-16 July 2010.

able that many research groups are unwilling to get involved in such a massive undertaking for relatively little reward.

The Manually Annotated Sub-Corpus (MASC) (Ide et al., 2008) project has been established to address many of these obstacles to the creation of large-scale, robust, multiply-annotated corpora. The project is providing appropriate data and annotations to serve as the base for a community-wide annotation effort, together with an infrastructure that enables the representation of internally-produced and contributed annotations in a single, usable format that can then be analyzed as it is or ported to any of a variety of other formats, thus enabling its immediate use with many common annotation platforms as well as off-the-shelf concordance and analysis software. The MASC project's aim is to offset some of the high costs of producing high quality linguistic annotations via a distribution of effort, and to solve some of the usability problems for annotations produced at different sites by harmonizing their representation formats.

The MASC project provides a resource that is significantly different from OntoNotes and similar corpora. It provides data from a much wider variety of genres than existing multiply-annotated corpora of English, and all of the data in the corpus are drawn from current American English so as to be most useful for NLP applications. Perhaps most importantly, the MASC project is committed to a fully open model of distribution, without restriction, for all data and annotations. It is also committed to incorporating diverse annotations contributed by the community, regardless of format, into the corpus. As such, MASC is the first large-scale, open, community-based effort to create a much-needed language resource for NLP. This paper describes the MASC project, its corpus and annotations, and serves as a call for contributions of data and annotations from the language processing community.

2 MASC: The Corpus

MASC is a balanced subset of 500K words of written texts and transcribed speech drawn primarily from the Open American National Corpus (OANC)[1]. The OANC is a 15 million word (and growing) corpus of American English produced since 1990, all of which is in the public domain or otherwise free of usage and redistribution restrictions.

Genre	No. texts	Total words
Email	2	468
Essay	4	17516
Fiction	4	20413
Gov't documents	1	6064
Journal	10	25635
Letters	31	10518
Newspaper/newswire	41	17951
Non-fiction	4	17118
Spoken	11	25783
Debate transcript	2	32325
Court transcript	1	20817
Technical	3	15417
Travel guides	4	12463
Total	118	222488

Table 1: MASC Composition (first 220K)

Where licensing permits, data for inclusion in MASC is drawn from sources that have already been heavily annotated by others. So far, the first 80K increment of MASC data includes a 40K subset consisting of OANC data that has been previously annotated for PropBank predicate argument structures, Pittsburgh Opinion annotation (opinions, evaluations, sentiments, etc.), TimeML time and events[2], and several other linguistic phenomena. It also includes a handful of small texts from the so-called Language Understanding (LU) Corpus[3] that has been annotated by multiple groups for a wide variety of phenomena, including events and committed belief. All of the first 80K increment is annotated for Penn Treebank syntax. The second 120K increment includes 5.5K words of *Wall Street Journal* texts that have been annotated by several projects, including Penn Treebank, PropBank, Penn Discourse Treebank, TimeML, and the Pittsburgh Opinion project. The composition of the 220K portion of the corpus annotated so far is shown in Table 1. The remaining 280K of the corpus fills out the genres that are under-represented in the first portion and includes a few additional genres such as blogs and tweets.

3 MASC Annotations

Annotations for a variety of linguistic phenomena, either manually produced or corrected from output of automatic annotation systems, are being added

[1]http://www.anc.org

[2]The TimeML annotations of the data are not yet completed.

[3]MASC contains about 2K words of the 10K LU corpus, eliminating non-English and translated LU texts as well as texts that are not free of usage and redistribution restrictions.

Annotation type	Method	No. texts	No. words
Token	Validated	118	222472
Sentence	Validated	118	222472
POS/lemma	Validated	118	222472
Noun chunks	Validated	118	222472
Verb chunks	Validated	118	222472
Named entities	Validated	118	222472
FrameNet frames	Manual	21	17829
HSPG	Validated	40*	30106
Discourse	Manual	40*	30106
Penn Treebank	Validated	97	87383
PropBank	Validated	92	50165
Opinion	Manual	97	47583
TimeBank	Validated	34	5434
Committed belief	Manual	13	4614
Event	Manual	13	4614
Coreference	Manual	2	1877

Table 2: Current MASC Annotations (* projected)

to MASC data in increments of roughly 100K words. To date, validated or manually produced annotations for 222K words have been made available.

The MASC project is itself producing annotations for portions of the corpus for WordNet senses and FrameNet frames and frame elements. To derive maximal benefit from the semantic information provided by these resources, the entire corpus is also annotated and manually validated for shallow parses (noun and verb chunks) and named entities (person, location, organization, date and time). Several additional types of annotation have either been contracted by the MASC project or contributed from other sources. The 220K words of MASC I and II include seventeen different types of linguistic annotation[4], shown in Table 2.

All MASC annotations, whether contributed or produced in-house, are transduced to the Graph Annotation Framework (GrAF) (Ide and Suderman, 2007) defined by ISO TC37 SC4's Linguistic Annotation Framework (LAF) (Ide and Romary, 2004). GrAF is an XML serialization of the LAF abstract model of annotations, which consists of a directed graph decorated with feature structures providing the annotation content. GrAF's primary role is to serve as a "pivot" format for transducing among annotations represented in different formats. However, because the underlying data structure is a graph, the GrAF representation itself can serve as the basis for analysis via application of graph-analytic algorithms such as common subtree detection.

The layering of annotations over MASC texts dictates the use of a stand-off annotation representation format, in which each annotation is contained in a separate document linked to the primary data. Each text in the corpus is provided in UTF-8 character encoding in a separate file, which includes no annotation or markup of any kind. Each file is associated with a set of GrAF standoff files, one for each annotation type, containing the annotations for that text. In addition to the annotation types listed in Table 2, a document containing annotation for logical structure (titles, headings, sections, etc. down to the level of paragraph) is included. Each text is also associated with (1) a header document that provides appropriate metadata together with machine-processable information about associated annotations and inter-relations among the annotation layers; and (2) a segmentation of the primary data into minimal regions, which enables the definition of different tokenizations over the text. Contributed annotations are also included in their original format, where available.

3.1 WordNet Sense Annotations

A focus of the MASC project is to provide corpus evidence to support an effort to harmonize sense distinctions in WordNet and FrameNet (Baker and Fellbaum, 2009), (Fellbaum and Baker, to appear). The WordNet and FrameNet teams have selected for this purpose 100 common polysemous words whose senses they will study in detail, and the MASC team is annotating occurrences of these words in the MASC. As a first step, fifty occurrences of each word are annotated using the WordNet 3.0 inventory and analyzed for problems in sense assignment, after which the WordNet team may make modifications to the inventory if needed. The revised inventory (which will be released as part of WordNet 3.1) is then used to annotate 1000 occurrences. Because of its small size, MASC typically contains less than 1000 occurrences of a given word; the remaining occurrences are therefore drawn from the 15 million words of the OANC. Furthermore, the FrameNet team is also annotating one hundred of the 1000 sentences for each word with FrameNet frames and frame elements, providing direct comparisons of WordNet and FrameNet sense assignments in

[4]This includes WordNet sense annotations, which are not listed in Table 2 because they are not applied to full texts; see Section 3.1 for a description of the WordNet sense annotations in MASC.

attested sentences.[5]

For convenience, the annotated sentences are provided as a stand-alone corpus, with the WordNet and FrameNet annotations represented in standoff files. Each sentence in this corpus is linked to its occurrence in the original text, so that the context and other annotations associated with the sentence may be retrieved.

3.2 Validation

Automatically-produced annotations for sentence, token, part of speech, shallow parses (noun and verb chunks), and named entities (person, location, organization, date and time) are hand-validated by a team of students. Each annotation set is first corrected by one student, after which it is checked (and corrected where necessary) by a second student, and finally checked by both automatic extraction of the annotated data and a third pass over the annotations by a graduate student or senior researcher. We have performed inter-annotator agreement studies for shallow parses in order to establish the number of passes required to achieve near-100% accuracy.

Annotations produced by other projects and the FrameNet and Penn Treebank annotations produced specifically for MASC are semi-automatically and/or manually produced by those projects and subjected to their internal quality controls. No additional validation is performed by the ANC project.

The WordNet sense annotations are being used as a base for an extensive inter-annotator agreement study, which is described in detail in (Passonneau et al., 2009), (Passonneau et al., 2010). All inter-annotator agreement data and statistics are published along with the sense tags. The release also includes documentation on the words annotated in each round, the sense labels for each word, the sentences for each word, and the annotator or annotators for each sense assignment to each word in context. For the multiply annotated data in rounds 2-4, we include raw tables for each word in the form expected by Ron Artstein's calculate_alpha.pl perl script[6], so that the agreement numbers can be regenerated.

[5] Note that several MASC texts have been fully annotated for FrameNet frames and frame elements, in addition to the WordNet-tagged sentences.

[6] http://ron.artstein.org/resources/calculate-alpha.perl

4 MASC Availability and Distribution

Like the OANC, MASC is distributed without license or other restrictions from the American National Corpus website[7]. It is also available from the Linguistic Data Consortium (LDC)[8] for a nominal processing fee.

In addition to enabling download of the entire MASC, we provide a web application that allows users to select some or all parts of the corpus and choose among the available annotations via a web interface (Ide et al., 2010). Once generated, the corpus and annotation bundle is made available to the user for download. Thus, the MASC user need never deal directly with or see the underlying representation of the stand-off annotations, but gains all the advantages that representation offers. The following output formats are currently available:

1. in-line XML (XCES[9]), suitable for use with the BNCs XAIRA search and access interface and other XML-aware software;
2. token / part of speech, a common input format for general-purpose concordance software such as MonoConc[10], as well as the Natural Language Toolkit (NLTK) (Bird et al., 2009);
3. CONLL IOB format, used in the Conference on Natural Language Learning shared tasks.[11]

5 Tools

The ANC project provides an API for GrAF annotations that can be used to access and manipulate GrAF annotations directly from Java programs and render GrAF annotations in a format suitable for input to the open source GraphViz[12] graph visualization application.[13] Beyond this, the ANC project does not provide specific tools for use of the corpus, but rather provides the data in formats suitable for use with a variety of available applications, as described in section 4, together with means to import GrAF annotations into major annotation software platforms. In particular, the ANC project provides plugins for the General

[7] http://www.anc.org

[8] http://www.ldc.upenn.edu

[9] XML Corpus Encoding Standard, http://www.xces.org

[10] http://www.athel.com/mono.html

[11] http://ifarm.nl/signll/conll

[12] http://www.graphviz.org/

[13] http://www.anc.org/graf-api

Architecture for Text Engineering (GATE) (Cunningham et al., 2002) to input and/or output annotations in GrAF format; a "CAS Consumer" to enable using GrAF annotations in the Unstructured Information Management Architecture (UIMA) (Ferrucci and Lally, 2004); and a corpus reader for importing MASC data and annotations into NLTK[14].

Because the GrAF format is isomorphic to input to many graph-analytic tools, existing graph-analytic software can also be exploited to search and manipulate MASC annotations. Trivial merging of GrAF-based annotations involves simply combining the graphs for each annotation, after which graph minimization algorithms[15] can be applied to collapse nodes with edges to common subgraphs to identify commonly annotated components. Graph-traversal and graph-coloring algorithms can also be applied in order to identify and generate statistics that could reveal interactions among linguistic phenomena that may have previously been difficult to observe. Other graph-analytic algorithms — including common sub-graph analysis, shortest paths, minimum spanning trees, connectedness, identification of articulation vertices, topological sort, graph partitioning, etc. — may also prove to be useful for mining information from a graph of annotations at multiple linguistic levels.

6 Community Contributions

The ANC project solicits contributions of annotations of any kind, applied to any part or all of the MASC data. Annotations may be contributed in any format, either inline or standoff. All contributed annotations are ported to GrAF standoff format so that they may be used with other MASC annotations and rendered in the various formats the ANC tools generate. To accomplish this, the ANC project has developed a suite of internal tools and methods for automatically transducing other annotation formats to GrAF and for rapid adaptation of previously unseen formats.

Contributions may be emailed to `anc@cs.vassar.edu` or uploaded via the ANC website[16]. The validity of annotations and supplemental documentation (if appropriate) are the responsibility of the contributor. MASC users may contribute evaluations and error reports for the various annotations on the ANC/MASC wiki[17].

Contributions of unvalidated annotations for MASC and OANC data are also welcomed and are distributed separately. Contributions of unencumbered texts in any genre, including stories, papers, student essays, poetry, blogs, and email, are also solicited via the ANC web site and the ANC FaceBook page[18], and may be uploaded at the contribution page cited above.

7 Conclusion

MASC is already the most richly annotated corpus of English available for widespread use. Because the MASC is an open resource that the community can continually enhance with additional annotations and modifications, the project serves as a model for community-wide resource development in the future. Past experience with corpora such as the *Wall Street Journal* shows that the community is eager to annotate available language data, and we anticipate even greater interest in MASC, which includes language data covering a range of genres that no existing resource provides. Therefore, we expect that as MASC evolves, more and more annotations will be contributed, thus creating a massive, inter-linked linguistic infrastructure for the study and processing of current American English in its many genres and varieties. In addition, by virtue of its WordNet and FrameNet annotations, MASC will be linked to parallel WordNets and FrameNets in languages other than English, thus creating a global resource for multi-lingual technologies, including machine translation.

Acknowledgments

The MASC project is supported by National Science Foundation grant CRI-0708952. The WordNet-FrameNet alignment work is supported by NSF grant IIS 0705155.

References

Collin F. Baker and Christiane Fellbaum. 2009. WordNet and FrameNet as complementary resources for annotation. In *Proceedings of the Third Linguistic*

[14] Available in September, 2010.

[15] Efficient algorithms for graph merging exist; see, e.g., (Habib et al., 2000).

[16] http://www.anc.org/contributions.html

[17] http://www.anc.org/masc-wiki

[18] http://www.facebook.com/pages/American-National-Corpus/42474226671

Annotation Workshop, pages 125–129, Suntec, Singapore, August. Association for Computational Linguistics.

Steven Bird, Ewan Klein, and Edward Loper. 2009. *Natural Language Processing with Python*. O'Reilly Media, 1st edition.

Hamish Cunningham, Diana Maynard, Kalina Bontcheva, and Valentin Tablan. 2002. GATE: A framework and graphical development environment for robust nlp tools and applications. In *Proceedings of ACL'02*.

Christiane Fellbaum and Collin Baker. to appear. Aligning verbs in WordNet and FrameNet. *Linguistics*.

David Ferrucci and Adam Lally. 2004. UIMA: An architectural approach to unstructured information processing in the corporate research environment. *Natural Language Engineering*, 10(3-4):327–348.

Michel Habib, Christophe Paul, and Laurent Viennot. 2000. Partition refinement techniques: an interesting algorithmic tool kit. *International Journal of Foundations of Computer Science*, 175.

Nancy Ide and Laurent Romary. 2004. International standard for a linguistic annotation framework. *Natural Language Engineering*, 10(3-4):211–225.

Nancy Ide and Keith Suderman. 2007. GrAF: A graph-based format for linguistic annotations. In *Proceedings of the Linguistic Annotation Workshop*, pages 1–8, Prague, Czech Republic, June. Association for Computational Linguistics.

Nancy Ide, Collin Baker, Christiane Fellbaum, Charles Fillmore, and Rebecca Passonneau. 2008. MASC: The Manually Annotated Sub-Corpus of American English. In *Proceedings of the Sixth International Conference on Language Resources and Evaluation (LREC)*, Marrakech, Morocco.

Nancy Ide, Keith Suderman, and Brian Simms. 2010. ANC2Go: A web application for customized corpus creation. In *Proceedings of the Seventh International Conference on Language Resources and Evaluation (LREC)*, Valletta, Malta, May. European Language Resources Association.

Mitchell P. Marcus, Mary Ann Marcinkiewicz, and Beatrice Santorini. 1993. Building a large annotated corpus of English: the Penn Treebank. *Computational Linguistics*, 19(2):313–330.

Rebecca J. Passonneau, Ansaf Salleb-Aouissi, and Nancy Ide. 2009. Making sense of word sense variation. In *SEW '09: Proceedings of the Workshop on Semantic Evaluations: Recent Achievements and Future Directions*, pages 2–9, Morristown, NJ, USA. Association for Computational Linguistics.

Rebecca Passonneau, Ansaf Salleb-Aouissi, Vikas Bhardwaj, and Nancy Ide. 2010. Word sense annotation of polysemous words by multiple annotators. In *Proceedings of the Seventh International Conference on Language Resources and Evaluation (LREC)*, Valletta, Malta.

Sameer S. Pradhan, Eduard Hovy, Mitch Marcus, Martha Palmer, Lance Ramshaw, and Ralph Weischedel. 2007. OntoNotes: A unified relational semantic representation. In *ICSC '07: Proceedings of the International Conference on Semantic Computing*, pages 517–526, Washington, DC, USA. IEEE Computer Society.

Correcting Errors in a Treebank Based on Synchronous Tree Substitution Grammar

Yoshihide Kato[1] and **Shigeki Matsubara**[2]
[1]Information Technology Center, Nagoya University
[2]Graduate School of Information Science, Nagoya University
Furo-cho, Chikusa-ku, Nagoya, 464-8601 Japan
yosihide@el.itc.nagoya-u.ac.jp

Abstract

This paper proposes a method of correcting annotation errors in a treebank. By using a synchronous grammar, the method transforms parse trees containing annotation errors into the ones whose errors are corrected. The synchronous grammar is automatically induced from the treebank. We report an experimental result of applying our method to the Penn Treebank. The result demonstrates that our method corrects syntactic annotation errors with high precision.

1 Introduction

Annotated corpora play an important role in the fields such as theoretical linguistic researches or the development of NLP systems. However, they often contain annotation errors which are caused by a manual or semi-manual mark-up process. These errors are problematic for corpus-based researches.

To solve this problem, several error detection and correction methods have been proposed so far (Eskin, 2000; Nakagawa and Matsumoto, 2002; Dickinson and Meurers, 2003a; Dickinson and Meurers, 2003b; Ule and Simov, 2004; Murata et al., 2005; Dickinson and Meurers, 2005; Boyd et al., 2008). These methods detect corpus positions which are marked up incorrectly, and find the correct labels (e.g. pos-tags) for those positions. However, the methods cannot correct errors in structural annotation. This means that they are insufficient to correct annotation errors in a treebank.

This paper proposes a method of correcting errors in structural annotation. Our method is based on a synchronous grammar formalism, called *synchronous tree substitution grammar* (STSG) (Eisner, 2003), which defines a tree-to-tree transformation. By using an STSG, our method transforms parse trees containing errors into the ones whose errors are corrected. The grammar is automatically induced from the treebank. To select STSG rules which are useful for error correction, we define a score function based on the occurrence frequencies of the rules. An experimental result shows that the selected rules archive high precision.

This paper is organized as follows: Section 2 gives an overview of previous work. Section 3 explains our method of correcting errors in a treebank. Section 4 reports an experimental result using the Penn Treebank.

2 Previous Work

This section summarizes previous methods for correcting errors in corpus annotation and discusses their problem.

Some research addresses the detection of errors in pos-annotation (Nakagawa and Matsumoto, 2002; Dickinson and Meurers, 2003a), syntactic annotation (Dickinson and Meurers, 2003b; Ule and Simov, 2004; Dickinson and Meurers, 2005), and dependency annotation (Boyd et al., 2008). These methods only detect corpus positions where errors occur. It is unclear how we can correct the errors.

Several methods can correct annotation errors (Eskin, 2000; Murata et al., 2005). These methods are to correct tag-annotation errors, that is, they simply suggest a candidate tag for each position where an error is detected. The methods cannot correct syntactic annotation errors, because syntactic annotation is structural. There is no approach to correct structural annotation errors.

To clarify the problem, let us consider an example. Figure 1 depicts two parse trees annotated according to the Penn Treebank annotation [1]. The

[1] 0 and *T* are null elements.

Proceedings of the ACL 2010 Conference Short Papers, pages 74–79,
Uppsala, Sweden, 11-16 July 2010.

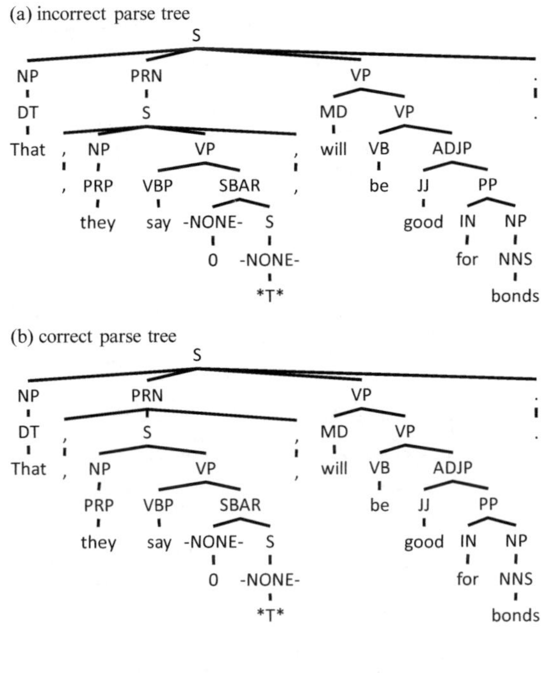

Figure 1: An example of a treebank error

parse tree (a) contains errors and the parse tree (b) is the corrected version. In the parse tree (a), the positions of the two subtrees (, ,) are erroneous. To correct the errors, we need to move the subtrees to the positions which are directly dominated by the node PRN. This example demonstrates that we need a framework of transforming tree structures to correct structural annotation errors.

3 Correcting Errors by Using Synchronous Grammar

To solve the problem described in Section 2, this section proposes a method of correcting structural annotation errors by using a synchronous tree substitution grammar (STSG) (Eisner, 2003). An STSG defines a tree-to-tree transformation. Our method induces an STSG which transforms parse trees containing errors into the ones whose errors are corrected.

3.1 Synchronous Tree Substitution Grammar

First of all, we describe the STSG formalism. An STSG defines a set of tree pairs. An STSG can be treated as a tree transducer which takes a tree as input and produces a tree as output. Each grammar rule consists of the following elements:

- a pair of trees called *elementary trees*

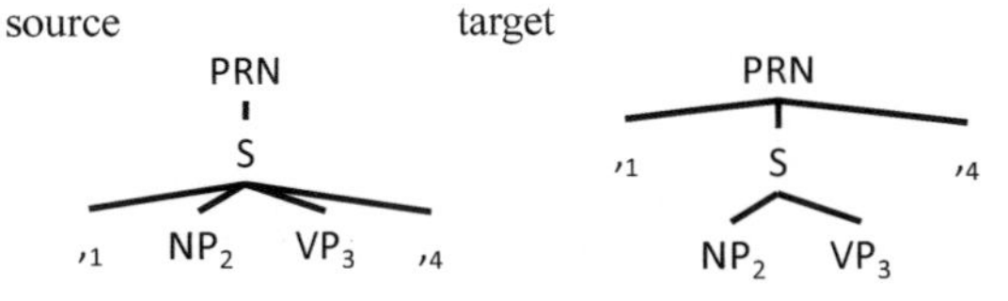

Figure 2: An example of an STSG rule

- a one-to-one alignment between nodes in the elementary trees

For a tree pair $\langle t, t' \rangle$, the tree t and t' are called *source* and *target*, respectively. The nonterminal leaves of elementary trees are called *frontier nodes*. There exists a one-to-one alignment between the frontier nodes in t and t'. The rule means that the structure which matches the source elementary tree is transformed into the structure which is represented by the target elementary tree. Figure 2 shows an example of an STSG rule. The subscripts indicate the alignment. This rule can correct the errors in the parse tree (a) depicted in Figure 1.

An STSG derives tree pairs. Any derivation process starts with the pair of nodes labeled with special symbols called *start symbols*. A derivation proceeds in the following steps:

1. Choose a pair of frontier nodes $\langle \eta, \eta' \rangle$ for which there exists an alignment.

2. Choose a rule $\langle t, t' \rangle$ s.t. $label(\eta) = root(t)$ and $label(\eta') = root(t')$ where $label(\eta)$ is the label of η and $root(t)$ is the root label of t.

3. Substitute t and t' into η and η', respectively.

Figure 3 shows a derivation process in an STSG.

In the rest of the paper, we focus on the rules in which the source elementary tree is not identical to its target, since such identical rules cannot contribute to error correction.

3.2 Inducing an STSG for Error Correction

This section describes a method of inducing an STSG for error correction. The basic idea of our method is similar to the method presented by Dickinson and Meurers (2003b). Their method detects errors by seeking word sequences satisfying the following conditions:

- The word sequence occurs more than once in the corpus.

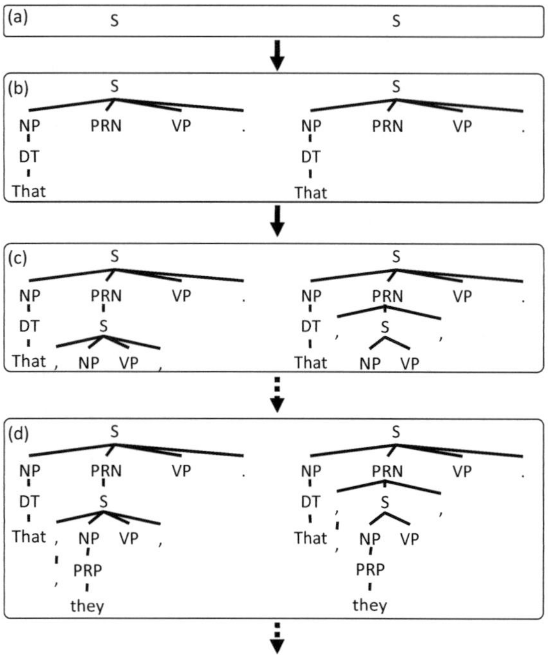

Figure 3: A derivation process of tree pairs in an STSG

- Different syntactic labels are assigned to the occurrences of the word sequence.

Unlike their method, our method seeks word sequences whose occurrences have different partial parse trees. We call a collection of these word sequences with partial parse trees *pseudo parallel corpus*. Moreover, our method extracts STSG rules which transform the one partial tree into the other.

3.2.1 Constructing a Pseudo Parallel Corpus

Our method firstly constructs a pseudo parallel corpus which represents a correspondence between parse trees containing errors and the ones whose errors are corrected. The procedure is as follows: Let T be the set of the parse trees occurring in the corpus. We write $Sub(\sigma)$ for the set which consists of the partial parse trees included in the parse tree σ. A pseudo parallel corpus $Para(T)$ is constructed as follows:

$$
\begin{aligned}
Para(T) \;=\; & \{\langle \tau, \tau' \rangle \mid \tau, \tau' \in \bigcup_{\sigma \in T} Sub(\sigma) \\
& \wedge \tau \neq \tau' \\
& \wedge yield(\tau) = yield(\tau') \\
& \wedge root(\tau) = root(\tau')\}
\end{aligned}
$$

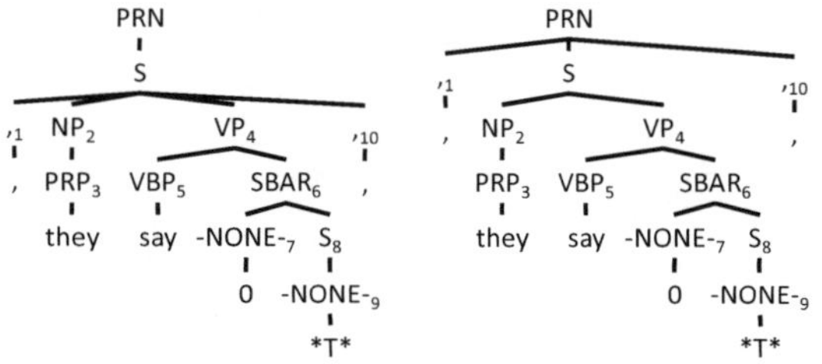

Figure 4: An example of a partial parse tree pair in a pseudo parallel corpus

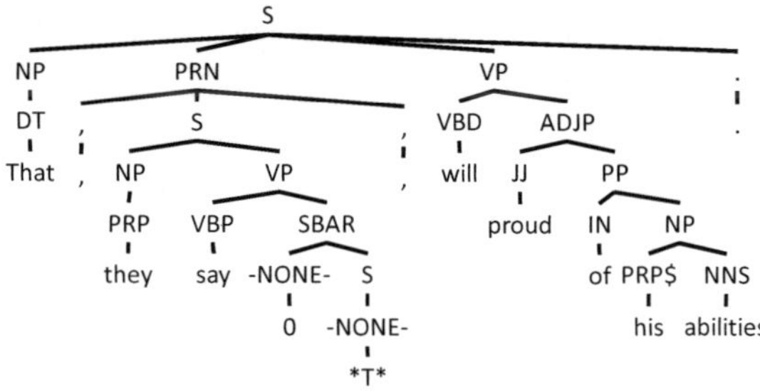

Figure 5: Another example of a parse tree containing a word sequence ", they say ,"

where $yield(\tau)$ is the word sequence dominated by τ.

Let us consider an example. If the parse trees depicted in Figure 1 exist in the treebank T, the pair of partial parse trees depicted in Figure 4 is an element of $Para(T)$. We also obtain this pair in the case where there exists not the parse tree (b) depicted in Figure 1 but the parse tree depicted in Figure 5, which contains the word sequence ", they say ,".

3.2.2 Inducing a Grammar from a Pseudo Parallel Corpus

Our method induces an STSG from the pseudo parallel corpus according to the method proposed by Cohn and Lapata (2009). Cohn and Lapata's method can induce an STSG which represents a correspondence in a parallel corpus. Their method firstly determine an alignment of nodes between pairs of trees in the parallel corpus and extracts STSG rules according to the alignments.

For partial parse trees τ and τ', we define a node alignment $C(\tau, \tau')$ as follows:

$$
\begin{aligned}
C(\tau, \tau') \;=\; & \{\langle \eta, \eta' \rangle \mid \eta \in Node(\tau) \\
& \wedge \eta' \in Node(\tau') \\
& \wedge \eta \text{ is not the root of } \tau
\end{aligned}
$$

$$\wedge\ \eta' \text{ is not the root of } \tau'$$
$$\wedge\ label(\eta) = label(\eta')$$
$$\wedge\ yield(\eta) = yield(\eta')\}$$

where $Node(\tau)$ is the set of the nodes in τ, and $yield(\eta)$ is the word sequence dominated by η. Figure 4 shows an example of a node alignment. The subscripts indicate the alignment.

An STSG rule is extracted by deleting nodes in a partial parse tree pair $\langle \tau, \tau' \rangle \in Para(T)$. The procedure is as follows:

- For each $\langle \eta, \eta' \rangle \in C(\tau, \tau')$, delete the descendants of η and η'.

For example, the rule shown in Figure 2 is extracted from the pair shown in Figure 4.

3.3 Rule Selection

Some rules extracted by the procedure in Section 3.2 are not useful for error correction, since the pseudo parallel corpus contains tree pairs whose source tree is correct or whose target tree is incorrect. The rules which are extracted from such pairs can be harmful. To select rules which are useful for error correction, we define a score function which is based on the occurrence frequencies of elementary trees in the treebank. The score function is defined as follows:

$$Score(\langle t, t' \rangle) = \frac{f(t')}{f(t) + f(t')}$$

where $f(\cdot)$ is the occurrence frequency in the treebank. The score function ranges from 0 to 1. We assume that the occurrence frequency of an elementary tree matching incorrect parse trees is very low. According to this assumption, the score function $Score(\langle t, t' \rangle)$ is high when the source elementary tree t matches incorrect parse trees and the target elementary tree t' matches correct parse trees. Therefore, STSG rules with high scores are regarded to be useful for error correction.

4 An Experiment

To evaluate the effectiveness of our method, we conducted an experiment using the Penn Treebank (Marcus et al., 1993).

We used 49208 sentences in Wall Street Journal sections. We induced STSG rules by applying our method to the corpus. We obtained 8776 rules. We

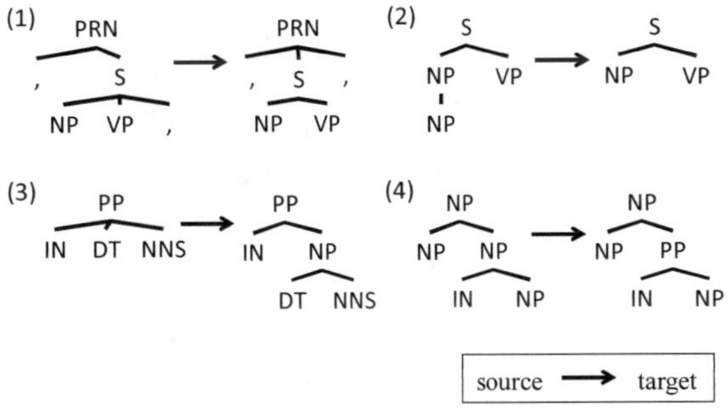

Figure 6: Examples of error correction rules induced from the Penn Treebank

measured the precision of the rules. The precision is defined as follows:

$$precision = \frac{\#\ of\ the\ positions\ where\ an\ error\ is\ corrected}{\#\ of\ the\ positions\ to\ which\ some\ rule\ is\ applied}$$

We manually checked whether each rule application corrected an error, because the corrected treebank does not exist[2]. Furthermore, we only evaluated the first 100 rules which are ordered by the score function described in Section 3.3, since it is time-consuming and expensive to evaluate all of the rules. These 100 rules were applied at 331 positions. The precision of the rules is 71.9%. For each rule, we measured the precision of it. 70 rules achieved 100% precision. These results demonstrate that our method can correct syntactic annotation errors with high precision. Moreover, 30 rules of the 70 rules transformed bracketed structures. This fact shows that the treebank contains structural errors which cannot be dealt with by the previous methods.

Figure 6 depicts examples of error correction rules which achieved 100% precision. Rule (1), (2) and (3) are rules which transform bracketed structures. Rule (4) simply replaces a node label. Rule (1) corrects an erroneous position of a comma (see Figure 7 (a)). Rule (2) deletes a useless node NP in a subject position (see Figure 7 (b)). Rule (3) inserts a node NP (see Figure 7 (c)). Rule (4) replaces a node label NP with the correct label PP (see Figure 7 (d)). These examples demonstrate that our method can correct syntactic annotation errors.

Figure 8 depicts an example where our method detected an annotation error but could not correct it. To correct the error, we need to attach the node

[2] This also means that we cannot measure the recall of the rules.

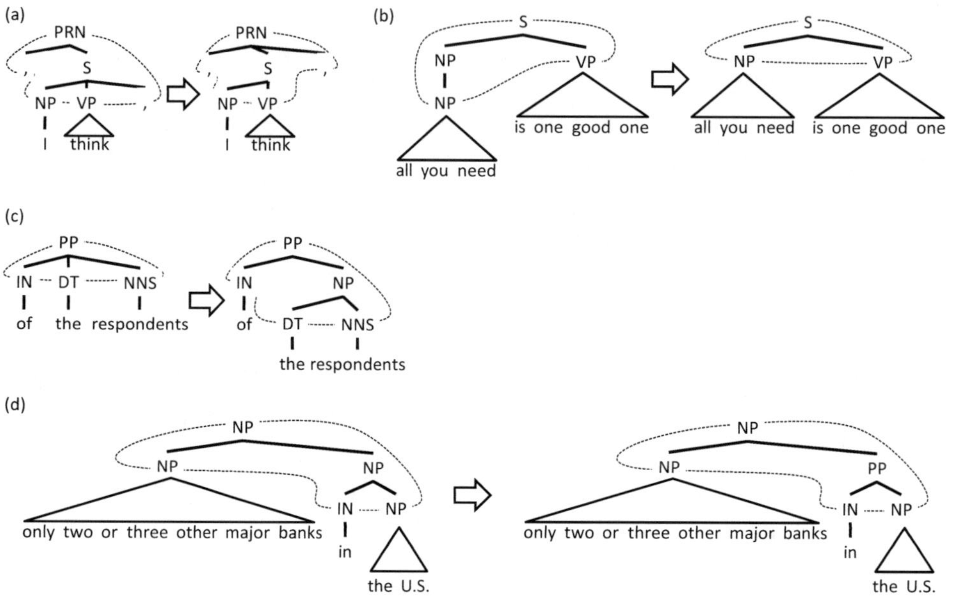

Figure 7: Examples of correcting syntactic annotation errors

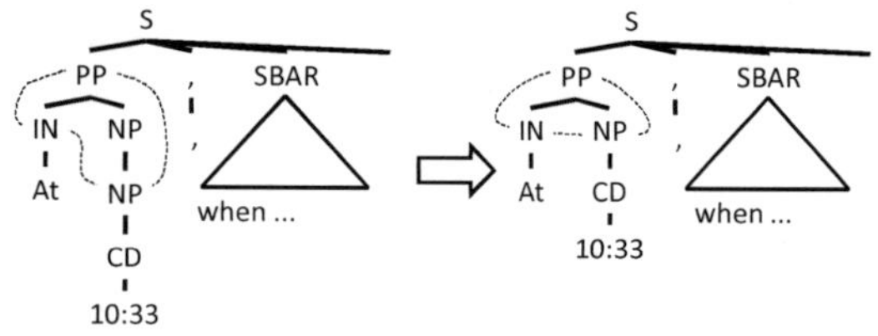

Figure 8: An example where our method detected an annotation error but could not correct it

SBAR under the node NP. We found that 22 of the rule applications were of this type.

Figure 9 depicts a false positive example where our method mistakenly transformed a correct syntactic structure. The score of the rule is very high, since the source elementary tree (TOP (NP NP VP .)) is less frequent. This example shows that our method has a risk of changing correct annotations of less frequent syntactic structures.

5 Conclusion

This paper proposes a method of correcting errors in a treebank by using a synchronous tree substitution grammar. Our method constructs a pseudo parallel corpus from the treebank and extracts STSG rules from the parallel corpus. The experimental result demonstrates that we can obtain error correction rules with high precision.

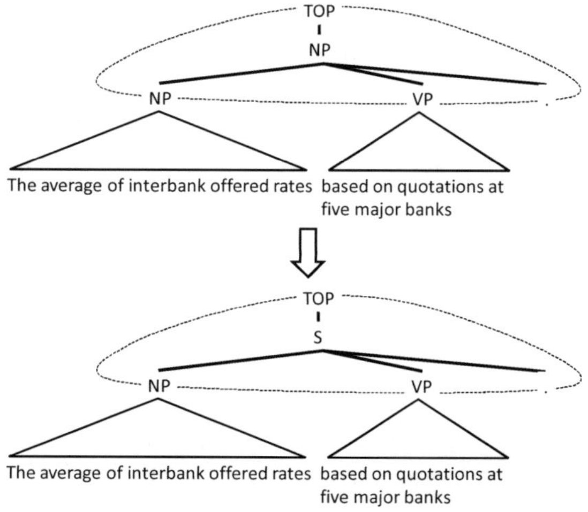

Figure 9: A false positive example where a correct syntactic structure was mistakenly transformed

In future work, we will explore a method of increasing the recall of error correction by constructing a wide-coverage STSG.

Acknowledgements

This research is partially supported by the Grant-in-Aid for Scientific Research (B) (No. 22300051) of JSPS and by the Kayamori Foundation of Informational Science Advancement.

References

Adriane Boyd, Markus Dickinson, and Detmar Meurers. 2008. On detecting errors in dependency treebanks. *Research on Language and Computation*, 6(2):113–137.

Trevor Cohn and Mirella Lapata. 2009. Sentence compression as tree transduction. *Journal of Artificial Intelligence Research*, 34(1):637–674.

Markus Dickinson and Detmar Meurers. 2003a. Detecting errors in part-of-speech annotation. In *Proceedings of the 10th Conference of the European Chapter of the Association for Computational Linguistics*, pages 107–114.

Markus Dickinson and Detmar Meurers. 2003b. Detecting inconsistencies in treebanks. In *Proceedings of the Second Workshop on Treebanks and Linguistic Theories*.

Markus Dickinson and W. Detmar Meurers. 2005. Prune diseased branches to get healthy trees! how to find erroneous local trees in a treebank and why it matters. In *Proceedings of the 4th Workshop on Treebanks and Linguistic Theories*.

Jason Eisner. 2003. Learning non-isomorphic tree mappings for machine translation. In *Proceedings of the 41st Annual Meeting of the Association for Computational Linguistics, Companion Volume*, pages 205–208.

Eleazar Eskin. 2000. Detecting errors within a corpus using anomaly detection. In *Proceedings of the 1st North American chapter of the Association for Computational Linguistics Conference*, pages 148–153.

Mitchell P. Marcus, Beatrice Santorini, and Mary Ann Marcinkiewicz. 1993. Building a large annotated corpus of English: the Penn Treebank. *Computational Linguistics*, 19(2):310–330.

Masaki Murata, Masao Utiyama, Kiyotaka Uchimoto, Hitoshi Isahara, and Qing Ma. 2005. Correction of errors in a verb modality corpus for machine translation with a machine-learning method. *ACM Transactions on Asian Language Information Processing*, 4(1):18–37.

Tetsuji Nakagawa and Yuji Matsumoto. 2002. Detecting errors in corpora using support vector machines. In *Proceedings of the 19th Internatinal Conference on Computatinal Linguistics*, pages 709–715.

Tylman Ule and Kiril Simov. 2004. Unexpected productions may well be errors. In *Proceedings of 4th International Conference on Language Resources and Evaluation*, pages 1795–1798.

Evaluating Machine Translations using mNCD

Marcus Dobrinkat and **Tero Tapiovaara** and **Jaakko Väyrynen**
Adaptive Informatics Research Centre
Aalto University School of Science and Technology
P.O. Box 15400, FI-00076 Aalto, Finland
{marcus.dobrinkat,jaakko.j.vayrynen,tero.tapiovaara}@tkk.fi

Kimmo Kettunen
Kymenlaakso University of Applied Sciences
P.O. Box 9, FI-48401 Kotka, Finland
kimmo.kettunen@kyamk.fi

Abstract

This paper introduces mNCD, a method for automatic evaluation of machine translations. The measure is based on normalized compression distance (NCD), a general information theoretic measure of string similarity, and flexible word matching provided by stemming and synonyms. The mNCD measure outperforms NCD in system-level correlation to human judgments in English.

1 Introduction

Automatic evaluation of machine translation (MT) systems requires automated procedures to ensure consistency and efficient handling of large amounts of data. In statistical MT systems, automatic evaluation of translations is essential for parameter optimization and system development. Human evaluation is too labor intensive, time consuming and expensive for daily evaluations. However, manual evaluation is important in the comparison of different MT systems and for the validation and development of automatic MT evaluation measures, which try to model human assessments of translations as closely as possible. Furthermore, the ideal evaluation method would be language independent, fast to compute and simple.

Recently, normalized compression distance (NCD) has been applied to the evaluation of machine translations. NCD is a general information theoretic measure of string similarity, whereas most MT evaluation measures, e.g., BLEU and METEOR, are specifically constructed for the task. Parker (2008) introduced BADGER, an MT evaluation measure that uses NCD and a language independent word normalization method. BADGER scores were directly compared against the scores of METEOR and word error rate (WER). The correlation between BADGER and METEOR were low and correlations between BADGER and WER high. Kettunen (2009) uses the NCD directly as an MT evaluation measure. He showed with a small corpus of three language pairs that NCD and METEOR 0.6 correlated for translations of 10–12 MT systems. NCD was not compared to human assessments of translations, but correlations of NCD and METEOR scores were very high for all the three language pairs.

Väyrynen et al. (2010) have extended the work by including NCD in the ACL WMT08 evaluation framework and showing that NCD is correlated to human judgments. The NCD measure did not match the performance of the state-of-the-art MT evaluation measures in English, but it presented a viable alternative to de facto standard BLEU (Papineni et al., 2001), which is simple and effective but has been shown to have a number of drawbacks (Callison-Burch et al., 2006).

Some recent advances in automatic MT evaluation have included non-binary matching between compared items (Banerjee and Lavie, 2005; Agarwal and Lavie, 2008; Chan and Ng, 2009), which is implicitly present in the string-based NCD measure. Our motivation is to investigate whether including additional language dependent resources would improve the NCD measure. We experiment with relaxed word matching using stemming and a lexical database to allow lexical changes. These additional modules attempt to make the reference sentences more similar to the evaluated translations on the string level. We report an experiment showing that document-level NCD and aggregated NCD scores for individual sentences produce very similar correlations to human judgments.

Proceedings of the ACL 2010 Conference Short Papers, pages 80–85,
Uppsala, Sweden, 11-16 July 2010.

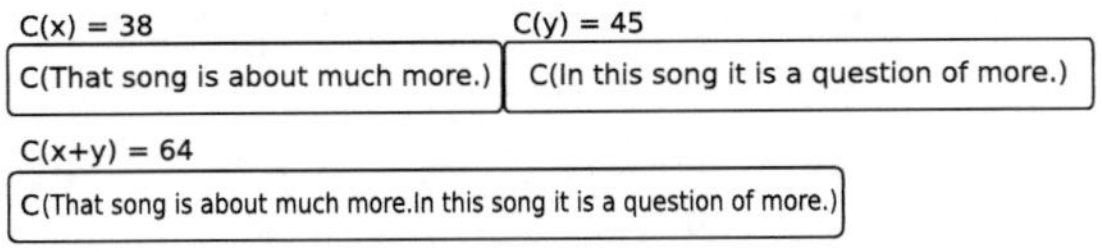

Figure 1: An example showing the compressed sizes of two strings separately and concatenated.

2 Normalized Compression Distance

Normalized compression distance (NCD) is a similarity measure based on the idea that a string x is similar to another string y when both share substrings. The description of y can reference shared substrings in the known x without repetition, indicating shared information. Figure 1 shows an example in which the compression of the concatenation of x and y results in a shorter output than individual compressions of x and y.

The normalized compression distance, as defined by Cilibrasi and Vitanyi (2005), is given in Equation 1, with $C(x)$ as length of the compression of x and $C(x, y)$ as the length of the compression of the concatenation of x and y.

$$NCD(x, y) = \frac{C(x, y) - \min\{C(x), C(y)\}}{\max\{C(x), C(y)\}} \tag{1}$$

NCD computes the distance as a score closer to one for very different strings and closer to zero for more similar strings.

NCD is an approximation of the uncomputable normalized information distance (NID), a general measure for the similarity of two objects. NID is based on the notion of Kolmogorov complexity $K(x)$, a theoretical measure for the information content of a string x, defined as the shortest universal Turing machine that prints x and stops (Solomonoff, 1964). NCD approximates NID by the use of a compressor $C(x)$ that is an upper bound of the Kolmogorov complexity $K(x)$.

3 mNCD

Normalized compression distance was not conceived with MT evaluation in mind, but rather it is a general measure of string similarity. Implicit non-binary matching with NCD is indicated by preliminary experiments which show that NCD is less sensitive to random changes on the character level than, for instance, BLEU, which only counts the exact matches between word n-grams. Thus comparison of sentences at the character level could account better for morphological changes.

Variation in language leads to several acceptable translations for each source sentence, which is why multiple reference translations are preferred in evaluation. Unfortunately, it is typical to have only one reference translation. Paraphrasing techniques can produce additional translation variants (Russo-Lassner et al., 2005; Kauchak and Barzilay, 2006). These can be seen as new reference translations, similar to pseudo references (Ma et al., 2007).

The proposed method, mNCD, works analogously to M-BLEU and M-TER, which use the flexible word matching modules from METEOR to find relaxed word-to-word alignments (Agarwal and Lavie, 2008). The modules are able to align words even if they do not share the same surface form, but instead have a common stem or are synonyms of each other. A similarized translation reference is generated by replacing words in the reference with their aligned counterparts from the translation hypothesis. The NCD score is computed between the translations and the similarized references to get the mNCD score.

Table 1 shows some hand-picked German–English candidate translations along with a) the reference translations including the 1-NCD score to easily compare with METEOR and b) the similarized references including the mNCD score. For comparison, the corresponding METEOR scores without implicit relaxed matching are shown.

4 Experiments

The proposed mNCD and the basic NCD measure were evaluated by computing correlation to human judgments of translations. A high correlation value between an MT evaluation measure and human judgments indicates that the measure is able to evaluate translations in a more similar way to humans.

Relaxed alignments with the METEOR modules `exact`, `stem` and `synonym` were created for English for the computation of the mNCD score. The `synonym` module was not available with other target languages.

4.1 Evaluation Data

The 2008 ACL Workshop on Statistical Machine Translation (Callison-Burch et al., 2008) shared task data includes translations from a total of 30 MT systems between English and five European languages, as well as automatic and human trans-

	Candidate C/ Reference R/ Similarized Reference S	1-NCD	METEOR
C	There is no effective means to stop a Tratsch, which was already included in the world.		
R	There is no `good way` to `halt` gossip that has already begun to spread.	.41	.31
S	There is no `effective means` to `stop` gossip that has already begun to spread.	.56	.55
C	Crisis, not only in America		
R	A Crisis `Not Only` in the `U.S.`	.51	.44
S	A Crisis `not only` in the `America`	.72	.56
C	Influence on the whole economy should not have this crisis.		
R	Nevertheless, the crisis should not have `influenced` the entire economy.	.60	.37
S	Nevertheless, the crisis should not have `Influence` the entire economy.	.62	.44
C	Or the lost tight meeting will be discovered at the hands of a gentlemen?		
R	Perhaps you `see` the pen you thought you lost lying on your colleague's desk.	.42	.09
S	Perhaps you `meeting` the pen you thought you lost lying on your colleague's desk.	.40	.13

Table 1: Example German–English translations showing the effect of relaxed matching in the 1-mNCD score (for rows S) compared with METEOR using the `exact` module only, since the modules `stem` and `synonym` are already used in the similarized reference. Replaced words are emphasized.

lation evaluations for the translations. There are several tasks, defined by the language pair and the domain of translated text.

The human judgments include three different categories. The RANK category has human quality rankings of five translations for one sentence from different MT systems. The CONST category contains rankings for short phrases (constituents), and the YES/NO category contains binary answers if a short phrase is an acceptable translation or not.

For the translation tasks into English, the relaxed alignment using a `stem` module and the `synonym` module affected 7.5 % of all words, whereas only 5.1 % of the words were changed in the tasks from English into the other languages.

The data was preprocessed in two different ways. For NCD we kept the data as is, which we called real casing (rc). Since the used METEOR align module lowercases all text, we restored the case information in mNCD by copying the correct case from the reference translation to the similarized reference, based on METEOR's alignment. The other way was to lowercase all data (lc).

4.2 System-level correlation

We follow the same evaluation methodology as in Callison-Burch et al. (2008), which allows us to measure how well MT evaluation measures correlate with human judgments on the system level.

Spearman's rank correlation coefficient ρ was calculated between each MT evaluation measure and human judgment category using the simplified equation

$$\rho = 1 - \frac{6 \sum_i d_i}{n(n^2-1)} \qquad (2)$$

where for each system i, d_i is the difference between the rank derived from annotators' input and the rank obtained from the measure. From the annotators' input, the n systems were ranked based on the number of times each system's output was selected as the best translation divided by the number of times each system was part of a judgment.

We computed system-level correlations for tasks with English, French, Spanish and German as the target language[1].

5 Results

We compare mNCD against NCD and relate their performance to other MT evaluation measures.

5.1 Block size effect on NCD scores

Väyrynen et al. (2010) computed NCD between a set of candidate translations and references at the same time regardless of the sentence alignments, analogously to document comparison. We experimented with segmentation of the candidate translations into smaller blocks, which were individually evaluated with NCD and aggregated into a single value with arithmetic mean. The resulting system-level correlations between NCD and human judgments are shown in Figure 2 as a function of the block size. The correlations are very similar with all block sizes, except for Spanish, where smaller block size produces higher correlation. An experiment with geometric mean produced similar results. The reported results with mNCD use maximum block size, similar to Väyrynen et al. (2010).

[1] The English-Spanish news task was left out as most measures had negative correlation with human judgments.

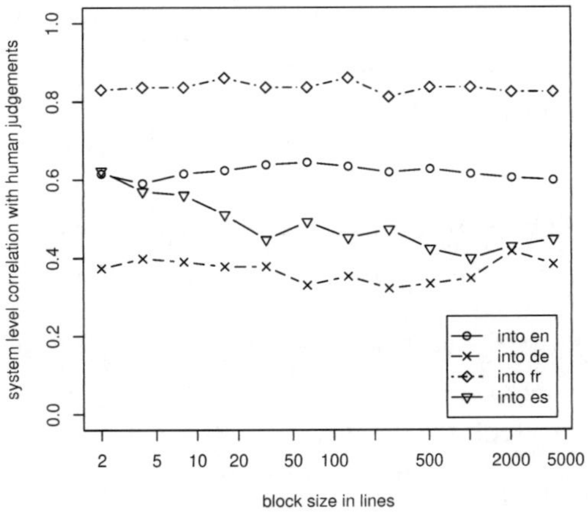

Figure 2: The block size has very little effect on the correlation between NCD and human judgments. The right side corresponds to document comparison and the left side to aggregated NCD scores for sentences.

5.2 mNCD against NCD

Table 2 shows the average system level correlation of different NCD and mNCD variants for translations into English. The two compressors that worked best in our experiments were PPMZ and bz2. PPMZ is slower to compute but performs slightly better compared to bz2, except for the lowercased CONST category.

Method	Parameters		RANK	CONST	YES/NO	Mean
mNCD	PPMZ	rc	**.69**	**.74**	**.80**	**.74**
NCD	PPMZ	rc	.60	.66	.71	.66
mNCD	bz2	rc	**.64**	**.73**	**.73**	**.70**
NCD	bz2	rc	.57	.64	.69	.64
mNCD	PPMZ	lc	**.66**	**.80**	**.79**	**.75**
NCD	PPMZ	lc	.56	.79	.75	.70
mNCD	bz2	lc	**.59**	**.85**	**.74**	**.73**
NCD	bz2	lc	.54	.82	.71	.69

Table 2: Mean system level correlations over all translation tasks into English for variants of mNCD and NCD. Higher values are emphasized. Parameters are the compressor PPMZ or bz2 and the preprocessing choice lowercasing (lc) or real casing (rc).

Method	Parameters		Target Lang Corr			
			EN	DE	FR	ES
mNCD	PPMZ	rc	**.69**	.37	.82	.38
NCD	PPMZ	rc	.60	.37	**.84**	**.39**
mNCD	bz2	rc	**.64**	.32	.75	.25
NCD	bz2	rc	.57	**.34**	**.85**	**.42**
mNCD	PPMZ	lc	**.66**	.33	**.79**	**.23**
NCD	PPMZ	lc	.56	**.37**	.77	.21
mNCD	bz2	lc	**.59**	.25	**.78**	**.16**
NCD	bz2	lc	.54	**.26**	.77	.15

Table 3: mNCD versus NCD system correlation RANK results with different parameters (the same as in Table 2) for each target language. Higher values are emphasized. Target languages DE, FR and ES use only the `stem` module.

Table 2 shows that real casing improves RANK correlation slightly throughout NCD and mNCD variants, whereas it reduces correlation in the categories CONST, YES/NO as well as the mean.

The best mNCD (PPMZ rc) improves the best NCD (PPMZ rc) method by 15% in the RANK category. In the CONST category the best mNCD (bz2 lc) improves the best NCD (bz2 lc) by 3.7%. For the total average, the best mNCD (PPMZ rc) improves the the best NCD (bz2 lc) by 7.2%.

Table 3 shows the correlation results for the RANK category by target language. As shown already in Table 2, mNCD clearly outperforms NCD for English. Correlations for other languages show mixed results and on average, mNCD gives lower correlations than NCD.

5.3 mNCD versus other methods

Table 4 presents the results for the selected mNCD (PPMZ rc) and NCD (bz2 rc) variants along with the correlations for other MT evaluation methods from the WMT'08 data, based on the results in Callison-Burch et al. (2008). The results are averages over language pairs into English, sorted by RANK, which we consider the most significant category. Although mNCD correlation with human evaluations improved over NCD, the ranking among other measures was not affected. Language and task specific results not shown here, reveal very low mNCD and NCD correlations in the Spanish-English news task, which significantly

Method	RANK	CONST	YES/NO	Mean
DP	.81	.66	.74	.73
ULCh	.80	.68	.78	.75
DR	.79	.53	.65	.66
meteor-ranking	.78	.55	.63	.65
ULC	.77	.72	.81	.76
posbleu	.75	.69	.78	.74
SR	.75	.66	.76	.72
posF4gram-gm	.74	.60	.71	.68
meteor-baseline	.74	.60	.63	.66
posF4gram-am	.74	.58	.69	.67
mNCD (PPMZ rc)	.69	.74	.80	.74
NCD (PPMZ rc)	.60	.66	.71	.66
mbleu	.50	.76	.70	.65
bleu	.50	.72	.74	.65
mter	.38	.74	.68	.60
svm-rank	.37	.10	.23	.23
Mean	.67	.62	.69	.66

Table 4: Average system-level correlations over translation tasks into English for NCD, mNCD and other MT evaluations measures

degrades the averages. Considering the mean of the categories instead, mNCD's correlation of .74 is third best together with 'posbleu'.

Table 5 shows the results from English. The table is shorter since many of the better MT measures use language specific linguistic resources that are not easily available for languages other than English. mNCD performs competitively only for French, otherwise it falls behind NCD and other methods as already shown earlier.

6 Discussion

We have introduced a new MT evaluation measure, mNCD, which is based on normalized compression distance and METEOR's relaxed alignment modules. The mNCD measure outperforms NCD in English with all tested parameter combinations, whereas results with other target languages are unclear. The improved correlations with mNCD did not change the position in the RANK category of the MT evaluation measures in the 2008 ACL WMT shared task.

The improvement in English was expected on the grounds of the synonym module, and indicated also by the larger number of affected words in the

Method	Target Lang Corr			
	DE	FR	ES	Mean
posbleu	.75	.80	.75	.75
posF4gram-am	.74	.82	.79	.74
posF4gram-gm	.74	.82	.79	.74
bleu	.47	.83	.80	.68
NCD (bz2 rc)	.34	.85	.42	.66
svm-rank	.44	.80	.80	.66
mbleu	.39	.77	.83	.63
mNCD (PPMZ rc)	.37	.82	.38	.63
meteor-baseline	.43	.61	.84	.58
meteor-ranking	.26	.70	.83	.55
mter	.26	.69	.73	.52
Mean	.47	.77	.72	.65

Table 5: Average system-level correlations for the RANK category from English for NCD, mNCD and other MT evaluation measures.

similarized references. We believe there is potential for improvement in other languages as well if synonym lexicons are available.

We have also extended the basic NCD measure to scale between a document comparison measure and aggregated sentence-level measure. The rather surprising result is that NCD produces quite similar scores with all block sizes. The different result with Spanish may be caused by differences in the data or problems in the calculations.

After using the same evaluation methodology as in Callison-Burch et al. (2008), we have doubts whether it presents the most effective method exploiting all the given human evaluations in the best way. The system-level correlation measure only awards the winner of the ranking of five different systems. If a system always scored second, it would never be awarded and therefore be overly penalized. In addition, the human knowledge that gave the lower rankings is not exploited.

In future work with mNCD as an MT evaluation measure, we are planning to evaluate synonym dictionaries for other languages than English. The synonym module for English does not distinguish between different senses of words. Therefore, synonym lexicons found with statistical methods might provide a viable alternative for manually constructed lexicons (Kauchak and Barzilay, 2006).

References

Abhaya Agarwal and Alon Lavie. 2008. METEOR, M-BLEU and M-TER: evaluation metrics for high-correlation with human rankings of machine translation output. In *StatMT '08: Proceedings of the Third Workshop on Statistical Machine Translation*, pages 115–118, Morristown, NJ, USA. Association for Computational Linguistics.

Satanjeev Banerjee and Alon Lavie. 2005. METEOR: An automatic metric for MT evaluation with improved correlation with human judgments. In *Proceedings of the ACL Workshop on Intrinsic and Extrinsic Evaluation Measures for Machine Translation and/or Summarization*, pages 65–72, Ann Arbor, Michigan, June. Association for Computational Linguistics.

Chris Callison-Burch, Miles Osborne, and Philipp Koehn. 2006. Re-evaluating the role of BLEU in machine translation research. In *Proceedings of EACL-2006*, pages 249–256.

Chris Callison-Burch, Cameron Fordyce, Philipp Koehn, Christoph Monz, and Josh Schroeder. 2008. Further meta-evalutation of machine translation. *ACL Workshop on Statistical Machine Translation.*

Yee Seng Chan and Hwee Tou Ng. 2009. MaxSim: performance and effects of translation fluency. *Machine Translation*, 23(2-3):157–168.

Rudi Cilibrasi and Paul Vitanyi. 2005. Clustering by compression. *IEEE Transactions on Information Theory*, 51:1523–1545.

David Kauchak and Regina Barzilay. 2006. Paraphrasing for automatic evaluation. In *Proceedings of the main conference on Human Language Technology Conference of the North American Chapter of the Association of Computational Linguistics*, pages 455–462, Morristown, NJ, USA. Association for Computational Linguistics.

Kimmo Kettunen. 2009. Packing it all up in search for a language independent MT quality measure tool. In *In Proceedings of LTC-09, 4th Language and Technology Conference*, pages 280–284, Poznan.

Yanjun Ma, Nicolas Stroppa, and Andy Way. 2007. Bootstrapping word alignment via word packing. In *Proceedings of the 45th Annual Meeting of the Association of Computational Linguistics*, pages 304–311, Prague, Czech Republic, June. Association for Computational Linguistics.

K. Papineni, S. Roukos, T. Ward, and W. Zhu. 2001. BLEU: a method for automatic evaluation of machine translation. Technical Report RC22176 (W0109-022), IBM Research Division, Thomas J. Watson Research Center.

Steven Parker. 2008. BADGER: A new machine translation metric. In *Metrics for Machine Translation Challenge 2008*, Waikiki, Hawai'i, October. AMTA.

Grazia Russo-Lassner, Jimmy Lin, and Philip Resnik. 2005. A paraphrase-based approach to machine translation evaluation. Technical Report LAMP-TR-125/CS-TR-4754/UMIACS-TR-2005-57, University of Maryland, College Park.

Ray Solomonoff. 1964. Formal theory of inductive inference. Part I. *Information and Control,*, 7(1):1–22.

Jaakko J. Väyrynen, Tero Tapiovaara, Kimmo Kettunen, and Marcus Dobrinkat. 2010. Normalized compression distance as an automatic MT evaluation metric. In *Proceedings of MT 25 years on*. To appear.

Tackling Sparse Data Issue in Machine Translation Evaluation *

Ondřej Bojar, Kamil Kos, and David Mareček
Charles University in Prague, Institute of Formal and Applied Linguistics
`{bojar,marecek}@ufal.mff.cuni.cz, kamilkos@email.cz`

Abstract

We illustrate and explain problems of n-grams-based machine translation (MT) metrics (e.g. BLEU) when applied to morphologically rich languages such as Czech. A novel metric SemPOS based on the deep-syntactic representation of the sentence tackles the issue and retains the performance for translation to English as well.

1 Introduction

Automatic metrics of machine translation (MT) quality are vital for research progress at a fast pace. Many automatic metrics of MT quality have been proposed and evaluated in terms of correlation with human judgments while various techniques of manual judging are being examined as well, see e.g. MetricsMATR08 (Przybocki et al., 2008)[1], WMT08 and WMT09 (Callison-Burch et al., 2008; Callison-Burch et al., 2009)[2].

The contribution of this paper is twofold. Section 2 illustrates and explains severe problems of a widely used BLEU metric (Papineni et al., 2002) when applied to Czech as a representative of languages with rich morphology. We see this as an instance of the sparse data problem well known for MT itself: too much detail in the formal representation leading to low coverage of e.g. a translation dictionary. In MT evaluation, too much detail leads to the lack of comparable parts of the hypothesis and the reference.

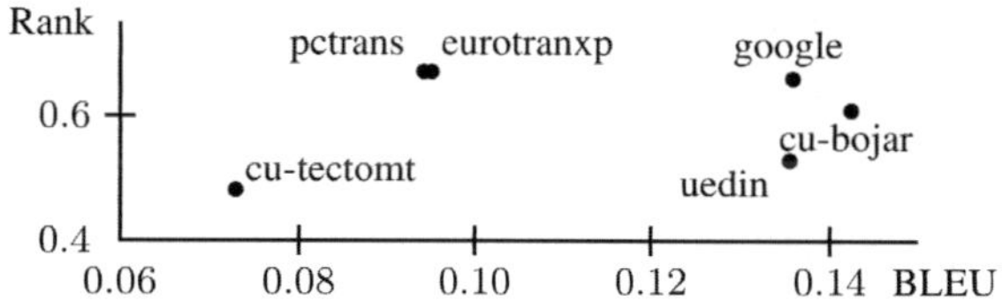

Figure 1: BLEU and human ranks of systems participating in the English-to-Czech WMT09 shared task.

Section 3 introduces and evaluates some new variations of SemPOS (Kos and Bojar, 2009), a metric based on the deep syntactic representation of the sentence performing very well for Czech as the target language. Aside from including dependency and n-gram relations in the scoring, we also apply and evaluate SemPOS for English.

2 Problems of BLEU

BLEU (Papineni et al., 2002) is an established language-independent MT metric. Its correlation to human judgments was originally deemed high (for English) but better correlating metrics (esp. for other languages) were found later, usually employing language-specific tools, see e.g. Przybocki et al. (2008) or Callison-Burch et al. (2009). The unbeaten advantage of BLEU is its simplicity.

Figure 1 illustrates a very low correlation to human judgments when translating to Czech. We plot the official BLEU score against the rank established as the percentage of sentences where a system ranked no worse than all its competitors (Callison-Burch et al., 2009). The systems developed at Charles University (cu-) are described in Bojar et al. (2009), uedin is a vanilla configuration of Moses (Koehn et al., 2007) and the remaining ones are commercial MT systems.

In a manual analysis, we identified the reasons for the low correlation: BLEU is overly sensitive to *sequences* and *forms* in the hypothesis matching

* This work has been supported by the grants EuroMatrixPlus (FP7-ICT-2007-3-231720 of the EU and 7E09003 of the Czech Republic), FP7-ICT-2009-4-247762 (Faust), GA201/09/H057, GAUK 1163/2010, and MSM 0021620838. We are grateful to the anonymous reviewers for further research suggestions.

[1] `http://nist.gov/speech/tests/metricsmatr/2008/results/`

[2] `http://www.statmt.org/wmt08` and `wmt09`

Proceedings of the ACL 2010 Conference Short Papers, pages 86–91,
Uppsala, Sweden, 11-16 July 2010.

Con-firmed	Error Flags	1-grams	2-grams	3-grams	4-grams
Yes	Yes	6.34%	1.58%	0.55%	0.29%
Yes	No	36.93%	13.68%	5.87%	2.69%
No	Yes	22.33%	41.83%	54.64%	63.88%
No	No	**34.40%**	**42.91%**	**38.94%**	**33.14%**
Total n-grams		35,531	33,891	32,251	30,611

Table 1: n-grams confirmed by the reference and containing error flags.

the reference translation. This focus goes directly against the properties of Czech: relatively free word order allows many permutations of words and rich morphology renders many valid word forms not confirmed by the reference.[3] These problems are to some extent mitigated if several reference translations are available, but this is often not the case.

Figure 2 illustrates the problem of "sparse data" in the reference. Due to the lexical and morphological variance of Czech, only a single word in each hypothesis matches a word in the reference. In the case of pctrans, the match is even a false positive, "do" (to) is a preposition that should be used for the "minus" phrase and not for the "end of the day" phrase. In terms of BLEU, both hypotheses are equally poor but 90% of their tokens were not evaluated.

Table 1 estimates the overall magnitude of this issue: For 1-grams to 4-grams in 1640 instances (different MT outputs and different annotators) of 200 sentences with manually flagged errors[4], we count how often the n-gram is confirmed by the reference and how often it contains an error flag. The suspicious cases are n-grams confirmed by the reference but still containing a flag (false positives) and n-grams not confirmed despite containing no error flag (false negatives).

Fortunately, there are relatively few false positives in n-gram based metrics: 6.3% of unigrams and far fewer higher n-grams.

The issue of false negatives is more serious and confirms the problem of sparse data if only one reference is available. 30 to 40% of n-grams do not contain any error and yet they are not confirmed by the reference. This amounts to 34% of running unigrams, giving enough space to differ in human judgments and still remain unscored.

Figure 3 documents the issue across languages: the lower the BLEU score itself (i.e. fewer confirmed n-grams), the lower the correlation to human judgments regardless of the target language (WMT09 shared task, 2025 sentences per language).

Figure 4 illustrates the overestimation of scores caused by too much attention to sequences of tokens. A phrase-based system like Moses (cu-bojar) can sometimes produce a long sequence of tokens exactly as required by the reference, leading to a high BLEU score. The framed words in the illustration are not confirmed by the reference, but the actual error in these words is very severe for comprehension: nouns were used twice instead of finite verbs, and a misleading translation of a preposition was chosen. The output by pctrans preserves the meaning much better despite not scoring in either of the finite verbs and producing far shorter confirmed sequences.

3 Extensions of SemPOS

SemPOS (Kos and Bojar, 2009) is inspired by metrics based on overlapping of linguistic features in the reference and in the translation (Giménez and Márquez, 2007). It operates on so-called "tectogrammatical" (deep syntactic) representation of the sentence (Sgall et al., 1986; Hajič et al., 2006), formally a dependency tree that includes only autosemantic (content-bearing) words.[5] SemPOS as defined in Kos and Bojar (2009) disregards the syntactic structure and uses the semantic part of speech of the words (noun, verb, etc.). There are 19 fine-grained parts of speech. For each semantic part of speech t, the overlapping $\mathrm{O}(t)$ is set to zero if the part of speech does not occur in the reference or the candidate set and otherwise it is computed as given in Equation 1 below.

[3]Condon et al. (2009) identify similar issues when evaluating translation to Arabic and employ rule-based normalization of MT output to improve the correlation. It is beyond the scope of this paper to describe the rather different nature of morphological richness in Czech, Arabic and also other languages, e.g. German or Finnish.

[4]The dataset with manually flagged errors is available at http://ufal.mff.cuni.cz/euromatrixplus/

[5]We use TectoMT (Žabokrtský and Bojar, 2008), http://ufal.mff.cuni.cz/tectomt/, for the linguistic pre-processing. While both our implementation of SemPOS as well as TectoMT are in principle freely available, a stable public version has yet to be released. Our plans include experiments with approximating the deep syntactic analysis with a simple tagger, which would also decrease the installation burden and computation costs, at the expense of accuracy.

SRC	Prague Stock Market falls to minus by the end of the trading day
REF	pražská burza se ke konci obchodování propadla do minusu
cu-bojar	praha stock market klesne k minus na konci obchodního dne
pctrans	praha trh cenných papírů padá minus do konce obchodního dne

Figure 2: Sparse data in BLEU evaluation: Large chunks of hypotheses are not compared at all. Only a single unigram in each hypothesis is confirmed in the reference.

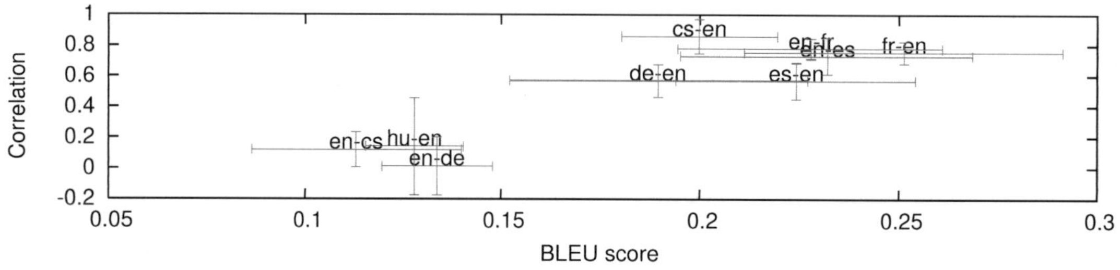

Figure 3: BLEU correlates with its correlation to human judgments. BLEU scores around 0.1 predict little about translation quality.

$$\mathrm{O}(t) = \frac{\sum_{i \in I} \sum_{w \in r_i \cap c_i} \min(\mathrm{cnt}(w,t,r_i), \mathrm{cnt}(w,t,c_i))}{\sum_{i \in I} \sum_{w \in r_i \cup c_i} \max(\mathrm{cnt}(w,t,r_i), \mathrm{cnt}(w,t,c_i))} \quad (1)$$

The semantic part of speech is denoted t; c_i and r_i are the candidate and reference translations of sentence i, and $\mathrm{cnt}(w,t,rc)$ is the number of words w with type t in rc (the reference or the candidate). The matching is performed on the level of lemmas, i.e. no morphological information is preserved in ws. See Figure 5 for an example; the sentence is the same as in Figure 4.

The final SemPOS score is obtained by macro-averaging over all parts of speech:

$$\text{SemPOS} = \frac{1}{|T|} \sum_{t \in T} \mathrm{O}(t) \quad (2)$$

where T is the set of all possible semantic parts of speech types. (The degenerate case of blank candidate and reference has SemPOS zero.)

3.1 Variations of SemPOS

This section describes our modifications of SemPOS. All methods are evaluated in Section 3.2.

Different Classification of Autosemantic Words. SemPOS uses semantic parts of speech to classify autosemantic words. The tectogrammatical layer offers also a feature called *Functor* describing the relation of a word to its governor similarly as semantic roles do. There are 67 functor types in total.

Using *Functor* instead of *SemPOS* increases the number of word classes that independently require a high overlap. For a contrast we also completely remove the classification and use only one global class (*Void*).

Deep Syntactic Relations in SemPOS. In SemPOS, an autosemantic word of a class is confirmed if its lemma matches the reference. We utilize the dependency relations at the tectogrammatical layer to validate valence by refining the overlap and requiring also the lemma of 1) the parent (denoted "par"), or 2) all the children regardless of their order (denoted "sons") to match.

Combining BLEU and SemPOS. One of the major drawbacks of *SemPOS* is that it completely ignores word order. This is too coarse even for languages with relatively free word order like Czech. Another issue is that it operates on lemmas and it completely disregards correct word forms. Thus, a weighted linear combination of SemPOS and BLEU (computed on the surface representation of the sentence) should compensate for this. For the purposes of the combination, we compute BLEU *only* on unigrams up to fourgrams (denoted BLEU_1, ..., BLEU_4) but including the brevity penalty as usual. Here we try only a few weight settings in the linear combination but given a held-out dataset, one could optimize the weights for the best performance.

SRC	Congress yields: US government can pump 700 billion dollars into banks
REF	kongres ustoupil : vláda usa může do bank napumpovat 700 miliard dolarů
cu-bojar	kongres výnosy : vláda usa může čerpadlo 700 miliard dolarů v bankách
pctrans	kongres vynáší : us vláda může čerpat 700 miliardu dolarů do bank

Figure 4: Too much focus on sequences in BLEU: pctrans' output is better but does not score well. BLEU gave credit to cu-bojar for 1, 3, 5 and 8 fourgrams, trigrams, bigrams and unigrams, resp., but only for 0, 0, 1 and 8 n-grams produced by pctrans. Confirmed sequences of tokens are underlined and important errors (not considered by BLEU) are framed.

REF	kongres/n ustoupit/v :/n vláda/n usa/n banka/n napumpovat/v 700/n miliarda/n dolar/n
cu-bojar	kongres/n výnos/n :/n vláda/n usa/n moci/v čerpadlo/n 700/n miliarda/n dolar/n banka/n
pctrans	kongres/n vynášet/v :/n us/n vláda/n čerpat/v 700/n miliarda/n dolar/n banka/n

Figure 5: SemPOS evaluates the overlap of lemmas of autosemantic words given their semantic part of speech (n, v, ...). Underlined words are confirmed by the reference.

SemPOS for English. The tectogrammatical layer is being adapted for English (Cinková et al., 2004; Hajič et al., 2009) and we are able to use the available tools to obtain all SemPOS features for English sentences as well.

3.2 Evaluation of SemPOS and Friends

We measured the metric performance on data used in MetricsMATR08, WMT09 and WMT08. For the evaluation of metric correlation with human judgments at the system level, we used the Pearson correlation coefficient ρ applied to ranks. In case of a tie, the systems were assigned the average position. For example if three systems achieved the same highest score (thus occupying the positions 1, 2 and 3 when sorted by score), each of them would obtain the average rank of $2 = \frac{1+2+3}{3}$. When correlating ranks (instead of exact scores) and with this handling of ties, the Pearson coefficient is equivalent to Spearman's rank correlation coefficient.

The MetricsMATR08 human judgments include preferences for pairs of MT systems saying which one of the two systems is better, while the WMT08 and WMT09 data contain system scores (for up to 5 systems) on the scale 1 to 5 for a given sentence. We assigned a human ranking to the systems based on the percent of time that their translations were judged to be better than or equal to the translations of any other system in the manual evaluation. We converted automatic metric scores to ranks.

Metrics' performance for translation to English and Czech was measured on the following testsets (the number of human judgments for a given source language in brackets):

To English: MetricsMATR08 (cn+ar: 1652), WMT08 News Articles (de: 199, fr: 251), WMT08 Europarl (es: 190, fr: 183), WMT09 (cz: 320, de: 749, es: 484, fr: 786, hu: 287)

To Czech: WMT08 News Articles (en: 267), WMT08 Commentary (en: 243), WMT09 (en: 1425)

The MetricsMATR08 testset contained 4 reference translations for each sentence whereas the remaining testsets only one reference.

Correlation coefficients for English are shown in Table 2. The best metric is Void_{par} closely followed by $\text{Void}_{\text{sons}}$. The explanation is that Void compared to SemPOS or Functor does not lose points by an erroneous assignment of the POS or the functor, and that Void_{par} profits from checking the dependency relations between autosemantic words. The combination of BLEU and SemPOS[6] outperforms both individual metrics, but in case of SemPOS only by a minimal difference. Additionally, we confirm that 4-grams alone have little discriminative power both when used as a metric of their own (BLEU_4) as well as in a linear combination with SemPOS.

The best metric for Czech (see Table 3) is a linear combination of SemPOS and 4-gram BLEU closely followed by other SemPOS and BLEU_n combinations. We assume this is because BLEU_4 can capture correctly translated fixed phrases, which is positively reflected in human judgments. Including BLEU_1 in the combination favors translations with word forms as expected by the refer-

[6]For each $n \in \{1, 2, 3, 4\}$, we show only the best weight setting for SemPOS and BLEU_n.

Metric	Avg	Best	Worst
Void$_{par}$	0.75	0.89	0.60
Void$_{sons}$	0.75	0.90	0.54
Void	0.72	0.91	0.59
Functor$_{sons}$	0.72	1.00	0.43
GTM	0.71	0.90	0.54
4·SemPOS+1·BLEU$_2$	0.70	0.93	0.43
SemPOS$_{par}$	0.70	0.93	0.30
1·SemPOS+4·BLEU$_3$	0.70	0.91	0.26
4·SemPOS+1·BLEU$_1$	0.69	0.93	0.43
NIST	0.69	0.90	0.53
SemPOS$_{sons}$	0.69	0.94	0.40
SemPOS	0.69	0.95	0.30
2·SemPOS+1·BLEU$_4$	0.68	0.91	0.09
BLEU$_1$	0.68	0.87	0.43
BLEU$_2$	0.68	0.90	0.26
BLEU$_3$	0.66	0.90	0.14
BLEU	0.66	0.91	0.20
TER	0.63	0.87	0.29
PER	0.63	0.88	0.32
BLEU$_4$	0.61	0.90	-0.31
Functor$_{par}$	0.57	0.83	-0.03
Functor	0.55	0.82	-0.09

Table 2: Average, best and worst system-level correlation coefficients for translation to English from various source languages evaluated on 10 different testsets.

Metric	Avg	Best	Worst
3·SemPOS+1·BLEU$_4$	0.55	0.83	0.14
2·SemPOS+1·BLEU$_2$	0.55	0.83	0.14
2·SemPOS+1·BLEU$_1$	0.53	0.83	0.09
4·SemPOS+1·BLEU$_3$	0.53	0.83	0.09
SemPOS	0.53	0.83	0.09
BLEU$_2$	0.43	0.83	0.09
SemPOS$_{par}$	0.37	0.53	0.14
Functor$_{sons}$	0.36	0.53	0.14
GTM	0.35	0.53	0.14
BLEU$_4$	0.33	0.53	0.09
Void	0.33	0.53	0.09
NIST	0.33	0.53	0.09
Void$_{sons}$	0.33	0.53	0.09
BLEU	0.33	0.53	0.09
BLEU$_3$	0.33	0.53	0.09
BLEU$_1$	0.29	0.53	-0.03
SemPOS$_{sons}$	0.28	0.42	0.03
Functor$_{par}$	0.23	0.40	0.14
Functor	0.21	0.40	0.09
Void$_{par}$	0.16	0.53	-0.08
PER	0.12	0.53	-0.09
TER	0.07	0.53	-0.23

Table 3: System-level correlation coefficients for English-to-Czech translation evaluated on 3 different testsets.

ence, thus allowing to spot bad word forms. In all cases, the linear combination puts more weight on SemPOS. Given the negligible difference between SemPOS alone and the linear combinations, we see that word forms are not the major issue for humans interpreting the translation—most likely because the systems so far often make more important errors. This is also confirmed by the observation that using BLEU alone is rather unreliable for Czech and BLEU-1 (which judges unigrams only) is even worse. Surprisingly BLEU-2 performed better than any other n-grams for reasons that have yet to be examined. The error metrics PER and TER showed the lowest correlation with human judgments for translation to Czech.

4 Conclusion

This paper documented problems of single-reference BLEU when applied to morphologically rich languages such as Czech. BLEU suffers from a sparse data problem, unable to judge the quality of tokens not confirmed by the reference. This is confirmed for other languages as well: the lower the BLEU score the lower the correlation to human judgments.

We introduced a refinement of SemPOS, an automatic metric of MT quality based on deep-syntactic representation of the sentence tackling the sparse data issue. SemPOS was evaluated on translation to Czech and to English, scoring better than or comparable to many established metrics.

References

Ondřej Bojar, David Mareček, Václav Novák, Martin Popel, Jan Ptáček, Jan Rouš, and Zdeněk Žabokrtský. 2009. English-Czech MT in 2008. In *Proceedings of the Fourth Workshop on Statistical Machine Translation*, Athens, Greece, March. Association for Computational Linguistics.

Chris Callison-Burch, Cameron Fordyce, Philipp Koehn, Christof Monz, and Josh Schroeder. 2008. Further meta-evaluation of machine translation. In *Proceedings of the Third Workshop on Statistical Machine Translation*, pages 70–106, Columbus, Ohio, June. Association for Computational Linguistics.

Chris Callison-Burch, Philipp Koehn, Christof Monz, and Josh Schroeder. 2009. Findings of the 2009 workshop on statistical machine translation. In *Proceedings of the Fourth Workshop on Statistical Machine Translation*, Athens, Greece. Association for Computational Linguistics.

Silvie Cinková, Jan Hajič, Marie Mikulová, Lucie Mladová, Anja Nedolužko, Petr Pajas, Jarmila Panevová, Jiří Semecký, Jana Šindlerová, Josef Toman, Zdeňka Urešová, and Zdeněk Žabokrtský. 2004. Annotation of English on the tectogrammatical level. Technical Report TR-2006-35, ÚFAL/CKL, Prague, Czech Republic, December.

Sherri Condon, Gregory A. Sanders, Dan Parvaz, Alan Rubenstein, Christy Doran, John Aberdeen, and Beatrice Oshika. 2009. Normalization for Automated Metrics: English and Arabic Speech Translation. In *MT Summit XII*.

Jesús Giménez and Lluís Márquez. 2007. Linguistic Features for Automatic Evaluation of Heterogenous MT Systems. In *Proceedings of the Second Workshop on Statistical Machine Translation*, pages 256–264, Prague, June. Association for Computational Linguistics.

Jan Hajič, Silvie Cinková, Kristýna Čermáková, Lucie Mladová, Anja Nedolužko, Petr Pajas, Jiří Semecký, Jana Šindlerová, Josef Toman, Kristýna Tomšů, Matěj Korvas, Magdaléna Rysová, Kateřina Veselovská, and Zdeněk Žabokrtský. 2009. Prague English Dependency Treebank 1.0. Institute of Formal and Applied Linguistics, Charles University in Prague, ISBN 978-80-904175-0-2, January.

Jan Hajič, Jarmila Panevová, Eva Hajičová, Petr Sgall, Petr Pajas, Jan Štěpánek, Jiří Havelka, Marie Mikulová, Zdeněk Žabokrtský, and Magda Ševčíková Razímová. 2006. Prague Dependency Treebank 2.0. LDC2006T01, ISBN: 1-58563-370-4.

Philipp Koehn, Hieu Hoang, Alexandra Birch, Chris Callison-Burch, Marcello Federico, Nicola Bertoldi, Brooke Cowan, Wade Shen, Christine Moran, Richard Zens, Chris Dyer, Ondřej Bojar, Alexandra Constantin, and Evan Herbst. 2007. Moses: Open Source Toolkit for Statistical Machine Translation. In *ACL 2007, Proceedings of the 45th Annual Meeting of the Association for Computational Linguistics Companion Volume Proceedings of the Demo and Poster Sessions*, pages 177–180, Prague, Czech Republic, June. Association for Computational Linguistics.

Kamil Kos and Ondřej Bojar. 2009. Evaluation of Machine Translation Metrics for Czech as the Target Language. *Prague Bulletin of Mathematical Linguistics*, 92.

Kishore Papineni, Salim Roukos, Todd Ward, and Wei-Jing Zhu. 2002. BLEU: a Method for Automatic Evaluation of Machine Translation. In *ACL 2002, Proceedings of the 40th Annual Meeting of the Association for Computational Linguistics*, pages 311–318, Philadelphia, Pennsylvania.

M. Przybocki, K. Peterson, and S. Bronsart. 2008. Official results of the NIST 2008 "Metrics for MAchine TRanslation" Challenge (MetricsMATR08).

Petr Sgall, Eva Hajičová, and Jarmila Panevová. 1986. *The Meaning of the Sentence and Its Semantic and Pragmatic Aspects*. Academia/Reidel Publishing Company, Prague, Czech Republic/Dordrecht, Netherlands.

Zdeněk Žabokrtský and Ondřej Bojar. 2008. TectoMT, Developer's Guide. Technical Report TR-2008-39, Institute of Formal and Applied Linguistics, Faculty of Mathematics and Physics, Charles University in Prague, December.

Exemplar-Based Models for Word Meaning In Context

Katrin Erk
Department of Linguistics
University of Texas at Austin
katrin.erk@mail.utexas.edu

Sebastian Padó
Institut für maschinelle Sprachverarbeitung
Stuttgart University
pado@ims.uni-stuttgart.de

Abstract

This paper describes ongoing work on distributional models for word meaning in context. We abandon the usual one-vector-per-word paradigm in favor of an exemplar model that activates only relevant occurrences. On a paraphrasing task, we find that a simple exemplar model outperforms more complex state-of-the-art models.

1 Introduction

Distributional models are a popular framework for representing word meaning. They describe a lemma through a high-dimensional vector that records co-occurrence with context features over a large corpus. Distributional models have been used in many NLP analysis tasks (Salton et al., 1975; McCarthy and Carroll, 2003; Salton et al., 1975), as well as for cognitive modeling (Baroni and Lenci, 2009; Landauer and Dumais, 1997; McDonald and Ramscar, 2001). Among their attractive properties are their simplicity and versatility, as well as the fact that they can be acquired from corpora in an unsupervised manner.

Distributional models are also attractive as a model of word meaning in context, since they do not have to rely on fixed sets of dictionary sense with their well-known problems (Kilgarriff, 1997; McCarthy and Navigli, 2009). Also, they can be used directly for testing paraphrase applicability (Szpektor et al., 2008), a task that has recently become prominent in the context of textual entailment (Bar-Haim et al., 2007). However, polysemy is a fundamental problem for distributional models. Typically, distributional models compute a single "type" vector for a target word, which contains co-occurrence counts for all the occurrences of the target in a large corpus. If the target is polysemous, this vector mixes contextual features for all the senses of the target. For example, among the top 20 features for *coach*, we get *match* and *team* (for the "trainer" sense) as well as *driver* and *car* (for the "bus" sense). This problem has typically been approached by modifying the type vector for a target to better match a given context (Mitchell and Lapata, 2008; Erk and Padó, 2008; Thater et al., 2009).

In the terms of research on human concept representation, which often employs feature vector representations, the use of type vectors can be understood as a *prototype*-based approach, which uses a single vector per category. From this angle, computing prototypes throws away much interesting distributional information. A rival class of models is that of *exemplar* models, which memorize each seen instance of a category and perform categorization by comparing a new stimulus to each remembered exemplar vector.

We can address the polysemy issue through an exemplar model by simply removing all exemplars that are "not relevant" for the present context, or conversely *activating* only the relevant ones. For the *coach* example, in the context of a text about motorways, presumably an instance like "The coach drove a steady 45 mph" would be activated, while "The team lost all games since the new coach arrived" would not.

In this paper, we present an exemplar-based distributional model for modeling word meaning in context, applying the model to the task of deciding paraphrase applicability. With a very simple vector representation and just using activation, we outperform the state-of-the-art prototype models. We perform an in-depth error analysis to identify stable parameters for this class of models.

2 Related Work

Among distributional models of word, there are some approaches that address polysemy, either by inducing a fixed clustering of contexts into senses (Schütze, 1998) or by dynamically modi-

Proceedings of the ACL 2010 Conference Short Papers, pages 92–97,
Uppsala, Sweden, 11-16 July 2010.

fying a word's type vector according to each given sentence context (Landauer and Dumais, 1997; Mitchell and Lapata, 2008; Erk and Padó, 2008; Thater et al., 2009). Polysemy-aware approaches also differ in their notion of *context*. Some use a bag-of-words representation of words in the current sentence (Schütze, 1998; Landauer and Dumais, 1997), some make use of syntactic context (Mitchell and Lapata, 2008; Erk and Padó, 2008; Thater et al., 2009). The approach that we present in the current paper computes a representation dynamically for each sentence context, using a simple bag-of-words representation of context.

In cognitive science, prototype models predict degree of category membership through similarity to a single prototype, while exemplar theory represents a concept as a collection of all previously seen exemplars (Murphy, 2002). Griffiths et al. (2007) found that the benefit of exemplars over prototypes grows with the number of available exemplars. The problem of representing meaning in context, which we consider in this paper, is closely related to the problem of *concept combination* in cognitive science, i.e., the derivation of representations for complex concepts (such as "metal spoon") given the representations of base concepts ("metal" and "spoon"). While most approaches to concept combination are based on prototype models, Voorspoels et al. (2009) show superior results for an exemplar model based on exemplar *activation*.

In NLP, exemplar-based (memory-based) models have been applied to many problems (Daelemans et al., 1999). In the current paper, we use an exemplar model for computing distributional representations for word meaning in context, using the context to *activate* relevant exemplars. Comparing representations of context, bag-of-words (BOW) representations are more informative and noisier, while syntax-based representations deliver sparser and less noisy information. Following the hypothesis that richer, topical information is more suitable for exemplar activation, we use BOW representations of sentential context in the current paper.

3 Exemplar Activation Models

We now present an exemplar-based model for meaning in context. It assumes that each target lemma is represented by a set of exemplars, where an exemplar is a sentence in which the target occurs, represented as a vector. We use lowercase letters for individual exemplars (vectors), and uppercase letters for sets of exemplars.

Sentential context	Paraphrase
After a fire extinguisher is used, it must always be **returned** for recharging and its use recorded.	bring back (3), take back (2), send back (1), give back (1)
We **return** to the young woman who is reading the Wrigley's wrapping paper.	come back (3), revert (1), revisit (1), go (1)

Table 1: The Lexical Substitution (LexSub) dataset.

We model polysemy by *activating* relevant exemplars of a lemma E in a given sentence context s. (Note that we use E to refer to both a lemma and its exemplar set, and that s can be viewed as just another exemplar vector.) In general, we define *activation* of a set E by exemplar s as

$$act(E, s) = \{e \in E \mid \mathrm{sim}(e, s) > \theta(E, s)\}$$

where E is an exemplar set, s is the "point of comparison", sim is some similarity measure such as Cosine or Jaccard, and $\theta(E, s)$ is a threshold. Exemplars belong to the activated set if their similarity to s exceeds $\theta(E, s)$.[1] We explore two variants of activation. In **kNN activation**, the k most similar exemplars to s are activated by setting θ to the similarity of the k-th most similar exemplar. In **q-percentage activation**, we activate the top $q\%$ of E by setting θ to the (100-q)-th percentile of the $sim(e, s)$ distribution. Note that, while in the kNN activation scheme the number of activated exemplars is the same for every lemma, this is not the case for percentage activation: There, a more frequent lemma (i.e., a lemma with more exemplars) will have more exemplars activated.

Exemplar activation for paraphrasing. A paraphrases is typically only applicable to a particular sense of a target word. Table 1 illustrates this on two examples from the Lexical Substitution (LexSub) dataset (McCarthy and Navigli, 2009), both featuring the target *return*. The right column lists appropriate paraphrases of *return* in each context (given by human annotators). [2] We apply the exemplar activation model to the task of predicting paraphrase felicity: Given a target lemma T in a particular sentential context s, and given a list of

[1]In principle, activation could be treated not just as binary inclusion/exclusion, but also as a graded weighting scheme. However, weighting schemes introduce a large number of parameters, which we wanted to avoid.

[2]Each annotator was allowed to give up to three paraphrases per target in context. As a consequence, the number of gold paraphrases per target sentence varies.

potential paraphrases of T, the task is to predict which of the paraphrases are applicable in s.

Previous approaches (Mitchell and Lapata, 2008; Erk and Padó, 2008; Erk and Padó, 2009; Thater et al., 2009) have performed this task by modifying the type vector for T to the context s and then comparing the resulting vector T' to the type vector of a paraphrase candidate P. In our exemplar setting, we select a contextually adequate subset of contexts in which T has been observed, using $T' = act(T, s)$ as a generalized representation of meaning of target T in the context of s.

Previous approaches used all of P as a representation for a paraphrase candidate P. However, P includes also irrelevant exemplars, while for a paraphrase to be judged as good, it is sufficient that one plausible reading exists. Therefore, we use $P' = act(P, s)$ to represent the paraphrase.

4 Experimental Evaluation

Data. We evaluate our model on predicting paraphrases from the Lexical Substitution (LexSub) dataset (McCarthy and Navigli, 2009). This dataset consists of 2000 instances of 200 target words in sentential contexts, with paraphrases for each target word instance generated by up to 6 participants. Paraphrases are ranked by the number of annotators that chose them (cf. Table 1). Following Erk and Padó (2008), we take the list of paraphrase candidates for a target as given (computed by pooling all paraphrases that LexSub annotators proposed for the target) and use the models to rank them for any given sentence context.

As exemplars, we create bag-of-words co-occurrence vectors from the BNC. These vectors represent instances of a target word by the other words in the same sentence, lemmatized and POS-tagged, minus stop words. E.g., if the lemma *gnurge* occurs twice in the BNC, once in the sentence "The dog will gnurge the other dog", and once in "The old windows gnurged", the exemplar set for *gnurge* contains the vectors *[dog-n: 2, other-a:1]* and *[old-a: 1, window-n: 1]*. For exemplar similarity, we use the standard Cosine similarity, and for the similarity of two exemplar sets, the Cosine of their centroids.

Evaluation. The model's prediction for an item is a list of paraphrases ranked by their predicted goodness of fit. To evaluate them against a weighted list of gold paraphrases, we follow Thater et al. (2009) in using Generalized Average Precision (GAP), which interpolates the precision values of top-n prediction lists for increasing n. Let $G = \langle q_1, \ldots, q_m \rangle$ be the list of gold paraphrases with gold weights $\langle y_1, \ldots, y_m \rangle$. Let $P = \langle p_1, \ldots, p_n \rangle$ be the list of model predictions as ranked by the model, and let $\langle x_1, \ldots, x_n \rangle$ be the *gold* weights associated with them (assume $x_i = 0$ if $p_i \notin G$), where $G \subseteq P$. Let $I(x_i) = 1$ if $p_i \in G$, and zero otherwise. We write $\overline{x_i} = \frac{1}{i} \sum_{k=1}^{i} x_k$ for the average gold weight of the first i model predictions, and analogously $\overline{y_i}$. Then

$$GAP(P, G) = \frac{1}{\sum_{j=1}^{m} I(y_j)\overline{y_j}} \sum_{i=1}^{n} I(x_i)\overline{x_i}$$

Since the model may rank multiple paraphrases the same, we average over 10 random permutations of equally ranked paraphrases. We report mean GAP over all items in the dataset.

para-meter	*actT*		*actP*	
	kNN	perc.	kNN	perc.
10	36.1	35.5	36.5	**38.6**
20	**36.2**	35.2	36.2	37.9
30	36.1	35.3	35.8	37.8
40	36.0	35.3	35.8	37.7
50	35.9	35.1	35.9	37.5
60	36.0	35.0	36.1	37.5
70	35.9	34.8	36.1	37.5
80	36.0	34.7	36.0	37.4
90	35.9	34.5	35.9	37.3
no act.	34.6		35.7	
random BL	28.5			

Table 2: Activation of T or P individually on the full LexSub dataset (GAP evaluation)

Results and Discussion. We first computed two models that activate either the paraphrase or the target, but not both. Model 1, *actT*, activates only the target, using the complete P as paraphrase, and ranking paraphrases by $sim(P, act(T, s))$. Model 2, *actP*, activates only the paraphrase, using s as the target word, ranking by $sim(act(P, s), s)$.

The results for these models are shown in Table 2, with both kNN and percentage activation: kNN activation with a parameter of 10 means that the 10 closest neighbors were activated, while percentage with a parameter of 10 means that the closest 10% of the exemplars were used. Note first that we computed a random baseline (last row) with a GAP of 28.5. The second-to-last row ("no activation") shows two more informed baselines.

The *actT* "no act" result (34.6) corresponds to a prototype-based model that ranks paraphrase candidates by the distance between their type vectors and the target's type vector. Virtually all exemplar models outperform this prototype model. Note also that both *actT* and *actP* show the best results for small values of the activation parameter. This indicates paraphrases can be judged on the basis of a rather small number of exemplars. Nevertheless, *actT* and *actP* differ with regard to the details of their optimal activation. For *actT*, a small absolute number of activated exemplars (here, 20) works best , while *actP* yields the best results for a small percentage of paraphrase exemplars. This can be explained by the different functions played by *actT* and *actP* (cf. Section 3): Activation of the paraphrase must allow a guess about whether there is reasonable interpretation of P in the context s. This appears to require a reasonably-sized sample from P. In contrast, target activation merely has to counteract the sparsity of s, and activation of too many exemplars from T leads to oversmoothing.

We obtained significances by computing 95% and 99% confidence intervals with bootstrap resampling. As a rule of thumb, we find that 0.4% difference in GAP corresponds to a significant difference at the 95% level, and 0.7% difference in GAP to significance at the 99% level. The four activation methods (i.e., columns in Table 2) are significantly different from each other, with the exception of the pair *actT*/kNN and *actP*/kNN (n.s.), so that we get the following order:

actP/perc $>$ *actP*/kNN $\approx$ *actT*/kNN $>$ *actT*/perc

where $>$ means "significantly outperforms". In particular, the best method (*actT*/kNN) outperforms all other methods at $p<0.01$. Here, the best parameter setting (10% activation) is also significantly better than the next-one one (20% activation). With the exception of *actT*/perc, all activation methods significantly outperform the best baseline (*actP*, no activation).

Based on these observations, we computed a third model, *actTP*, that activates both T (by kNN) and P (by percentage), ranking paraphrases by $sim(act(P, s), act(T, s))$. Table 3 shows the results. We find the overall best model at a similar location in parameter space as for *actT* and *actP* (cf. Table 2), namely by setting the activation parameters to small values. The sensitivity of the parameters changes considerably, though. When

P activation (%) $\Rightarrow$ T activation (kNN) $\Downarrow$	10	20	30
5	**38.2**	38.1	38.1
10	37.6	37.8	37.7
20	37.3	37.4	37.3
40	37.2	37.2	36.1

Table 3: Joint activation of P and T on the full LexSub dataset (GAP evaluation)

we fix the *actP* activation level, we find comparatively large performance differences between the T activation settings k=5 and k=10 (highly significant for 10% *actP*, and significant for 20% and 30% *actP*). On the other hand, when we fix the *actT* activation level, changes in *actP* activation generally have an insignificant impact.

Somewhat disappointingly, we are not able to surpass the best result for *actP* alone. This indicates that – at least in the current vector space – the sparsity of s is less of a problem than the "dilution" of s that we face when we representing the target word by exemplars of T close to s. Note, however, that the numerically worse performance of the best *actTP* model is still not significantly different from the best *actP* model.

Influence of POS and frequency. An analysis of the results by target part-of-speech showed that the globally optimal parameters also yield the best results for individual POS, even though there are substantial differences among POS. For *actT*, the best results emerge for all POS with kNN activation with k between 10 and 30. For k=20, we obtain a GAP of 35.3 (verbs), 38.2 (nouns), and 35.1 (adjectives). For *actP*, the best parameter for all POS was activation of 10%, with GAPs of 36.9 (verbs), 41.4 (nouns), and 37.5 (adjectives). Interestingly, the results for *actTP* (verbs: 38.4, nouns: 40.6, adjectives: 36.9) are better than *actP* for verbs, but worse for nouns and adjectives, which indicates that the sparsity problem might be more prominent than for the other POS. In all three models, we found a clear effect of target and paraphrase frequency, with deteriorating performance for the highest-frequency targets as well as for the lemmas with the highest average paraphrase frequency.

Comparison to other models. Many of the other models are syntax-based and are therefore only applicable to a subset of the LexSub data. We have re-evaluated our exemplar models on the subsets we used in Erk and Padó (2008, EP08, 367

	Models		
	EP08	EP09	TDP09
EP08 dataset	27.4	NA	NA
EP09 dataset	NA	32.2	36.5
	actT	*actP*	*actTP*
EP08 dataset	36.5	38.0	**39.9**
EP09 dataset	39.1	**39.9**	39.6

Table 4: Comparison to other models on two subsets of LexSub (GAP evaluation)

datapoints) and Erk and Padó (2009, EP09, 100 datapoints). The second set was also used by Thater et al. (2009, TDP09). The results in Table 4 compare these models against our best previous exemplar models and show that our models outperform these models across the board. [3] Due to the small sizes of these datasets, statistical significance is more difficult to attain. On EP09, the differences among our models are not significant, but the difference between them and the original EP09 model is.[4] On EP08, all differences are significant except for *actP* vs. *actTP*.

We note that both the EP08 and the EP09 datasets appear to be simpler to model than the complete Lexical Substitution dataset, at least by our exemplar-based models. This underscores an old insight: namely, that direct syntactic neighbors, such as arguments and modifiers, provide strong clues as to word sense.

5 Conclusions and Outlook

This paper reports on work in progress on an exemplar activation model as an alternative to one-vector-per-word approaches to word meaning in context. Exemplar activation is very effective in handling polysemy, even with a very simple (and sparse) bag-of-words vector representation. On both the EP08 and EP09 datasets, our models surpass more complex prototype-based approaches (Tab. 4). It is also noteworthy that the exemplar activation models work best when few exemplars are used, which bodes well for their efficiency.

We found that the best target representations result from activating a low absolute number of exemplars. Paraphrase representations are best activated with a percentage-based threshold. Overall, we found that paraphrase activation had a much larger impact on performance than target activation, and that drawing on target exemplars other than s to represent the target meaning in context improved over using s itself only for verbs (Tab. 3). This suggests the possibility of considering T's activated paraphrase candidates as the representation of T in the context s, rather than some vector of T itself, in the spirit of Kintsch (2001).

While it is encouraging that the best parameter settings involved the activation of only few exemplars, computation with exemplar models still requires the management of large numbers of vectors. The computational overhead can be reduced by using data structures that cut down on the number of vector comparisons, or by decreasing vector dimensionality (Gorman and Curran, 2006). We will experiment with those methods to determine the tradeoff of runtime and accuracy for this task.

Another area of future work is to move beyond bag-of-words context: It is known from WSD that syntactic and bag-of-words contexts provide complementary information (Florian et al., 2002; Szpektor et al., 2008), and we hope that they can be integrated in a more sophisticated exemplar model.

Finally, we will to explore task-based evaluations. Relation extraction and textual entailment in particular are tasks where similar models have been used before (Szpektor et al., 2008).

Acknowledgements. This work was supported in part by National Science Foundation grant IIS-0845925, and by a Morris Memorial Grant from the New York Community Trust.

References

R. Bar-Haim, I. Dagan, I. Greental, and E. Shnarch. 2007. Semantic inference at the lexical-syntactic level. In *Proceedings of AAAI*, pages 871–876, Vancouver, BC.

M. Baroni and A. Lenci. 2009. One distributional memory, many semantic spaces. In *Proceedings of the EACL Workshop on Geometrical Models of Natural Language Semantics*, Athens, Greece.

W. Daelemans, A. van den Bosch, and J. Zavrel. 1999. Forgetting exceptions is harmful in language learning. *Machine Learning*, 34(1/3):11–43. Special Issue on Natural Language Learning.

K. Erk and S. Padó. 2008. A structured vector space

[3]Since our models had the advantage of being tuned on the dataset, we also report the range of results across the parameters we tested. On the EP08 dataset, we obtained 33.1–36.5 for *actT*; 33.3–38.0 for *actP*; 37.7-39.9 for *actTP*. On the EP09 dataset, the numbers were 35.8–39.1 for *actT*; 38.1–39.9 for *actP*; 37.2–39.8 for *actTP*.

[4]We did not have access to the TDP09 predictions to do significance testing.

model for word meaning in context. In *Proceedings of EMNLP*, pages 897–906, Honolulu, HI.

K. Erk and S. Padó. 2009. Paraphrase assessment in structured vector space: Exploring parameters and datasets. In *Proceedings of the EACL Workshop on Geometrical Models of Natural Language Semantics*, Athens, Greece.

R. Florian, S. Cucerzan, C. Schafer, and D. Yarowsky. 2002. Combining classifiers for word sense disambiguation. *Journal of Natural Language Engineering*, 8(4):327–341.

J. Gorman and J. R. Curran. 2006. Scaling distributional similarity to large corpora. In *Proceedings of ACL*, pages 361–368, Sydney.

T. Griffiths, K. Canini, A. Sanborn, and D. J. Navarro. 2007. Unifying rational models of categorization via the hierarchical Dirichlet process. In *Proceedings of CogSci*, pages 323–328, Nashville, TN.

A. Kilgarriff. 1997. I don't believe in word senses. *Computers and the Humanities*, 31(2):91–113.

W. Kintsch. 2001. Predication. *Cognitive Science*, 25:173–202.

T. Landauer and S. Dumais. 1997. A solution to Platos problem: the latent semantic analysis theory of acquisition, induction, and representation of knowledge. *Psychological Review*, 104(2):211–240.

D. McCarthy and J. Carroll. 2003. Disambiguating nouns, verbs, and adjectives using automatically acquired selectional preferences. *Computational Linguistics*, 29(4):639–654.

D. McCarthy and R. Navigli. 2009. The English lexical substitution task. *Language Resources and Evaluation*, 43(2):139–159. Special Issue on Computational Semantic Analysis of Language: SemEval-2007 and Beyond.

S. McDonald and M. Ramscar. 2001. Testing the distributional hypothesis: The influence of context on judgements of semantic similarity. In *Proceedings of CogSci*, pages 611–616.

J. Mitchell and M. Lapata. 2008. Vector-based models of semantic composition. In *Proceedings of ACL*, pages 236–244, Columbus, OH.

G. L. Murphy. 2002. *The Big Book of Concepts*. MIT Press.

G Salton, A Wang, and C Yang. 1975. A vector-space model for information retrieval. *Journal of the American Society for Information Science*, 18:613–620.

H. Schütze. 1998. Automatic word sense discrimination. *Computational Linguistics*, 24(1):97–124.

I. Szpektor, I. Dagan, R. Bar-Haim, and J. Goldberger. 2008. Contextual preferences. In *Proceedings of ACL*, pages 683–691, Columbus, OH.

S. Thater, G. Dinu, and M. Pinkal. 2009. Ranking paraphrases in context. In *Proceedings of the ACL Workshop on Applied Textual Inference*, pages 44–47, Singapore.

W. Voorspoels, W. Vanpaemel, and G. Storms. 2009. The role of extensional information in conceptual combination. In *Proceedings of CogSci*.

A Structured Model for Joint Learning of Argument Roles and Predicate Senses

Yotaro Watanabe
Graduate School of Information Sciences
Tohoku University
6-6-05, Aramaki Aza Aoba, Aoba-ku,
Sendai 980-8579, Japan
yotaro-w@ecei.tohoku.ac.jp

Masayuki Asahara **Yuji Matsumoto**
Graduate School of Information Science
Nara Institute of Science and Technology
8916-5 Takayama, Ikoma,
Nara, 630-0192, Japan
{masayu-a, matsu}@is.naist.jp

Abstract

In predicate-argument structure analysis, it is important to capture non-local dependencies among arguments and inter-dependencies between the sense of a predicate and the semantic roles of its arguments. However, no existing approach explicitly handles both non-local dependencies and semantic dependencies between predicates and arguments. In this paper we propose a structured model that overcomes the limitation of existing approaches; the model captures both types of dependencies simultaneously by introducing four types of factors including a global factor type capturing non-local dependencies among arguments and a pairwise factor type capturing local dependencies between a predicate and an argument. In experiments the proposed model achieved competitive results compared to the state-of-the-art systems without applying any feature selection procedure.

1 Introduction

Predicate-argument structure analysis is a process of assigning *who* does *what* to *whom*, *where*, *when*, etc. for each predicate. Arguments of a predicate are assigned particular *semantic roles*, such as *Agent*, *Theme*, *Patient*, etc. Lately, predicate-argument structure analysis has been regarded as a task of assigning semantic roles of arguments as well as word senses of a predicate (Surdeanu et al., 2008; Hajič et al., 2009).

Several researchers have paid much attention to predicate-argument structure analysis, and the following two important factors have been shown. Toutanova et al. (2008), Johansson and Nugues (2008), and Björkelund et al. (2009) presented importance of capturing non-local dependencies of core arguments in predicate-argument structure analysis. They used argument sequences tied with a predicate sense (e.g. AGENT-buy.01/Active-PATIENT) as a feature for the re-ranker of the system where predicate sense and argument role candidates are generated by their pipelined architecture. They reported that incorporating this type of features provides substantial gain of the system performance.

The other factor is inter-dependencies between a predicate sense and argument roles, which relate to selectional preference, and motivated us to jointly identify a predicate sense and its argument roles. This type of dependencies has been explored by Riedel and Meza-Ruiz (2008; 2009b; 2009a), all of which use Markov Logic Networks (MLN). The work uses the global formulae that have atoms in terms of both a predicate sense and each of its argument roles, and the system identifies predicate senses and argument roles simultaneously.

Ideally, we want to capture both types of dependencies simultaneously. The former approaches can not explicitly include features that capture inter-dependencies between a predicate sense and its argument roles. Though these are implicitly incorporated by re-ranking where the most plausible assignment is selected from a small subset of predicate and argument candidates, which are generated independently. On the other hand, it is difficult to deal with core argument features in MLN. Because the number of core arguments varies with the role assignments, this type of features cannot be expressed by a single formula.

Thompson et al. (2010) proposed a generative model that captures both predicate senses and its argument roles. However, the first-order markov assumption of the model eliminates ability to capture non-local dependencies among arguments. Also, generative models are in general inferior to discriminatively trained linear or log-

Proceedings of the ACL 2010 Conference Short Papers, pages 98–102,
Uppsala, Sweden, 11-16 July 2010.

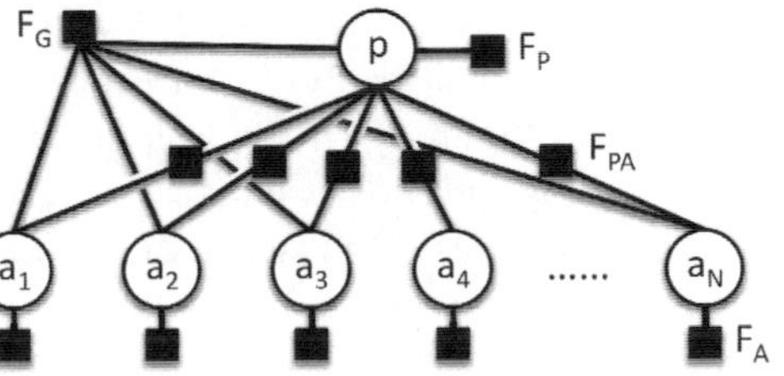

Figure 1: Undirected graphical model representation of the structured model

linear models.

In this paper we propose a structured model that overcomes limitations of the previous approaches. For the model, we introduce several types of features including those that capture both non-local dependencies of core arguments, and inter-dependencies between a predicate sense and its argument roles. By doing this, both tasks are mutually influenced, and the model determines the most plausible set of assignments of a predicate sense and its argument roles simultaneously. We present an exact inference algorithm for the model, and a large-margin learning algorithm that can handle both local and global features.

2 Model

Figure 1 shows the graphical representation of our proposed model. The node p corresponds to a predicate, and the nodes $a_1, ..., a_N$ to arguments of the predicate. Each node is assigned a particular predicate sense or an argument role label. The black squares are *factors* which provide scores of label assignments. In the model, the nodes for arguments depend on the predicate sense, and by influencing labels of a predicate sense and its argument roles, the most plausible label assignment of the nodes is determined considering all factors.

In this work, we use linear models. Let $\mathbf{x}$ be words in a sentence, p be a sense of a predicate in $\mathbf{x}$, and $\mathcal{A} = \{a_n\}_1^N$ be a set of possible role label assignments for $\mathbf{x}$. A predicate-argument structure is represented by a pair of p and $\mathcal{A}$. We define the score function for predicate-argument structures as $s(p, \mathcal{A}) = \sum_{F_k \in \mathcal{F}} F_k(\mathbf{x}, p, \mathcal{A})$. $\mathcal{F}$ is a set of all the factors, $F_k(\mathbf{x}, p, \mathcal{A})$ corresponds to a particular factor in Figure 1, and gives a score to a predicate or argument label assignments. Since we use linear models, $F_k(\mathbf{x}, p, \mathcal{A}) = \mathbf{w} \cdot \Phi_k(\mathbf{x}, p, \mathcal{A})$.

2.1 Factors of the Model

We define four types of factors for the model.

Predicate Factor F_P scores a sense of p, and does not depend on any arguments. The score function is defined by $F_P(\mathbf{x}, p, \mathcal{A}) = \mathbf{w} \cdot \Phi_P(\mathbf{x}, p)$.

Argument Factor F_A scores a label assignment of a particular argument $a \in \mathcal{A}$. The score is determined independently from a predicate sense, and is given by $F_A(\mathbf{x}, p, a) = \mathbf{w} \cdot \Phi_A(\mathbf{x}, a)$.

Predicate-Argument Pairwise Factor F_{PA} captures inter-dependencies between a predicate sense and one of its argument roles. The score function is defined as $F_{PA}(\mathbf{x}, p, a) = \mathbf{w} \cdot \Phi_{PA}(\mathbf{x}, p, a)$. The difference from F_A is that F_{PA} influences both the predicate sense and the argument role. By introducing this factor, the role label can be influenced by the predicate sense, and vise versa.

Global Factor F_G is introduced to capture plausibility of the whole predicate-argument structure. Like the other factors, the score function is defined as $F_G(\mathbf{x}, p, \mathcal{A}) = \mathbf{w} \cdot \Phi_G(\mathbf{x}, p, \mathcal{A})$. A possible feature that can be considered by this factor is the mutual dependencies among core arguments. For instance, if a predicate-argument structure has an agent (A0) followed by the predicate and a patient (A1), we encode the structure as a string *A0-PRED-A1* and use it as a feature. This type of features provide *plausibility* of predicate-argument structures. Even if the highest scoring predicate-argument structure with the other factors misses some core arguments, the global feature demands the model to fill the missing arguments.

The numbers of factors for each factor type are: F_P and F_G are 1, F_A and F_{PA} are $|\mathcal{A}|$. By integrating the all factors, the score function becomes $s(p, \mathcal{A}) = \mathbf{w} \cdot \Phi_P(\mathbf{x}, p) + \mathbf{w} \cdot \Phi_G(\mathbf{x}, p, \mathcal{A}) + \mathbf{w} \cdot \sum_{a \in \mathcal{A}} \{\Phi_A(\mathbf{x}, a) + \Phi_{PA}(\mathbf{x}, p, a)\}$.

2.2 Inference

The crucial point of the model is how to deal with the global factor F_G, because enumerating possible assignments is too costly. A number of methods have been proposed for the use of global features for linear models such as (Daumé III and Marcu, 2005; Kazama and Torisawa, 2007). In this work, we use the approach proposed in (Kazama and Torisawa, 2007). Although the approach is proposed for sequence labeling tasks, it can be easily extended to our structured model. That is, for each possible predicate sense p of the predicate, we provide N-best argument role assignments using three local factors F_P, F_A and F_{PA}, and then add scores of the global factor F_G, finally select the argmax from them. In this case, the argmax is selected from $|\mathcal{P}_l|N$ candidates.

2.3 Learning the Model

For learning of the model, we borrow a fundamental idea of Kazama and Torisawa's perceptron learning algorithm. However, we use a more sophisticated online-learning algorithm based on the Passive-Aggressive Algorithm (PA) (Crammer et al., 2006).

For the sake of simplicity, we introduce some notations. We denote a predicate-argument structure $\mathbf{y} = \langle p, \mathcal{A} \rangle$, a local feature vector as $\Phi_L(\mathbf{x}, \mathbf{y}) = \Phi_P(\mathbf{x}, p) + \sum_{a \in \mathcal{A}} \{\Phi_A(\mathbf{x}, a) + \Phi_{PA}(\mathbf{x}, p, a)\}$, a feature vector coupling both local and global features as $\Phi_{L+G}(\mathbf{x}, \mathbf{y}) = \Phi_L(\mathbf{x}, \mathbf{y}) + \Phi_G(\mathbf{x}, p, \mathcal{A})$, the argmax using Φ_{L+G} as $\hat{\mathbf{y}}^{L+G}$, the argmax using Φ_L as $\hat{\mathbf{y}}^L$. Also, we use a loss function $\rho(\mathbf{y}, \mathbf{y}')$, which is a cost function associated with $\mathbf{y}$ and $\mathbf{y}'$.

The margin perceptron learning proposed by Kazama and Torisawa can be seen as an optimization with the following two constrains.

(A) $\mathbf{w} \cdot \Phi_{L+G}(\mathbf{x}, \mathbf{y}) - \mathbf{w} \cdot \Phi_{L+G}(\mathbf{x}, \hat{\mathbf{y}}^{L+G}) \geq \rho(\mathbf{y}, \hat{\mathbf{y}}^{L+G})$

(B) $\mathbf{w} \cdot \Phi_L(\mathbf{x}, \mathbf{y}) - \mathbf{w} \cdot \Phi_L(\mathbf{x}, \hat{\mathbf{y}}^L) \geq \rho(\mathbf{y}, \hat{\mathbf{y}}^L)$

(A) is the constraint that ensures a sufficient margin $\rho(\mathbf{y}, \hat{\mathbf{y}}^{L+G})$ between $\mathbf{y}$ and $\hat{\mathbf{y}}^{L+G}$. (B) is the constraint that ensures a sufficient margin $\rho(\mathbf{y}, \hat{\mathbf{y}}^L)$ between $\mathbf{y}$ and $\hat{\mathbf{y}}^L$. The necessity of this constraint is that if we apply only (A), the algorithm does not guarantee a sufficient margin in terms of local features, and it leads to poor quality in the N-best assignments. The Kazama and Torisawa's perceptron algorithm uses constant values for the cost function $\rho(\mathbf{y}, \hat{\mathbf{y}}^{L+G})$ and $\rho(\mathbf{y}, \hat{\mathbf{y}}^L)$.

The proposed model is trained using the following optimization problem.

$$\mathbf{w}_{new} = \arg \min_{\mathbf{w}' \in \Re^n} \frac{1}{2} ||\mathbf{w}' - \mathbf{w}||^2 + C\xi$$

$$\begin{cases} \text{s.t. } l_{L+G} \leq \xi,\ \xi \geq 0 & \text{if } \hat{\mathbf{y}}^{L+G} \neq \mathbf{y} \\ \text{s.t. } l_L \leq \xi,\ \xi \geq 0 & \text{if } \hat{\mathbf{y}}^{L+G} = \mathbf{y} \neq \hat{\mathbf{y}}^L \end{cases} \quad (1)$$

$$l_{L+G} = \mathbf{w} \cdot \Phi_{L+G}(\mathbf{x}, \hat{\mathbf{y}}^{L+G}) - \mathbf{w} \cdot \Phi_{L+G}(\mathbf{x}, \mathbf{y}) + \rho(\mathbf{y}, \hat{\mathbf{y}}^{L+G}) \quad (2)$$

$$l_L = \mathbf{w} \cdot \Phi_L(\mathbf{x}, \hat{\mathbf{y}}^L) - \mathbf{w} \cdot \Phi_L(\mathbf{x}, \mathbf{y}) + \rho(\mathbf{y}, \hat{\mathbf{y}}^L) \quad (3)$$

l_{L+G} is the loss function for the case of using both local and global features, corresponding to the constraint (A), and l_L is the loss function for the case of using only local features, corresponding to the constraints (B) provided that (A) is satisfied.

2.4 The Role-less Argument Bias Problem

The fact that an argument candidate is not assigned any role (namely it is assigned the label "NONE") is unlikely to contribute predicate sense disambiguation. However, it remains possible that "NONE" arguments is biased toward a particular predicate sense by F_{PA} (i.e. $\mathbf{w} \cdot \Phi_{PA}(\mathbf{x}, sense_i, a_k\text{= "NONE"}) > \mathbf{w} \cdot \Phi_{PA}(\mathbf{x}, sense_j, a_k\text{= "NONE"})$.

In order to avoid this bias, we define a special sense label, $sense_{any}$, that is used to calculate the score for a predicate and a roll-less argument, regardless of the predicate's sense. We use the feature vector $\Phi_{PA}(\mathbf{x}, sense_{any}, a_k)$ if a_k= "NONE" and $\Phi_{PA}(\mathbf{x}, sense_i, a_k)$ otherwise.

3 Experiment

3.1 Experimental Settings

We use the CoNLL-2009 Shared Task dataset (Hajič et al., 2009) for experiments. It is a dataset for multi-lingual syntactic and semantic dependency parsing [1]. In the SRL-only challenge of the task, participants are required to identify predicate-argument structures of only the specified predicates. Therefore the problems to be solved are predicate sense disambiguation and argument role labeling. We use Semantic Labeled F1 for evaluation.

For generating N-bests, we used the beam-search algorithm, and the number of N-bests was set to $N = 64$. For learning of the joint model, the loss function $\rho(\mathbf{y}_t, \mathbf{y}')$ of the Passive-Aggressive Algorithm was set to the number of incorrect assignments of a predicate sense and its argument roles. Also, the number of iterations of the model used for testing was selected based on the performance on the development data.

Table 1 shows the features used for the structured model. The global features used for F_G are based on those used in (Toutanova et al., 2008; Johansson and Nugues, 2008), and the features

[1] The dataset consists of seven languages: Catalan, Chinese, Czech, English, German, Japanese and Spanish.

F_P	Plemma of the predicate and predicate's head, and ppos of the predicate Dependency label between the predicate and predicate's head The concatenation of the dependency labels of the predicate's dependents
F_A	Plemma and ppos of the predicate, the predicate's head, the argument candidate, and the argument's head Plemma and ppos of the leftmost/rightmost dependent and leftmost/rightmost sibling The dependency label of predicate, argument candidate and argument candidate's dependent The position of the argument candidate with respect to the predicate position in the dep. tree (e.g. CHILD) The position of the head of the dependency relation with respect to the predicate position in the sentence The left-to-right chain of the deplabels of the predicate's dependents Plemma, ppos and dependency label paths between the predicate and the argument candidates The number of dependency edges between the predicate and the argument candidate
F_{PA}	Plemma and plemma&ppos of the argument candidate Dependency label path between the predicate and the argument candidates
F_G	The sequence of the predicate and the argument labels in the predicate-argument structure (e.g. A0-PRED-A1) Whether the semantic roles defined in frames exist in the structure, (e.g. *CONTAINS:A1*) The conjunction of the predicate sense and the frame information (e.g. *wear.01&CONTAINS:A1*)

Table 1: Features for the Structured Model

	Avg.	Ca	Ch	Cz	En	Ge	Jp	Sp
F_P+F_A	79.17	78.00	76.02	85.24	83.09	76.76	77.27	77.83
F_P+F_A+F_{PA}	79.58	78.38	76.23	85.14	83.36	78.31	77.72	77.92
F_P+F_A+F_G	80.42	79.50	76.96	85.88	84.49	78.64	78.32	79.21
ALL	80.75	79.55	77.20	**85.94**	84.97	79.62	**78.69**	79.29
Björkelund	**80.80**	80.01	**78.60**	85.41	**85.63**	**79.71**	76.30	79.91
Zhao	80.47	**80.32**	77.72	85.19	85.44	75.99	78.15	**80.46**
Meza-Ruiz	77.46	78.00	77.73	75.75	83.34	73.52	76.00	77.91

Table 2: Results on the CoNLL-2009 Shared Task dataset (Semantic Labeled F1).

	SENSE	ARG
F_P+F_A	89.65	72.20
F_P+F_A+F_{PA}	89.78	72.74
F_P+F_A+F_G	89.83	74.11
ALL	90.15	74.46

Table 3: Predicate sense disambiguation and argument role labeling results (average).

used for F_{PA} are inspired by formulae used in the MLN-based SRL systems, such as (Meza-Ruiz and Riedel, 2009b). We used the same feature templates for all languages.

3.2 Results

Table 2 shows the results of the experiments, and also shows the results of the top 3 systems in the CoNLL-2009 Shared Task participants of the *SRL-only* system.

By incorporating F_{PA}, we achieved performance improvement for all languages. This results suggest that it is effective to capture local inter-dependencies between a predicate sense and one of its argument roles. Comparing the results with F_P+F_A and F_P+F_A+F_G, incorporating F_G also contributed performance improvements for all languages, especially the substantial F1 improvement of $+1.88$ is obtained in German.

Next, we compare our system with top 3 systems in the CoNLL-2009 Shared Task. By incorporating both F_{PA} and F_G, our joint model achieved competitive results compared to the top 2 systems (Björkelund and Zhao), and achieved the better results than the Meza-Ruiz's system [2]. The systems by Björkelund and Zhao applied feature selection algorithms in order to select the best set of feature templates for each language, requiring about 1 to 2 months to obtain the best feature set. On the other hand, our system achieved the competitive results with the top two systems, despite the fact that we used the same feature templates for all languages without applying any feature engineering procedure.

Table 3 shows the performances of predicate sense disambiguation and argument role labeling separately. In terms of sense disambiguation results, incorporating F_{PA} and F_G worked well. Although incorporating either of F_{PA} and F_G provided improvements of $+0.13$ and $+0.18$ on average, adding both factors provided improvements of $+0.50$. We compared the predicate sense dis-

[2]The result of Meza-Ruiz for Czech is substantially worse than the other systems because of inappropriate preprocessing for predicate sense disambiguation. Excepting Czech, the average F1 value of the Meza-Ruiz is 77.75, where as our system is 79.89.

ambiguation results of $F_P + F_A$ and ALL with the McNemar test, and the difference was statistically significant ($p < 0.01$). This result suggests that combination of these factors is effective for sense disambiguation.

As for argument role labeling results, incorporating F_{PA} and F_G contributed positively for all languages. Especially, we obtained a substantial gain (+4.18) in German. By incorporating F_{PA}, the system achieved the F1 improvements of $+0.54$ on average. This result shows that capturing inter-dependencies between a predicate and its arguments contributes to argument role labeling. By incorporating F_G, the system achieved the substantial improvement of F1 ($+1.91$).

Since both tasks improved by using all factors, we can say that the proposed joint model succeeded in *joint learning* of predicate senses and its argument roles.

4 Conclusion

In this paper, we proposed a structured model that captures both non-local dependencies between arguments, and inter-dependencies between a predicate sense and its argument roles. We designed a linear model-based structured model, and defined four types of factors: predicate factor, argument factor, predicate-argument pairwise factor and global factor for the model. In the experiments, the proposed model achieved competitive results compared to the state-of-the-art systems without any feature engineering.

A further research direction we are investigating is exploitation of unlabeled texts. Semi-supervised semantic role labeling methods have been explored by (Collobert and Weston, 2008; Deschacht and Moens, 2009; Fürstenau and Lapata, 2009), and they have achieved successful outcomes. However, we believe that there is still room for further improvement.

References

Anders Björkelund, Love Hafdell, and Pierre Nugues. 2009. Multilingual semantic role labeling. In *CoNLL-2009*.

Ronan Collobert and Jason Weston. 2008. A unified architecture for natural language processing: Deep neural networks with multitask learning. In *ICML 2008*.

Koby Crammer, Ofer Dekel, Joseph Keshet, Shai Shalev-Shwartz, and Yoram Singer. 2006. Online passive-aggressive algorithms. *JMLR*, 7:551–585.

Hal Daumé III and Daniel Marcu. 2005. Learning as search optimization: Approximate large margin methods for structured prediction. In *ICML-2005*.

Koen Deschacht and Marie-Francine Moens. 2009. Semi-supervised semantic role labeling using the latent words language model. In *EMNLP-2009*.

Hagen Fürstenau and Mirella Lapata. 2009. Graph alignment for semi-supervised semantic role labeling. In *EMNLP-2009*.

Jan Hajič, Massimiliano Ciaramita, Richard Johansson, Daisuke Kawahara, Maria Antònia Martí, Lluís Màrquez, Adam Meyers, Joakim Nivre, Sebastian Padó, Jan Štěpánek, Pavel Straňák, Mihai Surdeanu, Nianwen Xue, and Yi Zhang. 2009. The CoNLL-2009 shared task: Syntactic and semantic dependencies in multiple languages. In *CoNLL-2009*, Boulder, Colorado, USA.

Richard Johansson and Pierre Nugues. 2008. Dependency-based syntactic-semantic analysis with propbank and nombank. In *CoNLL-2008*.

Jun'Ichi Kazama and Kentaro Torisawa. 2007. A new perceptron algorithm for sequence labeling with non-local features. In *EMNLP-CoNLL 2007*.

Ivan Meza-Ruiz and Sebastian Riedel. 2009a. Jointly identifying predicates, arguments and senses using markov logic. In *HLT/NAACL-2009*.

Ivan Meza-Ruiz and Sebastian Riedel. 2009b. Multilingual semantic role labelling with markov logic. In *CoNLL-2009*.

Sebastian Riedel and Ivan Meza-Ruiz. 2008. Collective semantic role labelling with markov logic. In *CoNLL-2008*.

Mihai Surdeanu, Richard Johansson, Adam Meyers, Lluís Màrquez, and Joakim Nivre. 2008. The CoNLL-2008 shared task on joint parsing of syntactic and semantic dependencies. In *CoNLL-2008*.

Synthia A. Thompson, Roger Levy, and Christopher D. Manning. 2010. A generative model for semantic role labeling. In *Proceedings of the 48th Annual Meeting of the Association of Computational Linguistics (to appear)*.

Kristina Toutanova, Aria Haghighi, and Christopher D. Manning. 2008. A global joint model for semantic role labeling. *Computational Linguistics*, 34(2).

Semantics-Driven Shallow Parsing for Chinese Semantic Role Labeling

Weiwei Sun
Department of Computational Linguistics, Saarland University
German Research Center for Artificial Intelligence (DFKI)
D-66123, Saarbrücken, Germany
wsun@coli.uni-saarland.de

Abstract

One deficiency of current shallow parsing based Semantic Role Labeling (SRL) methods is that syntactic chunks are too small to effectively group words. To partially resolve this problem, we propose semantics-driven shallow parsing, which takes into account both syntactic structures and predicate-argument structures. We also introduce several new "path" features to improve shallow parsing based SRL method. Experiments indicate that our new method obtains a significant improvement over the best reported Chinese SRL result.

1 Introduction

In the last few years, there has been an increasing interest in Semantic Role Labeling (SRL) on several languages, which consists of recognizing arguments involved by predicates of a given sentence and labeling their semantic types. Both full parsing based and shallow parsing based SRL methods have been discussed for English and Chinese. In Chinese SRL, shallow parsing based methods that cast SRL as the classification of syntactic chunks into semantic labels has gained promising results. The performance reported in (Sun et al., 2009) outperforms the best published performance of full parsing based SRL systems.

Previously proposed shallow parsing takes into account only syntactic information and basic chunks are usually too small to group words into argument candidates. This causes one main deficiency of Chinese SRL. To partially resolve this problem, we propose a new shallow parsing. The new chunk definition takes into account both syntactic structure and predicate-argument structures of a given sentence. Because of the semantic information it contains, we call it semantics-driven shallow parsing. The key idea is to make basic chunks as large as possible but not overlap with arguments. Additionally, we introduce several new "path" features to express more structural information, which is important for SRL.

We present encouraging SRL results on Chinese PropBank (CPB) data. With semantics-driven shallow parsing, our SRL system achieves 76.10 F-measure, with gold segmentation and POS tagging. The performance further achieves 76.46 with the help of new "path" features. These results obtain significant improvements over the best reported SRL performance (74.12) in the literature (Sun et al., 2009).

2 Related Work

CPB is a project to add predicate-argument relations to the syntactic trees of the Chinese TreeBank (CTB). Similar to English PropBank, the arguments of a predicate are labeled with a contiguous sequence of integers, in the form of AN (N is a natural number); the adjuncts are annotated as such with the label AM followed by a secondary tag that represents the semantic classification of the adjunct. The assignment of argument labels is illustrated in Figure 1, where the predicate is the verb "提供/provide" For example, the noun phrase "保险公司/the insurance company" is labeled as *A0*, meaning that it is the *proto-Agent* of "提供".

Sun et al. (2009) explore the Chinese SRL problem on the basis of shallow syntactic information at the level of phrase chunks. They present a semantic chunking method to resolve SRL on basis of shallow parsing. Their method casts SRL as the classification of syntactic chunks with IOB2 representation for semantic roles (i.e. semantic

Proceedings of the ACL 2010 Conference Short Papers, pages 103–108,
Uppsala, Sweden, 11-16 July 2010.

WORD:	保险	公司	已	为	三峡	工程	提供	保险	服务
	insurance	company	already	for	Sanxia	Project	provide	insurance	service
POS:	[NN	NN]	[AD]	[P]	[NR]	[NN]	[VV]	[NN	NN]
SYN CH:	[NP]		[ADVP]	[PP	NP	NP]	[VP]	[NP]	
SEM CH:	B-A0		B-AM-ADV	B-A2	I-A2	I-A2	B-V	B-A1	
	The insurance company has provided insurance services for the Sanxia Project.								

Figure 1: An example from Chinese PropBank.

chunks). Two labeling strategies are presented: 1) directly tagging semantic chunks in one-stage, and 2) identifying argument boundaries as a chunking task and labeling their semantic types as a classification task. On the basis of syntactic chunks, they define semantic chunks which do not overlap nor embed using IOB2 representation. Syntactic chunks outside a chunk receive the tag O (Outside). For syntactic chunks forming a chunk of type *A**, the first chunk receives the *B-A** tag (Begin), and the remaining ones receive the tag *I-A** (Inside). Then a SRL system can work directly by using sequence tagging technique. Shallow chunk definition presented in (Chen et al., 2006) is used in their experiments. The definition of syntactic and semantic chunks is illustrated Figure 1. For example, "保险公司/the insurance company", consisting of two nouns, is a noun phrase; in the syntactic chunking stage, its two components "保险" and "公司" should be labeled as *B-NP* and *I-NP*. Because this phrase is the *Agent* of the predicate "提供/provide", it takes a semantic chunk label *B-A0*. In the semantic chunking stage, this phrase should be labeled as *B-A0*.

Their experiments on CPB indicate that according to current state-of-the-art of Chinese parsing, SRL systems on basis of full parsing do not perform better than systems based on shallow parsing. They report the best SRL performance with gold segmentation and POS tagging as inputs. This is very different from English SRL. In English SRL, previous work shows that full parsing, both constituency parsing and dependency parsing, is necessary.

Ding and Chang (2009) discuss semantic chunking methods without any parsing information. Different from (Sun et al., 2009), their method formulates SRL as the classification of words with semantic chunks. Comparison of experimental results in their work shows that parsing is necessary for Chinese SRL, and the semantic chunking methods on the basis of shallow parsing outperform the ones without any parsing.

Joint learning of syntactic and semantic structures is another hot topic in dependency parsing research. Some models have been well evaluated in CoNLL 2008 and 2009 shared tasks (Surdeanu et al., 2008; Hajič et al., 2009). The CoNLL 2008/2009 shared tasks propose a unified dependency-based formalism to model both syntactic dependencies and semantic roles for multiple languages. Several joint parsing models are presented in the shared tasks. Our focus is different from the shared tasks. In this paper, we hope to find better syntactic representation for semantic role labeling.

3 Semantics-Driven Shallow Parsing

3.1 Motivation

There are two main jobs of semantic chunking: 1) grouping words as argument candidate and 2) classifying semantic types of possible arguments. Previously proposed shallow parsing only considers syntactic information and basic chunks are usually too small to effectively group words. This causes one main deficiency of semantic chunking. E.g. the argument "为三峡工程/for the Sanxia Project" consists of three chunks, each of which only consists of one word. To rightly recognize this *A2*, Semantic chunker should rightly predict three chunk labels. Small chunks also make the important "path" feature sparse, since there are more chunks between a target chunk and the predicate in focus. In this section, we introduce a new chunk definition to improve shallow parsing based SRL, which takes both syntactic and predicate-argument structures into account. The key idea is to make syntactic chunks as large as possible for semantic chunking. The formal definition is as follows.

3.2 Chunk Bracketing

Given a sentence $s = w_1, ..., w_n$, let $c[i : j]$ denote a constituent that is made up of words between w_i and w_j (including w_i and w_j); let $p_v = \{c[i : j] | c[i : j]$ is an argument of $v\}$

	WORD	POS	TARGET	PROPOSITION				CHUNK 1	CHUNK 2
China	中国	NR	-	(A0*	*	*	*	B-NP	B-NP^S
tax	税务	NN	-	*	*	*	*	I-NP	I-NP^S
department	部门	NN	-	*)	*	*	*	I-NP	I-NP^S
stipulate	规定	VV	规定	(V*)	*	*	*	O	O
:	：	PU	-	*	*	*	*	O	O
owing	欠缴	VV	欠缴	(A1*	(V*)	*	(A0*	O	O
tax payment	税款	NN	-	*	(A1*)	*	*	B-NP	B-NP^VP
company	企业	NN	-	*	(A0*)	*	*	B-NP	B-NP^NP
Function Word	的	DEG	-	*	*	*	*	O	O
leaders	领导人	NN	-	*	*	*	*)	B-NP	B-NP^NP
not	不	AD	-	*	*	*	(AM-ADV*)	B-ADVP	B-ADVP^VP
can	得	VV	得	*	*	(V*)	*	O	O
leave the country	出境	VV	出境	*)	*	*	(V*)	B-VP	B-VP^VP

Figure 2: An example for definition of semantics-driven chunks with IOB2 representation.

denote one predicate-argument structure where v is the predicate in focus. Given a syntactic tree $\mathcal{T}_s = \{c[i:j] | c[i:j]$ is a constituent of $s\}$, and its all argument structures $\mathcal{P}_s = \{p_v|$ v is a verbal predicate in $s\}$, there is one and only one chunk set $\mathcal{C} = \{c[i:j]\}$ s.t.

1. $\forall c[i:j] \in \mathcal{C}$, $c[i:j] \in \mathcal{T}_s$;
2. $\forall c[i:j] \in \mathcal{C}$, $\forall c[i^v : j^v] \in \cup\mathcal{P}_s$, $j < i^v$ or $i > j^v$ or $i^v \leq i \leq j \leq j^v$;
3. $\forall c[i:j] \in \mathcal{C}$, the parent of $c[i:j]$ does not satisfy the condition 2.
4. $\forall \mathcal{C}'$ satisfies above conditions, $\mathcal{C}' \subset \mathcal{C}$.

The first condition guarantees that every chunk is a constituent. The second condition means that chunks do not overlap with arguments, and further guarantees that semantic chunking can recover all arguments with the last condition. The third condition makes new chunks as big as possible. The last one makes sure that $\mathcal{C}$ contains all sub-components of all arguments. Figure 2 is an example to illustrate our new chunk definition. For example, "中国/Chinese 税务/tax 部分/department" is a constituent of current sentence, and is also an argument of "规定/stipulate". If we take it as a chunk, it does not conflict with any other arguments, so it is a reasonable syntactic chunk. For the phrase "欠缴/owing 税款/tax payment", though it does not overlap with the first, third and fourth propositions, it is bigger than the argument "税款" (conflicting with condition 2) while labeling the predicate "欠缴", so it has to be separated into two chunks. Note that the third condition also guarantees the constituents in $\mathcal{C}$ does not overlap with each other since each one is as large as possible. So we can still formulate our new shallow parsing as an "IOB" sequence labeling problem.

3.3 Chunk Type

We introduce two types of chunks. The first is simply the phrase type, such as *NP*, *PP*, of current chunk. The column *CHUNK 1* illustrates this kind of chunk type definition. The second is more complicated. Inspired by (Klein and Manning, 2003), we split one phrase type into several subsymbols, which contain category information of current constituent's parent. For example, an *NP* immediately dominated by a *S*, will be substituted by *NP^S*. This strategy severely increases the number of chunk types and make it hard to train chunking models. To shrink this number, we linguistically use a cluster of CTB phrasal types, which was introduced in (Sun and Sui, 2009). The column *CHUNK 2* illustrates this definition. E.g., *NP^S* implicitly represents *Subject* while *NP^VP* represents *Object*.

3.4 New Path Features

The *Path* feature is defined as a chain of base phrases between the token and the predicate. At both ends, the chain is terminated with the POS tags of the predicate and the headword of the token. For example, the path feature of "保险公司" in Figure 1 is "公司-ADVP-PP-NP-NP-VV". Among all features, the "path" feature contains more structural information, which is very important for SRL. To better capture structural information, we introduce several new "path" features. They include:

- NP|PP|VP path: only syntactic chunks that takes tag *NP*, *PP* or *VP* are kept.

When labeling the predicate "出境/leave the country" in Figure 2, this feature of "中国税务部门/Chinese tax departments" is *NP+NP+NP+NP+VP*.

- V|的 path: a sequential container of POS tags of verbal words and "的"; This feature of "中国税务部门" is *NP+VV+VV+的+VV+VP*.

- O2POS path: if a word occupies a chunk label *O*, use its POS in the path feature. This feature of "中国税务部门" is *NP+VV+PU+VV+NP+NP+DEG+ADVP+VV+VP*.

4 Experiments and Analysis

4.1 Experimental Setting

Experiments in previous work are mainly based on CPB 1.0 and CTB 5.0. We use CoNLL-2005 shared task software to process CPB and CTB. To facilitate comparison with previous work, we use the same data setting with (Xue, 2008). Nearly all previous research on Chinese SRL evaluation use this setting, also including (Ding and Chang, 2008, 2009; Sun et al., 2009; Sun, 2010). The data is divided into three parts: files from chtb_081 to chtb_899 are used as training set; files from chtb_041 to chtb_080 as development set; files from chtb_001 to chtb_040, and chtb_900 to chtb_931 as test set. Both syntactic chunkers and semantic chunkers are trained and evaluated by using the same data set. By using CPB and CTB, we can extract gold standard semantics-driven shallow chunks according to our definition. We use this kind of gold chunks automatically generated from training data to train syntactic chunkers.

For both syntactic and semantic chunking, we used conditional random field model. Crfsgd[1], is used for experiments. Crfsgd provides a feature template that defines a set of strong word and POS features to do syntactic chunking. We use this feature template to resolve shallow parsing. For semantic chunking, we implement a similar *one-stage* shallow parsing based SRL system described in (Sun et al., 2009). There are two differences between our system and Sun et al.'s system. First, our system uses Start/End method to represent semantic chunks (Kudo and Matsumoto, 2001). Second, word formation features are not used.

Test	P(%)	R(%)	$F_{\beta=1}$
(Chen et al., 2006)	93.51	92.81	93.16
Overall (C1)	91.66	89.13	90.38
Bracketing (C1)	92.31	89.72	91.00
Overall (C2)	88.77	86.71	87.73
Bracketing (C2)	92.71	90.55	91.62

Table 1: Shallow parsing performance.

4.2 Syntactic Chunking Performance

Table 1 shows the performance of shallow syntactic parsing. Line *Chen et al., 2006* is the chunking performance evaluated on syntactic chunk definition proposed in (Chen et al., 2006). The second and third blocks present the chunking performance with new semantics-driven shallow parsing. The second block shows the overall performance when the first kind of chunks type is used, while the last block shows the performance when the more complex chunk type definition is used. For the semantic-driven parsing experiments, we add the *path* from current word to the first verb before or after as two new features. Line *Bracketing* evaluates the word grouping ability of these two kinds of chunks. In other words, detailed phrase types are not considered. Because the two new chunk definitions use the same chunk boundaries, the fourth and sixth lines are comparable. There is a clear decrease between the traditional shallow parsing (Chen et al., 2006) and ours. We think one main reason is that syntactic chunks in our new definition are larger than the traditional ones. An interesting phenomenon is that though the second kind of chunk type definition increases the complexity of the parsing job, it achieves better bracketing performance.

4.3 SRL Performance

Table 2 summarizes the SRL performance. Line *Sun et al., 2009* is the SRL performance reported in (Sun et al., 2009). To the author's knowledge, this is the best published SRL result in the literature. Line *SRL (Chen et al., 2006)* is the SRL performance of our system. These two systems are both evaluated by using syntactic chunking defined in (Chen et al., 2006). From the first block we can see that our semantic chunking system reaches the state-of-the-art. The second and third blocks in Table 2 present the performance with

[1] http://leon.bottou.org/projects/sgd

new shallow parsing. Line *SRL (C1)* and *SRL (C2)* show the overall performances with the first and second chunk definition. The lines following are the SRL performance when new "path" features are added. We can see that new "path" features are useful for semantic chunking.

Test	P(%)	R(%)	$F_{\beta=1}$
(Sun et al., 2009)	79.25	**69.61**	74.12
SRL [(Chen et al., 2006)]	**80.87**	68.74	**74.31**
SRL [C1]	80.23	71.00	75.33
+ NP|PP|VP path	80.25	71.19	75.45
+ V|的 path	80.78	71.67	75.96
+ O2POS path	80.44	71.59	75.76
+ All new path	80.73	72.08	76.16
SRL [C2]	80.87	71.86	76.10
+ All new path	**81.03**	**72.38**	**76.46**

Table 2: SRL performance on the test data. Items in the first column *SRL [(Chen et al., 2006)]*, *SRL [C1]* and *SRL [C2]* respetively denote the SRL systems based on shallow parsing defined in (Chen et al., 2006) and Section 3.

5 Conclusion

In this paper we propose a new syntactic shallow parsing for Chinese SRL. The new chunk definition contains both syntactic structure and predicate-argument structure information. To improve SRL, we also introduce several new "path" features. Experimental results show that our new chunk definition is more suitable for Chinese SRL. It is still an open question what kinds of syntactic information is most important for Chinese SRL. We suggest that our attempt at semantics-driven shallow parsing is a possible way to better exploit this problem.

Acknowledgments

The author is funded both by German Academic Exchange Service (DAAD) and German Research Center for Artificial Intelligence (DFKI).

The author would like to thank the anonymous reviewers for their helpful comments.

References

Wenliang Chen, Yujie Zhang, and Hitoshi Isahara. 2006. An empirical study of Chinese chunking. In *Proceedings of the COLING/ACL 2006 Main Conference Poster Sessions*, pages 97–104. Association for Computational Linguistics, Sydney, Australia.

Weiwei Ding and Baobao Chang. 2008. Improving Chinese semantic role classification with hierarchical feature selection strategy. In *Proceedings of the EMNLP 2008*, pages 324–333. Association for Computational Linguistics, Honolulu, Hawaii.

Weiwei Ding and Baobao Chang. 2009. Fast semantic role labeling for Chinese based on semantic chunking. In *ICCPOL '09: Proceedings of the 22nd International Conference on Computer Processing of Oriental Languages. Language Technology for the Knowledge-based Economy*, pages 79–90. Springer-Verlag, Berlin, Heidelberg.

Jan Hajič, Massimiliano Ciaramita, Richard Johansson, Daisuke Kawahara, Maria Antònia Martí, Lluís Màrquez, Adam Meyers, Joakim Nivre, Sebastian Padó, Jan Štěpánek, Pavel Straňák, Mihai Surdeanu, Nianwen Xue, and Yi Zhang. 2009. The CoNLL-2009 shared task: Syntactic and semantic dependencies in multiple languages. In *Proceedings of the 13th Conference on Computational Natural Language Learning (CoNLL-2009), June 4-5*. Boulder, Colorado, USA.

Dan Klein and Christopher D. Manning. 2003. Accurate unlexicalized parsing. In *Proceedings of the 41st Annual Meeting of the Association for Computational Linguistics*, pages 423–430. Association for Computational Linguistics, Sapporo, Japan.

Taku Kudo and Yuji Matsumoto. 2001. Chunking with support vector machines. In *NAACL '01: Second meeting of the North American Chapter of the Association for Computational Linguistics on Language technologies 2001*, pages 1–8. Association for Computational Linguistics, Morristown, NJ, USA.

Weiwei Sun. 2010. Improving Chinese semantic role labeling with rich features. In *Proceedings of the ACL 2010*.

Weiwei Sun and Zhifang Sui. 2009. Chinese function tag labeling. In *Proceedings of the 23rd Pacific Asia Conference on Language, Information and Computation*. Hong Kong.

Weiwei Sun, Zhifang Sui, Meng Wang, and Xin Wang. 2009. Chinese semantic role labeling with shallow parsing. In *Proceedings of the 2009 Conference on Empirical Methods in Natural Language Processing*, pages 1475–1483. Association for Computational Linguistics, Singapore.

Mihai Surdeanu, Richard Johansson, Adam Meyers, Lluís Màrquez, and Joakim Nivre. 2008. The conll 2008 shared task on joint parsing of syntactic and semantic dependencies. In *CoNLL 2008: Proceedings of the Twelfth Conference on Computational Natural Language Learning*, pages 159–177. Coling 2008 Organizing Committee, Manchester, England.

Nianwen Xue. 2008. Labeling Chinese predicates with semantic roles. *Comput. Linguist.*, 34(2):225–255.

Collocation Extraction beyond the Independence Assumption

Gerlof Bouma
Universität Potsdam, Department Linguistik
Campus Golm, Haus 24/35
Karl-Liebknecht-Straße 24–25
14476 Potsdam, Germany
gerlof.bouma@uni-potsdam.de

Abstract

In this paper we start to explore two-part collocation extraction association measures that do not estimate expected probabilities on the basis of the independence assumption. We propose two new measures based upon the well-known measures of mutual information and pointwise mutual information. Expected probabilities are derived from automatically trained Aggregate Markov Models. On three collocation gold standards, we find the new association measures vary in their effectiveness.

1 Introduction

Collocation extraction typically proceeds by scoring collocation candidates with an association measure, where high scores are taken to indicate likely collocationhood. Two well-known such measures are pointwise mutual information (PMI) and mutual information (MI). In terms of observing a combination of words w_1, w_2, these are:

$$i(w_1, w_2) = \log \frac{p(w_1, w_2)}{p(w_1)\, p(w_2)}, \tag{1}$$

$$I(w_1, w_2) = \sum_{\substack{x \in \{w_1, \neg w_1\} \\ y \in \{w_2, \neg w_2\}}} p(x, y)\, i(x, y). \tag{2}$$

PMI (1) is the logged ratio of the observed bigramme probability and the expected bigramme probability under independence of the two words in the combination. MI (2) is the expected outcome of PMI, and measures how much information of the distribution of one word is contained in the distribution of the other. PMI was introduced into the collocation extraction field by Church and Hanks (1990). Dunning (1993) proposed the use of the likelihood-ratio test statistic, which is equivalent to MI up to a constant factor.

Two aspects of (P)MI are worth highlighting. First, the observed occurrence probability p_{obs} is compared to the expected occurrence probability p_{exp}. Secondly, the independence assumption underlies the estimation of p_{exp}.

The first aspect is motivated by the observation that interesting combinations are often those that are *unexpectedly* frequent. For instance, the bigramme *of the* is uninteresting from a collocation extraction perspective, although it probably is amongst the most frequent bigrammes for any English corpus. However, we can expect to frequently observe the combination by mere chance, simply because its parts are so frequent. Looking at p_{obs} and p_{exp} together allows us to recognize these cases (Manning and Schütze (1999) and Evert (2007) for more discussion).

The second aspect, the independence assumption in the estimation of p_{exp}, is more problematic, however, even in the context of collocation extraction. As Evert (2007, p42) notes, the assumption of "independence is extremely unrealistic," because it ignores "a variety of syntactic, semantic and lexical restrictions." Consider an estimate for p_{exp}(*the the*). Under independence, this estimate will be high, as *the* itself is very frequent. However, with our knowledge of English syntax, we would say p_{exp}(*the the*) is low. The independence assumption leads to overestimated expectation and *the the* will need to be very frequent for it to show up as a likely collocation. A less contrived example of how the independence assumption might mislead collocation extraction is when bigramme distribution is influenced by compositional, non-collocational, semantic dependencies. Investigating adjective-noun combinations in a corpus, we might find that *beige cloth* gets a high PMI, whereas *beige thought* does not. This does not make the former a collocation or multiword unit. Rather, what we would measure is the tendency to use colours with visible things and not with abstract objects. Syntactic and semantic

Proceedings of the ACL 2010 Conference Short Papers, pages 109–114,
Uppsala, Sweden, 11-16 July 2010. ©2010 Association for Computational Linguistics

associations between words are real dependencies, but they need not be *collocational* in nature. Because of the independence assumption, PMI and MI measure these syntactic and semantic associations just as much as they measure collocational association. In this paper, we therefore experimentally investigate the use of a more informed p_{exp} in the context of collocation extraction.

2 Aggregate Markov Models

To replace p_{exp} under independence, one might consider models with explicit linguistic information, such as a POS-tag bigramme model. This would for instance give us a more realistic $p_{\text{exp}}(\textit{the the})$. However, lexical semantic information is harder to incorporate. We might not know exactly what factors are needed to estimate p_{exp} and even if we do, we might lack the resources to train the resulting models. The only thing we know about estimating p_{exp} is that we need more information than a unigramme model but less than a bigramme model (as this would make $p_{\text{obs}}/p_{\text{exp}}$ uninformative). Therefore, we propose to use Aggregate Markov Models (Saul and Pereira, 1997; Hofmann and Puzicha, 1998; Rooth et al., 1999; Blitzer et al., 2005)[1] for the task of estimating p_{exp}. In an AMM, bigramme probability is not directly modeled, but mediated by a hidden class variable c:

$$p_{\text{amm}}(w_2|w_1) = \sum_c p(c|w_1)p(w_2|c). \quad (3)$$

The number of classes in an AMM determines the amount of dependency that can be captured. In the case of just one class, AMM is equivalent to a unigramme model. AMMs become equivalent to the full bigramme model when the number of classes equals the size of the smallest of the vocabularies of the parts of the combination. Between these two extremes, AMMs can capture syntactic, lexical, semantic and even pragmatic dependencies.

AMMs can be trained with EM, using no more information than one would need for ML bigramme probability estimates. Specifications of the E- and M-steps can be found in any of the four papers cited above – here we follow Saul and Pereira (1997). At each iteration, the model components are updated according to:

$$p(c|w_1) \leftarrow \frac{\sum_w n(w_1, w)p(c|w_1, w)}{\sum_{w,c'} n(w_1, w)p(c'|w_1, w)}, \quad (4)$$

$$p(w_2|c) \leftarrow \frac{\sum_w n(w, w_2)p(c|w, w_2)}{\sum_{w,w'} n(w, w')p(c|w, w')}, \quad (5)$$

where $n(w_1, w_2)$ are bigramme counts and the posterior probability of a hidden category c is estimated by:

$$p(c|w_1, w_2) = \frac{p(c|w_1)p(w_2|c)}{\sum_{c'} p(c'|w_1)p(w_2|c')}. \quad (6)$$

Successive updates converge to a local maximum of the AMM's log-likelihood.

The definition of the counterparts to (P)MI without the independence assumption, the AMM-ratio and AMM-divergence, is now straightforward:

$$r_{\text{amm}}(w_1, w_2) = \log \frac{p(w_1, w_2)}{p(w_1)\, p_{\text{amm}}(w_2|w_1)}, \quad (7)$$

$$d_{\text{amm}}(w_1, w_2) = \sum_{\substack{x \in \{w_1, \neg w_1\} \\ y \in \{w_2, \neg w_2\}}} p(x, y)\, r_{\text{amm}}(x, y). \quad (8)$$

The free parameter in these association measures is the number of hidden classes in the AMM, that is, the amount of dependency between the bigramme parts used to estimate p_{exp}. Note that AMM-ratio and AMM-divergence with one hidden class are equivalent to PMI and MI, respectively. It can be expected that in different corpora and for different types of collocation, different settings of this parameter are suitable.

3 Evaluation

3.1 Data and procedure

We apply AMM-ratio and AMM-divergence to three collocation gold standards. The effectiveness of association measures in collocation extraction is measured by ranking collocation candidates after the scores defined by the measures, and calculating average precision of these lists against the gold standard annotation. We consider the newly proposed AMM-based measures for a varying number of hidden categories. The new measures are compared against two baselines: ranking by frequency (p_{obs}) and random ordering. Because AMM-ratio and -divergence with one hidden class boil down to PMI and MI (and thus log-likelihood ratio), the evaluation contains an implicit comparison with

[1] These authors use very similar models, but with differing terminology and with different goals. The term AMM is used in the first and fourth paper. In the second paper, the models are referred to as Separable Mixture Models. Their use in collocation extraction is to our knowledge novel.

these canonical measures, too. However, the results will not be state-of-the-art: for the datasets investigated below, there are more effective extraction methods based on supervised machine learning (Pecina, 2008).

The first gold standard used is the German adjective-noun dataset (Evert, 2008). It contains 1212 A-N pairs taken from a German newspaper corpus. We consider three subtasks, depending on how strict we define true positives. We used the bigramme frequency data included in the resource. We assigned all types with a token count ≤ 5 to one type, resulting in AMM training data of 10k As, 20k Ns and 446k A-N pair types.

The second gold standard consists of 5102 German PP-verb combinations, also sampled from newspaper texts (Krenn, 2008). The data contains annotation for support verb constructions (FVGs) and figurative expressions. This resource also comes with its own frequency data. After frequency thresholding, AMMs are trained on 46k PPs, 7.6k Vs, and 890k PP-V pair types.

Third and last is the English verb-particle construction (VPC) gold standard (Baldwin, 2008), consisting of 3078 verb-particle pairs and annotation for transitive and intransitive idiomatic VPCs. We extract frequency data from the BNC, following the methods described in Baldwin (2005). This results in two slightly different datasets for the two types of VPC. For the intransitive VPCs, we train AMMs on 4.5k Vs, 35 particles, and 43k pair types. For the transitive VPCs, we have 5k Vs, 35 particles and 54k pair types.

All our EM runs start with randomly initialized model vectors. In Section 3.3 we discuss the impact of model variation due to this random factor.

3.2 Results

German A-N collocations The top slice in Table 1 shows results for the three subtasks of the A-N dataset. We see that using AMM-based p_{exp} initially improves average precision, for each task and for both the ratio and the divergence measure. At their maxima, the informed measures outperform both baselines as well as PMI and MI/log-likelihood ratio (# classes=1). The AMM-ratio performs best for 16-class AMMs, the optimum for AMM-divergence varies slightly.

It is likely that the drop in performance for the larger AMM-based measures is due to the AMMs learning the collocations themselves. That is, the AMMs become rich enough to not only capture the broadly applicative distributional influences of syntax and semantics, but also provide accurate p_{exp}s for individual, distributionally deviant combinations – like collocations. An accurate p_{exp} results in a low association score.

One way of inspecting what kind of dependencies the AMMs pick up is to cluster the data with them. Following Blitzer et al. (2005), we take the 200 most frequent adjectives and assign them to the category that maximizes $p(c|w_1)$; likewise for nouns and $p(w_2|c)$. Four selected clusters (out of 16) are given in Table 2.[2] The esoteric class 1 contains ordinal numbers and nouns that one typically uses those with, including references to temporal concepts. Class 2 and 3 appear more semantically motivated, roughly containing human and collective denoting nouns, respectively. Class 4 shows a group of adjectives denoting colours and/or political affiliations and a less coherent set of nouns, although the noun cluster can be understood if we consider individual adjectives that are associated with this class. Our informal impression from looking at clusters is that this is a common situation: as a whole, a cluster cannot be easily characterized, although for subsets or individual pairs, one can get an intuition for why they are in the same class. Unfortunately, we also see that some actual collocations are clustered in class 4, such as *gelbe Karte* 'warning' (lit.: 'yellow card') and *dickes Auto* 'big (lit.: fat) car'.

German PP-Verb collocations The second slice in Table 1 shows that, for both subtypes of PP-V collocation, better p_{exp}-estimates lead to *decreased* average precision. The most effective AMM-ratio and -distance measures are those equivalent to (P)MI. Apparently, the better p_{exp}s are unfortunate for the extraction of the type of collocations in this dataset.

The poor performance of PMI on these data – clearly below frequency – has been noticed before by Krenn and Evert (2001). A possible explanation for the lack of improvement in the AMMs lies in the relatively high performing frequency baselines. The frequency baseline for FVGs is five times the

[2]An anonymous reviewer rightly warns against sketching an overly positive picture of the knowledge captured in the AMMs by only presenting a few clusters. However, the clustering performed here is only secondary to our main goal of improving collocation extraction. The model inspection should thus not be taken as an evaluation of the quality of the models as clustering models.

		# classes											
		1	2	4	8	16	32	64	128	256	512	Rnd	Frq
A-N													
category 1	r_{amm}	45.6	46.4	47.6	47.3	**48.3**	48.0	47.0	46.1	44.7	41.9	30.1	32.2
	d_{amm}	42.3	42.9	44.4	45.2	46.1	**46.5**	45.0	46.3	45.5	45.5		
category 1–2	r_{amm}	55.7	56.3	57.4	57.5	**58.1**	58.1	57.7	56.9	55.7	52.8	43.1	47.0
	d_{amm}	56.3	57.0	58.1	58.4	59.8	60.1	59.3	**60.6**	59.2	59.3		
category 1–3	r_{amm}	62.3	62.8	63.9	64.0	**64.4**	62.2	62.2	62.7	62.4	60.0	52.7	56.4
	d_{amm}	64.3	64.7	65.9	66.6	**66.7**	66.3	66.3	65.4	66.0	64.7		
PP-V													
figurative	r_{amm}	**7.5**	6.1	6.4	6.0	5.6	5.4	4.5	4.2	3.8	3.5	3.3	10.5
	d_{amm}	**14.4**	13.0	13.3	13.1	12.2	11.2	9.0	7.7	6.9	5.7		
FVG	r_{amm}	**4.1**	3.4	3.4	3.0	2.9	2.7	2.2	2.1	2.0	2.0	3.0	14.7
	d_{amm}	**15.3**	12.7	12.6	10.7	9.0	7.7	3.4	3.2	2.5	2.3		
VPC													
intransitive	r_{amm}	**9.3**	9.2	9.0	8.3	5.5	5.3					4.8	14.7
	d_{amm}	12.2	12.2	14.0	**16.3**	6.9	5.8						
transitive	r_{amm}	**16.4**	14.8	15.2	14.5	11.3	10.0					10.1	20.1
	d_{amm}	19.6	17.3	20.7	**23.8**	12.8	10.1						

Table 1: Average precision for AMM-based association measures and baselines on three datasets.

Cl	Adjective	Noun
1	*dritt* 'third', *erst* 'first', *fünft* 'fifth', *halb* 'half', *kommend* 'next', *laufend* 'current', *letzt* 'last', *nah* 'near', *paar* 'pair', *vergangen* 'last', *viert* 'fourth', *wenig* 'few', *zweit* 'second'	*Jahr* 'year', *Klasse* 'class', *Linie* 'line', *Mal* 'time', *Monat* 'month', *Platz* 'place', *Rang* 'grade', *Runde* 'round', *Saison* 'season', *Satz* 'sentence', *Schritt* 'step', *Sitzung* 'session', *Sonntag* 'Sunday', *Spiel* 'game', *Stunde* 'hour', *Tag* 'day', *Woche* 'week', *Wochenende* 'weekend'
2	*aktiv* 'active', *alt* 'old', *ausländisch* 'foreign', *betroffen* 'concerned', *jung* 'young', *lebend* 'alive', *meist* 'most', *unbekannt* 'unknown', *viel* 'many'	*Besucher* 'visitor', *Bürger* 'citizens', *Deutsche* 'German', *Frau* 'woman', *Gast* 'guest', *Jugendliche* 'youth', *Kind* 'child', *Leute* 'people', *Mädchen* 'girl', *Mann* 'man', *Mensch* 'human', *Mitglied* 'member'
3	*deutsch* 'German', *europäisch* 'European', *ganz* 'whole', *gesamt* 'whole', *international* 'international', *national* 'national', *örtlich* 'local', *ostdeutsch* 'East-German', *privat* 'private', *rein* 'pure', *sogenannt* 'so-called', *sonstig* 'other', *westlich* 'western'	*Betrieb* 'company', *Familie* 'family', *Firma* 'firm', *Gebiet* 'area', *Gesellschaft* 'society', *Land* 'country', *Mannschaft* 'team', *Markt* 'market', *Organisation* 'organisation', *Staat* 'state', *Stadtteil* 'city district', *System* 'system', *Team* 'team', *Unternehmen* 'enterprise', *Verein* 'club', *Welt* 'world'
4	*blau* 'blue', *dick* 'fat', *gelb* 'yellow', *grün* 'green', *linke* 'left', *recht* 'right', *rot* 'red', *schwarz* 'black', *white* 'weiß'	*Auge* 'eye', *Auto* 'car', *Haar* 'hair', *Hand* 'hand', *Karte* 'card', *Stimme* 'voice/vote'

Table 2: Selected adjective-noun clusters from a 16-class AMM.

random baseline, and MI does not outperform it by much. Since the AMMs provide a better fit for the more frequent pairs in the training data, they might end up providing too good p_{exp}-estimates for the true collocations from the beginning.

Further investigation is needed to find out whether this situation can be ameliorated and, if not, whether we can systematically identify for what kind of collocation extraction tasks using better p_{exp}s is simply not a good idea.

English Verb-Particle constructions The last gold standard is the English VPC dataset, shown in the bottom slice of Table 1. We have only used class-sizes up to 32, as there are only 35 particle types. We can clearly see the effect of the largest AMMs approaching the full bigramme model as average precision here approaches the random baseline. The VPC extraction task shows a difference between the two AMM-based measures: AMM-ratio does not improve at all, remaining below the frequency baseline. AMM-divergence, however, shows a slight decrease in precision first, but ends up performing above the frequency baseline for the 8-class AMMs in both subtasks.

Table 3 shows four clusters of verbs and particles. The large first cluster contains verbs that involve motion/displacement of the subject or object and associated particles, for instance *walk about* or *push away*. Interestingly, the description of the gold standard gives exactly such cases as negatives, since they constitute compositional verb-particle constructions (Baldwin, 2008). Classes 2 and 3 show syntactic dependencies, which helps

Cl	Verb	Particle
1	*break, bring, come, cut, drive, fall, get, go, lay, look, move, pass, push, put, run, sit, throw, turn, voice, walk*	*across, ahead, along, around, away, back, backward, down, forward, into, over, through, together*
2	*accord, add, apply, give, happen, lead, listen, offer, pay, present, refer, relate, return, rise, say, sell, send, speak, write*	*astray, to*
3	*know, talk, tell, think*	*about*
4	*accompany, achieve, affect, cause, create, follow, hit, increase, issue, mean, produce, replace, require, sign, support*	*by*

Table 3: Selected verb-particle clusters from an 8-class AMM on transitive data.

collocation extraction by decreasing the impact of verb-preposition associations that are due to PP-selecting verbs. Class 4 shows a third type of distributional generalization: the verbs in this class are all frequently used in the passive.

3.3 Variation due to local optima

We start each EM run with a random initialization of the model parameters. Since EM finds local rather than global optima, each run may lead to different AMMs, which in turn will affect AMM-based collocation extraction. To gain insight into this variation, we have trained 40 16-class AMMs on the A-N dataset. Table 4 gives five point summaries of the average precision of the resulting 40 'association measures'. Performance varies considerably, spanning 2–3 percentage points in each case. The models consistently outperform (P)MI in Table 1, though.

Several techniques might help to address this variation. One might try to find a good fixed way of initializing EM or to use EM variants that reduce the impact of the initial state (Smith and Eisner, 2004, a.o.), so that a run with the same data and the same number of classes will always learn (almost) the same model. On the assumption that an average over several runs will vary less than individual runs, we have also constructed a combined p_{exp} by averaging over 40 p_{exp}s. The last column in Table 4 shows this combined estimator leads to good extraction results.

		Variation in avg precision					
		min	q1	med	q3	max	Comb
A-N							
cat 1	r_{amm}	46.5	47.3	47.9	48.4	49.1	48.4
	d_{amm}	44.4	45.4	45.8	46.1	47.1	46.4
cat 1–2	r_{amm}	56.7	57.2	57.9	58.2	59.0	58.2
	d_{amm}	58.1	58.8	59.2	59.4	60.4	60.0
cat 1–3	r_{amm}	63.0	63.7	64.2	64.6	65.3	64.6
	d_{amm}	65.2	66.0	66.4	66.6	67.6	66.9

Table 4: Variation on A-N data over 40 EM runs and result of combining p_{exp}s.

4 Conclusions

In this paper, we have started to explore collocation extraction beyond the assumption of independence. We have introduced two new association measures that do away with this assumption in the estimation of expected probabilities. The success of using these association measures varies. It remains to be investigated whether they can be improved more.

A possible obstacle in the adoption of AMMs in collocation extraction is that we have not provided any heuristic for setting the number of classes for the AMMs. We hope to be able to look into this question in future research. Luckily, for the AN and VPC data, the best models are not that large (in the order of 8–32 classes), which means that model fitting is fast enough to experiment with different settings. In general, considering these smaller models might suffice for tasks that have a fairly restricted definition of collocation candidate, like the tasks in our evaluation do. Because AMM fitting is unsupervised, selecting a class size is in this respect no different from selecting a suitable association measure from the canon of existing measures.

Future research into association measures that are not based on the independence assumption will also include considering different EM variants and other automatically learnable models besides the AMMs used in this paper. Finally, the idea of using an informed estimate of expected probability in an association measure need not be confined to (P)MI, as there are many other measures that employ expected probabilities.

Acknowledgements

This research was carried out in the context of the SFB 632 *Information Structure*, subproject D4: *Methoden zur interaktiven linguistischen Korpusanalyse von Informationsstruktur*.

References

Timothy Baldwin. 2005. The deep lexical acquisition of english verb-particle constructions. *Computer Speech and Language, Special Issue on Multiword Expressions*, 19(4):398–414.

Timothy Baldwin. 2008. A resource for evaluating the deep lexical acquisition of English verb-particle constructions. In *Proceedings of the LREC 2008 Workshop Towards a Shared Task for Multiword Expressions (MWE 2008)*, pages 1–2, Marrakech.

John Blitzer, Amir Globerson, and Fernando Pereira. 2005. Distributed latent variable models of lexical co-occurrences. In *Tenth International Workshop on Artificial Intelligence and Statistics*.

Kenneth W. Church and Patrick Hanks. 1990. Word association norms, mutual information, and lexicography. *Computational Linguistics*, 16(1):22–29.

Ted Dunning. 1993. Accurate methods for the statistics of surprise and coincidence. *Computational Linguistics*, 19(1):61–74.

Stefan Evert. 2007. Corpora and collocations. Extended Manuscript of Chapter 58 of A. Lüdeling and M. Kytö, 2008, *Corpus Linguistics. An International Handbook*, Mouton de Gruyter, Berlin.

Stefan Evert. 2008. A lexicographic evaluation of German adjective-noun collocations. In *Proceedings of the LREC 2008 Workshop Towards a Shared Task for Multiword Expressions (MWE 2008)*, pages 3–6, Marrakech.

Thomas Hofmann and Jan Puzicha. 1998. Statistical models for co-occurrence data. Technical report, MIT. AI Memo 1625, CBCL Memo 159.

Brigitte Krenn and Stefan Evert. 2001. Can we do better than frequency? a case study on extracting PP-verb collocations. In *Proceedings of the ACL Workshop on Collocations*, Toulouse.

Brigitte Krenn. 2008. Description of evaluation resource – German PP-verb data. In *Proceedings of the LREC 2008 Workshop Towards a Shared Task for Multiword Expressions (MWE 2008)*, pages 7–10, Marrakech.

Chris Manning and Hinrich Schütze. 1999. *Foundations of Statistical Natural Language Processing*. MIT Press, Cambridge, MA.

Pavel Pecina. 2008. A machine learning approach to multiword expression extraction. In *Proceedings of the LREC 2008 Workshop Towards a Shared Task for Multiword Expressions (MWE 2008)*, pages 54–57, Marrakech.

Mats Rooth, Stefan Riester, Detlef Prescher, Glenn Carrol, and Franz Beil. 1999. Inducing a semantically annotated lexicon via em-based clustering. In *Proceedings of the 37th Annual Meeting of the Association for Computational Linguistics*, College Park, MD.

Lawrence Saul and Fernando Pereira. 1997. Aggregate and mixed-order markov models for statistical language processing. In *Proceedings of the Second Conference on Empirical Methods in Natural Language Processing*, pages 81–89.

Noah A. Smith and Jason Eisner. 2004. Annealing techniques for unsupervised statistical language learning. In *Proceedings of the 42nd Annual Meeting of the Association for Computational Linguistics*.

Automatic Collocation Suggestion in Academic Writing

Jian-Cheng Wu[1] **Yu-Chia Chang**[1,*] **Teruko Mitamura**[2] **Jason S. Chang**[1]

[1] National Tsing Hua University
Hsinchu, Taiwan
{wujc86, richtrf, jason.jschang}@gmail.com

[2] Carnegie Mellon University
Pittsburgh, United States
teruko@cs.cmu.edu

Abstract

In recent years, collocation has been widely acknowledged as an essential characteristic to distinguish native speakers from non-native speakers. Research on academic writing has also shown that collocations are not only common but serve a particularly important discourse function within the academic community. In our study, we propose a machine learning approach to implementing an online collocation writing assistant. We use a data-driven classifier to provide collocation suggestions to improve word choices, based on the result of classification. The system generates and ranks suggestions to assist learners' collocation usages in their academic writing with satisfactory results.

1 Introduction

The notion of collocation has been widely discussed in the field of language teaching for decades. It has been shown that collocation, a successive common usage of words in a chain, is important in helping language learners achieve native-like fluency. In the field of English for Academic Purpose, more and more researchers are also recognizing this important feature in academic writing. It is often argued that collocation can influence the effectiveness of a piece of writing and the lack of such knowledge might cause cumulative loss of precision (Howarth, 1998).

Many researchers have discussed the function of collocations in the highly conventionalized and specialized writing used within academia. Research also identified noticeable increases in the quantity and quality of collocational usage by native speakers (Howarth, 1998). Granger (1998) reported that learners underuse native-like collocations and overuse atypical word combinations. This disparity in collocation usage between native and non-native speakers is clear and should receive more attention from the language technology community.

To tackle such word usage problems, traditional language technology often employs a database of the learners' common errors that are manually tagged by teachers or specialists (e.g. Shei and Pain, 2000; Liu, 2002). Such system then identifies errors via string or pattern matching and offer only pre-stored suggestions. Compiling the database is time-consuming and not easily maintainable, and the usefulness is limited by the manual collection of pre-stored suggestions. Therefore, it is beneficial if a system can mainly use untagged data from a corpus containing correct language usages rather than the error-tagged data from a learner corpus. A large corpus of correct language usages is more readily available and useful than a small labeled corpus of incorrect language usages.

For this suggestion task, the large corpus not only provides us with a rich set of common collocations but also provides the context within which these collocations appear. Intuitively, we can take account of such context of collocation to generate more suitable suggestions. Contextual information in this sense often entails more linguistic clues to provide suggestions within sentences or paragraph. However, the contextual information is messy and complex and thus has long been overlooked or ignored. To date, most fashionable suggestion methods still rely upon the linguistic components within collocations as well as the linguistic relationship between misused words and their correct counterparts (Chang et al., 2008; Liu, 2009).

In contrast to other research, we employ contextual information to automate suggestions for verb-noun lexical collocation. Verb-noun collocations are recognized as presenting the most

* Corresponding author: Yu-chia Chang (Email address: richtrf@gmail.com)

Proceedings of the ACL 2010 Conference Short Papers, pages 115–119,
Uppsala, Sweden, 11-16 July 2010.

challenge to students (Howarth, 1996; Liu, 2002). More specifically, in this preliminary study we start by focusing on the word choice of verbs in collocations which are considered as the most difficult ones for learners to master (Liu, 2002; Chang, 2008). The experiment confirms that our collocation writing assistant proves the feasibility of using machine learning methods to automatically prompt learners with collocation suggestions in academic writing.

2 Collocation Checking and Suggestion

This study aims to develop a web service, *Collocation Inspector* (shown in Figure 1) that accepts sentences as input and generates the related candidates for learners.

In this paper, we focus on automatically providing academic collocation suggestions when users are writing up their abstracts. After an abstract is submitted, the system extracts linguistic features from the user's text for machine learning model. By using a corpus of published academic texts, we hope to match contextual linguistic clues from users' text to help elicit the most relevant suggestions. We now formally state the problem that we are addressing:

Problem Statement: Given a sentence *S* written by a learner and a reference corpus *RC*, our goal is to output a set of most probable suggestion candidates $c_1, c_2, \ldots, c_m$. For this, we train a classifier *MC* to map the context (represented as feature set $f_1, f_2, \ldots, f_n$) of each sentence in *RC* to the collocations. At run-time, we predict these collocations for *S* as suggestions.

2.1 Academic Collocation Checker Training Procedures

Sentence Parsing and Collocation Extraction: We start by collecting a large number of abstracts from the Web to develop a reference corpus for collocation suggestion. And we continue to identify collocations in each sentence for the subsequent processing.

Collocation extraction is an essential step in preprocessing data. We only expect to extract the collocation which comprises components having a syntactic relationship with one another. However, this extraction task can be complicated. Take the following scholarly sentence from the reference corpus as an example (example (1)):

```
(1) We introduce a novel method
for learning to find documents
on the web.
```

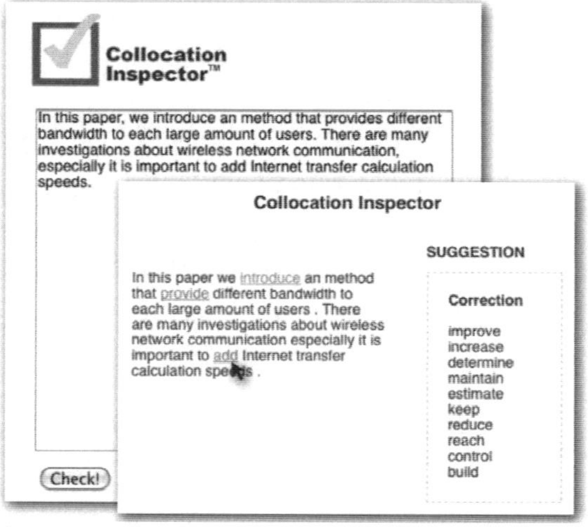

Figure 1. The interface for the collocation suggestion

```
nsubj (introduce-2, We-1)
det (method-5, a-3)
amod (method-5, novel-4)
dobj (introduce-2, method-5)
prepc_for (introduce-2, learning-7)
aux (find-9, to-8)
... ...
```

Figure 2. Dependency parsing of Example (1)

Traditionally, through part-of-speech tagging, we can obtain a tagged sentence as follows (example (2)). We can observe that the desired collocation "introduce method", conforming to "VERB+NOUN" relationship, exists within the sentence. However, the distance between these two words is often flexible, not necessarily rigid. Heuristically writing patterns to extract such verb and noun might not be effective. The patterns between them can be tremendously varied. In addition, some verbs and nouns are adjacent, but they might be intervened by clause and thus have no syntactic relation with one another (e.g. "propose model" in example (3)).

```
(2) We/PRP  introduce/VB  a/DT
novel/JJ  method/NN  for/IN
learning/VBG  to/TO  find/VB
documents/NNS  on/IN  the/DT
web/NN  ./.
```

```
(3) We proposed that the web-
based model would be more ef-
fective than corpus-based one.
```

A natural language parser can facilitate the extraction of the target type of collocations. Such parser is a program that works out the grammatical structure of sentences, for instance, by identifying which group of words go together or which word is the subject or object of a verb. In our study, we take advantage of a dependency parser, *Stanford Parser*, which extracts typed dependencies for certain grammatical relations (shown in Figure 2). Within the parsed sentence of example (1), we can notice that the extracted dependency "dobj (introduce-2, method-4)" meets the criterion.

Using a Classifier for the Suggestion task: A classifier is a function generally to take a set of attributes as an input and to provide a tagged class as an output. The basic way to build a classifier is to derive a regression formula from a set of tagged examples. And this trained classifier can thus make predication and assign a tag to any input data.

The suggestion task in this study will be seen as a classification problem. We treat the collocation extracted from each sentence as the class tag (see examples in Table 1). Hopefully, the system can learn the rules between tagged classes (i.e. collocations) and example sentences (i.e. scholarly sentences) and can predict which collocation is the most appropriate one given attributes extracted from the sentences.

Another advantage of using a classifier to automate suggestion is to provide alternatives with regard to the similar attributes shared by sentences. In Table 1, we can observe that these collocations exhibit a similar discourse function and can thus become interchangeable in these sentences. Therefore, based on the outputs along with the probability from the classifier, we can provide more than one adequate suggestions.

Feature Selection for Machine Learning: In the final stage of training, we build a statistical machine-learning model. For our task, we can use a supervised method to automatically learn the relationship between collocations and example sentences.

We choose Maximum Entropy (ME) as our training algorithm to build a collocation suggestion classifier. One advantage of an ME classifier is that in addition to assigning a classification it can provide the probability of each assignment. The ME framework estimates probabilities based on the principle of making as few assumptions as possible. Such constraints are derived from the training data, expressing relationships between features and outcomes.

Moreover, an effective feature selection can increase the precision of machine learning. In our study, we employ the contextual features which

Table 1. Example sentences and class tags (collocations)

Example Sentence	**Class tag**
We introduce a novel method for learning to find documents on the web.	introduce
We presented a method of improving Japanese dependency parsing by using large-scale statistical information.	present
In this paper, we will describe a method of identifying the syntactic role of antecedents, which consists of two phases	describe
In this paper, we suggest a method that automatically constructs an NE tagged corpus from the web to be used for learning of NER systems.	suggest

consist of two elements, the *head* and the *ngram* of context words:

Head: Each collocation comprises two parts, collocate and head. For example, in a given verb-noun collocation, the verb is the collocate as well as the target for which we provide suggestions; the noun serves as the head of collocation and convey the essential meaning of the collocation. We use the head as a feature to condition the classifier to generate candidates relevant to a given head.

Ngram: We use the context words around the target collocation by considering the corresponding unigrams and bigrams words within the sentence. Moreover, to ensure the relevance, those context words, before and after the punctuation marks enclosing the collocation in question, will be excluded. We use the parsed sentence from previous step (example (2)) to show the extracted context features[1] (example (4)):

```
(4) CN=method UniV_L=we
UniV_R=a UniV_R=novel UniN_L=a
UniN_L=novel UniN_R=for
UniN_R=learn BiV_R=a_novel
BiN_L=a_novel BiN_R=for_learn
BiV_I=we_a BiN_I=novel_for
```

[1] CN refers to the head within collocation. Uni and Bi indicate the unigram and bigram context words of window size two respectively. V and N differentiate the contexts related to verb or noun. The ending alphabets L, R, I show the position of the words in context, L = left, R = right, and I = in between.

2.2 Automatic Collocation Suggestion at Run-time

After the ME classifier is automatically trained, the model is used to find out the best collocation suggestion. Figure 3 shows the algorithm of producing suggestions for a given sentence. The input is a learner's sentence in an abstract, along with an ME model trained from the reference corpus.

In Step (1) of the algorithm, we parse the sentence for data preprocessing. Based on the parser output, we extract the collocation from a given sentence as well as generate features sets in Step (2) and (3). After that in Step (4), with the trained machine-learning model, we obtain a set of likely collocates with probability as predicted by the ME model. In Step (5), SuggestionFilter singles out the valid collocation and returns the best collocation suggestion as output in Step (6). For example, if a learner inputs the sentence like Example (5), the features and output candidates are shown in Table 2.

```
(5) There are many investiga-
tions about wireless network
communication, especially it is
important to add Internet
transfer calculation speeds.
```

Procedure CollocationSuggestion(*sent*, *MEmodel*)
(1) *parsedSen* = Parsing(*sent*)
(2) *extractedColl* = CollocationExtraction(*parsedSent*)
(3) *features* = AssignFeature(*ParsedSent*)
(4) *probCollection* = MEprob(*features*, *MEmodel*)
(5) *candidate* = SuggestionFilter(*probCollection*)
(6) Return candidate

Figure 3. Collocation Suggestion at Run-time

Table 2. An example from learner's sentence

Extracted Collocation	**Features**	**Ranked Candidates**
add speed	CN=speed UniV_L=important UniV_L=to UniV_R=internet UniV_R=transfer UniN_L=transfer UniN_L=calculation BiV_L=important_to BiV_R=internet_transfer BiN_L=transfer_calculation BiV_I=to_intenet	improve increase determine maintain … …

Table 3. MRR for different feature sets

Feature Sets Included In Classifier	**MRR**
Features of HEAD	0.407
Features of CONTEXT	0.469
Features of HEAD+CONTEXT	0.518

3 Experiment

From an online research database, *CiteSeer*, we have collected a corpus of 20,306 unique abstracts, which contained 95,650 sentences. To train a Maximum Entropy classifier, 46,255 collocations are extracted and 790 verbal collocates are identified as tagged classes for collocation suggestions. We tested the classifier on scholarly sentences in place of authentic student writings which were not available at the time of this pilot study. We extracted 364 collocations among 600 randomly selected sentences as the held out test data not overlapping with the training set. To automate the evaluation, we blank out the verb collocates within these sentences and treat these verbs directly as the only correct suggestions in question, although two or more suggestions may be interchangeable or at least appropriate. In this sense, our evaluation is an underestimate of the performance of the proposed method.

While evaluating the quality of the suggestions provided by our system, we used the mean reciprocal rank (MRR) of the first relevant suggestions returned so as to assess whether the suggestion list contains an answer and how far up the answer is in the list as a quality metric of the system output. Table 3 shows that the best MRR of our prototype system is 0.518. The results indicate that on average users could easily find answers (exactly reproduction of the blanked out collocates) in the first two to three ranking of suggestions. It is very likely that we get a much higher MMR value if we would go through the lists and evaluate each suggestion by hand. Moreover, in Table 3, we can further notice that contextual features are quite informative in comparison with the baseline feature set containing merely the feature of HEAD. Also the integrated feature set of HEAD and CONTEXT together achieves a more satisfactory suggestion result.

4 Conclusion

Many avenues exist for future research that are important for improving the proposed method. For example, we need to carry out the experiment on authentic learners' texts. We will conduct a user study to investigate whether our system would improve a learner's writing in a real setting. Additionally, adding classifier features based on the translation of misused words in learners' text could be beneficial (Chang et al.,

2008). The translation can help to resolve prevalent collocation misuses influenced by a learner's native language. Yet another direction of this research is to investigate if our methodology is applicable to other types of collocations, such as AN and PN in addition to VN dealt with in this paper.

In summary, we have presented an unsupervised method for suggesting collocations based on a corpus of abstracts collected from the Web. The method involves selecting features from the reference corpus of the scholarly texts. Then a classifier is automatically trained to determine the most probable collocation candidates with regard to the given context. The preliminary results show that it is beneficial to use classifiers for identifying and ranking collocation suggestions based on the context features.

Reference

Y. Chang, J. Chang, H. Chen, and H. Liou. 2008. An automatic collocation writing assistant for Taiwanese EFL learners: A case of corpus-based NLP technology. *Computer Assisted Language Learning*, 21(3), pages 283-299.

S. Granger. 1998. Prefabricated patterns in advanced EFL writing: collocations and formulae. In Cowie, A. (ed.) *Phraseology: theory, analysis and applications*. Oxford University Press, Oxford, pages 145-160.

P. Howarth. 1996. *Phraseology in English Academic Writing*. Tübingen: Max Niemeyer Verlag.

P. Howarth. 1998. The phraseology of learner's academic writing. In Cowie, A. (ed.) *Phraseology: theory, analysis and applications*. Oxford University Press, Oxford, pages 161-186.

D. Hawking and N. Craswell. 2002. Overview of the TREC-2001 Web track. In *Proceedings of the 10th Text Retrieval Conference (TREC 2001)*, pages 25-31.

L. E. Liu. 2002. A corpus-based lexical semantic investigation of verb-noun miscollocations in Taiwan learners' English. *Unpublished master's thesis*, Tamkang University, Taipei, January.

A. L. Liu, D. Wible, and N. L. Tsao. 2009. Automated suggestions for miscollocations. In *Proceedings of the Fourth Workshop on Innovative Use of NLP for Building Educational Applications*, pages 47-50.

C. C. Shei and H. Pain. 2000. An ESL writer's collocational aid. *Computer Assisted Language Learning*, 13, pages 167-182.

Event-based Hyperspace Analogue to Language for Query Expansion

Tingxu Yan
Tianjin University
Tianjin, China
sunriser2008@gmail.com

Tamsin Maxwell
University of Edinburgh
Edinburgh, United Kingdom
t.maxwell@ed.ac.uk

Dawei Song
Robert Gordon University
Aberdeen, United Kingdom
d.song@rgu.ac.uk

Yuexian Hou
Tianjin University
Tianjin, China
yxhou@tju.edu.cn

Peng Zhang
Robert Gordon University
Aberdeen, United Kingdom.
p.zhang1@rgu.ac.uk

Abstract

Bag-of-words approaches to information retrieval (IR) are effective but assume independence between words. The Hyperspace Analogue to Language (HAL) is a cognitively motivated and validated semantic space model that captures statistical dependencies between words by considering their co-occurrences in a surrounding window of text. HAL has been successfully applied to query expansion in IR, but has several limitations, including high processing cost and use of distributional statistics that do not exploit syntax. In this paper, we pursue two methods for incorporating syntactic-semantic information from textual 'events' into HAL. We build the HAL space directly from events to investigate whether processing costs can be reduced through more careful definition of word co-occurrence, and improve the quality of the pseudo-relevance feedback by applying event information as a constraint during HAL construction. Both methods significantly improve performance results in comparison with original HAL, and interpolation of HAL and relevance model expansion outperforms either method alone.

1 Introduction

Despite its intuitive appeal, the incorporation of linguistic and semantic word dependencies in IR has not been shown to significantly improve over a bigram language modeling approach (Song and Croft, 1999) that encodes word dependencies assumed from mere syntactic adjacency. Both the dependence language model for IR (Gao et al., 2004), which incorporates linguistic relations between non-adjacent words while limiting the generation of meaningless phrases, and the Markov Random Field (MRF) model, which captures short and long range term dependencies (Metzler and Croft, 2005; Metzler and Croft, 2007), consistently outperform a unigram language modelling approach but are closely approximated by a bigram language model that uses no linguistic knowledge. Improving retrieval performance through application of semantic and syntactic information beyond proximity and co-occurrence features is a difficult task but remains a tantalising prospect.

Our approach is like that of Gao et al. (2004) in that it considers semantic-syntactically determined relationships between words at the sentence level, but allows words to have more than one role, such as predicate and argument for different events, while link grammar (Sleator and Temperley, 1991) dictates that a word can only satisfy one connector in a disjunctive set. Compared to the MRF model, our approach is unsupervised where MRFs require the training of parameters using relevance judgments that are often unavailable in practical conditions.

Other work incorporating syntactic and linguistic information into IR includes early research by (Smeaton, O'Donnell and Kelledy, 1995), who employed tree structured analytics (TSAs) resembling dependency trees, the use of syntax to detect paraphrases for question answering (QA) (Lin and Pantel, 2001), and semantic role labelling in QA (Shen and Lapata, 2007).

Independent from IR, Pado and Lapata (2007) proposed a general framework for the construction of a semantic space endowed with syntactic

Proceedings of the ACL 2010 Conference Short Papers, pages 120–125,
Uppsala, Sweden, 11-16 July 2010. ©2010 Association for Computational Linguistics

information. This was represented by an undirected graph, where nodes stood for words, dependency edges stood for syntactical relations, and sequences of dependency edges formed paths that were weighted for each target word. Our work is in line with Pado and Lapata (2007) in constructing a semantic space with syntactic information, but builds our space from events, states and attributions as defined linguistically by Bach (1986). We call these simply *events*, and extract them automatically from predicate-argument structures and a dependency parse. We will use this space to perform query expansion in IR, a task that aims to find additional words related to original query terms, such that an expanded query including these words better expresses the information need. To our knowledge, the notion of events has not been applied to query expansion before.

This paper will outline the original HAL algorithm which serves as our baseline, and the event extraction process. We then propose two methods to arm HAL with event information: direct construction of HAL from events (eHAL-1), and treating events as constraints on HAL construction from the corpus (eHAL-2). Evaluation will compare results using original HAL, eHAL-1 and eHAL-2 with a widely used unigram language model (LM) for IR and a state of the art query expansion method, namely the Relevance Model (RM) (Lavrenko and Croft, 2001). We also explore whether a complementary effect can be achieved by combining HAL-based dependency modelling with the unigram-based RM.

2 HAL Construction

Semantic space models aim to capture the meanings of words using co-occurrence information in a text corpus. Two examples are the Hyperspace Analogue to Language (HAL) (Lund and Burgess, 1996), in which a word is represented by a vector of other words co-occurring with it in a sliding window, and Latent Semantic Analysis (LSA) (Deerwester, Dumais, Furnas, Landauer and Harshman, 1990; Landauer, Foltz and Laham, 1998), in which a word is expressed as a vector of documents (or any other syntactical units such as sentences) containing the word. In these semantic spaces, vector-based representations facilitate measurement of similarities between words. Semantic space models have been validated through various studies and demonstrate compatibility with human information processing. Recently, they have also been applied in IR, such as LSA for latent semantic indexing, and HAL for query expansion. For the purpose of this paper, we focus on HAL, which encodes word co-occurrence information explicitly and thus can be applied to query expansion in a straightforward way.

HAL is premised on context surrounding a word providing important information about its meaning (Harris, 1968). To be specific, an L-size sliding window moves across a large text corpus word-by-word. Any two words in the same window are treated as co-occurring with each other with a weight that is inversely proportional to their separation distance in the text. By accumulating co-occurrence information over a corpus, a word-by-word matrix is constructed, a simple illustration of which is given in Table 1. A single word is represented by a row vector and a column vector that capture the information before and after the word, respectively. In some applications, direction sensitivity is ignored to obtain a single vector representation of a word by adding corresponding row and column vectors (Bai et al., 2005).

	w_1	w_2	w_3	w_4	w_5	w_6
w_1						
w_2	5					
w_3	4	5				
w_4	3	4	5			
w_5	2	3	4	5		
w_6		2	3	4	5	

Table 1: A HAL space for the text "w_1 w_2 w_3 w_4 w_5 w_6" using a 5-word sliding window ($L = 5$).

HAL has been successfully applied to query expansion and can be incorporated into this task directly (Bai et al., 2005) or indirectly, as with the Information Flow method based on HAL (Bruza and Song, 2002). However, to date it has used only statistical information from co-occurrence patterns. We extend HAL to incorporate syntactic-semantic information.

3 Event Extraction

Prior to event extraction, predicates, arguments, part of speech (POS) information and syntactic dependencies are annotated using the best-performing joint syntactic-semantic parser from the CoNNL 2008 Shared Task (Johansson and

Nugues, 2008), trained on PropBank and NomBank data. The event extraction algorithm then instantiates the template *REL [modREL] Arg0 [modArg0] ...ArgN [modArgN]*, where *REL* is the predicate relation (or root verb if no predicates are identified), and *Arg0...ArgN* are its arguments. Modifiers (*mod*) are identified by tracing from predicate and argument heads along the dependency tree. All predicates are associated with at least one event unless both *Arg0* and *Arg1* are not identified, or the only argument is not a noun.

The algorithm checks for modifiers based on POS tag[1], tracing up and down the dependency tree, skipping over prepositions, coordinating conjunctions and words indicating apportionment, such as *'sample (of)'*. However, to constrain output the search is limited to a depth of one (with the exception of skipping). For example, given the phrase *'apples from the store nearby'* and an argument head *apples*, the first dependent, *store*, will be extracted but not *nearby*, which is the dependent of store. This can be detrimental when encountering compound nouns but does focus on core information. For verbs, modal dependents are not included in output.

Available paths up and down the dependency tree are followed until all branches are exhausted, given the rules outlined above. Tracing can result in multiple extracted events for one predicate and predicates may also appear as arguments in a different event, or be part of argument phrases. For this reason, events are constrained to cover only detail appearing above subsequent predicates in the tree, which simplifies the event structure. For example, the sentence *"Baghdad already has the facilities to continue producing massive quantities of its own biological and chemical weapons"* results in the event output: (1) *has Baghdad already facilities continue producing*; (2) *continue quantities producing massive*; (3) *producing quantities massive weapons biological*; (4) *quantities weapons biological massive*.

4 HAL With Events

4.1 eHAL-1: Construction From Events

Since events are extracted from documents, they form a reduced text corpus from which HAL can be built in a similar manner to the original HAL. We ignore the parameter of window length (L) and treat every event as a single window of length equal to the number of words in the event. Every pair of words in an event is considered to be co-occurrent with each other. The weight assigned to the association between each pair is simply set to one. With this scheme, all the events are traversed and the event-based HAL is constructed.

The advantage of this method is that it substantially reduces the processing time during HAL construction because only events are involved and there is no need to calculate weights per occurrence. Additional processing time is incurred in semantic role labelling (SRL) during event identification. However, the naive approach to extraction might be simulated with a combination of less costly chunking and dependency parsing, given that the word ordering information available with SRL is not utilised.

eHAL-1 combines syntactical and statistical information, but has a potential drawback in that only events are used during construction so some information existing in the co-occurrence patterns of the original text may be lost. This motivates the second method.

4.2 eHAL-2: Event-Based Filtering

This method attempts to include more statistical information in eHAL construction. The key idea is to decide whether a text segment in a corpus should be used for the HAL construction, based on how much event information it covers. Given a corpus of text and the events extracted from it, the eHAL-2 method runs as follows:

1. Select the events of length M or more and discard the others for efficiency;

2. Set an "inclusion criterion", which decides if a text segment, defined as a word sequence within an L-size sliding window, contains an event. For example, if 80% of the words in an event are contained in a text segment, it could be considered to "include" the event;

3. Move across the whole corpus word-by-word with an L-size sliding window. For each window, complete Steps 4-7;

4. For the current L-size text segment, check whether it includes an event according to the "inclusion criterion" (Step 2);

[1]To be specific, the modifiers include negation, as well as adverbs or particles for verbal heads, adjectives and nominal modifiers for nominal heads, and verbal or nominal dependents of modifiers, provided modifiers are not also identified as arguments elsewhere in the event.

5. If an event is included in the current text segment, check the following segments for a consecutive sequence of segments that also include this event. If the current segment includes more than one event, find the longest sequence of related text segments. An illustration is given in Figure 1 in which dark nodes stand for the words in a specific event and an 80% inclusion criterion is used.

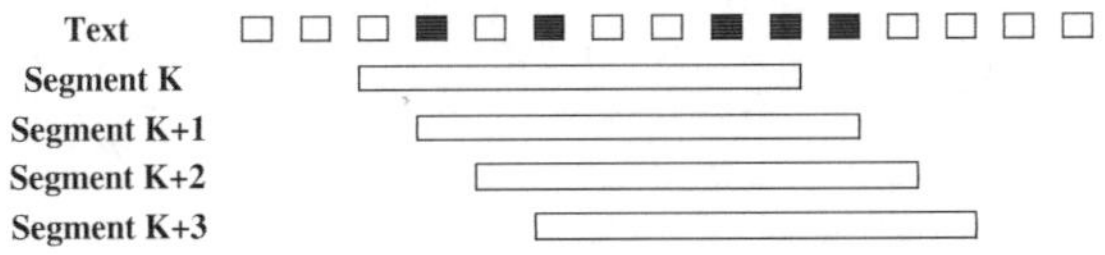

Figure 1: Consecutive segments for an event

6. Extract the full span of consecutive segments just identified and go to the next available text segment. Repeat Step 3;

7. When the scanning is done, construct HAL using the original HAL method over all extracted sequences.

With the guidance of event information, the procedure above keeps only those segments of text that include at least one event and discards the rest. It makes use of more statistical co-occurrence information than eHAL-1 by applying weights that are proportional to word separation distance. It also alleviates the identified drawback of eHAL-1 by using the full text surrounding events. A trade-off is that not all the events are included by the selected text segments, and thus some syntactical information may be lost. In addition, the parametric complexity and computational complexity are also higher than eHAL-1.

5 Evaluation

We empirically test whether our event-based HALs perform better than the original HAL, and standard LM and RM, using three TREC[2] collections: AP89 with Topics 1-50 (*title* field), AP8889 with Topics 101-150 (*title* field) and WSJ9092 with Topics 201-250 (*description* field). All the collections are stemmed, and stop words are removed, prior to retrieval using the Lemur Toolkit Version 4.11[3]. Initial retrieval is identical for all models evaluated: KL-divergence based LM smoothed using Dirichlet prior with μ set to 1000 as appropriate for TREC style title queries (Lavrenko, 2004). The top 50 returned documents form the basis for all pseudo-relevance feedback, with other parameters tuned separately for the RM and HAL methods.

For each dataset, the number of feedback terms for each method is selected optimally among 20, 40, 60, 80[4] and the interpolation and smoothing coefficient is set to be optimal in [0,1] with interval 0.1. For RM, we choose the first relevance model in Lavrenko and Croft (2001) with the document model smoothing parameter optimally set at 0.8. The number of feedback terms is fixed at 60 (for AP89 and WSJ9092) and 80 (for AP8889), and interpolation between the query and relevance models is set at 0.7 (for WSJ9092) and 0.9 (for AP89 and AP8889). The HAL-based query expansion methods add the top 80 expansion terms to the query with interpolation coefficient 0.9 for WSJ9092 and 1 (that is, no interpolation) for AP89 and AP8889. The other HAL-based parameters are set as follows: shortest event length $M = 5$, for eHAL-2 the "inclusion criterion" is 75% of words in an event, and for HAL and eHAL-2, window size $L = 8$. Top expansion terms are selected according to the formula:

$$P_{HAL}(t_j|\oplus t) = \frac{HAL(t_j|\oplus q)}{\sum\limits_{t_i} HAL(t_i|\oplus q)}$$

where $HAL(t_j|\oplus q)$ is the weight of t_j in the combined HAL vector $\oplus q$ (Bruza and Song, 2002) of original query terms. Mean Average Precision (MAP) is the performance indicator, and t-test (at the level of 0.05) is performed to measure the statistical significance of results.

Table 2 lists the experimental results[5]. It can be observed that all the three HAL-based query expansion methods improve performance over the LM and both eHALs achieve better performance than original HAL, indicating that the incorporation of event information is beneficial. In addition, eHAL-2 leads to better performance than eHAL-1, suggesting that use of linguistic information as a constraint on statistical processing, rather than the focus of extraction, is a more effective strategy. The results are still short of those achieved

[2]TREC stands for the Text REtrieval Conference series run by NIST. Please refer to http://trec.nist.gov/ for details.

[3]Available at http://www.lemurproject.org/

[4]For RM, feedback terms were also tested on larger numbers up to 1000 but only comparable result was observed.

[5]In Table 2, brackets show percent improvement of eHALs / RM over HAL / eHAL-2 respectively and * and # indicate the corresponding statistical significance.

Method	AP89	AP8889	WSJ9092
LM	0.2015	0.2290	0.2242
HAL	0.2299	0.2738	0.2346
eHAL-1	0.2364 (+2.83%)	0.2829 (+3.32%*)	0.2409 (+2.69%)
eHAL-2	0.2427 (+5.57%*)	0.2850 (+4.09%*)	0.2460 (+4.86%*)
RM	0.2611 (+7.58%#)	0.3178 (+11.5%#)	0.2676 (+8.78%#)

Table 2: Performance (MAP) comparison of query expansion using different HALs

with RM, but the gap is significantly reduced by incorporating event information here, suggesting this is a promising line of work. In addition, as shown in (Bai et al., 2005), the Information Flow method built upon the original HAL largely outperformed RM. We expect that eHAL would provide an even better basis for Information Flow, but this possibility is yet to be explored.

As is known, RM is a pure unigram model while HAL methods are dependency-based. They capture different information, hence it is natural to consider if their strengths might complement each other in a combined model. For this purpose, we design the following two schemes:

1. Apply RM to the feedback documents (original RM), the events extracted from these documents (eRM-1), and the text segments around each event (eRM-2), where the three sources are the same as used to produce HAL, eHAL-1 and eHAL-2 respectively;

2. Interpolate the expanded query model by RM with the ones generated by each HAL, represented by HAL+RM, eHAL-1+RM and eHAL-2+RM. The interpolation coefficient is again selected to achieve the optimal MAP.

The MAP comparison between the original RM and these new models are demonstrated in Table 3[6]. From the first three lines (Scheme 1), we can observe that in most cases the performance generally deteriorates when RM is directly run over the events and the text segments. The event information is more effective to express the information about the term dependencies while the unigram RM ignores this information and only takes the occurrence frequencies of individual words into account, which is not well-captured by the events. In contrast, the performance of Scheme 2 is more promising. The three methods outperform the original RM in most cases, but the improvement is not significant and it is also observed that there is little difference shown between RM with HAL and eHALs. The phenomenon implies more effective methods may be invented to complement the unigram models with the syntactical and statistical dependency information.

Method	AP89	AP8889	WSJ9092
RM	0.2611	0.3178	0.2676
eRM-1	0.2554 (-2.18%)	0.3150 (-0.88%)	0.2555 (-4.52%)
eRM-2	0.2605 (-0.23%)	0.3167 (-0.35%)	0.2626 (-1.87%)
HAL +RM	0.2640 (+1.11%)	0.3186 (+0.25%)	0.2727 (+1.19%)
eHAL-1 +RM	0.2600 (-0.42%)	0.3210 (+1.01%)	0.2734 (+2.17%)
eHAL-2 +RM	0.2636 (+0.96%)	0.3191 (+0.41%)	0.2735 (+2.20%)

Table 3: Performance (MAP) comparison of query expansion using the combination of RM and term dependencies

6 Conclusions

The application of original HAL to query expansion attempted to incorporate statistical word association information, but did not take into account the syntactical dependencies and had a high processing cost. By utilising syntactic-semantic knowledge from event modelling of pseudo-relevance feedback documents prior to computing the HAL space, we showed that processing costs might be reduced through more careful selection of word co-occurrences and that performance may be enhanced by effectively improving the quality of pseudo-relevance feedback documents. Both methods improved over original HAL query expansion. In addition, interpolation of HAL and RM expansion improved results over those achieved by either method alone.

Acknowledgments

This research is funded in part by the UK's Engineering and Physical Sciences Research Council, grant number: EP/F014708/2.

[6]For rows in Table 3, brackets show percent difference from original RM.

References

Bach E. The Algebra of Events. 1986. *Linguistics and Philosophy*, 9(1): pp. 5–16.

Bai J. and Song D. and Bruza P. and Nie J.-Y. and Cao G. Query Expansion using Term Relationships in Language Models for Information Retrieval 2005. In: *Proceedings of the 14th International ACM Conference on Information and Knowledge Management*, pp. 688–695.

Bruza P. and Song D. Inferring Query Models by Computing Information Flow. 2002. In: *Proceedings of the 11th International ACM Conference on Information and Knowledge Management*, pp. 206–269.

Deerwester S., Dumais S., Furnas G., Landauer T. and Harshman R. Indexing by latent semantic analysis. 1990. *Journal of the American Sociaty for Information Science*, 41(6): pp. 391–407.

Gao J. and Nie J. and Wu G. and Cao G. Dependence Language Model for Information Retrieval. 2004. In: *Proceedings of the 27th Annual International ACM SIGIR Conference on Research and Development in Information Retrieval*, pp. 170–177.

Harris Z. 1968. *Mathematical Structures of Language.*. Wiley, New York.

Johansson R. and Nugues P. Dependency-based Syntactic-semantic Analysis with PropBank and NomBank. 2008. In: *CoNLL '08: Proceedings of the Twelfth Conference on Computational Natural Language Learning*, pp. 183–187.

Landauer T., Foltz P. and Laham D. Introduction to Latent Semantic Analysis. 1998. *Discourse Processes*, 25: pp. 259–284.

Lavrenko V. 2004. *A Generative Theory of Relevance*, PhD thesis, University of Massachusetts, Amherst.

Lavrenko V. and Croft W. B. Relevance Based Language Models. 2001. In: *SIGIR '01: Proceedings of the 24th Annual International ACM SIGIR Conference on Research and Development in Information Retrieval*, pp. 120–127, New York, NY, USA, 2001. ACM.

Lin D. and Pantel P. DIRT - Discovery of Inference Rules from Text. 2001. In: *KDD '01: Proceedings of the Seventh ACM SIGKDD International Conference on Knowledge Discovery and Data Mining*, pp. 323–328, New York, NY, USA.

Lund K. and Burgess C. Producing High-dimensional Semantic Spaces from Lexical Co-occurrence. 1996. *Behavior Research Methods, Instruments & Computers*, 28: pp. 203–208. Prentice-Hall, Englewood Cliffs, NJ.

Metzler D. and Bruce W. B. A Markov Random Field Model for Term Dependencies 2005. In: *SIGIR '05: Proceedings of the 28th annual international ACM SIGIR conference on Research and development in information retrieval*, pp. 472–479, New York, NY, USA. ACM.

Metzler D. and Bruce W. B. Latent Concept Expansion using Markov Random Fields 2007. In: *SIGIR '07: Proceedings of the 30th Annual International ACM SIGIR Conference on Research and Development in Information Retrieval*, pp. 311–318, ACM, New York, NY, USA.

Pado S. and Lapata M. Dependency-Based Construction of Semantic Space Models. 2007. *Computational Linguistics*, 33: pp. 161–199.

Shen D. and Lapata M. Using Semantic Roles to Improve Question Answering. 2007. In: *Proceedings of the 2007 Joint Conference on Empirical Methods in Natural Language Processing and Computational Natural Language Learning*, pp. 12–21.

Sleator D. D. and Temperley D. Parsing English with a Link Grammar 1991. *Technical Report CMU-CS-91-196*, Department of Computer Science, Carnegie Mellon University.

Smeaton A. F., O'Donnell R. and Kelledy F. Indexing Structures Derived from Syntax in TREC-3: System Description. 1995. In: *The Third Text REtrieval Conference (TREC-3)*, pp. 55–67.

Song F. and Croft W. B. A General Language Model for Information Retrieval. 1999. In: *CIKM '99: Proceedings of the Eighth International Conference on Information and Knowledge Management*, pp. 316–321, New York, NY, USA, ACM.

Automatically Generating Term-frequency-induced Taxonomies

Karin Murthy **Tanveer A Faruquie** **L Venkata Subramaniam**
K Hima Prasad **Mukesh Mohania**
IBM Research - India
{karinmur|ftanveer|lvsubram|hkaranam|mkmukesh}@in.ibm.com

Abstract

We propose a novel method to automatically acquire a term-frequency-based taxonomy from a corpus using an unsupervised method. A term-frequency-based taxonomy is useful for application domains where the frequency with which terms occur on their own and in combination with other terms imposes a natural term hierarchy. We highlight an application for our approach and demonstrate its effectiveness and robustness in extracting knowledge from real-world data.

1 Introduction

Taxonomy deduction is an important task to understand and manage information. However, building taxonomies manually for specific domains or data sources is time consuming and expensive. Techniques to automatically deduce a taxonomy in an unsupervised manner are thus indispensable. Automatic deduction of taxonomies consist of two tasks: extracting relevant terms to represent concepts of the taxonomy and discovering relationships between concepts. For unstructured text, the extraction of relevant terms relies on information extraction methods (Etzioni et al., 2005).

The relationship extraction task can be classified into two categories. Approaches in the first category use lexical-syntactic formulation to define patterns, either manually (Kozareva et al., 2008) or automatically (Girju et al., 2006), and apply those patterns to mine instances of the patterns. Though producing accurate results, these approaches usually have low coverage for many domains and suffer from the problem of inconsistency between terms when connecting the instances as chains to form a taxonomy. The second category of approaches uses clustering to discover terms and the relationships between them (Roy and Subramaniam, 2006), even if those relationships do not explicitly appear in the text. Though these methods tackle inconsistency by addressing taxonomy deduction globally, the relationships extracted are often difficult to interpret by humans.

We show that for certain domains, the frequency with which terms appear in a corpus on their own and in conjunction with other terms induces a natural taxonomy. We formally define the concept of a term-frequency-based taxonomy and show its applicability for an example application. We present an unsupervised method to generate such a taxonomy from scratch and outline how domain-specific constraints can easily be integrated into the generation process. An advantage of the new method is that it can also be used to extend an existing taxonomy.

We evaluated our method on a large corpus of real-life addresses. For addresses from emerging geographies no standard postal address scheme exists and our objective was to produce a postal taxonomy that is useful in standardizing addresses (Kothari et al., 2010). Specifically, the experiments were designed to investigate the effectiveness of our approach on noisy terms with lots of variations. The results show that our method is able to induce a taxonomy without using any kind of lexical-semantic patterns.

2 Related Work

One approach for taxonomy deduction is to use explicit expressions (Iwaska et al., 2000) or lexical and semantic patterns such as *is a* (Snow et al., 2004), *similar usage* (Kozareva et al., 2008), *synonyms and antonyms* (Lin et al., 2003), *purpose* (Cimiano and Wenderoth, 2007), and *employed by* (Bunescu and Mooney, 2007) to extract and organize terms. The quality of extraction is often controlled using statistical measures (Pantel and Pennacchiotti, 2006) and external resources such as wordnet (Girju et al., 2006). However, there are

Proceedings of the ACL 2010 Conference Short Papers, pages 126–131,
Uppsala, Sweden, 11-16 July 2010. ©2010 Association for Computational Linguistics

domains (such as the one introduced in Section 3.2) where the text does not allow the derivation of linguistic relations.

Supervised methods for taxonomy induction provide training instances with global semantic information about concepts (Fleischman and Hovy, 2002) and use bootstrapping to induce new seeds to extract further patterns (Cimiano et al., 2005). Semi-supervised approaches start with known terms belonging to a category, construct context vectors of classified terms, and associate categories to previously unclassified terms depending on the similarity of their context (Tanev and Magnini, 2006). However, providing training data and hand-crafted patterns can be tedious. Moreover in some domains (such as the one presented in Section 3.2) it is not possible to construct a context vector or determine the replacement fit.

Unsupervised methods use clustering of word-context vectors (Lin, 1998), co-occurrence (Yang and Callan, 2008), and conjunction features (Caraballo, 1999) to discover implicit relationships. However, these approaches do not perform well for small corpora. Also, it is difficult to label the obtained clusters which poses challenges for evaluation. To avoid these problems, incremental clustering approaches have been proposed (Yang and Callan, 2009). Recently, lexical entailment has been used where the term is assigned to a category if its occurrence in the corpus can be replaced by the lexicalization of the category (Giuliano and Gliozzo, 2008). In our method, terms are incrementally added to the taxonomy based on their support and context.

Association rule mining (Agrawal and Srikant, 1994) discovers interesting relations between terms, based on the frequency with which terms appear together. However, the amount of patterns generated is often huge and constructing a taxonomy from all the patterns can be challenging. In our approach, we employ similar concepts but make taxonomy construction part of the relationship discovery process.

3 Term-frequency-induced Taxonomies

For some application domains, a taxonomy is induced by the frequency in which terms appear in a corpus on their own and in combination with other terms. We first introduce the problem formally and then motivate it with an example application.

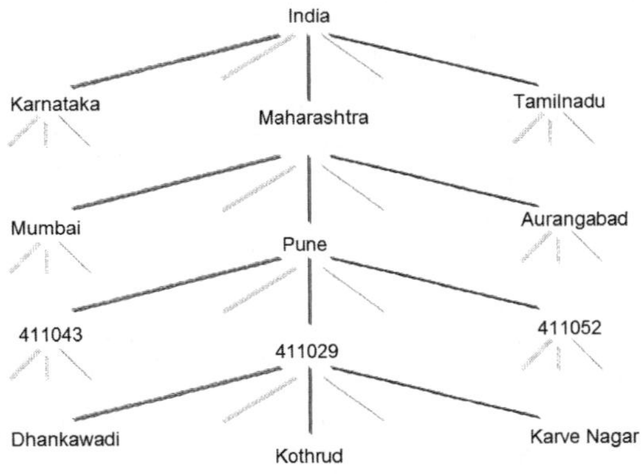

Figure 1: Part of an address taxonomy

3.1 Definition

Let C be a corpus of records r. Each record is represented as a set of terms t. Let $T = \{t \mid t \in r \wedge r \in C\}$ be the set of all terms of C. Let $f(t)$ denote the frequency of term t, that is the number of records in C that contain t. Let $F(t, T^+, T^-)$ denote the *frequency* of term t given a set of must-also-appear terms T^+ and a set of cannot-also-appear terms T^-. $F(t, T^+, T^-) = |\{r \in C \mid t \in r \wedge \forall t' \in T^+ : t' \in r \wedge \forall t' \in T^- : t' \notin r\}|$.

A term-frequency-induced taxonomy (TFIT), is an ordered tree over terms in T. For a node n in the tree, $n.t$ is the term at n, $A(n)$ the ancestors of n, and $P(n)$ the predecessors of n.

A TFIT has a root node with the special term $\perp$ and the conditional frequency ∞. The following condition is true for any other node n: $\forall t \in T, F(n.t, A(n), P(n)) \geq F(t, A(n), P(n))$. That is, each node's term has the highest conditional frequency in the context of the node's ancestors and predecessors. Only terms with a conditional frequency above zero are added to a TFIT.

We show in Section 4 how a TFIT taxonomy can be automatically induced from a given corpus. But before that, we show that TFITs are useful in practice and reflect a natural ordering of terms for application domains where the concept hierarchy is expressed through the frequency in which terms appear.

3.2 Example Domain: Address Data

An address taxonomy is a key enabler for address standardization. Figure 1 shows part of such an address taxonomy where the root contains the most generic term and leaf-level nodes contain the most specific terms. For emerging economies building a standardized address taxonomy is a huge chal-

Row	Term	Part of address	Category
1	D-15	house number	alphanumerical
2	Rawal	building name	proper noun
3	Complex	building name	proper noun
4	Behind	landmark	marker
5	Hotel	landmark	marker
6	Ruchira	landmark	proper noun
7	Katre	street	proper noun
8	Road	street	marker
9	Jeevan	area	proper noun
10	Nagar	area	marker
11	Andheri	city (taluk)	proper noun
12	East	city (taluk)	direction
13	Mumbai	district	proper noun
14	Maharashtra	state	proper noun
15	400069	ZIP code	6 digit string

Table 1: Example of a tokenized address

lenge. First, new areas and with it new addresses constantly emerge. Second, there are very limited conventions for specifying an address (Faruquie et al., 2010). However, while many developing countries do not have a postal taxonomy, there is often no lack of address data to learn a taxonomy from.

Column 2 of Table 1 shows an example of an Indian address. Although Indian addresses tend to follow the general principal that more specific information is mentioned earlier, there is no fixed order for different elements of an address. For example, the ZIP code of an address may be mentioned before or after the state information and, although ZIP code information is more specific than city information, it is generally mentioned later in the address. Also, while ZIP codes often exist, their use by people is very limited. Instead, people tend to mention copious amounts of landmark information (see for example rows 4-6 in Table 1).

Taking all this into account, there is often not enough structure available to automatically infer a taxonomy purely based on the structural or semantic aspects of an address. However, for address data, the general-to-specific concept hierarchy is reflected in the frequency with which terms appear on their own and together with other terms.

It mostly holds that $f(s) > f(d) > f(c) > f(z)$ where s is a state name, d is a district name, c is a city name, and z is a ZIP code. However, sometimes the name of a large city may be more frequent than the name of a small state. For example, in a given corpus, the term 'Houston' (a populous US city) may appear more frequent than the term 'Vermont' (a small US state). To avoid that 'Houston' is picked as a node at the first level of the taxonomy (which should only contain states), the conditional-frequency constraint introduced in Section 3.1 is enforced for each node in a TFIT. 'Houston's state 'Texas' (which is more frequent) is picked before 'Houston'. After 'Texas' is picked it appears in the "cannot-also-appear"' list for all further siblings on the first level, thus giving 'Houston' has a conditional frequency of zero.

We show in Section 5 that an address taxonomy can be inferred by generating a TFIT taxonomy.

4 Automatically Generating TFITs

We describe a basic algorithm to generate a TFIT and then show extensions to adapt to different application domains.

4.1 Base Algorithm

Algorithm 1 Algorithm for generating a TFIT.

// For initialization T^+, T^- are empty
// For initialization l,w are zero
genTFIT(T^+, T^-, C, l, w)
// select most frequent term
$t_{next} = t_j$ with $F(t_j, T^+, T^-)$ is maximal amongst all $t_j \in C$;
$f_{next} = F(t_{next}, T^+, T^-)$;
if $f_{next} \geq$ support **then**
  //Output node (t_j, l, w)
  ...
  // Generate child node
  genTFIT($T^+ \cup \{t_{next}\}, T^-, C, l+1, w$)
  // Generate sibling node
  genTFIT($T^+, T^- \cup \{t_{next}\}, C, l, w+1$)
end if

To generate a TFIT taxonomy as defined in Section 3.1 we recursively pick the most frequent term given previously chosen terms. The basic algorithm $genTFIT$ is sketched out in Algorithm 1. When $genTFIT$ is called the first time, T^+ and T^- are empty and both level l and width w are zero. With each call of $genTFIT$ a new node n in the taxonomy is created with (t, l, w) where t is the most frequent term given T^+ and T^- and l and w capture the position in the taxonomy. $genTFIT$ is recursively called to generate a child of n and a sibling for n.

The only input parameter required by our algorithm is $support$. Instead of adding all terms with a conditional frequency above zero, we only add terms with a conditional frequency equal to or higher than $support$. The $support$ parameter controls the precision of the resulting TFIT and also the runtime of the algorithm. Increasing $support$ increases the precision but also lowers the recall.

4.2 Integrating Constraints

Structural as well as semantic constraints can easily be integrated into the TFIT generation.

We distinguish between taxonomy-level and node-level structural constraints. For example, limiting the depth of the taxonomy by introducing a $maxLevel$ constraint and checking before each recursive call if $maxLevel$ is reached, is a taxonomy-level constraint. A node-level constraint applies to each node and affects the way the frequency of terms is determined.

For our example application, we introduce the following node-level constraint: at each node we only count terms that appear at specific positions in records with respect to the current level of the node. Specifically, we slide (or incrementally increase) a window over the address records starting from the end. For example, when picking the term 'Washington' as a state name, occurrences of 'Washington' as city or street name are ignored. Using a window instead of an exact position accounts for positional variability. Also, to accommodate varying amounts of landmark information we length-normalize the position of terms. That is, we divide all positions in an address by the average length of an address (which is 10 for our 40 Million addresses). Accordingly, we adjust the size of the window and use increments of 0.1 for sliding (or increasing) the window.

In addition to syntactical constraints, semantic constraints can be integrated by classifying terms for use when picking the next frequent term. In our example application, markers tend to appear much more often than any proper noun. For example, the term 'Road' appears in almost all addresses, and might be picked up as the most frequent term very early in the process. Thus, it is beneficial to ignore marker terms during taxonomy generation and adding them as a post-processing step.

4.3 Handling Noise

The approach we propose naturally handles noise by ignoring it, unless the noise level exceeds the support threshold. Misspelled terms are generally infrequent and will as such not become part of the taxonomy. The same applies to incorrect addresses. Incomplete addresses partially contribute to the taxonomy and only cause a problem if the same information is missing too often. For example, if more than $support$ addresses with the city 'Houston' are missing the state 'Texas', then 'Houston' may become a node at the first level and appear to be a state. Generally, such cases only appear at the far right of the taxonomy.

5 Evaluation

We present an evaluation of our approach for address data from an emerging economy. We implemented our algorithm in Java and store the records in a DB2 database. We rely on the DB2 optimizer to efficiently retrieve the next frequent term.

5.1 Dataset

The results are based on 40 Million Indian addresses. Each address record was given to us as a single string and was first tokenized into a sequence of terms as shown in Table 1. In a second step, we addressed spelling variations. There is no fixed way of transliterating Indian alphabets to English and most Indian proper nouns have various spellings in English. We used tools to detect synonyms with the same context to generate a list of rules to map terms to a standard form (Lin, 1998). For example, in Table 1 'Maharashtra' can also be spelled 'Maharastra'. We also used a list of keywords to classify some terms as markers such as 'Road' and 'Nagar' shown in Table 1.

Our evaluation consists of two parts. First, we show results for constructing a TFIT from scratch. To evaluate the precision and recall we also retrieved post office addresses from India Post[1], cleaned them, and organized them in a tree.

Second, we use our approach to enrich the existing hierarchy created from post office addresses with additional area terms. To validate the result, we also retrieved data about which area names appear within a ZIP code.[2] We also verified whether Google Maps shows an area on its map.[3]

5.2 Taxonomy Generation

We generated a taxonomy O using all 40 million addresses. We compare the terms assigned to category levels *district* and *taluk*[4] in O with the tree P constructed from post office addresses. Each district and taluk has at least one post office. Thus P covers all districts and taluks and allows us to test coverage and precision. We compute the precision and recall for each category level CL as

[1] http://www.indiapost.gov.in/Pin/pinsearch.aspx

[2] http://www.whereincity.com/india/pincode/search

[3] maps.google.com

[4] Administrative division in some South-Asian countries.

Support		Recall %	Precision %
100	District	93.9	57.4
	Taluk	50.9	60.5
200	District	87.9	64.4
	Taluk	49.6	66.1

Table 2: Precision and recall for categorizing terms belonging to the state Maharashtra

$$Recall_{CL} = \frac{\#\ correct\ paths\ from\ root\ to\ CL\ in\ O}{\#\ paths\ from\ root\ to\ CL\ in\ P}$$

$$Precision_{CL} = \frac{\#\ correct\ paths\ from\ root\ to\ CL\ in\ O}{\#\ paths\ from\ root\ to\ CL\ in\ O}$$

Table 2 shows precision and recall for district and taluk for the large state Maharashtra. Recall is good for district. For taluk it is lower because a major part of the data belongs to urban areas where taluk information is missing. The precision seems to be low but it has to be noted that in almost 75% of the addresses either district or taluk information is missing or noisy. Given that, we were able to recover a significant portion of the knowledge structure.

We also examined a branch for a smaller state (Kerala). Again, both districts and taluks appear at the next level of the taxonomy. For a support of 200 there are 19 entries in O of which all but two appear in P as district or taluk. One entry is a taluk that actually belongs to Maharashtra and one entry is a name variation of a taluk in P. There were not enough addresses to get a good coverage of all districts and taluks.

5.3 Taxonomy Augmentation

We used P and ran our algorithm for each branch in P to include area information. We focus our evaluation on the city Mumbai. The recall is low because many addresses do not mention a ZIP code or use an incorrect ZIP code. However, the precision is good implying that our approach works even in the presence of large amounts of noise.

Table 3 shows the results for ZIP code 400002 and 400004 for a support of 100. We get similar results for other ZIP codes. For each detected area we compared whether the area is also listed on whereincity.com, part of a post office name (PO), or shown on google maps. All but four areas found are confirmed by at least one of the three external sources. Out of the unconfirmed terms $Fanaswadi$ and $MarineDrive$ seem to be genuine area names but we could not confirm $DhakurdwarRoad$. The term th is due to our tokenization process. 16 correct terms out of 18 terms results in a precision of 89%.

Area	Whereincity	PO	Google
Bhuleshwar	yes	no	yes
Chira Bazar	yes	no	yes
Dhobi Talao	no	no	yes
Fanaswadi	no	no	no
Kalbadevi Road	yes	yes	yes
Marine Drive	no	no	no
Marine Lines	yes	yes	yes
Princess Street	no	no	yes
th	no	no	no
Thakurdwar Road	no	no	no
Zaveri Bazar	yes	no	yes
Charni Road	no	yes	no
Girgaon	yes	yes	yes
Khadilkar Road	yes	no	yes
Khetwadi Road	yes	no	no
Kumbharwada	no	no	yes
Opera House	no	yes	no
Prathna Samaj	yes	no	no

Table 3: Areas found for ZIP code 400002 (top) and 400004 (bottom)

We also ran experiments to measure the coverage of area detection for Mumbai without using ZIP codes. Initializing our algorithm with $Maharshtra$ and $Mumbai$ yielded over 100 areas with a support of 300 and more. However, again the precision is low because quite a few of those areas are actually taluk names.

Using a large number of addresses is necessary to achieve good recall and precision.

6 Conclusion

In this paper, we presented a novel approach to generate a taxonomy for data where terms exhibit an inherent frequency-based hierarchy. We showed that term frequency can be used to generate a meaningful taxonomy from address records. The presented approach can also be used to extend an existing taxonomy which is a big advantage for emerging countries where geographical areas evolve continuously.

While we have evaluated our approach on address data, it is applicable to all data sources where the inherent hierarchical structure is encoded in the frequency with which terms appear on their own and together with other terms. Preliminary experiments on real-time analyst's stock market tips [5] produced a taxonomy of (TV station, Analyst, Affiliation) with decent precision and recall.

[5] See Live Market voices at: http://money.rediff.com/money/jsp/markets_home.jsp

References

Rakesh Agrawal and Ramakrishnan Srikant. 1994. Fast algorithms for mining association rules in large databases. In *Proceedings of the 20th International Conference on Very Large Data Bases*, pages 487–499.

Razvan C. Bunescu and Raymond J. Mooney. 2007. Learning to extract relations from the web using minimal supervision. In *Proceedings of the 45th Annual Meeting of the Association of Computational Linguistics*, pages 576–583.

Sharon A. Caraballo. 1999. Automatic construction of a hypernym-labeled noun hierarchy from text. In *Proceedings of the 37th Annual Meeting of the Association for Computational Linguistics on Computational Linguistics*, pages 120–126.

Philipp Cimiano and Johanna Wenderoth. 2007. Automatic acquisition of ranked qualia structures from the web. In *Proceedings of the 45th Annual Meeting of the Association for Computational Linguistics*, pages 888–895.

Philipp Cimiano, Günter Ladwig, and Steffen Staab. 2005. Gimme' the context: context-driven automatic semantic annotation with c-pankow. In *Proceedings of the 14th International Conference on World Wide Web*, pages 332–341.

Oren Etzioni, Michael Cafarella, Doug Downey, Ana-Maria Popescu, Tal Shaked, Stephen Soderland, Daniel S. Weld, and Alexander Yates. 2005. Unsupervised named-entity extraction from the web: an experimental study. *Artificial Intelligence*, 165(1):91–134.

Tanveer A. Faruquie, K. Hima Prasad, L. Venkata Subramaniam, Mukesh K. Mohania, Girish Venkatachaliah, Shrinivas Kulkarni, and Pramit Basu. 2010. Data cleansing as a transient service. In *Proceedings of the 26th International Conference on Data Engineering*, pages 1025–1036.

Michael Fleischman and Eduard Hovy. 2002. Fine grained classification of named entities. In *Proceedings of the 19th International Conference on Computational Linguistics*, pages 1–7.

Roxana Girju, Adriana Badulescu, and Dan Moldovan. 2006. Automatic discovery of part-whole relations. *Computational Linguistics*, 32(1):83–135.

Claudio Giuliano and Alfio Gliozzo. 2008. Instance-based ontology population exploiting named-entity substitution. In *Proceedings of the 22nd International Conference on Computational Linguistics*, pages 265–272.

Lucja M. Iwaska, Naveen Mata, and Kellyn Kruger. 2000. Fully automatic acquisition of taxonomic knowledge from large corpora of texts. In Lucja M. Iwaska and Stuart C. Shapiro, editors, *Natural Language Processing and Knowledge Representation: Language for Knowledge and Knowledge for Language*, pages 335–345.

Govind Kothari, Tanveer A Faruquie, L V Subramaniam, K H Prasad, and Mukesh Mohania. 2010. Transfer of supervision for improved address standardization. In *Proceedings of the 20th International Conference on Pattern Recognition*.

Zornitsa Kozareva, Ellen Riloff, and Eduard Hovy. 2008. Semantic class learning from the web with hyponym pattern linkage graphs. In *Proceedings of the 46th Annual Meeting of the Association for Computational Linguistics: Human Language Technologies*, pages 1048–1056.

Dekang Lin, Shaojun Zhao, Lijuan Qin, and Ming Zhou. 2003. Identifying synonyms among distributionally similar words. In *Proceedings of the 18th International Joint Conference on Artificial Intelligence*, pages 1492–1493.

Dekang Lin. 1998. Automatic retrieval and clustering of similar words. In *Proceedings of the 17th International Conference on Computational Linguistics*, pages 768–774.

Patrick Pantel and Marco Pennacchiotti. 2006. Espresso: leveraging generic patterns for automatically harvesting semantic relations. In *Proceedings of the 21st International Conference on Computational Linguistics and the 44th Annual Meeting of the Association for Computational Linguistics*, pages 113–120.

Shourya Roy and L Venkata Subramaniam. 2006. Automatic generation of domain models for call centers from noisy transcriptions. In *Proceedings of the 21st International Conference on Computational Linguistics and the 44th Annual Meeting of the Association for Computational Linguistics*, pages 737–744.

Rion Snow, Daniel Jurafsky, and Andrew Y. Ng. 2004. Learning syntactic patterns for automatic hypernym discovery. In *Advances in Neural Information Processing Systems*, pages 1297–1304.

Hristo Tanev and Bernardo Magnini. 2006. Weakly supervised approaches for ontology population. In *Proceedings of the 11th Conference of the European Chapter of the Association for Computational Linguistics*, pages 3–7.

Hui Yang and Jamie Callan. 2008. Learning the distance metric in a personal ontology. In *Proceeding of the 2nd International Workshop on Ontologies and Information Systems for the Semantic Web*, pages 17–24.

Hui Yang and Jamie Callan. 2009. A metric-based framework for automatic taxonomy induction. In *Proceedings of the Joint Conference of the 47th Annual Meeting of the ACL and the 4th International Joint Conference on Natural Language Processing of the AFNLP*, pages 271–279.

Complexity assumptions in ontology verbalisation

Richard Power
Department of Computing
Open University, UK
r.power@open.ac.uk

Abstract

We describe the strategy currently pursued for verbalising OWL ontologies by sentences in Controlled Natural Language (i.e., combining *generic* rules for realising logical patterns with *ontology-specific* lexicons for realising atomic terms for individuals, classes, and properties) and argue that its success depends on assumptions about the complexity of terms and axioms in the ontology. We then show, through analysis of a corpus of ontologies, that although these assumptions could in principle be violated, they are overwhelmingly respected in practice by ontology developers.

1 Introduction

Since OWL (Web Ontology Language) was adopted as a standard in 2004, researchers have sought ways of mediating between the (decidedly cumbersome) raw code and the human users who aspire to view or edit it. Among the solutions that have been proposed are more readable coding formats such as Manchester OWL Syntax (Horridge et al., 2006), and graphical interfaces such as Protégé (Knublauch et al., 2004); more speculatively, several research groups have explored ways of mapping between OWL and controlled English, with the aim of presenting ontologies (both for viewing and editing) in natural language (Schwitter and Tilbrook, 2004; Sun and Mellish, 2006; Kaljurand and Fuchs, 2007; Hart et al., 2008). In this paper we uncover and test some assumptions on which this latter approach is based.

Historically, ontology verbalisation evolved from a more general tradition (predating OWL and the Semantic Web) that aimed to support knowledge formation by automatic interpretation of texts authored in Controlled Natural Languages (Fuchs and Schwitter, 1995). The idea is to establish a mapping from a formal language to a natural subset of English, so that any sentence conforming to the Controlled Natural Language (CNL) can be assigned a single interpretation in the formal language — and conversely, any well-formed statement in the formal language can be realised in the CNL. With the advent of OWL, some of these CNLs were rapidly adapted to the new opportunity: part of *Attempto Controlled English* (ACE) was mapped to OWL (Kaljurand and Fuchs, 2007), and *Processable English* (PENG) evolved to *Sydney OWL Syntax* (SOS) (Cregan et al., 2007). In addition, new CNLs were developed specifically for editing OWL ontologies, such as *Rabbit* (Hart et al., 2008) and *Controlled Language for Ontology Editing* (CLOnE) (Funk et al., 2007).

In detail, these CNLs display some variations: thus an inclusion relationship between the classes `Admiral` and `Sailor` would be expressed by the pattern 'Admirals are a type of sailor' in CLOnE, 'Every admiral is a kind of sailor' in Rabbit, and 'Every admiral is a sailor' in ACE and SOS. However, at the level of general strategy, all the CNLs rely on the same set of assumptions concerning the mapping from natural to formal language; for convenience we will refer to these assumptions as the *consensus model*. In brief, the consensus model assumes that when an ontology is verbalised in natural language, axioms are expressed by sentences, and atomic terms are expressed by entries from the lexicon. Such a model may fail in two ways: (1) an ontology might contain axioms that cannot be described transparently by a sentence (for instance, because they contain complex Boolean expressions that lead to structural ambiguity); (2) it might contain atomic terms for which no suitable lexical entry can be found. In the remainder of this paper we first describe the consensus model in more detail, then show that although

Proceedings of the ACL 2010 Conference Short Papers, pages 132–136,
Uppsala, Sweden, 11-16 July 2010. ©2010 Association for Computational Linguistics

Logic	OWL
$C \sqcap D$	`IntersectionOf(C D)`
$\exists P.C$	`SomeValuesFrom(P C)`
$C \sqsubseteq D$	`SubClassOf(C D)`
$a \in C$	`ClassAssertion(C a)`
$[a, b] \in P$	`PropertyAssertion(P a b)`

Table 1: Common OWL expressions

in principle it is vulnerable to both the problems just mentioned, in practice these problems almost never arise.

2 Consensus model

Atomic terms in OWL (or any other language implementing description logic) are principally of three kinds, denoting either individuals, classes or properties[1]. Individuals denote entities in the domain, such as Horatio Nelson or the Battle of Trafalgar; classes denote sets of entities, such as people or battles; and properties denote relations between individuals, such as the relation *victor of* between a person and a battle.

From these basic terms, a wide range of complex expressions may be constructed for classes, properties and axioms, of which some common examples are shown in table 1. The upper part of the table presents two class constructors (C and D denote any classes; P denotes any property); by combining them we could build the following expression denoting the class of persons that command fleets[2]:

$$Person \sqcap \exists \, CommanderOf.Fleet$$

The lower half of the table presents three axiom patterns for making statements about classes and individuals (a, b denote individuals); examples of their usage are as follows:

1. $Admiral \sqsubseteq \exists \, CommanderOf.Fleet$
2. $Nelson \in Admiral$
3. $[Nelson, Trafalgar] \in VictorOf$

Note that since class expressions contain classes as constituents, they can become indefinitely complex. For instance, given the intersection $A \sqcap B$ we could replace atomic class A by a constructed class, thus obtaining perhaps $(A_1 \sqcap A_2) \sqcap B$, and so on *ad infinitum*. Moreover, since most axiom patterns contain classes as constituents, they too can become indefinitely complex.

This sketch of knowledge representation in OWL illustrates the central distinction between logical functors (e.g., `IntersectionOf`, `SubClassOf`), which belong to the W3C standard (Motik et al., 2010), and atomic terms for individuals, classes and properties (e.g., `Nelson`, `Admiral`, `VictorOf`). Perhaps the fundamental design decision of the Semantic Web is that *all domain terms remain unstandardised*, leaving ontology developers free to conceptualise the domain in any way they see fit. In the consensus verbalisation model, this distinction is reflected by dividing linguistic resources into a *generic* grammar for realising logical patterns, and an *ontology-specific* lexicon for realising atomic terms.

Consider for instance $C \sqsubseteq D$, the axiom pattern for class inclusion. This purely logical pattern can often be mapped (following ACE and SOS) to the sentence pattern 'Every [C] is a [D]', where C and D will be realised by count nouns from the lexicon if they are atomic, or further grammatical rules if they are complex. The more specific pattern $C \sqsubseteq \exists P.D$ can be expressed better by a sentence pattern based on a verb frame ('Every [C] [P]s a [D]'). All these mappings depend entirely on the OWL logical functors, and will work with any lexicalisation of atomic terms that respects the syntactic constraints of the grammar, to yield verbalisations such as the following (for axioms 1-3 above):

1. Every admiral commands a fleet.
2. Nelson is an admiral.
3. Nelson is the victor of Trafalgar.

The CNLs we have cited are more sophisticated than this, allowing a wider range of linguistic patterns (e.g., adjectives for classes), but the basic assumptions are the same. The model provides satisfactory verbalisations for the simple examples considered so far, but what happens when the axioms and atomic terms become more complex?

3 Complex terms and axioms

The distribution of content among axioms depends to some extent on stylistic decisions by ontology developers, in particular with regard to ax-

[1] If data properties are used, there will also be terms for data types and literals (e.g., numbers and strings), but for simplicity these are not considered here.

[2] In description logic notation, the constructor $C \sqcap D$ forms the intersection of two classes and corresponds to Boolean conjunction, while the existential restriction $\exists P.C$ forms the class of individuals having the relation P to one or more members of class C. Thus $Person \sqcap \exists$ $CommanderOf.Fleet$ denotes the set of individuals x such that x is a person and x commands one or more fleets.

iom size. This freedom is possible because description logics (including OWL) allow equivalent formulations using a large number of short axioms at one extreme, and a small number of long ones at the other. For many logical patterns, rules can be stated for amalgamating or splitting axioms while leaving overall content unchanged (thus ensuring that exactly the same inferences are drawn by a reasoning engine); such rules are often used in reasoning algorithms. For instance, any set of `SubClassOf` axioms can be amalgamated into a single 'metaconstraint' (Horrocks, 1997) of the form $\top \sqsubseteq M$, where $\top$ is the class containing all individuals in the domain, and M is a class to which any individual respecting the axiom set must belong[3]. Applying this transformation even to only two axioms (verbalised by 1 and 2 below) will yield an outcome (verbalised by 3) that strains human comprehension:

1. Every admiral is a sailor.
2. Every admiral commands a fleet.
3. Everything is (a) either a non-admiral or a sailor, and (b) either a non-admiral or something that commands a fleet.

An example of axiom-splitting rules is found in a computational complexity proof for the description logic $\mathcal{EL}$+ (Baader et al., 2005), which requires class inclusion axioms to be rewritten to a maximally simple 'normal form' permitting only four patterns: $A_1 \sqsubseteq A_2$, $A_1 \sqcap A_2 \sqsubseteq A_3$, $A_1 \sqsubseteq \exists P.A_2$, and $\exists P.A_1 \sqsubseteq A_2$, where P and all A_N are atomic terms. However, this simplification of axiom structure can be achieved only by introducing new atomic terms. For example, to simplify an axiom of the form $A_1 \sqsubseteq \exists P.(A_2 \sqcap A_3)$, the rewriting rules must introduce a new term $A_{23} \equiv A_2 \sqcap A_3$, through which the axiom may be rewritten as $A_1 \sqsubseteq \exists P.A_{23}$ (along with some further axioms expressing the definition of A_{23}); depending on the expressions that they replace, the content of such terms may become indefinitely complex.

A trade-off therefore results. We can often find rules for refactoring an overcomplex axiom by a number of simpler ones, but only at the cost of introducing atomic terms for which no satisfactory lexical realisation may exist. In principle, therefore, there is no guarantee that OWL ontologies

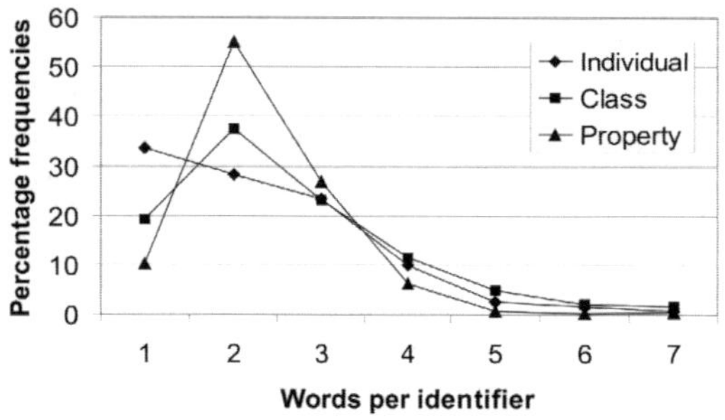

Figure 1: Identifier content

can be verbalised transparently within the assumptions of the consensus model.

4 Empirical studies of usage

We have shown that OWL syntax will permit atomic terms that cannot be lexicalised, and axioms that cannot be expressed clearly in a sentence. However, it remains possible that in practice, ontology developers use OWL in a constrained manner that favours verbalisation by the consensus model. This could happen either because the relevant constraints are psychologically intuitive to developers, or because they are somehow built into the editing tools that they use (e.g., Protégé). To investigate this possibility, we have carried out an exploratory study using a corpus of 48 ontologies mostly downloaded from the University of Manchester TONES repository (TONES, 2010). The corpus covers ontologies of varying expressivity and subject-matter, including some well-known tutorial examples (pets, pizzas) and topics of general interest (photography, travel, heraldry, wine), as well as some highly technical scientific material (mosquito anatomy, worm ontogeny, periodic table). Overall, our sample contains around 45,000 axioms and 25,000 atomic terms.

Our first analysis concerns identifier length, which we measure simply by counting the number of words in the identifying phrase. The program recovers the phrase by the following steps: (1) read an identifier (or label if one is provided[4]); (2) strip off the namespace prefix; (3) segment the resulting string into words. For the third step we

[3]For an axiom set $C_1 \sqsubseteq D_1, C_2 \sqsubseteq D_2 \ldots$, M will be $(\neg C_1 \sqcup D_1) \sqcap (\neg C_2 \sqcup D_2) \ldots$, where the class constructors $\neg C$ (complement of C) and $C \sqcup D$ (union of C and D) correspond to Boolean negation and disjunction.

[4]Some ontology developers use 'non-semantic' identifiers such as `#000123`, in which case the meaning of the identifier is indicated in an annotation assertion linking the identifier to a label.

Pattern	Frequency	Percentage
$C_A \sqsubseteq C_A$	18961	42.3%
$C_A \sqcap C_A \sqsubseteq \bot$	8225	18.3%
$C_A \sqsubseteq \exists P_A.C_A$	6211	13.9%
$[I, I] \in P_A$	4383	9.8%
$[I, L] \in D_A$	1851	4.1%
$I \in C_A$	1786	4.0%
$C_A \equiv C_A \sqcap \exists P_A.C_A$	500	1.1%
Other	2869	6.4%
Total	44786	100%

Table 2: Axiom pattern frequencies

assume that word boundaries are marked either by underline characters or by capital letters (e.g., `battle_of_trafalgar`, `BattleOfTrafalgar`), a rule that holds (in our corpus) almost without exception. The analysis (figure 1) reveals that phrase lengths are typically between one and four words (this was true of over 95% of individuals, over 90% of classes, and over 98% of properties), as in the following random selections:

> **Individuals**: beaujolais region, beringer, blue mountains, bondi beach
>
> **Classes**: abi graph plot, amps block format, abattoir, abbey church
>
> **Properties**: has activity, has address, has amino acid, has aunt in law

Our second analysis concerns axiom patterns, which we obtain by replacing all atomic terms with a symbol meaning either individual, class, property, datatype or literal. Thus for example the axioms $Admiral \sqsubseteq Sailor$ and $Dog \sqsubseteq Animal$ are both reduced to the form $C_A \sqsubseteq C_A$, where the symbol C_A means 'any atomic class term'. In this way we can count the frequencies of all the logical patterns in the corpus, abstracting from the domain-specific identifier names. The results (table 2) show an overwhelming focus on a small number of simple logical patterns[5]. Concerning class constructors, the most common by far were intersection ($C \sqcap C$) and existential restriction ($\exists P.C$); universal restriction ($\forall P.C$) was relatively rare, so that for example the pattern $C_A \sqsubseteq \forall P_A.C_A$ occurred only 54 times (0.1%)[6].

[5]Most of these patterns have been explained already; the others are disjoint classes ($C_A \sqcap C_A \sqsubseteq \bot$), equivalent classes ($C_A \equiv C_A \sqcap \exists P_A.C_A$) and data property assertion ($[I, L] \in D_A$). In the latter pattern, D_A denotes a data property, which differs from an object property (P_A) in that it ranges over literals (L) rather than individuals (I).

[6]If $C \sqsubseteq \exists P.D$ means 'Every admiral commands a fleet', $C \sqsubseteq \forall P.D$ will mean 'Every admiral commands only fleets' (this will remain true if some admirals do not command anything at all).

The preference for simple patterns was confirmed by an analysis of argument structure for the OWL functors (e.g., `SubClassOf`, `IntersectionOf`) that take classes as arguments. Overall, 85% of arguments were atomic terms rather than complex class expressions. Interestingly, there was also a clear effect of argument *position*, with the first argument of a functor being atomic rather than complex in as many as 99.4% of cases[7].

5 Discussion

Our results indicate that although in principle the consensus model cannot guarantee transparent realisations, in practice these are almost always attainable, since ontology developers overwhelmingly favour terms and axioms with relatively simple content. In an analysis of around 50 ontologies we have found that over 90% of axioms fit a mere seven patterns (table 2); the following examples show that each of these patterns can be verbalised by a clear unambiguous sentence – provided, of course, that no problems arise in lexicalising the atomic terms:

1. Every admiral is a sailor
2. No sailor is a landlubber
3. Every admiral commands a fleet
4. Nelson is the victor of Trafalgar
5. Trafalgar is dated 1805
6. Nelson is an admiral
7. An admiral is defined as a person that commands a fleet

However, since identifiers containing 3-4 words are fairly common (figure 1), we need to consider whether these formulations will remain transparent when combined with more complex lexical entries. For instance, a travel ontology in our corpus contains an axiom (fitting pattern 4) which our prototype verbalises as follows:

> 4'. West Yorkshire has as boundary the West Yorkshire Greater Manchester Boundary Fragment

The lexical entries here are far from ideal: 'has as boundary' is clumsy, and 'the West Yorkshire Greater Manchester Boundary Fragment' has as

[7]One explanation for this result could be that developers (or development tools) treat axioms as having a topic-comment structure, where the topic is usually the first argument; we intend to investigate this possibility in a further study.

many as six content words (and would benefit from hyphens). We assess the sentence as ugly but understandable, but to draw more definite conclusions one would need to perform a different kind of empirical study using human readers.

6 Conclusion

We conclude (a) that existing ontologies can be mostly verbalised using the consensus model, and (b) that an editing tool based on relatively simple linguistic patterns would not inconvenience ontology developers, but merely enforce constraints that they almost always respect anyway. These conclusions are based on analysis of identifier and axiom patterns in a corpus of ontologies; they need to be complemented by studies showing that the resulting verbalisations are understood by ontology developers and other users.

Acknowledgments

The research described in this paper was undertaken as part of the SWAT project (Semantic Web Authoring Tool), which is supported by the UK Engineering and Physical Sciences Research Council (EPSRC) grants G033579/1 (Open University) and G032459/1 (University of Manchester). Thanks are due to the anonymous ACL reviewers and to colleagues on the SWAT project for their comments and suggestions.

References

F. Baader, I. R. Horrocks, and U. Sattler. 2005. Description logics as ontology languages for the semantic web. *Lecture Notes in Artificial Intelligence*, 2605:228–248.

Anne Cregan, Rolf Schwitter, and Thomas Meyer. 2007. Sydney OWL Syntax - towards a Controlled Natural Language Syntax for OWL 1.1. In *OWLED*.

Norbert Fuchs and Rolf Schwitter. 1995. Specifying logic programs in controlled natural language. In *CLNLP-95*.

Adam Funk, Valentin Tablan, Kalina Bontcheva, Hamish Cunningham, Brian Davis, and Siegfried Handschuh. 2007. CLOnE: Controlled Language for Ontology Editing. In *6th International and 2nd Asian Semantic Web Conference (ISWC2007+ASWC2007)*, pages 141–154, November.

Glen Hart, Martina Johnson, and Catherine Dolbear. 2008. Rabbit: Developing a control natural language for authoring ontologies. In *ESWC*, pages 348–360.

Matthew Horridge, Nicholas Drummond, John Goodwin, Alan Rector, Robert Stevens, and Hai Wang. 2006. The Manchester OWL syntax. In *OWL: Experiences and Directions (OWLED'06)*, Athens, Georgia. CEUR.

Ian Horrocks. 1997. *Optimising Tableaux Decision Procedures for Description Logics*. Ph.D. thesis, University of Manchester.

K. Kaljurand and N. Fuchs. 2007. Verbalizing OWL in Attempto Controlled English. In *Proceedings of OWL: Experiences and Directions*, Innsbruck, Austria.

Holger Knublauch, Ray W. Fergerson, Natalya Fridman Noy, and Mark A. Musen. 2004. The Protégé OWL Plugin: An Open Development Environment for Semantic Web Applications. In *International Semantic Web Conference*, pages 229–243.

Boris Motik, Peter F. Patel-Schneider, and Bijan Parsia. 2010. OWL 2 web ontology language: Structural specification and functional-style syntax. http://www.w3.org/TR/owl2-syntax/. 21st April 2010.

R. Schwitter and M. Tilbrook. 2004. Controlled natural language meets the semantic web. In *Proceedings of the Australasian Language Technology Workshop*, pages 55–62, Macquarie University.

X. Sun and C. Mellish. 2006. Domain Independent Sentence Generation from RDF Representations for the Semantic Web. In *Proceedings of the Combined Workshop on Language-Enabled Educational Technology and Development and Evaluation of Robust Spoken Dialogue Systems (ECAI06)*, Riva del Garda, Italy.

TONES. 2010. The TONES ontology repository. http://owl.cs.manchester.ac.uk/repository/browser. Last accessed: 21st April 2010.

Word Alignment with Synonym Regularization

Hiroyuki Shindo, Akinori Fujino, and **Masaaki Nagata**
NTT Communication Science Laboratories, NTT Corp.
2-4 Hikaridai Seika-cho Soraku-gun Kyoto 619-0237 Japan
{shindo,a.fujino}@cslab.kecl.ntt.co.jp
nagata.masaaki@lab.ntt.co.jp

Abstract

We present a novel framework for word alignment that incorporates synonym knowledge collected from monolingual linguistic resources in a bilingual probabilistic model. Synonym information is helpful for word alignment because we can expect a synonym to correspond to the same word in a different language. We design a generative model for word alignment that uses synonym information as a regularization term. The experimental results show that our proposed method significantly improves word alignment quality.

1 Introduction

Word alignment is an essential step in most phrase and syntax based statistical machine translation (SMT). It is an inference problem of word correspondences between different languages given parallel sentence pairs. Accurate word alignment can induce high quality phrase detection and translation probability, which leads to a significant improvement in SMT performance. Many word alignment approaches based on generative models have been proposed and they learn from bilingual sentences in an unsupervised manner (Vogel et al., 1996; Och and Ney, 2003; Fraser and Marcu, 2007).

One way to improve word alignment quality is to add linguistic knowledge derived from a monolingual corpus. This monolingual knowledge makes it easier to determine corresponding words correctly. For instance, functional words in one language tend to correspond to functional words in another language (Deng and Gao, 2007), and the syntactic dependency of words in each language can help the alignment process (Ma et al., 2008). It has been shown that such *grammatical* information works as a constraint in word alignment models and improves word alignment quality.

A large number of monolingual *lexical* semantic resources such as WordNet (Miller, 1995) have been constructed in more than fifty languages (Sagot and Fiser, 2008). They include word-level relations such as synonyms, hypernyms and hyponyms. Synonym information is particularly helpful for word alignment because we can expect a synonym to correspond to the same word in a different language. In this paper, we explore a method for using synonym information effectively to improve word alignment quality.

In general, synonym relations are defined in terms of word sense, not in terms of word form. In other words, synonym relations are usually context or domain dependent. For instance, 'head' and 'chief' are synonyms in contexts referring to working environment, while 'head' and 'forefront' are synonyms in contexts referring to physical positions. It is difficult, however, to imagine a context where 'chief' and 'forefront' are synonyms. Therefore, it is easy to imagine that simply replacing all occurrences of 'chief' and 'forefront' with 'head' do sometimes harm with word alignment accuracy, and we have to model either the context or senses of words.

We propose a novel method that incorporates synonyms from monolingual resources in a bilingual word alignment model. We formulate a synonym pair generative model with a topic variable and use this model as a regularization term with a bilingual word alignment model. The topic variable in our synonym model is helpful for disambiguating the meanings of synonyms. We extend HM-BiTAM, which is a HMM-based word alignment model with a latent topic, with a novel synonym pair generative model. We applied the proposed method to an English-French word alignment task and successfully improved the word

Proceedings of the ACL 2010 Conference Short Papers, pages 137–141,
Uppsala, Sweden, 11-16 July 2010.

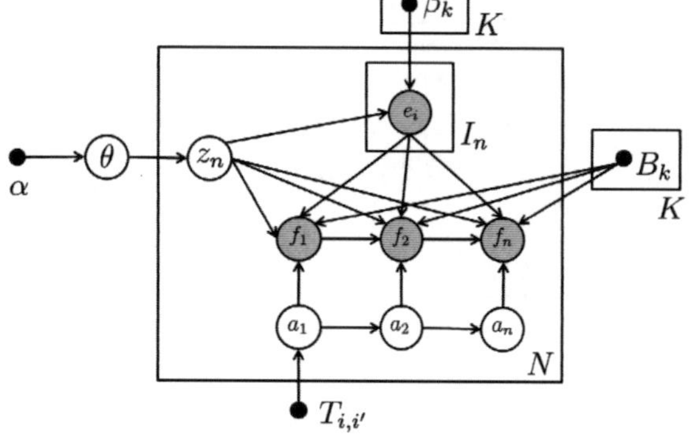

Figure 1: Graphical model of HM-BiTAM

alignment quality.

2 Bilingual Word Alignment Model

In this section, we review a conventional generative word alignment model, HM-BiTAM (Zhao and Xing, 2008).

HM-BiTAM is a bilingual generative model with topic z, alignment a and topic weight vector θ as latent variables. Topic variables such as 'science' or 'economy' assigned to individual sentences help to disambiguate the meanings of words. HM-BiTAM assumes that the nth bilingual sentence pair, (E_n, F_n), is generated under a given latent topic $z_n \in \{1, \ldots, k, \ldots, K\}$, where K is the number of latent topics. Let N be the number of sentence pairs, and I_n and J_n be the lengths of E_n and F_n, respectively. In this framework, all of the bilingual sentence pairs $\{E, F\} = \{(E_n, F_n)\}_{n=1}^{N}$ are generated as follows.

1. $\theta \sim Dirichlet\,(\alpha)$: sample topic-weight vector
2. For each sentence pair (E_n, F_n)
   (a) $z_n \sim Multinomial\,(\theta)$: sample the topic
   (b) $e_{n,i:I_n}\,|z_n \sim p\,(E_n\,|z_n; \beta)$: sample English words from a monolingual unigram model given topic z_n
   (c) For each position $j_n = 1, \ldots, J_n$
      i. $a_{j_n} \sim p\,(a_{j_n}\,|a_{j_n-1}; T)$: sample an alignment link a_{j_n} from a first order Markov process
      ii. $f_{j_n} \sim p\,(f_{j_n}\,|E_n, a_{j_n}, z_n; B)$: sample a target word f_{j_n} given an aligned source word and topic

where alignment $a_{j_n} = i$ denotes source word e_i and target word f_{j_n} are aligned. α is a parameter over the topic weight vector θ, $\beta = \{\beta_{k,e}\}$ is the source word probability given the kth topic: $p\,(e\,|z = k)$. $B = \{B_{f,e,k}\}$ represents the word translation probability from e to f under the kth topic: $p\,(f\,|e, z = k)$. $T = \{T_{i,i'}\}$ is a state transition probability of a first order Markov process. Fig. 1 shows a graphical model of HM-BiTAM.

The total likelihood of bilingual sentence pairs $\{E, F\}$ can be obtained by marginalizing out latent variables z, a and θ,

$$p\,(F, E; \Psi) = \sum_{z} \sum_{a} \int p\,(F, E, z, a, \theta; \Psi)\, d\theta, \quad (1)$$

where $\Psi = \{\alpha, \beta, T, B\}$ is a parameter set. In this model, we can infer word alignment a by maximizing the likelihood above.

3 Proposed Method

3.1 Synonym Pair Generative Model

We design a generative model for synonym pairs $\{f, f'\}$ in language F, which assumes that the synonyms are collected from monolingual linguistic resources. We assume that each synonym pair (f, f') is generated independently given the same 'sense' s. Under this assumption, the probability of synonym pair (f, f') can be formulated as,

$$p\,(f, f') \propto \sum_{s} p\,(f\,|s)\, p\,(f'\,|s)\, p\,(s)\,. \quad (2)$$

We define a pair (e, k) as a representation of the sense s, where e and k are a word in a different language E and a latent topic, respectively. It has been shown that a word e in a different language is an appropriate representation of s in synonym modeling (Bannard and Callison-Burch, 2005). We assume that adding a latent topic k for the sense is very useful for disambiguating word meaning, and thus that (e, k) gives us a good approximation of s. Under this assumption, the synonym pair generative model can be defined as follows.

$$p\left(\{f, f'\}; \tilde{\Psi}\right) \propto \prod_{(f,f')} \sum_{e,k} p(f|e, k; \tilde{\Psi}) p(f'|e, k; \tilde{\Psi}) p(e, k; \tilde{\Psi}), (3)$$

where $\tilde{\Psi}$ is the parameter set of our model.

3.2 Word Alignment with Synonym Regularization

In this section, we extend the bilingual generative model (HM-BiTAM) with our synonym pair model. Our expectation is that synonym pairs

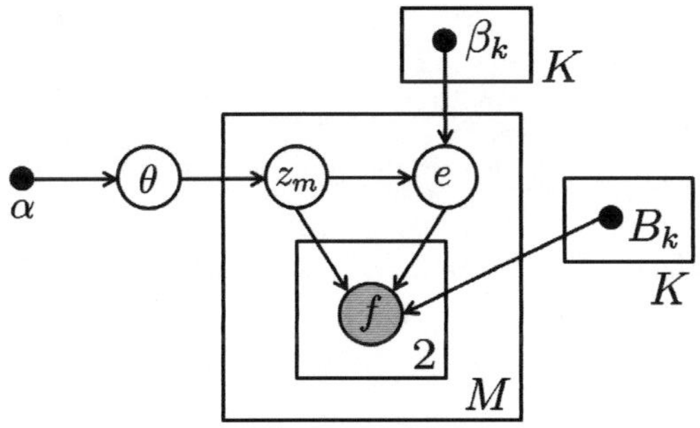

Figure 2: Graphical model of synonym pair generative process

correspond to the same word in a different language, thus they make it easy to infer accurate word alignment. HM-BiTAM and the synonym model share parameters in order to incorporate monolingual synonym information into the bilingual word alignment model. This can be achieved via reparameterizing $\widetilde{\Psi}$ in eq. 3 as,

$$p\left(f\left|e,k;\widetilde{\Psi}\right.\right) \equiv p\left(f\left|e,k;B\right.\right), \quad (4)$$

$$p\left(e,k;\widetilde{\Psi}\right) \equiv p\left(e\left|k;\beta\right.\right)p\left(k;\alpha\right). \quad (5)$$

Overall, we re-define the synonym pair model with the HM-BiTAM parameter set Ψ,

$$p(\{f,f'\};\Psi) \propto \frac{1}{\sum_{k'}\alpha_{k'}} \prod_{(f,f')} \sum_{k,e} \alpha_k \beta_{k,e} B_{f,e,k} B_{f',e,k}. \quad (6)$$

Fig. 2 shows a graphical model of the synonym pair generative process. We estimate the parameter values to maximize the likelihood of HM-BiTAM with respect to bilingual sentences and that of the synonym model with respect to synonym pairs collected from monolingual resources. Namely, the parameter estimate, $\hat{\Psi}$, is computed as

$$\hat{\Psi} = \arg\max_{\Psi} \left\{\log p(F,E;\Psi) + \zeta \log p(\{f,f'\};\Psi)\right\}, \quad (7)$$

where ζ is a regularization weight that should be set for training. We can expect that the second term of eq. 7 to constrain parameter set Ψ and avoid overfitting for the bilingual word alignment model. We resort to the variational EM approach (Bernardo et al., 2003) to infer $\hat{\Psi}$ following HM-BiTAM. We omit the parameter update equation due to lack of space.

4 Experiments

4.1 Experimental Setting

For an empirical evaluation of the proposed method, we used a bilingual parallel corpus of English-French Hansards (Mihalcea and Pedersen, 2003). The corpus consists of over 1 million sentence pairs, which include 447 manually word-aligned sentences. We selected 100 sentence pairs randomly from the manually word-aligned sentences as development data for tuning the regularization weight ζ, and used the 347 remaining sentence pairs as evaluation data. We also randomly selected 10k, 50k, and 100k sized sentence pairs from the corpus as additional training data. We ran the unsupervised training of our proposed word alignment model on the additional training data and the 347 sentence pairs of the evaluation data. Note that manual word alignment of the 347 sentence pairs was not used for the unsupervised training. After the unsupervised training, we evaluated the word alignment performance of our proposed method by comparing the manual word alignment of the 347 sentence pairs with the prediction provided by the trained model.

We collected English and French synonym pairs from WordNet 2.1 (Miller, 1995) and WOLF 0.1.4 (Sagot and Fiser, 2008), respectively. WOLF is a semantic resource constructed from the Princeton WordNet and various multilingual resources. We selected synonym pairs where both words were included in the bilingual training set.

We compared the word alignment performance of our model with that of GIZA++ 1.03 [1] (Vogel et al., 1996; Och and Ney, 2003), and HM-BiTAM (Zhao and Xing, 2008) implemented by us. GIZA++ is an implementation of IBM-model 4 and HMM, and HM-BiTAM corresponds to $\zeta = 0$ in eq. 7. We adopted $K = 3$ topics, following the setting in (Zhao and Xing, 2006).

We trained the word alignment in two directions: English to French, and French to English. The alignment results for both directions were refined with 'GROW' heuristics to yield high precision and high recall in accordance with previous work (Och and Ney, 2003; Zhao and Xing, 2006). We evaluated these results for precision, recall, F-measure and alignment error rate (AER), which are standard metrics for word alignment accuracy (Och and Ney, 2000).

[1] http://fjoch.com/GIZA++.html

10k		Precision	Recall	F-measure	AER
GIZA++	standard	0.856	0.718	0.781	0.207
	with SRH	0.874	0.720	0.789	0.198
HM-BiTAM	standard	0.869	0.788	0.826	0.169
	with SRH	0.884	0.790	0.834	0.160
Proposed		**0.941**	**0.808**	**0.870**	**0.123**

(a)

50k		Precision	Recall	F-measure	AER
GIZA++	standard	0.905	0.770	0.832	0.156
	with SRH	0.903	0.759	0.825	0.164
HM-BiTAM	standard	0.901	0.814	0.855	0.140
	with SRH	0.899	0.808	0.853	0.145
Proposed		**0.947**	**0.824**	**0.881**	**0.112**

(b)

100k		Precision	Recall	F-measure	AER
GIZA++	standard	0.925	0.791	0.853	0.136
	with SRH	**0.934**	0.803	0.864	0.126
HM-BiTAM	standard	0.898	0.851	0.874	0.124
	with SRH	0.909	0.860	0.879	0.114
Proposed		0.927	**0.862**	**0.893**	**0.103**

(c)

Table 1: Comparison of word alignment accuracy. The best results are indicated in bold type. The additional data set sizes are (a) 10k, (b) 50k, (c) 100k.

4.2 Results and Discussion

Table 1 shows the word alignment accuracy of the three methods trained with 10k, 50k, and 100k additional sentence pairs. For all settings, our proposed method outperformed other conventional methods. This result shows that synonym information is effective for improving word alignment quality as we expected.

As mentioned in Sections 1 and 3.1, the main idea of our proposed method is to introduce *latent topics* for modeling synonym pairs, and then to utilize the synonym pair model for the regularization of word alignment models. We expect the latent topics to be useful for modeling polysemous words included in synonym pairs and to enable us to incorporate synonym information effectively into word alignment models. To confirm the effect of the synonym pair model with latent topics, we also tested GIZA++ and HM-BiTAM with what we call *Synonym Replacement Heuristics (SRH)*, where all of the synonym pairs in the bilingual training sentences were simply replaced with a representative word. For instance, the words 'sick' and 'ill' in the bilingual sentences were replaced with the word 'sick'. As shown in Table 2, the number of vocabularies in the English and French data sets decreased as a result of employing the SRH.

# vocabularies		10k	50k	100k
English	standard	8578	16924	22817
	with SRH	5435	7235	13978
French	standard	10791	21872	30294
	with SRH	9737	20077	27970

Table 2: The number of vocabularies in the 10k, 50k and 100k data sets.

We show the performance of GIZA++ and HM-BiTAM with the SRH in the lines entitled "with SRH" in Table 1. The GIZA++ and HM-BiTAM with the SRH slightly outperformed the *standard* GIZA++ and HM-BiTAM for the 10k and 100k data sets, but underperformed with the 50k data set. We assume that the SRH mitigated the overfitting of these models into low-frequency word pairs in bilingual sentences, and then improved the word alignment performance. The SRH regards all of the different words coupled with the same word in the synonym pairs as synonyms. For instance, the words 'head', 'chief' and 'forefront' in the bilingual sentences are replaced with 'chief', since ('head', 'chief') and ('head', 'forefront') are synonyms. Obviously, ('chief', 'forefront') are not synonyms, which is detrimented to word alignment.

The proposed method consistently outperformed GIZA++ and HM-BiTAM with the SRH in 10k, 50k and 100k data sets in F-measure. The synonym pair model in our proposed method can automatically learn that ('head', 'chief') and ('head', 'forefront') are individual synonyms with different meanings by assigning these pairs to different topics. By sharing latent topics between the synonym pair model and the word alignment model, the synonym information incorporated in the synonym pair model is used directly for training word alignment model. The experimental results show that our proposed method was effective in improving the performance of the word alignment model by using synonym pairs including such *ambiguous* synonym words.

Finally, we discuss the data set size used for unsupervised training. As shown in Table 1, using a large number of additional sentence pairs improved the performance of all the models. In all our experimental settings, all the additional sentence pairs and the evaluation data were selected from the Hansards data set. These experimental results show that a larger number of sentence pairs was more effective in improving word alignment performance when the sentence pairs were collected from a *homogeneous* data source. However, in practice, it might be difficult to collect a large number of such homogeneous sentence pairs for a specific target domain and language pair. One direction for future work is to confirm the effect of the proposed method when training the word alignment model by using a large number of sentence pairs collected from various data sources including many topics for a specific language pair.

5 Conclusions and Future Work

We proposed a novel framework that incorporates synonyms from monolingual linguistic resources in a word alignment generative model. This approach utilizes both bilingual and monolingual synonym resources effectively for word alignment. Our proposed method uses a latent topic for bilingual sentences and monolingual synonym pairs, which is helpful in terms of word sense disambiguation. Our proposed method improved word alignment quality with both small and large data sets. Future work will involve examining the proposed method for different language pairs such as English-Chinese and English-Japanese and evaluating the impact of our proposed method on SMT performance. We will also apply our proposed method to a larger data sets of multiple domains since we can expect a further improvement in word alignment accuracy if we use more bilingual sentences and more monolingual knowledge.

References

C. Bannard and C. Callison-Burch. 2005. Paraphrasing with bilingual parallel corpora. In *Proceedings of the 43rd Annual Meeting on Association for Computational Linguistics*, pages 597–604. Association for Computational Linguistics Morristown, NJ, USA.

J. M. Bernardo, M. J. Bayarri, J. O. Berger, A. P. Dawid, D. Heckerman, A. F. M. Smith, and M. West. 2003. The variational bayesian EM algorithm for incomplete data: with application to scoring graphical model structures. In *Bayesian Statistics 7: Proceedings of the 7th Valencia International Meeting, June 2-6, 2002*, page 453. Oxford University Press, USA.

Y. Deng and Y. Gao. 2007. Guiding statistical word alignment models with prior knowledge. In *Proceedings of the 45th Annual Meeting of the Association of Computational Linguistics*, pages 1–8, Prague, Czech Republic, June. Association for Computational Linguistics.

A. Fraser and D. Marcu. 2007. Getting the structure right for word alignment: LEAF. In *Proceedings of the 2007 Joint Conference on Empirical Methods in Natural Language Processing and Computational Natural Language Learning (EMNLP-CoNLL)*, pages 51–60, Prague, Czech Republic, June. Association for Computational Linguistics.

Y. Ma, S. Ozdowska, Y. Sun, and A. Way. 2008. Improving word alignment using syntactic dependencies. In *Proceedings of the ACL-08: HLT Second Workshop on Syntax and Structure in Statistical Translation (SSST-2)*, pages 69–77, Columbus, Ohio, June. Association for Computational Linguistics.

R. Mihalcea and T. Pedersen. 2003. An evaluation exercise for word alignment. In *Proceedings of the HLT-NAACL 2003 Workshop on building and using parallel texts: data driven machine translation and beyond-Volume 3*, page 10. Association for Computational Linguistics.

G. A. Miller. 1995. WordNet: a lexical database for English. *Communications of the ACM*, 38(11):41.

F. J. Och and H. Ney. 2000. Improved statistical alignment models. In *Proceedings of the 38th Annual Meeting on Association for Computational Linguistics*, pages 440–447. Association for Computational Linguistics Morristown, NJ, USA.

F. J. Och and H. Ney. 2003. A systematic comparison of various statistical alignment models. *Computational Linguistics*, 29(1):19–51.

B. Sagot and D. Fiser. 2008. Building a free French wordnet from multilingual resources. In *Proceedings of Ontolex.*

S. Vogel, H. Ney, and C. Tillmann. 1996. HMM-based word alignment in statistical translation. In *Proceedings of the 16th Conference on Computational Linguistics-Volume 2*, pages 836–841. Association for Computational Linguistics Morristown, NJ, USA.

B. Zhao and E. P. Xing. 2006. BiTAM: Bilingual topic admixture models for word alignment. In *Proceedings of the COLING/ACL on Main Conference Poster Sessions*, page 976. Association for Computational Linguistics.

B. Zhao and E. P. Xing. 2008. HM-BiTAM: Bilingual topic exploration, word alignment, and translation. In *Advances in Neural Information Processing Systems 20*, pages 1689–1696, Cambridge, MA. MIT Press.

Better Filtration and Augmentation for Hierarchical Phrase-Based Translation Rules

Zhiyang Wang † **Yajuan Lü** † **Qun Liu** † **Young-Sook Hwang** ‡

†Key Lab. of Intelligent Information Processing
Institute of Computing Technology
Chinese Academy of Sciences
P.O. Box 2704, Beijing 100190, China
wangzhiyang@ict.ac.cn

‡HILab Convergence Technology Center
C&I Business
SKTelecom
11, Euljiro2-ga, Jung-gu, Seoul 100-999, Korea
yshwang@sktelecom.com

Abstract

This paper presents a novel filtration criterion to restrict the rule extraction for the hierarchical phrase-based translation model, where a bilingual but relaxed well-formed dependency restriction is used to filter out bad rules. Furthermore, a new feature which describes the regularity that the source/target dependency edge triggers the target/source word is also proposed. Experimental results show that, the new criteria weeds out about 40% rules while with translation performance improvement, and the new feature brings another improvement to the baseline system, especially on larger corpus.

1 Introduction

Hierarchical phrase-based (HPB) model (Chiang, 2005) is the state-of-the-art statistical machine translation (SMT) model. By looking for phrases that contain other phrases and replacing the subphrases with nonterminal symbols, it gets hierarchical rules. Hierarchical rules are more powerful than conventional phrases since they have better generalization capability and could capture long distance reordering. However, when the training corpus becomes larger, the number of rules will grow exponentially, which inevitably results in slow and memory-consuming decoding.

In this paper, we address the problem of reducing the hierarchical translation rule table resorting to the dependency information of bilingual languages. We only keep rules that both sides are *relaxed-well-formed* (RWF) dependency structure (see the definition in Section 3), and discard others which do not satisfy this constraint. In this way, about 40% bad rules are weeded out from the original rule table. However, the performance is even better than the traditional HPB translation system.

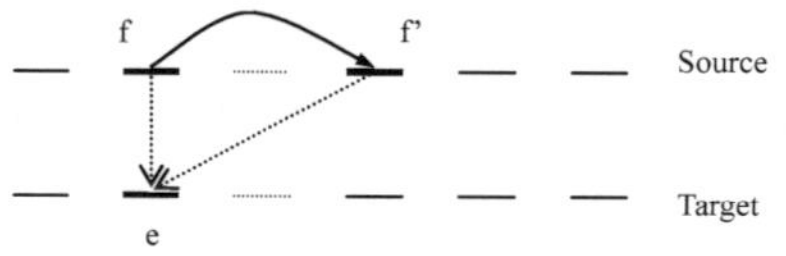

Figure 1: Solid wire reveals the dependency relation pointing from the child to the parent. Target word e is triggered by the source word f and it's head word f', $p(e|f \rightarrow f')$.

Based on the *relaxed-well-formed* dependency structure, we also introduce a new linguistic feature to enhance translation performance. In the traditional phrase-based SMT model, there are always lexical translation probabilities based on IBM model 1 (Brown et al., 1993), i.e. $p(e|f)$, namely, the target word e is triggered by the source word f. Intuitively, however, the generation of e is not only involved with f, sometimes may also be triggered by other context words in the source side. Here we assume that the dependency edge ($f \rightarrow f'$) of word f generates target word e (we call it head word trigger in Section 4). Therefore, two words in one language trigger one word in another, which provides a more sophisticated and better choice for the target word, i.e. Figure 1. Similarly, the dependency feature works well in Chinese-to-English translation task, especially on large corpus.

2 Related Work

In the past, a significant number of techniques have been presented to reduce the hierarchical rule table. He et al. (2009) just used the key phrases of source side to filter the rule table without taking advantage of any linguistic information. Iglesias et al. (2009) put rules into syntactic classes based on the number of non-terminals and patterns, and applied various filtration strategies to improve the rule table quality. Shen et al. (2008) discarded

Proceedings of the ACL 2010 Conference Short Papers, pages 142–146,
Uppsala, Sweden, 11-16 July 2010. ©2010 Association for Computational Linguistics

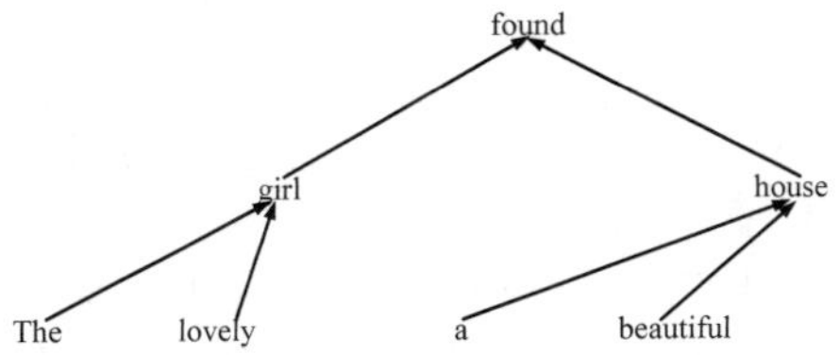

Figure 2: An example of dependency tree. The corresponding plain sentence is *The lovely girl found a beautiful house*.

most entries of the rule table by using the constraint that rules of the target-side are well-formed (WF) dependency structure, but this filtering led to degradation in translation performance. They obtained improvements by adding an additional dependency language model. The basic difference of our method from (Shen et al., 2008) is that we keep rules that both sides should be *relaxed-well-formed* dependency structure, not just the target side. Besides, our system complexity is not increased because no additional language model is introduced.

The feature of head word trigger which we apply to the log-linear model is motivated by the trigger-based approach (Hasan and Ney, 2009). Hasan and Ney (2009) introduced a second word to trigger the target word without considering any linguistic information. Furthermore, since the second word can come from any part of the sentence, there may be a prohibitively large number of parameters involved. Besides, He et al. (2008) built a maximum entropy model which combines rich context information for selecting translation rules during decoding. However, as the size of the corpus increases, the maximum entropy model will become larger. Similarly, In (Shen et al., 2009), context language model is proposed for better rule selection. Taking the dependency edge as condition, our approach is very different from previous approaches of exploring context information.

3 Relaxed-well-formed Dependency Structure

Dependency models have recently gained considerable interest in SMT (Ding and Palmer, 2005; Quirk et al., 2005; Shen et al., 2008). Dependency tree can represent richer structural information. It reveals long-distance relation between words and directly models the semantic structure of a sentence without any constituent labels. Figure 2 shows an example of a dependency tree. In this example, the word *found* is the root of the tree.

Shen et al. (2008) propose the well-formed dependency structure to filter the hierarchical rule table. A well-formed dependency structure could be either a single-rooted dependency tree or a set of sibling trees. Although most rules are discarded with the constraint that the target side should be well-formed, this filtration leads to degradation in translation performance.

As an extension of the work of (Shen et al., 2008), we introduce the so-called *relaxed-well-formed* dependency structure to filter the hierarchical rule table. Given a sentence $S = w_1w_2...w_n$. Let $d_1d_2...d_n$ represent the position of parent word for each word. For example, $d_3 = 4$ means that w_3 depends on w_4. If w_i is a root, we define $d_i = -1$.

Definition A dependency structure $w_i...w_j$ is a *relaxed-well-formed* structure, where there is $h \notin [i, j]$, all the words $w_i...w_j$ are directly or indirectly depended on w_h or -1 (here we define $h = -1$). If and only if it satisfies the following conditions

- $d_h \notin [i, j]$
- $\forall k \in [i, j],\ d_k \in [i, j]\ or\ d_k = h$

From the definition above, we can see that the *relaxed-well-formed* structure obviously covers the well-formed one. In this structure, we don't constrain that all the children of the sub-root should be complete. Let's review the dependency tree in Figure 2 as an example. Except for the well-formed structure, we could also extract *girl found a beautiful house*. Therefore, if the modifier *The lovely* changes to *The cute*, this rule also works.

4 Head Word Trigger

(Koehn et al., 2003) introduced the concept of lexical weighting to check how well words of the phrase translate to each other. Source word f aligns with target word e, according to the IBM model 1, the lexical translation probability is $p(e|f)$. However, in the sense of dependency relationship, we believe that the generation of the target word e, is not only triggered by the aligned source word f, but also associated with f 's head word f'. Therefore, the lexical translation probability becomes $p(e|f \rightarrow f')$, which of course allows for a more fine-grained lexical choice of the target word. More specifically, the probability could be estimated by the maximum likelihood (MLE) approach,

$$p(e|f \rightarrow f') = \frac{count(e, f \rightarrow f')}{\sum_{e'} count(e', f \rightarrow f')} \quad (1)$$

Given a phrase pair $\overline{f}$, $\overline{e}$ and word alignment a, and the dependent relation of the source sentence d_1^J (J is the length of the source sentence, I is the length of the target sentence). Therefore, given the lexical translation probability distribution $p(e|f \rightarrow f')$, we compute the feature score of a phrase pair ($\overline{f}$, $\overline{e}$) as

$$p(\overline{e}|\overline{f}, d_1^J, a) = \Pi_{i=1}^{|\overline{e}|} \frac{1}{|\{j|(j,i) \in a\}|} \sum_{\forall (j,i) \in a} p(e_i|f_j \rightarrow f_{d_j}) \quad (2)$$

Now we get $p(\overline{e}|\overline{f}, d_1^J, a)$, we could obtain $p(\overline{f}|\overline{e}, d_1^I, a)$ (d_1^I represents dependent relation of the target side) in the similar way. This new feature can be easily integrated into the log-linear model as lexical weighting does.

5 Experiments

In this section, we describe the experimental setting used in this work, and verify the effect of the *relaxed-well-formed* structure filtering and the new feature, head word trigger.

5.1 Experimental Setup

Experiments are carried out on the NIST[1] Chinese-English translation task with two different size of training corpora.

- **FBIS**: We use the FBIS corpus as the first training corpus, which contains 239K sentence pairs with 6.9M Chinese words and 8.9M English words.
- **GQ**: This is manually selected from the LDC[2] corpora. GQ contains 1.5M sentence pairs with 41M Chinese words and 48M English words. In fact, FBIS is the subset of GQ.

For language model, we use the SRI Language Modeling Toolkit (Stolcke, 2002) to train a 4-gram model on the first 1/3 of the Xinhua portion of GIGAWORD corpus. And we use the NIST 2002 MT evaluation test set as our development set, and NIST 2004, 2005 test sets as our blind test sets. We evaluate the translation quality using *case-insensitive* BLEU metric (Papineni et al., 2002) without dropping OOV words, and the feature weights are tuned by minimum error rate training (Och, 2003).

In order to get the dependency relation of the training corpus, we re-implement a beam-search style monolingual dependency parser according to (Nivre and Scholz, 2004). Then we use the same method suggested in (Chiang, 2005) to extract SCFG grammar rules within dependency constraint on both sides except that unaligned words are allowed at the edge of phrases. Parameters of head word trigger are estimated as described in Section 4. As a default, the maximum initial phrase length is set to 10 and the maximum rule length of the source side is set to 5. Besides, we also re-implement the decoder of Hiero (Chiang, 2007) as our baseline. In fact, we just exploit the dependency structure during the rule extraction phase. Therefore, we don't need to change the main decoding algorithm of the SMT system.

5.2 Results on FBIS Corpus

A series of experiments was done on the FBIS corpus. We first parse the bilingual languages with monolingual dependency parser respectively, and then only retain the rules that both sides are in line with the constraint of dependency structure. In Table 1, the *relaxed-well-formed* structure filtered out 35% of the rule table and the well-formed discarded 74%. *RWF* extracts additional 39% compared to *WF*, which can be seen as some kind of evidence that the rules we additional get seem common in the sense of linguistics. Compared to (Shen et al., 2008), we just use the dependency structure to constrain rules, not to maintain the tree structures to guide decoding.

Table 2 shows the translation result on FBIS. We can see that the *RWF* structure constraint can improve translation quality substantially both at development set and different test sets. On the Test04 task, it gains +0.86% BLEU, and +0.84% on Test05. Besides, we also used Shen et al. (2008)'s *WF* structure to filter both sides. Although it discard about 74% of the rule table, the

[1] www.nist.gov/speech/tests/mt

[2] It consists of six LDC corpora: LDC2002E18, LDC2003E07, LDC2003E14, Hansards part of LDC2004T07, LDC2004T08, LDC2005T06.

System	Rule table size
HPB	30,152,090
RWF	19,610,255
WF	7,742,031

Table 1: Rule table size with different constraint on FBIS. Here *HPB* refers to the baseline hierarchal phrase-based system, *RWF* means *relaxed-well-formed* constraint and *WF* represents the well-formed structure.

System	Dev02	Test04	Test05
HPB	0.3285	0.3284	0.2965
WF	0.3125	0.3218	0.2887
RWF	0.3326	**0.3370****	**0.3050**
RWF+Tri	0.3281	/	0.2965

Table 2: Results of FBIS corpus. Here *Tri* means the feature of head word trigger on both sides. And we don't test the new feature on Test04 because of the bad performance on development set. * or ** = significantly better than baseline ($p < 0.05$ or 0.01, respectively).

over-all BLEU is decreased by 0.66%-0.78% on the test sets.

As for the feature of head word trigger, it seems not work on the FBIS corpus. On Test05, it gets the same score with the baseline, but lower than *RWF* filtering. This may be caused by the data sparseness problem, which results in inaccurate parameter estimation of the new feature.

5.3 Result on GQ Corpus

In this part, we increased the size of the training corpus to check whether the feature of head word trigger works on large corpus.

We get 152M rule entries from the GQ corpus according to (Chiang, 2007)'s extraction method. If we use the *RWF* structure to constrain both sides, the number of rules is 87M, about 43% of rule entries are discarded. From Table 3, the new feature works well on two different test sets. The gain is +2.21% BLEU on Test04, and +1.33% on Test05. Compared to the result of the baseline, only using the *RWF* structure to filter performs the same as the baseline on Test05, and +0.99% gains on Test04.

System	Dev02	Test04	Test05
HPB	0.3473	0.3386	0.3206
RWF	0.3539	**0.3485****	**0.3228**
RWF+Tri	0.3540	**0.3607****	**0.3339***

Table 3: Results of GQ corpus. * or ** = significantly better than baseline ($p < 0.05$ or 0.01, respectively).

6 Conclusions

This paper proposes a simple strategy to filter the hierarchal rule table, and introduces a new feature to enhance the translation performance. We employ the *relaxed-well-formed* dependency structure to constrain both sides of the rule, and about 40% of rules are discarded with improvement of the translation performance. In order to make full use of the dependency information, we assume that the target word e is triggered by dependency edge of the corresponding source word f. And this feature works well on large parallel training corpus.

How to estimate the probability of head word trigger is very important. Here we only get the parameters in a generative way. In the future, we we are plan to exploit some discriminative approach to train parameters of this feature, such as EM algorithm (Hasan et al., 2008) or maximum entropy (He et al., 2008).

Besides, the quality of the parser is another effect for this method. As the next step, we will try to exploit bilingual knowledge to improve the monolingual parser, i.e. (Huang et al., 2009).

Acknowledgments

This work was partly supported by National Natural Science Foundation of China Contract 60873167. It was also funded by SK Telecom, Korea under the contract 4360002953. We show our special thanks to Wenbin Jiang and Shu Cai for their valuable suggestions. We also thank the anonymous reviewers for their insightful comments.

References

Peter F. Brown, Vincent J. Della Pietra, Stephen A. Della Pietra, and Robert L. Mercer. 1993. The mathematics of statistical machine translation: parameter estimation. *Comput. Linguist.*, 19(2):263–311.

David Chiang. 2005. A hierarchical phrase-based model for statistical machine translation. In *ACL*

'05: Proceedings of the 43rd Annual Meeting on Association for Computational Linguistics, pages 263–270.

David Chiang. 2007. Hierarchical phrase-based translation. *Comput. Linguist.*, 33(2):201–228.

Yuan Ding and Martha Palmer. 2005. Machine translation using probabilistic synchronous dependency insertion grammars. In *ACL '05: Proceedings of the 43rd Annual Meeting on Association for Computational Linguistics*, pages 541–548.

Saša Hasan and Hermann Ney. 2009. Comparison of extended lexicon models in search and rescoring for smt. In *NAACL '09: Proceedings of Human Language Technologies: The 2009 Annual Conference of the North American Chapter of the Association for Computational Linguistics, Companion Volume: Short Papers*, pages 17–20.

Saša Hasan, Juri Ganitkevitch, Hermann Ney, and Jesús Andrés-Ferrer. 2008. Triplet lexicon models for statistical machine translation. In *EMNLP '08: Proceedings of the Conference on Empirical Methods in Natural Language Processing*, pages 372–381.

Zhongjun He, Qun Liu, and Shouxun Lin. 2008. Improving statistical machine translation using lexicalized rule selection. In *COLING '08: Proceedings of the 22nd International Conference on Computational Linguistics*, pages 321–328.

Zhongjun He, Yao Meng, Yajuan Lü, Hao Yu, and Qun Liu. 2009. Reducing smt rule table with monolingual key phrase. In *ACL-IJCNLP '09: Proceedings of the ACL-IJCNLP 2009 Conference Short Papers*, pages 121–124.

Liang Huang, Wenbin Jiang, and Qun Liu. 2009. Bilingually-constrained (monolingual) shift-reduce parsing. In *EMNLP '09: Proceedings of the 2009 Conference on Empirical Methods in Natural Language Processing*, pages 1222–1231.

Gonzalo Iglesias, Adrià de Gispert, Eduardo R. Banga, and William Byrne. 2009. Rule filtering by pattern for efficient hierarchical translation. In *EACL '09: Proceedings of the 12th Conference of the European Chapter of the Association for Computational Linguistics*, pages 380–388.

Philipp Koehn, Franz Josef Och, and Daniel Marcu. 2003. Statistical phrase-based translation. In *NAACL '03: Proceedings of the 2003 Conference of the North American Chapter of the Association for Computational Linguistics on Human Language Technology*, pages 48–54.

Joakim Nivre and Mario Scholz. 2004. Deterministic dependency parsing of english text. In *COLING '04: Proceedings of the 20th international conference on Computational Linguistics*, pages 64–70.

Franz Josef Och. 2003. Minimum error rate training in statistical machine translation. In *ACL '03: Proceedings of the 41st Annual Meeting on Association for Computational Linguistics*, pages 160–167.

Kishore Papineni, Salim Roukos, Todd Ward, and Wei-Jing Zhu. 2002. Bleu: a method for automatic evaluation of machine translation. In *ACL '02: Proceedings of the 40th Annual Meeting on Association for Computational Linguistics*, pages 311–318.

Chris Quirk, Arul Menezes, and Colin Cherry. 2005. Dependency treelet translation: syntactically informed phrasal smt. In *ACL '05: Proceedings of the 43rd Annual Meeting on Association for Computational Linguistics*, pages 271–279.

Libin Shen, Jinxi Xu, and Ralph Weischedel. 2008. A new string-to-dependency machine translation algorithm with a target dependency language model. In *Proceedings of ACL-08: HLT*, pages 577–585.

Libin Shen, Jinxi Xu, Bing Zhang, Spyros Matsoukas, and Ralph Weischedel. 2009. Effective use of linguistic and contextual information for statistical machine translation. In *EMNLP '09: Proceedings of the 2009 Conference on Empirical Methods in Natural Language Processing*, pages 72–80.

Andreas Stolcke. 2002. Srilman extensible language modeling toolkit. In *In Proceedings of the 7th International Conference on Spoken Language Processing (ICSLP 2002)*, pages 901–904.

Fixed Length Word Suffix for Factored Statistical Machine Translation

Narges Sharif Razavian
School of Computer Science
Carnegie Mellon Universiy
Pittsburgh, USA
nsharifr@cs.cmu.edu

Stephan Vogel
School of Computer Science
Carnegie Mellon Universiy
Pittsburgh, USA
stephan.vogel@cs.cmu.edu

Abstract

Factored Statistical Machine Translation extends the Phrase Based SMT model by allowing each word to be a vector of factors. Experiments have shown effectiveness of many factors, including the Part of Speech tags in improving the grammaticality of the output. However, high quality part of speech taggers are not available in open domain for many languages. In this paper we used fixed length word suffix as a new factor in the Factored SMT, and were able to achieve significant improvements in three set of experiments: large NIST Arabic to English system, medium WMT Spanish to English system, and small TRANSTAC English to Iraqi system.

1 Introduction

Statistical Machine Translation(SMT) is currently the state of the art solution to the machine translation. Phrase based SMT is also among the top performing approaches available as of today. This approach is a purely lexical approach, using surface forms of the words in the parallel corpus to generate the translations and estimate probabilities. It is possible to incorporate syntactical information into this framework through different ways. Source side syntax based re-ordering as preprocessing step, dependency based reordering models, cohesive decoding features are among many available successful attempts for the integration of syntax into the translation model. Factored translation modeling is another way to achieve this goal. These models allow each word to be represented as a vector of factors rather than a single surface form. Factors can represent richer expression power on each word. Any factors such as word stems, gender, part of speech, tense, etc. can be easily used in this framework.

Previous work in factored translation modeling have reported consistent improvements from Part of Speech(POS) tags, morphology, gender, and case factors (Koehn et. a. 2007). In another work, Birch et. al. 2007 have achieved improvement using Combinational Categorial Grammar (CCG) super-tag factors. Creating the factors is done as a preprocessing step, and so far, most of the experiments have assumed existence of external tools for the creation of these factors (i. e. Part of speech taggers, CCG parsers, etc.). Unfortunately high quality language processing tools, especially for the open domain, are not available for most languages.

While linguistically identifiable representations (i.e. POS tags, CCG supertags, etc) have been very frequently used as factors in many applications including MT, simpler representations have also been effective in achieving the same result in other application areas. Grzymala-Busse and Old 1997, DINCER et.al. 2008, were able to use fixed length suffixes as features for training a POS tagging. In another work Saberi and Perrot 1999 showed that reversing middle chunks of the words while keeping the first and last part intact, does not decrease listeners' recognition ability. This result is very relevant to Machine Translation, suggesting that inaccurate context which is usually modeled with n-gram language models, can still be as effective as accurate surface forms. Another research (Rawlinson 1997) confirms this finding; this time in textual domain, observing that randomization of letters in the middle of words has little or no effect on the ability of skilled readers to understand the text. These results suggest that the inexpensive representational factors which do not need unavailable tools might also be worth investigating.

These results encouraged us to introduce language independent simple factors for machine translation. In this paper, following the work of Grzymala-Busse et. al. we used fixed length suf-

Proceedings of the ACL 2010 Conference Short Papers, pages 147–150,
Uppsala, Sweden, 11-16 July 2010. ©2010 Association for Computational Linguistics

fix as word factor, to lower the perplexity of the language model, and have the factors roughly function as part of speech tags, thus increasing the grammaticality of the translation results. We were able to obtain consistent, significant improvements over our baseline in 3 different experiments, large NIST Arabic to English system, medium WMT Spanish to English system, and small TRANSTAC English to Iraqi system.

The rest of this paper is as follows. Section 2 briefly reviews the Factored Translation Models. In section 3 we will introduce our model, and section 4 will contain the experiments and the analysis of the results, and finally, we will conclude this paper in section 5.

2 Factored Translation Model

Statistical Machine Translation uses the log linear combination of a number of features, to compute the highest probable hypothesis as the translation.

$$e = \text{argmax}_{\mathbf{e}}\ p(\mathbf{e}|\mathbf{f}) = \text{argmax}_{\mathbf{e}}\ p\ exp\ \Sigma_{i=1}^{n}\ \lambda_i\ h_i(\boldsymbol{e},\boldsymbol{f})$$

In phrase based SMT, assuming the source and target phrase segmentation as $\{(f_i,e_i)\}$, the most important features include: the Language Model feature $h_{lm}(\boldsymbol{e},\boldsymbol{f}) = p_{lm}(\boldsymbol{e})$; the phrase translation feature $h_t(\mathbf{e},\mathbf{f})$ defined as product of translation probabilities, lexical probabilities and phrase penalty; and the reordering probability, $h_d(\mathbf{e},\mathbf{f})$, usually defined as $\pi_{i=1}^{n}\ d(start_i,end_{i-1})$ over the source phrase reordering events.

Factored Translation Model, recently introduced by (Koehn et. al. 2007), allow words to have a vector representation. The model can then extend the definition of each of the features from a uni-dimensional value to an arbitrary joint and conditional combination of features. Phrase based SMT is in fact a special case of Factored SMT.

The factored features are defined as an extension of phrase translation features. The function $\tau(f_j,e_j)$, which was defined for a phrase pair before, can now be extended as a log linear combination $\Sigma_f\ \tau_f(\underline{f}_{jf},\underline{e}_{jf})$. The model also allows for a generation feature, defining the relationship between final surface form and target factors. Other features include additional language model features over individual factors, and factored reordering features.

Figure 1 shows an example of a possible factored model.

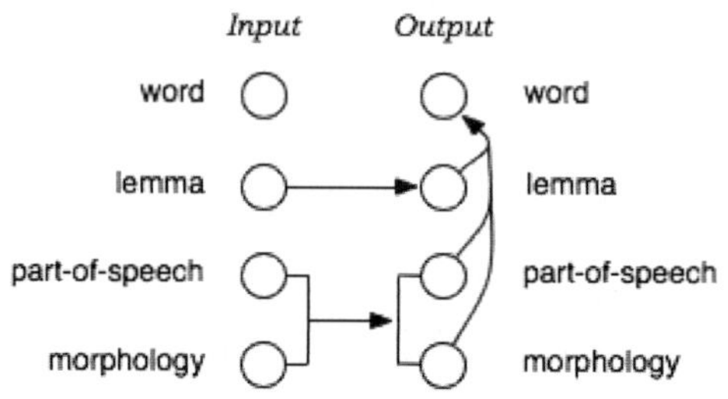

Figure 1: An example of a Factored Translation and Generation Model

In this particular model, words on both source and target side are represented as a vector of four factors: surface form, lemma, part of speech (POS) and the morphology. The target phrase is generated as follows: Source word lemma generates target word lemma. Source word's Part of speech and morphology together generate the target word's part of speech and morphology, and from its lemma, part of speech and morphology the surface form of the target word is finally generated. This model has been able to result in higher translation BLEU score as well as grammatical coherency for English to German, English to Spanish, English to Czech, English to Chinese, Chinese to English and German to English.

3 Fixed Length Suffix Factors for Factored Translation Modeling

Part of speech tagging, constituent and dependency parsing, combinatory categorical grammar super tagging are used extensively in most applications when syntactic representations are needed. However training these tools require medium size treebanks and tagged data, which for most languages will not be available for a while. On the other hand, many simple words features, such as their character n-grams, have in fact proven to be comparably as effective in many applications.

(Keikha et. al. 2008) did an experiment on text classification on noisy data, and compared several word representations. They compared surface form, stemmed words, character n-grams, and semantic relationships, and found that for noisy and open domain text, character-ngrams outperform other representations when used for text classification. In another work (Dincer et al 2009) showed that using fixed length word ending outperforms whole word representation for training a part of speech tagger for Turkish language.

Based on this result, we proposed a suffix factored model for translation, which is shown in Figure 2.

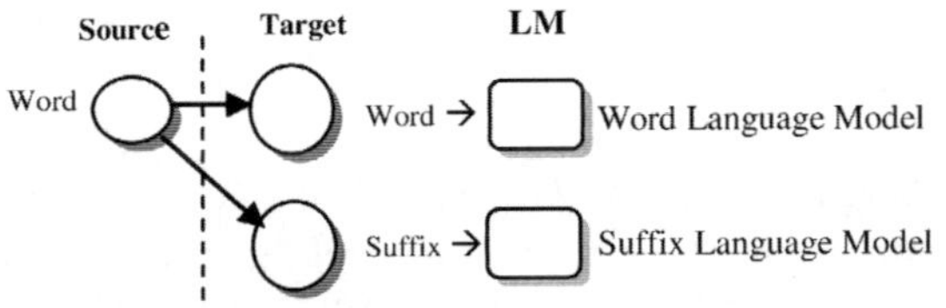

Figure 2: Suffix Factored model: Source word determines factor vectors (target word, target word suffix) and each factor will be associated with its language model.

Based on this model, the final probability of the translation hypothesis will be the log linear combination of phrase probabilities, reordering model probabilities, and each of the language models' probabilities.

$$P(e|f) \sim p_{lm\text{-}word}(e_{word}) * p_{lm\text{-}suffix}(e_{suffix}) \\ * \Sigma_{i=1}^{n}\ p(e_{word\text{-}j}\ \&\ e_{suffix\text{-}j}|f_j) \\ * \Sigma_{i=1}^{n}\ p(f_j \mid e_{word\text{-}j}\ \&\ e_{suffix\text{-}j})$$

Where $p_{lm\text{-}word}$ is the n-gram language model probability over the word surface sequence, with the language model built from the surface forms. Similarly, $p_{lm\text{-}suffix}(e_{suffix})$ is the language model probability over suffix sequences. $p(e_{word\text{-}j}\ \&\ e_{suffix\text{-}j}|f_j)$ *and* $p(f_j \mid e_{word\text{-}j}\ \&\ e_{suffix\text{-}j})$ are translation probabilities for each phrase pair i , used in by the decoder. This probability is estimated after the phrase extraction step which is based on grow-diag heuristic at this stage.

4 Experiments and Results

We used Moses implementation of the factored model for training the feature weights, and SRI toolkit for building n-gram language models. The baseline for all systems included the moses system with lexicalized re-ordering, SRI 5-gram language models.

4.1 Small System from Dialog Domain: English to Iraqi

This system was TRANSTAC system, which was built on about 650K sentence pairs with the average sentence length of 5.9 words. After choosing length 3 for suffixes, we built a new parallel corpus, and SRI 5-gram language models for each factor. Vocabulary size for the surface form was 110K whereas the word suffixes had about 8K distinct words. Table 1 shows the result (BLEU Score) of the system compared to the baseline.

System	Tune on Set-July07	Test on Set-June08	Test on Set-Nov08
Baseline	27.74	21.73	15.62
Factored	28.83	22.84	16.41
Improvement	1.09	1.11	0.79

Table 1: BLEU score, English to Iraqi Transtac system, comparing Factored and Baseline systems.

As you can see, this improvement is consistent over multiple unseen datasets. Arabic cases and numbers show up as the word suffix. Also, verb numbers usually appear partly as word suffix and in some cases as word prefix. Defining a language model over the word endings increases the probability of sequences which have this case and number agreement, favoring correct agreements over the incorrect ones.

4.2 Medium System on Travel Domain: Spanish to English

This system is the WMT08 system, on a corpus of 1.2 million sentence pairs with average sentence length 27.9 words. Like the previous experiment, we defined the 3 character suffix of the words as the second factor, and built the language model and reordering model on the joint event of (surface, suffix) pairs. We built 5-gram language models for each factor. The system had about 97K distinct vocabulary in the surface language model, which was reduced to 8K using the suffix corpus. Having defined the baseline, the system results are as follows.

System	Tune-WMT06	Test set-WMT08
Baseline	33.34	32.53
Factored	33.60	32.84
Improvement	0.26	0.32

Table 2: BLEU score, Spanish to English WMT system, comparing Factored and Baseline systems.

Here, we see improvement with the suffix factors compared to the baseline system. Word endings in English language are major indicators of word's part of speech in the sentence. In fact most common stemming algorithm, Porter's Stemmer, works by removing word's suffix. Having a language model on these suffixes pushes the common patterns of these suffixes to the top, making the more grammatically coherent sentences to achieve a better probability.

4.3 Large NIST 2009 System: Arabic to English

We used NIST2009 system as our baseline in this experiment. The corpus had about 3.8 Million sentence pairs, with average sentence length of 33.4 words. The baseline defined the lexicalized reordering model. As before we defined 3 character long word endings, and built 5-gram SRI language models for each factor. The result of this experiment is shown in table 3.

System	Tune on MT06	Test on Dev07 News Wire	Test on Dev07 Weblog	Test on MT08
Baseline	43.06	48.87	37.84	41.70
Factored	44.20	50.39	39.93	42.74
Improvement	1.14	1.52	2.09	1.04

Table 3: BLEU score, Arabic to English NIST 2009 system, comparing Factored and Baseline systems.

This result confirms the positive effect of the suffix factors even on large systems. As mentioned before we believe that this result is due to the ability of the suffix to reduce the word into a very simple but rough grammatical representation. Defining language models for this factor forces the decoder to prefer sentences with more probable suffix sequences, which is believed to increase the grammaticality of the result. Future error analysis will show us more insight of the exact effect of this factor on the outcome.

5 Conclusion

In this paper we introduced a simple yet very effective factor: fixed length word suffix, to use in Factored Translation Models. This simple factor has been shown to be effective as a rough replacement for part of speech. We tested our factors in three experiments in a small, English to Iraqi system, a medium sized system of Spanish to English, and a large system, NIST09 Arabic to English. We observed consistent and significant improvements over the baseline. This result, obtained from the language independent and inexpensive factor, shows promising new opportunities for all language pairs.

References

Birch, A., Osborne, M., and Koehn, P. CCG supertags in factored statistical machine translation. Proceedings of the Second Workshop on Statistical Machine Translation, pages 9–16, Prague, Czech Republic. Association for Computational Linguistics, 2007.

Dincer T., Karaoglan B. and Kisla T., A Suffix Based Part-Of-Speech Tagger For Turkish, Fifth International Conference on Information Technology: New Generations, 2008.

Grzymala-Busse J.W., Old L.J. A machine learning experiment to determine part of speech from word-endings, Lecture Notes in Computer Science, Communications Session 6B Learning and Discovery Systems, 1997.

Keikha M., Sharif Razavian N, Oroumchian F., and Seyed Razi H., Document Representation and Quality of Text: An Analysis, Chapter 12, Survey of Text Mining II, Springer London, 2008.

Koehn Ph., Hoang H., Factored Translation Models, Proceedings of 45th Annual Meeting of the Association for Computational Linguistics (ACL), 2007.

Rawlinson G. E., The significance of letter position in word recognition, PhD Thesis, Psychology Department, University of Nottingham, Nottingham UK, 1976.

Saberi K and Perrot D R, Cognitive restoration of reversed speech, Nature (London) 1999.

Unsupervised Discourse Segmentation of Documents with Inherently Parallel Structure

Minwoo Jeong and **Ivan Titov**
Saarland University
Saarbrücken, Germany
{m.jeong|titov}@mmci.uni-saarland.de

Abstract

Documents often have inherently parallel structure: they may consist of a text and commentaries, or an abstract and a body, or parts presenting alternative views on the same problem. Revealing relations between the parts by jointly segmenting and predicting links between the segments, would help to visualize such documents and construct friendlier user interfaces. To address this problem, we propose an unsupervised Bayesian model for joint discourse segmentation and alignment. We apply our method to the "English as a second language" podcast dataset where each episode is composed of two parallel parts: a story and an explanatory lecture. The predicted topical links uncover hidden relations between the stories and the lectures. In this domain, our method achieves competitive results, rivaling those of a previously proposed supervised technique.

1 Introduction

Many documents consist of parts exhibiting a high degree of parallelism: e.g., abstract and body of academic publications, summaries and detailed news stories, etc. This is especially common with the emergence of the Web 2.0 technologies: many texts on the web are now accompanied with comments and discussions. Segmentation of these parallel parts into coherent fragments and discovery of hidden relations between them would facilitate the development of better user interfaces and improve the performance of summarization and information retrieval systems.

Discourse segmentation of the documents composed of parallel parts is a novel and challenging problem, as previous research has mostly focused on the linear segmentation of isolated texts (e.g., (Hearst, 1994)). The most straightforward approach would be to use a pipeline strategy, where an existing segmentation algorithm finds discourse boundaries of each part independently, and then the segments are aligned. Or, conversely, a sentence-alignment stage can be followed by a segmentation stage. However, as we will see in our experiments, these strategies may result in poor segmentation and alignment quality.

To address this problem, we construct a non-parametric Bayesian model for joint segmentation and alignment of parallel parts. In comparison with the discussed pipeline approaches, our method has two important advantages: (1) it leverages the lexical cohesion phenomenon (Halliday and Hasan, 1976) in modeling the parallel parts of documents, and (2) ensures that the effective number of segments can grow adaptively. Lexical cohesion is an idea that topically-coherent segments display compact lexical distributions (Hearst, 1994; Utiyama and Isahara, 2001; Eisenstein and Barzilay, 2008). We hypothesize that not only isolated fragments but also each group of linked fragments displays a compact and consistent lexical distribution, and our generative model leverages this inter-part cohesion assumption.

In this paper, we consider the dataset of "English as a second language" (ESL) podcast[1], where each episode consists of two parallel parts: a *story* (an example monologue or dialogue) and an explanatory *lecture* discussing the meaning and usage of English expressions appearing in the story. Fig. 1 presents an example episode, consisting of two parallel parts, and their hidden topical relations.[2] From the figure we may conclude that there is a tendency of word repetition between each pair of aligned segments, illustrating our hypothesis of compactness of their joint distribution. Our goal is

[1] http://www.eslpod.com/

[2] Episode no. 232 post on Jan. 08, 2007.

Proceedings of the ACL 2010 Conference Short Papers, pages 151–155,
Uppsala, Sweden, 11-16 July 2010.

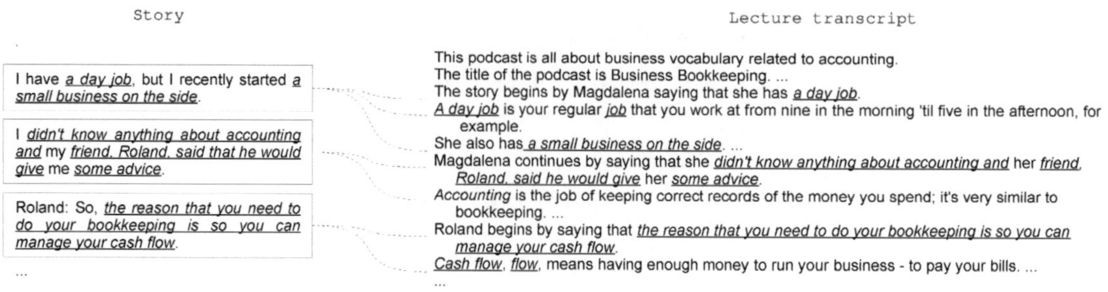

Figure 1: An example episode of ESL podcast. Co-occurred words are represented in *italic* and underline.

to divide the lecture transcript into discourse units and to align each unit to the related segment of the story. Predicting these structures for the ESL podcast could be the first step in development of an e-learning system and a podcast search engine for ESL learners.

2 Related Work

Discourse segmentation has been an active area of research (Hearst, 1994; Utiyama and Isahara, 2001; Galley et al., 2003; Malioutov and Barzilay, 2006). Our work extends the Bayesian segmentation model (Eisenstein and Barzilay, 2008) for isolated texts, to the problem of segmenting parallel parts of documents.

The task of aligning each sentence of an abstract to one or more sentences of the body has been studied in the context of summarization (Marcu, 1999; Jing, 2002; Daumé and Marcu, 2004). Our work is different in that we do not try to extract the most relevant sentence but rather aim to find coherent fragments with maximally overlapping lexical distributions. Similarly, the query-focused summarization (e.g., (Daumé and Marcu, 2006)) is also related but it focuses on sentence extraction rather than on joint segmentation.

We are aware of only one previous work on joint segmentation and alignment of multiple texts (Sun et al., 2007) but their approach is based on similarity functions rather than on modeling lexical cohesion in the generative framework. Our application, the analysis of the ESL podcast, was previously studied in (Noh et al., 2010). They proposed a supervised method which is driven by pairwise classification decisions. The main drawback of their approach is that it neglects the discourse structure and the lexical cohesion phenomenon.

3 Model

In this section we describe our model for discourse segmentation of documents with inherently parallel structure. We start by clarifying our assumptions about their structure.

We assume that a document $\boldsymbol{x}$ consists of K parallel parts, that is, $\boldsymbol{x} = \{\boldsymbol{x}^{(k)}\}_{k=1:K}$, and each part of the document consists of segments, $\boldsymbol{x}^{(k)} = \{\boldsymbol{s}_i^{(k)}\}_{i=1:I}$. Note that the effective number of fragments I is unknown. Each segment can either be specific to this part (drawn from a *part-specific* language model $\phi_i^{(k)}$) or correspond to the entire document (drawn from a *document-level* language model $\phi_i^{(doc)}$). For example, the first and the second sentences of the lecture transcript in Fig. 1 are part-specific, whereas other linked sentences belong to the document-level segments. The document-level language models define topical links between segments in different parts of the document, whereas the part-specific language models define the linear segmentation of the remaining unaligned text.

Each document-level language model corresponds to the set of aligned segments, at most one segment per part. Similarly, each part-specific language model corresponds to a single segment of the single corresponding part. Note that all the documents are modeled independently, as we aim not to discover collection-level topics (as e.g. in (Blei et al., 2003)), but to perform joint discourse segmentation and alignment.

Unlike (Eisenstein and Barzilay, 2008), we cannot make an assumption that the number of segments is known a-priori, as the effective number of part-specific segments can vary significantly from document to document, depending on their size and structure. To tackle this problem, we use Dirichlet processes (DP) (Ferguson, 1973) to define priors on the number of segments. We incorporate them in our model in a similar way as it is done for the Latent Dirichlet Allocation (LDA) by Yu et al. (2005). Unlike the standard LDA, the topic proportions are chosen not from a Dirichlet prior but from the marginal distribution $GEM(\alpha)$ defined by the *stick breaking* construction (Sethuraman, 1994), where α is the concentration parameter of the underlying DP distribution. $GEM(\alpha)$ defines a distribution of partitions of the unit interval into a countable number of parts.

The formal definition of our model is as follows:

- Draw the document-level topic proportions $\boldsymbol{\beta}^{(doc)} \sim GEM(\alpha^{(doc)})$.
- Choose the document-level language model $\phi_i^{(doc)} \sim Dir(\gamma^{(doc)})$ for $i \in \{1, 2, \ldots\}$.
- Draw the part-specific topic proportions $\boldsymbol{\beta}^{(k)} \sim GEM(\alpha^{(k)})$ for $k \in \{1, \ldots, K\}$.
- Choose the part-specific language models $\phi_i^{(k)} \sim Dir(\gamma^{(k)})$ for $k \in \{1, \ldots, K\}$ and $i \in \{1, 2, \ldots\}$.
- For each part k and each sentence n:
  - Draw type $t_n^{(k)} \sim Unif(Doc, Part)$.
  - If ($t_n^{(k)} = Doc$); draw topic $z_n^{(k)} \sim \boldsymbol{\beta}^{(doc)}$; generate words $\boldsymbol{x}_n^{(k)} \sim Mult(\phi^{(doc)}_{z_n^{(k)}})$
  - Otherwise; draw topic $z_n^{(k)} \sim \boldsymbol{\beta}^{(k)}$; generate words $\boldsymbol{x}_n^{(k)} \sim Mult(\phi^{(k)}_{z_n^{(k)}})$.

The priors $\gamma^{(doc)}$, $\gamma^{(k)}$, $\alpha^{(doc)}$ and $\alpha^{(k)}$ can be estimated at learning time using non-informative hyperpriors (as we do in our experiments), or set manually to indicate preferences of segmentation granularity.

At inference time, we enforce each latent topic $z_n^{(k)}$ to be assigned to a contiguous span of text, assuming that coherent topics are not recurring across the document (Halliday and Hasan, 1976). It also reduces the search space and, consequently, speeds up our sampling-based inference by reducing the time needed for Monte Carlo chains to mix. In fact, this constraint can be integrated in the model definition but it would significantly complicate the model description.

4 Inference

As exact inference is intractable, we follow Eisenstein and Barzilay (2008) and instead use a Metropolis-Hastings (MH) algorithm. At each iteration of the MH algorithm, a new potential alignment-segmentation pair $(\boldsymbol{z}', \boldsymbol{t}')$ is drawn from a proposal distribution $Q(\boldsymbol{z}', \boldsymbol{t}'|\boldsymbol{z}, \boldsymbol{t})$, where $(\boldsymbol{z}, \boldsymbol{t})$

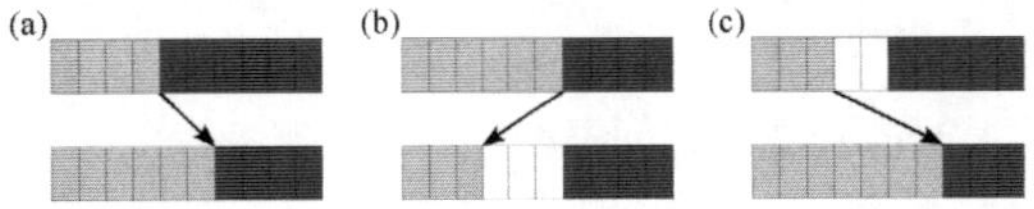

Figure 2: Three types of moves: (a) shift, (b) split and (c) merge.

is the current segmentation and its type. The new pair $(\boldsymbol{z}', \boldsymbol{t}')$ is accepted with the probability

$$\min\left(1, \frac{P(\boldsymbol{z}', \boldsymbol{t}', \boldsymbol{x})Q(\boldsymbol{z}', \boldsymbol{t}'|\boldsymbol{z}, \boldsymbol{t})}{P(\boldsymbol{z}, \boldsymbol{t}, \boldsymbol{x})Q(\boldsymbol{z}, \boldsymbol{t}|\boldsymbol{z}', \boldsymbol{t}')}\right).$$

In order to implement the MH algorithm for our model, we need to define the set of potential *moves* (i.e. admissible changes from $(\boldsymbol{z}, \boldsymbol{t})$ to $(\boldsymbol{z}', \boldsymbol{t}')$), and the proposal distribution Q over these moves. If the actual number of segments is known and only a linear discourse structure is acceptable, then a single move, *shift* of the segment border (Fig. 2(a)), is sufficient (Eisenstein and Barzilay, 2008). In our case, however, a more complex set of moves is required.

We make two assumptions which are motivated by the problem considered in Section 5: we assume that (1) we are given the number of document-level segments and also that (2) the aligned segments appear in the same order in each part of the document. With these assumptions in mind, we introduce two additional moves (Fig. 2(b) and (c)):

- *Split move*: select a segment, and split it at one of the spanned sentences; if the segment was a document-level segment then one of the fragments becomes the same document-level segment.
- *Merge move*: select a pair of adjacent segments where at least one of the segments is part-specific, and merge them; if one of them was a document-level segment then the new segment has the same document-level topic.

All the moves are selected with the uniform probability, and the distance c for the shift move is drawn from the proposal distribution proportional to $c^{-1/c_{max}}$. The moves are selected independently for each part.

Although the above two assumptions are not crucial as a simple modification to the set of moves would support both introduction and deletion of document-level fragments, this modification was not necessary for our experiments.

5 Experiment

5.1 Dataset and setup

Dataset We apply our model to the ESL podcast dataset (Noh et al., 2010) of 200 episodes, with an average of 17 sentences per story and 80 sentences per lecture transcript. The gold standard alignments assign each fragment of the story to a segment of the lecture transcript. We can induce segmentations at different levels of granularity on both the story and the lecture side. However, given that the segmentation of the story was obtained by an automatic sentence splitter, there is no reason to attempt to reproduce this segmentation. Therefore, for quantitative evaluation purposes we follow Noh et al. (2010) and restrict our model to alignment structures which agree with the given segmentation of the story. For all evaluations, we apply standard stemming algorithm and remove common stop words.

Evaluation metrics To measure the quality of segmentation of the lecture transcript, we use two standard metrics, P_k (Beeferman et al., 1999) and WindowDiff (WD) (Pevzner and Hearst, 2002), but both metrics disregard the alignment links (i.e. the topic labels). Consequently, we also use the macro-averaged F_1 score on pairs of aligned span, which measures both the segmentation and alignment quality.

Baseline Since there has been little previous research on this problem, we compare our results against two straightforward unsupervised baselines. For the first baseline, we consider the pairwise sentence alignment (SentAlign) based on the unigram and bigram overlap. The second baseline is a pipeline approach (Pipeline), where we first segment the lecture transcript with BayesSeg (Eisenstein and Barzilay, 2008) and then use the pairwise alignment to find their best alignment to the segments of the story.

Our model We evaluate our joint model of segmentation and alignment both with and without the split/merge moves. For the model without these moves, we set the desired number of segments in the lecture to be equal to the actual number of segments in the story I. In this setting, the moves can only adjust positions of the segment borders. For the model with the split/merge moves, we start with the same number of segments I but it can be increased or decreased during inference. For evaluation of our model, we run our inference algorithm from five random states, and take the 100,000th iteration of each chain as a sample. Results are the average over these five runs. Also we perform L-BFGS optimization to automatically adjust the non-informative hyperpriors after each 1,000 iterations of sampling.

Method	P_k	WD	$1 - F_1$
Uniform	0.453	0.458	0.682
SentAlign	0.446	0.547	0.313
Pipeline (I)	0.250	0.249	0.443
Pipeline ($2I$+1)	0.268	0.289	0.318
Our model (I)	0.193	0.204	0.254
+split/merge	**0.181**	**0.193**	**0.239**

Table 1: Results on the ESL podcast dataset. For all metrics, lower values are better.

5.2 Result

Table 1 summarizes the obtained results. 'Uniform' denotes the minimal baseline which uniformly draws a random set of I spans for each lecture, and then aligns them to the segments of the story preserving the linear order. Also, we consider two variants of the pipeline approach: segmenting the lecture on I and $2I + 1$ segments, respectively.[3] Our joint model substantially outperforms the baselines. The difference is statistically significant with the level $p < .01$ measured with the paired t-test. The significant improvement over the pipeline results demonstrates benefits of joint modeling for the considered problem. Moreover, additional benefits are obtained by using the DP priors and the split/merge moves (the last line in Table 1). Finally, our model significantly outperforms the previously proposed supervised model (Noh et al., 2010): they report micro-averaged F_1 score 0.698 while our best model achieves 0.778 with the same metric. This observation confirms that lexical cohesion modeling is crucial for successful discourse analysis.

6 Conclusions

We studied the problem of joint discourse segmentation and alignment of documents with inherently parallel structure and achieved favorable results on the ESL podcast dataset outperforming the cascaded baselines. Accurate prediction of these hidden relations would open interesting possibilities

[3]The use of the DP priors and the split/merge moves on the first stage of the pipeline did not result in any improvement in accuracy.

for construction of friendlier user interfaces. One example being an application which, given a user-selected fragment of the abstract, produces a summary from the aligned segment of the document body.

Acknowledgment

The authors acknowledge the support of the Excellence Cluster on Multimodal Computing and Interaction (MMCI), and also thank Mikhail Kozhevnikov and the anonymous reviewers for their valuable comments, and Hyungjong Noh for providing their data.

References

Doug Beeferman, Adam Berger, and John Lafferty. 1999. Statistical models for text segmentation. *Computational Linguistics*, 34(1–3):177–210.

David M. Blei, Andrew Ng, and Michael I. Jordan. 2003. Latent dirichlet allocation. *JMLR*, 3:993–1022.

Hal Daumé and Daniel Marcu. 2004. A phrase-based hmm approach to document/abstract alignment. In *Proceedings of EMNLP*, pages 137–144.

Hal Daumé and Daniel Marcu. 2006. Bayesian query-focused summarization. In *Proceedings of ACL*, pages 305–312.

Jacob Eisenstein and Regina Barzilay. 2008. Bayesian unsupervised topic segmentation. In *Proceedings of EMNLP*, pages 334–343.

Thomas S. Ferguson. 1973. A Bayesian analysis of some non-parametric problems. *Annals of Statistics*, 1:209–230.

Michel Galley, Kathleen R. McKeown, Eric Fosler-Lussier, and Hongyan Jing. 2003. Discourse segmentation of multi-party conversation. In *Proceedings of ACL*, pages 562–569.

M. A. K. Halliday and Ruqaiya Hasan. 1976. *Cohesion in English*. Longman.

Marti Hearst. 1994. Multi-paragraph segmentation of expository text. In *Proceedings of ACL*, pages 9–16.

Hongyan Jing. 2002. Using hidden Markov modeling to decompose human-written summaries. *Computational Linguistics*, 28(4):527–543.

Igor Malioutov and Regina Barzilay. 2006. Minimum cut model for spoken lecture segmentation. In *Proceedings of ACL*, pages 25–32.

Daniel Marcu. 1999. The automatic construction of large-scale corpora for summarization research. In *Proceedings of ACM SIGIR*, pages 137–144.

Hyungjong Noh, Minwoo Jeong, Sungjin Lee, Jonghoon Lee, and Gary Geunbae Lee. 2010. Script-description pair extraction from text documents of English as second language podcast. In *Proceedings of the 2nd International Conference on Computer Supported Education*.

Lev Pevzner and Marti Hearst. 2002. A critique and improvement of an evaluation metric for text segmentation. *Computational Linguistics*, 28(1):19–36.

Jayaram Sethuraman. 1994. A constructive definition of Dirichlet priors. *Statistica Sinica*, 4:639–650.

Bingjun Sun, Prasenjit Mitra, C. Lee Giles, John Yen, and Hongyuan Zha. 2007. Topic segmentation with shared topic detection and alignment of multiple documents. In *Proceedings of ACM SIGIR*, pages 199–206.

Masao Utiyama and Hitoshi Isahara. 2001. A statistical model for domain-independent text segmentation. In *Proceedings of ACL*, pages 491–498.

Kai Yu, Shipeng Yu, and Vokler Tresp. 2005. Dirichlet enhanced latent semantic analysis. In *Proceedings of AISTATS*.

Coreference Resolution with Reconcile

Veselin Stoyanov
Center for Language and Speech Processing
Johns Hopkins Univ.
Baltimore, MD
ves@cs.jhu.edu

Claire Cardie
Department of Computer Science
Cornell University
Ithaca, NY
cardie@cs.cornell.edu

Nathan Gilbert
Ellen Riloff
School of Computing
University of Utah
Salt Lake City, UT
ngilbert@cs.utah.edu
riloff@cs.utah.edu

David Buttler
David Hysom
Lawrence Livermore National Laboratory
Livermore, CA
buttler1@llnl.gov
hysom1@llnl.gov

Abstract

Despite the existence of several noun phrase coreference resolution data sets as well as several formal evaluations on the task, it remains frustratingly difficult to compare results across different coreference resolution systems. This is due to the high cost of implementing a complete end-to-end coreference resolution system, which often forces researchers to substitute available gold-standard information in lieu of implementing a module that would compute that information. Unfortunately, this leads to inconsistent and often unrealistic evaluation scenarios.

With the aim to facilitate consistent and realistic experimental evaluations in coreference resolution, we present Reconcile, an infrastructure for the development of learning-based noun phrase (NP) coreference resolution systems. Reconcile is designed to facilitate the rapid creation of coreference resolution systems, easy implementation of new feature sets and approaches to coreference resolution, and empirical evaluation of coreference resolvers across a variety of benchmark data sets and standard scoring metrics. We describe Reconcile and present experimental results showing that Reconcile can be used to create a coreference resolver that achieves performance comparable to state-of-the-art systems on six benchmark data sets.

1 Introduction

Noun phrase coreference resolution (or simply coreference resolution) is the problem of identifying all noun phrases (NPs) that refer to the same entity in a text. The problem of coreference resolution is fundamental in the field of natural language processing (NLP) because of its usefulness for other NLP tasks, as well as the theoretical interest in understanding the computational mechanisms involved in government, binding and linguistic reference.

Several formal evaluations have been conducted for the coreference resolution task (e.g., MUC-6 (1995), ACE NIST (2004)), and the data sets created for these evaluations have become standard benchmarks in the field (e.g., MUC and ACE data sets). However, it is still frustratingly difficult to compare results across different coreference resolution systems. Reported coreference resolution scores vary wildly across data sets, evaluation metrics, and system configurations.

We believe that one root cause of these disparities is the high cost of implementing an end-to-end coreference resolution system. Coreference resolution is a complex problem, and successful systems must tackle a variety of non-trivial subproblems that are central to the coreference task — e.g., mention/markable detection, anaphor identification — and that require substantial implementation efforts. As a result, many researchers exploit gold-standard annotations, when available, as a substitute for component technologies to solve these subproblems. For example, many published research results use gold standard annotations to identify NPs (substituting for mention/markable detection), to distinguish anaphoric NPs from non-anaphoric NPs (substituting for anaphoricity determination), to identify named entities (substituting for named entity recognition), and to identify the semantic types of NPs (substituting for semantic class identification). Unfortunately, the use of gold standard annotations for key/critical component technologies leads to an unrealistic evaluation setting, and makes it impossible to directly compare results against coreference resolvers that solve all of these subproblems from scratch.

Comparison of coreference resolvers is further hindered by the use of several competing (and non-trivial) evaluation measures, and data sets that have substantially different task definitions and annotation formats. Additionally, coreference resolution is a pervasive problem in NLP and many NLP applications could benefit from an effective coreference resolver that can be easily configured and customized.

To address these issues, we have created a platform for coreference resolution, called Reconcile, that can serve as a software infrastructure to support the creation of, experimentation with, and evaluation of coreference resolvers. Reconcile was designed with the following seven desiderata in mind:

- implement the basic underlying software ar-

Proceedings of the ACL 2010 Conference Short Papers, pages 156–161,
Uppsala, Sweden, 11-16 July 2010. ©2010 Association for Computational Linguistics

chitecture of contemporary state-of-the-art learning-based coreference resolution systems;

- support experimentation on most of the standard coreference resolution data sets;
- implement most popular coreference resolution scoring metrics;
- exhibit state-of-the-art coreference resolution performance (i.e., it can be configured to create a resolver that achieves performance close to the best reported results);
- can be easily extended with new methods and features;
- is relatively fast and easy to configure and run;
- has a set of pre-built resolvers that can be used as black-box coreference resolution systems.

While several other coreference resolution systems are publicly available (e.g., Poesio and Kabadjov (2004), Qiu et al. (2004) and Versley et al. (2008)), none meets all seven of these desiderata (see Related Work). Reconcile is a modular software platform that abstracts the basic architecture of most contemporary supervised learning-based coreference resolution systems (e.g., Soon et al. (2001), Ng and Cardie (2002), Bengtson and Roth (2008)) and achieves performance comparable to the state-of-the-art on several benchmark data sets. Additionally, Reconcile can be easily reconfigured to use different algorithms, features, preprocessing elements, evaluation settings and metrics.

In the rest of this paper, we review related work (Section 2), describe Reconcile's organization and components (Section 3) and show experimental results for Reconcile on six data sets and two evaluation metrics (Section 4).

2 Related Work

Several coreference resolution systems are currently publicly available. JavaRap (Qiu et al., 2004) is an implementation of the Lappin and Leass' (1994) Resolution of Anaphora Procedure (RAP). JavaRap resolves only pronouns and, thus, it is not directly comparable to Reconcile. GuiTaR (Poesio and Kabadjov, 2004) and BART (Versley et al., 2008) (which can be considered a successor of GuiTaR) are both modular systems that target the full coreference resolution task. As such, both systems come close to meeting the majority of the desiderata set forth in Section 1. BART, in particular, can be considered an alternative to Reconcile, although we believe that Reconcile's approach is more flexible than BART's. In addition, the architecture and system components of Reconcile (including a comprehensive set of features that draw on the expertise of state-of-the-art supervised learning approaches, such as Bengtson and Roth (2008)) result in performance closer to the state-of-the-art.

Coreference resolution has received much research attention, resulting in an array of approaches, algorithms and features. Reconcile is modeled after typical supervised learning approaches to coreference resolution (e.g. the architecture introduced by Soon et al. (2001)) because of the popularity and relatively good performance of these systems.

However, there have been other approaches to coreference resolution, including unsupervised and semi-supervised approaches (e.g. Haghighi and Klein (2007)), structured approaches (e.g. McCallum and Wellner (2004) and Finley and Joachims (2005)), competition approaches (e.g. Yang et al. (2003)) and a bell-tree search approach (Luo et al. (2004)). Most of these approaches rely on some notion of pairwise feature-based similarity and can be directly implemented in Reconcile.

3 System Description

Reconcile was designed to be a research testbed capable of implementing most current approaches to coreference resolution. Reconcile is written in Java, to be portable across platforms, and was designed to be easily reconfigurable with respect to subcomponents, feature sets, parameter settings, etc.

Reconcile's architecture is illustrated in Figure 1. For simplicity, Figure 1 shows Reconcile's operation during the classification phase (i.e., assuming that a trained classifier is present).

The basic architecture of the system includes five major steps. Starting with a corpus of documents together with a manually annotated coreference resolution answer key[1], Reconcile performs

[1]Only required during training.

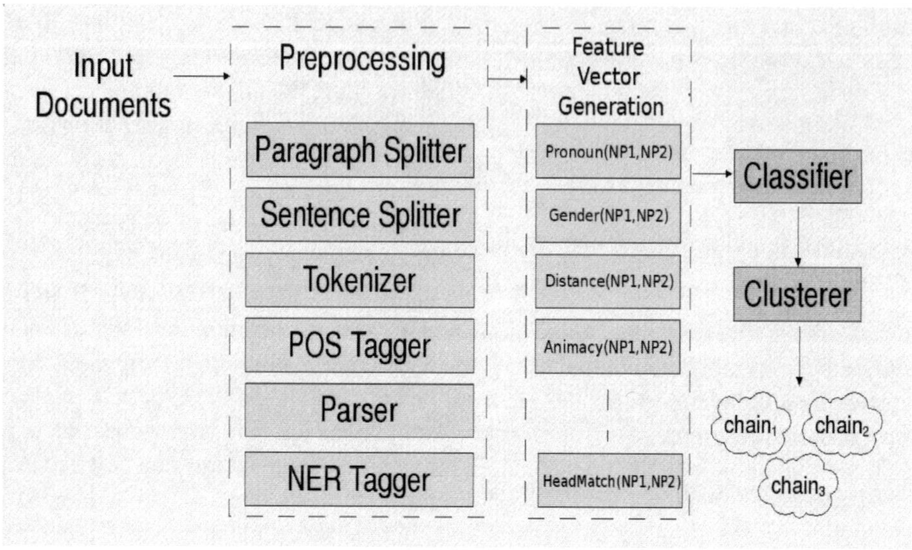

Figure 1: The Reconcile classification architecture.

the following steps, in order:

1. **Preprocessing.** All documents are passed through a series of (external) linguistic processors such as tokenizers, part-of-speech taggers, syntactic parsers, etc. These components produce annotations of the text. Table 1 lists the preprocessors currently interfaced in Reconcile. Note that Reconcile includes several in-house NP detectors, that conform to the different data sets' definitions of what constitutes a NP (e.g., MUC vs. ACE). All of the extractors utilize a syntactic parse of the text and the output of a Named Entity (NE) extractor, but extract different constructs as specialized in the corresponding definition. The NP extractors successfully recognize about 95% of the NPs in the MUC and ACE gold standards.

2. **Feature generation.** Using annotations produced during preprocessing, Reconcile produces feature vectors for pairs of NPs. For example, a feature might denote whether the two NPs agree in number, or whether they have any words in common. Reconcile includes over 80 features, inspired by other successful coreference resolution systems such as Soon et al. (2001) and Ng and Cardie (2002).

3. **Classification.** Reconcile learns a classifier that operates on feature vectors representing pairs of NPs and it is trained to assign a score indicating the likelihood that the NPs in the pair are coreferent.

4. **Clustering.** A clustering algorithm consolidates the predictions output by the classifier and forms the final set of coreference clusters (chains).[2]

5. **Scoring.** Finally, during testing Reconcile runs scoring algorithms that compare the chains produced by the system to the gold-standard chains in the answer key.

Task	Systems
Sentence splitter	UIUC (CC Group, 2009) OpenNLP (Baldridge, J., 2005)
Tokenizer	OpenNLP (Baldridge, J., 2005)
POS Tagger	OpenNLP (Baldridge, J., 2005) + the two parsers below
Parser	Stanford (Klein and Manning, 2003) Berkeley (Petrov and Klein, 2007)
Dep. parser	Stanford (Klein and Manning, 2003)
NE Recognizer	OpenNLP (Baldridge, J., 2005) Stanford (Finkel et al., 2005)
NP Detector	In-house

Table 1: Preprocessing components available in Reconcile.

Each of the five steps above can invoke different components. Reconcile's modularity makes it

[2]Some structured coreference resolution algorithms (e.g., McCallum and Wellner (2004) and Finley and Joachims (2005)) combine the classification and clustering steps above. Reconcile can easily accommodate this modification.

Step	Available modules
Classification	various learners in the Weka toolkit libSVM (Chang and Lin, 2001) SVM$_{light}$ (Joachims, 2002)
Clustering	Single-link Best-First Most Recent First
Scoring	MUC score (Vilain et al., 1995) B^3 score (Bagga and Baldwin, 1998) CEAF score (Luo, 2005)

Table 2: Available implementations for different modules available in Reconcile.

easy for new components to be implemented and existing ones to be removed or replaced. Reconcile's standard distribution comes with a comprehensive set of implemented components – those available for steps 2–5 are shown in Table 2. Reconcile contains over 38,000 lines of original Java code. Only about 15% of the code is concerned with running existing components in the preprocessing step, while the rest deals with NP extraction, implementations of features, clustering algorithms and scorers. More details about Reconcile's architecture and available components and features can be found in Stoyanov et al. (2010).

4 Evaluation

4.1 Data Sets

Reconcile incorporates the six most commonly used coreference resolution data sets, two from the MUC conferences (MUC-6, 1995; MUC-7, 1997) and four from the ACE Program (NIST, 2004). For ACE, we incorporate only the newswire portion. When available, Reconcile employs the standard test/train split. Otherwise, we randomly split the data into a training and test set following a 70/30 ratio. Performance is evaluated according to the B^3 and MUC scoring metrics.

4.2 The $Reconcile_{2010}$ Configuration

Reconcile can be easily configured with different algorithms for markable detection, anaphoricity determination, feature extraction, etc., and run against several scoring metrics. For the purpose of this sample evaluation, we create only one particular instantiation of Reconcile, which we will call $Reconcile_{2010}$ to differentiate it from the general platform. $Reconcile_{2010}$ is configured using the following components:

1. **Preprocessing**
   (a) **Sentence Splitter:** *OpenNLP*
   (b) **Tokenizer:** *OpenNLP*
   (c) **POS Tagger:** *OpenNLP*
   (d) **Parser:** *Berkeley*
   (e) **Named Entity Recognizer:** *Stanford*
2. **Feature Set** - A hand-selected subset of 60 out of the more than 80 features available. The features were selected to include most of the features from Soon et al. Soon et al. (2001), Ng and Cardie (2002) and Bengtson and Roth (2008).
3. **Classifier** - *Averaged Perceptron*
4. **Clustering** - *Single-link* - Positive decision threshold was tuned by cross validation of the training set.

4.3 Experimental Results

The first two rows of Table 3 show the performance of $Reconcile_{2010}$. For all data sets, B^3 scores are higher than MUC scores. The MUC score is highest for the MUC6 data set, while B^3 scores are higher for the ACE data sets as compared to the MUC data sets.

Due to the difficulties outlined in Section 1, results for Reconcile presented here are directly comparable only to a limited number of scores reported in the literature. The bottom three rows of Table 3 list these comparable scores, which show that $Reconcile_{2010}$ exhibits state-of-the-art performance for supervised learning-based coreference resolvers. A more detailed study of Reconcile-based coreference resolution systems in different evaluation scenarios can be found in Stoyanov et al. (2009).

5 Conclusions

Reconcile is a general architecture for coreference resolution that can be used to easily create various coreference resolvers. Reconcile provides broad support for experimentation in coreference resolution, including implementation of the basic architecture of contemporary state-of-the-art coreference systems and a variety of individual modules employed in these systems. Additionally, Reconcile handles all of the formatting and scoring peculiarities of the most widely used coreference resolution data sets (those created as part of the MUC and ACE conferences) and, thus, allows for easy implementation and evaluation across these data sets. We hope that Reconcile will support experimental research in coreference resolution and provide a state-of-the-art coreference resolver for both researchers and application developers. We believe that in this way Reconcile will facilitate meaningful and consistent comparisons of coreference resolution systems. The full Reconcile release is available for download at `http://www.cs.utah.edu/nlp/reconcile/`.

System	Score	Data sets					
		MUC6	MUC7	ACE-2	ACE03	ACE04	ACE05
$Reconcile_{2010}$	MUC	68.50	62.80	65.99	67.87	62.03	67.41
	B^3	70.88	65.86	78.29	79.39	76.50	73.71
Soon et al. (2001)	MUC	62.6	60.4	–	–	–	–
Ng and Cardie (2002)	MUC	70.4	63.4	–	–	–	–
Yang et al. (2003)	MUC	71.3	60.2	–	–	–	–

Table 3: Scores for Reconcile on six data sets and scores for comparable coreference systems.

Acknowledgments

This research was supported in part by the National Science Foundation under Grant # 0937060 to the Computing Research Association for the CIFellows Project, Lawrence Livermore National Laboratory subcontract B573245, Department of Homeland Security Grant N0014-07-1-0152, and Air Force Contract FA8750-09-C-0172 under the DARPA Machine Reading Program.

The authors would like to thank the anonymous reviewers for their useful comments.

References

A. Bagga and B. Baldwin. 1998. Algorithms for scoring coreference chains. In *Linguistic Coreference Workshop at the Language Resources and Evaluation Conference*.

Baldridge, J. 2005. The OpenNLP project. http://opennlp.sourceforge.net/.

E. Bengtson and D. Roth. 2008. Understanding the value of features for coreference resolution. In *Proceedings of the 2008 Conference on Empirical Methods in Natural Language Processing (EMNLP)*.

CC Group. 2009. Sentence Segmentation Tool. http://l2r.cs.uiuc.edu/ cogcomp/atool.php?tkey=SS.

C. Chang and C. Lin. 2001. LIBSVM: a Library for Support Vector Machines. Available at `http://www.csie.ntu.edu.tw/cjlin/libsvm`.

J. Finkel, T. Grenager, and C. Manning. 2005. Incorporating Non-local Information into Information Extraction Systems by Gibbs Sampling. In *Proceedings of the 21st International Conference on Computational Linguistics and 44th Annual Meeting of the ACL*.

T. Finley and T. Joachims. 2005. Supervised clustering with support vector machines. In *Proceedings of the Twenty-second International Conference on Machine Learning (ICML 2005)*.

A. Haghighi and D. Klein. 2007. Unsupervised Coreference Resolution in a Nonparametric Bayesian Model. In *Proceedings of the 45th Annual Meeting of the ACL*.

T. Joachims. 2002. SVM_{Light}, http://svmlight.joachims.org.

D. Klein and C. Manning. 2003. Fast Exact Inference with a Factored Model for Natural Language Parsing. In *Advances in Neural Information Processing (NIPS 2003)*.

S. Lappin and H. Leass. 1994. An algorithm for pronominal anaphora resolution. *Computational Linguistics*, 20(4):535–561.

X. Luo, A. Ittycheriah, H. Jing, N. Kambhatla, and S. Roukos. 2004. A mention-synchronous coreference resolution algorithm based on the bell tree. In *Proceedings of the 42nd Annual Meeting of the ACL*.

X. Luo. 2005. On Coreference Resolution Performance Metrics. In *Proceedings of Human Language Technology Conference and Conference on Empirical Methods in Natural Language Processing (HLT/EMNLP)*.

A. McCallum and B. Wellner. 2004. Conditional Models of Identity Uncertainty with Application to Noun Coreference. In *Advances in Neural Information Processing (NIPS 2004)*.

MUC-6. 1995. Coreference Task Definition. In *Proceedings of the Sixth Message Understanding Conference (MUC-6)*.

MUC-7. 1997. Coreference Task Definition. In *Proceedings of the Seventh Message Understanding Conference (MUC-7)*.

V. Ng and C. Cardie. 2002. Improving Machine Learning Approaches to Coreference Resolution. In *Proceedings of the 40th Annual Meeting of the ACL*.

NIST. 2004. *The ACE Evaluation Plan*. NIST.

S. Petrov and D. Klein. 2007. Improved Inference for Unlexicalized Parsing. In *Proceedings of the Joint Meeting of the Human Language Technology Conference and the North American Chapter of the Association for Computational Linguistics (HLT-NAACL 2007)*.

M. Poesio and M. Kabadjov. 2004. A general-purpose, off-the-shelf anaphora resolution module: implementation and preliminary evaluation. In *Proceedings of the Language Resources and Evaluation Conference*.

L. Qiu, M.-Y. Kan, and T.-S. Chua. 2004. A public reference implementation of the rap anaphora resolution algorithm. In *Proceedings of the Language Resources and Evaluation Conference*.

W. Soon, H. Ng, and D. Lim. 2001. A Machine Learning Approach to Coreference of Noun Phrases. *Computational Linguistics*, 27(4):521–541.

V. Stoyanov, N. Gilbert, C. Cardie, and E. Riloff. 2009. Conundrums in noun phrase coreference resolution: Making sense of the state-of-the-art. In *Proceedings of ACL/IJCNLP*.

V. Stoyanov, C. Cardie, N. Gilbert, E. Riloff, D. Buttler, and D. Hysom. 2010. Reconcile: A coreference resolution research platform. Technical report, Cornell University.

Y. Versley, S. Ponzetto, M. Poesio, V. Eidelman, A. Jern, J. Smith, X. Yang, and A. Moschitti. 2008. BART: A modular toolkit for coreference resolution. In *Proceedings of the Language Resources and Evaluation Conference*.

M. Vilain, J. Burger, J. Aberdeen, D. Connolly, and L. Hirschman. 1995. A Model-Theoretic Coreference Scoring Theme. In *Proceedings of the Sixth Message Understanding Conference (MUC-6)*.

X. Yang, G. Zhou, J. Su, and C. Tan. 2003. Coreference resolution using competition learning approach. In *Proceedings of the 41st Annual Meeting of the ACL*.

Predicate Argument Structure Analysis using Transformation-based Learning

Hirotoshi Taira **Sanae Fujita** **Masaaki Nagata**
NTT Communication Science Laboratories
2-4, Hikaridai, Seika-cho, Souraku-gun, Kyoto 619-0237, Japan
{taira,sanae}@cslab.kecl.ntt.co.jp nagata.masaaki@lab.ntt.co.jp

Abstract

Maintaining high annotation consistency in large corpora is crucial for statistical learning; however, such work is hard, especially for tasks containing semantic elements. This paper describes predicate argument structure analysis using transformation-based learning. An advantage of transformation-based learning is the readability of learned rules. A disadvantage is that the rule extraction procedure is time-consuming. We present incremental-based, transformation-based learning for semantic processing tasks. As an example, we deal with Japanese predicate argument analysis and show some tendencies of annotators for constructing a corpus with our method.

1 Introduction

Automatic predicate argument structure analysis (PAS) provides information of "who did what to whom" and is an important base tool for such various text processing tasks as machine translation information extraction (Hirschman et al., 1999), question answering (Narayanan and Harabagiu, 2004; Shen and Lapata, 2007), and summarization (Melli et al., 2005). Most recent approaches to predicate argument structure analysis are statistical machine learning methods such as support vector machines (SVMs)(Pradhan et al., 2004). For predicate argument structure analysis, we have the following representative large corpora: FrameNet (Fillmore et al., 2001), PropBank (Palmer et al., 2005), and NomBank (Meyers et al., 2004) in English, the Chinese PropBank (Xue, 2008) in Chinese, the GDA Corpus (Hashida, 2005), Kyoto Text Corpus Ver.4.0 (Kawahara et al., 2002), and the NAIST Text Corpus (Iida et al., 2007) in Japanese.

The construction of such large corpora is strenuous and time-consuming. Additionally, maintaining high annotation consistency in such corpora is crucial for statistical learning; however, such work is hard, especially for tasks containing semantic elements. For example, in Japanese corpora, distinguishing true dative (or indirect object) arguments from time-type argument is difficult because the arguments of both types are often accompanied with the 'ni' case marker.

A problem with such statistical learners as SVM is the lack of interpretability; if accuracy is low, we cannot identify the problems in the annotations.

We are focusing on transformation-based learning (TBL). An advantage for such learning methods is that we can easily interpret the learned model. The tasks in most previous research are such simple tagging tasks as part-of-speech tagging, insertion and deletion of parentheses in syntactic parsing, and chunking (Brill, 1995; Brill, 1993; Ramshaw and Marcus, 1995). Here we experiment with a complex task: Japanese PASs. TBL can be slow, so we proposed an incremental training method to speed up the training. We experimented with a Japanese PAS corpus with a graph-based TBL. From the experiments, we interrelated the annotation tendency on the dataset.

The rest of this paper is organized as follows. Section 2 describes Japanese predicate structure, our graph expression of it, and our improved method. The results of experiments using the NAIST Text Corpus, which is our target corpus, are reported in Section 3, and our conclusion is provided in Section 4.

2 Predicate argument structure and graph transformation learning

First, we illustrate the structure of a Japanese sentence in Fig. 1. In Japanese, we can divide a sentence into *bunsetsu* phrases (BP). A BP usually consists of one or more content words and zero,

Proceedings of the ACL 2010 Conference Short Papers, pages 162–167,
Uppsala, Sweden, 11-16 July 2010. ©2010 Association for Computational Linguistics

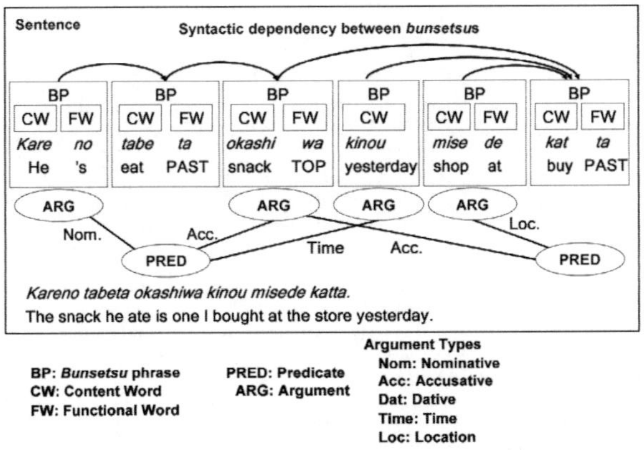

Figure 1: Graph expression for PAS

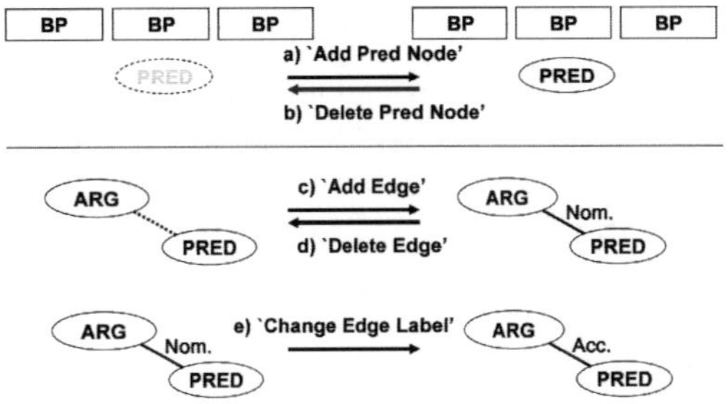

Figure 2: Transform types

one, or more than one functional words. Syntactic dependency between *bunsetsu* phrases can be defined. Japanese dependency parsers such as Cabocha (Kudo and Matsumoto, 2002) can extract BPs and their dependencies with about 90% accuracy.

Since predicates and arguments in Japanese are mainly annotated on the head content word in each BP, we can deal with BPs as candidates of predicates or arguments. In our experiments, we mapped each BP to an argument candidate node of graphs. We also mapped each predicate to a predicate node. Each predicate-argument relation is identified by an edge between a predicate and an argument, and the argument type is mapped to the edge label. In our experiments below, we defined five argument types: nominative (subjective), accusative (direct objective), dative (indirect objective), time, and location. We use five transformation types: a) add or b) delete a predicate node, c) add or d) delete an edge between an predicate and an argument node, e) change a label (= an argument type) to another label (Fig. 2). We explain the existence of an edge between a predicate and an argument labeled t candidate node as that the predicate and the argument have a t type relationship.

Transformation-based learning was proposed by (Brill, 1995). Below we explain our learning strategy when we directly adapt the learning method to our graph expression of PASs. First, unstructured texts from the training data are inputted. After pre-processing, each text is mapped to an initial graph. In our experiments, the initial graph has argument candidate nodes with corresponding BPs and no predicate nodes or edges. Next, comparing the current graphs with the gold standard graph structure in the training data, we find the different statuses of the nodes and edges among the graphs. We extract such transformation rule candidates as 'add node' and 'change edge label' with constraints, including 'the corresponding BP includes a verb' and 'the argument candidate and the predicate node have a syntactic dependency.' The extractions are executed based on the rule templates given in advance. Each extracted rule is evaluated for the current graphs, and error reduction is calculated. The best rule for the reduction is selected as a new rule and inserted at the bottom of the current rule list. The new rule is applied to the current graphs, which are transferred to other graph structures. This procedure is iterated until the total errors for the gold standard graphs become zero. When the process is completed, the rule list is the final model. In the test phase, we iteratively transform nodes and edges in the graphs mapped from the test data, based on rules in the model like decision lists. The last graph after all rule adaptations is the system output of the PAS.

In this procedure, the calculation of error reduction is very time-consuming, because we have to check many constraints from the candidate rules for all training samples. The calculation order is $O(MN)$, where M is the number of articles and N is the number of candidate rules. Additionally, an edge rule usually has three types of constraints: 'pred node constraint,' 'argument candidate node constraint,' and 'relation constraint.' The number of combinations and extracted rules are much larger than one of the rules for the node rules. Ramshaw et al. proposed an index-based efficient reduction method for the calculation of error reduction (Ramshaw and Marcus, 1994). However, in PAS tasks, we need to check the exclusiveness of the argument types (for example, a predicate argument structure does not have two nominative arguments), and we cannot directly use the method. Jijkoun et al. only used candidate rules that happen in the current and gold standard graphs and used SVM learning for constraint checks (Jijkoun and de Rijke, 2007). This method is effective for achieving high accuracy; however, it loses the readability of the rules. This is contrary to our aim to extract readable rules.

To reduce the calculations while maintaining readability, we propose an incremental method and describe its procedure below. In this procedure, we first have PAS graphs for only one article. After the total errors among the current and gold standard graphs become zero in the article, we proceed to the next article. For the next article, we first adapt the rules learned from the previous article. After that, we extract new rules from the two articles until the total errors for the articles become zero. We continue these processes until the last article. Additionally, we count the number of rule occurrences and only use the rule candidates that happen more than once, because most such rules harm the accuracy. We save and use these rules again if the occurrence increases.

3 Experiments

3.1 Experimental Settings

We used the articles in the NAIST Text Corpus version 1.4β (Iida et al., 2007) based on the *Mainichi Shinbun* Corpus (Mainichi, 1995), which were taken from news articles published in the Japanese *Mainichi Shinbun* newspaper. We used articles published on January 1st for training examples and on January 3rd for test examples. Three original argument types are defined in the NAIST Text Corpus: nominative (or subjective), accusative (or direct object), and dative (or indirect object). For evaluation of the difficult annotation cases, we also added annotations for 'time' and 'location' types by ourselves. We show the dataset distribution in Table 1. We extracted the BP units and dependencies among these BPs from the dataset using Cabocha, a Japanese dependency parser, as pre-processing. After that, we adapted our incremental learning to the training data. We used two constraint templates in Tables 2 and 3 for predicate nodes and edges when extracting the rule candidates.

Table 1: Data distribution

	Training	Test
# of Articles	95	74
# of Sentences	1,129	687
# of Predicates	3,261	2,038
# of Arguments	3,877	2,468
Nom.	1,717	971
Acc.	1,012	701
Dat.	632	376
Time	371	295
Loc.	145	125

Table 4: Total performances (F1-measure (%))

Type	System	P	R	F1
Pred.	Baseline	89.4	85.1	87.2
	Our system	**91.8**	**85.3**	**88.4**
Arg.	Baseline	79.3	59.5	68.0
	Our system	**81.9**	**62.4**	**70.8**

3.2 Results

Our incremental method takes an hour. In comparison, the original TBL cannot even extract one rule in a day. The results of predicate and argument type predictions are shown in Table 4. Here, 'Baseline' is the baseline system that predicts the BSs that contain verbs, adjectives, and *da* form nouns ('to be' in English) as predicates and predicts argument types for BSs having syntactical dependency with a predicted predicate BS, based on the following rules: 1) BSs containing nominative (*ga*) / accusative (*wo*) / dative (*ni*) case markers are predicted to be nominative, accusative, and dative, respectively. 2) BSs containing a topic case marker (*wa*) are predicted to be nominative. 3) When a word sense category from a Japanese ontology of the head word in BS belongs to a 'time' or 'location' category, the BS is predicted to be a 'time' and 'location' type argument. In all precision, recall, and F1-measure, our system outperformed the baseline system.

Next, we show our system's learning curve in Fig. 3. The number of final rules was 68. This indicates that the first twenty rules are mainly effective rules for the performance. The curve also shows that no overfitting happened. Next, we show the performance for every argument type in Table 5. 'TBL,' which stands for 'transformation-based learning,' is our system. In this table, the performance of the dative and time types improved, even though they are difficult to distinguish. On the other hand, the performance of the location type argument in our system is very low. Our method learns rules as decreasing errors of

Table 2: Predicate node constraint templates

Pred. Node Constraint Template		Rule Example	
Constraint	Description	Pred. Node Constraint	Operation
pos1	noun, verb, adjective, etc.	pos1='ADJECTIVE'	add pred node
pos2	independent, attached word, etc.	pos2='DEPENDENT WORD'	del pred node
pos1 & pos2	above two features combination	pos1='VERB' & pos2='ANCILLARY WORD'	add pred node
'da'	*da* form (copula)	'da form'	add pred node
lemma	word base form	lemma='%'	add pred node

Table 3: Edge constraint templates

Edge Constraint Template			Rule Example	
Arg. Cand. Const.	Pred. Node Const.	Relation Const.	Edge Constraint	Operation
FW (=func. word)	*	dep(arg → pred)	FW of Arg. ='*wa*(TOP)' & dep(arg → pred)	add NOM edge
*	FW	dep(arg ← pred)	FW of Pred. ='*na*(ADNOMINAL)' & dep(arg ← pred)	add NOM edge
SemCat (=semantic category)	*	dep(arg → pred)	SemCat of Arg. = 'TIME' & dep(arg → pred)	add TIME edge
FW	passive form	dep(arg → pred)	FW of Arg. ='*ga*(NOM) & Pred.: passive form	chg edge label NOM → ACC
*	kform (= type of inflected form)	*	kform of Pred. = continuative 'ta' form	add NOM edge
SemCat	Pred. SemCat	*	SemCat of Arg. = 'HUMAN' & Pred. SemCat = 'PHYSICAL MOVE'	add NOM edge

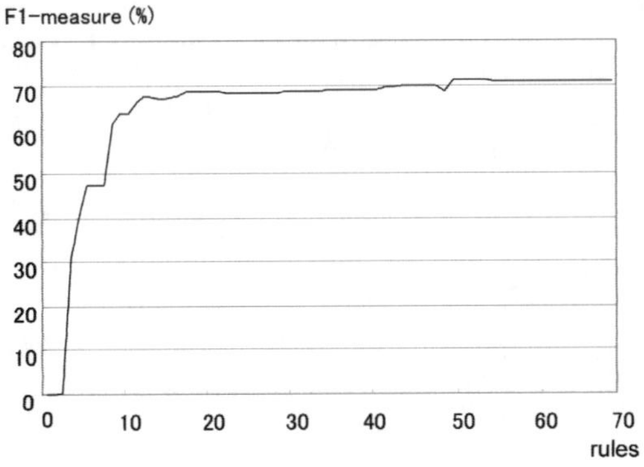

Figure 3: Learning curves: x-axis = number of rules; y-axis: F1-measure (%)

all arguments, and the performance of the location type argument is probably sacrificed for total error reduction because the number of location type arguments is much smaller than the number of other argument types (Table 1), and the improvement of the performance-based learning for location type arguments is relatively low. To confirm this, we performed an experiment in which we gave the rules of the baseline system to our system as initial rules and subsequently performed our incremental learning. 'Base + TBL' shows the experiment. The performance for the location type argument improved drastically. However, the total performance of the arguments was below the original TBL. Moreover, the 'Base + TBL' performance surpassed the baseline system. This indicates that our system learned a reasonable model.

Finally, we show some interesting extracted rules in Fig. 4. The first rule stands for an expression where the sentence ends with the performance of something, which is often seen in Japanese newspaper articles. The second and third rules represent that annotators of this dataset tend to annotate time types for which the semantic category of the argument is time, even if the argument looks like the dat. type, and annotators tend to annotate dat. type for arguments that have an dat.

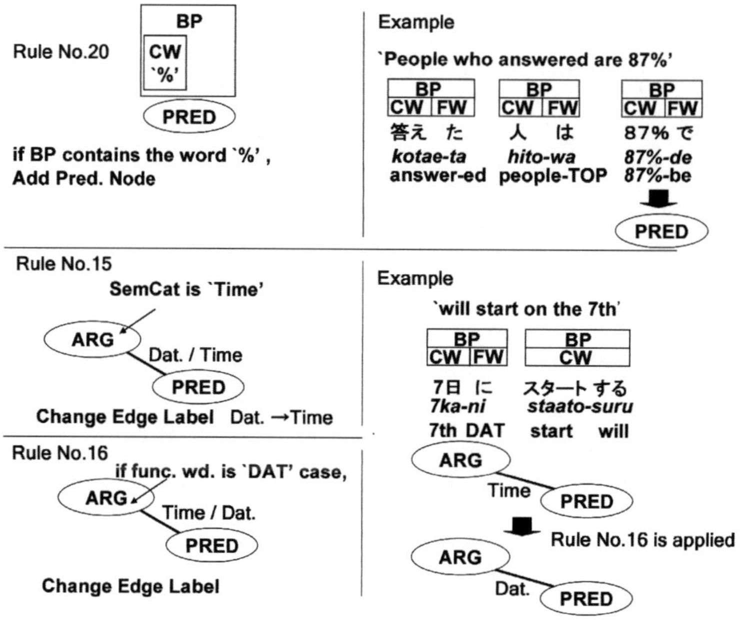

Figure 4: Examples of extracted rules

Table 5: Results for every arg. type (F-measure (%))

System	Args.	Nom.	Acc.	Dat.	Time	Loc.
Base	68.0	**65.8**	79.6	70.5	51.5	**38.0**
TBL	**70.8**	64.9	**86.4**	**74.8**	**59.6**	1.7
Base + TBL	69.5	63.9	85.8	67.8	55.8	37.4

type case marker.

4 Conclusion

We performed experiments for Japanese predicate argument structure analysis using transformation-based learning and extracted rules that indicate the tendencies annotators have. We presented an incremental procedure to speed up rule extraction. The performance of PAS analysis improved, especially, the dative and time types, which are difficult to distinguish. Moreover, when time expressions are attached to the 'ni' case, the learned model showed a tendency to annotate them as dative arguments in the used corpus. Our method has potential for dative predictions and interpreting the tendencies of annotator inconsistencies.

Acknowledgments

We thank Kevin Duh for his valuable comments.

References

Eric Brill. 1993. Transformation-based error-driven parsing. In *Proc. of the Third International Workshop on Parsing Technologies*.

Eric Brill. 1995. Transformation-based error-driven learning and natural language processing: A case study in part-of-speech tagging. *Computational Linguistics*, 21(4):543–565.

Charles J. Fillmore, Charles Wooters, and Collin F. Baker. 2001. Building a large lexical databank which provides deep semantics. In *Proc. of the Pacific Asian Conference on Language, Information and Computation (PACLING)*.

Kouichi Hashida. 2005. Global document annotation (GDA) manual. http://i-content.org/GDA/.

Lynette Hirschman, Patricia Robinson, Lisa Ferro, Nancy Chinchor, Erica Brown, Ralph Grishman, and Beth Sundheim. 1999. Hub-4 Event'99 general guidelines. http://www.itl.nist.gov/iaui/894.02/related_projects/muc/.

Ryu Iida, Mamoru Komachi, Kentaro Inui, and Yuji Matsumoto. 2007. Annotating a Japanese text corpus with predicate-argument and coreference relations. In *Proc. of ACL 2007 Workshop on Linguistic Annotation*, pages 132–139.

Valentin Jijkoun and Maarten de Rijke. 2007. Learning to transform linguistic graphs. In *Proc. of the Second Workshop on TextGraphs: Graph-Based Algorithms for Natural Language Processing (TextGraphs-2)*, pages 53–60. Association for Computational Linguistics.

Daisuke Kawahara, Sadao Kurohashi, and Koichi Hashida. 2002. Construction of a Japanese relevance-tagged corpus (in Japanese). *Proc. of the 8th Annual Meeting of the Association for Natural Language Processing*, pages 495–498.

Taku Kudo and Yuji Matsumoto. 2002. Japanese dependency analysis using cascaded chunking. In *Proc. of the 6th Conference on Natural Language Learning 2002 (CoNLL 2002).*

Mainichi. 1995. *CD Mainichi Shinbun 94.* Nichigai Associates Co.

Gabor Melli, Yang Wang, Yudong Liu, Mehdi M. Kashani, Zhongmin Shi, Baohua Gu, Anoop Sarkar, and Fred Popowich. 2005. Description of SQUASH, the SFU question answering summary handler for the DUC-2005 summarization task. In *Proc. of DUC 2005.*

Adam Meyers, Ruth Reeves, Catherine Macleod, Rachel Szekely, Veronika Zielinska, Brian Young, and Ralph Grishman. 2004. The NomBank project: An interim report. In *Proc. of HLT-NAACL 2004 Workshop on Frontiers in Corpus Annotation.*

Srini Narayanan and Sanda Harabagiu. 2004. Question answering based on semantic structures. In *Proc. of the 20th International Conference on Computational Linguistics (COLING).*

M. Palmer, P. Kingsbury, and D. Gildea. 2005. The proposition bank: An annotated corpus of semantic roles. *Computational Linguistics*, 31(1):71–106.

Sameer Pradhan, Waybe Ward, Kadri Hacioglu, James Martin, and Dan Jurafsky. 2004. Shallow semantic parsing using support vector machines. In *Proc. of the Human Language Technology Conference/North American Chapter of the Association of Computational Linguistics HLT/NAACL 2004.*

Lance Ramshaw and Mitchell Marcus. 1994. Exploring the statistical derivation of transformational rule sequences for part-of-speech tagging. In *The Balancing Act: Proc. of the ACL Workshop on Combining Symbolic and Statistical Approaches to Language.*

Lance Ramshaw and Mitchell Marcus. 1995. Text chunking using transformation-based learning. In *Proc. of the third workshop on very large corpora*, pages 82–94.

Dan Shen and Mirella Lapata. 2007. Using semantic roles to improve question answering. In *Proc. of the 2007 Joint Conference on Empirical Methods in Natural Language Processing and Computational Natural Language Learning (EMNLP/CoNLL)*, pages 12–21.

Nianwen Xue. 2008. Labeling Chinese predicates with semantic roles. *Computational Linguistics*, 34(2):224–255.

Improving Chinese Semantic Role Labeling with Rich Syntactic Features

Weiwei Sun*
Department of Computational Linguistics, Saarland University
German Research Center for Artificial Intelligence (DFKI)
D-66123, Saarbrücken, Germany
wsun@coli.uni-saarland.de

Abstract

Developing features has been shown crucial to advancing the state-of-the-art in Semantic Role Labeling (SRL). To improve Chinese SRL, we propose a set of additional features, some of which are designed to better capture structural information. Our system achieves 93.49 F-measure, a significant improvement over the best reported performance 92.0. We are further concerned with the effect of parsing in Chinese SRL. We empirically analyze the two-fold effect, grouping words into constituents and providing syntactic information. We also give some preliminary linguistic explanations.

1 Introduction

Previous work on Chinese Semantic Role Labeling (SRL) mainly focused on how to implement SRL methods which are successful on English. Similar to English, parsing is a *standard* pre-processing for Chinese SRL. Many features are extracted to represent constituents in the input parses (Sun and Jurafsky, 2004; Xue, 2008; Ding and Chang, 2008). By using these features, semantic classifiers are trained to predict whether a constituent fills a semantic role. Developing features that capture the right kind of information encoded in the input parses has been shown crucial to advancing the state-of-the-art. Though there has been some work on feature design in Chinese SRL, information encoded in the syntactic trees is not fully exploited and requires more research effort. In this paper, we propose a set of additional features, some of which are designed to better capture structural information of sub-trees in a given parse. With help of these new features, our system achieves 93.49 F-measure with hand-crafted parses. Comparison with the best reported results, 92.0 (Xue, 2008), shows that these features yield a significant improvement of the state-of-the-art.

We further analyze the effect of syntactic parsing in Chinese SRL. The main effect of parsing in SRL is two-fold. First, grouping words into constituents, parsing helps to find argument candidates. Second, parsers provide semantic classifiers plenty of syntactic information, not to only recognize arguments from all candidate constituents but also to classify their detailed semantic types. We empirically analyze each effect in turn. We also give some preliminary linguistic explanations for the phenomena.

2 Chinese SRL

The Chinese PropBank (CPB) is a semantic annotation for the syntactic trees of the Chinese TreeBank (CTB). The arguments of a predicate are labeled with a contiguous sequence of integers, in the form of AN (N is a natural number); the adjuncts are annotated as such with the label AM followed by a secondary tag that represents the semantic classification of the adjunct. The assignment of semantic roles is illustrated in Figure 1, where the predicate is the verb "调查/investigate". E.g., the NP "事故原因/the cause of the accident" is labeled as *A1*, meaning that it is the *Patient*.

In previous research, SRL methods that are successful on English are adopted to resolve Chinese SRL (Sun and Jurafsky, 2004; Xue, 2008; Ding and Chang, 2008, 2009; Sun et al., 2009; Sun, 2010). Xue (2008) produced complete and systematic research on full parsing based methods.

*The work was partially completed while this author was at Peking University.

Proceedings of the ACL 2010 Conference Short Papers, pages 168–172,
Uppsala, Sweden, 11-16 July 2010.

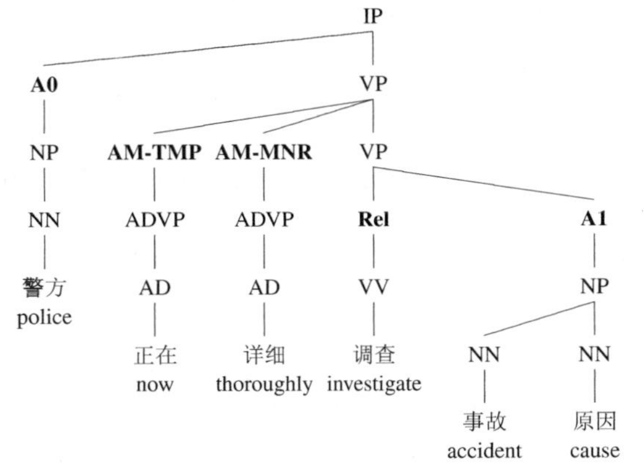

Figure 1: An example sentence: *The police are thoroughly investigating the cause of the accident.*

Their method divided SRL into three sub-tasks: 1) pruning with a heuristic rule, 2) Argument Identification (AI) to recognize arguments, and 3) Semantic Role Classification (SRC) to predict semantic types. The main two sub-tasks, AI and SRC, are formulated as two classification problems. Ding and Chang (2008) divided SRC into two sub-tasks in sequence: Each argument should first be determined whether it is a core argument or an adjunct, and then be classified into fine-grained categories. However, delicately designed features are more important and our experiments suggest that by using rich features, a better SRC solver can be directly trained without using hierarchical architecture. There are also some attempts at relaxing the necessity of using full syntactic parses, and semantic chunking methods have been introduced by (Sun et al., 2009; Sun, 2010; Ding and Chang, 2009).

2.1 Our System

We implement a three-stage (i.e. pruning, AI and SRC) SRL system. In the pruning step, our system keeps all constituents (except punctuations) that c-command[1] current predicate in focus as argument candidates. In the AI step, a lot of syntactic features are extracted to distinguish argument and non-argument. In other words, a binary classifier is trained to classify each argument candidate as either an argument or not. Finally, a multi-class classifier is trained to label each argument recognized in the former stage with a specific semantic role label. In both AI and SRC, the main job is to select strong syntactic features.

[1]See (Sun et al., 2008) for detailed definition.

3 Features

A majority of features used in our system are a combination of features described in (Xue, 2008; Ding and Chang, 2008) as well as the word formation and coarse frame features introduced in (Sun et al., 2009), the c-command thread features proposed in (Sun et al., 2008). We give a brief description of features used in previous work, but explain new features in details. For more information, readers can refer to relevant papers and our source codes[2] that are well commented. To conveniently illustrate, we denote a candidate constituent c_k with a fixed context $w_{i-1}[_{c_k} w_i ... w_h ... w_j] w_{j+1}$, where w_h is the head word of c_k, and denote predicate in focus with a context $w^v_{-2} w^v_{-1} w^v w^v_{+1} w^v_{+2}$, where w^v is the predicate in focus.

3.1 Baseline Features

The following features are introduced in previous Chinese SRL systems. We use them as baseline.

Word content of w^v, w_h, w_i, w_j and w_i+w_j; *POS tag* of w^v, w_h. *subcategorization frame*, *verb class* of w^v; *position*, *phrase type* c_k, *path* from c_k to w^v (from (Xue, 2008; Ding and Chang, 2008))

First character, *last character* and *word length* of w^v, *first character+length*, *last character+word length*, *first character+position*, *last character+position*, *coarse frame*, *frame+*w^v, *frame+left character*, *frame+verb class*, *frame+*c_k (from (Sun et al., 2009)).

Head word POS, *head word* of PP phrases, *category* of c_k's lift and right siblings, *CFG rewrite rule* that expands c_k and c_k's parent (from (Ding and Chang, 2008)).

3.2 New Word Features

We introduce some new features which can be extracted without syntactic structure. We denote them as word features. They include:

Word content of w^v_{-1}, w^v_{+1}, w_{i-1} and w_{j+1}; *POS tag* of w^v_{-1}, w^v_{+1}, w^v_{-2}, w^v_{+2}, w_{i-1}, w_i, w_j, w_{j+1}, w_{i+2} and w_{j-2}.

Length of c_k: how many words are there in c^k.

Word before "LC": If the POS of w_j is "LC" (localizer), we use w_{j-1} and its POS tag as two new features.

NT: Does c_k contain a word with POS "NT" (temporal noun)?

[2]Available at `http://code.google.com/p/csrler/`.

Combination features: w_i's POS+w_j's POS, w_v+*Position*

3.3 New Syntactic Features

Taking complex syntax trees as inputs, the classifiers should characterize their structural properties. We put forward a number of new features to encode the structural information.

Category of c_k's parent; *head word* and *POS of head word* of parent, left sibling and right sibling of c_k.

Lexicalized Rewrite rules: Conjuction of rewrite rule and head word of its corresponding RHS. These features of candidate (lrw-c) and its parent (lrw-p) are used. For example, this *lrw-c* feature of the NP "事故原因" in Figure 1 is $NP \rightarrow NN + NN$(原因).

Partial Path: Path from the c_k or w^v to the lowest common ancestor of c_k and w^v. One *path* feature, hence, is divided into *left path* and *right path*.

Clustered Path: We use the manually created clusters (see (Sun and Sui, 2009)) of categories of all nodes in the *path* (cpath) and *right path*.

C-commander thread between c_k and w^v (cct): (proposed by (Sun et al., 2008)). For example, this feature of the NP "警方" in Figure 1 is $NP + ADVP + ADVP + VV$.

Head Trace: The sequential container of the head down upon the phrase (from (Sun and Sui, 2009)). We design two kinds of traces (htr-p, htr-w): one uses POS of the head word; the other uses the head word word itself. E.g., the head word of 事故原因 is "原因" therefore these feature of this *NP* are *NP*↓*NN* and *NP*↓原因.

Combination features: *verb class*+c_k, w_h+w^v, w_h+*Position*, w_h+w^v+*Position*, *path*+w^v, w_h+*right path*, w^v+*left path*, *frame*+w^v+w_h, and w^v+cct.

4 Experiments and Analysis

4.1 Experimental Setting

To facilitate comparison with previous work, we use CPB 1.0 and CTB 5.0, the same data setting with (Xue, 2008). The data is divided into three parts: files from 081 to 899 are used as training set; files from 041 to 080 as development set; files from 001 to 040, and 900 to 931 as test set. Nearly all previous research on constituency based SRL evaluation use this setting, also including (Ding and Chang, 2008, 2009; Sun et al., 2009; Sun, 2010). All parsing and SRL experiments use this data setting. To resolve classification problems, we use a linear SVM classifier SVM_{lin}[3], along with One-Vs-All approach for multi-class classification. To evaluate SRL with automatic parsing, we use a state-of-the-art parser, Bikel parser[4] (Bikel, 2004). We use gold segmentation and POS as input to the Bikel parser and use it parsing results as input to our SRL system. The overall LP/LR/F performance of Bikel parser is 79.98%/82.95%/81.43.

4.2 Overall Performance

Table 1 summarizes precision, recall and F-measure of AI, SRC and the whole task (AI+SRC) of our system respectively. The forth line is the best published SRC performance reported in (Ding and Chang, 2008), and the sixth line is the best SRL performance reported in (Xue, 2008). Other lines show the performance of our system. These results indicate a significant improvement over previous systems due to the new features.

Test	P(%)	R(%)	F/A
AI	98.56	97.91	98.24
SRC	- -	- -	**95.04**
(Ding and Chang, 2008)	- -	- -	94.68
AI + SRC	**93.80**	**93.18**	**93.49**
(Xue, 2008)	93.0	91.0	92.0

Table 1: SRL performance on the test data with gold standard parses.

4.3 Two-fold Effect of Parsing in SRL

The effect of parsing in SRL is two-fold. On the one hand, SRL systems should group words as argument candidates, which are also constituents in a given sentence. Full parsing provides boundary information of all constituents. As arguments should c-command the predicate, a full parser can further prune a majority of useless constituents. In other words, parsing can effectively supply SRL with argument candidates. Unfortunately, it is very hard to rightly produce full parses for Chinese text. On the other hand, given a constituent, SRL systems should identify whether it is an argument and further predict detailed semantic types if

[3] http://people.cs.uchicago.edu/~vikass/svmlin.html

[4] http://www.cis.upenn.edu/~dbikel/software.html

Task	Parser	Bracket	Feat	P(%)	R(%)	F/A
AI	- -	Gold	W	82.44	86.78	84.55
	CTB	Gold	W+S	98.69	98.11	98.40
	Bikel	Bikel	W+S	77.54	71.62	74.46
SRC	- -	Gold	W	- -	- -	93.93
	CTB	Gold	W+S	- -	- -	95.80
	Bikel	Gold	W+S	- -	- -	92.62

Table 2: Classification perfromance on development data. In the *Feat* column, *W* means word features; *W+S* means word and syntactic feautres.

it is an argument. For the two classification problems, parsing can provide complex syntactic information such as *path* features.

4.3.1 The Effect of Parsing in AI

In AI, full parsing is very important for both grouping words and classification. Table 2 summarizes relative experimental results. Line 2 is the AI performance when gold candidate boundaries and word features are used; Line 3 is the performance with additional syntactic features. Line 4 shows the performance by using automatic parses generated by Bikel parser. We can see that: 1) word features only cannot train good classifiers to identify arguments; 2) it is very easy to recognize arguments with good enough syntactic parses; 3) there is a severe performance decline when automatic parses are used. The third observation is a similar conclusion in English SRL. However this problem in Chinese is much more serious due to the state-of-the-art of Chinese parsing.

Information theoretic criteria are popular criteria in variable selection (Guyon and Elisseeff, 2003). This paper uses empirical mutual information between each variable and the target, $I(X,Y) = \sum_{x \in X, y \in Y} p(x,y) \log \frac{p(x,y)}{p(x)p(y)}$, to roughly rank the importance of features. Table 3 shows the ten most useful features in AI. We can see that the most important features all based on full parsing information. Nine of these top 10 useful features are our new features.

Rank	Feature	Rank	Feature
1	w^v_cct	2	‡ w_h+w^v+Position
3	htr-w	4	htr-p
5	path	6	‡ w_h+w^v
7	cpath	8	cct
9	path+w^v	10	lrw-p

Table 3: Top 10 useful features for AI. ‡ means *word features*.

4.3.2 The Effect of Parsing in SRC

The second block in Table 2 summarizes the SRC performance with gold argument boundaries. Line 5 is the accuracy when word features are used; Line 6 is the accuracy when additional syntactic features are added; The last row is the accuracy when syntactic features used are extracted from automatic parses (*Bikel+Gold*). We can see that different from AI, word features only can train reasonable good semantic classifiers. The comparison between Line 5 and 7 suggests that with parsing errors, automatic parsed syntactic features cause noise to the semantic role classifiers.

4.4 Why Word Features Are Effective for SRC?

Rank	Feature	Rank	Feature
1	‡frame+w_h+w^v	2	‡w_h+w^v+position
3	‡w_h+w^v	4	w^v+cct
5	lrw-p	6	†w_i+w_j
7	lrw-c	8	‡w_h+Postion
9	†frame+w^v	10	htr-p

Table 4: Top 10 useful features for SRC.

Table 4 shows the ten most useful features in SRC. We can see that two of these ten features are word features (denoted by †). Namely, word features play a more important role in SRC than in AI. Though the other eight features are based on full parsing, four of them (denoted by ‡) use the head word which can be well approximated by word features, according to some language specific properties. The head rules described in (Sun and Jurafsky, 2004) are very popular in Chinese parsing research, such as in (Duan et al., 2007; Zhang and Clark, 2008). From these head rules, we can see that head words of most phrases in Chinese are located at the first or the last position. We implement these rules on Chinese Tree Bank and find that 84.12% [5] nodes realize their heads as either their first or last word. Head position suggests that boundary words are good approximation of head word features. If head words have good approximation word features, then it is not strange that the four features denoted by ‡ can be effectively represented by word features. Similar with feature effect in AI, most of most useful features in SRC are our new features.

[5]This statistics excludes all empty categories in CTB.

5 Conclusion

This paper proposes an additional set of features to improve Chinese SRL. These new features yield a significant improvement over the best published performance. We further analyze the effect of parsing in Chinese SRL, and linguistically explain some phenomena. We found that (1) full syntactic information playes an essential role only in AI and that (2) due to the head word position distribution, SRC is easy to resolve in Chinese SRL.

Acknowledgments

The author is funded both by German Academic Exchange Service (DAAD) and German Research Center for Artificial Intelligence (DFKI).

The author would like to thank the anonymous reviewers for their helpful comments.

References

Daniel M. Bikel. 2004. A distributional analysis of a lexicalized statistical parsing model. In Dekang Lin and Dekai Wu, editors, *Proceedings of EMNLP 2004*, pages 182–189. Association for Computational Linguistics, Barcelona, Spain.

Weiwei Ding and Baobao Chang. 2008. Improving Chinese semantic role classification with hierarchical feature selection strategy. In *Proceedings of the EMNLP 2008*, pages 324–333. Association for Computational Linguistics, Honolulu, Hawaii.

Weiwei Ding and Baobao Chang. 2009. Fast semantic role labeling for Chinese based on semantic chunking. In *ICCPOL '09: Proceedings of the 22nd International Conference on Computer Processing of Oriental Languages. Language Technology for the Knowledge-based Economy*, pages 79–90. Springer-Verlag, Berlin, Heidelberg.

Xiangyu Duan, Jun Zhao, and Bo Xu. 2007. Probabilistic models for action-based Chinese dependency parsing. In *ECML '07: Proceedings of the 18th European conference on Machine Learning*, pages 559–566. Springer-Verlag, Berlin, Heidelberg.

Isabelle Guyon and André Elisseeff. 2003. An introduction to variable and feature selection. *Journal of Machine Learning Research*, 3:1157–1182.

Honglin Sun and Daniel Jurafsky. 2004. Shallow semantc parsing of Chinese. In Daniel Marcu Susan Dumais and Salim Roukos, editors, *HLT-NAACL 2004: Main Proceedings*.

Weiwei Sun. 2010. Semantics-driven shallow parsing for Chinese semantic role labeling. In *Proceedings of the ACL 2010*.

Weiwei Sun and Zhifang Sui. 2009. Chinese function tag labeling. In *Proceedings of the 23rd Pacific Asia Conference on Language, Information and Computation*. Hong Kong.

Weiwei Sun, Zhifang Sui, and Haifeng Wang. 2008. Prediction of maximal projection for semantic role labeling. In *Proceedings of the 22nd International Conference on Computational Linguistics*.

Weiwei Sun, Zhifang Sui, Meng Wang, and Xin Wang. 2009. Chinese semantic role labeling with shallow parsing. In *Proceedings of the 2009 Conference on Empirical Methods in Natural Language Processing*, pages 1475–1483. Association for Computational Linguistics, Singapore.

Nianwen Xue. 2008. Labeling Chinese predicates with semantic roles. *Comput. Linguist.*, 34(2):225–255.

Yue Zhang and Stephen Clark. 2008. A tale of two parsers: Investigating and combining graph-based and transition-based dependency parsing. In *Proceedings of the 2008 Conference on Empirical Methods in Natural Language Processing*, pages 562–571. Association for Computational Linguistics, Honolulu, Hawaii.

Balancing User Effort and Translation Error in Interactive Machine Translation Via Confidence Measures

Jesús González-Rubio
Inst. Tec. de Informática
Univ. Politéc. de Valencia
46021 Valencia, Spain
jegonzalez@iti.upv.es

Daniel Ortiz-Martínez
Dpto. de Sist Inf. y Comp.
Univ. Politéc. de Valencia
46021 Valencia, Spain
dortiz@dsic.upv.es

Francisco Casacuberta
Dpto. de Sist Inf. y Comp.
Univ. Politéc. de Valencia
46021 Valencia, Spain
fcn@dsic.upv.es

Abstract

This work deals with the application of confidence measures within an interactive-predictive machine translation system in order to reduce human effort. If a small loss in translation quality can be tolerated for the sake of efficiency, user effort can be saved by interactively translating only those initial translations which the confidence measure classifies as incorrect. We apply confidence estimation as a way to achieve a balance between user effort savings and final translation error. Empirical results show that our proposal allows to obtain almost perfect translations while significantly reducing user effort.

1 Introduction

In *Statistical Machine Translation* (SMT), the translation is modelled as a decission process. For a given source string $f_1^J = f_1 \dots f_j \dots f_J$, we seek for the target string $e_1^I = e_1 \dots e_i \dots e_I$ which maximises posterior probability:

$$\hat{e}_1^{\hat{I}} = \underset{I, e_1^I}{\operatorname{argmax}}\, Pr(e_1^I | f_1^J) \,. \qquad (1)$$

Within the *Interactive-predictive Machine Translation* (IMT) framework, a state-of-the-art SMT system is employed in the following way: For a given source sentence, the SMT system fully automatically generates an initial translation. A human translator checks this translation from left to right, correcting the first error. The SMT system then proposes a new extension, taking the correct prefix $e_1^i = e_1 \dots e_i$ into account. These steps are repeated until the whole input sentence has been correctly translated. In the resulting decision rule, we maximise over all possible extensions e_{i+1}^I of e_1^i:

$$\hat{e}_{i+1}^{\hat{I}} = \underset{I, e_{i+1}^I}{\operatorname{argmax}}\, Pr(e_{i+1}^I | e_1^i, f_1^J) \,. \qquad (2)$$

An implementation of the IMT famework was performed in the TransType project (Foster et al., 1997; Langlais et al., 2002) and further improved within the TransType2 project (Esteban et al., 2004; Barrachina et al., 2009).

IMT aims at reducing the effort and increasing the productivity of translators, while preserving high-quality translation. In this work, we integrate *Confidence Measures* (CMs) within the IMT framework to further reduce the user effort. As will be shown, our proposal allows to balance the ratio between user effort and final translation error.

1.1 Confidence Measures

Confidence estimation have been extensively studied for speech recognition. Only recently have researchers started to investigate CMs for MT (Gandrabur and Foster, 2003; Blatz et al., 2004; Ueffing and Ney, 2007).

Different TransType-style MT systems use confidence information to improve translation prediction accuracy (Gandrabur and Foster, 2003; Ueffing and Ney, 2005). In this work, we propose a focus shift in which CMs are used to modify the interaction between the user and the system instead of modify the IMT translation predictions.

To compute CMs we have to select suitable confidence features and define a binary classifier. Typically, the classification is carried out depending on whether the confidence value exceeds a given threshold or not.

2 IMT with Sentence CMs

In the conventional IMT scenario a human translator and a SMT system collaborate in order to obtain the translation the user has in mind. Once the user has interactively translated the source sentences, the output translations are error-free. We propose an alternative scenario where not all the source sentences are interactively translated by the user. Specifically, only those source sentences

Proceedings of the ACL 2010 Conference Short Papers, pages 173–177,
Uppsala, Sweden, 11-16 July 2010. ©2010 Association for Computational Linguistics

whose initial fully automatic translation are incorrect, according to some quality criterion, are interactively translated. We propose to use CMs as the quality criterion to classify those initial translations.

Our approach implies a modification of the user-machine interaction protocol. For a given source sentence, the SMT system generates an initial translation. Then, if the CM classifies this translation as correct, we output it as our final translation. On the contrary, if the initial translation is classified as incorrect, we perform a conventional IMT procedure, validating correct prefixes and generating new suffixes, until the sentence that the user has in mind is reached.

In our scenario, we allow the final translations to be different from the ones the user has in mind. This implies that the output may contain errors. If a small loss in translation can be tolerated for the sake of efficiency, user effort can be saved by interactively translating only those sentences that the CMs classify as incorrect.

It is worth of notice that our proposal can be seen as a generalisation of the conventional IMT approach. Varying the value of the CM classification threshold, we can range from a fully automatic SMT system where all sentences are classified as correct to a conventional IMT system where all sentences are classified as incorrect.

2.1 Selecting a CM for IMT

We compute sentence CMs by combining the scores given by a word CM based on the IBM model 1 (Brown et al., 1993), similar to the one described in (Blatz et al., 2004). We modified this word CM by replacing the *average* by the *maximal* lexicon probability, because the average is dominated by this maximum (Ueffing and Ney, 2005). We choose this word CM because it can be calculated very fast during search, which is crucial given the time constraints of the IMT systems. Moreover, its performance is similar to that of other word CMs as results presented in (Blatz et al., 2003; Blatz et al., 2004) show. The word confidence value of word e_i, $c_w(e_i)$, is given by

$$c_w(e_i) = \max_{0 \leq j \leq J} p(e_i|f_j) \,, \tag{3}$$

where $p(e_i|f_j)$ is the IBM model 1 lexicon probability, and f_0 is the empty source word.

From this word CM, we compute two sentence CMs which differ in the way the word confidence

		Spanish	English
Train	Sentences	214.5K	
	Running words	5.8M	5.2M
	Vocabulary	97.4K	83.7K
Dev.	Sentences	400	
	Running words	11.5K	10.1K
	Perplexity (trigrams)	46.1	59.4
Test	Sentences	800	
	Running words	22.6K	19.9K
	Perplexity (trigrams)	45.2	60.8

Table 1: Statistics of the Spanish–English EU corpora. K and M denote thousands and millions of elements respectively.

scores $c_w(e_i)$ are combined:

MEAN CM ($c_M(e_1^I)$) is computed as the geometric mean of the confidence scores of the words in the sentence:

$$c_M(e_1^I) = \sqrt[I]{\prod_{i=1}^{I} c_w(e_i)} \,. \tag{4}$$

RATIO CM ($c_R(e_1^I)$) is computed as the percentage of words classified as correct in the sentence. A word is classified as correct if its confidence exceeds a word classification threshold τ_w.

$$c_R(e_1^I) = \frac{|\{e_i \,/\, c_w(e_i) > \tau_w\}|}{I} \tag{5}$$

After computing the confidence value, each sentence is classified as either correct or incorrect, depending on whether its confidence value exceeds or not a sentence clasiffication threshold τ_s. If $\tau_s = 0.0$ then all the sentences will be classified as correct whereas if $\tau_s = 1.0$ all the sentences will be classified as incorrect.

3 Experimentation

The aim of the experimentation was to study the possibly trade-off between saved user effort and translation error obtained when using sentence CMs within the IMT framework.

3.1 System evaluation

In this paper, we report our results as measured by *Word Stroke Ratio* (WSR) (Barrachina et al., 2009). WSR is used in the context of IMT to measure the effort required by the user to generate her

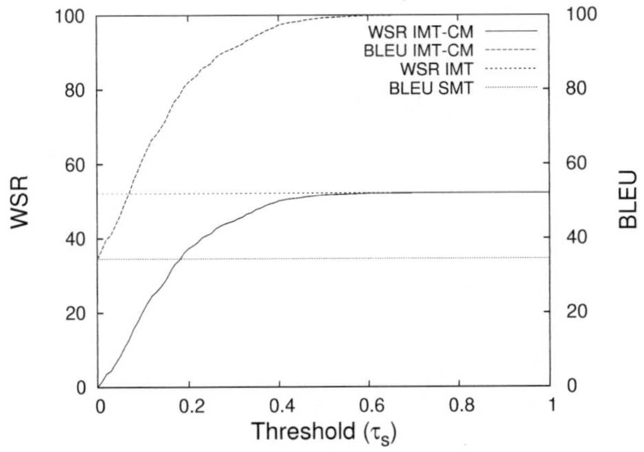

Figure 1: BLEU translation scores versus WSR for different values of the sentence classification threshold using the MEAN CM.

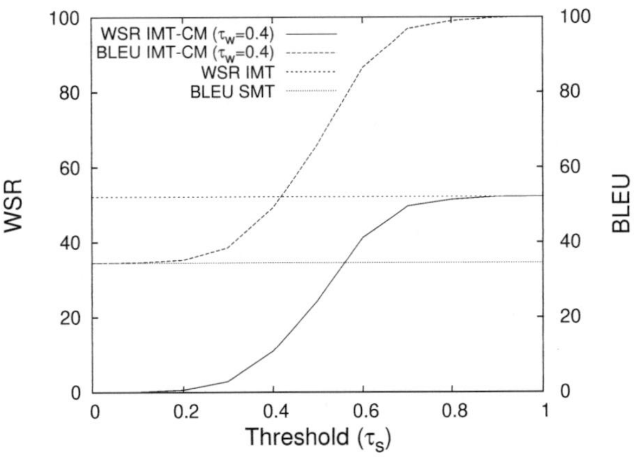

Figure 2: BLEU translation scores versus WSR for different values of the sentence classification threshold using the RATIO CM with $\tau_w = 0.4$.

translations. WSR is computed as the ratio between the number of word-strokes a user would need to achieve the translation she has in mind and the total number of words in the sentence. In this context, a word-stroke is interpreted as a single action, in which the user types a complete word, and is assumed to have constant cost.

Additionally, and because our proposal allows differences between its output and the reference translation, we will also present translation quality results in terms of *BiLingual Evaluation Understudy* (BLEU) (Papineni et al., 2002). BLEU computes a geometric mean of the precision of n-grams multiplied by a factor to penalise short sentences.

3.2 Experimental Setup

Our experiments were carried out on the EU corpora (Barrachina et al., 2009). The EU corpora were extracted from the Bulletin of the European Union. The EU corpora is composed of sentences given in three different language pairs. Here, we will focus on the Spanish–English part of the EU corpora. The corpus is divided into training, development and test sets. The main figures of the corpus can be seen in Table 1.

As a first step, be built a SMT system to translate from Spanish into English. This was done by means of the Thot toolkit (Ortiz et al., 2005), which is a complete system for building phrase-based SMT models. This toolkit involves the estimation, from the training set, of different statistical models, which are in turn combined in a log-linear fashion by adjusting a weight for each of them by means of the MERT (Och, 2003) procedure, optimising the BLEU score on the development set.

The IMT system which we have implemented relies on the use of word graphs (Ueffing et al., 2002) to efficiently compute the suffix for a given prefix. A word graph has to be generated for each sentence to be interactively translated. For this purpose, we used a multi-stack phrase-based decoder which will be distributed in the near future together with the Thot toolkit. We discarded to use the state-of-the-art Moses toolkit (Koehn et al., 2007) because preliminary experiments performed with it revealed that the decoder by Ortiz-Martínez et al. (2005) performs better in terms of WSR when used to generate word graphs for their use in IMT (Sanchis-Trilles et al., 2008). Moreover, the performance difference in regular SMT is negligible. The decoder was set to only consider monotonic translation, since in real IMT scenarios considering non-monotonic translation leads to excessive response time for the user.

Finally, the obtained word graphs were used within the IMT procedure to produce the reference translations in the test set, measuring WSR and BLEU.

3.3 Results

We carried out a series of experiments ranging the value of the sentence classification threshold τ_s, between 0.0 (equivalent to a fully automatic SMT system) and 1.0 (equivalent to a conventional IMT system), for both the MEAN and RATIO CMs. For each threshold value, we calculated the effort of the user in terms of WSR, and the translation quality of the final output as measured by BLEU.

src-1	DECLARACIÓN (No 17) relativa al derecho de acceso a la información	
ref-1	DECLARATION (No 17) on the right of access to information	
tra-1	DECLARATION (No 17) on the right of access to information	
src-2	Conclusiones del Consejo sobre el comercio electrónico y los impuestos indirectos.	
ref-2	Council conclusions on electronic commerce and indirect taxation.	
tra-2	Council conclusions on e-commerce and indirect taxation.	
src-3	participación de los países candidatos en los programas comunitarios.	
ref-3	participation of the applicant countries in Community programmes.	
tra-3	countries' involvement in Community programmes.	

Example 1: Examples of initial fully automatically generated sentences classified as correct by the CMs.

Figure 1 shows WSR (WSR IMT-CM) and BLEU (BLEU IMT-CM) scores obtained varying τ_s for the MEAN CM. Additionally, we also show the BLEU score (BLEU SMT) obtained by a fully automatic SMT system as translation quality baseline, and the WSR score (WSR IMT) obtained by a conventional IMT system as user effort baseline. This figure shows a continuous transition between the fully automatic SMT system and the conventional IMT system. This transition occurs when ranging τ_s between 0.0 and 0.6. This is an undesired effect, since for almost a half of the possible values for τ_s there is no change in the behaviour of our proposed IMT system.

The RATIO CM confidence values depend on a word classification threshold τ_w. We have carried out experimentation ranging τ_w between 0.0 and 1.0 and found that this value can be used to solve the above mentioned undesired effect for the MEAN CM. Specifically, varying the value of τ_w we can stretch the interval in which the transition between the fully automatic SMT system and the conventional IMT system is produced, allowing us to obtain smother transitions. Figure 2 shows WSR and BLEU scores for different values of the sentence classification threshold τ_s using $\tau_w = 0.4$. We show results only for this value of τ_w due to paper space limitations and because $\tau_w = 0.4$ produced the smoothest transition. According to Figure 2, using a sentence classification threshold value of 0.6 we obtain a WSR reduction of 20% relative and an almost perfect translation quality of 87 BLEU points.

It is worth of notice that the final translations are compared with only one reference, therefore, the reported translation quality scores are clearly pessimistic. Better results are expected using a multi-reference corpus. Example 1 shows the source sentence (src), the reference translation (ref) and the final translation (tra) for three of the initial fully automatically generated translations that were classified as correct by our CMs, and thus, were not interactively translated by the user. The first translation (tra-1) is identical to the corresponding reference translation (ref-1). The second translation (tra-2) corresponds to a correct translation of the source sentence (src-2) that is different from the corresponding reference (ref-2). Finally, the third translation (tra-3) is an example of a slightly incorrect translation.

4 Concluding Remarks

In this paper, we have presented a novel proposal that introduces sentence CMs into an IMT system to reduce user effort. Our proposal entails a modification of the user-machine interaction protocol that allows to achieve a balance between the user effort and the final translation error.

We have carried out experimentation using two different sentence CMs. Varying the value of the sentence classification threshold, we can range from a fully automatic SMT system to a conventional IMT system. Empirical results show that our proposal allows to obtain almost perfect translations while significantly reducing user effort.

Future research aims at the investigation of improved CMs to be integrated in our IMT system.

Acknowledgments

Work supported by the EC (FEDER/FSE) and the Spanish MEC/MICINN under the MIPRCV "Consolider Ingenio 2010" program (CSD2007-00018), the iTransDoc (TIN2006-15694-CO2-01) and iTrans2 (TIN2009-14511) projects and the FPU scholarship AP2006-00691. Also supported by the Spanish MITyC under the erudito.com (TSI-020110-2009-439) project and by the Generalitat Valenciana under grant Prometeo/2009/014.

References

S. Barrachina, O. Bender, F. Casacuberta, J. Civera, E. Cubel, S. Khadivi, A. Lagarda, H. Ney, J. Tomás, and E. Vidal. 2009. Statistical approaches to computer-assisted translation. *Computational Linguistics*, 35(1):3–28.

J. Blatz, E. Fitzgerald, G. Foster, S. Gandrabur, C. Goutte, A. Kulesza, A. Sanchis, and N. Ueffing. 2003. Confidence estimation for machine translation.

J. Blatz, E. Fitzgerald, G. Foster, S. Gandrabur, C. Goutte, A. Kuesza, A. Sanchis, and N. Ueffing. 2004. Confidence estimation for machine translation. In *Proc. COLING*, page 315.

P. F. Brown, S. A. Della Pietra, V. J. Della Pietra, and R. L. Mercer. 1993. The Mathematics of Statistical Machine Translation: Parameter Estimation. *Computational Linguistics*, 19(2):263–311.

J. Esteban, J. Lorenzo, A. Valderrábanos, and G. Lapalme. 2004. Transtype2: an innovative computer-assisted translation system. In *Proc. ACL*, page 1.

G. Foster, P. Isabelle, and P. Plamondon. 1997. Target-text mediated interactive machine translation. *Machine Translation*, 12:12–175.

S. Gandrabur and G. Foster. 2003. Confidence estimation for text prediction. In *Proc. CoNLL*, pages 315–321.

P. Koehn, H. Hoang, A. Birch, C. Callison-Burch, M. Federico, N. Bertoldi, B. Cowan, W. Shen, C. Moran, R. Zens, C. Dyer, O. Bojar, A. Constantin, and E. Herbst. 2007. Moses: Open source toolkit for statistical machine translation. In *Proc. ACL*, pages 177–180.

P. Langlais, G. Lapalme, and M. Loranger. 2002. Transtype: Development-evaluation cycles to boost translator's productivity. *Machine Translation*, 15(4):77–98.

F. J. Och. 2003. Minimum error rate training in statistical machine translation. In *Proc. ACL*, pages 160–167.

D. Ortiz, I. García-Varea, and F. Casacuberta. 2005. Thot: a toolkit to train phrase-based statistical translation models. In *Proc. MT Summit*, pages 141–148.

K. Papineni, S. Roukos, T. Ward, and W. Zhu. 2002. BLEU: a method for automatic evaluation of MT. In *Proc. ACL*, pages 311–318.

G. Sanchis-Trilles, D. Ortiz-Martínez, J. Civera, F. Casacuberta, E. Vidal, and H. Hoang. 2008. Improving interactive machine translation via mouse actions. In *Proc. EMNLP*, pages 25–27.

N. Ueffing and H. Ney. 2005. Application of word-level confidence measures in interactive statistical machine translation. In *Proc. EAMT*, pages 262–270.

N. Ueffing and H. Ney. 2007. Word-level confidence estimation for machine translation. *Comput. Linguist.*, 33(1):9–40.

N. Ueffing, F.J. Och, and H. Ney. 2002. Generation of word graphs in statistical machine translation. In *Proc. EMNLP*, pages 156–163.

Improving Arabic-to-English Statistical Machine Translation by Reordering Post-verbal Subjects for Alignment

Marine Carpuat **Yuval Marton** **Nizar Habash**
Columbia University
Center for Computational Learning Systems
475 Riverside Drive, New York, NY 10115
{marine,ymarton,habash}@ccls.columbia.edu

Abstract

We study the challenges raised by Arabic verb and subject detection and reordering in Statistical Machine Translation (SMT). We show that post-verbal subject (VS) constructions are hard to translate because they have highly ambiguous reordering patterns when translated to English. In addition, implementing reordering is difficult because the boundaries of VS constructions are hard to detect accurately, even with a state-of-the-art Arabic dependency parser. We therefore propose to reorder VS constructions into SV order for SMT word alignment only. This strategy significantly improves BLEU and TER scores, even on a strong large-scale baseline and despite noisy parses.

1 Introduction

Modern Standard Arabic (MSA) is a morpho-syntactically complex language, with different phenomena from English, a fact that raises many interesting issues for natural language processing and Arabic-to-English statistical machine translation (SMT). While comprehensive Arabic preprocessing schemes have been widely adopted for handling Arabic morphology in SMT (e.g., Sadat and Habash (2006), Zollmann et al. (2006), Lee (2004)), syntactic issues have not received as much attention by comparison (Green et al. (2009), Crego and Habash (2008), Habash (2007)). Arabic verbal constructions are particularly challenging since subjects can occur in pre-verbal (SV), post-verbal (VS) or pro-dropped ("null subject") constructions. As a result, training data for learning verbal construction translations is split between the different constructions and their patterns; and complex reordering schemas are needed in order to translate them into primarily pre-verbal subject languages (SVO) such as English.

These issues are particularly problematic in phrase-based SMT (Koehn et al., 2003). Standard phrase-based SMT systems memorize phrasal translation of verb and subject constructions as observed in the training bitext. They do not capture any generalizations between occurrences in VS and SV orders, even for the same verbs. In addition, their distance-based reordering models are not well suited to handling complex reordering operations which can include long distance dependencies, and may vary by context. Despite these limitations, phrase-based SMT systems have achieved competitive results in Arabic-to-English benchmark evaluations.[1] However, error analysis shows that verbs are still often dropped or incorrectly translated, and subjects are split or garbled in translation. This suggests that better syntactic modeling should further improve SMT.

We attempt to get a better understanding of translation patterns for Arabic verb constructions, particularly VS constructions, by studying their occurrence and reordering patterns in a hand-aligned Arabic-English parallel treebank. Our analysis shows that VS reordering rules are not straightforward and that SMT should therefore benefit from direct modeling of Arabic verb subject translation. In order to detect VS constructions, we use our state-of-the-art Arabic dependency parser, which is essentially the CATIBEX baseline in our subsequent parsing work in Marton et al. (2010), and is further described there. We show that VS subjects and their exact boundaries are hard to identify accurately. Given the noise in VS detection, existing strategies for source-side reordering (e.g., Xia and McCord (2004), Collins et al. (2005), Wang et al. (2007)) or using de-

[1] http://www.itl.nist.gov/iad/mig/tests/mt/2009/ResultsRelease/currentArabic.html

Proceedings of the ACL 2010 Conference Short Papers, pages 178–183,
Uppsala, Sweden, 11-16 July 2010.

Table 1: How are Arabic SV and VS translated in the manually word-aligned Arabic-English parallel treebank? We check whether V and S are translated in a "monotone" or "inverted" order for all VS and SV constructions. "Overlap" represents instances where translations of the Arabic verb and subject have some English words in common, and are not monotone nor inverted.

	gold reordering	all verbs	%
SV	monotone	2588	**98.2**
SV	inverted	15	0.5
SV	overlap	35	1.3
SV	total	2638	100
VS	monotone	1700	27.3
VS	inverted	4033	**64.7**
VS	overlap	502	8.0
VS	total	6235	100

pendency parses as cohesion constraints in decoding (e.g., Cherry (2008); Bach et al. (2009)) are not effective at this stage. While these approaches have been successful for language pairs such as German-English for which syntactic parsers are more developed and relevant reordering patterns might be less ambiguous, their impact potential on Arabic-English translation is still unclear.

In this work, we focus on VS constructions only, and propose a new strategy in order to benefit from their noisy detection: for the word alignment stage only, we reorder phrases detected as VS constructions into an SV order. Then, for phrase extraction, weight optimization and decoding, we use the original (non-reordered) text. This approach significantly improves both BLEU and TER on top of strong medium and large-scale phrase-based SMT baselines.

2 VS reordering in gold Arabic-English translation

We use the manually word-aligned parallel Arabic-English Treebank (LDC2009E82) to study how Arabic VS constructions are translated into English by humans. Given the gold Arabic syntactic parses and the manual Arabic-English word alignments, we can determine the gold reorderings for SV and VS constructions. We extract VS representations from the gold constituent parses by deterministic conversion to a simplified dependency structure, CATiB (Habash and Roth, 2009) (see Section 3). We then check whether the English translations of the Arabic verb and the Arabic subject occur in the same order as in Arabic (monotone) or not (inverted). Table 1 summarizes the reordering patterns for each category. As expected, 98% of Arabic SV are translated in a monotone order in English. For VS constructions, the picture is surprisingly more complex. The monotone VS translations are mostly explained by changes to passive voice or to non-verbal constructions (such as nominalization) in the English translation.

In addition, Table 1 shows that verb subjects occur more frequently in VS order (70%) than in SV order (30%). These numbers do not include prodropped ("null subject") constructions.

3 Arabic VS construction detection

Even if the SMT system had perfect knowledge of VS reordering, it has to accurately detect VS constructions and their spans in order to apply the reordering correctly. For that purpose, we use our state-of-ther-art parsing model, which is essentially the CATIBEX baseline model in Marton et al. (2010), and whose details we summarize next. We train a syntactic dependency parser, MaltParser v1.3 with the Nivre "eager" algorithm (Nivre, 2003; Nivre et al., 2006; Nivre, 2008) on the training portion of the Penn Arabic Treebank part 3 v3.1, hereafter PATB3 (Maamouri et al., 2008; Maamouri et al., 2009). The training / development split is the same as in Zitouni et al. (2006). We convert the PATB3 representation into the succinct CATiB format, with 8 dependency relations and 6 POS tags, which we then extend to a set of 44 tags using regular expressions of the basic POS and the normalized surface word form, similarly to Marton et al. (2010), following Habash and Roth (2009). We normalize Alif Maqsura to Ya, and Hamzated Alifs to bare Alif, as is commonly done in Arabic SMT.

For analysis purposes, we evaluate our subject and verb detection on the development part of PATB3 using gold POS tags. There are various ways to go about it. We argue that combined detection statistics of constructions of verbs and their subjects (VATS), for which we achieve an F-score of 74%, are more telling for the task at hand.[2]

[2]We divert from the CATiB representation in that a non-matrix subject of a pseudo verb (*An* and her sisters) is treated as a subject of the verb that is under the same pseudo verb. This treatment of said subjects is comparable to the PATB's.

These scores take into account the spans of both the subject and the specific verb it belongs to, and potentially reorder with. We also provide statistics of VS detection separately (F-score 63%), since we only handle VS here. This low score can be explained by the difficulty in detecting the post-verbal subject's end boundary, and the correct verb the subject belongs to. The SV construction scores are higher, presumably since the pre-verbal subject's end is bounded by the verb it belongs to. See Table 2.

Although not directly comparable, our VS scores are similar to those of Green et al. (2009). Their VS detection technique with conditional random fields (CRF) is different from ours in bypassing full syntactic parsing, and in only detecting maximal (non-nested) subjects of verb-initial clauses. Additionally, they use a different training / test split of the PATB data (parts 1, 2 and 3). They report 65.9% precision and 61.3% F-score. Note that a closer score comparison should take into account their reported verb detection accuracy of 98.1%.

Table 2: Precision, Recall and F-scores for constructions of Arabic verbs and their subjects, evaluated on our development part of PATB3.

construction	P	R	F
VATS (verbs & their subj.)	73.84	74.37	74.11
VS	66.62	59.41	62.81
SV	86.75	61.07	71.68
VNS (verbs w/ null subj.)	76.32	92.04	83.45
verbal subj. exc. null subj.	72.46	60.18	65.75
verbal subj. inc. null subj.	73.97	74.50	74.23
verbs with non-null subj.	91.94	76.17	83.31
SV or VS	72.19	59.95	65.50

4 Reordering Arabic VS for SMT word alignment

Based on these analyses, we propose a new method to help phrase-based SMT systems deal with Arabic-English word order differences due to VS constructions. As in related work on syntactic reordering by preprocessing, our method attempts to make Arabic and English word order closer to each other by reordering Arabic VS constructions into SV. However, unlike in previous work, the reordered Arabic sentences are used only for word alignment. Phrase translation extraction and decoding are performed on the original Arabic word order. Preliminary experiments on an earlier version of the large-scale SMT system described in Section 6 showed that forcing reordering of all VS constructions at training and test time does not have a consistent impact on translation quality: for instance, on the NIST MT08-NW test set, TER slightly improved from 44.34 to 44.03, while BLEU score decreased from 49.21 to 49.09.

Limiting reordering to alignment allows the system to be more robust and recover from incorrect changes introduced either by incorrect VS detection, or by incorrect reordering of a correctly detected VS. Given a parallel sentence (a, e), we proceed as follows:

1. automatically tag VS constructions in a
2. generate new sentence $a' = reorder(a)$ by reordering Arabic VS into SV
3. get word alignment wa' on new sentence pair (a', e)
4. using mapping from a to a', get corresponding word alignment $wa = unreorder(wa')$ for the original sentence pair (a, e)

5 Experiment set-up

We use the open-source Moses toolkit (Koehn et al., 2007) to build two phrase-based SMT systems trained on two different data conditions:

- **medium-scale** the bitext consists of 12M words on the Arabic side (LDC2007E103). The language model is trained on the English side of the large bitext.
- **large-scale** the bitext consists of several newswire LDC corpora, and has 64M words on the Arabic side. The language model is trained on the English side of the bitext augmented with Gigaword data.

Except from this difference in training data, the two systems are identical. They use a standard phrase-based architecture. The parallel corpus is word-aligned using the GIZA++ (Och and Ney, 2003), which sequentially learns word alignments for the IBM1, HMM, IBM3 and IBM4 models. The resulting alignments in both translation directions are intersected and augmented using the grow-diag-final-and heuristic (Koehn et al., 2007). Phrase translations of up to 10 words are extracted in the Moses phrase-table. We apply statistical significance tests to prune unreliable phrase-pairs and score remaining phrase-table entries (Chen et al., 2009). We use a 5-gram language model with modified Kneser-Ney smoothing. Feature weights are tuned to maximize BLEU on the NIST MT06 test set.

For all systems, the English data is tokenized using simple punctuation-based rules. The Arabic side is segmented according to the Arabic Treebank (PATB3) tokenization scheme (Maamouri et al., 2009) using the MADA+TOKAN morphological analyzer and tokenizer (Habash and Rambow, 2005). MADA-produced Arabic lemmas are used for word alignment.

6 Results

We evaluate translation quality using both BLEU (Papineni et al., 2002) and TER (Snover et al., 2006) scores on three standard evaluation test sets from the NIST evaluations, which yield more than 4400 test sentences with 4 reference translations. On this large data set, our VS reordering method remarkably yields statistically significant improvements in BLEU and TER on the medium and large SMT systems at the 99% confidence level (Table 3).

Table 3: Evaluation on all test sets: on the total of 4432 test sentences, improvements are statistically significant at the 99% level using bootstrap resampling (Koehn, 2004)

system	BLEU r4n4 (%)	TER (%)
medium baseline	44.35	48.34
+ VS reordering	44.65 (+0.30)	47.78 (-0.56)
large baseline	51.45	42.45
+ VS reordering	51.70 (+0.25)	42.21 (-0.24)

Results per test set are reported in Table 4. TER scores are improved in all 10 test configurations, and BLEU scores are improved in 8 out of the 10 configurations. Results on the MT08 test set show that improvements are obtained both on newswire and on web text as measured by TER (but not BLEU score on the web section.) It is worth noting that consistent improvements are obtained even on the large-scale system, and that both baselines are full-fledged systems, which include lexicalized reordering and large 5-gram language models.

Analysis shows that our VS reordering technique improves word alignment coverage (yielding 48k and 330k additional links on the medium and large scale systems respectively). This results in larger phrase-tables which improve translation quality.

7 Related work

To the best of our knowledge, the only other approach to detecting and using Arabic verb-subject constructions for SMT is that of Green et al. (2009) (see Section 3), which failed to improve Arabic-English SMT. In contrast with our reordering approach, they integrate subject span information as a log-linear model feature which encourages a phrase-based SMT decoder to use phrasal translations that do not break subject boundaries.

Syntactically motivated reordering for phrase-based SMT has been more successful on language pairs other than Arabic-English, perhaps due to more accurate parsers and less ambiguous reordering patterns than for Arabic VS. For instance, Collins et al. (2005) apply six manually defined transformations to German parse trees which improve German-English translation by 0.4 BLEU on the Europarl task. Xia and McCord (2004) learn reordering rules for French to English translations, which arguably presents less syntactic distortion than Arabic-English. Zhang et al. (2007) limit reordering to decoding for Chinese-English SMT using a lattice representation. Cherry (2008) uses dependency parses as cohesion constraints in decoding for French-English SMT.

For Arabic-English phrase-based SMT, the impact of syntactic reordering as preprocessing is less clear. Habash (2007) proposes to learn syntactic reordering rules targeting Arabic-English word order differences and integrates them as deterministic preprocessing. He reports improvements in BLEU compared to phrase-based SMT limited to monotonic decoding, but these improvements do not hold with distortion. Instead of applying reordering rules deterministically, Crego and Habash (2008) use a lattice input to represent alternate word orders which improves a ngram-based SMT system. But they do not model VS constructions explicitly.

Most previous syntax-aware word alignment models were specifically designed for syntax-based SMT systems. These models are often bootstrapped from existing word alignments, and could therefore benefit from our VS reordering approach. For instance, Fossum et al. (2008) report improvements ranging from 0.1 to 0.5 BLEU on Arabic translation by learning to delete alignment

Table 4: VS reordering improves BLEU and TER scores in almost all test conditions on 5 test sets, 2 metrics, and 2 MT systems

BLEU r4n4 (%)					
test set	MT03	MT04	MT05	MT08nw	MT08wb
medium baseline	45.95	44.94	48.05	44.86	32.05
+ VS reordering	46.33 (+0.38)	45.03 (+0.09)	48.69 (+0.64)	45.06 (+0.20)	31.96 (-0.09)
large baseline	52.3	52.45	54.66	52.60	39.22
+ VS reordering	52.63 (+0.33)	52.34 (-0.11)	55.29 (+0.63)	52.85 (+0.25)	39.87 (+0.65)
TER (%)					
test set	MT03	MT04	MT05	MT08nw	MT08wb
medium baseline	48.77	46.45	45.00	47.74	58.02
+ VS reordering	48.31 (-0.46)	46.10 (-0.35)	44.29 (-0.71)	47.11 (-0.63)	57.30 (-0.72)
large baseline	43.33	40.42	39.15	41.81	52.05
+ VS reordering	42.95 (-0.38)	40.40 (-0.02)	38.75 (-0.40)	41.51 (-0.30)	51.86 (-0.19)

links if they degrade their syntax-based translation system. Departing from commonly-used alignment models, Hermjakob (2009) aligns Arabic and English content words using pointwise mutual information, and in this process indirectly uses English sentences reordered into VS order to collect cooccurrence counts. The approach outperforms GIZA++ on a small-scale translation task, but the impact of reordering alone is not evaluated.

8 Conclusion and future work

We presented a novel method for improving overall SMT quality using a noisy syntactic parser: we use these parses to reorder VS constructions into SV for word alignment only. This approach increases word alignment coverage and significantly improves BLEU and TER scores on two strong SMT baselines.

In subsequent work, we show that matrix (main-clause) VS constructions are reordered much more frequently than non-matrix VS, and that limiting reordering to matrix VS constructions for word alignment further improves translation quality (Carpuat et al., 2010). In the future, we plan to improve robustness to parsing errors by using not just one, but multiple subject boundary hypotheses. We will also investigate the integration of VS reordering in SMT decoding.

Acknowledgements

The authors would like to thank Mona Diab, Owen Rambow, Ryan Roth, Kristen Parton and Joakim Nivre for helpful discussions and assistance. This material is based upon work supported by the Defense Advanced Research Projects Agency (DARPA) under GALE Contract No HR0011-08-C-0110. Any opinions, findings and conclusions or recommendations expressed in this material are those of the authors and do not necessarily reflect the views of DARPA.

References

Nguyen Bach, Stephan Vogel, and Colin Cherry. 2009. Cohesive constraints in a beam search phrase-based decoder. In *Proceedings of the 10th Meeting of the North American Chapter of the Association for Computational Linguistics, Companion Volume: Short Papers*, pages 1–4.

Marine Carpuat, Yuval Marton, and Nizar Habash. 2010. Reordering matrix post-verbal subjects for arabic-to-english smt. In *Proceedings of the Conference Traitement Automatique des Langues Naturelles (TALN)*.

Boxing Chen, George Foster, and Roland Kuhn. 2009. Phrase translation model enhanced with association based features. In *Proceedings of MT-Summit XII*, Ottawa, Ontario, September.

Colin Cherry. 2008. Cohesive phrase-based decoding for statistical machine translation. In *Proceedings of the 46th Annual Meeting of the Association for Computational Linguistics (ACL)*, pages 72–80, Columbus, Ohio, June.

Michael Collins, Philipp Koehn, and Ivona Kucerova. 2005. Clause restructuring for statistical machine translation. In *Proceedings of the 43rd Annual Meeting of the Association for Computational Linguistics (ACL)*, pages 531–540, Ann Arbor, MI, June.

Josep M. Crego and Nizar Habash. 2008. Using shallow syntax information to improve word alignment and reordering for SMT. In *Proceedings of the Third Workshop on Statistical Machine Translation*, pages 53–61, June.

Victoria Fossum, Kevin Knight, and Steven Abney. 2008. Using syntax to improve word alignment precision for syntax-based machine translation. In *Proceedings of the Third Workshop on Statistical Machine Translation*, pages 44–52.

Spence Green, Conal Sathi, and Christopher D. Manning. 2009. NP subject detection in verb-initial Arabic clauses.

In *Proceedings of the Third Workshop on Computational Approaches to Arabic Script-based Languages (CAASL3)*.

Nizar Habash and Owen Rambow. 2005. Arabic Tokenization, Part-of-Speech Tagging and Morphological Disambiguation in One Fell Swoop. In *Proceedings of the 43rd Annual Meeting of the Association for Computational Linguistics (ACL'05)*, pages 573–580, Ann Arbor, Michigan, June.

Nizar Habash and Ryan Roth. 2009. CATiB: The Columbia Arabic treebank. In *Proceedings of the ACL-IJCNLP 2009 Conference Short Papers*, pages 221–224, Suntec, Singapore, August. Association for Computational Linguistics.

Nizar Habash. 2007. Syntactic preprocessing for statistical machine translation. In *Proceedings of the Machine Translation Summit (MT-Summit)*, Copenhagen.

Ulf Hermjakob. 2009. Improved word alignment with statistics and linguistic heuristics. In *Proceedings of the 2009 Conference on Empirical Methods in Natural Language Processing*, pages 229–237, Singapore, August.

Philipp Koehn, Franz Och, and Daniel Marcu. 2003. Statistical phrase-based translation. In *Proceedings of HLT/NAACL-2003*, Edmonton, Canada, May.

Philipp Koehn, Hieu Hoang, Alexandra Birch, Chris Callison-Burch, Marcello Federico, Nicola Bertoldi, Brooke Cowan, Wade Shen, Christine Moran, Richard Zens, Chris Dyer, Ondrej Bojar, Alexandra Constantin, and Evan Herbst. 2007. Moses: Open source toolkit for statistical machine translation. In *Annual Meeting of the Association for Computational Linguistics (ACL), demonstration session*, Prague, Czech Republic, June.

Philipp Koehn. 2004. Statistical significance tests for machine translation evaluation. In *Proceedings of the 2004 Conference on Empirical Methods in Natural Language Processing (EMNLP-2004)*, Barcelona, Spain, July.

Young-Suk Lee. 2004. Morphological analysis for statistical machine translation. In *Proceedings of the Human Language Technology Conference of the NAACL*, pages 57–60, Boston, MA.

Mohamed Maamouri, Ann Bies, and Seth Kulick. 2008. Enhancing the arabic treebank: a collaborative effort toward new annotation guidelines. In *Proceedings of the Sixth International Language Resources and Evaluation (LREC'08)*, Marrakech, Morocco.

Mohamed Maamouri, Ann Bies, Seth Kulick, Fatma Gaddeche, Wigdan Mekki, Sondos Krouna, and Basma Bouziri. 2009. The penn arabic treebank part 3 version 3.1. Linguistic Data Consortium LDC2008E22.

Yuval Marton, Nizar Habash, and Owen Rambow. 2010. Improving arabic dependency parsing with lexical and inflectional morphological features. In *Proceedings of the 11th Meeting of the North American Chapter of the Association for Computational Linguistics (NAACL) workshop on Statistical Parsing of Morphologically Rich Languages (SPMRL)*, Los Angeles.

Joakim Nivre, Johan Hall, and Jens Nilsson. 2006. MaltParser: A Data-Driven Parser-Generator for Dependency Parsing. In *Proceedings of the Conference on Language Resources and Evaluation (LREC)*.

Joakim Nivre. 2003. An efficient algorithm for projective dependency parsing. In *Proceedings of the 8th International Conference on Parsing Technologies (IWPT)*, pages 149–160, Nancy, France.

Joakim Nivre. 2008. Algorithms for Deterministic Incremental Dependency Parsing. *Computational Linguistics*, 34(4).

Franz Josef Och and Hermann Ney. 2003. A systematic comparison of various statistical alignment models. *Computational Linguistics*, 29(1):19–52.

Kishore Papineni, Salim Roukos, Todd Ward, and Wei-Jing Zhu. 2002. BLEU: a method for automatic evaluation of machine translation. In *Proceedings of the 40th Annual Meeting of the Association for Computational Linguistics*.

Fatiha Sadat and Nizar Habash. 2006. Combination of arabic preprocessing schemes for statistical machine translation. In *Proceedings of the 21st International Conference on Computational Linguistics and the 44th annual meeting of the Association for Computational Linguistics*, pages 1–8, Morristown, NJ, USA.

Matthew Snover, Bonnie Dorr, Richard Schwartz, Linnea Micciulla, and John Makhoul. 2006. A study of translation edit rate with targeted human annotation. In *Proceedings of AMTA*, pages 223–231, Boston, MA.

Chao Wang, Michael Collins, and Philipp Koehn. 2007. Chinese syntactic reordering for statistical machine translation. In *Proceedings of the 2007 Joint Conference on Empirical Methods in Natural Language Processing and Computational Natural Language Learning (EMNLP-CoNLL)*, pages 737–745.

Fei Xia and Michael McCord. 2004. Improving a statistical mt system with automatically learned rewrite patterns. In *Proceedings of COLING 2004*, pages 508–514, Geneva, Switzerland, August.

Yuqi Zhang, Richard Zens, and Hermann Ney. 2007. Chunk-level reordering of source language sentences with automatically learned rules for statistical machine translation. In *Human Language Technology Conf. / North American Chapter of the Assoc. for Computational Linguistics Annual Meeting*, Rochester, NY, April.

Imed Zitouni, Jeffrey S. Sorensen, and Ruhi Sarikaya. 2006. Maximum Entropy Based Restoration of Arabic Diacritics. In *Proceedings of COLING-ACL, the joint conference of the International Committee on Computational Linguistics and the Association for Computational Linguistics*, pages 577–584, Sydney, Australia.

Andreas Zollmann, Ashish Venugopal, and Stephan Vogel. 2006. Bridging the inflection morphology gap for arabic statistical machine translation. In *Proceedings of the Human Language Technology Conference of the NAACL, Companion Volume: Short Papers*, pages 201–204, New York City, USA.

Learning Common Grammar from Multilingual Corpus

Tomoharu Iwata **Daichi Mochihashi** **Hiroshi Sawada**
NTT Communication Science Laboratories
2-4 Hikaridai, Seika-cho, Soraku-gun, Kyoto, Japan
{iwata,daichi,sawada}@cslab.kecl.ntt.co.jp

Abstract

We propose a corpus-based probabilistic framework to extract hidden common syntax across languages from non-parallel multilingual corpora in an unsupervised fashion. For this purpose, we assume a generative model for multilingual corpora, where each sentence is generated from a language dependent probabilistic context-free grammar (PCFG), and these PCFGs are generated from a prior grammar that is common across languages. We also develop a variational method for efficient inference. Experiments on a non-parallel multilingual corpus of eleven languages demonstrate the feasibility of the proposed method.

1 Introduction

Languages share certain common properties (Pinker, 1994). For example, the word order in most European languages is subject-verb-object (SVO), and some words with similar forms are used with similar meanings in different languages. The reasons for these common properties can be attributed to: 1) a common ancestor language, 2) borrowing from nearby languages, and 3) the innate abilities of humans (Chomsky, 1965).

We assume hidden commonalities in syntax across languages, and try to extract a common grammar from non-parallel multilingual corpora. For this purpose, we propose a generative model for multilingual grammars that is learned in an unsupervised fashion. There are some computational models for capturing commonalities at the phoneme and word level (Oakes, 2000; Bouchard-Côté et al., 2008), but, as far as we know, no attempt has been made to extract commonalities in syntax level from non-parallel and non-annotated multilingual corpora.

In our scenario, we use probabilistic context-free grammars (PCFGs) as our monolingual grammar model. We assume that a PCFG for each language is generated from a general model that are common across languages, and each sentence in multilingual corpora is generated from the language dependent PCFG. The inference of the general model as well as the multilingual PCFGs can be performed by using a variational method for efficiency. Our approach is based on a Bayesian multitask learning framework (Yu et al., 2005; Daumé III, 2009). Hierarchical Bayesian modeling provides a natural way of obtaining a joint regularization for individual models by assuming that the model parameters are drawn from a common prior distribution (Yu et al., 2005).

2 Related work

The unsupervised grammar induction task has been extensively studied (Carroll and Charniak, 1992; Stolcke and Omohundro, 1994; Klein and Manning, 2002; Klein and Manning, 2004; Liang et al., 2007). Recently, models have been proposed that outperform PCFG in the grammar induction task (Klein and Manning, 2002; Klein and Manning, 2004). We used PCFG as a first step for capturing commonalities in syntax across languages because of its simplicity. The proposed framework can be used for probabilistic grammar models other than PCFG.

Grammar induction using bilingual parallel corpora has been studied mainly in machine translation research (Wu, 1997; Melamed, 2003; Eisner, 2003; Chiang, 2005; Blunsom et al., 2009; Snyder et al., 2009). These methods require sentence-aligned parallel data, which can be costly to obtain and difficult to scale to many languages. On the other hand, our model does not require sentences to be aligned. Moreover, since the complexity of our model increases linearly with the number of languages, our model is easily applicable to cor-

Proceedings of the ACL 2010 Conference Short Papers, pages 184–188,
Uppsala, Sweden, 11-16 July 2010. ©2010 Association for Computational Linguistics

pora of more than two languages, as we will show in the experiments. To our knowledge, the only grammar induction work on non-parallel corpora is (Cohen and Smith, 2009), but their method does not model a common grammar, and requires prior information such as part-of-speech tags. In contrast, our method does not require any such prior information.

3 Proposed Method

3.1 Model

Let $\boldsymbol{X} = \{\boldsymbol{X}_l\}_{l \in \boldsymbol{L}}$ be a non-parallel and non-annotated multilingual corpus, where $\boldsymbol{X}_l$ is a set of sentences in language l, and $\boldsymbol{L}$ is a set of languages. The task is to learn multilingual PCFGs $\boldsymbol{G} = \{G_l\}_{l \in \boldsymbol{L}}$ and a common grammar that generates these PCFGs. Here, $\boldsymbol{G}_l = (\boldsymbol{K}, \boldsymbol{W}_l, \boldsymbol{\Phi}_l)$ represents a PCFG of language l, where $\boldsymbol{K}$ is a set of nonterminals, $\boldsymbol{W}_l$ is a set of terminals, and $\boldsymbol{\Phi}_l$ is a set of rule probabilities. Note that a set of nonterminals $\boldsymbol{K}$ is shared among languages, but a set of terminals $\boldsymbol{W}_l$ and rule probabilities $\boldsymbol{\Phi}_l$ are specific to the language. For simplicity, we consider Chomsky normal form grammars, which have two types of rules: emissions rewrite a nonterminal as a terminal $A \to w$, and binary productions rewrite a nonterminal as two nonterminals $A \to BC$, where $A, B, C \in \boldsymbol{K}$ and $w \in \boldsymbol{W}_l$.

The rule probabilities for each nonterminal A of PCFG G_l in language l consist of: 1) $\boldsymbol{\theta}_{Al} = \{\theta_{lAt}\}_{t \in \{0,1\}}$, where θ_{lA0} and θ_{lA1} represent probabilities of choosing the emission rule and the binary production rule, respectively, 2) $\phi_{lA} = \{\phi_{lABC}\}_{B,C \in \boldsymbol{K}}$, where ϕ_{lABC} represents the probability of nonterminal production $A \to BC$, and 3) $\boldsymbol{\psi}_{lA} = \{\psi_{lAw}\}_{w \in \boldsymbol{W}_l}$, where ψ_{lAw} represents the probability of terminal emission $A \to w$. Note that $\theta_{lA0} + \theta_{lA1} = 1$, $\theta_{lAt} \geq 0$, $\sum_{B,C} \phi_{lABC} = 1$, $\phi_{lABC} \geq 0$, $\sum_w \psi_{lAw} = 1$, and $\psi_{lAw} \geq 0$. In the proposed model, multinomial parameters $\boldsymbol{\theta}_{lA}$ and ϕ_{lA} are generated from Dirichlet distributions that are common across languages: $\theta_{lA} \sim \text{Dir}(\boldsymbol{\alpha}^{\theta}_{A})$ and $\boldsymbol{\phi}_{lA} \sim \text{Dir}(\boldsymbol{\alpha}^{\phi}_{A})$, since we assume that languages share a common syntax structure. $\boldsymbol{\alpha}^{\theta}_{A}$ and $\boldsymbol{\alpha}^{\phi}_{A}$ represent the parameters of a common grammar. We use the Dirichlet prior because it is the conjugate prior for the multinomial distribution. In summary, the proposed model assumes the following generative process for a multilingual corpus,

1. For each nonterminal $A \in \boldsymbol{K}$:
   (a) For each rule type $t \in \{0, 1\}$:
      i. Draw common rule type parameters $\alpha^{\theta}_{At} \sim \text{Gam}(a^{\theta}, b^{\theta})$
   (b) For each nonterminal pair (B, C):
      i. Draw common production parameters $\alpha^{\phi}_{ABC} \sim \text{Gam}(a^{\phi}, b^{\phi})$
2. For each language $l \in \boldsymbol{L}$:
   (a) For each nonterminal $A \in \boldsymbol{K}$:
      i. Draw rule type parameters $\theta_{lA} \sim \text{Dir}(\boldsymbol{\alpha}^{\theta}_{A})$
      ii. Draw binary production parameters $\boldsymbol{\phi}_{lA} \sim \text{Dir}(\boldsymbol{\alpha}^{\phi}_{A})$
      iii. Draw emission parameters $\boldsymbol{\psi}_{lA} \sim \text{Dir}(\alpha^{\psi})$
   (b) For each node i in the parse tree:
      i. Choose rule type $t_{li} \sim \text{Mult}(\boldsymbol{\theta}_{lz_i})$
      ii. If $t_{li} = 0$:
         A. Emit terminal $x_{li} \sim \text{Mult}(\boldsymbol{\psi}_{lz_i})$
      iii. Otherwise:
         A. Generate children nonterminals $(z_{lL(i)}, z_{lR(i)}) \sim \text{Mult}(\boldsymbol{\phi}_{lz_i})$,

where $L(i)$ and $R(i)$ represent the left and right children of node i. Figure 1 shows a graphical model representation of the proposed model, where the shaded and unshaded nodes indicate observed and latent variables, respectively.

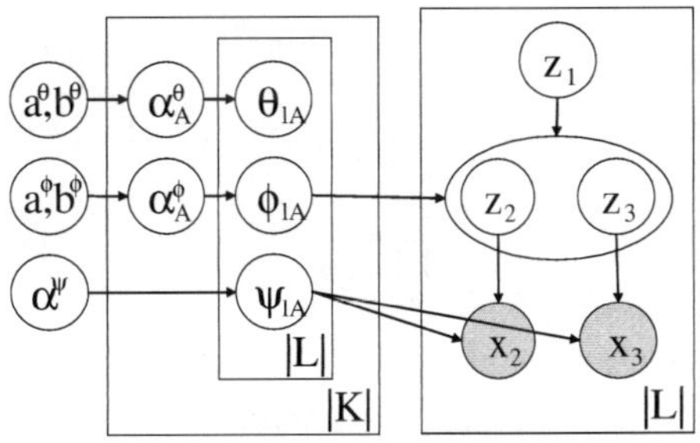

Figure 1: Graphical model.

3.2 Inference

The inference of the proposed model can be efficiently computed using a variational Bayesian method. We extend the variational method to the monolingual PCFG learning of Kurihara and Sato (2004) for multilingual corpora. The goal is to estimate posterior $p(\boldsymbol{Z}, \boldsymbol{\Phi}, \boldsymbol{\alpha}|\boldsymbol{X})$, where $\boldsymbol{Z}$ is a set of parse trees, $\boldsymbol{\Phi} = \{\boldsymbol{\Phi}_l\}_{l \in \boldsymbol{L}}$ is a set of language dependent parameters, $\boldsymbol{\Phi}_l = \{\boldsymbol{\theta}_{lA}, \boldsymbol{\phi}_{lA}, \boldsymbol{\psi}_{lA}\}_{A \in \boldsymbol{K}}$, and $\boldsymbol{\alpha} = \{\boldsymbol{\alpha}^{\theta}_{A}, \boldsymbol{\alpha}^{\phi}_{A}\}_{A \in \boldsymbol{K}}$ is a set of common parameters. In the variational method, posterior $p(\boldsymbol{Z}, \boldsymbol{\Phi}, \boldsymbol{\alpha}|\boldsymbol{X})$ is approximated by a tractable variational distribution $q(\boldsymbol{Z}, \boldsymbol{\Phi}, \boldsymbol{\alpha})$.

We use the following variational distribution,

$$q(\boldsymbol{Z},\boldsymbol{\Phi},\boldsymbol{\alpha}) = \prod_{A} q(\boldsymbol{\alpha}^{\theta}_{A})q(\boldsymbol{\alpha}^{\phi}_{A})\prod_{l,d} q(\boldsymbol{z}_{ld}) \times \prod_{l,A} q(\boldsymbol{\theta}_{lA})q(\boldsymbol{\phi}_{lA})q(\boldsymbol{\psi}_{lA}), \quad (1)$$

where we assume that hyperparameters $q(\boldsymbol{\alpha}^{\theta}_{A})$ and $q(\boldsymbol{\alpha}^{\phi}_{A})$ are degenerated, or $q(\boldsymbol{\alpha}) = \delta_{\boldsymbol{\alpha}^*}(\boldsymbol{\alpha})$, and infer them by point estimation instead of distribution estimation. We find an approximate posterior distribution that minimizes the Kullback-Leibler divergence from the true posterior. The variational distribution of the parse tree of the dth sentence in language l is obtained as follows,

$$q(\boldsymbol{z}_{ld}) \propto \prod_{A\to BC}\left(\pi^{\theta}_{lA1}\pi^{\phi}_{lABC}\right)^{C(A\to BC;\boldsymbol{z}_{ld},l,d)} \times \prod_{A\to w}\left(\pi^{\theta}_{lA0}\pi^{\psi}_{lAw}\right)^{C(A\to w;\boldsymbol{z}_{ld},l,d)}, \quad (2)$$

where $C(r;\boldsymbol{z},l,d)$ is the count of rule r that occurs in the dth sentence of language l with parse tree $\boldsymbol{z}$. The multinomial weights are calculated as follows,

$$\pi^{\theta}_{lAt} = \exp\left(\mathbb{E}_{q(\boldsymbol{\theta}_{lA})}\left[\log\theta_{lAt}\right]\right), \quad (3)$$

$$\pi^{\phi}_{lABC} = \exp\left(\mathbb{E}_{q(\boldsymbol{\phi}_{lA})}\left[\log\phi_{lABC}\right]\right), \quad (4)$$

$$\pi^{\psi}_{lAw} = \exp\left(\mathbb{E}_{q(\boldsymbol{\psi}_{lA})}\left[\log\psi_{lAw}\right]\right). \quad (5)$$

The variational Dirichlet parameters for $q(\boldsymbol{\theta}_{lA}) = \mathrm{Dir}(\boldsymbol{\gamma}^{\theta}_{lA})$, $q(\boldsymbol{\phi}_{lA}) = \mathrm{Dir}(\boldsymbol{\gamma}^{\phi}_{lA})$, and $q(\boldsymbol{\psi}_{lA}) = \mathrm{Dir}(\boldsymbol{\gamma}^{\psi}_{lA})$, are obtained as follows,

$$\gamma^{\theta}_{lAt} = \alpha^{\theta}_{At} + \sum_{d,\boldsymbol{z}_{ld}} q(\boldsymbol{z}_{ld})C(A,t;\boldsymbol{z}_{ld},l,d), \quad (6)$$

$$\gamma^{\phi}_{lABC} = \alpha^{\phi}_{ABC} + \sum_{d,\boldsymbol{z}_{ld}} q(\boldsymbol{z}_{ld})C(A\to BC;\boldsymbol{z}_{ld},l,d), \quad (7)$$

$$\gamma^{\psi}_{lAw} = \alpha^{\psi} + \sum_{d,\boldsymbol{z}_{ld}} q(\boldsymbol{z}_{ld})C(A\to w;\boldsymbol{z}_{ld},l,d), \quad (8)$$

where $C(A,t;\boldsymbol{z},l,d)$ is the count of rule type t that is selected in nonterminal A in the dth sentence of language l with parse tree $\boldsymbol{z}$.

The common rule type parameter α^{θ}_{At} that minimizes the KL divergence between the true posterior and the approximate posterior can be obtained by using the fixed-point iteration method described in (Minka, 2000). The update rule is as follows,

$$\alpha^{\theta(\mathrm{new})}_{At} \leftarrow \frac{a^{\theta}-1+\alpha^{\theta}_{At}L\left(\Psi(\sum_{t'}\alpha^{\theta}_{At'})-\Psi(\alpha^{\theta}_{At})\right)}{b^{\theta}+\sum_{l}\left(\Psi(\sum_{t'}\gamma^{\theta}_{lAt'})-\Psi(\gamma^{\theta}_{lAt})\right)}, \quad (9)$$

where L is the number of languages, and $\Psi(x) = \frac{\partial\log\Gamma(x)}{\partial x}$ is the digamma function. Similarly, the common production parameter α^{ϕ}_{ABC} can be updated as follows,

$$\alpha^{\phi(\mathrm{new})}_{ABC} \leftarrow \frac{a^{\phi}-1+\alpha^{\phi}_{ABC}LJ_{ABC}}{b^{\phi}+\sum_{l}J'_{lABC}}, \quad (10)$$

where $J_{ABC} = \Psi(\sum_{B',C'}\alpha^{\phi}_{AB'C'}) - \Psi(\alpha^{\phi}_{ABC})$, and $J'_{lABC} = \Psi(\sum_{B',C'}\gamma^{\phi}_{lAB'C'}) - \Psi(\gamma^{\phi}_{lABC})$.

Since factored variational distributions depend on each other, an optimal approximated posterior can be obtained by updating parameters by (2) - (10) alternatively until convergence. The updating of language dependent distributions by (2) - (8) is also described in (Kurihara and Sato, 2004; Liang et al., 2007) while the updating of common grammar parameters by (9) and (10) is new. The inference can be carried out efficiently using the inside-outside algorithm based on dynamic programming (Lari and Young, 1990).

After the inference, the probability of a common grammar rule $A \to BC$ is calculated by $\hat{\phi}_{A\to BC} = \hat{\theta}_1\hat{\phi}_{ABC}$, where $\hat{\theta}_1 = \alpha^{\theta}_1/(\alpha^{\theta}_0+\alpha^{\theta}_1)$ and $\hat{\phi}_{ABC} = \alpha^{\phi}_{ABC}/\sum_{B',C'}\alpha^{\phi}_{AB'C'}$ represent the mean values of θ_{l0} and ϕ_{lABC}, respectively.

4 Experimental results

We evaluated our method by employing the EuroParl corpus (Koehn, 2005). The corpus consists of the proceedings of the European Parliament in eleven western European languages: Danish (da), German (de), Greek (el), English (en), Spanish (es), Finnish (fi), French (fr), Italian (it), Dutch (nl), Portuguese (pt), and Swedish (sv), and it contains roughly 1,500,000 sentences in each language. We set the number of nonterminals at $|\boldsymbol{K}| = 20$, and omitted sentences with more than ten words for tractability. We randomly sampled 100,000 sentences for each language, and analyzed them using our method. It should be noted that our random samples are not sentence-aligned.

Figure 2 shows the most probable terminals of emission for each language and nonterminal with a high probability of selecting the emission rule.

2: verb and auxiliary verb (V)

```
[da] det jeg vi der de derfor dette forhandlingen hvad
[de] ist sind haben wird hat müssen möchte meine werden kann
[el] , είναι για να πρέπει δεν και αυτό με ότι
[en] is are , will have has must was should you
[es] es hay gracias mañana qué tiene tenemos trata lugar son
[fi] on ei ovat olisi oli toimitetaan eivät voi koskee voidaan
[fr] ' ne est n' en a lieu aura vous avons
[it] , è che non si discussione svolgerà presidente ' sono
[nl] is zijn moeten heeft hebben moet kan zal wil wordt
[pt] , que é não senhor parlamento de aprova amanhã com
[sv] det jag vi detta vad därför de debatten ni den
```

5: noun (N)

```
[da] det dem her dette sig dag os noget betænkningen over
[de] abstimmung aussprache kommission bericht frage parlament
[el] θέμα έκθεση τροπολογία κ. Επιτροπή ψήφισμα πρόταση
[en] vote debate president commission much like council minutes
[es] debate presidente informe parlamento ello comisario sr.
[fi] unionin " yhteisön hetkellä enemmän uudelleen kerran heidän
[fr] vote débat parlement rapport commission question président
[it] votazione parlamento commissione relazione risoluzione
[nl] debat stemming commissie parlement verslag voorzitter
[pt] votação comissão questão relatório situação sessão proposta
[sv] det rum damer här detta oss sig frågan första dem
```

7: subject (SBJ)

```
[da] er har vil skal kan må var finder bør ville
[de] ich wir das , es sie - dies vielen (
[el] , θα δεν ψηφοφορία ότι Σώμα πολύ αυτό Πρόεδρε Το
[en] we i that it this there what ( thank they
[es] no se ¿ esto por lo me pero muchas tendrá
[fi] , että puhemies kiitoksia mietintö joka parlamentin mitä
[fr] nous je il c' cela j' ce l mais vous
[it] non ( la e questo ma si vorrei signor mi
[nl] dat ik wij het er we dit u daar wat
[pt] o , que encerrado presidente terá obrigado lugar isso não
[sv] är har måste kommer kan vill skall finns skulle var
```

9: preposition (PR)

```
[da] , af for i og til på med om fra
[de] und , in für auf von zu mit an auch
[el] και / ( σε , που από είναι των για
[en] to of in , for not and on with take
[es] , de que a en por con y para sobre
[fi] ja euroopan , on kuin / : tai ovat eikä
[fr] , de à que pour sur dans d' et par
[it] di e della del in a ( dell' dei da
[nl] van in , voor en op met aan over maar
[pt] de da do e para em dos / é com
[sv] i och för av till på om med som :
```

11: punctuation (.)

```
[da] . ? ) ! : f.eks. ... sessionen vedtoges bl.a.
[de] . ! ? ) : protokolls ... sitzungsperiode " ···
[el] . ) ! ; : κ. πρακτικών ... π.μ. κ.κ.
[en] . ? ) ! a.m. : p.m. ... ' ;
[es] . ? ) ! : ... ; » " anterior
[fi] . ? ) ! : ... " ···; ääntä
[fr] . ? ) ! la : ... » ; ···
[it] . ? ) ! : sessione ... " ; precedente
[nl] . ? ) ! : zitting ... gesloten " onderbroken
[pt] . ? ) ! : ... " anterior ; urgentes
[sv] . ! ) ? : protokoll ... sessionen t.ex. "
```

13: determiner (DT)

```
[da] ikke at en den også de et gerne det være
[de] die der eine den das ein diese im des dieser
[el] να το την η τη τις είναι τα στην μια
[en] the a be mr very an been not no in
[es] el ha este señor un se hemos debemos han debe
[fi] ole myös kuitenkin vielä hyvin siis erittäin nyt jo vain
[fr] le la les l' une cette un ce ces des
[it] la il l' un una le in i a gli
[nl] de het een deze dit geen die onze mijn mijnheer
[pt] a o uma um os de as esta este em
[sv] att inte en mycket också ett för vara om äga
```

Figure 2: Probable terminals of emission for each language and nonterminal.

$0 \to 16\ 11$	(R $\to$ S .)	0.11
$16 \to 7\ 6$	(S $\to$ SBJ VP)	0.06
$6 \to 2\ 12$	(VP $\to$ V NP)	0.04
$12 \to 13\ 5$	(NP $\to$ DT N)	0.19
$15 \to 17\ 19$	(NP $\to$ NP N)	0.07
$17 \to 5\ 9$	(NP $\to$ N PR)	0.07
$15 \to 13\ 5$	(NP $\to$ DT N)	0.06

Figure 3: Examples of inferred common grammar rules in eleven languages, and their probabilities. Hand-provided annotations have the following meanings, R: root, S: sentence, NP: noun phrase, VP: verb phrase, and others appear in Figure 2.

We named nonterminals by using grammatical categories after the inference. We can see that words in the same grammatical category clustered across languages as well as within a language. Figure 3 shows examples of inferred common grammar rules with high probabilities. Grammar rules that seem to be common to European languages have been extracted.

5 Discussion

We have proposed a Bayesian hierarchical PCFG model for capturing commonalities at the syntax level for non-parallel multilingual corpora. Although our results have been encouraging, a number of directions remain in which we must extend our approach. First, we need to evaluate our model quantitatively using corpora with a greater diversity of languages. Measurement examples include the perplexity, and machine translation score. Second, we need to improve our model. For example, we can infer the number of nonterminals with a nonparametric Bayesian model (Liang et al., 2007), infer the model more robustly based on a Markov chain Monte Carlo inference (Johnson et al., 2007), and use probabilistic grammar models other than PCFGs. In our model, all the multilingual grammars are generated from a general model. We can extend it hierarchically using the coalescent (Kingman, 1982). That model may help to infer an evolutionary tree of languages in terms of grammatical structure without the etymological information that is generally used (Gray and Atkinson, 2003). Finally, the proposed approach may help to indicate the presence of a universal grammar (Chomsky, 1965), or to find it.

References

Phil Blunsom, Trevor Cohn, and Miles Osborne. 2009. Bayesian synchronous grammar induction. In D. Koller, D. Schuurmans, Y. Bengio, and L. Bottou, editors, *Advances in Neural Information Processing Systems 21*, pages 161–168.

Alexandre Bouchard-Côté, Percy Liang, Thomas Griffiths, and Dan Klein. 2008. A probabilistic approach to language change. In J.C. Platt, D. Koller, Y. Singer, and S. Roweis, editors, *Advances in Neural Information Processing Systems 20*, pages 169–176, Cambridge, MA. MIT Press.

Glenn Carroll and Eugene Charniak. 1992. Two experiments on learning probabilistic dependency grammars from corpora. In *Working Notes of the Workshop Statistically-Based NLP Techniques*, pages 1–13. AAAI.

David Chiang. 2005. A hierarchical phrase-based model for statistical machine translation. In *ACL '05: Proceedings of the 43rd Annual Meeting on Association for Computational Linguistics*, pages 263–270, Morristown, NJ, USA. Association for Computational Linguistics.

Norm Chomsky. 1965. *Aspects of the Theory of Syntax*. MIT Press.

Shay B. Cohen and Noah A. Smith. 2009. Shared logistic normal distributions for soft parameter tying in unsupervised grammar induction. In *NAACL '09: Proceedings of Human Language Technologies: The 2009 Annual Conference of the North American Chapter of the Association for Computational Linguistics*, pages 74–82, Morristown, NJ, USA. Association for Computational Linguistics.

Hal Daumé III. 2009. Bayesian multitask learning with latent hierarchies. In *Proceedings of the Twenty-Fifth Annual Conference on Uncertainty in Artificial Intelligence (UAI-09)*, pages 135–142, Corvallis, Oregon. AUAI Press.

Jason Eisner. 2003. Learning non-isomorphic tree mappings for machine translation. In *ACL '03: Proceedings of the 41st Annual Meeting on Association for Computational Linguistics*, pages 205–208, Morristown, NJ, USA. Association for Computational Linguistics.

Russell D. Gray and Quentin D. Atkinson. 2003. Language-tree divergence times support the Anatolian theory of Indo-European origin. *Nature*, 426(6965):435–439, November.

Mark Johnson, Thomas Griffiths, and Sharon Goldwater. 2007. Bayesian inference for PCFGs via Markov chain Monte Carlo. In *Human Language Technologies 2007: The Conference of the North American Chapter of the Association for Computational Linguistics; Proceedings of the Main Conference*, pages 139–146, Rochester, New York, April. Association for Computational Linguistics.

J. F. C. Kingman. 1982. The coalescent. *Stochastic Processes and their Applications*, 13:235–248.

Dan Klein and Christopher D. Manning. 2002. A generative constituent-context model for improved grammar induction. In *ACL '02: Proceedings of the 40th Annual Meeting on Association for Computational Linguistics*, pages 128–135, Morristown, NJ, USA. Association for Computational Linguistics.

Dan Klein and Christopher D. Manning. 2004. Corpus-based induction of syntactic structure: models of dependency and constituency. In *ACL '04: Proceedings of the 42nd Annual Meeting on Association for Computational Linguistics*, page 478, Morristown, NJ, USA. Association for Computational Linguistics.

Philipp Koehn. 2005. Europarl: A parallel corpus for statistical machine translation. In *Proceedings of the 10th Machine Translation Summit*, pages 79–86.

Kenichi Kurihara and Taisuke Sato. 2004. An application of the variational Bayesian approach to probabilistic context-free grammars. In *International Joint Conference on Natural Language Processing Workshop Beyond Shallow Analysis*.

K. Lari and S.J. Young. 1990. The estimation of stochastic context-free grammars using the inside-outside algorithm. *Computer Speech and Language*, 4:35–56.

Percy Liang, Slav Petrov, Michael I. Jordan, and Dan Klein. 2007. The infinite PCFG using hierarchical dirichlet processes. In *EMNLP '07: Proceedings of the Empirical Methods on Natural Language Processing*, pages 688–697.

I. Dan Melamed. 2003. Multitext grammars and synchronous parsers. In *NAACL '03: Proceedings of the 2003 Conference of the North American Chapter of the Association for Computational Linguistics on Human Language Technology*, pages 79–86, Morristown, NJ, USA. Association for Computational Linguistics.

Thomas Minka. 2000. Estimating a Dirichlet distribution. Technical report, M.I.T.

Michael P. Oakes. 2000. Computer estimation of vocabulary in a protolanguage from word lists in four daughter languages. *Journal of Quantitative Linguistics*, 7(3):233–243.

Steven Pinker. 1994. *The Language Instinct: How the Mind Creates Language*. HarperCollins, New York.

Benjamin Snyder, Tahira Naseem, and Regina Barzilay. 2009. Unsupervised multilingual grammar induction. In *Proceedings of the Joint Conference of the 47th Annual Meeting of the ACL and the 4th International Joint Conference on Natural Language Processing of the AFNLP*, pages 73–81, Suntec, Singapore, August. Association for Computational Linguistics.

Andreas Stolcke and Stephen M. Omohundro. 1994. Inducing probabilistic grammars by Bayesian model merging. In *ICGI '94: Proceedings of the Second International Colloquium on Grammatical Inference and Applications*, pages 106–118, London, UK. Springer-Verlag.

Dekai Wu. 1997. Stochastic inversion transduction grammars and bilingual parsing of parallel corpora. *Comput. Linguist.*, 23(3):377–403.

Kai Yu, Volker Tresp, and Anton Schwaighofer. 2005. Learning gaussian processes from multiple tasks. In *ICML '05: Proceedings of the 22nd International Conference on Machine Learning*, pages 1012–1019, New York, NY, USA. ACM.

Tree-Based Deterministic Dependency Parsing — An Application to Nivre's Method —

Kotaro Kitagawa **Kumiko Tanaka-Ishii**
Graduate School of Information Science and Technology,
The University of Tokyo
kitagawa@cl.ci.i.u-tokyo.ac.jp kumiko@i.u-tokyo.ac.jp

Abstract

Nivre's method was improved by enhancing deterministic dependency parsing through application of a tree-based model. The model considers all words necessary for selection of parsing actions by including words in the form of trees. It chooses the most probable head candidate from among the trees and uses this candidate to select a parsing action.

In an evaluation experiment using the Penn Treebank (WSJ section), the proposed model achieved higher accuracy than did previous deterministic models. Although the proposed model's worst-case time complexity is $O(n^2)$, the experimental results demonstrated an average parsing time not much slower than $O(n)$.

1 Introduction

Deterministic parsing methods achieve both effective time complexity and accuracy not far from those of the most accurate methods. One such deterministic method is Nivre's method, an incremental parsing method whose time complexity is linear in the number of words (Nivre, 2003). Still, deterministic methods can be improved. As a specific example, Nivre's model greedily decides the parsing action only from two words and their locally relational words, which can lead to errors.

In the field of Japanese dependency parsing, Iwatate et al. (2008) proposed a tournament model that takes all head candidates into account in judging dependency relations. This method assumes backward parsing because the Japanese dependency structure has a head-final constraint, so that any word's head is located to its right.

Here, we propose a tree-based model, applicable to any projective language, which can be considered as a kind of generalization of Iwatate's idea. Instead of selecting a parsing action for two words, as in Nivre's model, our tree-based model first chooses the most probable head candidate from among the trees through a tournament and then decides the parsing action between two trees.

Global-optimization parsing methods are another common approach (Eisner, 1996; McDonald et al., 2005). Koo et al. (2008) studied semi-supervised learning with this approach. Hybrid systems have improved parsing by integrating outputs obtained from different parsing models (Zhang and Clark, 2008).

Our proposal can be situated among global-optimization parsing methods as follows. The proposed tree-based model is deterministic but takes a step towards global optimization by widening the search space to include all necessary words connected by previously judged head-dependent relations, thus achieving a higher accuracy yet largely retaining the speed of deterministic parsing.

2 Deterministic Dependency Parsing

2.1 Dependency Parsing

A dependency parser receives an input sentence $x = w_1, w_2, \ldots, w_n$ and computes a dependency graph $G = (W, A)$. The set of nodes $W = \{w_0, w_1, \ldots, w_n\}$ corresponds to the words of a sentence, and the node w_0 is the root of G. A is the set of arcs (w_i, w_j), each of which represents a dependency relation where w_i is the *head* and w_j is the *dependent*.

In this paper, we assume that the resulting dependency graph for a sentence is well-formed and projective (Nivre, 2008). G is well-formed if and only if it satisfies the following three conditions of being **single-headed**, **acyclic**, and **rooted**.

2.2 Nivre's Method

An incremental dependency parsing algorithm was first proposed by (Covington, 2001). After

Proceedings of the ACL 2010 Conference Short Papers, pages 189–193,
Uppsala, Sweden, 11-16 July 2010. ©2010 Association for Computational Linguistics

Table 1: Transitions for Nivre's method and the proposed method.

		Transition	Precondition
Nivre's Method	Left-Arc	$(\sigma\|w_i, w_j\|\beta, A) \Rightarrow (\sigma, w_j\|\beta, A \cup \{(w_j, w_i)\})$	$i \neq 0 \wedge \neg\exists w_k\ (w_k, w_i) \in A$
	Right-Arc	$(\sigma\|w_i, w_j\|\beta, A) \Rightarrow (\sigma\|w_i\|w_j, \beta, A \cup \{(w_i, w_j)\})$	
	Reduce	$(\sigma\|w_i, \beta, A) \Rightarrow (\sigma, \beta, A)$	$\exists w_k\ (w_k, w_i) \in A$
	Shift	$(\sigma, w_j\|\beta, A) \Rightarrow (\sigma\|w_j, \beta, A)$	
Proposed Method	Left-Arc	$(\sigma\|t_i, t_j\|\beta, A) \Rightarrow (\sigma, t_j\|\beta, A \cup \{(w_j, w_i)\})$	$i \neq 0$
	Right-Arc	$(\sigma\|t_i, t_j\|\beta, A) \Rightarrow (\sigma\|t_i, \beta, A \cup \{(mphc(t_i, t_j), w_j)\})$	
	Shift	$(\sigma, t_j\|\beta, A) \Rightarrow (\sigma\|t_j, \beta, A)$	

studies taking data-driven approaches, by (Kudo and Matsumoto, 2002), (Yamada and Matsumoto, 2003), and (Nivre, 2003), the deterministic incremental parser was generalized to a state transition system in (Nivre, 2008).

Nivre's method applying an arc-eager algorithm works by using a stack of words denoted as σ, for a buffer β initially containing the sentence x. Parsing is formulated as a quadruple (S, T_s, s_{init}, S_t), where each component is defined as follows:

- S is a set of states, each of which is denoted as $(\sigma, \beta, A) \in S$.
- T_s is a set of transitions, and each element of T_s is a function $t_s : S \rightarrow S$.
- $s_{init} = ([w_0], [w_1, \ldots, w_n], \phi)$ is the initial state.
- S_t is a set of terminal states.

Syntactic analysis generates a sequence of optimal transitions t_s provided by an oracle $o : S \rightarrow T_s$, applied to a target consisting of the stack's top element w_i and the first element w_j in the buffer. The oracle is constructed as a classifier trained on treebank data. Each transition is defined in the upper block of Table 1 and explained as follows:

Left-Arc Make w_j the head of w_i and pop w_i, where w_i is located at the stack top (denoted as $\sigma|w_i$), when the buffer head is w_j (denoted as $w_j|\beta$).

Right-Arc Make w_i the head of w_j, and push w_j.

Reduce Pop w_i, located at the stack top.

Shift Push the word w_j, located at the buffer head, onto the stack top.

The method explained thus far has the following drawbacks.

Locality of Parsing Action Selection

The dependency relations are greedily determined, so when the transition Right-Arc adds a dependency arc (w_i, w_j), a more probable head of w_j located in the stack is disregarded as a candidate.

Features Used for Selecting Reduce

The features used in (Nivre and Scholz, 2004) to define a state transition are basically obtained from the two target words w_i and w_j, and their related words. These words are not sufficient to select Reduce, because this action means that w_j has no dependency relation with any word in the stack.

Preconditions

When the classifier selects a transition, the resulting graph satisfies well-formedness and projectivity only under the preconditions listed in Table 1. Even though the parsing seems to be formulated as a four-class classifier problem, it is in fact formed of two types of three-class classifiers.

Solving these problems and selecting a more suitable dependency relation requires a parser that considers more global dependency relations.

3 Tree-Based Parsing Applied to Nivre's Method

3.1 Overall Procedure

Tree-based parsing uses trees as the procedural elements instead of words. This allows enhancement of previously proposed deterministic models such as (Covington, 2001; Yamada and Matsumoto, 2003). In this paper, we show the application of tree-based parsing to Nivre's method. The parser is formulated as a state transition system (S, T_s, s_{init}, S_t), similarly to Nivre's parser, but σ and β for a state $s = (\sigma, \beta, A) \in S$ denote a stack of trees and a buffer of trees, respectively. A tree $t_i \in T$ is defined as the tree rooted by the word w_i, and the initial state is $s_{init} = ([t_0], [t_1, \ldots, t_n], \phi)$, which is formed from the input sentence x.

The state transitions T_s are decided through the following two steps.

1. **Select the most probable head candidate (MPHC)**: For the tree t_i located at the stack top, search for and select the MPHC for w_j, which is the root word of t_j located at the buffer head. This procedure is denoted as a

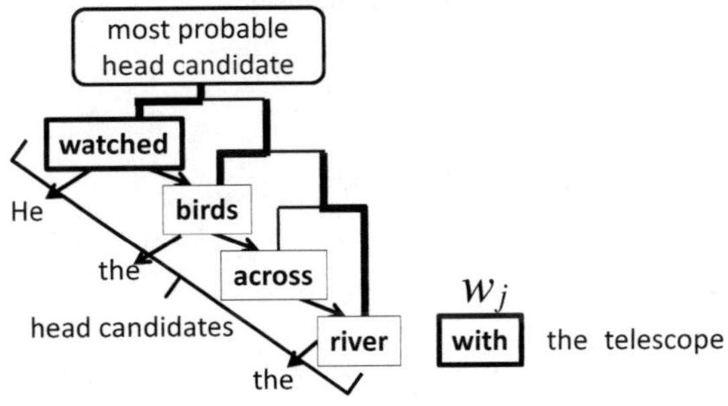

Figure 1: Example of a tournament.

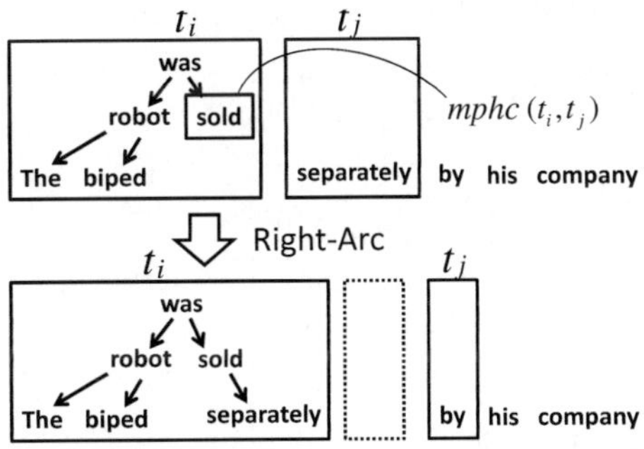

Figure 2: Example of the transition Right.

function $mphc(t_i, t_j)$, and its details are explained in §3.2.

2. **Select a transition:** Choose a transition, by using an oracle, from among the following three possibilities (explained in detail in §3.3):

   Left-Arc Make w_j the head of w_i and pop t_i, where t_i is at the stack top (denoted as $\sigma|t_i$, with the tail being σ), when the buffer head is t_j (denoted as $t_j|\beta$).

   Right-Arc Make the MPHC the head of w_j, and pop the MPHC.

   Shift Push the tree t_j located at the buffer head onto the stack top.

These transitions correspond to three possibilities for the relation between t_i and t_j: (1) a word of t_i is a dependent of a word of t_j; (2) a word of t_j is a dependent of a word of t_i; or (3) the two trees are not related.

The formulations of these transitions in the lower block of Table 1 correspond to Nivre's transitions of the same name, except that here a transition is applied to a tree. This enhancement from words to trees allows removal of both the Reduce transition and certain preconditions.

3.2 Selection of Most Probable Head Candidate

By using $mphc(t_i, t_j)$, a word located far from w_j (the head of t_j) can be selected as the head candidate in t_i. This selection process decreases the number of errors resulting from greedy decision considering only a few candidates.

Various procedures can be considered for implementing $mphc(t_i, t_j)$. One way is to apply the tournament procedure to the words in t_i. The tournament procedure was originally introduced for parsing methods in Japanese by (Iwatate et al., 2008). Since the Japanese language has the head-final property, the tournament model itself constitutes parsing, whereas for parsing a general projective language, the tournament model can only be used as part of a parsing algorithm.

Figure 1 shows a tournament for the example of "with," where the word "watched" finally wins. Although only the words on the left-hand side of tree t_j are searched, this does not mean that the tree-based method considers only one side of a dependency relation. For example, when we apply the tree-based parsing to Yamada's method, the search problems on both sides are solved.

To implement $mphc(t_i, t_j)$, a binary classifier is built to judge which of two given words is more appropriate as the head for another input word. This classifier concerns three words, namely, the two words l (left) and r (right) in t_i, whose appropriateness as the head is compared for the dependent w_j. All word pairs of l and r in t_i are compared repeatedly in a "tournament," and the survivor is regarded as the MPHC of w_j.

The classifier is generated through learning of training examples for all t_i and w_j pairs, each of which generates examples comparing the true head and other (inappropriate) heads in t_i. Table 2 lists the features used in the classifier. Here, lex(X) and pos(X) mean the surface form and part of speech of X, respectively. X^{left} means the dependents of X located on the left-hand side of X, while X^{right} means those on the right. Also, X^{head} means the head of X. The feature design concerns three additional words occurring after w_j, as well, denoted as $w_{j+1}, w_{j+2}, w_{j+3}$.

3.3 Transition Selection

A transition is selected by a three-class classifier after deciding the MPHC, as explained in §3.1. Table 1 lists the three transitions and one precon-

Table 2: Features used for a tournament.

pos(l), lex(l) pos(l^{head}), pos(l^{left}), pos(l^{right})
pos(r), lex(r) pos(r^{head}), pos(r^{left}), pos(r^{right})
pos(w_j), lex(w_j), pos(w_j^{left})
pos(w_{j+1}), lex(w_{j+1}), pos(w_{j+2}), lex(w_{j+2}) pos(w_{j+3}), lex(w_{j+3})

Table 3: Features used for a state transition.

pos(w_i), lex(w_i) pos(w_i^{left}), pos(w_i^{right}), lex(w_i^{left}), lex(w_i^{right})
pos(MPHC), lex(MPHC) pos(MPHC^{head}), pos(MPHC^{left}), pos(MPHC^{right}) lex(MPHC^{head}), lex(MPHC^{left}), lex(MPHC^{right})
pos(w_j), lex(w_j), pos(w_j^{left}), lex(w_j^{left})
pos(w_{j+1}), lex(w_{j+1}), pos(w_{j+2}), lex(w_{j+2}), pos(w_{j+3}), lex(w_{j+3})

dition. The transition Shift indicates that the target trees t_i and t_j have no dependency relations. The transition Right-Arc indicates generation of the dependent-head relation between w_j and the result of $mphc(t_i, t_j)$, i.e., the MPHC for w_j. Figure 2 shows an example of this transition. The transition Left-Arc indicates generation of the dependency relation in which w_j is the head of w_i. While Right-Arc requires searching for the MPHC in t_i, this is not the case for Left-Arc[1].

The key to obtaining an accurate tree-based parsing model is to extend the search space while at the same time providing ways to narrow down the space and find important information, such as the MPHC, for proper judgment of transitions.

The three-class classifier is constructed as follows. The dependency relation between the target trees is represented by the three words w_i, MPHC, and w_j. Therefore, the features are designed to incorporate these words, their relational words, and the three words next to w_j. Table 3 lists the exact set of features used in this work. Since this transition selection procedure presumes selection of the MPHC, the result of $mphc(t_i, t_j)$ is also incorporated among the features.

4 Evaluation

4.1 Data and Experimental Setting

In our experimental evaluation, we used Yamada's head rule to extract unlabeled dependencies from the Wall Street Journal section of a Penn Treebank. Sections 2-21 were used as the training data, and section 23 was used as the test data. This test data was used in several other previous works, enabling mutual comparison with the methods reported in those works.

The SVM^{light} package[2] was used to build the support vector machine classifiers. The binary classifier for MPHC selection and the three-class classifier for transition selection were built using a cubic polynomial kernel. The parsing speed was evaluated on a Core2Duo (2.53 GHz) machine.

4.2 Parsing Accuracy

We measured the ratio of words assigned correct heads to all words (accuracy), and the ratio of sentences with completely correct dependency graphs to all sentences (complete match). In the evaluation, we consistently excluded punctuation marks.

Table 4 compares our results for the proposed method with those reported in some previous works using equivalent training and test data. The first column lists the four previous methods and our method, while the second through fourth columns list the accuracy, complete match accuracy, and time complexity, respectively, for each method. Here, we obtained the scores for the previous works from the corresponding articles listed in the first column. Note that every method used different features, which depend on the method.

The proposed method achieved higher accuracy than did the previous deterministic models. Although the accuracy of our method did not reach that of (McDonald and Pereira, 2006), the scores were competitive even though our method is deterministic. These results show the capability of the tree-based approach in effectively extending the search space.

4.3 Parsing Time

Such extension of the search space also concerns the speed of the method. Here, we compare its computational time with that of Nivre's method. We re-implemented Nivre's method to use SVMs with cubic polynomial kernel, similarly to our

[1] The head word of w_i can only be w_j without searching within t_j, because the relations between the other words in t_j and w_i have already been inferred from the decisions made within previous transitions. If t_j has a child w_k that could become the head of w_i under projectivity, this w_k must be located between w_i and w_j. The fact that w_k's head is w_j means that there were two phases before t_i and t_j (i.e., w_i and w_j) became the target:

- t_i and t_k became the target, and Shift was selected.
- t_k and t_j became the target, and Left-Arc was selected.

The first phase precisely indicates that w_i and w_k are unrelated.

[2] http://svmlight.joachims.org/

Table 4: Dependency parsing performance.

	Accuracy	Complete match	Time complexity	Global vs. deterministic	Learning method
McDonald & Pereira (2006)	91.5	42.1	$O(n^3)$	global	MIRA
McDonald et al. (2005)	90.9	37.5	$O(n^3)$	global	MIRA
Yamada & Matsumoto (2003)	90.4	38.4	$O(n^2)$	deterministic	support vector machine
Goldberg & Elhadad (2010)	89.7	37.5	$O(n \log n)$	deterministic	structured perceptron
Nivre (2004)	87.1	30.4	$O(n)$	deterministic	memory based learning
Proposed method	91.3	41.7	$O(n^2)$	deterministic	support vector machine

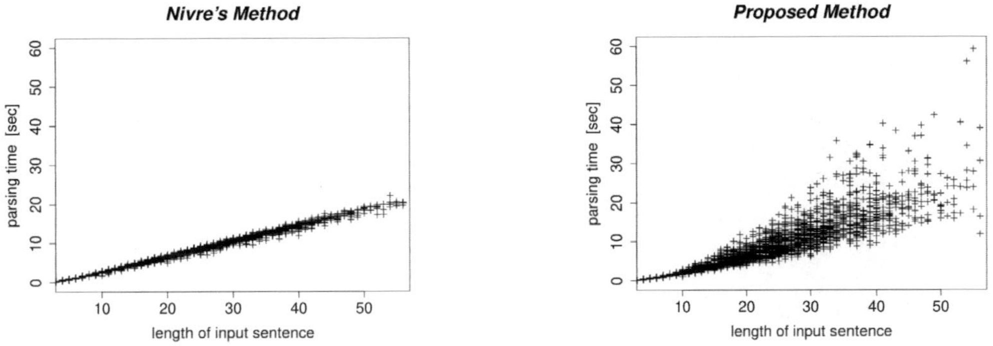

Figure 3: Parsing time for sentences.

method. Figure 3 shows plots of the parsing times for all sentences in the test data. The average parsing time for our method was 8.9 sec, whereas that for Nivre's method was 7.9 sec.

Although the worst-case time complexity for Nivre's method is $O(n)$ and that for our method is $O(n^2)$, worst-case situations (e.g., all words having heads on their left) did not appear frequently. This can be seen from the sparse appearance of the upper bound in the second figure.

5 Conclusion

We have proposed a tree-based model that decides head-dependency relations between trees instead of between words. This extends the search space to obtain the best head for a word within a deterministic model. The tree-based idea is potentially applicable to various previous parsing methods; in this paper, we have applied it to enhance Nivre's method.

Our tree-based model outperformed various deterministic parsing methods reported previously. Although the worst-case time complexity of our method is $O(n^2)$, the average parsing time is not much slower than $O(n)$.

References

Xavier Carreras. 2007. Experiments with a higher-order projective dependency parse. *Proceedings of the CoNLL Shared Task Session of EMNLP-CoNLL*, pp. 957-961.

Michael A. Covington. 2001. A fundamental algorithm for dependency parsing. *Proceedings of ACM*, pp. 95-102.

Jason M. Eisner. 1996. Three new probabilistic models for dependency parsing: An exploration. *Proceedings of COLING*, pp. 340-345.

Yoav Goldberg and Michael Elhadad. 2010. An Efficient Algorithm for Easy-First Non-Directional Dependency Parsing. *Proceedings of NAACL*.

Masakazu Iwatate, Masayuki Asahara, and Yuji Matsumoto. 2008. Japanese dependency parsing using a tournament model. *Proceedings of COLING*, pp. 361–368.

Terry Koo, Xavier Carreras, and Michael Collins. 2008. Simple semi-supervised dependency parsing. *Proceedings of ACL*, pp. 595–603.

Taku Kudo and Yuji Matsumoto. 2002. Japanese dependency analysis using cascaded chunking *Proceedings of CoNLL*, pp. 63–69.

Ryan McDonald, Koby Crammer, and Fernando Pereira. 2005. Online large-margin training of dependency parsers. *Proceedings of ACL*, pp. 91–98.

Ryan McDonald and Fernando Pereira. 2006. Online learning of approximate dependency parsing algorithms. *Proceedings of the EACL*, pp. 81–88.

Joakim Nivre. 2003. An efficient algorithm for projective dependency parsing. *Proceedings of IWPT*, pp. 149–160.

Joakim Nivre. 2008. Algorithms for deterministic incremental dependency parsing. *Computational Linguistics*, vol. 34, num. 4, pp. 513–553.

Joakim Nivre and Mario Scholz. 2004. Deterministic dependency parsing of English text. *Proceedings of COLING*, pp. 64–70.

Hiroyasu Yamada and Yuji Matsumoto. 2003. Statistical dependency analysis with support vector machines. *Proceedings of IWPT*, pp. 195–206.

Yue Zhang and Stephen Clark. 2008. A tale of two parsers: investigating and combining graph-based and transition-based dependency parsing using beamsearch. *Proceedings of EMNLP*, pp. 562–571.

Sparsity in Dependency Grammar Induction

Jennifer Gillenwater and **Kuzman Ganchev**
University of Pennsylvania
Philadelphia, PA, USA
{jengi,kuzman}@cis.upenn.edu

João Graça
L^2F INESC-ID
Lisboa, Portugal
joao.graca@l2f.inesc-id.pt

Fernando Pereira
Google Inc.
Mountain View, CA, USA
pereira@google.com

Ben Taskar
University of Pennsylvania
Philadelphia, PA, USA
taskar@cis.upenn.edu

Abstract

A strong inductive bias is essential in unsupervised grammar induction. We explore a particular sparsity bias in dependency grammars that encourages a small number of unique dependency types. Specifically, we investigate sparsity-inducing penalties on the posterior distributions of parent-child POS tag pairs in the posterior regularization (PR) framework of Graça et al. (2007). In experiments with 12 languages, we achieve substantial gains over the standard expectation maximization (EM) baseline, with average improvement in attachment accuracy of 6.3%. Further, our method outperforms models based on a standard Bayesian sparsity-inducing prior by an average of 4.9%. On English in particular, we show that our approach improves on several other state-of-the-art techniques.

1 Introduction

We investigate an unsupervised learning method for dependency parsing models that imposes sparsity biases on the dependency types. We assume a corpus annotated with POS tags, where the task is to induce a dependency model from the tags for corpus sentences. In this setting, the *type* of a dependency is defined as a pair: tag of the dependent (also known as the child), and tag of the head (also known as the parent). Given that POS tags are designed to convey information about grammatical relations, it is reasonable to assume that only some of the possible dependency types will be realized for a given language. For instance, in English it is ungrammatical for nouns to dominate verbs, adjectives to dominate adverbs, and determiners to dominate almost any part of speech. Thus, the realized dependency types should be a sparse subset of all possible types.

Previous work in unsupervised grammar induction has tried to achieve sparsity through priors. Liang et al. (2007), Finkel et al. (2007) and Johnson et al. (2007) proposed hierarchical Dirichlet process priors. Cohen et al. (2008) experimented with a discounting Dirichlet prior, which encourages a standard dependency parsing model (see Section 2) to limit the number of dependent types for each head type.

Our experiments show a more effective sparsity pattern is one that limits the total number of unique head-dependent tag pairs. This kind of sparsity bias avoids inducing competition between dependent types for each head type. We can achieve the desired bias with a constraint on model posteriors during learning, using the posterior regularization (PR) framework (Graça et al., 2007). Specifically, to implement PR we augment the maximum marginal likelihood objective of the dependency model with a term that penalizes head-dependent tag distributions that are too permissive.

Although not focused on sparsity, several other studies use soft parameter sharing to couple different types of dependencies. To this end, Cohen et al. (2008) and Cohen and Smith (2009) investigated logistic normal priors, and Headden III et al. (2009) used a backoff scheme. We compare to their results in Section 5.

The remainder of this paper is organized as fol-

Proceedings of the ACL 2010 Conference Short Papers, pages 194–199,
Uppsala, Sweden, 11-16 July 2010. ©2010 Association for Computational Linguistics

lows. Section 2 and 3 review the models and several previous approaches for learning them. Section 4 describes learning with PR. Section 5 describes experiments across 12 languages and Section 6 analyzes the results. For additional details on this work see Gillenwater et al. (2010).

2 Parsing Model

The models we use are based on the generative dependency model with valence (DMV) (Klein and Manning, 2004). For a sentence with tags $\mathbf{x}$, the root POS $r(\mathbf{x})$ is generated first. Then the model decides whether to generate a right dependent conditioned on the POS of the root and whether other right dependents have already been generated for this head. Upon deciding to generate a right dependent, the POS of the dependent is selected by conditioning on the head POS and the directionality. After stopping on the right, the root generates left dependents using the mirror reversal of this process. Once the root has generated all its dependents, the dependents generate their own dependents in the same manner.

2.1 Model Extensions

For better comparison with previous work we implemented three model extensions, borrowed from Headden III et al. (2009). The first extension alters the stopping probability by conditioning it not only on whether there are *any* dependents in a particular direction already, but also on *how many* such dependents there are. When we talk about models with maximum stop valency $V_s = S$, this means it distinguishes S different cases: $0, 1, \ldots, S-2$, and $\geq S-1$ dependents in a given direction. The basic DMV has $V_s = 2$.

The second model extension we implement is analogous to the first, but applies to dependent tag probabilities instead of stop probabilities. Again, we expand the conditioning such that the model considers how many other dependents were already generated in the same direction. When we talk about a model with maximum child valency $V_c = C$, this means we distinguish C different cases. The basic DMV has $V_c = 1$. Since this extension to the dependent probabilities dramatically increases model complexity, the third model extension we implement is to add a backoff for the dependent probabilities that does not condition on the identity of the parent POS (see Equation 2).

More formally, under the extended DMV the probability of a sentence with POS tags $\mathbf{x}$ and dependency tree $\mathbf{y}$ is given by:

$$p_\theta(\mathbf{x}, \mathbf{y}) = p_{root}(r(\mathbf{x})) \times \prod_{y \in \mathbf{y}} p_{stop}(false \mid y_p, y_d, y_{v_s}) p_{child}(y_c \mid y_p, y_d, y_{v_c}) \times \prod_{x \in \mathbf{x}} p_{stop}(true \mid x, left, x_{v_l})\, p_{stop}(true \mid x, right, x_{v_r}) \quad (1)$$

where y is the dependency of y_c on head y_p in direction y_d, and y_{v_c}, y_{v_s}, x_{v_r}, and x_{v_l} indicate valence. For the third model extension, the backoff to a probability not dependent on parent POS can be formally expressed as:

$$\lambda p_{child}(y_c \mid y_p, y_d, y_{v_c}) + (1-\lambda) p_{child}(y_c \mid y_d, y_{v_c}) \quad (2)$$

for $\lambda \in [0, 1]$. We fix $\lambda = 1/3$, which is a crude approximation to the value learned by Headden III et al. (2009).

3 Previous Learning Approaches

In our experiments, we compare PR learning to standard expectation maximization (EM) and to Bayesian learning with a sparsity-inducing prior. The EM algorithm optimizes marginal likelihood $\mathcal{L}(\theta) = \log \sum_{\mathbf{Y}} p_\theta(\mathbf{X}, \mathbf{Y})$, where $\mathbf{X} = \{\mathbf{x}^1, \ldots, \mathbf{x}^n\}$ denotes the entire unlabeled corpus and $\mathbf{Y} = \{\mathbf{y}^1, \ldots, \mathbf{y}^n\}$ denotes a set of corresponding parses for each sentence. Neal and Hinton (1998) view EM as block coordinate ascent on a function that lower-bounds $\mathcal{L}(\theta)$. Starting from an initial parameter estimate θ^0, the algorithm iterates two steps:

$$\mathbf{E}: q^{t+1} = \arg\min_q \mathbf{KL}(q(\mathbf{Y}) \parallel p_{\theta^t}(\mathbf{Y} \mid \mathbf{X})) \quad (3)$$

$$\mathbf{M}: \theta^{t+1} = \arg\max_\theta \mathbf{E}_{q^{t+1}} [\log p_\theta(\mathbf{X}, \mathbf{Y})] \quad (4)$$

Note that the E-step just sets $q^{t+1}(\mathbf{Y}) = p_{\theta^t}(\mathbf{Y}|\mathbf{X})$, since it is an unconstrained minimization of a KL-divergence. The PR method we present modifies the E-step by adding constraints.

Besides EM, we also compare to learning with several Bayesian priors that have been applied to the DMV. One such prior is the Dirichlet, whose hyperparameter we will denote by α. For $\alpha < 0.5$, this prior encourages parameter sparsity. Cohen et al. (2008) use this method with $\alpha = 0.25$ for training the DMV and achieve improvements over basic EM. In this paper we will refer to our own implementation of the Dirichlet prior as the "discounting Dirichlet" (DD) method. In addition to the Dirichlet, other types of priors have been applied, in particular logistic normal priors (LN) and shared logistic normal priors (SLN) (Cohen et al., 2008; Cohen and Smith, 2009). LN and SLN aim to tie parameters together. Essentially, this has a similar goal to sparsity-inducing methods in that it posits a more concise explanation for the grammar of a language. Headden III et al. (2009) also implement a sort of parameter tying for the E-DMV through a learning a backoff distribution on child probabilities. We compare against results from all these methods.

4 Learning with Sparse Posteriors

We would like to penalize models that predict a large number of distinct dependency types. To enforce this penalty, we use the posterior regularization (PR) framework (Graça et al., 2007). PR is closely related to generalized expectation constraints (Mann and McCallum, 2007; Mann and McCallum, 2008; Bellare et al., 2009), and is also indirectly related to a Bayesian view of learning with constraints on posteriors (Liang et al., 2009). The PR framework uses constraints on posterior expectations to guide parameter estimation. Here, PR allows a natural and tractable representation of sparsity constraints based on edge type counts that cannot easily be encoded in model parameters. We use a version of PR where the desired bias is a penalty on the log likelihood (see Ganchev et al. (2010) for more details). For a distribution p_θ, we define a penalty as the (generic) β-norm of expectations of some features ϕ:

$$||\mathbf{E}_{p_\theta}[\phi(\mathbf{X}, \mathbf{Y})]||_\beta \tag{5}$$

For computational tractability, rather than penalizing the model's posteriors directly, we use an auxiliary distribution q, and penalize the marginal log-likelihood of a model by the KL-divergence of p_θ from q, plus the penalty term with respect to q. For a fixed set of model parameters θ the full PR penalty term is:

$$\min_q \mathbf{KL}(q(\mathbf{Y}) \parallel p_\theta(\mathbf{Y}|\mathbf{X})) \; + \; \sigma\, ||\mathbf{E}_q[\phi(\mathbf{X}, \mathbf{Y})]||_\beta \tag{6}$$

where σ is the strength of the regularization. PR seeks to maximize $\mathcal{L}(\theta)$ minus this penalty term. The resulting objective can be optimized by a variant of the EM (Dempster et al., 1977) algorithm used to optimize $\mathcal{L}(\theta)$.

4.1 ℓ_1/ℓ_∞ Regularization

We now define precisely how to count dependency types. For each child tag c, let i range over an enumeration of all occurrences of c in the corpus, and let p be another tag. Let the indicator $\phi_{cpi}(\mathbf{X}, \mathbf{Y})$ have value 1 if p is the parent tag of the ith occurrence of c, and value 0 otherwise. The number of unique dependency types is then:

$$\sum_{cp} \max_i \phi_{cpi}(\mathbf{X}, \mathbf{Y}) \tag{7}$$

Note there is an asymmetry in this count: occurrences of child type c are enumerated with i, but all occurrences of parent type p are or-ed in ϕ_{cpi}. That is, $\phi_{cpi} = 1$ if *any* occurrence of p is the parent of the ith occurrence of c. We will refer to PR training with this constraint as PR-AS. Instead of counting pairs of a child token and a parent type, we can alternatively count pairs of a child token and a parent token by letting p range over all *tokens* rather than *types*. Then each potential dependency corresponds to a different indicator ϕ_{cpij}, and the penalty is symmetric with respect to parents and children. We will refer to PR training with this constraint as PR-S. Both approaches perform very well, so we report results for both.

Equation 7 can be viewed as a mixed-norm penalty on the features ϕ_{cpi} or ϕ_{cpij}: the sum corresponds to an ℓ_1 norm and the max to an ℓ_∞ norm. Thus, the quantity we want to minimize fits precisely into the PR penalty framework. Formally, to optimize the PR objective, we complete the following E-step:

$$\arg\min_q \mathbf{KL}(q(\mathbf{Y})||p_\theta(\mathbf{Y}|\mathbf{X})) + \sigma \sum_{cp} \max_i \mathbf{E}_q[\phi(\mathbf{X}, \mathbf{Y})], \tag{8}$$

which can equivalently be written as:

$$\begin{aligned} \min_{q(\mathbf{Y}),\xi_{cp}} \quad & \mathbf{KL}(q(\mathbf{Y}) \parallel p_\theta(\mathbf{Y}|\mathbf{X})) + \sigma \sum_{cp} \xi_{cp} \\ \text{s.t.} \quad & \xi_{cp} \leq \mathbf{E}_q[\phi(\mathbf{X}, \mathbf{Y})] \end{aligned} \tag{9}$$

where ξ_{cp} corresponds to the maximum expectation of ϕ over all instances of c and p. Note that the projection problem can be solved efficiently in the dual (Ganchev et al., 2010).

5 Experiments

We evaluate on 12 languages. Following the example of Smith and Eisner (2006), we strip punctuation from the sentences and keep only sentences of length ≤ 10. For simplicity, for all models we use the "harmonic" initializer from Klein

Model	EM	PR	Type	σ
DMV	45.8	**62.1**	PR-S	140
2-1	45.1	**62.7**	PR-S	100
2-2	54.4	**62.9**	PR-S	80
3-3	55.3	**64.3**	PR-S	140
4-4	55.1	**64.4**	PR-AS	140

Table 1: Attachment accuracy results. **Column 1**: V_c-V_s used for the E-DMV models. **Column 3**: Best PR result for each model, which is chosen by applying each of the two types of constraints (PR-S and PR-AS) and trying $\sigma \in \{80, 100, 120, 140, 160, 180\}$. **Columns 4 & 5**: Constraint type and σ that produced the values in column 3.

Learning Method	Accuracy		
	≤ 10	≤ 20	all
PR-S ($\sigma = 140$)	**62.1**	**53.8**	**49.1**
LN families	59.3	45.1	39.0
SLN TieV & N	61.3	47.4	41.4
PR-AS ($\sigma = 140$)	64.4	55.2	50.5
DD ($\alpha = 1$, λ learned)	**65.0** (± 5.7)		

Table 2: Comparison with previous published results. Rows 2 and 3 are taken from Cohen et al. (2008) and Cohen and Smith (2009), and row 5 from Headden III et al. (2009).

and Manning (2004), which we refer to as K&M. We always train for 100 iterations and evaluate on the test set using Viterbi parses. Before evaluating, we smooth the resulting models by adding e^{-10} to each learned parameter, merely to remove the chance of zero probabilities for unseen events. (We did not tune this as it should make very little difference for final parses.) We score models by their attachment accuracy — the fraction of words assigned the correct parent.

5.1 Results on English

We start by comparing English performance for EM, PR, and DD. To find α for DD we searched over five values: $\{0.01, 0.1, 0.25, 1\}$. We found 0.25 to be the best setting for the DMV, the same as found by Cohen et al. (2008). DD achieves accuracy 46.4% with this α. For the E-DMV we tested four model complexities with valencies V_c-V_s of 2-1, 2-2, 3-3, and 4-4. DD's best accuracy was 53.6% with the 4-4 model at $\alpha = 0.1$. A comparison between EM and PR is shown in Table 1. PR-S generally performs better than the PR-AS for English. Comparing PR-S to EM, we also found PR-S is always better, independent of the particular σ, with improvements ranging from 2% to 17%. Note that in this work we do not perform the PR projection at test time; we found it detrimental, probably due to a need to set the (corpus-size-dependent) σ differently for the test set. We also note that development likelihood and the best setting for σ are not well-correlated, which unfortunately makes it hard to pick these parameters without some supervision.

5.2 Comparison with Previous Work

In this section we compare to previously published unsupervised dependency parsing results for English. It might be argued that the comparison is unfair since we do supervised selection of model complexity and regularization strength. However, we feel the comparison is not so unfair as we perform only a very limited search of the model-σ space. Specifically, the only values of σ we search over are $\{80, 100, 120, 140, 160, 180\}$.

First, we consider the top three entries in Table 2, which are for the basic DMV. The first entry was generated using our implementation of PR-S. The second two entries are logistic normal and shared logistic normal parameter tying results (Cohen et al., 2008; Cohen and Smith, 2009). The PR-S result is the clear winner, especially as length of test sentences increases. For the bottom two entries in the table, which are for the E-DMV, the last entry is best, corresponding to using a DD prior with $\alpha = 1$ (non-sparsifying), but with a special "random pools" initialization and a learned weight λ for the child backoff probability. The result for PR-AS is well within the variance range of this last entry, and thus we conjecture that combining PR-AS with random pools initialization and learned λ would likely produce the best-performing model of all.

5.3 Results on Other Languages

Here we describe experiments on 11 additional languages. For each we set σ and model complexity (DMV versus one of the four E-DMV experimented with previously) based on the best configuration found for English. This likely will not result in the ideal parameters for all languages, but provides a realistic test setting: a user has available a labeled corpus in one language, and would like to induce grammars for many other languages. Table 3 shows the performance for all models and training procedures. We see that the sparsifying methods tend to improve over EM most of the time. For the basic DMV, average improvements are 1.6% for DD, 6.0% for PR-S, and 7.5% for PR-AS. PR-AS beats PR-S in 8 out of 12 cases,

	Bg	Cz	De	Dk	En	Es	Jp	Nl	Pt	Se	Si	Tr
	DMV Model											
EM	37.8	29.6	35.7	**47.2**	45.8	40.3	52.8	37.1	35.7	39.4	42.3	46.8
DD 0.25	39.3	30.0	38.6	43.1	46.4	47.5	57.8	35.1	38.7	40.2	48.8	43.8
PR-S 140	53.7	31.5	**39.6**	44.0	**62.1**	61.1	58.8	31.0	47.0	**42.2**	39.9	51.4
PR-AS 140	**54.0**	**32.0**	**39.6**	42.4	61.9	**62.4**	**60.2**	**37.9**	**47.8**	38.7	**50.3**	**53.4**
	Extended Model											
EM (3,3)	41.7	48.9	40.1	46.4	55.3	44.3	48.5	**47.5**	35.9	**48.6**	47.5	46.2
DD 0.1 (4,4)	47.6	48.5	42.0	44.4	53.6	48.9	57.6	45.2	48.3	47.6	35.6	48.9
PR-S 140 (3,3)	59.0	**54.7**	**47.4**	45.8	64.3	**57.9**	**60.8**	33.9	**54.3**	45.6	49.1	56.3
PR-AS 140 (4,4)	**59.8**	54.6	45.7	**46.6**	**64.4**	**57.9**	59.4	38.8	49.5	41.4	**51.2**	**56.9**

Table 3: Attachment accuracy results. The parameters used are the best settings found for English. Values for hyperparameters (α or σ) are given after the method name. For the extended model (V_c, V_s) are indicated in parentheses. En is the English Penn Treebank (Marcus et al., 1993) and the other 11 languages are from the CoNLL X shared task: Bulgarian [Bg] (Simov et al., 2002), Czech [Cz] (Bohomovà et al., 2001), German [De] (Brants et al., 2002), Danish [Dk] (Kromann et al., 2003), Spanish [Es] (Civit and Martí, 2004), Japanese [Jp] (Kawata and Bartels, 2000), Dutch [Nl] (Van der Beek et al., 2002), Portuguese [Pt] (Afonso et al., 2002), Swedish [Se] (Nilsson et al., 2005), Slovene [Sl] (Džeroski et al., 2006), and Turkish [Tr] (Oflazer et al., 2003).

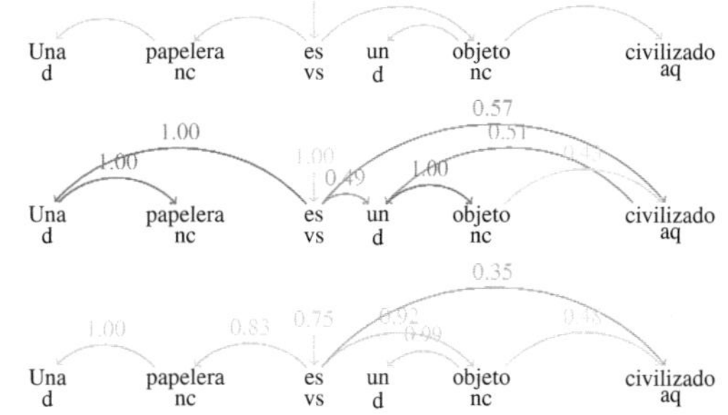

Figure 1: Posterior edge probabilities for an example sentence from the Spanish test corpus. At the top are the gold dependencies, the middle are EM posteriors, and bottom are PR posteriors. Green indicates correct dependencies and red indicates incorrect dependencies. The numbers on the edges are the values of the posterior probabilities.

though the average increase is only 1.5%. PR-S is also better than DD for 10 out of 12 languages. If we instead consider these methods for the E-DMV, DD performs worse, just 1.4% better than the E-DMV EM, while both PR-S and PR-AS continue to show substantial average improvements over EM, 6.5% and 6.3%, respectively.

6 Analysis

One common EM error that PR fixes in many languages is the directionality of the noun-determiner relation. Figure 1 shows an example of a Spanish sentence where PR significantly outperforms EM because of this. Sentences such as "Lleva tiempo entenderlos" which has tags "main-verb common-noun main-verb" (no determiner tag) provide an explanation for PR's improvement—when PR sees that sometimes nouns can appear without determiners but that the opposite situation does not occur, it shifts the model parameters to make nouns the parent of determiners instead of the reverse. Then it does not have to pay the cost of assigning a parent with a new tag to cover each noun that doesn't come with a determiner.

7 Conclusion

In this paper we presented a new method for unsupervised learning of dependency parsers. In contrast to previous approaches that constrain model parameters, we constrain model posteriors. Our approach consistently outperforms the standard EM algorithm and a discounting Dirichlet prior.

We have several ideas for further improving our constraints, such as: taking into account the directionality of the edges, using different regularization strengths for the root probabilities than for the child probabilities, and working directly on word types rather than on POS tags. In the future, we would also like to try applying similar constraints to the more complex task of joint induction of POS tags and dependency parses.

Acknowledgments

J. Gillenwater was supported by NSF-IGERT 0504487. K. Ganchev was supported by ARO MURI SUBTLE W911NF-07-1-0216. J. Graça was supported by FCT fellowship SFRH/BD/27528/2006 and by FCT project CMU-PT/HuMach/0039/2008. B. Taskar was partly supported by DARPA CSSG and ONR Young Investigator Award N000141010746.

References

S. Afonso, E. Bick, R. Haber, and D. Santos. 2002. Floresta Sinta(c)tica: a treebank for Portuguese. In *Proc. LREC*.

K. Bellare, G. Druck, and A. McCallum. 2009. Alternating projections for learning with expectation constraints. In *Proc. UAI*.

A. Bohomovà, J. Hajic, E. Hajicova, and B. Hladka. 2001. The prague dependency treebank: Three-level annotation scenario. In Anne Abeillé, editor, *Treebanks: Building and Using Syntactically Annotated Corpora*.

S. Brants, S. Dipper, S. Hansen, W. Lezius, and G. Smith. 2002. The TIGER treebank. In *Proc. Workshop on Treebanks and Linguistic Theories*.

M. Civit and M.A. Martí. 2004. Building cast3lb: A Spanish Treebank. *Research on Language & Computation*.

S.B. Cohen and N.A. Smith. 2009. The shared logistic normal distribution for grammar induction. In *Proc. NAACL*.

S.B. Cohen, K. Gimpel, and N.A. Smith. 2008. Logistic normal priors for unsupervised probabilistic grammar induction. In *Proc. NIPS*.

A.P. Dempster, N.M. Laird, and D.B. Rubin. 1977. Maximum likelihood from incomplete data via the EM algorithm. *Journal of the Royal Statistical Society*, 39(1):1–38.

S. Džeroski, T. Erjavec, N. Ledinek, P. Pajas, Z. Žabokrtsky, and A. Žele. 2006. Towards a Slovene dependency treebank. In *Proc. LREC*.

J. Finkel, T. Grenager, and C. Manning. 2007. The infinite tree. In *Proc. ACL*.

K. Ganchev, J. Graça, J. Gillenwater, and B. Taskar. 2010. Posterior regularization for structured latent variable models. *Journal of Machine Learning Research*.

J. Gillenwater, K. Ganchev, J. Graça, F. Pereira, and B. Taskar. 2010. Posterior sparsity in unsupervised dependency parsing. Technical report, MS-CIS-10-19, University of Pennsylvania.

J. Graça, K. Ganchev, and B. Taskar. 2007. Expectation maximization and posterior constraints. In *Proc. NIPS*.

W.P. Headden III, M. Johnson, and D. McClosky. 2009. Improving unsupervised dependency parsing with richer contexts and smoothing. In *Proc. NAACL*.

M. Johnson, T.L. Griffiths, and S. Goldwater. 2007. Adaptor grammars: A framework for specifying compositional nonparametric Bayesian models. In *Proc. NIPS*.

Y. Kawata and J. Bartels. 2000. Stylebook for the Japanese Treebank in VERBMOBIL. Technical report, Eberhard-Karls-Universitat Tubingen.

D. Klein and C. Manning. 2004. Corpus-based induction of syntactic structure: Models of dependency and constituency. In *Proc. ACL*.

M.T. Kromann, L. Mikkelsen, and S.K. Lynge. 2003. Danish Dependency Treebank. In *Proc. TLT*.

P. Liang, S. Petrov, M.I. Jordan, and D. Klein. 2007. The infinite PCFG using hierarchical Dirichlet processes. In *Proc. EMNLP*.

P. Liang, M.I. Jordan, and D. Klein. 2009. Learning from measurements in exponential families. In *Proc. ICML*.

G. Mann and A. McCallum. 2007. Simple, robust, scalable semi-supervised learning via expectation regularization. In *Proc. ICML*.

G. Mann and A. McCallum. 2008. Generalized expectation criteria for semi-supervised learning of conditional random fields. In *Proc. ACL*.

M. Marcus, M. Marcinkiewicz, and B. Santorini. 1993. Building a large annotated corpus of English: The Penn Treebank. *Computational Linguistics*, 19(2):313–330.

R. Neal and G. Hinton. 1998. A new view of the EM algorithm that justifies incremental, sparse and other variants. In M. I. Jordan, editor, *Learning in Graphical Models*, pages 355–368. MIT Press.

J. Nilsson, J. Hall, and J. Nivre. 2005. MAMBA meets TIGER: Reconstructing a Swedish treebank from antiquity. *NODALIDA Special Session on Treebanks*.

K. Oflazer, B. Say, D.Z. Hakkani-Tür, and G. Tür. 2003. Building a Turkish treebank. *Treebanks: Building and Using Parsed Corpora*.

K. Simov, P. Osenova, M. Slavcheva, S. Kolkovska, E. Balabanova, D. Doikoff, K. Ivanova, A. Simov, E. Simov, and M. Kouylekov. 2002. Building a linguistically interpreted corpus of bulgarian: the bultreebank. In *Proc. LREC*.

N. Smith and J. Eisner. 2006. Annealing structural bias in multilingual weighted grammar induction. In *Proc. ACL*.

L. Van der Beek, G. Bouma, R. Malouf, and G. Van Noord. 2002. The Alpino dependency treebank. *Language and Computers*.

Top-Down K-Best A* Parsing

Adam Pauls and **Dan Klein**
Computer Science Division
University of California at Berkeley
{adpauls,klein}@cs.berkeley.edu

Chris Quirk
Microsoft Research
Redmond, WA, 98052
chrisq@microsoft.com

Abstract

We propose a top-down algorithm for extracting k-best lists from a parser. Our algorithm, TKA* is a variant of the k-best A* (KA*) algorithm of Pauls and Klein (2009). In contrast to KA*, which performs an inside and outside pass before performing k-best extraction bottom up, TKA* performs only the inside pass before extracting k-best lists top down. TKA* maintains the same optimality and efficiency guarantees of KA*, but is simpler to both specify and implement.

1 Introduction

Many situations call for a parser to return a k-best list of parses instead of a single best hypothesis.[1] Currently, there are two efficient approaches known in the literature. The k-best algorithm of Jiménez and Marzal (2000) and Huang and Chiang (2005), referred to hereafter as LAZY, operates by first performing an exhaustive Viterbi inside pass and then lazily extracting k-best lists in top-down manner. The k-best A* algorithm of Pauls and Klein (2009), hereafter KA*, computes Viterbi inside *and* outside scores before extracting k-best lists bottom up.

Because these additional passes are only partial, KA* can be significantly faster than LAZY, especially when a heuristic is used (Pauls and Klein, 2009). In this paper, we propose TKA*, a top-down variant of KA* that, like LAZY, performs only an inside pass before extracting k-best lists top-down, but maintains the same optimality and efficiency guarantees as KA*. This algorithm can be seen as a generalization of the lattice k-best algorithm of Soong and Huang (1991) to parsing. Because TKA* eliminates the outside pass from KA*, TKA* is simpler both in implementation and specification.

[1] See Huang and Chiang (2005) for a review.

2 Review

Because our algorithm is very similar to KA*, which is in turn an extension of the (1-best) A* parsing algorithm of Klein and Manning (2003), we first introduce notation and review those two algorithms before presenting our new algorithm.

2.1 Notation

Assume we have a PCFG[2] $\mathcal{G}$ and an input sentence $s_0 \dots s_{n-1}$ of length n. The grammar $\mathcal{G}$ has a set of symbols denoted by capital letters, including a distinguished goal (root) symbol G. Without loss of generality, we assume Chomsky normal form: each non-terminal rule r in $\mathcal{G}$ has the form $r = A \rightarrow B\ C$ with weight w_r. *Edges* are labeled spans $e = (A, i, j)$. *Inside derivations* of an edge (A, i, j) are trees with root nonterminal A, spanning $s_i \dots s_{j-1}$. The weight (negative log-probability) of the best (minimum) inside derivation for an edge e is called the Viterbi inside score $\beta(e)$, and the weight of the best derivation of $G \rightarrow s_0 \dots s_{i-1}\ A\ s_j \dots s_{n-1}$ is called the Viterbi outside score $\alpha(e)$. The goal of a k-best parsing algorithm is to compute the k best (minimum weight) inside derivations of the edge $(G, 0, n)$.

We formulate the algorithms in this paper in terms of prioritized weighted deduction rules (Shieber et al., 1995; Nederhof, 2003). A *prioritized weighted deduction rule* has the form

$$\phi_1 : w_1, \dots, \phi_n : w_n \xrightarrow{p(w_1,\dots,w_n)} \phi_0 : g(w_1, \dots, w_n)$$

where $\phi_1, \dots, \phi_n$ are the *antecedent items* of the deduction rule and ϕ_0 is the *conclusion item*. A deduction rule states that, given the antecedents $\phi_1, \dots, \phi_n$ with weights $w_1, \dots, w_n$, the conclusion ϕ_0 can be formed with weight $g(w_1, \dots, w_n)$ and priority $p(w_1, \dots, w_n)$.

[2] While we present the algorithm specialized to parsing with a PCFG, this algorithm generalizes to a wide range of

Proceedings of the ACL 2010 Conference Short Papers, pages 200–204,
Uppsala, Sweden, 11-16 July 2010. ©2010 Association for Computational Linguistics

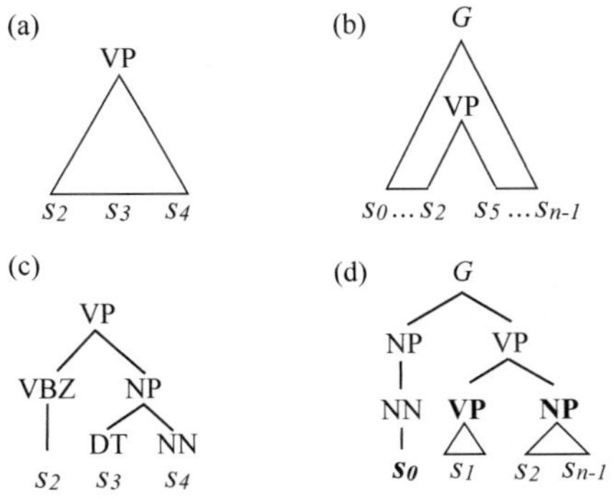

Figure 1: Representations of the different types of items used in parsing. (a) An inside edge item $I(\text{VP}, 2, 5)$. (b) An outside edge item $O(\text{VP}, 2, 5)$. (c) An inside derivation item: $D(T^{\text{VP}}, 2, 5)$. (d) An outside derivation item: $Q(T^{G}_{\text{VP}}, 1, 2, \{(NP, 2, n)\}$. The edges in boldface are frontier edges.

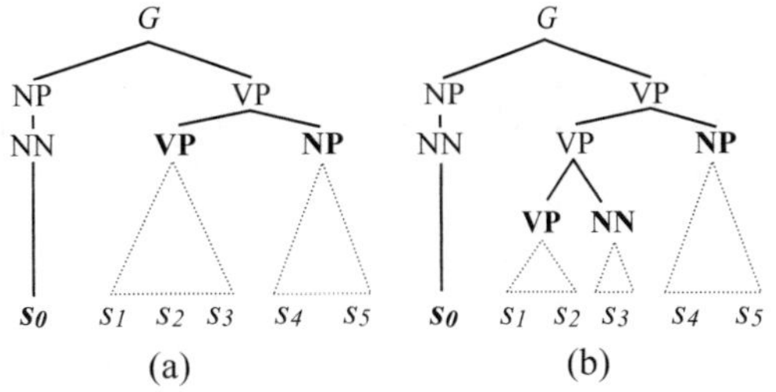

Figure 2: (a) An outside derivation item before expansion at the edge $(\text{VP}, 1, 4)$. (b) A possible expansion of the item in (a) using the rule VP→ VP NN. Frontier edges are marked in boldface.

These deduction rules are "executed" within a generic agenda-driven algorithm, which constructs items in a prioritized fashion. The algorithm maintains an *agenda* (a priority queue of items), as well as a *chart* of items already processed. The fundamental operation of the algorithm is to pop the highest priority item ϕ from the agenda, put it into the chart with its current weight, and apply deduction rules to form any items which can be built by combining ϕ with items already in the chart. When the resulting items are either new or have a weight smaller than an item's best score so far, they are put on the agenda with priority given by $p(\cdot)$. Because all antecedents must be constructed before a deduction rule is executed, we sometimes refer to particular conclusion item as "waiting" on another item before it can be built.

2.2 A*

A* parsing (Klein and Manning, 2003) is an algorithm for computing the 1-best parse of a sentence. A* operates on items called *inside edge items* $I(A, i, j)$, which represent the many possible inside derivations of an edge (A, i, j). Inside edge items are constructed according to the IN deduction rule of Table 1. This deduction rule constructs inside edge items in a bottom-up fashion, combining items representing smaller edges $I(B, i, k)$ and $I(C, k, j)$ with a grammar rule $r = A \rightarrow B\ C$ to form a larger item $I(A, i, j)$. The weight of a newly constructed item is given by the sum of the weights of the antecedent items and the grammar rule r, and its priority is given by its weight plus a *heuristic* $h(A, i, j)$. For consistent and admissible heuristics $h(\cdot)$, this deduction rule guarantees that when an inside edge item is removed from the agenda, its current weight is its true Viterbi inside score.

The heuristic h controls the speed of the algorithm. It can be shown that an edge e satisfying $\beta(e) + h(A, i, j) > \beta(G, 0, n)$ will never be removed from the agenda, allowing some edges to be safely pruned during parsing. The more closely $h(e)$ approximates the Viterbi outside cost $\alpha(e)$, the more items are pruned.

2.3 KA*

The use of inside edge items in A* exploits the optimal substructure property of derivations – since a best derivation of a larger edge is always composed of best derivations of smaller edges, it is only necessary to compute the best way of building a particular inside edge item. When finding k-best lists, this is no longer possible, since we are interested in suboptimal derivations.

Thus, KA*, the k-best extension of A*, must search not in the space of inside edge items, but rather in the space of *inside derivation items* $D(T^A, i, j)$, which represent specific derivations of the edge (A, i, j) using tree T^A. However, the number of inside derivation items is exponential in the length of the input sentence, and even with a very accurate heuristic, running A* directly in this space is not feasible.

Fortunately, Pauls and Klein (2009) show that with a *perfect* heuristic, that is, $h(e) = \alpha(e)\ \forall e$, A* search on inside derivation items will only remove items from the agenda that participate in the true k-best lists (up to ties). In order to compute this perfect heuristic, KA* makes use of *outside edge items* $O(A, i, j)$ which represent the many possible derivations of $G \rightarrow$

hypergraph search problems as shown in Klein and Manning (2001).

IN*†:		$I(B,i,l) : w_1$	$I(C,l,j) : w_2$	$\xrightarrow{w_1+w_2+w_r+h(A,i,j)}$	$I(A,i,j) : w_1 + w_2 + w_r$
IN-D†:	$O(A,i,j) : w_1$	$D(T^B,i,l) : w_2$	$D(T^C,l,j) : w_3$	$\xrightarrow{w_2+w_3+w_r+w_1}$	$D(T^A,i,j) : w_2 + w_3 + w_r$
OUT-L†:	$O(A,i,j) : w_1$	$I(B,i,l) : w_2$	$I(C,l,j) : w_3$	$\xrightarrow{w_1+w_3+w_r+w_2}$	$O(B,i,l) : w_1 + w_3 + w_r$
OUT-R†:	$O(A,i,j) : w_1$	$I(B,i,l) : w_2$	$I(C,l,j) : w_3$	$\xrightarrow{w_1+w_2+w_r+w_3}$	$O(C,l,j) : w_1 + w_2 + w_r$
OUT-D*:	$Q(T_A^G,i,j,\mathcal{F}) : w_1$	$I(B,i,l) : w_2$	$I(C,l,j) : w_3$	$\xrightarrow{w_1+w_r+w_2+w_3+\beta(\mathcal{F})}$	$Q(T_B^G,i,l,\mathcal{F}_C) : w_1 + w_r$

Table 1: The deduction rules used in this paper. Here, r is the rule $A \rightarrow B\ C$. A superscript * indicates that the rule is used in TKA*, and a superscript † indicates that the rule is used in KA*. In IN-D, the tree T_A is rooted at (A,i,j) and has children T^B and T^C. In OUT-D, the tree T_B^G is the tree T_A^G extended at (A,i,j) with rule r, $\mathcal{F}_C$ is the list $\mathcal{F}$ with (C,l,j) prepended, and $\beta(\mathcal{F})$ is $\sum_{e\in\mathcal{F}}\beta(e)$. Whenever the left child $I(B,i,l)$ of an application of OUT-D represents a terminal, the next edge is removed from $\mathcal{F}$ and is used as the new point of expansion.

$s_1 \dots s_i\ A\ s_{j+1} \dots s_n$ (see Figure 1(b)).

Outside items are built using the OUT-L and OUT-R deduction rules shown in Table 1. OUT-L and OUT-R combine, in a top-down fashion, an outside edge over a larger span and inside edge over a smaller span to form a new outside edge over a smaller span. Because these rules make reference to inside edge items $I(A,i,j)$, these items must also be built using the IN deduction rules from 1-best A*. Outside edge items must thus wait until the necessary inside edge items have been built. The outside pass is initialized with the item $O(G,0,n)$ when the inside edge item $I(G,0,n)$ is popped from the agenda.

Once we have started populating outside scores using the outside deductions, we can initiate a search on inside derivation items.[3] These items are built bottom-up using the IN-D deduction rule. The crucial element of this rule is that derivation items for a particular edge wait until the exact outside score of that edge has been computed. The algorithm terminates when k derivation items rooted at $(G,0,n)$ have been popped from the agenda.

3 TKA*

KA* efficiently explores the space of inside derivation items because it waits for the exact Viterbi outside cost before building each derivation item. However, these outside costs and associated deduction items are only auxiliary quantities used to guide the exploration of inside derivations: they allow KA* to prioritize currently constructed inside derivation items (i.e., constructed derivations of the goal) by their optimal completion costs. Outside costs are thus only necessary because we construct partial derivations bottom-up; if we constructed partial derivations in a top-down fashion, all we would need to compute optimal completion costs are Viterbi inside scores, and we could forget the outside pass.

TKA* does exactly that. Inside edge items are constructed in the same way as KA*, but once the inside edge item $I(G,0,n)$ has been discovered, TKA* begins building partial derivations from the goal outwards. We replace the inside derivation items of KA* with *outside derivation items*, which represent trees rooted at the goal and expanding downwards. These items bottom out in a list of edges called the *frontier* edges. See Figure 1(d) for a graphical representation. When a frontier edge represents a single word in the input, i.e. is of the form $(s_i, i, i+1)$, we say that edge is *complete*. An outside derivation can be expanded by applying a rule to one of its incomplete frontier edges; see Figure 2. In the same way that inside derivation items wait on exact outside scores before being built, outside derivation items wait on the inside edge items of all frontier edges before they can be constructed.

Although building derivations top-down obviates the need for a 1-best outside pass, it raises a new issue. When building derivations bottom-up, the only way to expand a particular partial inside derivation is to combine it with another partial inside derivation to build a bigger tree. In contrast, an outside derivation item can be expanded anywhere along its frontier. Naively building derivations top-down would lead to a prohibitively large number of expansion choices.

We solve this issue by always expanding the left-most incomplete frontier edge of an outside derivation item. We show the deduction rule OUT-D which performs this deduction in Figure 1(d). We denote an outside derivation item as $Q(T_A^G, i, j, \mathcal{F})$, where T_A^G is a tree rooted at the goal with left-most incomplete edge (A,i,j), and $\mathcal{F}$ is the list of incomplete frontier edges excluding (A,i,j), ordered from left to right. Whenever the application of this rule "completes" the left-

[3] We stress that the order of computation is entirely specified by the deduction rules – we only speak about e.g. "initiating a search" as an appeal to intuition.

most edge, the next edge is removed from $\mathcal{F}$ and is used as the new point of expansion. Once all frontier edges are complete, the item represents a correctly scored derivation of the goal, explored in a pre-order traversal.

3.1 Correctness

It should be clear that expanding the left-most incomplete frontier edge first eventually explores the same set of derivations as expanding all frontier edges simultaneously. The only worry in fixing this canonical order is that we will somehow explore the Q items in an incorrect order, possibly building some complete derivation Q'_C before a more optimal complete derivation Q_C. However, note that all items Q along the left-most construction of Q_C have priority equal to or better than any less optimal complete derivation Q'_C. Therefore, when Q'_C is enqueued, it will have lower priority than all Q; Q'_C will therefore not be dequeued until all Q – and hence Q_C – have been built.

Furthermore, it can be shown that the top-down expansion strategy maintains the same efficiency and optimality guarantees as KA* for all item types: for consistent heuristics h, the first k entirely complete outside derivation items are the true k-best derivations (modulo ties), and that only derivation items which participate in those k-best derivations will be removed from the queue (up to ties).

3.2 Implementation Details

Building derivations bottom-up is convenient from an indexing point of view: since larger derivations are built from smaller ones, it is not necessary to construct the larger derivation from scratch. Instead, one can simply construct a new tree whose children point to the old trees, saving both memory and CPU time.

In order keep the same efficiency when building trees top-down, a slightly different data structure is necessary. We represent top-down derivations as a lazy list of expansions. The top node T_G^G is an empty list, and whenever we expand an outside derivation item $Q(T_A^G, i, j, \mathcal{F})$ with a rule $r = A \rightarrow B\ C$ and split point l, the resulting derivation T_B^G is a new list item with (r, l) as the head data, and T_A^G as its tail. The tree can be reconstructed later by recursively reconstructing the parent, and adding the edges (B, i, l) and (C, l, j) as children of (A, i, j).

3.3 Advantages

Although our algorithm eliminates the 1-best outside pass of KA*, in practice, even for $k = 10^4$, the 1-best inside pass remains the overwhelming bottleneck (Pauls and Klein, 2009), and our modifications leave that pass unchanged.

However, we argue that our implementation is simpler to specify and implement. In terms of deduction rules, our algorithm eliminates the 2 outside deduction rules and replaces the IN-D rule with the OUT-D rule, bringing the total number of rules from four to two.

The ease of specification translates directly into ease of implementation. In particular, if high-quality heuristics are not available, it is often more efficient to implement the 1-best inside pass as an exhaustive dynamic program, as in Huang and Chiang (2005). In this case, one would only need to implement a single, agenda-based k-best extraction phase, instead of the 2 needed for KA*.

3.4 Performance

The contribution of this paper is theoretical, not empirical. We have argued that TKA* is simpler than TKA*, but we do not expect it to do any more or less work than KA*, modulo grammar specific optimizations. Therefore, we simply verify, like KA*, that the additional work of extracting k-best lists with TKA* is negligible compared to the time spent building 1-best inside edges.

We examined the time spent building 100-best lists for the same experimental setup as Pauls and Klein (2009).[4] On 100 sentences, our implementation of TKA* constructed 3.46 billion items, of which about 2% were outside derivation items. Our implementation of KA* constructed 3.41 billion edges, of which about 0.1% were outside edge items or inside derivation items. In other words, the cost of k-best extraction is dwarfed by the the 1-best inside edge computation in both cases. The reason for the slight performance advantage of KA* is that our implementation of KA* uses lazy optimizations discussed in Pauls and Klein (2009), and while such optimizations could easily be incorporated in TKA*, we have not yet done so in our implementation.

[4]This setup used 3- and 6-round state-split grammars from Petrov et al. (2006), the former used to compute a heuristic for the latter, tested on sentences of length up to 25.

4 Conclusion

We have presented TKA*, a simplification to the KA* algorithm. Our algorithm collapses the 1-best outside and bottom-up derivation passes of KA* into a single, top-down pass without sacrificing efficiency or optimality. This reduces the number of non base-case deduction rules, making TKA* easier both to specify and implement.

Acknowledgements

This project is funded in part by the NSF under grant 0643742 and an NSERC Postgraduate Fellowship.

References

Liang Huang and David Chiang. 2005. Better k-best parsing. In *Proceedings of the International Workshop on Parsing Technologies (IWPT)*, pages 53–64.

Víctor M. Jiménez and Andrés Marzal. 2000. Computation of the n best parse trees for weighted and stochastic context-free grammars. In *Proceedings of the Joint IAPR International Workshops on Advances in Pattern Recognition*, pages 183–192, London, UK. Springer-Verlag.

Dan Klein and Christopher D. Manning. 2001. Parsing and hypergraphs. In *Proceedings of the International Workshop on Parsing Technologies (IWPT)*, pages 123–134.

Dan Klein and Christopher D. Manning. 2003. A* parsing: Fast exact Viterbi parse selection. In *Proceedings of the Human Language Technology Conference and the North American Association for Computational Linguistics (HLT-NAACL)*, pages 119–126.

Mark-Jan Nederhof. 2003. Weighted deductive parsing and Knuth's algorithm. *Computationl Linguistics*, 29(1):135–143.

Adam Pauls and Dan Klein. 2009. K-best A* parsing. In *Proccedings of the Association for Computational Linguistics (ACL)*.

Slav Petrov, Leon Barrett, Romain Thibaux, and Dan Klein. 2006. Learning accurate, compact, and interpretable tree annotation. In *Proccedings of the Association for Computational Linguistics (ACL)*.

Stuart M. Shieber, Yves Schabes, and Fernando C. N. Pereira. 1995. Principles and implementation of deductive parsing. *Journal of Logic Programming*, 24:3–36.

Frank K. Soong and Eng-Fong Huang. 1991. A tree-trellis based fast search for finding the n best sentence hypotheses in continuous speech recognition. In *Proceedings of the Workshop on Speech and Natural Language*.

Simple semi-supervised training of part-of-speech taggers

Anders Søgaard
Center for Language Technology
University of Copenhagen
soegaard@hum.ku.dk

Abstract

Most attempts to train part-of-speech taggers on a mixture of labeled and unlabeled data have failed. In this work stacked learning is used to reduce tagging to a classification task. This simplifies semi-supervised training considerably. Our prefered semi-supervised method combines tri-training (Li and Zhou, 2005) and disagreement-based co-training. On the Wall Street Journal, we obtain an error reduction of 4.2% with SVMTool (Gimenez and Marquez, 2004).

1 Introduction

Semi-supervised part-of-speech (POS) tagging is relatively rare, and the main reason seems to be that results have mostly been negative. Merialdo (1994), in a now famous negative result, attempted to improve HMM POS tagging by expectation maximization with unlabeled data. Clark et al. (2003) reported positive results with little labeled training data but negative results when the amount of labeled training data increased; the same seems to be the case in Wang et al. (2007) who use co-training of two diverse POS taggers. Huang et al. (2009) present positive results for self-training a simple bigram POS tagger, but results are considerably below state-of-the-art.

Recently researchers have explored alternative methods. Suzuki and Isozaki (2008) introduce a semi-supervised extension of conditional random fields that combines supervised and unsupervised probability models by so-called MDF parameter estimation, which reduces error on Wall Street Journal (WSJ) standard splits by about 7% relative to their supervised baseline. Spoustova et al. (2009) use a new pool of unlabeled data tagged by an ensemble of state-of-the-art taggers in every training step of an averaged perceptron POS tagger with 4–5% error reduction. Finally, Søgaard (2009) stacks a POS tagger on an unsupervised clustering algorithm trained on large amounts of unlabeled data with mixed results.

This work combines a new semi-supervised learning method to POS tagging, namely tri-training (Li and Zhou, 2005), with stacking on unsupervised clustering. It is shown that this method can be used to improve a state-of-the-art POS tagger, SVMTool (Gimenez and Marquez, 2004). Finally, we introduce a variant of tri-training called tri-training with disagreement, which seems to perform equally well, but which imports much less unlabeled data and is therefore more efficient.

2 Tagging as classification

This section describes our dataset and our input tagger. We also describe how stacking is used to reduce POS tagging to a classification task. Finally, we introduce the supervised learning algorithms used in our experiments.

2.1 Data

We use the POS-tagged WSJ from the Penn Treebank Release 3 (Marcus et al., 1993) with the standard split: Sect. 0–18 is used for training, Sect. 19–21 for development, and Sect. 22–24 for testing. Since we need to train our classifiers on material distinct from the training material for our input POS tagger, we save Sect. 19 for training our classifiers. Finally, we use the (untagged) Brown corpus as our unlabeled data. The number of tokens we use for training, developing and testing the classifiers, and the amount of unlabeled data available to it, are thus:

	tokens
train	44,472
development	103,686
test	129,281
unlabeled	1,170,811

Proceedings of the ACL 2010 Conference Short Papers, pages 205–208,
Uppsala, Sweden, 11-16 July 2010.

The amount of unlabeled data available to our classifiers is thus a bit more than 25 times the amount of labeled data.

2.2 Input tagger

In our experiments we use SVMTool (Gimenez and Marquez, 2004) with model type 4 run incrementally in both directions. SVMTool has an accuracy of 97.15% on WSJ Sect. 22-24 with this parameter setting. Gimenez and Marquez (2004) report that SVMTool has an accuracy of 97.16% with an optimized parameter setting.

2.3 Classifier input

The way classifiers are constructed in our experiments is very simple. We train SVMTool and an unsupervised tagger, Unsupos (Biemann, 2006), on our training sections and apply them to the development, test and unlabeled sections. The results are combined in tables that will be the input of our classifiers. Here is an excerpt:[1]

Gold standard	SVMTool	Unsupos
DT	DT	17
NNP	NNP	27
NNP	NNS	17*
NNP	NNP	17
VBD	VBD	26

Each row represents a word and lists the gold standard POS tag, the predicted POS tag and the word cluster selected by Unsupos. For example, the first word is labeled 'DT', which SVMTool correctly predicts, and it belongs to cluster 17 of about 500 word clusters. The first column is blank in the table for the unlabeled section.

Generally, the idea is that a classifier will learn to trust SVMTool in some cases, but that it may also learn that if SVMTool predicts a certain tag for some word cluster the correct label is another tag. This way of combining taggers into a single end classifier can be seen as a form of stacking (Wolpert, 1992). It has the advantage that it reduces POS tagging to a classification task. This may simplify semi-supervised learning considerably.

2.4 Learning algorithms

We assume some knowledge of supervised learning algorithms. Most of our experiments are implementations of wrapper methods that call off-the-shelf implementations of supervised learning algorithms. Specifically we have experimented with support vector machines (SVMs), decision trees, bagging and random forests. Tri-training, explained below, is a semi-supervised learning method which requires large amounts of data. Consequently, we only used very fast learning algorithms in the context of tri-training. On the development section, decisions trees performed better than bagging and random forests. The decision tree algorithm is the C4.5 algorithm first introduced in Quinlan (1993). We used SVMs with polynomial kernels of degree 2 to provide a stronger stacking-only baseline.

3 Tri-training

This section first presents the tri-training algorithm originally proposed by Li and Zhou (2005) and then considers a novel variant: tri-training with disagreement.

Let L denote the labeled data and U the unlabeled data. Assume that three classifiers c_1, c_2, c_3 (same learning algorithm) have been trained on three bootstrap samples of L. In tri-training, an unlabeled datapoint in U is now labeled for a classifier, say c_1, if the other two classifiers agree on its label, i.e. c_2 and c_3. Two classifiers inform the third. If the two classifiers agree on a labeling, there is a good chance that they are right. The algorithm stops when the classifiers no longer change. The three classifiers are combined by majority voting. Li and Zhou (2005) show that under certain conditions the increase in classification noise rate is compensated by the amount of newly labeled data points.

The most important condition is that the three classifiers are diverse. If the three classifiers are identical, tri-training degenerates to self-training. Diversity is obtained in Li and Zhou (2005) by training classifiers on bootstrap samples. In their experiments, they consider classifiers based on the C4.5 algorithm, BP neural networks and naive Bayes classifiers. The algorithm is sketched in a simplified form in Figure 1; see Li and Zhou (2005) for all the details.

Tri-training has to the best of our knowledge not been applied to POS tagging before, but it has been applied to other NLP classification tasks, incl. Chinese chunking (Chen et al., 2006) and question classification (Nguyen et al., 2008).

[1]The numbers provided by Unsupos refer to clusters; "*" marks out-of-vocabulary words.

```
1: for i ∈ {1..3} do
2:   S_i ← bootstrap_sample(L)
3:   c_i ← train_classifier(S_i)
4: end for
5: repeat
6:   for i ∈ {1..3} do
7:     for x ∈ U do
8:       L_i ← ∅
9:       if c_j(x) = c_k(x)(j, k ≠ i) then
10:        L_i ← L_i ∪ {(x, c_j(x))}
11:      end if
12:    end for
13:    c_i ← train_classifier(L ∪ L_i)
14:  end for
15: until none of c_i changes
16: apply majority vote over c_i
```

Figure 1: Tri-training (Li and Zhou, 2005).

3.1 Tri-training with disagreement

We introduce a possible improvement of the tri-training algorithm: If we change lines 9–10 in the algorithm in Figure 1 with the lines:

```
if c_j(x) = c_k(x) ≠ c_i(x)(j, k ≠ i) then
  L_i ← L_i ∪ {(x, c_j(x))}
end if
```

two classifiers, say c_1 and c_2, only label a datapoint for the third classifier, c_3, if c_1 and c_2 agree on its label, but c_3 *disagrees*. The intuition is that we only want to strengthen a classifier in its weak points, and we want to avoid skewing our labeled data by easy data points. Finally, since tri-training with disagreement imports less unlabeled data, it is much more efficient than tri-training. No one has to the best of our knowledge applied tri-training with disagreement to real-life classification tasks before.

4 Results

Our results are presented in Figure 2. The stacking result was obtained by training a SVM on top of the predictions of SVMTool and the word clusters of Unsupos. SVMs performed better than decision trees, bagging and random forests on our development section, but improvements on test data were modest. Tri-training refers to the original algorithm sketched in Figure 1 with C4.5 as learning algorithm. Since tri-training degenerates to self-training if the three classifiers are trained on the same sample, we used our implementation of tri-training to obtain self-training results and validated our results by a simpler implementation. We varied poolsize to optimize self-training. Finally, we list results for a technique called co-forests (Li and Zhou, 2007), which is a recent alternative to tri-training presented by the same authors, and for tri-training with disagreement (tri-disagr). The p-values are computed using 10,000 stratified shuffles.

Tri-training and tri-training with disagreement gave the best results. Note that since tri-training leads to much better results than stacking alone, it is unlabeled data that gives us most of the improvement, not the stacking itself. The difference between tri-training and self-training is near-significant (p <0.0150). It seems that tri-training with disagreement is a competitive technique in terms of accuracy. The main advantage of tri-training with disagreement compared to ordinary tri-training, however, is that it is very efficient. This is reflected by the average number of tokens in L_i over the three learners in the worst round of learning:

	av. tokens in L_i
tri-training	1,170,811
tri-disagr	173

Note also that self-training gave very good results. Self-training was, again, much slower than tri-training with disagreement since we had to train on a large pool of unlabeled data (but only once). Of course this is not a standard self-training set-up, but self-training informed by unsupervised word clusters.

4.1 Follow-up experiments

SVMTool is one of the most accurate POS taggers available. This means that the predictions that are added to the labeled data are of very high quality. To test if our semi-supervised learning methods were sensitive to the quality of the input taggers we repeated the self-training and tri-training experiments with a less competitive POS tagger, namely the maximum entropy-based POS tagger first described in (Ratnaparkhi, 1998) that comes with the maximum entropy library in (Zhang, 2004). Results are presented as the second line in Figure 2. Note that error reduction is much lower in this case.

	BL	stacking	tri-tr.	self-tr.	co-forests	tri-disagr	error red.	p-value
SVMTool	97.15%	97.19%	**97.27%**	97.26%	97.13%	**97.27%**	4.21%	<0.0001
MaxEnt	96.31%	-	**96.36%**	**96.36%**	96.28%	**96.36%**	1.36%	<0.0001

Figure 2: Results on Wall Street Journal Sect. 22-24 with different semi-supervised methods.

5 Conclusion

This paper first shows how stacking can be used to reduce POS tagging to a classification task. This reduction seems to enable robust semi-supervised learning. The technique was used to improve the accuracy of a state-of-the-art POS tagger, namely SVMTool. Four semi-supervised learning methods were tested, incl. self-training, tri-training, co-forests and tri-training with disagreement. All methods increased the accuracy of SVMTool significantly. Error reduction on Wall Street Journal Sect. 22-24 was 4.2%, which is comparable to related work in the literature, e.g. Suzuki and Isozaki (2008) (7%) and Spoustova et al. (2009) (4–5%).

References

Chris Biemann. 2006. Unsupervised part-of-speech tagging employing efficient graph clustering. In *COLING-ACL Student Session*, Sydney, Australia.

Wenliang Chen, Yujie Zhang, and Hitoshi Isahara. 2006. Chinese chunking with tri-training learning. In *Computer processing of oriental languages*, pages 466–473. Springer, Berlin, Germany.

Stephen Clark, James Curran, and Mike Osborne. 2003. Bootstrapping POS taggers using unlabeled data. In *CONLL*, Edmonton, Canada.

Jesus Gimenez and Lluis Marquez. 2004. SVMTool: a general POS tagger generator based on support vector machines. In *LREC*, Lisbon, Portugal.

Zhongqiang Huang, Vladimir Eidelman, and Mary Harper. 2009. Improving a simple bigram HMM part-of-speech tagger by latent annotation and self-training. In *NAACL-HLT*, Boulder, CO.

Ming Li and Zhi-Hua Zhou. 2005. Tri-training: exploiting unlabeled data using three classifiers. *IEEE Transactions on Knowledge and Data Engineering*, 17(11):1529–1541.

Ming Li and Zhi-Hua Zhou. 2007. Improve computer-aided diagnosis with machine learning techniques using undiagnosed samples. *IEEE Transactions on Systems, Man and Cybernetics*, 37(6):1088–1098.

Mitchell Marcus, Mary Marcinkiewicz, and Beatrice Santorini. 1993. Building a large annotated corpus of English: the Penn Treebank. *Computational Linguistics*, 19(2):313–330.

Bernard Merialdo. 1994. Tagging English text with a probabilistic model. *Computational Linguistics*, 20(2):155–171.

Tri Nguyen, Le Nguyen, and Akira Shimazu. 2008. Using semi-supervised learning for question classification. *Journal of Natural Language Processing*, 15:3–21.

Ross Quinlan. 1993. *Programs for machine learning*. Morgan Kaufmann.

Adwait Ratnaparkhi. 1998. *Maximum entropy models for natural language ambiguity resolution*. Ph.D. thesis, University of Pennsylvania.

Anders Søgaard. 2009. Ensemble-based POS tagging of italian. In *IAAI-EVALITA*, Reggio Emilia, Italy.

Drahomira Spoustova, Jan Hajic, Jan Raab, and Miroslav Spousta. 2009. Semi-supervised training for the averaged perceptron POS tagger. In *EACL*, Athens, Greece.

Jun Suzuki and Hideki Isozaki. 2008. Semi-supervised sequential labeling and segmentation using giga-word scale unlabeled data. In *ACL*, pages 665–673, Columbus, Ohio.

Wen Wang, Zhongqiang Huang, and Mary Harper. 2007. Semi-supervised learning for part-of-speech tagging of Mandarin transcribed speech. In *ICASSP*, Hawaii.

David Wolpert. 1992. Stacked generalization. *Neural Networks*, 5:241–259.

Le Zhang. 2004. Maximum entropy modeling toolkit for Python and C++. University of Edinburgh.

Efficient Optimization of an MDL-Inspired Objective Function for Unsupervised Part-of-Speech Tagging

Ashish Vaswani[1] **Adam Pauls**[2] **David Chiang**[1]

[1]Information Sciences Institute
University of Southern California
4676 Admiralty Way, Suite 1001
Marina del Rey, CA 90292
{avaswani,chiang}@isi.edu

[2]Computer Science Division
University of California at Berkeley
Soda Hall
Berkeley, CA 94720
adpauls@eecs.berkeley.edu

Abstract

The Minimum Description Length (MDL) principle is a method for model selection that trades off between the explanation of the data by the model and the complexity of the model itself. Inspired by the MDL principle, we develop an objective function for generative models that captures the description of the data by the model (log-likelihood) and the description of the model (model size). We also develop a efficient general search algorithm based on the MAP-EM framework to optimize this function. Since recent work has shown that minimizing the model size in a Hidden Markov Model for part-of-speech (POS) tagging leads to higher accuracies, we test our approach by applying it to this problem. The search algorithm involves a simple change to EM and achieves high POS tagging accuracies on both English and Italian data sets.

1 Introduction

The Minimum Description Length (MDL) principle is a method for model selection that provides a generic solution to the overfitting problem (Barron et al., 1998). A formalization of Ockham's Razor, it says that the parameters are to be chosen that minimize the description length of the data given the model plus the description length of the model itself.

It has been successfully shown that minimizing the model size in a Hidden Markov Model (HMM) for part-of-speech (POS) tagging leads to higher accuracies than simply running the Expectation-Maximization (EM) algorithm (Dempster et al., 1977). Goldwater and Griffiths (2007) employ a Bayesian approach to POS tagging and use sparse Dirichlet priors to minimize model size. More recently, Ravi and Knight (2009) alternately minimize the model using an integer linear program and maximize likelihood using EM to achieve the highest accuracies on the task so far. However, in the latter approach, because there is no single objective function to optimize, it is not entirely clear how to generalize this technique to other problems. In this paper, inspired by the MDL principle, we develop an objective function for generative models that captures both the description of the data by the model (log-likelihood) and the description of the model (model size). By using a simple prior that encourages sparsity, we cast our problem as a search for the maximum *a posteriori* (MAP) hypothesis and present a variant of EM to approximately search for the minimum-description-length model. Applying our approach to the POS tagging problem, we obtain higher accuracies than both EM and Bayesian inference as reported by Goldwater and Griffiths (2007). On a Italian POS tagging task, we obtain even larger improvements. We find that our objective function correlates well with accuracy, suggesting that this technique might be useful for other problems.

2 MAP EM with Sparse Priors

2.1 Objective function

In the unsupervised POS tagging task, we are given a word sequence $\mathbf{w} = w_1, \ldots, w_N$ and want to find the best tagging $\mathbf{t} = t_1, \ldots, t_N$, where $t_i \in \mathcal{T}$, the tag vocabulary. We adopt the problem formulation of Merialdo (1994), in which we are given a dictionary of possible tags for each word type.

We define a bigram HMM

$$P(w, t \mid \theta) = \prod_{i=1}^{N} P(\mathbf{w}, \mathbf{t} \mid \theta) \cdot P(t_i \mid t_{i-1}) \qquad (1)$$

In maximum likelihood estimation, the goal is to

Proceedings of the ACL 2010 Conference Short Papers, pages 209–214,
Uppsala, Sweden, 11-16 July 2010. ©2010 Association for Computational Linguistics

find parameter estimates

$$\hat{\theta} = \arg\max_{\theta} \log P(\mathbf{w} \mid \theta) \quad (2)$$

$$= \arg\max_{\theta} \log \sum_{\mathbf{t}} P(\mathbf{w}, \mathbf{t} \mid \theta) \quad (3)$$

The EM algorithm can be used to find a solution. However, we would like to maximize likelihood and minimize the size of the model simultaneously. We define the size of a model as the number of non-zero probabilities in its parameter vector. Let $\theta_1, \ldots, \theta_n$ be the components of θ. We would like to find

$$\hat{\theta} = \arg\min_{\theta} (-\log P(\mathbf{w} \mid \theta) + \alpha \|\theta\|_0) \quad (4)$$

where $\|\theta\|_0$, called the L0 norm of θ, simply counts the number of non-zero parameters in θ. The hyperparameter α controls the tradeoff between likelihood maximization and model minimization. Note the similarity of this objective function with MDL's, where α would be the space (measured in nats) needed to describe one parameter of the model.

Unfortunately, minimization of the L0 norm is known to be NP-hard (Hyder and Mahata, 2009). It is not smooth, making it unamenable to gradient-based optimization algorithms. Therefore, we use a smoothed approximation,

$$\|\theta\|_0 \approx \sum_i \left(1 - e^{\frac{-\theta_i}{\beta}}\right) \quad (5)$$

where $0 < \beta \leq 1$ (Mohimani et al., 2007). For smaller values of β, this closely approximates the desired function (Figure 1). Inverting signs and ignoring constant terms, our objective function is now:

$$\hat{\theta} = \arg\max_{\theta} \left(\log P(\mathbf{w} \mid \theta) + \alpha \sum_i e^{\frac{-\theta_i}{\beta}}\right) \quad (6)$$

We can think of the approximate model size as a kind of prior:

$$P(\theta) = \frac{\exp \alpha \sum_i e^{\frac{-\theta_i}{\beta}}}{Z} \quad (7)$$

$$\log P(\theta) = \alpha \cdot \sum_i e^{\frac{-\theta_i}{\beta}} - \log Z \quad (8)$$

where $Z = \int_{d\theta} \exp \alpha \sum_i e^{\frac{-\theta_i}{\beta}}$ is a normalization constant. Then our goal is to find the maximum

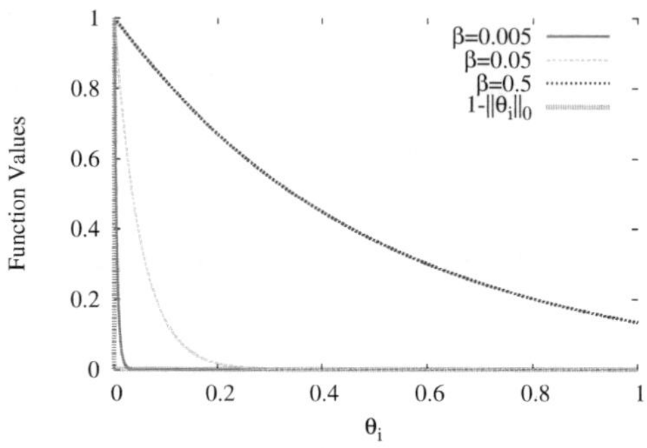

Figure 1: Ideal model-size term and its approximations.

a posterior parameter estimate, which we find using MAP-EM (Bishop, 2006):

$$\hat{\theta} = \arg\max_{\theta} \log P(\mathbf{w}, \theta) \quad (9)$$

$$= \arg\max_{\theta} (\log P(\mathbf{w} \mid \theta) + \log P(\theta)) \quad (10)$$

Substituting (8) into (10) and ignoring the constant term $\log Z$, we get our objective function (6) again.

We can exercise finer control over the sparsity of the tag-bigram and channel probability distributions by using a different α for each:

$$\arg\max_{\theta} \Bigg(\log P(\mathbf{w} \mid \theta) + \alpha_c \sum_{w,t} e^{\frac{-P(w|t)}{\beta}} + \alpha_t \sum_{t,t'} e^{\frac{-P(t'|t)}{\beta}}\Bigg) \quad (11)$$

In our experiments, we set $\alpha_c = 0$ since previous work has shown that minimizing the number of tag n-gram parameters is more important (Ravi and Knight, 2009; Goldwater and Griffiths, 2007).

A common method for preferring smaller models is minimizing the L1 norm, $\sum_i |\theta_i|$. However, for a model which is a product of multinomial distributions, the L1 norm is a constant.

$$\sum_i |\theta_i| = \sum_i \theta_i$$

$$= \sum_t \left(\sum_w P(w \mid t) + \sum_{t'} P(t' \mid t)\right)$$

$$= 2|\mathcal{T}|$$

Therefore, we cannot use the L1 norm as part of the size term as the result will be the same as the EM algorithm.

2.2 Parameter optimization

To optimize (11), we use MAP EM, which is an iterative search procedure. The E step is the same as in standard EM, which is to calculate $P(\mathbf{t} \mid \mathbf{w}, \theta^t)$, where the θ^t are the parameters in the current iteration t. The M step in iteration $(t+1)$ looks like

$$\theta^{t+1} = \arg\max_{\theta} \left(E_{P(\mathbf{t}|\mathbf{w},\theta^t)} [\log P(\mathbf{w}, \mathbf{t} \mid \theta)] + \alpha_t \sum_{t,t'} e^{\frac{-P(t'|t)}{\beta}} \right) \quad (12)$$

Let $C(t, w; \mathbf{t}, \mathbf{w})$ count the number of times the word w is tagged as t in $\mathbf{t}$, and $C(t, t'; \mathbf{t})$ the number of times the tag bigram (t, t') appears in $\mathbf{t}$. We can rewrite the M step as

$$\theta^{t+1} = \arg\max_{\theta} \Bigg(\sum_t \sum_w E[C(t,w)] \log P(w \mid t) + \sum_t \sum_{t'} \left(E[C(t,t')] \log P(t' \mid t) + \alpha_t e^{\frac{-P(t'|t)}{\beta}} \right) \Bigg) \quad (13)$$

subject to the constraints $\sum_w P(w \mid t) = 1$ and $\sum_{t'} P(t' \mid t) = 1$. Note that we can optimize each term of both summations over t separately. For each t, the term

$$\sum_w E[C(t,w)] \log P(w \mid t) \quad (14)$$

is easily optimized as in EM: just let $P(w \mid t) \propto E[C(t,w)]$. But the term

$$\sum_{t'} \left(E[C(t,t')] \log P(t' \mid t) + \alpha_t e^{\frac{-P(t'|t)}{\beta}} \right) \quad (15)$$

is trickier. This is a non-convex optimization problem for which we invoke a publicly available constrained optimization tool, ALGENCAN (Andreani et al., 2007). To carry out its optimization, ALGENCAN requires computation of the following in every iteration:

- **Objective function**, defined in equation (15). This is calculated in polynomial time using dynamic programming.
- **Constraints**: $g_t = \sum_{t'} P(t' \mid t) - 1 = 0$ for each tag $t \in \mathcal{T}$. Also, we constrain $P(t' \mid t)$ to the interval $[\epsilon, 1]$.[1]
- **Gradient of objective function**:

$$\frac{\partial F}{\partial P(t' \mid t)} = \frac{E[C(t,t')]}{P(t' \mid t)} - \frac{\alpha_t}{\beta} e^{\frac{-P(t'|t)}{\beta}} \quad (16)$$

- **Gradient of equality constraints**:

$$\frac{\partial g_t}{\partial P(t'' \mid t')} = \begin{cases} 1 & \text{if } t = t' \\ 0 & \text{otherwise} \end{cases} \quad (17)$$

- **Hessian of objective function**, which is not required but greatly speeds up the optimization:

$$\frac{\partial^2 F}{\partial P(t' \mid t) \partial P(t' \mid t)} = -\frac{E[C(t,t')]}{P(t' \mid t)^2} + \alpha_t \frac{e^{\frac{-P(t'|t)}{\beta}}}{\beta^2} \quad (18)$$

  The other second-order partial derivatives are all zero, as are those of the equality constraints.

We perform this optimization for each instance of (15). These optimizations could easily be performed in parallel for greater scalability.

3 Experiments

We carried out POS tagging experiments on English and Italian.

3.1 English POS tagging

To set the hyperparameters α_t and β, we prepared three held-out sets H_1, H_2, and H_3 from the Penn Treebank. Each H_i comprised about 24,000 words annotated with POS tags. We ran MAP-EM for 100 iterations, with uniform probability initialization, for a suite of hyperparameters and averaged their tagging accuracies over the three held-out sets. The results are presented in Table 2. We then picked the hyperparameter setting with the highest average accuracy. These were $\alpha_t = 80, \beta = 0.05$. We then ran MAP-EM again on the test data with these hyperparameters and achieved a tagging accuracy of 87.4% (see Table 1). This is higher than the 85.2% that Goldwater and Griffiths (2007) obtain using Bayesian methods for inferring both POS tags and hyperparameters. It is much higher than the 82.4% that standard EM achieves on the test set when run for 100 iterations.

Using $\alpha_t = 80, \beta = 0.05$, we ran multiple random restarts on the test set (see Figure 2). We find that the objective function correlates well with accuracy, and picking the point with the highest objective function value achieves 87.1% accuracy.

[1] We must have $\epsilon > 0$ because of the $\log P(t' \mid t)$ term in equation (15). It seems reasonable to set $\epsilon \ll \frac{1}{N}$; in our experiments, we set $\epsilon = 10^{-7}$.

α_t	0.75	0.5	0.25	0.075	β 0.05	0.025	0.0075	0.005	0.0025
10	82.81	82.78	83.10	83.50	83.76	83.70	84.07	83.95	83.75
20	82.78	82.82	83.26	83.60	83.89	84.88	83.74	84.12	83.46
30	82.78	83.06	83.26	83.29	84.50	84.82	84.54	83.93	83.47
40	82.81	83.13	83.50	83.98	84.23	85.31	85.05	83.84	83.46
50	82.84	83.24	83.15	84.08	82.53	84.90	84.73	83.69	82.70
60	83.05	83.14	83.26	83.30	82.08	85.23	85.06	83.26	82.96
70	83.09	83.10	82.97	82.37	83.30	86.32	83.98	83.55	82.97
80	83.13	83.15	82.71	83.00	**86.47**	86.24	83.94	83.26	82.93
90	83.20	83.18	82.53	84.20	86.32	84.87	83.49	83.62	82.03
100	83.19	83.51	82.84	84.60	86.13	85.94	83.26	83.67	82.06
110	83.18	83.53	83.29	84.40	86.19	85.18	80.76	83.32	82.05
120	83.08	83.65	83.71	84.11	86.03	85.39	80.66	82.98	82.20
130	83.10	83.19	83.52	84.02	85.79	85.65	80.08	82.04	81.76
140	83.11	83.17	83.34	85.26	85.86	85.84	79.09	82.51	81.64
150	83.14	83.20	83.40	85.33	85.54	85.18	78.90	81.99	81.88

Table 2: Average accuracies over three held-out sets for English.

system	accuracy (%)
Standard EM	82.4
+ random restarts	84.5
(Goldwater and Griffiths, 2007)	85.2
our approach	87.4
+ random restarts	87.1

Table 1: MAP-EM with a L0 norm achieves higher tagging accuracy on English than (2007) and much higher than standard EM.

system	zero parameters	bigram types
maximum possible	1389	–
EM, 100 iterations	444	924
MAP-EM, 100 iterations	695	648

Table 3: MAP-EM with a smoothed L0 norm yields much smaller models than standard EM.

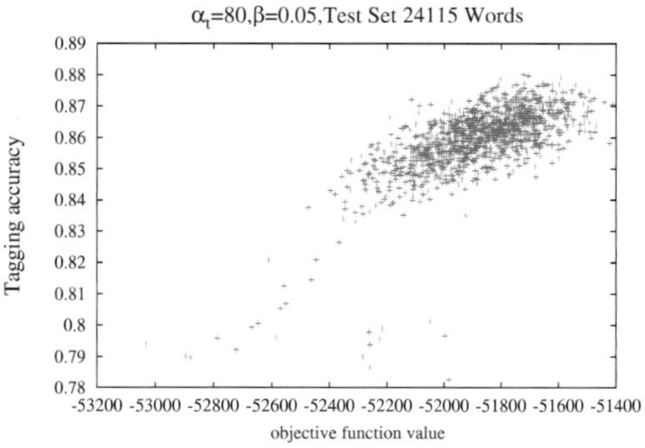

Figure 2: Tagging accuracy vs. objective function for 1152 random restarts of MAP-EM with smoothed L0 norm.

We also carried out the same experiment with standard EM (Figure 3), where picking the point with the highest corpus probability achieves 84.5% accuracy.

We also measured the minimization effect of the sparse prior against that of standard EM. Since our method lower-bounds all the parameters by ϵ, we consider a parameter θ_i as a zero if $\theta_i \leq \epsilon$. We also measured the number of unique tag bigram types in the Viterbi tagging of the word sequence. Table 3 shows that our method produces much smaller models than EM, and produces Viterbi taggings with many fewer tag-bigram types.

3.2 Italian POS tagging

We also carried out POS tagging experiments on an Italian corpus from the Italian Turin University Treebank (Bos et al., 2009). This test set comprises 21,878 words annotated with POS tags and a dictionary for each word type. Since this is all the available data, we could not tune the hyperparameters on a held-out data set. Using the hyperparameters tuned on English ($\alpha_t = 80, \beta = 0.05$), we obtained 89.7% tagging accuracy (see Table 4), which was a large improvement over 81.2% that standard EM achieved. When we tuned the hyperparameters on the test set, the best setting ($\alpha_t = 120, \beta = 0.05$ gave an accuracy of 90.28%.

4 Conclusion

A variety of other techniques in the literature have been applied to this unsupervised POS tagging task. Smith and Eisner (2005) use conditional random fields with contrastive estimation to achieve

α_t	β								
	0.75	0.5	0.25	0.075	0.05	0.025	0.0075	0.005	0.0025
10	81.62	81.67	81.63	82.47	82.70	84.64	84.82	84.96	84.90
20	81.67	81.63	81.76	82.75	84.28	84.79	85.85	88.49	85.30
30	81.66	81.63	82.29	83.43	85.08	88.10	86.16	88.70	88.34
40	81.64	81.79	82.30	85.00	86.10	88.86	89.28	88.76	88.80
50	81.71	81.71	78.86	85.93	86.16	88.98	88.98	89.11	88.01
60	81.65	82.22	78.95	86.11	87.16	89.35	88.97	88.59	88.00
70	81.69	82.25	79.55	86.32	89.79	89.37	88.91	85.63	87.89
80	81.74	82.23	80.78	86.34	89.70	89.58	88.87	88.32	88.56
90	81.70	81.85	81.00	86.35	90.08	89.40	89.09	88.09	88.50
100	81.70	82.27	82.24	86.53	90.07	88.93	89.09	88.30	88.72
110	82.19	82.49	82.22	86.77	90.12	89.22	88.87	88.48	87.91
120	82.23	78.60	82.76	86.77	**90.28**	89.05	88.75	88.83	88.53
130	82.20	78.60	83.33	87.48	90.12	89.15	89.30	87.81	88.66
140	82.24	78.64	83.34	87.48	90.12	89.01	88.87	88.99	88.85
150	82.28	78.69	83.32	87.75	90.25	87.81	88.50	89.07	88.41

Table 4: Accuracies on test set for Italian.

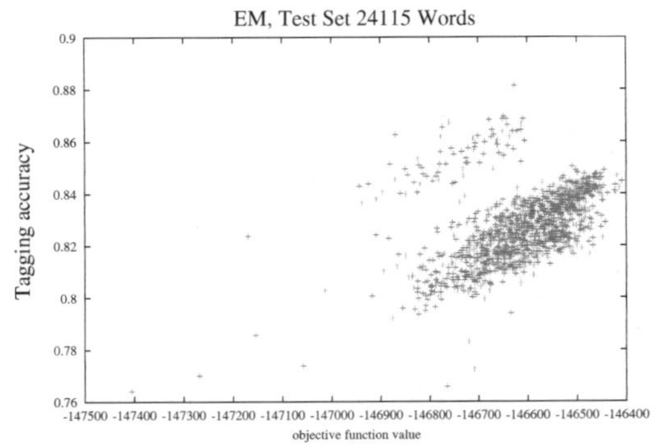

Figure 3: Tagging accuracy vs. likelihood for 1152 random restarts of standard EM.

88.6% accuracy. Goldberg et al. (2008) provide a linguistically-informed starting point for EM to achieve 91.4% accuracy. More recently, Chiang et al. (2010) use GIbbs sampling for Bayesian inference along with automatic run selection and achieve 90.7%.

In this paper, our goal has been to investigate whether EM can be extended in a generic way to use an MDL-like objective function that simultaneously maximizes likelihood and minimizes model size. We have presented an efficient search procedure that optimizes this function for generative models and demonstrated that maximizing this function leads to improvement in tagging accuracy over standard EM. We infer the hyperparameters of our model using held out data and achieve better accuracies than (Goldwater and Griffiths, 2007). We have also shown that the objective function correlates well with tagging accuracy supporting the MDL principle. Our approach performs quite well on POS tagging for both English and Italian. We believe that, like EM, our method can benefit from more unlabeled data, and there is reason to hope that the success of these experiments will carry over to other tasks as well.

Acknowledgements

We would like to thank Sujith Ravi, Kevin Knight and Steve DeNeefe for their valuable input, and Jason Baldridge for directing us to the Italian POS data. This research was supported in part by DARPA contract HR0011-06-C-0022 under subcontract to BBN Technologies and DARPA contract HR0011-09-1-0028.

References

R. Andreani, E. G. Birgin, J. M. Martnez, and M. L. Schuverdt. 2007. On Augmented Lagrangian methods with general lower-level constraints. *SIAM Journal on Optimization*, 18:1286–1309.

A. Barron, J. Rissanen, and B. Yu. 1998. The minimum description length principle in coding and modeling. *IEEE Transactions on Information Theory*, 44(6):2743–2760.

C. Bishop. 2006. *Pattern Recognition and Machine Learning*. Springer.

J. Bos, C. Bosco, and A. Mazzei. 2009. Converting a dependency treebank to a categorical grammar treebank for italian. In *Eighth International Workshop on Treebanks and Linguistic Theories (TLT8)*.

D. Chiang, J. Graehl, K. Knight, A. Pauls, and S. Ravi. 2010. Bayesian inference for Finite-State transducers. In *Proceedings of the North American Association of Computational Linguistics*.

A. P. Dempster, N. M. Laird, and D. B. Rubin. 1977. Maximum likelihood from incomplete data via the EM algorithm. *Computational Linguistics*, 39(4):1–38.

Y. Goldberg, M. Adler, and M. Elhadad. 2008. EM can find pretty good HMM POS-taggers (when given a good start). In *Proceedings of the ACL.*

S. Goldwater and T. L. Griffiths. 2007. A fully Bayesian approach to unsupervised part-of-speech tagging. In *Proceedings of the ACL.*

M. Hyder and K. Mahata. 2009. An approximate L0 norm minimization algorithm for compressed sensing. In *Proceedings of the 2009 IEEE International Conference on Acoustics, Speech and Signal Processing*.

B. Merialdo. 1994. Tagging English text with a probabilistic model. *Computational Linguistics*, 20(2):155–171.

H. Mohimani, M. Babaie-Zadeh, and C. Jutten. 2007. Fast sparse representation based on smoothed L0 norm. In *Proceedings of the 7th International Conference on Independent Component Analysis and Signal Separation (ICA2007).*

S. Ravi and K. Knight. 2009. Minimized models for unsupervised part-of-speech tagging. In *Proceedings of ACL-IJCNLP.*

N. Smith. and J. Eisner. 2005. Contrastive estimation: Training log-linear models on unlabeled data. In *Proceedings of the ACL.*

SVD and Clustering for Unsupervised POS Tagging

Michael Lamar*
Division of Applied Mathematics
Brown University
Providence, RI, USA
mlamar@dam.brown.edu

Yariv Maron*
Gonda Brain Research Center
Bar-Ilan University
Ramat-Gan, Israel
syarivm@yahoo.com

Mark Johnson
Department of Computing
Faculty of Science
Macquarie University
Sydney, Australia
mjohnson@science.mq.edu.au

Elie Bienenstock
Division of Applied Mathematics
and Department of Neuroscience
Brown University
Providence, RI, USA
elie@brown.edu

Abstract

We revisit the algorithm of Schütze (1995) for unsupervised part-of-speech tagging. The algorithm uses reduced-rank singular value decomposition followed by clustering to extract latent features from context distributions. As implemented here, it achieves state-of-the-art tagging accuracy at considerably less cost than more recent methods. It can also produce a range of finer-grained taggings, with potential applications to various tasks.

1 Introduction

While supervised approaches are able to solve the part-of-speech (POS) tagging problem with over 97% accuracy (Collins 2002; Toutanova et al. 2003), unsupervised algorithms perform considerably less well. These models attempt to tag text without resources such as an annotated corpus, a dictionary, etc. The use of singular value decomposition (SVD) for this problem was introduced in Schütze (1995). Subsequently, a number of methods for POS tagging without a dictionary were examined, e.g., by Clark (2000), Clark (2003), Haghighi and Klein (2006), Johnson (2007), Goldwater and Griffiths (2007), Gao and Johnson (2008), and Graça et al. (2009). The latter two, using Hidden Markov Models (HMMs), exhibit the highest performances to date for fully unsupervised POS tagging.

The revisited SVD-based approach presented here, which we call "two-step SVD" or SVD2, has four important characteristics. First, it achieves state-of-the-art tagging accuracy. Second, it requires drastically less computational effort than the best currently available models. Third, it demonstrates that state-of-the-art accuracy can be realized without disambiguation, *i.e.*, without attempting to assign different tags to different tokens of the same type. Finally, with no significant increase in computational cost, SVD2 can create much finer-grained labelings than typically produced by other algorithms. When combined with some minimal supervision in post-processing, this makes the approach useful for tagging languages that lack the resources required by fully supervised models.

2 Methods

Following the original work of Schütze (1995), we begin by constructing a right context matrix, R, and a left context matrix, L. R_{ij} counts the number of times in the corpus a token of word type i is immediately followed by a token of word type j. Similarly, L_{ij} counts the number of times a token of type i is preceded by a token of type j. We truncate these matrices, including, in the right and left contexts, only the w_1 most frequent word types. The resulting L and R are of dimension $N_{\text{types}} \times w_1$, where N_{types} is the number of word types (spelling forms) in the corpus, and w_1 is set to 1000. (The full $N_{\text{types}} \times N_{\text{types}}$ context matrices satisfy $R = L^T$.)

* These authors contributed equally.

Proceedings of the ACL 2010 Conference Short Papers, pages 215–219,
Uppsala, Sweden, 11-16 July 2010.

Next, both context matrices are factored using singular value decomposition:

$$L = U_L S_L V_L^T$$
$$R = U_R S_R V_R^T.$$

The diagonal matrices S_L and S_R (each of rank 1000) are reduced down to rank $r_1 = 100$ by replacing the 900 smallest singular values in each matrix with zeros, yielding S_L^* and S_R^*. We then form a pair of latent-descriptor matrices defined by:

$$L^* = U_L S_L^*$$
$$R^* = U_R S_R^*.$$

Row i in matrix L^* (resp. R^*) is the left (resp. right) latent descriptor for word type i. We next include a normalization step in which each row in each of L^* and R^* is scaled to unit length, yielding matrices L^{**} and R^{**}. Finally, we form a single descriptor matrix D by concatenating these matrices into $D = [L^{**} R^{**}]$. Row i in matrix D is the complete latent descriptor for word type i; this latent descriptor sits on the Cartesian product of two 100-dimensional unit spheres, hereafter the *2-sphere*.

We next categorize these descriptors into $k_1 = 500$ groups, using a k-means clustering algorithm. Centroid initialization is done by placing the k initial centroids on the descriptors of the k most frequent words in the corpus. As the descriptors sit on the 2-sphere, we measure the proximity of a descriptor to a centroid by the dot product between them; this is equal to the sum of the cosines of the angles—computed on the left and right parts—between them. We update each cluster's centroid as the weighted average of its constituents, the weight being the frequency of the word type; the centroids are then scaled, so they sit on the 2-sphere. Typically, only a few dozen iterations are required for full convergence of the clustering algorithm.

We then apply a second pass of this entire SVD-and-clustering procedure. In this second pass, we use the $k_1 = 500$ clusters from the first iteration to assemble a new pair of context matrices. Now, R_{ij} counts all the cluster-j (j=1... k_1) words to the right of word i, and L_{ij} counts all the cluster-j words to the left of word i. The new matrices L and R have dimension $N_{types} \times k_1$.

As in the first pass, we perform reduced-rank SVD, this time down to rank $r_2 = 300$, and we again normalize the descriptors to unit length, yielding a new pair of latent descriptor matrices L^{**} and R^{**}. Finally, we concatenate L^{**} and R^{**} into a single matrix of descriptors, and cluster these descriptors into k_2 groups, where k_2 is the desired number of induced tags. We use the same weighted k-means algorithm as in the first pass, again placing the k initial centroids on the descriptors of the k most frequent words in the corpus. The final tag of any token in the corpus is the cluster number of its type.

3 Data and Evaluation

We ran the SVD2 algorithm described above on the full Wall Street Journal part of the Penn Treebank (1,173,766 tokens). Capitalization was ignored, resulting in $N_{types} = 43{,}766$, with only a minor effect on accuracy. Evaluation was done against the POS-tag annotations of the 45-tag PTB tagset (hereafter PTB45), and against the Smith and Eisner (2005) coarse version of the PTB tagset (hereafter PTB17). We selected the three evaluation criteria of Gao and Johnson (2008): M-to-1, 1-to-1, and VI. M-to-1 and 1-to-1 are the tagging accuracies under the best many-to-one map and the greedy one-to-one map respectively; VI is a map-free information-theoretic criterion—see Gao and Johnson (2008) for details. Although we find M-to-1 to be the most reliable criterion of the three, we include the other two criteria for completeness.

In addition to the best M-to-1 map, we also employ here, for large values of k_2, a *prototype-based* M-to-1 *map*. To construct this map, we first find, for each induced tag t, the word type with which it co-occurs most frequently; we call this word type the *prototype* of t. We then query the annotated data for the most common gold tag for each prototype, and we map induced tag t to this gold tag. This prototype-based M-to-1 map produces accuracy scores no greater—typically lower—than the best M-to-1 map. We discuss the value of this approach as a minimally-supervised post-processing step in Section 5.

4 Results

Low-*k* performance. Here we present the performance of the SVD2 model when k_2, the number of induced tags, is the same or roughly the same as the number of tags in the gold standard—hence small. Table 1 compares the performance of SVD2 to other leading models. Following Gao and Johnson (2008), the number of induced tags is 17 for PTB17 evaluation and 50 for PTB45 evaluation. Thus, with the exception of Graça et al. (2009) who use 45 induced tags for PTB45, the number of induced tags is the same across each column of Table 1.

Model	M-to-1		1-to-1		VI	
	PTB17	PTB45	PTB17	PTB45	PTB17	PTB45
SVD2	**0.730**	**0.660**	0.513	0.467	**3.02**	**3.84**
HMM-EM	0.647	0.621	0.431	0.405	3.86	4.48
HMM-VB	0.637	0.605	0.514	0.461	3.44	4.28
HMM-GS	0.674	**0.660**	0.466	**0.499**	3.46	4.04
HMM-Sparse(32)	0.702(2.2)	0.654(1.0)	0.495	0.445		
VEM (10^{-1},10^{-1})	0.682(0.8)	0.546(1.7)	**0.528**	0.460		

Table 1. Tagging accuracy under the best M-to-1 map, the greedy 1-to-1 map, and VI, for the full PTB45 tagset and the reduced PTB17 tagset. HMM-EM, HMM-VB and HMM-GS show the best results from Gao and Johnson (2008); HMM-Sparse(32) and VEM (10^{-1},10^{-1}) show the best results from Graça et al. (2009).

The performance of SVD2 compares favorably to the HMM models. Note that SVD2 is a deterministic algorithm. The table shows, in parentheses, the standard deviations reported in Graça et al. (2009). For the sake of comparison with Graça et al. (2009), we also note that, with $k_2 = 45$, SVD2 scores 0.659 on PTB45. The NVI scores (Reichart and Rappoport 2009) corresponding to the VI scores for SVD2 are 0.938 for PTB17 and 0.885 for PTB45. To examine the sensitivity of the algorithm to its four parameters, w_1, r_1, k_1, and r_2, we changed each of these parameters separately by a multiplicative factor of either 0.5 or 2; in neither case did M-to-1 accuracy drop by more than 0.014.

This performance was achieved despite the fact that the SVD2 tagger is mathematically much simpler than the other models. Our MATLAB implementation of SVD2 takes only a few minutes to run on a desktop computer, in contrast to HMM training times of several hours or days (Gao and Johnson 2008; Johnson 2007).

High-*k* performance. Not suffering from the same computational limitations as other models, SVD2 can easily accommodate high numbers of induced tags, resulting in fine-grained labelings. The value of this flexibility is discussed in the next section. Figure 1 shows, as a function of k_2, the tagging accuracy of SVD2 under both the best and the prototype-based M-to-1 maps (see Section 3), for both the PTB45 and the PTB17 tagsets. The horizontal one-tag-per-word-type line in each panel is the theoretical upper limit for tagging accuracy in non-disambiguating models (such as SVD2). This limit is the fraction of all tokens in the corpus whose gold tag is the most frequent for their type.

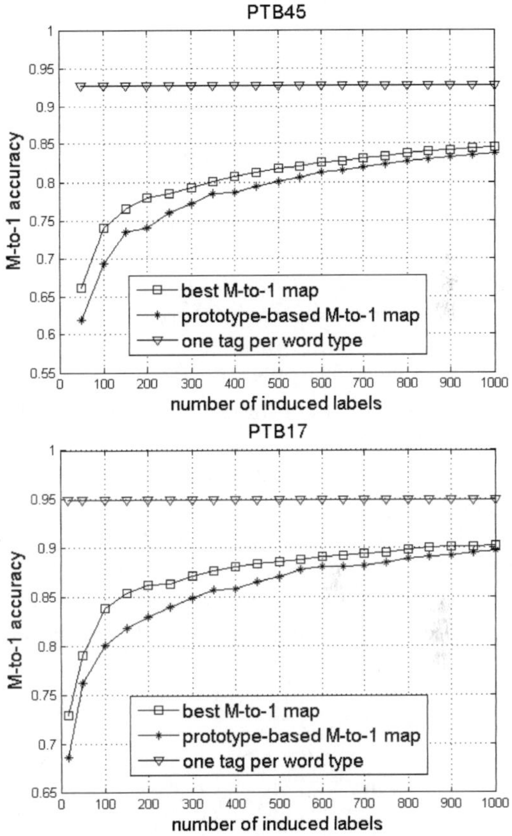

Figure 1. Performance of the SVD2 algorithm as a function of the number of induced tags. Top: PTB45; bottom: PTB17. Each plot shows the tagging accuracy under the best and the prototype-based M-to-1 maps, as well as the upper limit for non-disambiguating taggers.

5 Discussion

At the heart of the algorithm presented here is the reduced-rank SVD method of Schütze (1995), which transforms bigram counts into latent descriptors. In view of the present work, which achieves state-of-the-art performance when evaluation is done with the criteria now in common use, Schütze's original work should rightly be praised as ahead of its time. The SVD2 model presented here differs from Schütze's work in many details of implementation—not all of which are explicitly specified in Schütze (1995). In what follows, we discuss the features of SVD2 that are most critical to its performance. Failure to incorporate any one of them significantly reduces the performance of the algorithm (M-to-1 reduced by 0.04 to 0.08).

First, the reduced-rank left-singular vectors (for the right and left context matrices) are scaled, *i.e.*, multiplied, by the singular values. While the resulting descriptors, the rows of L^* and R^*, live in a much lower-dimensional space than the original context vectors, they are mapped by an angle-preserving map (defined by the matrices of right-singular vectors V_L and V_R) into vectors in the original space. These mapped vectors best approximate (in the least-squares sense) the original context vectors; they have the same geometric relationships as their equivalent high-dimensional images, making them good candidates for the role of word-type descriptors.

A second important feature of the SVD2 algorithm is the unit-length normalization of the latent descriptors, along with the computation of cluster centroids as the weighted averages of their constituent vectors. Thanks to this combined device, rare words are treated equally to frequent words regarding the length of their descriptor vectors, yet contribute less to the placement of centroids.

Finally, while the usual drawback of *k*-means-clustering algorithms is the dependency of the outcome on the initial—usually random—placement of centroids, our initialization of the *k* centroids as the descriptors of the *k* most frequent word types in the corpus makes the algorithm fully deterministic, and improves its performance substantially: M-to-1 PTB45 by 0.043, M-to-1 PTB17 by 0.063.

As noted in the Results section, SVD2 is fairly robust to changes in all four parameters w_1, r_1, k_1, and r_2. The values used here were obtained by a coarse, greedy strategy, where each parameter was optimized independently. It is worth noting that dispensing with the second pass altogether, *i.e.*, clustering directly the latent descriptor vectors obtained in the first pass into the desired number of induced tags, results in a drop of Many-to-1 score of only 0.021 for the PTB45 tagset and 0.009 for the PTB17 tagset.

Disambiguation. An obvious limitation of SVD2 is that it is a non-disambiguating tagger, assigning the same label to all tokens of a type. However, this limitation *per se* is unlikely to be the main obstacle to the improvement of low-*k* performance, since, as is well known, the theoretical upper limit for the tagging accuracy of non-disambiguating models (shown in Fig. 1) is much higher than the current state-of-the-art for unsupervised taggers, whether disambiguating or not.

To further gain insight into how successful current models are at disambiguating when they have the power to do so, we examined a collection of HMM-VB runs (Gao and Johnson 2008) and asked how the accuracy scores would change if, after training was completed, the model were forced to assign the same label to all tokens of the same type. To answer this question, we determined, for each word type, the *modal* HMM state, *i.e.*, the state most frequently assigned by the HMM to tokens of that type. We then relabeled all words with their modal label. The effect of thus eliminating the disambiguation capacity of the model was to slightly *increase* the tagging accuracy under the best M-to-1 map for every HMM-VB run (the average increase was 0.026 for PTB17, and 0.015 for PTB45). We view this as a further indication that, in the current state of the art and with regards to tagging accuracy, limiting oneself to non-disambiguating models may not adversely affect performance.

To the contrary, this limitation may actually benefit an approach such as SVD2. Indeed, on difficult learning tasks, simpler models often behave better than more powerful ones (Geman et al. 1992). HMMs are powerful since they can, in theory, induce both a system of tags and a system of contextual patterns that allow them to disambiguate word types in terms of these tags. However, carrying out both of these unsupervised learning tasks *at once* is problematic in view of the very large number of parameters to be estimated compared to the size of the training data set.

The POS-tagging subtask of disambiguation may then be construed as a challenge in its own right: demonstrate *effective* disambiguation in an unsupervised model. Specifically, show that tagging accuracy *decreases* when the model's disambiguation capacity is removed, by re-labeling all tokens with their modal label, defined above.

We believe that the SVD2 algorithm presented here could provide a launching pad for an approach that would successfully address the disambiguation challenge. It would do so by allowing a gradual and carefully controlled amount of ambiguity into an initially non-disambiguating model. This is left for future work.

Fine-grained labeling. An important feature of the SVD2 algorithm is its ability to produce a fine-grained labeling of the data, using a number of clusters much larger than the number of tags in a syntax-motivated POS-tag system. Such fine-grained labelings can capture additional linguistic features. To achieve a fine-grained labeling, only the final clustering step in the SVD2 algorithm needs to be changed; the computational cost this entails is negligible. A high-quality fine-grained labeling, such as achieved by the SVD2 approach, may be of practical interest as an input to various types of unsupervised grammar-induction algorithms (Headden et al. 2008). This application is left for future work.

Prototype-based tagging. One potentially important practical application of a high-quality fine-grained labeling is its use for languages which lack any kind of annotated data. By first applying the SVD2 algorithm, word types are grouped together into a few hundred clusters. Then, a prototype word is automatically extracted from each cluster. This produces, in a completely unsupervised way, a list of only a few hundred words that need to be hand-tagged by an expert. The results shown in Fig. 1 indicate that these prototype tags can then be used to tag the entire corpus with only a minor decrease in accuracy compared to the best M-to-1 map—the construction of which requires a fully annotated corpus. Fig. 1 also indicates that, with only a few hundred prototypes, the gap left between the accuracy thus achieved and the upper bound for non-disambiguating models is fairly small.

References

Alexander Clark. 2000. Inducing syntactic categories by context distribution clustering. In *The Fourth Conference on Natural Language Learning*.

Alexander Clark. 2003. Combining distributional and morphological information for part of speech induction. In *10th Conference of the European Chapter of the Association for Computational Linguistics*, pages 59–66.

Michael Collins. 2002. Discriminative training methods for hidden markov models: Theory and experiments with perceptron algorithms. In *Proceedings of the ACL-02 conference on Empirical methods in natural language processing – Volume 10*.

Jianfeng Gao and Mark Johnson. 2008. A comparison of bayesian estimators for unsupervised Hidden Markov Model POS taggers. In *Proceedings of the 2008 Conference on Empirical Methods in Natural Language Processing*, pages 344–352.

Stuart Geman, Elie Bienenstock and René Doursat. 1992. Neural Networks and the Bias/Variance Dilemma. *Neural Computation*, 4 (1), pages 1–58.

Sharon Goldwater and Tom Griffiths. 2007. A fully Bayesian approach to unsupervised part-of-speech tagging. In *Proceedings of the 45th Annual Meeting of the Association of Computational Linguistics*, pages 744–751.

João V. Graça, Kuzman Ganchev, Ben Taskar, and Fernando Pereira. 2009. Posterior vs. Parameter Sparsity in Latent Variable Models. In Neural Information Processing Systems Conference (NIPS).

Aria Haghighi and Dan Klein. 2006. Prototype-driven learning for sequence models. In *Proceedings of the Human Language Technology Conference of the NAACL, Main Conference*, pages 320–327, New York City, USA, June. Association for Computational Linguistics.

William P. Headden, David McClosky, and Eugene Charniak. 2008. Evaluating unsupervised part-of-speech tagging for grammar induction. In *Proceedings of the International Conference on Computational Linguistics (COLING '08)*.

Mark Johnson. 2007. Why doesn't EM find good HMM POS-taggers? In Proceedings of the 2007 Joint Conference on Empirical Methods in Natural Language Processing and Computational Natural Language Learning (EMNLP-CoNLL), pages 296–305.

Marina Meilă. 2003. Comparing clusterings by the variation of information. In Bernhard Schölkopf and Manfred K. Warmuth, editors, *COLT 2003: The Sixteenth Annual Conference on Learning Theory*, volume 2777 of *Lecture Notes in Computer Science*, pages 173–187. Springer.

Roi Reichart and Ari Rappoport. 2009. The NVI Clustering Evaluation Measure. In *Proceedings of the Thirteenth Conference on Computational Natural Language Learning (CoNLL)*, pages 165–173.

Hinrich Schütze. 1995. Distributional part-of-speech tagging. In Proceedings of the seventh conference on European chapter of the Association for Computational Linguistics, pages 141–148.

Noah A. Smith and Jason Eisner. 2005. Contrastive estimation: Training log-linear models on unlabeled data. In *Proceedings of the 43rd Annual Meeting of the Association for Computational Linguistics (ACL'05)*, pages 354–362.

Kristina Toutanova, Dan Klein, Christopher D. Manning and Yoram Singer. 2003. Feature-rich part-of-speech tagging with a cyclic dependency network. In *Proceedings of HLT-NAACL* 2003, pages 252-259.

Intelligent Selection of Language Model Training Data

Robert C. Moore **William Lewis**
Microsoft Research
Redmond, WA 98052, USA
{bobmoore,wilewis}@microsoft.com

Abstract

We address the problem of selecting non-domain-specific language model training data to build auxiliary language models for use in tasks such as machine translation. Our approach is based on comparing the cross-entropy, according to domain-specific and non-domain-specifc language models, for each sentence of the text source used to produce the latter language model. We show that this produces better language models, trained on less data, than both random data selection and two other previously proposed methods.

1 Introduction

Statistical N-gram language models are widely used in applications that produce natural-language text as output, particularly speech recognition and machine translation. It seems to be a universal truth that output quality can always be improved by using more language model training data, but only if the training data is reasonably well-matched to the desired output. This presents a problem, because in virtually any particular application the amount of in-domain data is limited.

Thus it has become standard practice to combine in-domain data with other data, either by combining N-gram counts from in-domain and other data (usually weighting the counts in some way), or building separate language models from different data sources, interpolating the language model probabilities either linearly or log-linearly. Log-linear interpolation is particularly popular in statistical machine translation (e.g., Brants et al., 2007), because the interpolation weights can easily be discriminatively trained to optimize an end-to-end translation objective function (such as BLEU) by making the log probability according to each language model a separate feature function in the overall translation model.

The normal practice when using multiple languages models in machine translation seems to be to train models on as much data as feasible from each source, and to depend on feature weight optimization to down-weight the impact of data that is less well-matched to the translation application. In this paper, however, we show that for a data source that is not entirely in-domain, we can improve the match between the language model from that data source and the desired application output by intelligently selecting a subset of the available data as language model training data. This not only produces a language model better matched to the domain of interest (as measured in terms of perplexity on held-out in-domain data), but it reduces the computational resources needed to exploit a large amount of non-domain-specific data, since the resources needed to filter a large amount of data are much less (especially in terms of memory) than those required to build a language model from all the data.

2 Approaches to the Problem

Our approach to the problem assumes that we have enough in-domain data to train a reasonable in-domain language model, which we then use to help score text segments from other data sources, and we select segments based on a score cutoff optimized on held-out in-domain data.

We are aware of two comparable previous approaches. Lin et al. (1997) and Gao et al. (2002) both used a method similar to ours, in which the metric used to score text segments is their perplexity according to the in-domain language model. The candidate text segments with perplexity less than some threshold are selected.

The second previous approach does not explicitly make use of an in-domain language model, but is still applicable to our scenario. Klakow (2000) estimates a unigram language model from the entire non-domain-specific corpus to be selected

Proceedings of the ACL 2010 Conference Short Papers, pages 220–224,
Uppsala, Sweden, 11-16 July 2010.

from, and scores each candidate text segment from that corpus by the change in the log likelihood of the in-domain data according to the unigram model, if that segment were removed from the corpus used to estimate the unigram model. Those segments whose removal would decrease the log likelihood of the in-domain data more than some threshold are selected.

Our method is a fairly simple variant of scoring by perplexity according to an in-domain language model. First, note that selecting segments based on a perplexity threshold is equivalent to selecting based on a cross-entropy threshold. Perplexity and cross-entropy are monotonically related, since the perplexity of a string s according to a model M is simply $b^{H_M(s)}$, where $H_M(s)$ is the cross-entropy of s according to M and b is the base with respect to which the cross-entropy is measured (e.g., bits or nats). However, instead of scoring text segments by perplexity or cross-entropy according to the in-domain language model, we score them by the difference of the cross-entropy of a text segment according to the in-domain language model and the cross-entropy of the text segment according to a language model trained on a random sample of the data source from which the text segment is drawn.

To state this formally, let I be an in-domain data set and N be a non-domain-specific (or otherwise not entirely in-domain) data set. Let $H_I(s)$ be the per-word cross-entropy, according to a language model trained on I, of a text segment s drawn from N. Let $H_N(s)$ be the per-word cross-entropy of s according to a language model trained on a random sample of N. We partition N into text segments (e.g., sentences), and score the segments according to $H_I(s) - H_N(s)$, selecting all text segments whose score is less than a threshold T.

This method can be justified by reasoning simliar to that used to derive methods for training binary text classifiers without labeled negative examples (Denis et al., 2002; Elkin and Noto, 2008). Let us imagine that our non-domain-specific corpus N contains an in-domain subcorpus N_I, drawn from the same distribution as our in-domain corpus I. Since N_I is statistically just like our in-domain data I, it would seem to be a good candidate for the data that we want to extract from N. By a simple variant of Bayes rule, the probability $P(N_I|s, N)$ of a text segment s, drawn randomly from N, being in N_I is given by

$$P(N_I|s, N) = \frac{P(s|N_I, N)P(N_I|N)}{P(s|N)}$$

Since N_I is a subset of N, $P(s|N_I, N) = P(s|N_I)$, and by our assumption about the relationship of I and N_I, $P(s|N_I) = P(s|I)$. Hence,

$$P(N_I|s, N) = \frac{P(s|I)P(N_I|N)}{P(s|N)}$$

If we could estimate all the probabilities in the right-hand side of this equation, we could use it to select text segments that have a high probability of being in N_I.

We can estimate $P(s|I)$ and $P(s|N)$ by training language models on I and a sample of N, respectively. That leaves us only $P(N_I|N)$, to estimate, but we really don't care what $P(N_I|N)$ is, because knowing that would still leave us wondering what threshold to set on $P(N_I|s, N)$. We don't care about classification accuracy; we care only about the quality of the resulting language model, so we might as well just attempt to find a threshold on $P(s|I)/P(s|N)$ that optimizes the fit of the resulting language model to held-out in-domain data.

Equivalently, we can work in the log domain with the quantity $\log(P(s|I)) - \log(P(s|N))$. This gets us very close to working with the difference in cross-entropies, because $H_I(s) - H_N(s)$ is just a length-normalized version of $\log(P(s|I)) - \log(P(s|N))$, with the sign reversed. The reason that we need to normalize for length is that the value of $\log(P(s|I)) - \log(P(s|N))$ tends to correlate very strongly with text segment length. If the candidate text segments vary greatly in length—e.g., if we partition N into sentences—this correlation can be a serious problem.

We estimated this effect on a 1000-sentence sample of our experimental data described below, and found the correlation between sentence log probability difference and sentence length to be $r = -0.92$, while the cross-entropy difference was almost uncorrelated with sentence length ($r = 0.04$). Hence, using sentence probability ratios or log probability differences as our scoring function would result in selecting disproportionately very short sentences. We tested this in an experiment not described here in detail, and found it not to be significantly better as a selection criterion than random selection.

Corpus	Sentence count	Token count
Gigaword	133,310,562	3,445,946,266
Europarl train	1,651,392	48,230,859
Europarl test	2,000	55,566

Table 1: Corpus size statistics

3 Experiments

We have empirically evaluated our proposed method for selecting data from a non-domain-specific source to model text in a specific domain. For the in-domain corpus, we chose the English side of the English-French parallel text from release v5 of the Europarl corpus (Koehn, 2005). This consists of proceedings of the European Parliament from 1999 through 2009. We used the text from 1999 through 2008 as in-domain training data, and we used the first 2000 sentences from January 2009 as test data. For the non-domain-specific corpus, we used the LDC English Gigaword Third Edition (LDC Catalog No.: LDC2007T07).

We used a simple tokenization scheme on all data, splitting on white space and on boundaries between alphanumeric and nonalphanumeric (e.g., punctuation) characters. With this tokenization, the sizes of our data sets in terms of sentences and tokens are shown in Table 1. The token counts include added end-of-sentence tokens.

To implement our data selection method we required one language model trained on the Europarl training data and one trained on the Gigaword data. To make these language models comparable, and to show the feasibility of optimizing the fit to the in-domain data without training a model on the entire Gigaword corpus, we trained the Gigaword language model for data selection on a random sample of the Gigaword corpus of a similar size to that of the Europarl training data: 1,874,051 sentences, 48,459,945 tokens.

To further increase the comparability of these Europarl and Gigaword language models, we restricted the vocabulary of both models to the tokens appearing at least twice in the Europarl training data, treating all other tokens as instances of <UNK>. With this vocabulary, 4-gram language models were trained on both the Europarl training data and the Gigaword random sample using backoff absolute discounting (Ney et al. 1994), with a discount of 0.7 used for all N-gram lengths. The discounted probability mass at the unigram level was added to the probability of <UNK>. A count cutoff of 2 occurrences was applied to the trigrams and 4-grams in estimating these models.

We computed the cross-entropy of each sentence in the Gigaword corpus according to both models, and scored each sentence by the difference in cross-entropy, $H_{Ep}(s) - H_{Gw}(s)$. We then selected subsets of the Gigaword data corresponding to 8 cutoff points in the cross-entropy difference scores, and trained 4-gram models (again using absolute discounting with a discount of 0.7) on each of these subsets and on the full Gigaword corpus. These language models were estimated without restricting the vocabulary or applying count cutoffs, but the only parameters computed were those needed to determine the perplexity of the held-out Europarl test set, which saves a substantial amount of computation in determining the optimal selection threshold.

We compared our selection method to three other methods. As a baseline, we trained language models on random subsets of the Gigaword corpus of approximately equal size to the data sets produced by the cutoffs we selected for the cross-entropy difference scores. Next, we scored all the Gigaword sentences by the cross-entropy according to the Europarl-trained model alone. As we noted above, this is equivalent to the in-domain perplexity scoring method used by Lin et al. (1997) and Gao et al. (2002). Finally, we implemented Klakow's (2000) method, scoring each Gigaword sentence by removing it from the Gigaword corpus and computing the difference in the log likelihood of the Europarl corpus according to unigram models trained on the Gigaword corpus with and without that sentence. With the latter two methods, we chose cutoff points in the resulting scores to produce data sets approximately equal in size to those obtained using our selection method.

4 Results

For all four selection methods, plots of test set perplexity vs. the number of training data tokens selected are displayed in Figure 1. (Note that the training data token counts are displayed on a logarithmic scale.) The test set perplexity for the language model trained on the full Gigaword corpus is 135. As we might expect, reducing training data by random sampling always increases perplexity. Selecting Gigaword sentences by their

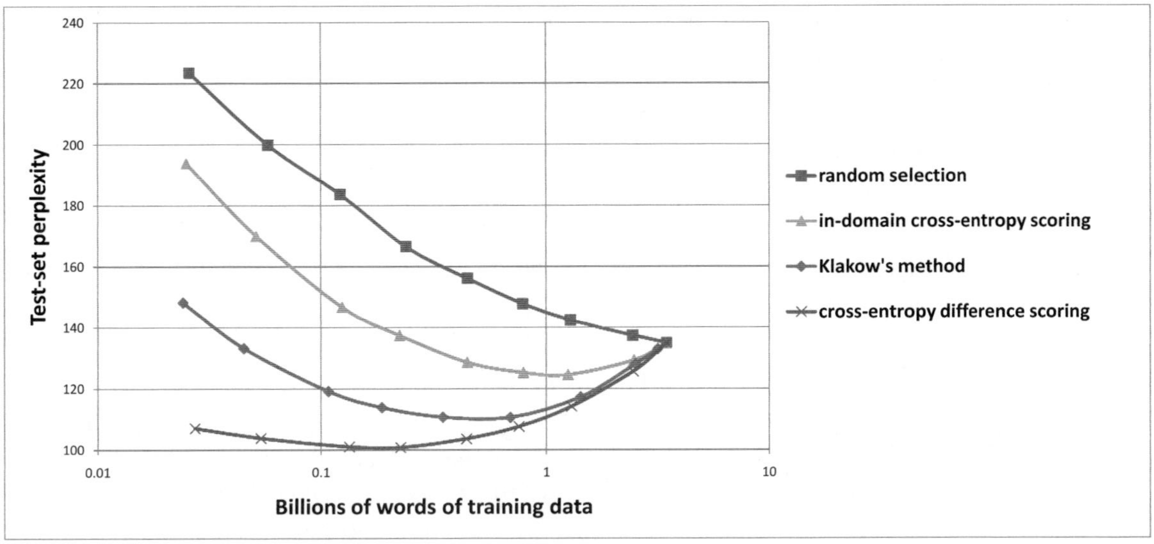

Figure 1: Test set perplexity vs. training set size

Selection Method	Original LM PPL	Modified LM PPL
in-domain cross-entropy scoring	124.4	124.8
Klakow's method	110.5	110.8
cross-entropy difference scoring	100.7	101.9

Table 2: Results adjusted for vocabulary coverage

cross-entropy according to the Europarl-trained model is effective in reducing both test set perplexity and training corpus size, with an optimum perplexity of 124, obtained with a model built from 36% of the Gigaword corpus. Klakow's method is even more effective, with an optimum perplexity of 111, obtained with a model built from 21% of the Gigaword corpus. The cross-entropy difference selection method, however, is yet more effective, with an optimum perplexity of 101, obtained with a model built from less than 7% of the Gigaword corpus.

The comparisons implied by Figure 1, however, are only approximate, because each perplexity (even along the same curve) is computed with respect to a different vocabulary, resulting in a different out-of-vocabulary (OOV) rate. OOV tokens in the test data are excluded from the perplexity computation, so the perplexity measurements are not strictly comparable.

Out of the 55566 test set tokens, the number of OOV tokens ranges from 418 (0.75%), for the smallest training set based on in-domain cross-entropy scoring, to 20 (0.03%), for training on the full Gigaword corpus. If we consider only the training sets that appear to produce the lowest perplexity for each selection method, however, the spread of OOV counts is much narrower, ranging 53 (0.10%) for best training set based on cross-entropy difference scoring, to 20 (0.03%), for random selection.

To control for the difference in vocabulary, we estimated a modified 4-gram language model for each selection method (other than random selection) using the training set that appeared to produce the lowest perplexity for that selection method in our initial experiments. In the modified language models, the unigram model based on the selected training set is smoothed by absolute discounting, and backed-off to an unsmoothed unigram model based on the full Gigaword corpus. This produces language models that are normalized over the same vocabulary as a model trained on the full Gigaword corpus; thus the test set has the same OOVs for each model.

Test set perplexity for each of these modifed language models is compared to that of the original version of the model in Table 2. It can be seen that adjusting the vocabulary in this way, so that all models are based on the same vocabulary, yields only very small changes in the measured test-set perplexity, and these differences are much smaller than the differences between the different selection methods, whichever way the vocabulary of the language models is determined.

5 Conclusions

The cross-entropy difference selection method introduced here seems to produce language models that are both a better match to texts in a restricted domain, and require less data for training, than any of the other data selection methods tested. This study is preliminary, however, in that we have not yet shown improved end-to-end task performance applying this approach, such as improved BLEU scores in a machine translation task. However, we believe there is reason to be optimistic about this. When a language model trained on non-domain-specific data is used in a statistical translation model as a separate feature function (as is often the case), lower perplexity on in-domain target language test data derived from reference translations corresponds directly to assigning higher language model feature scores to those reference translations, which should in turn lead to translation system output that matches reference translations better.

References

Thorsten Brants, Ashok C. Popat, Peng Xu, Franz J. Och, and Jeffrey Dean. 2007. Large language models in machine translation. In *Proceedings of the Joint Conference on Empirical Methods in Natural Language Processing and Computational Natural Language Learning*, June 28–30, Prague, Czech Republic, 858–867.

François Denis, Remi Gilleron, and Marc Tommasi. 2002. Text classification from positive and unlabeled examples. In *The 9th International Conference on Information Processing and Management of Uncertainty in Knowledge-Based Systems (IPMU 2002)*, 1927–1934.

Charles Elkin and Keith Noto. 2008. Learning classifiers from only positive and unlabeled data. In *KDD 2008*, August 24–27, Las Vegas, Nevada, USA, 213–220.

Jianfeng Gao, Joshua Goodman, Mingjing Li, and Kai-Fu Lee. 2002. Toward a unified approach to statistical language modeling for Chinese. *ACM Transactions on Asian Language Information Processing*, 1(1):3–33.

Dietrich Klakow. 2000. Selecting articles from the language model training corpus. In *ICASSP 2000*, June 5–9, Istanbul, Turkey, vol. 3, 1695–1698.

Philipp Koehn. 2005. Europarl: a parallel corpus for statistical machine translation. In *MT Summit X*, September 12–16, Phuket, Thailand, 79–86.

Sung-Chien Lin, Chi-Lung Tsai, Lee-Feng Chien, Ker-Jiann Chen, and Lin-Shan Lee. 1997. Chinese language model adaptation based on document classification and multiple domain-specific language models. In *EUROSPEECH-1997*, 1463–1466.

Hermann Ney, Ute Essen, and Reinhard Kneser. 1994. On structuring dependencies in stochastic language modelling. *Computer Speech and Language*, 8:1–38.

Blocked Inference in Bayesian Tree Substitution Grammars

Trevor Cohn
Department of Computer Science
University of Sheffield
T.Cohn@dcs.shef.ac.uk

Phil Blunsom
Computing Laboratory
University of Oxford
Phil.Blunsom@comlab.ox.ac.uk

Abstract

Learning a tree substitution grammar is very challenging due to derivational ambiguity. Our recent approach used a Bayesian non-parametric model to induce good derivations from treebanked input (Cohn et al., 2009), biasing towards small grammars composed of small generalisable productions. In this paper we present a novel training method for the model using a blocked Metropolis-Hastings sampler in place of the previous method's local Gibbs sampler. The blocked sampler makes considerably larger moves than the local sampler and consequently converges in less time. A core component of the algorithm is a grammar transformation which represents an infinite tree substitution grammar in a finite context free grammar. This enables efficient blocked inference for training and also improves the parsing algorithm. Both algorithms are shown to improve parsing accuracy.

1 Introduction

Tree Substitution Grammar (TSG) is a compelling grammar formalism which allows nonterminal rewrites in the form of trees, thereby enabling the modelling of complex linguistic phenomena such as argument frames, lexical agreement and idiomatic phrases. A fundamental problem with TSGs is that they are difficult to estimate, even in the supervised scenario where treebanked data is available. This is because treebanks are typically not annotated with their TSG derivations (how to decompose a tree into elementary tree fragments); instead the derivation needs to be inferred.

In recent work we proposed a TSG model which infers an optimal decomposition under a non-parametric Bayesian prior (Cohn et al., 2009). This used a Gibbs sampler for training, which repeatedly samples for every node in every training tree a binary value indicating whether the node is or is not a substitution point in the tree's derivation. Aggregated over the whole corpus, these values and the underlying trees specify the weighted grammar. Local Gibbs samplers, although conceptually simple, suffer from slow convergence (a.k.a. poor mixing). The sampler can get easily stuck because many locally improbable decisions are required to escape from a locally optimal solution. This problem manifests itself both locally to a sentence and globally over the training sample. The net result is a sampler that is non-convergent, overly dependent on its initialisation and cannot be said to be sampling from the posterior.

In this paper we present a blocked Metropolis-Hasting sampler for learning a TSG, similar to Johnson et al. (2007). The sampler jointly updates all the substitution variables in a tree, making much larger moves than the local single-variable sampler. A critical issue when developing a Metroplis-Hastings sampler is choosing a suitable proposal distribution, which must have the same support as the true distribution. For our model the natural proposal distribution is a MAP point estimate, however this cannot be represented directly as it is infinitely large. To solve this problem we develop a grammar transformation which can succinctly represent an infinite TSG in an equivalent finite Context Free Grammar (CFG). The transformed grammar can be used as a proposal distribution, from which samples can be drawn in polynomial time. Empirically, the blocked sampler converges in fewer iterations and in less time than the local Gibbs sampler. In addition, we also show how the transformed grammar can be used for parsing, which yields theoretical and empirical improvements over our previous method which truncated the grammar.

Proceedings of the ACL 2010 Conference Short Papers, pages 225–230,
Uppsala, Sweden, 11-16 July 2010.

2 Background

A *Tree Substitution Grammar* (TSG; Bod et al. (2003)) is a 4-tuple, $G = (T, N, S, R)$, where T is a set of *terminal symbols*, N is a set of *nonterminal symbols*, $S \in N$ is the distinguished *root nonterminal* and R is a set of productions (rules). The productions take the form of tree fragments, called *elementary trees* (ETs), in which each internal node is labelled with a nonterminal and each leaf is labelled with either a terminal or a nonterminal. The *frontier nonterminal* nodes in each ET form the sites into which other ETs can be substituted. A *derivation* creates a tree by recursive substitution starting with the root symbol and finishing when there are no remaining frontier nonterminals. Figure 1 (left) shows an example derivation where the arrows denote substitution. A *Probabilistic Tree Substitution Grammar* (PTSG) assigns a probability to each rule in the grammar, where each production is assumed to be conditionally independent given its root nonterminal. A derivation's probability is the product of the probabilities of the rules therein.

In this work we employ the same non-parametric TSG model as Cohn et al. (2009), which we now summarise. The inference problem within this model is to identify the posterior distribution of the elementary trees $\mathbf{e}$ given whole trees $\mathbf{t}$. The model is characterised by the use of a Dirichlet Process (DP) prior over the grammar. We define the distribution over elementary trees $\mathbf{e}$ with root nonterminal symbol c as

$$\begin{aligned} G_c | \alpha_c, P_0 &\sim \text{DP}(\alpha_c, P_0(\cdot|c)) \\ e|c &\sim G_c \end{aligned}$$

where $P_0(\cdot|c)$ (the *base distribution*) is a distribution over the infinite space of trees rooted with c, and α_c (the *concentration parameter*) controls the model's tendency towards either reusing elementary trees or creating novel ones as each training instance is encountered.

Rather than representing the distribution G_c explicitly, we integrate over all possible values of G_c. The key result required for inference is that the conditional distribution of e_i, given $\mathbf{e}_{-i}, = e_1 \dots e_n \backslash e_i$ and the root category c is:

$$p(e_i | \mathbf{e}_{-i}, c, \alpha_c, P_0) = \frac{n^{-i}_{e_i,c}}{n^{-i}_{\cdot,c} + \alpha_c} + \frac{\alpha_c P_0(e_i|c)}{n^{-i}_{\cdot,c} + \alpha_c} \quad (1)$$

where $n^{-i}_{e_i,c}$ is the number number of times e_i has been used to rewrite c in $\mathbf{e}_{-i}$, and $n^{-i}_{\cdot,c} = \sum_e n^{-i}_{e,c}$

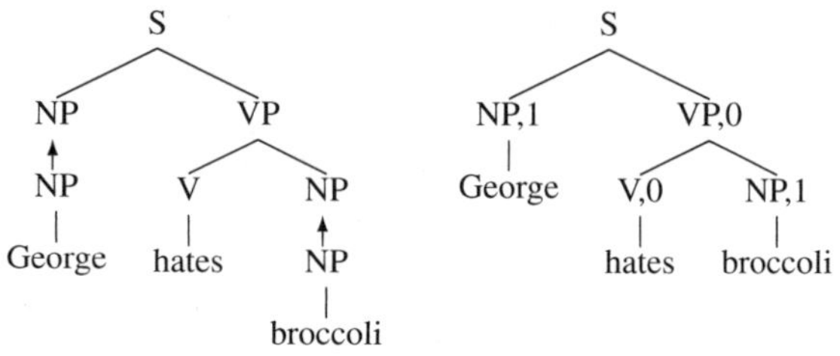

Figure 1: TSG derivation and its corresponding Gibbs state for the local sampler, where each node is marked with a binary variable denoting whether it is a substitution site.

is the total count of rewriting c. Henceforth we omit the $-i$ sub-/super-script for brevity.

A primary consideration is the definition of P_0. Each e_i can be generated in one of two ways: by drawing from the base distribution, where the probability of any particular tree is proportional to $\alpha_c P_0(e_i|c)$, or by drawing from a cache of previous expansions of c, where the probability of any particular expansion is proportional to the number of times that expansion has been used before. In Cohn et al. (2009) we presented base distributions that favour small elementary trees which we expect will generalise well to unseen data. In this work we show that if P_0 is chosen such that it decomposes with the CFG rules contained within each elementary tree,[1] then we can use a novel dynamic programming algorithm to sample derivations without ever enumerating all the elementary trees in the grammar.

The model was trained using a local Gibbs sampler (Geman and Geman, 1984), a Markov chain Monte Carlo (MCMC) method in which random variables are repeatedly sampled conditioned on the values of all other random variables in the model. To formulate the local sampler, we associate a binary variable with each non-root internal node of each tree in the training set, indicating whether that node is a substitution point or not (illustrated in Figure 1). The sampler then visits each node in a random schedule and resamples that node's substitution variable, where the probability of the two different configurations are given by (1). Parsing was performed using a Metropolis-Hastings sampler to draw derivation samples for a string, from which the best tree was recovered. However the sampler used for parsing was biased

[1]Both choices of base distribution in Cohn et al. (2009) decompose into CFG rules. In this paper we focus on the better performing one, P_0^C, which combines a PCFG applied recursively with a stopping probability, s, at each node.

because it used as its proposal distribution a truncated grammar which excluded all but a handful of the unseen elementary trees. Consequently the proposal had smaller support than the true model, voiding the MCMC convergence proofs.

3 Grammar Transformation

We now present a blocked sampler using the Metropolis-Hastings (MH) algorithm to perform sentence-level inference, based on the work of Johnson et al. (2007) who presented a MH sampler for a Bayesian PCFG. This approach repeats the following steps for each sentence in the training set: 1) run the inside algorithm (Lari and Young, 1990) to calculate marginal expansion probabilities under a MAP approximation, 2) sample an analysis top-down and 3) accept or reject using a Metropolis-Hastings (MH) test to correct for differences between the MAP proposal and the true model. Though our model is similar to Johnson et al. (2007)'s, we have an added complication: the MAP grammar cannot be estimated directly. This is a consequence of the base distribution having infinite support (assigning non-zero probability to infinitely many unseen tree fragments), which means the MAP has an infinite rule set. For example, if our base distribution licences the CFG production NP → NP PP then our TSG grammar will contain the infinite set of elementary trees NP → NP PP, NP → (NP NP PP) PP, NP → (NP (NP NP PP) PP) PP, ... with decreasing but non-zero probability.

However, we can represent the infinite MAP using a grammar transformation inspired by Goodman (2003), which represents the MAP TSG in an equivalent finite PCFG.[2] Under the transformed PCFG inference is efficient, allowing its use as the proposal distribution in a blocked MH sampler. We represent the MAP using the grammar transformation in Table 1 which separates the $n_{e,c}$ and P_0 terms in (1) into two separate CFGs, A and B. Grammar A has productions for every ET with $n_{e,c} \geq 1$ which are assigned unsmoothed probabilities: omitting the P_0 term from (1).[3] Grammar B has productions for every CFG production licensed under P_0; its productions are denoted using primed (') nonterminals. The rule $c \rightarrow c'$ bridges from A to B, weighted by the smoothing term excluding P_0, which is computed recursively via child productions. The remaining rules in grammar B correspond to every CFG production in the underlying PCFG base distribution, coupled with the binary decision whether or not nonterminal children should be substitution sites (frontier nonterminals). This choice affects the rule probability by including a s or $1 - s$ factor, and child substitution sites also function as a bridge back from grammar B to A. In this way there are often two equivalent paths to reach the same chart cell using the same elementary tree – via grammar A using observed TSG productions and via grammar B using P_0 backoff; summing these yields the desired net probability.

For every ET, e, rewriting c with non-zero count:	
$c \rightarrow \text{sign}(e)$	$\frac{n^-_{e,c}}{n^-_{\cdot,c}+\alpha_c}$
For every internal node e_i in e with children $e_{i,1}, \ldots, e_{i,n}$	
$\text{sign}(e_i) \rightarrow \text{sign}(e_{i,1}) \ldots \text{sign}(e_{i,n})$	1
For every nonterminal, c:	
$c \rightarrow c'$	$\frac{\alpha_c}{n^-_{\cdot,c}+\alpha_c}$
For every pre-terminal CFG production, $c \rightarrow t$:	
$c' \rightarrow t$	$P_{CFG}(c \rightarrow t)$
For every unary CFG production, $c \rightarrow a$:	
$c' \rightarrow a$	$P_{CFG}(c \rightarrow a)s_a$
$c' \rightarrow a'$	$P_{CFG}(c \rightarrow a)(1 - s_a)$
For every binary CFG production, $c \rightarrow ab$:	
$c' \rightarrow ab$	$P_{CFG}(c \rightarrow ab)s_a s_b$
$c' \rightarrow ab'$	$P_{CFG}(c \rightarrow ab)s_a(1 - s_b)$
$c' \rightarrow a'b$	$P_{CFG}(c \rightarrow ab)(1 - s_a)s_b$
$c' \rightarrow a'b'$	$P_{CFG}(c \rightarrow ab)(1 - s_a)(1 - s_b)$

Table 1: Grammar transformation rules to map a MAP TSG into a CFG. Production probabilities are shown to the right of each rule. The sign(e) function creates a unique string signature for an ET e (where the signature of a frontier node is itself) and s_c is the Bernoulli probability of c being a substitution variable (and stopping the P_0 recursion).

Figure 2 shows an example of the transformation of an elementary tree with non-zero count, $n_{e,c} \geq 1$, into the two types of CFG rules. Both parts are capable of parsing the string NP, saw, NP into a S, as illustrated in Figure 3; summing the probability of both analyses gives the model probability from (1). Note that although the probabilities exactly match the true model for a single elementary tree, the probability of derivations composed of many elementary trees may not match because the model's caching behaviour has been suppressed, i.e., the counts, n, are not incremented during the course of a derivation.

For training we define the MH sampler as follows. First we estimate the MAP grammar over

[2] Backoff DOP uses a similar packed representation to encode the set of smaller subtrees for a given elementary tree (Sima'an and Buratto, 2003), which are used to smooth its probability estimate.

[3] The transform assumes inside inference. For Viterbi replace the probability for $c \rightarrow \text{sign}(e)$ with $\frac{n^-_{e,c}+\alpha_c P_0(e|c)}{n^-_{\cdot,c}+\alpha_c}$.

S → NP VP{V{saw},NP}	$\frac{n^-_{e,S}}{n^-_{\cdot,S}+\alpha_S}$
VP{V{saw},NP} → V{saw} NP	1
V{saw} → saw	1
S → S'	$\frac{\alpha_S}{n^-_{\cdot,S}+\alpha_S}$
S' → NP VP'	P_{CFG}(S → NP VP)$s_{NP}(1 - s_{VP})$
VP' → V' NP	P_{CFG}(VP → V NP)$(1 - s_V)s_{NP}$
V' → saw	P_{CFG}(V → saw)

Figure 2: Example of the transformed grammar for the ET (S NP (VP (V saw) NP)). Taking the product of the rule scores above the line yields the left term in (1), and the product of the scores below the line yields the right term.

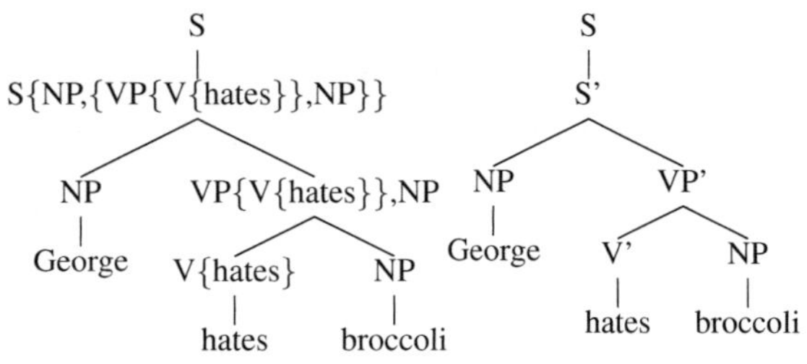

Figure 3: Example trees under the grammar transform, which both encode the same TSG derivation from Figure 1. The left tree encodes that the S → NP (VP (V hates) NP elementary tree was drawn from the cache, while for the right tree this same elementary tree was drawn from the base distribution (the left and right terms in (1), respectively).

the derivations of training corpus excluding the current tree, which we represent using the PCFG transformation. The next step is to sample derivations for a given tree, for which we use a constrained variant of the inside algorithm (Lari and Young, 1990). We must ensure that the TSG derivation produces the given tree, and therefore during inside inference we only consider spans that are constituents in the tree and are labelled with the correct nonterminal. Nonterminals are said to match their primed and signed counterparts, e.g., NP′ and NP{DT,NN{car}} both match NP. Under the tree constraints the time complexity of inside inference is linear in the length of the sentence. A derivation is then sampled from the inside chart using a top-down traversal (Johnson et al., 2007), and converted back into its equivalent TSG derivation. The derivation is scored with the true model and accepted or rejected using the MH test; accepted samples then replace the current derivation for the tree, and rejected samples leave the previous derivation unchanged. These steps are then repeated for another tree in the training set, and the process is then repeated over the full training set many times.

Parsing The grammar transform is not only useful for training, but also for parsing. To parse a sentence we sample a number of TSG derivations from the MAP which are then accepted or rejected into the full model using a MH step. The samples are obtained from the same transformed grammar but adapting the algorithm for an unsupervised setting where parse trees are not available. For this we use the standard inside algorithm applied to the sentence, omitting the tree constraints, which has time complexity cubic in the length of the sentence. We then sample a derivation from the inside chart and perform the MH acceptance test. This setup is theoretically more appealing than our previous approach in which we truncated the approximation grammar to exclude most of the zero count rules (Cohn et al., 2009). We found that both the maximum probability derivation and tree were considerably worse than a tree constructed to maximise the expected number of correct CFG rules (MER), based on Goodman's (2003) algorithm for maximising labelled recall. For this reason we the MER parsing algorithm using sampled Monte Carlo estimates for the marginals over CFG rules at each sentence span.

4 Experiments

We tested our model on the Penn treebank using the same data setup as Cohn et al. (2009). Specifically, we used only section 2 for training and section 22 (devel) for reporting results. Our models were all sampled for 5k iterations with hyperparameter inference for α_c and s_c $\forall$ $c \in N$, but in contrast to our previous approach we did not use annealing which we did not find to help generalisation accuracy. The MH acceptance rates were in excess of 99% across both training and parsing. All results are averages over three runs.

For training the blocked MH sampler exhibits faster convergence than the local Gibbs sampler, as shown in Figure 4. Irrespective of the initialisation the blocked sampler finds higher likelihood states in many fewer iterations (the same trend continues until iteration 5k). To be fair, the blocked sampler is slower per iteration (roughly 50% worse) due to the higher overheads of the grammar transform and performing dynamic programming (despite nominal optimisation).[4] Even after accounting for the time differ-

[4]The speed difference diminishes with corpus size: on sections 2–22 the blocked sampler is only 19% slower per

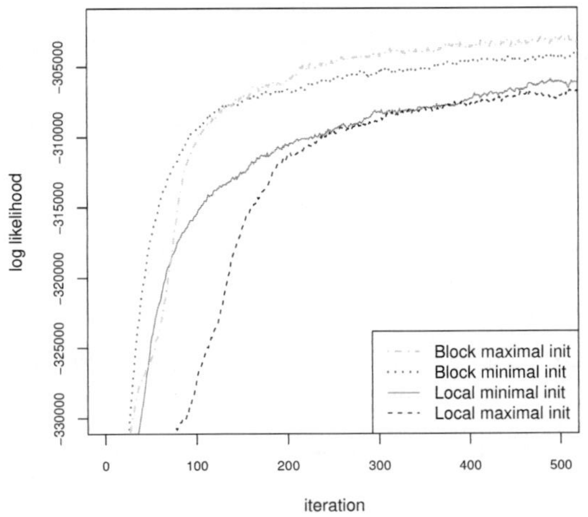

Figure 4: Training likelihood vs. iteration. Each sampling method was initialised with both minimal and maximal elementary trees.

Training	truncated	transform
Local minimal init	77.63	77.98
Local maximal init	77.19	77.71
Blocked minimal init	77.98	78.40
Blocked maximal init	77.67	78.24

Table 2: Development F1 scores using the truncated parsing algorithm and the novel grammar transform algorithm for four different training configurations.

ence the blocked sampler is more effective than the local Gibbs sampler. Training likelihood is highly correlated with generalisation F1 (Pearson's correlation efficient of 0.95), and therefore improving the sampler convergence will have immediate effects on performance.

Parsing results are shown in Table 2.[5] The blocked sampler results in better generalisation F1 scores than the local Gibbs sampler, irrespective of the initialisation condition or parsing method used. The use of the grammar transform in parsing also yields better scores irrespective of the underlying model. Together these results strongly advocate the use of the grammar transform for inference in infinite TSGs.

We also trained the model on the standard Penn treebank training set (sections 2–21). We initialised the model with the final sample from a run on the small training set, and used the blocked sampler for 6500 iterations. Averaged over three runs, the test F1 (section 23) was 85.3 an improvement over our earlier 84.0 (Cohn et al., 2009) although still well below state-of-the-art parsers. We conjecture that the performance gap is due to the model using an overly simplistic treatment of unknown words, and also a further mixing problems with the sampler. For the full data set the counts are much larger in magnitude which leads to stronger modes. The sampler has difficulty escaping such modes and therefore is slower to mix. One way to solve the mixing problem is for the sampler to make more global moves, e.g., with table label resampling (Johnson and Goldwater, 2009) or split-merge (Jain and Neal, 2000). Another way is to use a variational approximation instead of MCMC sampling (Wainwright and Jordan, 2008).

iteration than the local sampler.

[5]Our baseline 'Local maximal init' slightly exceeds previously reported score of 76.89% (Cohn et al., 2009).

5 Discussion

We have demonstrated how our grammar transformation can implicitly represent an exponential space of tree fragments efficiently, allowing us to build a sampler with considerably better mixing properties than a local Gibbs sampler. The same technique was also shown to improve the parsing algorithm. These improvements are in no way limited to our particular choice of a TSG parsing model, many hierarchical Bayesian models have been proposed which would also permit similar optimised samplers. In particular models which induce segmentations of complex structures stand to benefit from this work; Examples include the word segmentation model of Goldwater et al. (2006) for which it would be trivial to adapt our technique to develop a blocked sampler. Hierarchical Bayesian segmentation models have also become popular in statistical machine translation where there is a need to learn phrasal translation structures that can be decomposed at the word level (DeNero et al., 2008; Blunsom et al., 2009; Cohn and Blunsom, 2009). We envisage similar representations being applied to these models to improve their mixing properties.

A particularly interesting avenue for further research is to employ our blocked sampler for unsupervised grammar induction. While it is difficult to extend the local Gibbs sampler to the case where the tree is not observed, the dynamic program for our blocked sampler can be easily used for unsupervised inference by omitting the tree matching constraints.

References

Phil Blunsom, Trevor Cohn, Chris Dyer, and Miles Osborne. 2009. A Gibbs sampler for phrasal synchronous grammar induction. In *Proceedings of the Joint Conference of the 47th Annual Meeting of the ACL and the 4th International Joint Conference on Natural Language Processing of the AFNLP (ACL-IJCNLP)*, pages 782–790, Suntec, Singapore, August.

Rens Bod, Remko Scha, and Khalil Sima'an, editors. 2003. *Data-oriented parsing*. Center for the Study of Language and Information - Studies in Computational Linguistics. University of Chicago Press.

Trevor Cohn and Phil Blunsom. 2009. A Bayesian model of syntax-directed tree to string grammar induction. In *Proceedings of the 2009 Conference on Empirical Methods in Natural Language Processing (EMNLP)*, pages 352–361, Singapore, August.

Trevor Cohn, Sharon Goldwater, and Phil Blunsom. 2009. Inducing compact but accurate tree-substitution grammars. In *Proceedings of Human Language Technologies: The 2009 Annual Conference of the North American Chapter of the Association for Computational Linguistics (HLT-NAACL)*, pages 548–556, Boulder, Colorado, June.

John DeNero, Alexandre Bouchard-Côté, and Dan Klein. 2008. Sampling alignment structure under a Bayesian translation model. In *Proceedings of the 2008 Conference on Empirical Methods in Natural Language Processing*, pages 314–323, Honolulu, Hawaii, October.

Stuart Geman and Donald Geman. 1984. Stochastic relaxation, Gibbs distributions and the Bayesian restoration of images. *IEEE Transactions on Pattern Analysis and Machine Intelligence*, 6:721–741.

Sharon Goldwater, Thomas L. Griffiths, and Mark Johnson. 2006. Contextual dependencies in unsupervised word segmentation. In *Proceedings of the 21st International Conference on Computational Linguistics and 44th Annual Meeting of the Association for Computational Linguistics*, pages 673–680, Sydney, Australia, July.

Joshua Goodman. 2003. Efficient parsing of DOP with PCFG-reductions. In Bod et al. (Bod et al., 2003), chapter 8.

Sonia Jain and Radford M. Neal. 2000. A split-merge Markov chain Monte Carlo procedure for the Dirichlet process mixture model. *Journal of Computational and Graphical Statistics*, 13:158–182.

Mark Johnson and Sharon Goldwater. 2009. Improving nonparameteric bayesian inference: experiments on unsupervised word segmentation with adaptor grammars. In *Proceedings of Human Language Technologies: The 2009 Annual Conference of the North American Chapter of the Association for Computational Linguistics*, pages 317–325, Boulder, Colorado, June.

Mark Johnson, Thomas Griffiths, and Sharon Goldwater. 2007. Bayesian inference for PCFGs via Markov chain Monte Carlo. In *Proceedings of Human Language Technologies 2007: The Conference of the North American Chapter of the Association for Computational Linguistics*, pages 139–146, Rochester, NY, April.

Karim Lari and Steve J. Young. 1990. The estimation of stochastic context-free grammars using the inside-outside algorithm. *Computer Speech and Language*, 4:35–56.

Khalil Sima'an and Luciano Buratto. 2003. Backoff parameter estimation for the dop model. In Nada Lavrac, Dragan Gamberger, Ljupco Todorovski, and Hendrik Blockeel, editors, *ECML*, volume 2837 of *Lecture Notes in Computer Science*, pages 373–384. Springer.

Martin J Wainwright and Michael I Jordan. 2008. *Graphical Models, Exponential Families, and Variational Inference*. Now Publishers Inc., Hanover, MA, USA.

Online Generation of Locality Sensitive Hash Signatures

Benjamin Van Durme
HLTCOE
Johns Hopkins University
Baltimore, MD 21211 USA

Ashwin Lall
College of Computing
Georgia Institute of Technology
Atlanta, GA 30332 USA

Abstract

Motivated by the recent interest in streaming algorithms for processing large text collections, we revisit the work of Ravichandran et al. (2005) on using the Locality Sensitive Hash (LSH) method of Charikar (2002) to enable fast, approximate comparisons of vector cosine similarity. For the common case of feature updates being additive over a data stream, we show that LSH signatures can be maintained *online*, without additional approximation error, and with lower memory requirements than when using the standard *offline* technique.

1 Introduction

There has been a surge of interest in adapting results from the streaming algorithms community to problems in processing large text collections. The term *streaming* refers to a model where data is made available sequentially, and it is assumed that resource limitations preclude storing the entirety of the data for offline (batch) processing. Statistics of interest are approximated via online, randomized algorithms. Examples of text applications include: collecting approximate counts (Talbot, 2009; Van Durme and Lall, 2009a), finding top-n elements (Goyal et al., 2009), estimating term co-occurrence (Li et al., 2008), adaptive language modeling (Levenberg and Osborne, 2009), and building top-k ranklists based on pointwise mutual information (Van Durme and Lall, 2009b).

Here we revisit the work of Ravichandran et al. (2005) on building word similarity measures from large text collections by using the Locality Sensitive Hash (LSH) method of Charikar (2002). For the common case of feature updates being additive over a data stream (such as when tracking lexical co-occurrence), we show that LSH signatures can be maintained online, without additional approximation error, and with lower memory requirements than when using the standard offline technique.

We envision this method being used in conjunction with dynamic clustering algorithms, for a variety of applications. For example, Petrovic et al. (2010) made use of LSH signatures generated over individual *tweets*, for the purpose of *first story detection*. Streaming LSH should allow for the clustering of Twitter *authors*, based on the tweets they generate, with signatures continually updated over the Twitter stream.

2 Locality Sensitive Hashing

We are concerned with computing the *cosine similarity* of feature vectors, defined for a pair of vectors $\vec{u}$ and $\vec{v}$ as the dot product normalized by their lengths:

$$\text{cosine}-\text{similarity}(\vec{u},\vec{v}) = \frac{\vec{u}\cdot\vec{v}}{|\vec{u}||\vec{v}|}.$$

This similarity is the cosine of the angle between these high-dimensional vectors and attains a value of one (i.e., $\cos(0)$) when the vectors are parallel and zero (i.e., $\cos(\pi/2)$) when orthogonal.

Building on the seminal work of Indyk and Motwani (1998) on *locality sensitive hashing* (LSH), Charikar (2002) presented an LSH that maps high-dimensional vectors to a much smaller dimensional space while still preserving (cosine) similarity between vectors in the original space. The LSH algorithm computes a succinct signature of the feature set of the words in a corpus by computing d independent dot products of each feature vector $\vec{v}$ with a random unit vector $\vec{r}$, i.e., $\sum_i v_i r_i$, and retaining the sign of the d resulting products. Each entry of $\vec{r}$ is drawn from the distribution $N(0,1)$, the normal distribution with zero mean and unit variance. Charikar's algorithm makes use of the fact (proved by Goemans and Williamson

Proceedings of the ACL 2010 Conference Short Papers, pages 231–235,
Uppsala, Sweden, 11-16 July 2010.

(1995) for an unrelated application) that the angle between any two vectors summarized in this fashion is proportional to the expected Hamming distance of their signature vectors. Hence, we can retain length d bit-signatures in the place of high dimensional feature vectors, while preserving the ability to (quickly) approximate cosine similarity in the original space.

Ravichandran et al. (2005) made use of this algorithm to reduce the computation in searching for similar nouns by first computing signatures for each noun and then computing similarity over the signatures rather than the original feature space.

3 Streaming Algorithm

In this work, we focus on features that can be maintained additively, such as raw frequencies.[1] Our streaming algorithm for this problem makes use of the simple fact that the dot product of the feature vector with random vectors is a linear operation. This permits us to replace the $v_i \cdot r_i$ operation by v_i individual additions of r_i, once for each time the feature is encountered in the stream (where v_i is the frequency of a feature and r_i is the randomly chosen Gaussian-distributed value associated with this feature). The result of the final computation is identical to the dot products computed by the algorithm of Charikar (2002), but the processing can now be done online. A similar technique, for stable random projections, was independently discussed by Li et al. (2008).

Since each feature may appear multiple times in the stream, we need a consistent way to retrieve the random values drawn from $N(0,1)$ associated with it. To avoid the expense of computing and storing these values explicitly, as is the norm, we propose the use of a precomputed pool of random values drawn from this distribution that we can then hash into. Hashing into a fixed pool ensures that the same feature will consistently be associated with the same value drawn from $N(0,1)$. This introduces some weak dependence in the random vectors, but we will give some analysis showing that this should have very limited impact on the cosine similarity computation, which we further support with experimental evidence (see Table 3).

Our algorithm traverses a stream of words and

Algorithm 1 STREAMING LSH ALGORITHM

Parameters:
m : size of pool
d : number of bits (size of resultant signature)
s : a random seed
$h_1, ..., h_d$: hash functions mapping $\langle s, f_i \rangle$ to $\{0, \ldots, m-1\}$

INITIALIZATION:
Initialize floating point array $P[0, \ldots, m-1]$
Initialize H, a hashtable mapping words to floating point arrays of size d
for $i := 0 \ldots m-1$ **do**
  $P[i]$:= random sample from $N(0,1)$, using s as seed

ONLINE:
for each word w in the stream **do**
  for each feature f_i associated with w **do**
    for $j := 1 \ldots d$ **do**
      $H[w][j] := H[w][j] + P[h_j(s, f_i)]$

SIGNATURECOMPUTATION:
for each $w \in H$ **do**
  for $i := 1 \ldots d$ **do**
    if $H[w][i] > 0$ **then**
      $S[w][i] := 1$
    else
      $S[w][i] := 0$

maintains some state for each possible word that it encounters (cf. Algorithm 1). In particular, the state maintained for each word is a vector of floating point numbers of length d. Each element of the vector holds the (partial) dot product of the feature vector of the word with a random unit vector. Updating the state for a feature seen in the stream for a given word simply involves incrementing each position in the word's vector by the random value associated with the feature, accessed by hash functions h_1 through h_d. At any point in the stream, the vector for each word can be processed (in time $O(d)$) to create a signature computed by checking the sign of each component of its vector.

3.1 Analysis

The update cost of the streaming algorithm, per word in the stream, is $O(df)$, where d is the target signature size and f is the number of features associated with each word in the stream.[2] This results in an overall cost of $O(ndf)$ for the streaming algorithm, where n is the length of the stream. The memory footprint of our algorithm is $O(n_0 d + m)$, where n_0 is the number of distinct words in the stream and m is the size of the pool of normally distributed values. In comparison, the original LSH algorithm computes signatures at a cost of $O(nf + n_0 dF)$ updates and $O(n_0 F + dF + n_0 d)$ memory, where F is the (large) number of unique

[1] Note that Ravichandran et al. (2005) used pointwise mutual information features, which are not additive since they require a global statistic to compute.

[2] For the bigram features used in § 4, $f = 2$.

features. Our algorithm is superior in terms of memory (because of the pooling trick), and has the benefit of supporting similarity queries online.

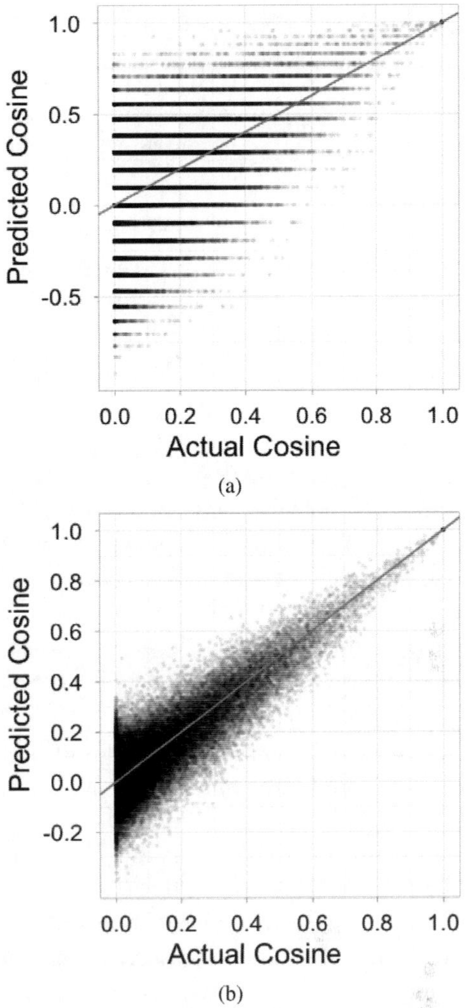

Figure 1: Predicted versus actual cosine values for 50,000 pairs, using LSH signatures generated online, with $d = 32$ in Fig. 1(a) and $d = 256$ in Fig. 1(b).

3.2 Pooling Normally-distributed Values

We now discuss why it is possible to use a fixed pool of random values instead of generating unique ones for each feature. Let g be the c.d.f. of the distribution $N(0, 1)$. It is easy to see that picking $x \in (0, 1)$ uniformly results in $g^{-1}(x)$ being chosen with distribution $N(0, 1)$. Now, if we select for our pool the values

$$g^{-1}(1/m), g^{-1}(2/m), \ldots, g^{-1}(1 - 1/m),$$

for some sufficiently large m, then this is identical to sampling from $N(0, 1)$ with the caveat that the accuracy of the sample is limited. More precisely, the deviation from sampling from this pool is off from the actual value by at most

$$\max_{i=1,\ldots,m-2} \{g^{-1}((i+1)/m) - g^{-1}(i/m)\}.$$

By choosing m to be sufficiently large, we can bound the error of the approximate sample from a true sample (i.e., the loss in precision expressed above) to be a small fraction (e.g., 1%) of the actual value. This would result in the same relative error in the computation of the dot product (i.e., 1%), which would almost never affect the sign of the final value. Hence, pooling as above should give results almost identical to the case where all the random values were chosen independently. Finally, we make the observation that, for large m, randomly choosing m values from $N(0, 1)$ results in a set of values that are distributed very similarly to the pool described above. An interesting avenue for future work is making this analysis more mathematically precise.

3.3 Extensions

Decay The algorithm can be extended to support *temporal decay* in the stream, where recent observations are given higher relative weight, by multiplying the current sums by a decay value (e.g., 0.9) on a regular interval (e.g., once an hour, once a day, once a week, etc.).

Distributed The algorithm can be easily distributed across multiple machines in order to process different parts of a stream, or multiple different streams, in parallel, such as in the context of the MapReduce framework (Dean and Ghemawat, 2004). The underlying operation is a linear operator that is easily composed (i.e., via addition), and the randomness between machines can be tied based on a shared seed s. At any point in processing the stream(s), current results can be aggregated by summing the d-dimensional vectors for each word, from each machine.

4 Experiments

Similar to the experiments of Ravichandran et al. (2005), we evaluated the fidelity of signature generation in the context of calculating distributional similarity between words across a large text collection: in our case, articles taken from the NYTimes portion of the Gigaword corpus (Graff, 2003). The collection was processed as a stream, sentence by sentence, using bigram fea-

d	16	32	64	128	256
SLSH	0.2885	0.2112	0.1486	0.1081	0.0769
LSH	0.2892	0.2095	0.1506	0.1083	0.0755

Table 1: Mean absolute error when using signatures generated online (StreamingLSH), compared to offline (LSH).

tures. This gave a stream of 773,185,086 tokens, with 1,138,467 unique types. Given the number of types, this led to a (sparse) feature space with dimension on the order of 2.5 million.

After compiling signatures, fifty-thousand $\langle x, y \rangle$ pairs of types were randomly sampled by selecting x and y each independently, with replacement, from those types with at least 10 tokens in the stream (where 310,327 types satisfied this constraint). The true cosine values between each such x and y was computed based on offline calculation, and compared to the cosine similarity predicted by the Hamming distance between the signatures for x and y. Unless otherwise specified, the random pool size was fixed at $m = 10,000$.

Figure 1 visually reaffirms the trade-off in LSH between the number of bits and the accuracy of cosine prediction across the range of cosine values. As the underlying vectors are strictly positive, the true cosine is restricted to $[0, 1]$. Figure 2 shows the absolute error between truth and prediction for a similar sample, measured using signatures of a variety of bit lengths. Here we see horizontal bands arising from truly orthogonal vectors leading to step-wise absolute error values tracked to Hamming distance.

Table 1 compares the online and batch LSH algorithms, giving the mean absolute error between predicted and actual cosine values, computed for the fifty-thousand element sample, using signatures of various lengths. These results confirm that we achieve the same level of accuracy with online updates as compared to the standard method.

Figure 3 shows how a pool size as low as $m = 100$ gives reasonable variation in random values, and that $m = 10,000$ is sufficient. When using a standard 32 bit floating point representation, this is just 40 KBytes of memory, as compared to, e.g., the 2.5 GBytes required to store 256 random vectors each containing 2.5 million elements.

Table 2 is based on taking an example for each of three part-of-speech categories, and reporting the resultant top-5 words as according to approximated cosine similarity. Depending on the intended application, these results indicate a range

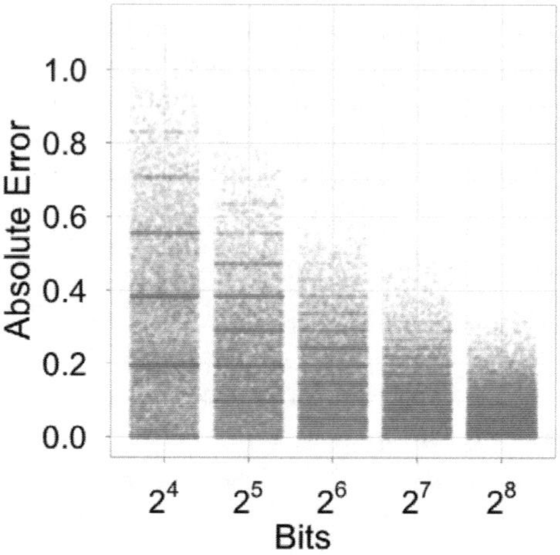

Figure 2: Absolute error between predicted and true cosine for a sample of pairs, when using signatures of length $\log_2(d) \in \{4, 5, 6, 7, 8\}$, drawn with added *jitter* to avoid overplotting.

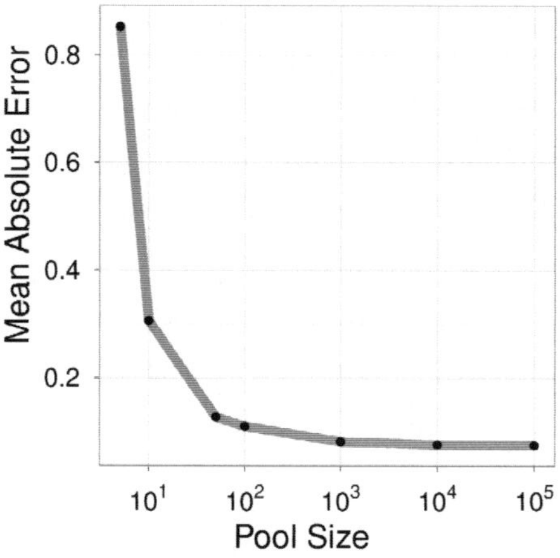

Figure 3: Error versus pool size, when using $d = 256$.

of potentially sufficient signature lengths.

5 Conclusions

We have shown that when updates to a feature vector are additive, it is possible to convert the offline LSH signature generation method into a streaming algorithm. In addition to allowing for online querying of signatures, our approach leads to space efficiencies, as it does not require the explicit representation of either the feature vectors, nor the random matrix. Possibilities for future work include the pairing of this method with algorithms for dynamic clustering, as well as exploring algorithms for different distances (e.g., L_2) and estimators (e.g., asymmetric estimators (Dong et al., 2009)).

London
Milan$_{.97}$, **Madrid**$_{.96}$, **Stockholm**$_{.96}$, **Manila**$_{.95}$, **Moscow**$_{.95}$
ASHER$_{0}$, Champaign$_{0}$, MANS$_{0}$, NOBLE$_{0}$, come$_{0}$
Prague$_{1}$, Vienna$_{1}$, suburban$_{1}$, synchronism$_{1}$, Copenhagen$_{2}$
Frankfurt$_{4}$, Prague$_{4}$, Taszar$_{5}$, Brussels$_{6}$, Copenhagen$_{6}$
Prague$_{12}$, Stockholm$_{12}$, Frankfurt$_{14}$, Madrid$_{14}$, Manila$_{14}$
Stockholm$_{20}$, Milan$_{22}$, Madrid$_{24}$, Taipei$_{24}$, Frankfurt$_{25}$
in
during$_{.99}$, **on**$_{.98}$, **beneath**$_{.98}$, **from**$_{.98}$, **onto**$_{.97}$
Across$_{0}$, Addressing$_{0}$, Addy$_{0}$, Against$_{0}$, Allmon$_{0}$
aboard$_{0}$, mishandled$_{0}$, overlooking$_{0}$, Addressing$_{1}$, Rejecting$_{1}$
Rejecting$_{2}$, beneath$_{2}$, during$_{2}$, from$_{3}$, hamstringing$_{3}$
during$_{4}$, beneath$_{5}$, of$_{6}$, on$_{7}$, overlooking$_{7}$
during$_{10}$, on$_{13}$, beneath$_{15}$, of$_{17}$, overlooking$_{17}$
sold
deployed$_{.84}$, **presented**$_{.83}$, **sacrificed**$_{.82}$, **held**$_{.82}$, **installed**$_{.82}$
Bustin$_{0}$, Diors$_{0}$, Draining$_{0}$, Kosses$_{0}$, UNA$_{0}$
delivered$_{2}$, held$_{2}$, marks$_{2}$, seared$_{2}$, Ranked$_{3}$
delivered$_{5}$, rendered$_{5}$, presented$_{6}$, displayed$_{7}$, exhibited$_{7}$
held$_{18}$, rendered$_{18}$, presented$_{19}$, deployed$_{20}$, displayed$_{20}$
presented$_{41}$, rendered$_{42}$, held$_{47}$, leased$_{47}$, reopened$_{47}$

Table 2: Top-5 items based on true cosine (bold), then using minimal Hamming distance, given in top-down order when using signatures of length $\log_2(d) \in \{4, 5, 6, 7, 8\}$. Ties broken lexicographically. Values given as subscripts.

Acknowledgments

Thanks to Deepak Ravichandran, Miles Osborne, Sasa Petrovic, Ken Church, Glen Coppersmith, and the anonymous reviewers for their feedback. This work began while the first author was at the University of Rochester, funded by NSF grant IIS-1016735. The second author was supported in part by NSF grant CNS-0905169, funded under the American Recovery and Reinvestment Act of 2009.

References

Moses Charikar. 2002. Similarity estimation techniques from rounding algorithms. In *Proceedings of STOC*.

Jeffrey Dean and Sanjay Ghemawat. 2004. MapReduce: Simplified Data Processing on Large Clusters. In *Proceedings of OSDI*.

Wei Dong, Moses Charikar, and Kai Li. 2009. Asymmetric distance estimation with sketches for similarity search in high-dimensional spaces. In *Proceedings of SIGIR*.

Michel X. Goemans and David P. Williamson. 1995. Improved approximation algorithms for maximum cut and satisfiability problems using semidefinite programming. *JACM*, 42:1115–1145.

Amit Goyal, Hal Daumé III, and Suresh Venkatasubramanian. 2009. Streaming for large scale NLP: Language Modeling. In *Proceedings of NAACL*.

David Graff. 2003. English Gigaword. Linguistic Data Consortium, Philadelphia.

Piotr Indyk and Rajeev Motwani. 1998. Approximate nearest neighbors: towards removing the curse of dimensionality. In *Proceedings of STOC*.

Abby Levenberg and Miles Osborne. 2009. Stream-based Randomised Language Models for SMT. In *Proceedings of EMNLP*.

Ping Li, Kenneth W. Church, and Trevor J. Hastie. 2008. One Sketch For All: Theory and Application of Conditional Random Sampling. In *Advances in Neural Information Processing Systems 21*.

Sasa Petrovic, Miles Osborne, and Victor Lavrenko. 2010. Streaming First Story Detection with application to Twitter. In *Proceedings of NAACL*.

Deepak Ravichandran, Patrick Pantel, and Eduard Hovy. 2005. Randomized Algorithms and NLP: Using Locality Sensitive Hash Functions for High Speed Noun Clustering. In *Proceedings of ACL*.

David Talbot. 2009. Succinct approximate counting of skewed data. In *Proceedings of IJCAI*.

Benjamin Van Durme and Ashwin Lall. 2009a. Probabilistic Counting with Randomized Storage. In *Proceedings of IJCAI*.

Benjamin Van Durme and Ashwin Lall. 2009b. Streaming Pointwise Mutual Information. In *Advances in Neural Information Processing Systems 22*.

Optimizing Question Answering Accuracy by Maximizing Log-Likelihood

Matthias H. Heie, Edward W. D. Whittaker and Sadaoki Furui
Department of Computer Science
Tokyo Institute of Technology
Tokyo 152-8552, Japan
{heie,edw,furui}@furui.cs.titech.ac.jp

Abstract

In this paper we demonstrate that there is a strong correlation between the Question Answering (QA) accuracy and the log-likelihood of the answer typing component of our statistical QA model. We exploit this observation in a clustering algorithm which optimizes QA accuracy by maximizing the log-likelihood of a set of question-and-answer pairs. Experimental results show that we achieve better QA accuracy using the resulting clusters than by using manually derived clusters.

1 Introduction

Question Answering (QA) distinguishes itself from other information retrieval tasks in that the system tries to return accurate answers to queries posed in natural language. Factoid QA limits itself to questions that can usually be answered with a few words. Typically factoid QA systems employ some form of question type analysis, so that a question such as *What is the capital of Japan?* will be answered with a geographical term. While many QA systems use hand-crafted rules for this task, such an approach is time-consuming and doesn't generalize well to other languages. Machine learning methods have been proposed, such as question classification using support vector machines (Zhang and Lee, 2003) and language modeling (Merkel and Klakow, 2007). In these approaches, question categories are predefined and a classifier is trained on manually labeled data. This is an example of supervised learning. In this paper we present an unsupervised method, where we attempt to cluster question-and-answer (q-a) pairs without any predefined question categories, hence no manually class-labeled questions are used.

We use a statistical QA framework, described in Section 2, where the system is trained with clusters of q-a pairs. This framework was used in several TREC evaluations where it placed in the top 10 of participating systems (Whittaker et al., 2006). In Section 3 we show that answer accuracy is strongly correlated with the log-likelihood of the q-a pairs computed by this statistical model. In Section 4 we propose an algorithm to cluster q-a pairs by maximizing the log-likelihood of a disjoint set of q-a pairs. In Section 5 we evaluate the QA accuracy by training the QA system with the resulting clusters.

2 QA system

In our QA framework we choose to model only the probability of an answer A given a question Q, and assume that the answer A depends on two sets of features: $W = W(Q)$ and $X = X(Q)$:

$$P(A|Q) = P(A|W, X), \qquad (1)$$

where W represents a set of $|W|$ features describing the question-type part of Q such as *who*, *when*, *where*, *which*, etc., and X is a set of features which describes the "information-bearing" part of Q, i.e. what the question is actually about and what it refers to. For example, in the questions *Where is Mount Fuji?* and *How high is Mount Fuji?*, the question type features W differ, while the information-bearing features X are identical. Finding the best answer $\hat{A}$ involves a search over all A for the one which maximizes the probability of the above model, i.e.:

$$\hat{A} = \arg\max_A P(A|W, X). \qquad (2)$$

Given the correct probability distribution, this will give us the optimal answer in a maximum likelihood sense. Using Bayes' rule, assuming uniform $P(A)$ and that W and X are independent of each other given A, in addition to ignoring $P(W, X)$ since it is independent of A, enables us to rewrite Eq. (2) as

Proceedings of the ACL 2010 Conference Short Papers, pages 236–240,
Uppsala, Sweden, 11-16 July 2010.

$$\hat{A} = \arg\max_{A} \underbrace{P(A \mid X)}_{\substack{retrieval\\ model}} \cdot \underbrace{P(W \mid A)}_{\substack{filter\\ model}}. \quad (3)$$

2.1 Retrieval Model

The retrieval model $P(A|X)$ is essentially a language model which models the probability of an answer sequence A given a set of information-bearing features $X = \{x_1, \ldots, x_{|X|}\}$. This set is constructed by extracting single-word features from Q that are not present in a stop-list of high-frequency words. The implementation of the retrieval model used for the experiments described in this paper, models the proximity of A to features in X. It is not examined further here; see (Whittaker et al., 2005) for more details.

2.2 Filter Model

The question-type feature set $W = \{w_1, \ldots, w_{|W|}\}$ is constructed by extracting n-tuples ($n = 1, 2, \ldots$) such as *where*, *in what* and *when were* from the input question Q. We limit ourselves to extracting single-word features. The 2522 most frequent words in a collection of example questions are considered in-vocabulary words; all other words are out-of-vocabulary words, and substituted with $\langle UNK \rangle$.

Modeling the complex relationship between W and A directly is non-trivial. We therefore introduce an intermediate variable $C_E = \{c_1, \ldots, c_{|C_E|}\}$, representing a set of classes of example q-a pairs. In order to construct these classes, given a set $E = \{t_1, \ldots, t_{|E|}\}$ of example q-a pairs, we define a mapping function $f : E \mapsto C_E$ which maps each example q-a pair t_j for $j = 1 \ldots |E|$ into a particular class $f(t_j) = c_e$. Thus each class c_e may be defined as the union of all component q-a features from each t_j satisfying $f(t_j) = c_e$. Hence each class c_e constitutes a cluster of q-a pairs. Finally, to facilitate modeling we say that W is conditionally independent of A given c_e so that,

$$P(W \mid A) = \sum_{e=1}^{|C_E|} P(W \mid c_W^e) \cdot P(c_A^e \mid A), \quad (4)$$

where c_W^e and c_A^e refer to the subsets of question-type features and example answers for the class c_e, respectively.

$P(W \mid c_W^e)$ is implemented as trigram language models with backoff smoothing using absolute discounting (Huang et al., 2001).

Due to data sparsity, our set of example q-a pairs cannot be expected to cover all the possible answers to questions that may ever be asked. We therefore employ answer class modeling rather than answer word modeling by expanding Eq. (4) as follows:

$$P(W \mid A) = \sum_{e=1}^{|C_E|} P(W \mid c_W^e) \cdot \sum_{a=1}^{|K_A|} P(c_A^e \mid k_a) P(k_a \mid A), \quad (5)$$

where k_a is a concrete class in the set of $|K_A|$ answer classes K_A. These classes are generated using the Kneser-Ney clustering algorithm, commonly used for generating class definitions for class language models (Kneser and Ney, 1993).

In this paper we restrict ourselves to single-word answers; see (Whittaker et al., 2005) for the modeling of multi-word answers. We estimate $P(c_A^e \mid k_A)$ as

$$P(c_A^e \mid k_A) = \frac{f(k_A, c_A^e)}{\sum_{g=1}^{|C_E|} f(k_A, c_A^g)}, \quad (6)$$

where

$$f(k_A, c_A^e) = \frac{\sum_{\forall i: i \in c_A^e} \delta(i \in k_A)}{|c_A^e|}, \quad (7)$$

and $\delta(\cdot)$ is a discrete indicator function which equals 1 if its argument evaluates true and 0 if false.

$P(k_a \mid A)$ is estimated as

$$P(k_a \mid A) = \frac{1}{\sum_{\forall j: j \in K_a} \delta(A \in j)}. \quad (8)$$

3 The Relationship between Mean Reciprocal Rank and Log-Likelihood

We use Mean Reciprocal Rank (MRR) as our metric when evaluating the QA accuracy on a set of questions $G = \{g_1 \ldots g_{|G|}\}$:

$$MRR = \frac{\sum_{i=1}^{|G|} 1/R_i}{|G|}, \quad (9)$$

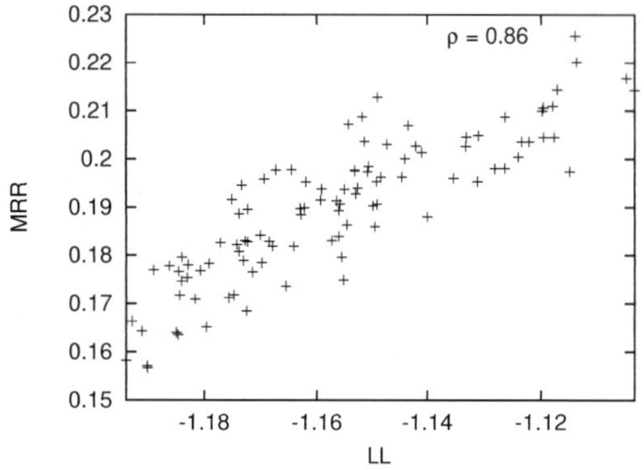

Figure 1: MRR vs. LL (average per q-a pair) for 100 random cluster configurations.

where R_i is the rank of the highest ranking correct candidate answer for g_i.

Given a set $D = (d_1...d_{|D|})$ of q-a pairs disjoint from the q-a pairs in C_E, we can, using Eq. (5), calculate the log-likelihood as

$$\begin{aligned} LL &= \sum_{d=1}^{|D|} \log P(W_d|A_d) \\ &= \sum_{d=1}^{|D|} \log \sum_{e=1}^{|C_E|} P(W_d \mid c_W^e) \cdot \\ & \quad \sum_{a=1}^{|K_A|} P(c_A^e \mid k_a) P(k_a \mid A_d). \end{aligned} \tag{10}$$

To examine the relationship between MRR and LL, we randomly generate configurations C_E, with a fixed cluster size of 4, and plot the resulting MRR and LL, computed on the same data set D, as data points in a scatter plot, as seen in Figure 1. We find that LL and MRR are strongly correlated, with a correlation coefficient $\rho = 0.86$.

This observation indicates that we should be able to improve the answer accuracy of the QA system by optimizing the LL of the filter model in isolation, similar to how, in automatic speech recognition, the LL of the language model can be optimized in isolation to improve the speech recognition accuracy (Huang et al., 2001).

4 Clustering algorithm

Using the observation that LL is correlated with MRR on the same data set, we expect that optimizing LL on a development set (LL_{dev}) will also improve MRR on an evaluation set (MRR_{eval}). Hence we propose the following greedy algorithm to maximize LL_{dev}:

init: $c_1 \in C_E$ contains all training pairs $|E|$
while $improvement > threshold$ **do**
  $best\_LL_{dev} \leftarrow -\infty$
  for all $j = 1...|E|$ **do**
    $original\_cluster = f(t_j)$
    Take t_j out of $f(t_j)$
    for $e = -1, 1...|C_E|, |C_E| + 1$ **do**
      Put t_j in c_e
      Calculate LL_{dev}
      if $LL_{dev} > best\_LL_{dev}$ **then**
        $best\_LL_{dev} \leftarrow LL_{dev}$
        $best\_cluster \leftarrow e$
        $best\_pair \leftarrow j$
      end if
      Take t_j out of c_e
    end for
    Put t_j back in $original\_cluster$
  end for
  Take t_{best_pair} out of $f(t_{best\_pair})$
  Put t_{best_pair} into $c_{best\_cluster}$
end while

In this algorithm, c_{-1} indicates the set of training pairs outside the cluster configuration, thus every training pair will not necessarily be included in the final configuration. $c_{|C|+1}$ refers to a new, empty cluster, hence this algorithm automatically finds the optimal number of clusters as well as the optimal configuration of them.

5 Experiments

5.1 Experimental Setup

For our data sets, we restrict ourselves to questions that start with *who*, *when* or *where*. Furthermore, we only use q-a pairs which can be answered with a single word. As training data we use questions and answers from the Knowledge-Master collection[1]. Development/evaluation questions are the questions from TREC QA evaluations from TREC 2002 to TREC 2006, the answers to which are to be retrieved from the AQUAINT corpus. In total we have 2016 q-a pairs for training and 568 questions for development/evaluation. We are able to retrieve the correct answer for 317 of the development/evaluation questions, thus the theoretical upper bound for our experiments is an answer accuracy of $MRR = 0.558$.

Accuracy is evaluated using 5-fold (rotating) cross-validation, where in each fold the TREC QA data is partitioned into a development set of

[1] http://www.greatauk.com/

Configuration	LL_{eval}	MRR_{eval}	#clusters
manual	-1.18	0.262	3
all-in-one	-1.32	0.183	1
one-in-each	-0.87	0.263	2016
automatic	-0.24	0.281	4

Table 1: LL_{eval} (average per q-a pair) and MRR_{eval} (over all held-out TREC years), and number of clusters (median of the cross-evaluation folds) for the various configurations.

4 years' data and an evaluation set of one year's data. For each TREC question the top 50 documents from the AQUAINT corpus are retrieved using Lucene[2]. We use the QA system described in Section 2 for QA evaluation. Our evaluation metric is MRR_{eval}, and LL_{dev} is our optimization criterion, as motivated in Section 3.

Our baseline system uses manual clusters. These clusters are obtained by putting all *who* q-a pairs in one cluster, all *when* pairs in a second and all *where* pairs in a third. We compare this baseline with using clusters resulting from the algorithm described in Section 4. We run this algorithm until there are no further improvements in LL_{dev}. Two other cluster configurations are also investigated: all q-a pairs in one cluster (all-in-one), and each q-a pair in its own cluster (one-in-each). The all-in-one configuration is equivalent to not using the filter model, i.e. answer candidates are ranked solely by the retrieval model. The one-in-each configuration was shown to perform well in the TREC 2006 QA evaluation (Whittaker et al., 2006), where it ranked 9th among 27 participants on the factoid QA task.

5.2 Results

In Table 1, we see that the manual clusters (baseline) achieves an MRR_{eval} of 0.262, while the clusters resulting from the clustering algorithm give an MRR_{eval} of 0.281, which is a relative improvement of 7%. This improvement is statistically significant at the 0.01 level using the Wilcoxon signed-rank test. The one-in-each cluster configuration achieves an MRR_{eval} of 0.263, which is not a statistically significant improvement over the baseline. The all-in-one cluster configuration (i.e. no filter model) has the lowest accuracy, with an MRR_{eval} of 0.183.

[2] http://lucene.apache.org/

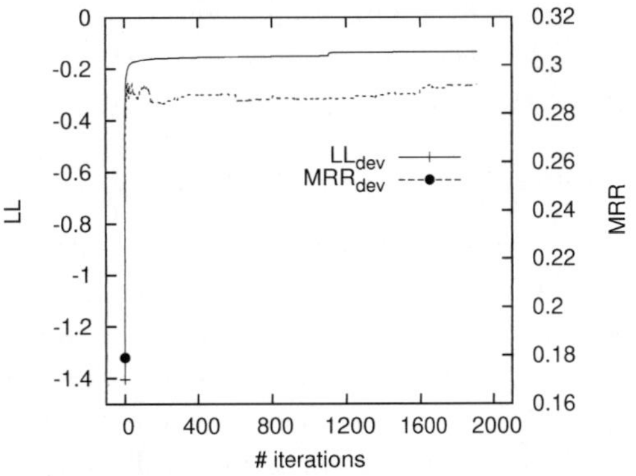

(a) Development set, 4 year's TREC.

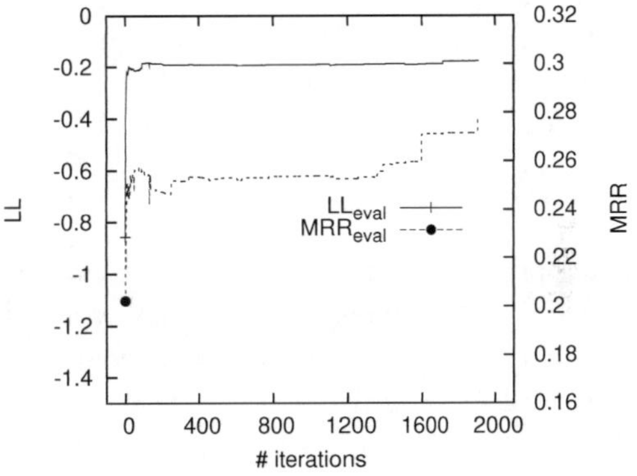

(b) Evaluation set, 1 year's TREC.

Figure 2: MRR and LL (average per q-a pair) vs. number of algorithm iterations for one cross-validation fold.

6 Discussion

Manual inspection of the automatically derived clusters showed that the algorithm had constructed configurations where typically *who*, *when* and *where* q-a pairs were put in separate clusters, as in the manual configuration. However, in some cases both *who* and *where* q-a pairs occurred in the same cluster, so as to better answer questions like *Who won the World Cup?*, where the answer could be a country name.

As can be seen from Table 1, there are only 4 clusters in the automatic configuration, compared to 2016 in the one-in-each configuration. Since the computational complexity of the filter model described in Section 2.2 is linear in the number of clusters, a beneficial side effect of our clustering procedure is a significant reduction in the computational requirement of the filter model.

In Figure 2 we plot LL and MRR for one of the cross-validation folds over multiple iterations (the *while* loop) of the clustering algorithm in Section 4. It can clearly be seen that the optimization of LL_{dev} leads to improvement in MRR_{eval}, and that LL_{eval} is also well correlated with MRR_{eval}.

7 Conclusions and Future Work

In this paper we have shown that the log-likelihood of our statistical model is strongly correlated with answer accuracy. Using this information, we have clustered training q-a pairs by maximizing log-likelihood on a disjoint development set of q-a pairs. The experiments show that with these clusters we achieve better QA accuracy than using manually clustered training q-a pairs.

In future work we will extend the types of questions that we consider, and also allow for multi-word answers.

Acknowledgements

The authors wish to thank Dietrich Klakow for his discussion at the concept stage of this work. The anonymous reviewers are also thanked for their constructive feedback.

References

[Huang et al.2001] Xuedong Huang, Alex Acero and Hsiao-Wuen Hon. 2001. *Spoken Language Processing*. Prentice-Hall, Upper Saddle River, NJ, USA.

[Kneser and Ney1993] Reinhard Kneser and Hermann Ney. 1993. Improved Clustering Techniques for Class-based Statistical Language Modelling. *Proceedings of the European Conference on Speech Communication and Technology (EUROSPEECH)*.

[Merkel and Klakow2007] Andreas Merkel and Dietrich Klakow. 2007. Language Model Based Query Classification. *Proceedings of the European Conference on Information Retrieval (ECIR)*.

[Whittaker et al.2005] Edward Whittaker, Sadaoki Furui and Dietrich Klakow. 2005. A Statistical Classification Approach to Question Answering using Web Data. *Proceedings of the International Conference on Cyberworlds*.

[Whittaker et al.2006] Edward Whittaker, Josef Novak, Pierre Chatain and Sadaoki Furui. 2006. TREC 2006 Question Answering Experiments at Tokyo Institute of Technology. *Proceedings of The Fifteenth Text REtrieval Conference (TREC)*.

[Zhang and Lee2003] Dell Zhang and Wee Sun Lee. 2003. Question Classification using Support Vector Machines. *Proceedings of the Special Interest Group on Information Retrieval (SIGIR)*.

Generating Entailment Rules from FrameNet

Roni Ben Aharon
Department of Computer Science
Bar-Ilan University
Ramat Gan, Israel
r.ben.aharon@gmail.com

Idan Szpektor
Yahoo! Research
Haifa, Israel
idan@yahoo-inc.com

Ido Dagan
Department of Computer Science
Bar-Ilan University
Ramat Gan, Israel
dagan@cs.biu.ac.il

Abstract

Many NLP tasks need accurate knowledge for semantic inference. To this end, mostly WordNet is utilized. Yet WordNet is limited, especially for inference between predicates. To help filling this gap, we present an algorithm that generates inference rules between predicates from FrameNet. Our experiment shows that the novel resource is effective and complements WordNet in terms of rule coverage.

1 Introduction

Many text understanding applications, such as Question Answering (QA) and Information Extraction (IE), need to infer a target textual meaning from other texts. This need was proposed as a generic semantic inference task under the Textual Entailment (TE) paradigm (Dagan et al., 2006).

A fundamental component in semantic inference is the utilization of knowledge resources. However, a major obstacle to improving semantic inference performance is the lack of such knowledge (Bar-Haim et al., 2006; Giampiccolo et al., 2007). We address one prominent type of inference knowledge known as *entailment rules*, focusing specifically on rules between predicates, such as '*cure X* $\Rightarrow$ *X recover*'.

We aim at highly accurate rule acquisition, for which utilizing manually constructed sources seem appropriate. The most widely used manual resource is WordNet (Fellbaum, 1998). Yet it is incomplete for generating entailment rules between predicates (Section 2.1). Hence, other manual resources should also be targeted.

In this work[1], we explore how FrameNet (Baker et al., 1998) could be effectively used for generating entailment rules between predicates. FrameNet is a manually constructed database based on Frame Semantics. It models the semantic argument structure of predicates in terms of prototypical situations called *frames*.

Prior work utilized FrameNet's argument mapping capabilities but took entailment relations from other resources, namely WordNet. We propose a novel method for generating entailment rules from FrameNet by detecting the entailment relations implied in FrameNet. We utilize FrameNet's annotated sentences and relations between frames to extract both the entailment relations and their argument mappings.

Our analysis shows that the rules generated by our algorithm have a reasonable "per-rule" accuracy of about 70%[2]. We tested the generated rule-set on an entailment testbed derived from an IE benchmark and compared it both to WordNet and to state-of-the-art rule generation from FrameNet. Our experiment shows that our method outperforms prior work. In addition, our rule-set's performance is comparable to WordNet and it is complementary to WordNet when uniting the two resources. Finally, additional analysis shows that our rule-set accuracy is 90% in practical use.

2 Background

2.1 Entailment Rules and their Acquisition

To generate entailment rules, two issues should be addressed: a) identifying the lexical entailment relations between predicates, e.g. '*cure* $\Rightarrow$ *recover*'; b) mapping argument positions, e.g. '*cure X* $\Rightarrow$ *X recover*'. The main approach for generating highly accurate rule-sets is to use manually constructed resources. To this end, most systems mainly utilize WordNet (Fellbaum, 1998), being the most prominent lexical resource with broad coverage of predicates. Furthermore, some of its

[1]The detailed description of our work can be found in (Ben Aharon, 2010).

[2]The rule-set is available at: http://www.cs.biu.ac.il/~nlp/downloads

Proceedings of the ACL 2010 Conference Short Papers, pages 241–246,
Uppsala, Sweden, 11-16 July 2010. ©2010 Association for Computational Linguistics

relations capture types of entailment relations, including *synonymy*, *hypernymy*, *morphologically-derived*, *entailment* and *cause*.

Yet, WordNet is limited for entailment rule generation. First, many entailment relations, notably for the WordNet *entailment* and *cause* relation types, are missing, e.g. '*elect* ⇒ *vote*'. Furthermore, WordNet does not include argument mapping between related predicates. Thus, only *substitutable* WordNet relations (*synonymy* and *hypernymy*), for which argument positions are preserved, could be used to generate entailment rules. The other *non-substitutable* relations, e.g. *cause* ('*kill* ⇒ *die*') and *morphologically-derived* ('*meet.v* ⇔ *meeting.n*'), cannot be used.

2.2 FrameNet

FrameNet (Baker et al., 1998) is a knowledge-base of *frames*, describing prototypical situations. Frames can be related to each other by inter-frame relations, e.g. *Inheritance*, *Precedence*, *Usage* and *Perspective*.

For each frame, several semantic roles are specified, called *frame elements* (FEs), denoting the participants in the situation described. Each FE may be labeled as *core* if it is central to the frame. For example, some core FEs of the *Commerce_pay* frame are *Buyer* and *Goods*, while a non-core FE is *Place*. Each FE may also be labeled with a semantic type, e.g. *Sentient*, *Event*, and *Time*.

A frame includes a list of predicates that can evoke the described situation, called *lexical units* (LUs). LUs are mainly verbs but may also be nouns or adjectives. For example, the frame *Commerce_pay* lists the LUs *pay.v* and *payment.n*.

Finally, FrameNet contains annotated sentences that represent typical LU occurrences in texts. Each annotation refers to one LU in a specific frame and the FEs of the frame that occur in the sentence. An example sentence is "I_{Buyer} *have to* *pay* *the bills*$_{Money}$". Each sentence is accompanied by a *valence pattern*, which provides, among other info, grammatical functions of the core FEs with respect to the LU. The valence pattern of the above sentence is *[(Buyer Subj), (Money Obj)]*.

2.3 Using FrameNet for Semantic Inference

To the best of our knowledge, the only work that utilized FrameNet for entailment rule generation is LexPar (Coyne and Rambow, 2009). LexPar first identifies lexical entailment relations by going over all LU pairs which are either in the same frame or whose frames are related by one of FrameNet's inter-frame relations. Each candidate pair is considered entailing if the two LUs are either synonyms or in a direct hypernymy relation in WordNet (providing the vast majority of LexPar's relations), or if their related frames are connected via the *Perspective* relation in FrameNet.

Then, argument mappings between each entailing LU pair are extracted based on the core FEs that are shared between the two LUs. The syntactic positions of the shared FEs are taken from the valence patterns of the LUs. A LexPar rule example is presented in Figure 3 (top part).

Since most of LexPar's entailment relations are based on WordNet's relations, LexPar's rules could be viewed as an intersection of WordNet and FrameNet lexical relations, accompanied with argument mappings taken from FrameNet.

3 Rule Extraction from FrameNet

The above prior work identified lexical entailment relations mainly from WordNet, which limits the use of FrameNet in two ways. First, some relations that appear in FrameNet are missed because they do not appear in WordNet. Second, unlike FrameNet, WordNet does not include argument mappings for its relations. Thus, prior work for rule generation considered only substitutable relations from WordNet (*synonyms* and *hypernyms*), not utilizing FrameNet's capability to map arguments of non-substitutable relations.

Our goal in this paper is to generate entailment rules solely from the information within FrameNet. We present a novel algorithm for generating entailment rules from FrameNet, called *FRED* (**Fr**ameNet **E**ntailment-rule **D**erivation), which operates in three steps: a) extracting templates for each LU; b) detecting lexical entailment relations between pairs of LUs; c) generating entailment rules by mapping the arguments between two LUs in each entailing pair.

3.1 Template Extraction

Many LUs in FrameNet are accompanied by annotated sentences (Section 2.2). From each sentence of a given LU, we extract one template for each annotated FE in the sentence. Each template includes the LU, one argument corresponding to the target FE and their syntactic relation in the sentence parse-tree. We focus on extracting unary templates, as they can describe any ar-

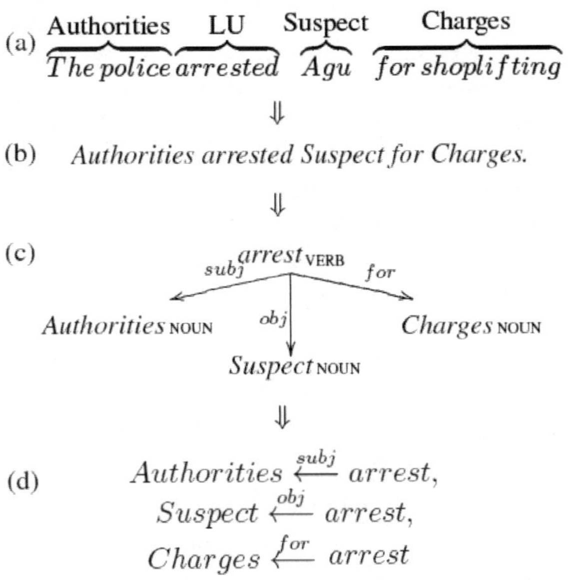

Figure 1: Template extraction for a sentence containing the LU *'arrest'*.

gument mapping by decomposing templates with several arguments into unary ones (Szpektor and Dagan, 2008). Figure 1 exemplifies this process.

As a pre-parsing step, all FE phrases in a given sentence are replaced by their related FE names, excluding syntactic information such as prepositions or possessives (step (b) in Figure 1). Then, the sentence is parsed using the Minipar dependency parser (Lin, 1998) (step (c)). Finally, a path in the parse-tree is extracted between each FE node and the node of the LU (step (d)). Each extracted path is converted into a template by replacing the FE node with an argument variable.

We simplify each extracted path by removing nodes along the path that are not part of the syntactic relation between the LU and the FE, such as conjunctions and other FE nodes. For example, *'*$Authorities \overset{subj}{\longleftarrow}$ enter $\overset{conj}{\longrightarrow}$ *arrest'* is simplified into *'*$Authorities \overset{subj}{\longleftarrow}$ *arrest'*.

Some templates originated from different annotated sentences share the same LU and syntactic structure, but differ in their FEs. Usually, one of these templates is incorrect, due to erroneous parse (e.g. *'*$Suspect \overset{obj}{\longleftarrow}$ *arrest'* is a correct template, in contrast to *'*$Charges \overset{obj}{\longleftarrow}$ *arrest'*). We thus keep only the most frequently annotated template out of the identical templates, assuming it is the correct one.

3.2 Identifying Lexical Entailment Relations

FrameNet groups LUs in frames and describes relations between frames. However, relations between LUs are not explicitly defined. We next describe how we automatically extract several types of lexical entailment relations between LUs using two approaches.

In the first approach, LUs in the same frame that are morphological derivations of each other, e.g. *'negotiation.n'* and *'negotiate.v'*, are marked as paraphrases. We take morphological derivation information from the CATVAR database (Habash and Dorr, 2003).

The second approach is based on our observation that some LUs express the prototypical situation that their frame describes, which we denote *dominant LUs*. For example, the LU *'recover'* is dominant for the *Recovery* frame. We mark LUs as dominant if they are morphologically derived from the frame's name.

Our assumption is that since dominant LUs express the frame's generic meaning, their meaning is likely to be entailed by the other LUs in this frame. Consequently, we generate such lexical rules between any dominant LU and any other LU in a given frame, e.g. '*heal* ⇒ *recover*' and '*convalescence* ⇒ *recover*' for the *Recovery* frame.

In addition, we assume that if two frames are related by some type of entailment relation, their dominant LUs are also related by the same relation. Accordingly, we extract entailment relations between dominant LUs of frames that are connected via the *Inheritance*, *Cause* and *Perspective* relations, where *Inheritance* and *Cause* generate directional entailment relations (e.g. '*choose* ⇒ *decide*' and '*cure* ⇒ *recover*', respectively) while *Perspective* generates bidirectional paraphrase relations (e.g. '*transfer* ⇔ *receive*').

Finally, we generate the transitive closure of the set of lexical relations identified by the above methods. For example, the combination of '*sell* ⇔ *buy*' and '*buy* ⇒ *get*' generates '*sell* ⇒ *get*'.

3.3 Generating Entailment Rules

The final step in the FRED algorithm generates lexical syntactic entailment rules from the extracted templates and lexical entailment relations.

For each identified lexical relation '*left* ⇒ *right*' between two LUs, the set of FEs that are shared by both LUs is collected. Then, for each shared FE, we take the list of templates that connect this FE

Lexical Relation:
cure ⇒ recovery

Templates:

$Patient \xleftarrow{obj} cure$	(cure *Patient*)
$Affliction \xleftarrow{of} cure$	(cure of *Affliction*)
$Patient \xleftarrow{gen} recovery$	(*Patient*'s recovery)
$Patient \xleftarrow{of} recovery$	(recovery of *Patient*)
$Affliction \xleftarrow{from} recovery$	(recovery from *Affliction*)

Intra-LU Entailment Rules:
$Patient \xleftarrow{gen} recovery \Longleftrightarrow Patient \xleftarrow{of} recovery$

Inter-LU Entailment Rules:
$Patient \xleftarrow{obj} cure \Longrightarrow Patient \xleftarrow{gen} recovery$
$Patient \xleftarrow{obj} cure \Longrightarrow Patient \xleftarrow{of} recovery$
$Affliction \xleftarrow{of} cure \Longrightarrow Affliction \xleftarrow{from} recovery$

Figure 2: Some entailment rules generated for the lexical relation '*cure.v ⇒ recovery.n*'.

Configuration	R (%)	P (%)	F1
No-Rules	13.8	57.7	20.9
LexPar	14.1	42.9	17.4
WordNet	18.3	32.2	17.8
FRED	17.6	55.1	24.6
FRED ∪ WordNet	21.8	33.3	20.9

Table 1: Macro average Recall (R), Precision (P) and F1 results for the tested configurations.

to each of the LUs, denoted by T^{fe}_{left} and T^{fe}_{right}. Finally, for each template pair, $l \in T^{fe}_{left}$ and $r \in T^{fe}_{right}$, the rule '$l \Rightarrow r$' is generated. In addition, we generate paraphrase rules between the various templates including the same FE and the same LU. Figure 2 illustrates this process.

To improve rule quality, we filter out rules that map FEs of adjunct-like semantic types, such as *Time* and *Location*, since different templates of such FEs may have different semantic meanings (e.g. '$Time \xleftarrow{before} arrive$' '$Time \xleftarrow{after} arrive$'). Thus, it is hard to identify those template pairs that correctly map these FEs for entailment.

We manually evaluated a random sample of 250 rules from the resulting rule-set, out of which we judged 69% as correct.

4 Application-based Evaluation

4.1 Experimental Setup

We would like to evaluate the overall utility of our resource for NLP applications, assessing the correctness of the actual rule applications performed in practice, as well as to compare its performance to related resources. To this end, we follow the experimental setup presented in (Szpektor and Dagan, 2009), which utilized the ACE 2005 event dataset[3] as a testbed for entailment rule-sets. We briefly describe this setup here.

The task is to extract argument mentions for 26 events, such as *Sue* and *Attack*, from the ACE annotated corpus, using a given tested entailment rule-set. Each event is represented by a set of unary *seed templates*, one for each event argument. Some seed templates for *Attack* are '*Attacker*$\xleftarrow{subj}$attack' and 'attack$\xrightarrow{obj}$*Target*'.

Argument mentions are found in the ACE corpus by matching either the seed templates or templates entailing them found in the tested rule-set. We manually added for each event its relevant WordNet synset-ids and FrameNet frame-ids, so only rules fitting the event target meaning will be extracted from the tested rule-sets.

4.2 Tested Configurations

We evaluated several rule-set configurations:

No-Rules The system matches only the seed templates directly, without any additional rules.

WordNet Rules are generated from WordNet 3.0, using only the *synonymy* and *hypernymy* relations (see Section 2.1). Transitive chaining of relations is allowed (Moldovan and Novischi, 2002).

LexPar Rules are generated from the publicly available LexPar database. We generated unary rules from each LexPar rule based on a manually constructed mapping from FrameNet grammatical functions to Minipar dependency relations. Figure 3 presents an example of this procedure.

FRED Rules are generated by our algorithm.

FRED ∪ WordNet The union of the rule-sets of FRED and WordNet.

4.3 Results

Each configuration was tested on each ACE event. We measured *recall*, *precision* and *F1*. Table 1 reports macro averages of the three measures over the 26 ACE events.

As expected, using *No-Rules* achieves the highest precision and the lowest recall compared to all other configurations. When adding LexPar rules,

[3] `http://projects.ldc.upenn.edu/ace/`

LexPar rule:
Lexemes: arrest $\longrightarrow$ apprehend
Valencies: [(Authorities Subj), (Suspect Obj), (Offense (for))] $\Longrightarrow$ [(Authorities Subj), (Suspect Obj), (Offense (in))]

Generated unary rules:
$X \overset{subj}{\longleftarrow}$ arrest $\Longrightarrow X \overset{subj}{\longleftarrow}$ apprehend , arrest $\overset{obj}{\longrightarrow} Y \Longrightarrow$ apprehend $\overset{obj}{\longrightarrow} Y$, arrest $\overset{for}{\longrightarrow} Z \Longrightarrow$ apprehend $\overset{in}{\longrightarrow} Z$

Figure 3: An example for generation of unary entailment rules from a LexPar rule.

only a slight increase in recall is gained. This shows that the subset of WordNet rules captured by LexPar (Section 2.3) might be too small for the ACE application setting.

When using all WordNet's substitutable relations, a substantial relative increase in recall is achieved (32%). Yet, precision decreases dramatically (relative decrease of 44%), causing an overall decrease in F1. Most errors are due to correct WordNet rules whose LHS is ambiguous. Since we do not apply a WSD module, these rules are also incorrectly applied to other senses of the LHS. While this phenomenon is common to all rule-sets, WordNet suffers from it the most since it contains many infrequent word senses.

Our main result is that using FRED's rule-set, recall increases significantly, a relative increase of 27% compared to No-Rules, while precision hardly decreases. Hence, overall F1 is the highest compared to all other configurations (a relative increase of 17% compared to No-Rules). The improvement in F1 is statistically significant compared to all other configurations, according to the two-sided Wilcoxon signed rank test at the level of 0.01 (Wilcoxon, 1945).

FRED preforms significantly better than LexPar in both recall, precision and F1 (a relative increase of 25%, 28% and 41% respectively). For example, LexPar hardly utilizes FrameNet's argument mapping capabilities since most of its rules are based on a sub-set of WordNet's substitutable relations.

FRED's precision is substantially higher than WordNet. This mostly results from the fact that FrameNet mainly contains common senses of predicates while WordNet includes many rare word senses; which, as said above, harms precision when WSD is not applied. Error analysis showed that only 7.5% of incorrect extractions are due to erronous rules in FRED, while the majority of errors are due to sense mismatch or syntactic matching errors of the seed templates ot entailing templates in texts.

FRED's Recall is somewhat lower than WordNet, since FrameNet is a much smaller resource. Yet, its rules are mostly complementary to those from WordNet. This added value is demonstrated by the 19% recall increase for the union of FRED and WordNet rule-sets compared to WordNet alone. FRED provides mainly argument mappings for non-substitutable WordNet relations, e.g. '*attack.n on X ⇒ attack.v X*', but also lexical relations that are missing from WordNet, e.g. '*ambush.v ⇒ attack.v*'.

Overall, our experiment shows that the rule-base generated by FRED seems an appropriate complementary resource to the widely used WordNet-based rules in semantic inference and expansion over predicates. This suggestion is especially appealing since our rule-set performs well even when a WSD module is not applied.

5 Conclusions

We presented FRED, a novel algorithm for generating entailment rules solely from the information contained in FrameNet. Our experiment showed that FRED's rules perform substantially better than LexPar, the only prior rule-set derived from FrameNet. In addition, FRED's rule-set largely complements the rules generated from WordNet because it contains argument mappings between non-substitutable predicates, which are missing from WordNet, as well as lexical relations that are not included in WordNet.

In future work we plan to investigate combining FrameNet and WordNet rule-sets in a transitive manner, instead of their simple union.

Acknowledgments

This work was partially supported by the Rector's research grant of Bar-Ilan University, the PASCAL-2 Network of Excellence of the European Community FP7-ICT-2007-1-216886 and the Israel Science Foundation grant 1112/08.

References

Collin Baker, Charles Fillmore, and John Lowe. 1998. The berkeley framenet project. In *Proceedings of COLING-ACL*, Montreal, Canada.

Roy Bar-Haim, Ido Dagan, Bill Dolan, Lisa Ferro, Danilo Giampiccolo, Bernardo Magnini, and Idan Szpektor. 2006. The second pascal recognising textual entailment challenge. In *Second PASCAL Challenge Workshop for Recognizing Textual Entailment*.

Roni Ben Aharon. 2010. Generating entailment rules from framenet. Master's thesis, Bar-Ilan University.

Robert Coyne and Owen Rambow. 2009. Lexpar: A freely available english paraphrase lexicon automatically extracted from framenet. In *Proceedings of the Third IEEE International Conference on Semantic Computing*.

Ido Dagan, Oren Glickman, and Bernardo Magnini. 2006. The pascal recognising textual entailment challenge. In *Lecture Notes in Computer Science*, volume 3944, pages 177–190.

Christiane Fellbaum, editor. 1998. *WordNet: An Electronic Lexical Database*. MIT Press, Cambridge, Massachusetts.

Danilo Giampiccolo, Bernardo Magnini, Ido Dagan, and Bill Dolan. 2007. The third pascal recognizing textual entailment challenge. In *Proceedings of the ACL-PASCAL Workshop on Textual Entailment and Paraphrasing*.

Nizar Habash and Bonnie Dorr. 2003. A categorial variation database for english. In *Proceedings of the North American Association for Computational Linguistics (NAACL '03)*, pages 96–102, Edmonton, Canada. Association for Computational Linguistics.

Dekang Lin. 1998. Dependency-based evaluation of minipar. In *Proceedings of the Workshop on Evaluation of Parsing Systems at LREC*.

Dan Moldovan and Adrian Novischi. 2002. Lexical chains for question answering. In *Proceedings of COLING*.

Idan Szpektor and Ido Dagan. 2008. Learning entailment rules for unary templates. In *Proceedings of the 22nd International Conference on Computational Linguistics (Coling 2008)*, pages 849–856, Manchester, UK, August.

Idan Szpektor and Ido Dagan. 2009. Augmenting wordnet-based inference with argument mapping. In *Proceedings of the 2009 Workshop on Applied Textual Inference*, pages 27–35, Suntec, Singapore, August.

Frank Wilcoxon. 1945. Individual comparisons by ranking methods. *Biometrics Bulletin*, 1(6):80–83.

Don't 'have a clue'? Unsupervised co-learning of downward-entailing operators

Cristian Danescu-Niculescu-Mizil and Lillian Lee
Department of Computer Science, Cornell University
cristian@cs.cornell.edu, llee@cs.cornell.edu

Abstract

Researchers in textual entailment have begun to consider inferences involving *downward-entailing operators*, an interesting and important class of lexical items that change the way inferences are made. Recent work proposed a method for learning English downward-entailing operators that requires access to a high-quality collection of *negative polarity items* (NPIs). However, English is one of the very few languages for which such a list exists. We propose the first approach that can be applied to the many languages for which there is no pre-existing high-precision database of NPIs. As a case study, we apply our method to Romanian and show that our method yields good results. Also, we perform a cross-linguistic analysis that suggests interesting connections to some findings in linguistic typology.

1 Introduction

Cristi:	*"Nicio" ... is that adjective you've mentioned.*
Anca:	*A negative pronominal adjective.*
Cristi:	*You mean there are people who analyze that kind of thing?*
Anca:	*The Romanian Academy.*
Cristi:	*They're crazy.*

—From the movie *Police, adjective*

Downward-entailing operators are an interesting and varied class of lexical items that change the default way of dealing with certain types of inferences. They thus play an important role in understanding natural language [6, 18–20, etc.].

We explain what downward entailing means by first demonstrating the "default" behavior, which is *upward entailing*. The word 'observed' is an example upward-entailing operator: the statement

(i) 'Witnesses <u>observed</u> opium use.'
implies
(ii) 'Witnesses <u>observed</u> narcotic use.'

but not vice versa (we write i $\Rightarrow$ ($\not\Leftarrow$) ii). That is, the truth value is preserved if we replace the argument of an upward-entailing operator by a superset (a more general version); in our case, the set 'opium use' was replaced by the superset 'narcotic use'.

Downward-entailing (DE) (also known as *downward monotonic* or *monotone decreasing*) operators violate this default inference rule: with DE operators, reasoning instead goes from "sets to subsets". An example is the word 'bans':

'The law [bans] opium use'
$\not\Rightarrow$ ($\Leftarrow$)
'The law [bans] narcotic use'.

Although DE behavior represents an exception to the default, DE operators are as a class rather common. They are also quite diverse in sense and even part of speech. Some are simple negations, such as 'not', but some other English DE operators are 'without', 'reluctant to', 'to doubt', and 'to allow'.[1] This variety makes them hard to extract automatically.

Because DE operators violate the default "sets to supersets" inference, identifying them can potentially improve performance in many NLP tasks. Perhaps the most obvious such tasks are those involving textual entailment, such as question answering, information extraction, summarization, and the evaluation of machine translation [4]. Researchers are in fact beginning to build textual-entailment systems that can handle inferences involving downward-entailing operators other than simple negations, although these systems almost all rely on small handcrafted lists of DE operators [1–3, 15, 16].[2] Other application areas are natural-language generation and human-computer interaction, since downward-entailing inferences induce

[1]Some examples showing different constructions for analyzing these operators: 'The defendant does not own a blue car' $\not\Rightarrow$ ($\Leftarrow$) 'The defendant does not own a car'; 'They are reluctant to tango' $\not\Rightarrow$ ($\Leftarrow$) 'They are reluctant to dance'; 'Police doubt Smith threatened Jones' $\not\Rightarrow$ ($\Leftarrow$) 'Police doubt Smith threatened Jones or Brown'; 'You are allowed to use Mastercard' $\not\Rightarrow$ ($\Leftarrow$) 'You are allowed to use any credit card'.

[2]The exception [2] employs the list automatically derived by Danescu-Niculescu-Mizil, Lee, and Ducott [5], described later.

Proceedings of the ACL 2010 Conference Short Papers, pages 247–252,
Uppsala, Sweden, 11-16 July 2010. ©2010 Association for Computational Linguistics

greater cognitive load than inferences in the opposite direction [8].

Most NLP systems for the applications mentioned above have only been deployed for a small subset of languages. A key factor is the lack of relevant resources for other languages. While one approach would be to separately develop a method to acquire such resources for each language individually, we instead aim to ameliorate the resource-scarcity problem in the case of DE operators wholesale: we propose a single unsupervised method that can extract DE operators in any language for which raw text corpora exist.

Overview of our work Our approach takes the English-centric work of Danescu-Niculescu-Mizil et al. [5] — DLD09 for short — as a starting point, as they present the first and, until now, only algorithm for automatically extracting DE operators from data. However, our work departs significantly from DLD09 in the following key respect.

DLD09 critically depends on access to a high-quality, carefully curated collection of *negative polarity items (NPIs)* — lexical items such as 'any', 'ever', or the idiom 'have a clue' that tend to occur only in negative environments (see §2 for more details). DLD09 use NPIs as signals of the occurrence of downward-entailing operators. However, almost every language other than English lacks a high-quality accessible NPI list.

To circumvent this problem, we introduce a knowledge-lean *co-learning* approach. Our algorithm is initialized with a very small seed set of NPIs (which we describe how to generate), and then iterates between (a) discovering a set of DE operators using a collection of *pseudo-NPIs* — a concept we introduce — and (b) using the newly-acquired DE operators to detect new pseudo-NPIs.

Why this isn't obvious Although the algorithmic idea sketched above seems quite simple, it is important to note that prior experiments in that direction have not proved fruitful. Preliminary work on learning (German) NPIs using a small list of simple known DE operators did not yield strong results [14]. Hoeksema [10] discusses why NPIs might be hard to learn from data.[3] We circumvent this problem because we are not interested in learning NPIs per se; rather, for our purposes, pseudo-NPIs suffice. Also, our preliminary work determined that one of the most famous co-learning algorithms, *hubs and authorities* or *HITS* [11], is poorly suited to our problem.[4]

Contributions To begin with, we apply our algorithm to produce the first large list of DE operators for a language other than English. In our case study on Romanian (§4), we achieve quite high precisions at k (for example, iteration achieves a precision at 30 of 87%).

Auxiliary experiments explore the effects of using a large but noisy NPI list, should one be available for the language in question. Intriguingly, we find that co-learning new pseudo-NPIs provides better results.

Finally (§5), we engage in some cross-linguistic analysis based on the results of applying our algorithm to English. We find that there are some suggestive connections with findings in linguistic typology.

Appendix available A more complete account of our work and its implications can be found in a version of this paper containing appendices, available at www.cs.cornell.edu/~cristian/acl2010/.

2 DLD09: successes and challenges

In this section, we briefly summarize those aspects of the DLD09 method that are important to understanding how our new co-learning method works.

DE operators and NPIs Acquiring DE operators is challenging because of the complete lack of annotated data. DLD09's insight was to make use of *negative polarity items (NPIs)*, which are words or phrases that tend to occur only in negative contexts. The reason they did so is that Ladusaw's hypothesis [7, 13] asserts that *NPIs only occur within the scope of DE operators*. Figure 1 depicts examples involving the English NPIs 'any'[5] and 'have a clue' (in the idiomatic sense) that illustrate this relationship. Some other English NPIs are 'ever', 'yet' and 'give a damn'.

Thus, NPIs can be treated as clues that a DE operator might be present (although DE operators may also occur without NPIs).

[3]In fact, humans can have trouble agreeing on NPI-hood; for instance, Lichte and Soehn [14] mention doubts about over half of Kürschner [12]'s 344 manually collected German NPIs.

[4]We explored three different edge-weighting schemes based on co-occurrence frequencies and seed-set membership, but the results were extremely poor; HITS invariably retrieved very frequent words.

[5]The *free-choice* sense of 'any', as in 'I can skim any paper in five minutes', is a known exception.

DE operators	NPIs: any^3	NPIs: *have a clue*, idiomatic sense
not or n't	✓ We do n't have *any* apples	✓ We do n't *have a clue*
doubt	✓I doubt they have *any* apples	✓ I doubt they *have a clue*
no DE operator	× They have *any* apples	× They *have a clue*

Figure 1: Examples consistent with Ladusaw's hypothesis that NPIs can only occur within the scope of DE operators. A ✓ denotes an acceptable sentence; a × denotes an unacceptable sentence.

DLD09 algorithm Potential DE operators are collected by extracting those words that appear in an NPI's context at least once.[6] Then, the potential DE operators x are ranked by

$$f(x) := \frac{\text{fraction of NPI contexts that contain } x}{\text{relative frequency of } x \text{ in the corpus}},$$

which compares x's probability of occurrence conditioned on the appearance of an NPI with its probability of occurrence overall.[7]

The method just outlined requires access to a list of NPIs. DLD09's system used a subset of John Lawler's carefully curated and "moderately complete" list of English NPIs.[8] The resultant rankings of candidate English DE operators were judged to be of high quality.

The challenge in porting to other languages: cluelessness Can the unsupervised approach of DLD09 be successfully applied to languages other than English? Unfortunately, for most other languages, it does not seem that large, high-quality NPI lists are available.

One might wonder whether one can circumvent the NPI-acquisition problem by simply translating a known English NPI list into the target language. However, NPI-hood need not be preserved under translation [17]. Thus, for most languages, we lack the critical clues that DLD09 depends on.

3 Getting a clue

In this section, we develop an iterative co-learning algorithm that can extract DE operators in the many languages where a high-quality NPI database is not available, using Romanian as a case study.

3.1 Data and evaluation paradigm

We used Rada Mihalcea's corpus of ≈1.45 million sentences of raw Romanian newswire articles.

Note that we cannot evaluate impact on textual inference because, to our knowledge, no publicly available textual-entailment system or evaluation data for Romanian exists. We therefore examine the system outputs directly to determine whether the top-ranked items are actually DE operators or not. Our evaluation metric is precision at k of a given system's ranked list of candidate DE operators; it is not possible to evaluate recall since no list of Romanian DE operators exists (a problem that is precisely the motivation for this paper).

To evaluate the results, two native Romanian speakers labeled the system outputs as being "DE", "not DE" or "Hard (to decide)". The labeling protocol, which was somewhat complex to prevent bias, is described in the externally-available appendices (§7.1). The complete system output and annotations are publicly available at: http://www.cs.cornell.edu/~cristian/acl2010/.

3.2 Generating a seed set

Even though, as discussed above, the translation of an NPI need not be an NPI, a preliminary review of the literature indicates that in many languages, there is some NPI that can be translated as 'any' or related forms like 'anybody'. Thus, with a small amount of effort, one can form a minimal NPI seed set for the DLD09 method by using an appropriate target-language translation of 'any'. For Romanian, we used 'vreo' and 'vreun', which are the feminine and masculine translations of English 'any'.

3.3 DLD09 using the Romanian seed set

We first check whether DLD09 with the two-item seed set described in §3.2 performs well on Romanian. In fact, the results are fairly poor:

[6]DLD09 policies: (a) "NPI context" was defined as the part of the sentence to the left of the NPI up to the first comma, semi-colon or beginning of sentence; (b) to encourage the discovery of new DE operators, those sentences containing one of a list of 10 well-known DE operators were discarded. For Romanian, we treated only negations ('nu' and 'n-') and questions as well-known environments.

[7]DLD09 used an additional *distilled* score, but we found that the distilled score performed worse on Romanian.

[8]http://www-personal.umich.edu/~jlawler/aue/npi.html

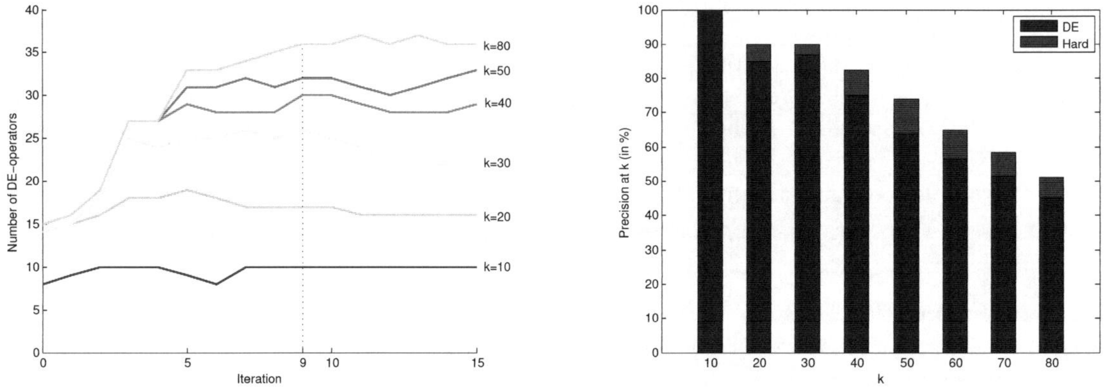

Figure 2: **Left:** Number of DE operators in the top k results returned by the co-learning method at each iteration. Items labeled "Hard" are not included. Iteration 0 corresponds to DLD09 applied to {'vreo', 'vreun'}. Curves for $k = 60$ and 70 omitted for clarity. **Right:** Precisions at k for the results of the 9th iteration. The bar divisions are: DE (blue/darkest/largest) and Hard (red/lighter, sometimes non-existent).

for example, the precision at 30 is below 50%. (See blue/dark bars in figure 3 in the externally-available appendices for detailed results.)

This relatively unsatisfactory performance may be a consequence of the very small size of the NPI list employed, and may therefore indicate that it would be fruitful to investigate automatically extending our list of clues.

3.4 Main idea: a co-learning approach

Our main insight is that not only can NPIs be used as clues for finding DE operators, as shown by DLD09, but conversely, DE operators (if known) can potentially be used to discover new NPI-like clues, which we refer to as *pseudo-NPIs* (or *pNPIs* for short). By "NPI-like" we mean, "serve as possible indicators of the presence of DE operators, regardless of whether they are actually restricted to negative contexts, as true NPIs are". For example, in English newswire, the words 'allegation' or 'rumor' tend to occur mainly in DE contexts, like 'denied' or 'dismissed', even though they are clearly not true NPIs (the sentence 'I heard a rumor' is fine). Given this insight, we approach the problem using an *iterative co-learning* paradigm that integrates the search for new DE operators with a search for new pNPIs.

First, we describe an algorithm that is the "reverse" of DLD09 (henceforth *rDLD*), in that it retrieves and ranks pNPIs assuming a given list of DE operators. Potential pNPIs are collected by extracting those words that appear in a DE context (defined here, to avoid the problems of parsing or scope determination, as the part of the sentence to the right of a DE operator, up to the first comma, semi-colon or end of sentence); these candidates x are then ranked by

$$f_r(x) := \frac{\text{fraction of DE contexts that contain } x}{\text{relative frequency of } x \text{ in the corpus}}.$$

Then, our *co-learning* algorithm consists of the iteration of the following two steps:

- (*DE learning*) Apply DLD09 using a set $\mathcal{N}$ of pseudo-NPIs to retrieve a list of candidate DE operators ranked by f (defined in Section 2). Let $\mathcal{D}$ be the top n candidates in this list.
- (*pNPI learning*) Apply rDLD using the set $\mathcal{D}$ to retrieve a list of pNPIs ranked by f_r; extend $\mathcal{N}$ with the top n_r pNPIs in this list. Increment n.

Here, $\mathcal{N}$ is initialized with the NPI seed set. At each iteration, we consider the output of the algorithm to be the ranked list of DE operators retrieved in the DE-learning step. In our experiments, we initialized n to 10 and set n_r to 1.

4 Romanian results

Our results show that there is indeed favorable synergy between DE-operator and pNPI retrieval. Figure 2 plots the number of correctly retrieved DE operators in the top k outputs at each iteration. The point at iteration 0 corresponds to a datapoint already discussed above, namely, DLD09 applied to the two 'any'-translation NPIs. Clearly, we see general substantial improvement over DLD09, although the increases level off in later iterations.

(Determining how to choose the optimal number of iterations is a subject for future research.)

Additional experiments, described in the externally-available appendices (§7.2), suggest that pNPIs can even be more effective clues than a noisy list of NPIs. (Thus, a larger seed set does not necessarily mean better performance.) pNPIs also have the advantage of being derivable automatically, and might be worth investigating from a linguistic perspective in their own right.

5 Cross-linguistic analysis

Applying our algorithm to English: connections to linguistic typology So far, we have made no assumptions about the language on which our algorithm is applied. A valid question is, does the quality of the results vary with choice of application language? In particular, what happens if we run our algorithm on English?

Note that in some sense, this is a perverse question: the motivation behind our algorithm is the non-existence of a high-quality list of NPIs for the language in question, and English is essentially the only case that does not fit this description. On the other hand, the fact that DLD09 applied their method for extraction of DE operators to English necessitates some form of comparison, for the sake of experimental completeness.

We thus ran our algorithm on the English BLLIP newswire corpus with seed set {'any'} . We observe that, surprisingly, the iterative addition of pNPIs has very little effect: the precisions at k are good at the beginning and stay about the same across iterations (for details see figure 5 in in the externally-available appendices). Thus, on English, co-learning does not hurt performance, which is good news; but unlike in Romanian, it does not lead to improvements.

Why is English 'any' seemingly so "powerful", in contrast to Romanian, where iterating beyond the initial 'any' translations leads to better results? Interestingly, findings from linguistic typology may shed some light on this issue. Haspelmath [9] compares the functions of indefinite pronouns in 40 languages. He shows that English is one of the minority of languages (11 out of 40)[9] in which there exists an indefinite pronoun series that occurs in all (Haspelmath's) classes of DE contexts, and thus can constitute a sufficient seed on its own. In the other languages (including Romanian),[10] no indirect pronoun can serve as a sufficient seed. So, we expect our method to be viable for all languages; while the iterative discovery of pNPIs is not necessary (although neither is it harmful) for the subset of languages for which a sufficient seed exists, such as English, it is essential for the languages for which, like Romanian, 'any'-equivalents do not suffice.

Using translation Another interesting question is whether directly translating DE operators from English is an alternative to our method. First, we emphasize that there exists no complete list of English DE operators (the largest available collection is the one extracted by DLD09). Second, we do not know whether DE operators in one language translate into DE operators in another language. Even if that were the case, and we somehow had access to ideal translations of DLD09's list, there would still be considerable value in using our method: 14 (39%) of our top 36 highest-ranked Romanian DE operators for iteration 9 do not, according to the Romanian-speaking author, have English equivalents appearing on DLD09's 90-item list. Some examples are: 'abţinut' (abstained), 'criticat' (criticized) and 'reacţionat' (reacted). Therefore, a significant fraction of the DE operators derived by our co-learning algorithm would have been missed by the translation alternative even under ideal conditions.

6 Conclusions

We have introduced the first method for discovering downward-entailing operators that is universally applicable. Previous work on automatically detecting DE operators assumed the existence of a high-quality collection of NPIs, which renders it inapplicable in most languages, where such a resource does not exist. We overcome this limitation by employing a novel *co-learning* approach, and demonstrate its effectiveness on Romanian.

Also, we introduce the concept of *pseudo-NPIs*. Auxiliary experiments described in the externally-available appendices show that pNPIs are actually more effective seeds than a noisy "true" NPI list.

Finally, we noted some cross-linguistic differences in performance, and found an interesting connection between these differences and Haspelmath's [9] characterization of cross-linguistic variation in the occurrence of indefinite pronouns.

[9]English, Ancash Quechua, Basque, Catalan, French, Hindi/Urdu, Irish, Portuguese, Swahili, Swedish, Turkish.

[10]Examples: Chinese, German, Italian, Polish, Serbian.

Acknowledgments We thank Tudor Marian for serving as an annotator, Rada Mihalcea for access to the Romanian newswire corpus, and Claire Cardie, Yejin Choi, Effi Georgala, Mark Liberman, Myle Ott, João Paula Muchado, Stephen Purpura, Mark Yatskar, Ainur Yessenalina, and the anonymous reviewers for their helpful comments. Supported by NSF grant IIS-0910664.

References

[1] Roy Bar-Haim, Jonathan Berant, Ido Dagan, Iddo Greental, Shachar Mirkin, Eyal Shnarch, and Idan Szpektor. Efficient semantic deduction and approximate matching over compact parse forests. In *Proceedings of the Text Analysis Conference (TAC)*, 2008.

[2] Eric Breck. A simple system for detecting non-entailment. In *Proceedings of the Text Analysis Conference (TAC)*, 2009.

[3] Christos Christodoulopoulos. Creating a natural logic inference system with combinatory categorial grammar. Master's thesis, University of Edinburgh, 2008.

[4] Ido Dagan, Oren Glickman, and Bernardo Magnini. The PASCAL Recognising Textual Entailment challenge. In *Machine Learning Challenges, Evaluating Predictive Uncertainty, Visual Object Classification and Recognizing Textual Entailment, First PASCAL Machine Learning Challenges Workshop*, pages 177–190. Springer, 2006.

[5] Cristian Danescu-Niculescu-Mizil, Lillian Lee, and Richard Ducott. Without a 'doubt'? Unsupervised discovery of downward-entailing operators. In *Proceedings of NAACL HLT*, 2009.

[6] David Dowty. The role of negative polarity and concord marking in natural language reasoning. In Mandy Harvey and Lynn Santelmann, editors, *Proceedings of SALT IV*, pages 114–144, 1994.

[7] Gilles Fauconnier. Polarity and the scale principle. In *Proceedings of the Chicago Linguistic Society (CLS)*, pages 188–199, 1975. Reprinted in Javier Gutierrez-Rexach (ed.), *Semantics: Critical Concepts in Linguistics*, 2003.

[8] Bart Geurts and Frans van der Slik. Monotonicity and processing load. *Journal of Semantics*, 22(1):97–117, 2005.

[9] Martin Haspelmath. *Indefinite Pronouns*. Oxford University Press, 2001.

[10] Jack Hoeksema. Corpus study of negative polarity items. *IV-V Jornades de corpus linguistics 1996-1997*, 1997. http://odur.let.rug.nl/~hoeksema/docs/barcelona.html.

[11] Jon Kleinberg. Authoritative sources in a hyperlinked environment. In *Proceedings of the 9th ACM-SIAM Symposium on Discrete Algorithms (SODA)*, pages 668–677, 1998. Extended version in *Journal of the ACM*, 46:604–632, 1999.

[12] Wilfried Kürschner. *Studien zur Negation im Deutschen*. Narr, 1983.

[13] William A. Ladusaw. *Polarity Sensitivity as Inherent Scope Relations*. Garland Press, New York, 1980. Ph.D. thesis date 1979.

[14] Timm Lichte and Jan-Philipp Soehn. The retrieval and classification of Negative Polarity Items using statistical profiles. In Sam Featherston and Wolfgang Sternefeld, editors, *Roots: Linguistics in Search of its Evidential Base*, pages 249–266. Mouton de Gruyter, 2007.

[15] Bill MacCartney and Christopher D. Manning. Modeling semantic containment and exclusion in natural language inference. In *Proceedings of COLING*, pages 521–528, 2008.

[16] Rowan Nairn, Cleo Condoravdi, and Lauri Karttunen. Computing relative polarity for textual inference. In *Proceedings of Inference in Computational Semantics (ICoS)*, 2006.

[17] Frank Richter, Janina Radó, and Manfred Sailer. Negative polarity items: Corpus linguistics, semantics, and psycholinguistics: Day 2: Corpus linguistics. Tutorial slides: http://www.sfs.uni-tuebingen.de/~fr/esslli/08/byday/day2/day2-part1.pdf, 2008.

[18] Víctor Sánchez Valencia. *Studies on natural logic and categorial grammar*. PhD thesis, University of Amsterdam, 1991.

[19] Johan van Benthem. *Essays in Logical Semantics*. Reidel, Dordrecht, 1986.

[20] Ton van der Wouden. *Negative contexts: Collocation, polarity and multiple negation*. Routledge, 1997.

Vocabulary Choice as an Indicator of Perspective

Beata Beigman Klebanov, Eyal Beigman, Daniel Diermeier
Northwestern University and Washington University in St. Louis
beata,d-diermeier@northwestern.edu, beigman@wustl.edu

Abstract

We establish the following characteristics of the task of perspective classification: (a) using term frequencies in a document does not improve classification achieved with absence/presence features; (b) for datasets allowing the relevant comparisons, a small number of top features is found to be as effective as the full feature set and indispensable for the best achieved performance, testifying to the existence of perspective-specific keywords. We relate our findings to research on word frequency distributions and to discourse analytic studies of perspective.

1 Introduction

We address the task of perspective classification. Apart from the spatial sense not considered here, perspective can refer to an agent's role (doctor vs patient in a dialogue), or understood as "a particular way of thinking about something, especially one that is influenced by one's beliefs or experiences," stressing the manifestation of one's broader perspective in some specific issue, or "the state of one's ideas, the facts known to one, etc., in having a meaningful interrelationship," stressing the meaningful connectedness of one's stances and pronouncements on possibly different issues.[1]

Accordingly, one can talk about, say, opinion on a particular proposed legislation on abortion within pro-choice or pro-life perspectives; in this case, perspective essentially boils down to opinion in a particular debate. Holding the issue constant but relaxing the requirement of a debate on a specific document, we can consider writings from pro- and con- perspective, in, for example, the death penalty controversy over a course of a period of time. Relaxing the issue specificity somewhat, one can talk about perspectives of people on two sides of a conflict; this is not opposition or support for any particular proposal, but ideas about a highly related cluster of issues, such as Israeli and Palestinian perspectives on the conflict in all its manifestations. Zooming out even further, one can talk about perspectives due to certain life contingencies, such as being born and raised in a particular culture, region, religion, or political tradition, such perspectives manifesting themselves in certain patterns of discourse on a wide variety of issues, for example, views on political issues in the Middle East from Arab vs Western observers.

In this article, we consider perspective at all the four levels of abstraction. We apply the same types of models to all, in order to discover any common properties of perspective classification. We contrast it with text categorization and with opinion classification by employing models routinely used for such tasks. Specifically, we consider models that use term frequencies as features (usually found to be superior for text categorization) and models that use term absence/presence (usually found to be superior for opinion classification). We motivate our hypothesis that presence/absence features would be as good as or better than frequencies, and test it experimentally. Secondly, we investigate the question of feature redundancy often observed in text categorization.

2 Vocabulary Selection

A line of inquiry going back at least to Zipf strives to characterize word frequency distributions in texts and corpora; see Baayen (2001) for a survey. One of the findings in this literature is that a multinomial (called "urn model" by Baayen) is not a good model for word frequency distributions. Among the many proposed remedies (Baayen, 2001; Jansche, 2003; Baroni and Evert, 2007; Bhat and Sproat, 2009), we would like to draw attention to the following insight articulated

[1] Google English Dictionary, Dictionary.com

Proceedings of the ACL 2010 Conference Short Papers, pages 253–257,
Uppsala, Sweden, 11-16 July 2010.

most clearly in Jansche (2003). Estimation is improved if texts are construed as being generated by two processes, one choosing which words would appear at all in the text, and then, for words that have been chosen to appear, how many times they would in fact appear. Jansche (2003) describes a two-stage generation process: (1) Toss a z-biased coin; if it comes up heads, generate 0; if it comes up tails, (2) generate according to $F(\theta)$, where $F(\theta)$ is a negative binomial distribution and z is a parameter controlling the extent of zero-inflation.

The postulation of two separate processes is effective for predicting word frequencies, but is there any meaning to the two processes? The first process of deciding on the vocabulary, or word types, for the text – what is its function? Jansche (2003) suggests that the zero-inflation component takes care of the multitude of vocabulary words that are not "on topic" for the given text, including taboo words, technical jargon, proper names. This implies that words that are chosen to appear are all "on topic". Indeed, text segmentation studies show that tracing recurrence of words in a text permits topical segmentation (Hearst, 1997; Hoey, 1991). Yet, if a person compares abortion to *infanticide* – are we content with describing this word as being merely "on topic," that is, having a certain probability of occurrence once the topic of abortion comes up? In fact, it is only likely to occur if the speaker holds a pro-life perspective, while a pro-choicer would avoid this term.

We therefore hypothesize that the choice of vocabulary is not only a matter of topic but also of perspective, while word *recurrence* has mainly to do with the topical composition of the text. Therefore, tracing word frequencies is not going to be effective for perspective classification beyond noting the mere presence/absence of words, differently from the findings in text categorization, where frequency-based features usually do better than boolean features for sufficiently large vocabulary sizes (McCallum and Nigam, 1998).

3 Data

Partial Birth Abortion (PBA) debates: We use transcripts of the debates on Partial Birth Abortion Ban Act on the floors of the US House and Senate in 104-108 Congresses (1995-2003). Similar legislation was proposed multiple times, passed the legislatures, and, after having initially been vetoed by President Clinton, was signed into law by President Bush in 2003. We use data from 278 legislators, with 669 speeches in all. We take only one speech per speaker per year; since many serve multiple years, each speaker is represented with 1 to 5 speeches. We perform 10-fold cross-validation splitting by speakers, so that all speeches by the same speaker are assigned to the same fold and testing is always inter-speaker.

When deriving the label for perspective, it is important to differentiate between a particular legislation and a pro-choice / pro-life perspective. A pro-choice person might still support the bill: "I am pro-choice, but believe late-term abortions are wrong. Abortion is a very personal decision and a woman's right to choose whether to terminate a pregnancy subject to the restrictions of Roe v. Wade must be protected. In my judgment, however, the use of this particular procedure cannot be justified." (Rep. Shays, R-CT, 2003). To avoid inconsistency between vote and perspective, we use data from pro-choice and pro-life non-governmental organizations, NARAL and NRLC, that track legislators' votes on abortion-related bills, showing the percentage of times a legislator supported the side the organization deems consistent with its perspective. We removed 22 legislators with a mixed record, that is, those who gave 20-60% support to one of the positions.[2]

Death Penalty (DP) blogs: We use University of Maryland Death Penalty Corpus (Greene and Resnik, 2009) of 1085 texts from a number of pro- and anti-death penalty websites. We report 4-fold cross-validation (DP-4) using the folds in Greene and Resnik (2009), where training and testing data come from different websites for each of the sides, as well as 10-fold cross-validation performance on the entire corpus, irrespective of the site.[3]

Bitter Lemons (BL): We use the GUEST part of the BitterLemons corpus (Lin et al., 2006), containing 296 articles published in 2001-2005 on http://www.bitterlemons.org by more than 200 different Israeli and Palestinian writers on issues related to the conflict.

Bitter Lemons International (BL-I): We collected 150 documents each by a different per-

[2]Ratings are from: http://www.OnTheIssues.org/. We further excluded data from Rep. James Moran, D-VA, as he changed his vote over the years. For legislators rated by neither NRLC nor NARAL, we assumed the vote aligns with the perspective.

[3]The 10-fold setting yields almost perfect performance likely due to site-specific features beyond perspective per se, hence we do not use this setting in subsequent experiments.

son from either Arab or Western perspectives on Middle Eastern affairs in 2003-2009 from http://www.bitterlemons-international.org/. The writers and interviewees on this site are usually former diplomats or government officials, academics, journalists, media and political analysts.[4] The specific issues cover a broad spectrum, including public life, politics, wars and conflicts, education, trade relations in and between countries like Lebanon, Jordan, Iraq, Egypt, Yemen, Morocco, Saudi Arabia, as well as their relations with the US and members of the European Union.

3.1 Pre-processing

We are interested in perspective manifestations using common English vocabulary. To avoid the possibility that artifacts such as names of senators or states drive the classification, we use as features words that contain only lowercase letters, possibly hyphenated. No stemming is performed, and no stopwords are excluded.[5]

Table 1: Summary of corpora

Data	#Docs	#Features	# CV folds
PBA	669	9.8 K	10
BL	296	10 K	10
BL-I	150	9 K	10
DP	1085	25 K	4

4 Models

For generative models, we use two versions of Naive Bayes models termed *multi-variate Bernoulli* (here, NB-BOOL) and *multinomial* (here, NB-COUNT), respectively, in McCallum and Nigam (1998) study of event models for text categorization. The first records presence/absence of a word in a text, while the second records the number of occurrences. McCallum and Nigam (1998) found NB-COUNT to do better than NB-BOOL for sufficiently large vocabulary sizes for text categorization by topic. For discriminative models, we use linear SVM, with presence-absence, normalized frequency, and tfidf feature weighting. Both types of models are commonly used for text classification tasks. For example, Lin et al. (2006) use NB-COUNT and SVM-NORMF for perspective classification; Pang et al. (2002) consider most and Yu et al. (2008) all of the above for related tasks of movie review and political party classification. We use SVM^{light} (Joachims, 1999) for SVM and WEKA toolkit (Witten and Frank, 2005; Hall et al., 2009) for both version of Naive Bayes. Parameter optimization for all SVM models is performed using grid search on the training data separately for each partition into train and test data.[6]

5 Results

Table 2 summarizes the cross-validation results for the four datasets discussed above. Notably, the SVM-BOOL model is either the best or not significantly different from the best performing model, although the competitors use more detailed textual information, namely, the count of each word's appearance in the text, either raw (NB-COUNT), normalized (SVM-NORMF), or combined with document frequency (SVM-TFIDF).

Table 2: Classification accuracy. Scores significantly different from the best performance (p_{2t}<0.05 on paired t-test) are given an asterisk.

Data	NB		SVM		
	BOOL	COUNT	BOOL	NORMF	TFIDF
PBA	*0.93	0.96	0.96	0.96	0.97
DP-4	0.82	0.82	0.83	0.82	0.72[7]
DP-10	*0.88	*0.93	0.98	*0.97	*0.97
BL	0.89	0.88	0.89	0.86	0.84
BL-I	0.68	0.66	0.73	0.65	0.65

We conclude that there is no evidence for the relevance of the frequency composition of the text for perspective classification, for all levels of venue- and topic-control, from the tightest (PBA debates) to the loosest (Western vs Arab authors on Middle Eastern affairs). This result is a clear indication that perspective classification is quite different from text categorization by topic, where count-based features usually perform better than boolean features. On the other hand, we have not

[4]We excluded Israeli, Turkish, Iranian, Pakistani writers as not clearly representing either perspective.

[5]We additionally removed words containing *support*, *oppos*, *sustain*, *overrid* from the PBA data, in order not to inflate the performance on perspective classification due to the explicit reference to the upcoming vote.

[6]Parameter c controlling the trade-off between errors on training data and margin is optimized for all datasets, with the grid $c = \{10^{-6}, 10^{-5}, \ldots, 10^{5}\}$. On the DP data parameter j controlling penalties for misclassification of positive and negative cases is optimized as well ($j = \{10^{-2}, 10^{-1}, \ldots, 10^{2}\}$), since datasets are unbalanced (for example, there is a fold with 27%-73% split).

[7]Here SVM-TFIDF is doing somewhat better than SVM-BOOL on one of the folds and much worse on two other folds; paired t-test with just 4 pairs of observations does not detect a significant difference.

observed that boolean features are reliably better than count-based features, as reported for the sentiment classification task in the movie review domain (Pang et al., 2002).

We note the low performance on BL-I, which could testify to a low degree of lexical consolidation in the Arab vs Western perspectives (more on this below). It is also possible that the small size of BL-I leads to overfitting and low accuracies. However, PBA subset with only 151 items (only 2002 and 2003 speeches) is still 96% classifiable, so size alone does not explain low BL-I performance.

6 Consolidation of perspective

We explore feature redundancy in perspective classification.We first investigate retention of only N best features, then elimination thereof. As a proxy of feature quality, we use the weight assigned to the feature by the SVM-BOOL model based on the training data. Thus, to get the performance with N best features, we take the $\frac{N}{2}$ highest and lowest weight features, for the positive and negative classes, respectively, and retrain SVM-BOOL with these features only.[8]

Table 3: Consolidation of perspective. Nbest shows the smallest N and its proportion out of all features for which the performance of SVM-BOOL with only the best N features is not significantly inferior (p_{1t}>0.1) to that of the full feature set. No-Nbest shows the largest number N for which a model *without* N best features is not significantly inferior to the full model. N=$\{50, 100, 150, \ldots, 1000\}$; for DP and BL-I, additionally N=$\{1050, 1100, ..., 1500\}$; for PBA, additionally N=$\{10, 20, 30, 40\}$.

Data	Nbest		No-Nbest	
	N	%	N	%
PBA	250	2.6%	10	<1%
BL	500	4.9%	100	<1%
DP	100	<1%	1250	5.2%
BL-I	200	2.2%	950	11%

We observe that it is generally sufficient to use a small percentage of the available words to obtain the same classification accuracy as with the full feature set, even in high-accuracy cases such as PBA and BL. The effectiveness of a small subset of features is consistent with the observation in the discourse analysis studies that rivals in long-lasting controversies tend to consolidate their vocabulary and signal their perspective with certain *stigma words* and *banner words*, that is, specific keywords used by a discourse community to implicate adversaries and to create sympathy with own perspective, respectively (Teubert, 2001). Thus, in abortion debates, using *infanticide* as a synonym for abortion is a pro-life stigma. Note that this does not mean the rest of the features are not informative for classification, only that they are redundant with respect to a small percentage of top weight features.

When N best features are eliminated, performance goes down significantly with even smaller N for PBA and BL datasets. Thus, top features are not only effective, they are also crucial for accurate classification, as their discrimination capacity is not replicated by any of the other vocabulary words. This finding is consistent with Lin and Hauptmann (2006) study of perspective vs topic classification: While topical differences between two corpora are manifested in difference in distributions of great many words, they observed little perspective-based variation in distributions of most words, apart from certain words that are preferentially used by adherents of one or the other perspective on the given topic.

For DP and BL-I datasets, the results seem to suggest perspectives with more diffused keyword distribution (No-NBest figures are higher). We note, however, that feature redundancy experiments are confounded in these cases by either a low power of the paired t-test with only 4 pairs (DP) or by a high variance in performance among the 10 folds (BL-I), both of which lead to numerically large discrepancy in performance that is not deemed significant, making it easy to "match" the full set performance with small-N best features as well as without large-N best features. Better comparisons are needed in order to verify the hypothesis of low consolidation.

In future work, we plan to experiment with additional features. For example, Greene and Resnik (2009) reported higher classification accuracies for the DP-4 data using syntactic frames in which a selected group of words appeared, rather than mere presence/absence of the words. Another direction is exploring words as members of semantic fields – while word use might be insufficiently consistent within a perspective, selection of a semantic domain might show better consistency.

[8] We experimented with the mutual information based feature selection as well, with generally worse results.

References

Herald Baayen. 2001. *Word frequency distributions*. Dordrecht: Kluwer.

Marco Baroni and Stefan Evert. 2007. Words and Echoes: Assessing and Mitigating the Non-Randomness Problem in Word Frequency Distribution Modeling. In *Proceedings of the ACL*, pages 904–911, Prague, Czech Republic.

Suma Bhat and Richard Sproat. 2009. Knowing the Unseen: Estimating Vocabulary Size over Unseen Samples. In *Proceedings of the ACL*, pages 109–117, Suntec, Singapore, August.

Stephan Greene and Philip Resnik. 2009. More than Words: Syntactic Packaging and Implicit Sentiment. In *Proceedings of HLT-NAACL*, pages 503–511, Boulder, CO, June.

Mark Hall, Eibe Frank, Geoffrey Holmes, Bernhard Pfahringe, Peter Reutemann, and Ian H. Witten. 2009. The WEKA data mining software: An update. *SIGKDD Explorations*, 11(1).

Marti Hearst. 1997. TextTiling: Segmenting Text into Multi-Paragraph Subtopic Passages. *Computational Linguistics*, 23(1):33–64.

Michael Hoey. 1991. *Patterns of Lexis in Text*. Oxford University Press.

Martin Jansche. 2003. Parametric Models of Linguistic Count Data. In *Proceedings of the ACL*, pages 288–295, Sapporo, Japan, July.

Thorsten Joachims. 1999. Making large-scale SVM learning practical. In B. Schlkopf, C. Burges, and A. Smola, editors, *Advances in Kernel Methods - Support Vector Learning*. MIT Press.

Wei-Hao Lin and Alexander Hauptmann. 2006. Are these documents written from different perspectives? A test of different perspectives based on statistical distribution divergence. In *Proceedings of the ACL*, pages 1057–1064, Morristown, NJ, USA.

Wei-Hao Lin, Theresa Wilson, Janyce Wiebe, and Alexander Hauptmann. 2006. Which side are you on? Identifying perspectives at the document and sentence levels. In *Proceedings of CoNLL*, pages 109–116, Morristown, NJ, USA.

Andrew McCallum and Kamal Nigam. 1998. A comparison of event models for Naive Bayes text classification. In *Proceedings of AAAI-98 Workshop on Learning for Text Categorization*, pages 41–48, Madison, WI, July.

Bo Pang, Lillian Lee, and Shivakumar Vaithyanathan. 2002. Thumbs up? Sentiment Classification using Machine Learning Techniques. In *Proceedings of EMNLP*, Philadelphia, PA, July.

Wolfgang Teubert. 2001. A Province of a Federal Superstate, Ruled by an Unelected Bureaucracy – Keywords of the Euro-Sceptic Discourse in Britain. In Andreas Musolff, Colin Good, Petra Points, and Ruth Wittlinger, editors, *Attitudes towards Europe: Language in the unification process*, pages 45–86. Ashgate Publishing Ltd, Hants, England.

Ian H. Witten and Eibe Frank. 2005. *Data Mining: Practical Machine Learning Tools and Techniques*. Morgan Kaufmann, 2 edition.

Bei Yu, Stefan Kaufmann, and Daniel Diermeier. 2008. Classifying party affiliation from political speech. *Journal of Information Technology and Politics*, 5(1):33–48.

Cross Lingual Adaptation: An Experiment on Sentiment Classifications

Bin Wei
University of Rochester
Rochester, NY, USA.
bwei@cs.rochester.edu

Christopher Pal
École Polytechnique de Montréal
Montréal, QC, Canada.
christopher.pal@polymtl.ca

Abstract

In this paper, we study the problem of using an annotated corpus in English for the same natural language processing task in another language. While various machine translation systems are available, automated translation is still far from perfect. To minimize the noise introduced by translations, we propose to use only key 'reliable" parts from the translations and apply structural correspondence learning (SCL) to find a low dimensional representation shared by the two languages. We perform experiments on an English-Chinese sentiment classification task and compare our results with a previous co-training approach. To alleviate the problem of data sparseness, we create extra pseudo-examples for SCL by making queries to a search engine. Experiments on real-world on-line review data demonstrate the two techniques can effectively improve the performance compared to previous work.

1 Introduction

In this paper we are interested in the problem of transferring knowledge gained from data gathered in one language to another language. A simple and straightforward solution for this problem might be to use automatic machine translations. However, while machine translation has been the subject of a great deal of development in recent years, many of the recent gains in performance manifest as syntactically as opposed to semantically correct sentences. For example, "PIANYI" is a word mainly used in positive comments in Chinese but its translation from the online Google translator is always "cheap", a word typically used in a negative context in English. To reduce this kind of error introduced by the translator, Wan in (Wan, 2009) applied a co-training scheme. In this setting classifiers are trained in both languages and the two classifiers teach each other for the unlabeled examples. The co-training approach manages to boost the performance as it allows the text similarity in the target language to compete with the "fake" similarity from the translated texts. However, the translated texts are still used as training data and thus can potentially mislead the classifier. As we are not really interested in predicting something on the language created by the translator, but rather on the real one, it may be better to further diminish the role of the translated texts in the learning process. Motivated by this observation, we suggest here to view this problem as a special case of domain adaptation, in the source domain, we mainly observe English features, while in the other domain mostly features from Chinese. The problem we address is how to associate the features under a unified setting.

There has been a lot of work in domain adaption for NLP (Dai et al., 2007)(Jiang and Zhai, 2007) and one suitable choice for our problem is the approach based on structural correspondence learning (SCL) as in (Blitzer et al., 2006) and (Blitzer et al., 2007b). The key idea of SCL is to identify a low-dimensional representations that capture correspondence between features from both domains (x_s and x_t in our case) by modeling their correlations with some special pivot features. The SCL approach is a good fit for our problem as it performs knowledge transfer through identifying important features. In the cross-lingual setting, we can restrict the translated texts by using them only through the pivot features. We believe this form is more robust to errors in the language produced by the translator.

Adapting language resources and knowledge to a new language was first studied for general text categorization and information retrieval as in (Bel

Proceedings of the ACL 2010 Conference Short Papers, pages 258–262,
Uppsala, Sweden, 11-16 July 2010.

et al., 2003), where the authors translate a keyword lexicon to perform cross-lingual text categorization. In (Mihalcea et al., 2007), different shortcomings of lexicon-based translation scheme was discussed for the more semantic-oriented task subjective analysis, instead the authors proposed to use a parallel-corpus, apply the classifier in the source language and use the corresponding sentences in the target language to train a new classifier. With the rapid development of automatic machine translations, translating the whole corpus becomes a plausible option. One can either choose to translate a corpus in the target language and apply the classifier in the source language to obtain labeled data, or directly translated the existing data set to the new language. Various experiments of the first strategy are performed in (Banea et al., 2008) for the subjective analysis task and an average 65 F1 score was reported. In (Wan, 2008), the authors propose to combine both strategies with ensemble learning and train a bi-lingual classifier.

In this paper, we are also interested in exploring whether a search engine can be used to improve the performance of NLP systems through reducing the effect of data sparseness. As the SCL algorithm we use here is based on co-occurrence statistics, we adopt a simple approach of creating pseudo-examples from the query counts returned by Google.

2 Our Approach

To begin, we give a formal definition of the problem we are considering. Assume we have two languages l_s and l_t and denote features in these two languages as x_s and x_t respectively. We also have text-level translations and we use $x_{t'}$ for features in the translations from l_s to l_t and $x_{s'}$ for the other direction. Let y be the output variable we want to predict, we have labeled examples (y, x_s) and some unlabeled examples (x_t). Our task is to train a classifier for (y, x_t). In this paper, we consider the binary sentiment classification (positive or negative) problem where l_s and l_t correspond to English and Chinese (for general sentiment analysis, we refer the readers to the various previous studies as in (Turney, 2002),(Pang et al., 2002),and (McDonald et al., 2007)). With these definitions in place, we now describe our approach in further detail.

2.1 Structural Correspondence Learning(SCL)

Due to space limitations, we give a very brief overview of the SCL framework here. For a detailed illustration, please refer to (Ando and Zhang, 2005). When SCL is used in a domain adaptation problem, one first needs to find a set of pivot features x_p. These pivot features should behave in a similar manner in both domains, and can be used as "references" to estimate how much other features may contribute when used in a classifier to predict a target variable. These features can either be identified with heuristics (Blitzer et al., 2006) or by automatic selection (Blitzer et al., 2007b). Take sentiment classification as an example, "very good" and "awful" are good pivot features, if a certain feature in the target domain co-occurs often with "very good" but infrequently with "awful", we could expect this feature will play a similar role as "very good" in the final classifier but a different role from "awful". We can make this observation purely based on the co-occurrence between these features. No hand-labeling is required and this specific feature doesn't need to be present in our labeled training data of the source domain.

The SCL approach of (Ando and Zhang, 2005) formulates the above idea by constructing a set of linear predictors for each of the pivot features. Each of these linear predictor is binary like whether "very good" occurs in the text and we have a set of training instances $(1|0, \{x_i\})$. The weight matrix of these linear predictors will encode the co-occurrence statistics between an ordinary feature and the pivot features. As the co-occurrence data are generally very sparse for a typical NLP task, we usually compress the weight matrix using the singular vector decomposition and only selects the top k eigenvectors v_k. This matrix w of the k vectors $\{v_k\}$ gives a mapping from the original feature space to a lower dimensional representation and is shown in (Ando and Zhang, 2005) to be the optimal choice of dimension k under common loss functions. In the next step we can then train a classifier on the extended feature $(x, w * x)$ in the source domain. As w groups the features from different domains with similar behavior relative to the pivot features together, if such a classifier has good performance on the source domain, it will likely do well on the target domain as well.

2.2 SCL for the Cross-lingual Adaptation

Viewing our task as a domain adaptation problem. The source domain correspond to English reviews and the target domain for Chinese ones. The full feature vector is (x_s, x_t). The difficulty we are facing is, due to noise in the translations, the conditional probabilities $p(y|x_s)$ and the one in the translated texts $p(y|x_{s'})$ may be quite different. Consider the following two straightforward strategies of using automatic machine translations: one can translate the original English labeled data (y, x_s) into $(y, x_{t'})$ in Chinese and train a classifier, or one can train a classifier on (y, x_s) and translate x_t in Chinese into $x_{s'}$ in English so as to use the classifier. But as the conditional distribution can be quite different for the original language and the pseudo language produced by the machine translators, these two strategies give poor performance as reported in (Wan, 2009).

Our solution to this problem is simple: instead of using all the features as $(x_s, x_{t'})$ and $(x_{s'}, x_t)$, we only preserves the pivot features in the translated texts $x_{s'}$ and $x_{t'}$ respectively and discard the other features produced by the translator. So, now we will have (x_s, x_{tp}) and (x_{sp}, x_t) where $x_{(s|t)p}$ are pivot features in the source and the target languages. In other words, when we use the SCL on our problem, the translations are only used to decide if a certain pivot feature occurs or not in the training of the linear predictors. All the other non-pivot features in the translators are blocked to reduce the noise.

In the original SCL as we mentioned earlier, the final classifier is trained on the extended features $(x, w * x)$. However, as mentioned above we will only use the pivot features. To represent this constraint, we can modify the vector to be $(w_p * x, w * x)$ where w_p is a constant matrix that only selects the pivot features. This modification will not affect the deduction procedure and results in (Ando and Zhang, 2005). Experiments show that using only pivot features actually outperforms the full feature setting.

For the selection of the pivot features, we follow the automatic selection method proposed in (Blitzer et al., 2007a). We first select some candidates that occur at least some constant number of times in reviews of the two languages. Then, we rank these features according to their conditional entropy to the labels on the training set. In table 1, we give some of the pivot features with English translations associated with the Chinese pivot features. As we can see from the table, although we only have text-level translations we still get some features with similar meaning from different languages, just like performing an alignment of words.

English Pivot Features
"poor quality", "not buy", "easy use", "very easy" "excellent", "perfect", "still very", "garbage", "poor", "not work", "not to", "very comfortable"
Chinese Pivot Features
wanmei(perfect), xiaoguo hen(effect is very...) tisheng(improve),feichang hao(very good), cha(poor), shushi(comfortable), chuse(excellent)

Table 1: Some pivot features.

2.3 Utilizing the Search Engine

Data sparseness is a common problem in NLP tasks. On the other hand, search engines nowadays usually index a huge amount of web pages. We now show how they can also be used as a valuable data source in a less obvious way. Previous studies like (Bollegala, 2007) have shown that search engine results can be comparable to language statistics from a large scale corpus for some NLP tasks like word sense disambiguation. For our problem, we use the query counts returned by a search engine to compute the correlations between a normal feature and the pivot features.

Consider the word "PIANYI" which is mostly used in positive comments, the query "CHANPIN(product) PING(comment) CHA(bad) PIANYI" has 2,900,000 results, while "CHANPIN(product) PING(comment) HAO(good) PIANYI" returns 57,400,000 pages. The results imply the word "PIANYI" is closer to the pivot feature "good" and it behaves less similar with the pivot feature "bad".

To add the query counts into the SCL scheme, we create pseudo examples when training linear predictors for pivot features. To construct a pseudo-positive example between a certain feature x_i and a certain pivot feature x_p, we simply query the term $x_i x_p$ and get a count c_1. We also query x_p alone and get another count c_2.Then we can create an example $(1, \{0, ..., 0, x_i = \frac{c_1}{c_2}, 0, ..., 0\})$. The pseudo-negative examples are created similarly. These pseudo examples are equivalent to texts with a single word and the count is used to approximate the empirical expectation. As an initial experiment, we select 10,000 Chinese features that occur more than once in the Chinese unlabeled data set but not frequent enough to be captured by the original SCL. And we also select the top 20 most informative Chinese pivot features to perform the queries.

3 Experiment

3.1 Data Set

For comparsion, we use the same data set in (Wan, 2009):

Test Set(Labeled Chinese Reviews): The data set contains a total of 886 labeled product reviews in Chinese (451 positive reviews and 435 negative ones). These reviews are extracted from a popular Chinese IT product website IT168 [1]. The reviews are mainly about electronic devices like mp3 players, mobile phones, digital cameras and computers.

Training Set(Labeled English Reviews): This is the data set used in the domain adaption experiment of (Blitzer et al., 2007b). It contains four major categories: books, DVDs, electronics and kitchen appliances. The data set consists of 8000 reviews with 4000 positive and 4000 negative, It is a public data set available on the web [2].

Unlabeled Set (Unlabeled Chinese Reviews): 1000 Chinese reviews downloaded from the same website as the Chinese training set. They are of the same domain as the test set.

We translate each English review into Chinese and vice versus through the public Google Translation service. Also following the setting in (Wan, 2009), we only use the Chinese unlabeled data and English training sets for our SCL training procedures. The test set is blind to the training stage.

The features we used are bigrams and unigrams in the two languages as in (Wan, 2009). In Chinese, we first apply the stanford Chinese word segmenter [3] to segment the reviews. Bigrams refers to a single Chinese word and a bigram refers to two adjacent Chinese words. The features are also pre-processed and normalized as in (Blitzer et al., 2007b).

[1]http://www.it168.com

[2]http://www.cis.upenn.edu/ mdredze/datasets/sentiment/

[3]http://nlp.stanford.edu/software/segmenter.shtml

Models	Precision	Recall	F-Score
CoTrain	0.768	0.905	0.831
SCL-B	0.772	0.914	0.837
SCL-C	0.764	0.896	0.825
SCL-O	0.760	0.909	0.828
SCL-E	0.801	0.909	0.851

Table 2: Results on the Positive Reviews

Models	Precision	Recall	F-Score
CoTrain	0.879	0.717	0.790
SCL-B	0.931	0.752	0.833
SCL-C	0.908	0.743	0.817
SCL-O	0.928	0.739	0.823
SCL-E	0.928	0.796	0.857

Table 3: Results on the Negative Reviews

3.2 Comparisons

We compare our procedure with the co-training scheme reported in (Wan, 2009):

CoTrain: The method with the best performance in (Wan, 2009). Two standard SVMs are trained using the co-training scheme for the Chinese views and the English views. And the results of the two SVMs are combined to give the final output.

SCL-B: The basic SCL procedure as explained.

SCL-O: The basic SCL except that we use all features from the translated texts instead of only the pivot features.

SCL-C: The training procedure is still the same as **SCL-B** except in the test time we only use the Chinese pivot features and neglect the English pivot features from translations.

SCL-E: The same as **SCL-B** except that in the training of linear pivot predictors, we also use the pseudo examples constructed from queries of the search engine.

Table 2 and 3 give results measured on the positive labeled reviews and negative reviews separately. Table 4 gives the overall accuracy on the whole 886 reviews. Our basic SCL approach **SCL-B** outperforms the original **Co-Training** approach by 2.2% in the overall accuracy. We can

CoTrain	SCL-B	SCL-O	SCL-C	SCL-E
0.813	0.835	0.826	0.822	0.854

Table 4: Overall Accuracy of Different Methods

also notice that using all the features including the ones from translations actually deteriorate the performance from 0.835 to 0.826.

The model incorporating the co-occurrence count information from the search engine has the best overall performance of 0.857. It is interesting to note that the simple scheme we have adopted increased the recall performance on the negative reviews significantly. After examining the reviews, we find the negative part contains some idioms and words mainly used on the internet and the query count seems to be able to capture their usage.

Finally, as our final goal is to train a Chinese sentiment classifier, it will be best if our model can only rely on the Chinese features. The **SCL-C** model improves the performance from the **Co-Training** method a little but not as much as the $SCL-B$ and the $SCL-O$ approaches. This observation suggests that the translations are still helpful for the cross-lingual adaptation problem as the translators perform some implicit semantic mapping.

4 Conclusion

In this paper, we are interested in adapting existing knowledge to a new language. We show that instead of fully relying on automatic translation, which may be misleading for a highly semantic task like the sentiment analysis, using techniques like SCL to connect the two languages through feature-level mapping seems a more suitable choice. We also perform an initial experiment using the co-occurrence statistics from a search engine to handle the data sparseness problem in the adaptation process, and the result is encouraging.

As future research we believe a promising avenue of exploration is to construct a probabilistic version of the SCL approach which could offer a more explicit model of the relations between the two domains and the relations between the search engine results and the model parameters. Also, in the current work, we select the pivot features by simple ranking with mutual information, which only considers the distribution information. Incorporating the confidence from the translator may further improve the performance.

References

Rie Kubota Ando and Tong Zhang. 2005. A framework for learning predictive structures from multiple tasks and unlabeled data. *Journal of Machine Learning Research.*

Carmen Banea, Rada Mihalcea, Janyce Wiebe, and Samer Hassan. 2008. Multilingual subjectivity analysis using machine translation. In *Proceedings of EMNLP.*

Nuria Bel, Cornelis H. A. Koster, and Marta Villegas. 2003. Cross-lingual text categorization. In *Research and AdvancedTechnology for Digital Libraries.*

John Blitzer, Ryan McDonald, and Fernando Pereira. 2006. Domain adaptation with structural correspondence learning. In *Proceedings of EMNLP.*

John Blitzer, Koby Crammer, Alex Kulesza, Fernando Pereira, and Jennifer Wortman. 2007a. Learning bounds for domain adaptation. In *Proceedings of NIPS.*

John Blitzer, Mark Dredze, and Fernando Pereira. 2007b. Biographies, bollywood, boom-boxes and blenders: Domain adaptation for sentiment classification. In *Proceedings of ACL.*

Danushka Bollegala. 2007. Measuring semantic similarity between words using web search engines. In *Proceedings of WWW 07.*

Wenyuan Dai, Gui-Rong Xue, Qiang Yang, and Yong Yu. 2007. Co-clustering based classification for out-of-domain documents. In *Proceedings of KDD.*

Jing Jiang and ChengXiang Zhai. 2007. A two-stage approach to domain adaptation for statistical classifiers. In *Proceedings of CIKM.*

Ryan T. McDonald, Kerry Hannan, Tyler Neylon, Mike Wells, and Jeffrey C. Reynar. 2007. Structured models for fine-to-coarse sentiment analysis. In *Proceedings of ACL.*

Rada Mihalcea, Carmen Banea, and Janyce Wiebe. 2007. Learning multilingual subjective language via cross-lingual projections. In *Proceedings of ACL.*

Bo Pang, Lillian Lee, and Shivakumar Vaithyanathan. 2002. Thumbs up? sentiment classification using machine learning techniques. In *Proceedings of EMNLP.*

Peter D. Turney. 2002. Thumbs up or thumbs down? semantic orientation applied to unsupervised classification of reviews. In *Proceedings of ACL.*

Xiaojun Wan. 2008. Using bilingual knowledge and ensemble techniques for unsupervised chinese sentiment analysis. In *Proceedings of EMNLP.*

Xiaojun Wan. 2009. Co-training for cross-lingual sentiment classification. In *Proceedings of ACL.*

Using Anaphora Resolution to Improve Opinion Target Identification in Movie Reviews

Niklas Jakob
Technische Universität Darmstadt
Hochschulstraße 10, 64289 Darmstadt

Iryna Gurevych
Technische Universität Darmstadt
Hochschulstraße 10, 64289 Darmstadt

http://www.ukp.tu-darmstadt.de/people

Abstract

Current work on automatic opinion mining has ignored opinion targets expressed by anaphorical pronouns, thereby missing a significant number of opinion targets. In this paper we empirically evaluate whether using an off-the-shelf anaphora resolution algorithm can improve the performance of a baseline opinion mining system. We present an analysis based on two different anaphora resolution systems. Our experiments on a movie review corpus demonstrate, that an unsupervised anaphora resolution algorithm significantly improves the opinion target extraction. We furthermore suggest domain and task specific extensions to an off-the-shelf algorithm which in turn yield significant improvements.

1 Introduction

Over the last years the task of opinion mining (OM) has been the topic of many publications. It has been approached with different goals in mind: Some research strived to perform subjectivity analysis at the document or sentence level, without focusing on what the individual opinions uttered in the document are about. Other approaches focused on extracting individual opinion words or phrases and what they are about. This aboutness has been referred to as the *opinion target* or opinion topic in the literature from the field. In this work our goal is to extract *opinion target - opinion word* pairs from sentences from movie reviews. A challenge which is frequently encountered in text mining tasks at this level of granularity is, that entities are being referred to by anaphora. In the task of OM, it can therefore also be necessary to analyze more than the content of one individual sentence when extracting opinion targets. Consider this example sentence: *"Simply put, it's unfathomable that this movie cracks the Top 250. It is absolutely awful."*. If one wants to extract what the opinion in the second sentence is about, an algorithm which resolves the anaphoric reference to the opinion target is required.

The extraction of such anaphoric opinion targets has been noted as an open issue multiple times in the OM context (Zhuang et al., 2006; Hu and Liu, 2004; Nasukawa and Yi, 2003). It is not a marginal phenomenon, since Kessler and Nicolov (2009) report that in their data, 14% of the opinion targets are pronouns. However, the task of resolving anaphora to mine opinion targets has not been addressed and evaluated yet to the best of our knowledge.

In this work, we investigate whether anaphora resolution (AR) can be successfully integrated into an OM algorithm and whether we can achieve an improvement regarding the OM in doing so. This paper is structured as follows: Section 2 discusses the related work on opinion target identification and OM on movie reviews. Section 3 outlines the OM algorithm we employed by us, while in Section 4 we discuss two different algorithms for AR which we experiment with. Finally, in Section 5 we present our experimental work including error analysis and discussion, and we conclude in Section 6.

2 Related Work

We split the description of the related work in two parts: In Section 2.1 we discuss the related work on OM with a focus on approaches for opinion target identification. In Section 2.2 we elaborate on findings from related OM research which also worked with movie reviews as this is our target domain in the present paper.

2.1 Opinion Target Identification

The extraction of opinions and especially opinion targets has been performed with quite diverse

Proceedings of the ACL 2010 Conference Short Papers, pages 263–268,
Uppsala, Sweden, 11-16 July 2010.

approaches. Initial approaches combined statistical information and basic linguistic features such as part-of-speech tags. The goal was to identify the opinion targets, here in form of products and their attributes, without a pre-built knowledge base which models the domain. For the target candidate identification, simple part-of-speech patterns were employed. The relevance ranking and extraction was then performed with different statistical measures: Pointwise Mutual Information (Popescu and Etzioni, 2005), the Likelihood Ratio Test (Yi et al., 2003) and Association Mining (Hu and Liu, 2004). A more linguistically motivated approach was taken by Kim and Hovy (2006) through identifying opinion holders and targets with semantic role labeling. This approach was promising, since their goal was to extract opinions from professionally edited content i.e. newswire.

Zhuang et al. (2006) present an algorithm for the extraction of *opinion target - opinion word* pairs. The opinion word and target candidates are identified in the annotated corpus and their extraction is then performed by applying possible paths connecting them in a dependency graph. These paths are combined with part-of-speech information and also learned from the annotated corpus.

To the best of our knowledge, there is currently only one system which integrates coreference information in OM. The algorithm by Stoyanov and Cardie (2008) identifies coreferring targets in newspaper articles. A candidate selection or extraction step for the opinion targets is not required, since they rely on manually annotated targets and focus solely on the coreference resolution. However they do not resolve pronominal anaphora in order to achieve that.

2.2 Opinion Mining on Movie Reviews

There is a huge body of work on OM in movie reviews which was sparked by the dataset from Pang and Lee (2005). This dataset consists of sentences which are annotated as expressing positive or negative opinions. An interesting insight was gained from the document level sentiment analysis on movie reviews in comparison to documents from other domains: Turney (2002) observes that the movie reviews are hardest to classify since the review authors tend to give information about the storyline of the movie which often contain characterizations, such as *"bad guy"* or *"violent scene"*. These statements however do not reflect any opinions of the reviewers regarding the movie. Zhuang et al. (2006) also observe that movie reviews are different from e.g. customer reviews on Amazon.com. This is reflected in their experiments, in which their system outperforms the system by Hu and Liu (2004) which attributes an opinion target to the opinion word which is closest regarding word distance in a sentence. The sentences in the movie reviews tend to be more complex, which can also be explained by their origin. The reviews were taken from the Internet Movie Database[1], on which the users are given a set of guidelines on how to write a review. Due to these insights, we are confident that the overall textual quality of the movie reviews is high enough for linguistically more advanced technologies such as parsing or AR to be successfully applied.

3 Opinion Target Identification

3.1 Dataset

Currently the only freely available dataset annotated with opinions including annotated anaphoric opinion targets is a corpus of movie reviews by Zhuang et al. (2006). Kessler and Nicolov (2009) describe a collection of product reviews in which anaphoric opinion targets are also annotated, but it is not available to the public (yet). Zhuang et al. (2006) used a subset of the dataset they published (1829 documents), namely 1100 documents, however they do not state which documents comprise this subset used in their evaluation. In our experiments, we therefore use the complete dataset available, detailed in Table 1. As shown, roughly 9.5% of the opinion targets are referred to by pronouns. Table 2 outlines detailed statistics on which pronouns occur as opinion targets.

Table 1: Dataset Statistics

# Documents	1829
# Sentences	24918
# Tokens	273715
# Target + Opinion Pairs	5298
# Targets which are Pronouns	504
# Pronouns	$>$ 11000

3.2 Baseline Opinion Mining

We reimplemented the algorithm presented by Zhuang et al. (2006) as the baseline for our

[1] http://www.imdb.com (IMDB)

Table 2: Pronouns as Opinion Targets

it	274	he	58	she	22	they	22
this	77	his	26	her	10		
		him	15				

experiments. Their approach is a supervised one. The annotated dataset is split in five folds, of which four are used as the training data. In the first step, opinion target and opinion word candidates are extracted from the training data. Frequency counts of the annotated opinion targets and opinion words are extracted from four training folds. The most frequently occurring opinion targets and opinion words are selected as candidates. Then the annotated sentences are parsed and a graph containing the words of the sentence is created, which are connected by the dependency relations between them. For each *opinion target - opinion word* pair, the shortest path connecting them is extracted from the dependency graph. A path consists of the part-of-speech tags of the nodes and the dependency types of the edges.
In order to be able to identify rarely occurring opinion targets which are not in the candidate list, they expand it by crawling the cast and crew names of the movies from the IMDB. How this crawling and extraction is done is not explained.

4 Algorithms for Anaphora Resolution

As pointed out by Charniak and Elsner (2009) there are hardly any freely available systems for AR. Although Charniak and Elsner (2009) present a machine-learning based algorithm for AR, they evaluate its performance in comparison to three non machine-learning based algorithms, since those are the only ones available. They observe that the best performing baseline algorithm (OpenNLP) is hardly documented. The algorithm with the next-to-highest results in (Charniak and Elsner, 2009) is MARS (Mitkov, 1998) from the GuiTAR (Poesio and Kabadjov, 2004) toolkit. This algorithm is based on statistical analysis of the antecedent candidates. Another promising algorithm for AR employs a rule based approach for antecedent identification. The CogNIAC algorithm (Baldwin, 1997) was designed for high-precision AR. This approach seems like an adequate strategy for our OM task, since in the dataset used in our experiments only a small fraction of the total number of pronouns are actual opinion targets (see Table 1). We extended the CogNIAC implementation to also resolve *"it"* and *"this"* as anaphora candidates, since off-the-shelf it only resolves personal pronouns. We will refer to this extension with **[id]**. Both algorithms follow the common approach that noun phrases are antecedent candidates for the anaphora. In our experiments we employed both the MARS and the CogNIAC algorithm, for which we created three extensions which are detailed in the following.

4.1 Extensions of CogNIAC

We identified a few typical sources of errors in a preliminary error analysis. We therefore suggest three extensions to the algorithm which are on the one hand possible in the OM setting and on the other hand represent special features of the target discourse type: **[1.]** We observed that the Stanford Named Entity Recognizer (Finkel et al., 2005) is superior to the *Person* detection of the (MUC6 trained) CogNIAC implementation. We therefore filter out *Person* antecedent candidates which the Stanford NER detects for the impersonal and demonstrative pronouns and *Location & Organization* candidates for the personal pronouns. This way the input to the AR is optimized. **[2.]** The second extension exploits the fact that reviews from the IMDB exhibit certain contextual properties. They are gathered and to be presented in the context of one particular entity (=movie). The context or topic under which it occurs is therefore typically clear to the reader and is therefore not explicitly introduced in the discourse. This is equivalent to the situational context we often refer to in dialogue. In the reviews, the authors often refer to the movie or film as a whole by a pronoun. We exploit this by an additional rule which resolves an impersonal or demonstrative pronoun to *"movie"* or *"film"* if there is no other (matching) antecedent candidate in the previous two sentences. **[3.]** The rules by which CogNIAC resolves anaphora were designed so that anaphora which have ambiguous antecedents are left unresolved. This strategy should lead to a high precision AR, but at the same time it can have a negative impact on the recall. In the OM context, it happens quite frequently that the authors comment on the entity they want to criticize in a series of arguments. In such argument chains, we try to solve cases of antecedent ambiguity by analyzing the opinions: If there are ambiguous antecedent candidates for a pronoun, we check whether there is an opinion uttered in the previous sentence. If this is the case and if the opinion target matches the pronoun regarding gender and number, we resolve the pronoun to the antecedent which was the previous opinion target.

In the results of our experiments in Section 5, we will refer to the configurations using these extensions with the numbers attributed to them above.

5 Experimental Work

To integrate AR in the OM algorithm, we add the antecedents of the pronouns annotated as opinion targets to the target candidate list. Then we extract the dependency paths connecting pronouns and opinion words and add them to the list of valid paths. When we run the algorithm, we extract anaphora which were resolved, if they occur with a valid dependency path to an opinion word. In such a case, the anaphor is substituted for its antecedent and thus extracted as part of an *opinion target - opinion word* pair.

To reproduce the system by Zhuang et al. (2006), we substitute the cast and crew list employed by them (see Section 3.2), with a NER component (Finkel et al., 2005). One aspect regarding the extraction of *opinion target - opinion word* pairs remains open in Zhuang et al. (2006): The dependency paths only identify connections between pairs of single words. However, almost 50% of the opinion target candidates are multiword expressions. Zhuang et al. (2006) do not explain how they extract multiword opinion targets with the dependency paths. In our experiments, we require a dependency path to be found to each word of a multiword target candidate for it to be extracted. Furthermore, Zhuang et al. (2006) do not state whether in their evaluation annotated multiword targets are treated as a single unit which needs to be extracted, or whether a partial matching is employed in such cases. We require all individual words of a multiword expression to be extracted by the algorithm. As mentioned above, the dependency path based approach will only identify connections between pairs of single words. We therefore employ a merging step, in which we combine adjacent opinion targets to a multiword expression. We have compiled two result sets: Table 3 shows the results of the overall OM in a five-fold cross-validation. Table 4 gives a detailed overview of the AR for opinion target identification summed up over all folds. In Table 4, a true positive refers to an extracted pronoun which was annotated as an opinion target and is resolved to the correct antecedent. A false positive subsumes two error classes: A pronoun which was not annotated as an opinion target but extracted as such, or a pronoun which is resolved to an incorrect antecedent.

As shown in Table 3, the recall of our reimplementation is slightly higher than the recall reported in Zhuang et al. (2006). However, our precision and thus f-measure are lower. This can be attributed to the different document sets used in our experiments (see Section 3.1), or our substitution of the list of peoples' names with the NER component, or differences regarding the evaluation strategy as mentioned above.

We observe that the MARS algorithm yields an improvement regarding recall compared to the baseline system. However, it also extracts a high number of false positives for both the personal and impersonal / demonstrative pronouns. This is due to the fact that the MARS algorithm is designed for robustness and always resolves a pronoun to an antecedent.

CogNIAC in its off-the-shelf configuration already yields significant improvements over the baseline regarding f-measure[2]. Our CogNIAC extension [id] improves recall slightly in comparison to the off-the-shelf system. As shown in Table 4, the algorithm extracts impersonal and demonstrative pronouns with lower precision than personal pronouns. Our error analysis shows that this is mostly due to the *Person / Location / Organization* classification of the CogNIAC implementation. The names of actors and movies are thus often misclassified. Extension [1] mitigates this problem, since it increases precision (Table 3 row 6), while not affecting recall. The overall improvement of our extensions [id] + [1] is however not statistically significant in comparison to off-the-shelf CogNIAC.

Our extensions [2] and [3] in combination with [id] each increase recall at the expense of precision. The improvement in f-measure of CogNIAC [id] + [3] over the off-the-shelf system is statistically significant. The best overall results regarding f-measure are reached if we combine all our extensions of the CogNIAC algorithm. The results of this configuration show that the positive effects of extensions [2] and [3] are complemen-

[2]Significance of improvements was tested using a paired two-tailed t-test and $p \leq 0.05$ (*) and $p \leq 0.01$ (**)

Table 3: Op. Target - Op. Word Pair Extraction

Configuration	Reca.	Prec.	F-Meas.
Results in Zhuang et al.	0.548	0.654	0.596
Our Reimplementation	0.554	0.523	0.538
MARS off-the-shelf	0.595	0.467	0.523
CogNIAC off-the-shelf	0.586	**0.534**	0.559**
CogNIAC+[id]	0.594	0.516	0.552
CogNIAC+[id]+[1]	0.594	0.533	0.561
CogNIAC+[id]+[2]	0.603	0.501	0.547
CogNIAC+[id]+[3]	0.613	0.521	0.563*
CogNIAC+[id]+[1]+[2]+[3]	**0.614**	0.531	**0.569***

Table 4: Results of AR for Opinion Targets

Algorithm	Pers.[1]		Imp. & Dem.[1]	
	TP[2]	FP[2]	TP	FP
MARS off-the-shelf	102	164	115	623
CogNIAC off-the-shelf	117	95	0	0
CogNIAC+[id]	117	95	105	180
CogNIAC+[id]+[1]	117	41	105	51
CogNIAC+[id]+[2]	117	95	153	410
CogNIAC+[id]+[3]	131	103	182	206
CogNIAC+[id]+[1]+[2]+[3]	124	64	194	132

[1] **pers**onal, **imp**ersonal & **dem**onstrative pronouns
[2] true **p**ositives, **f**alse **p**ositives

tary regarding the extraction of impersonal and demonstrative pronouns. This configuration yields statistically significant improvements regarding f-measure over the off-the-shelf CogNIAC configuration, while also having the overall highest recall.

5.1 Error Analysis

When extracting opinions from movie reviews, we observe the same challenge as Turney (2002): The users often characterize events in the storyline or roles the characters play. These characterizations contain the same words which are also used to express opinions. Hence these combinations are frequently but falsely extracted as *opinion target - opinion word* pairs, negatively affecting the precision. The algorithm cannot distinguish them from opinions expressing the stance of the author. Overall, the recall of the baseline is rather low. This is due to the fact that the algorithm only learns a subset of the opinion words and opinion targets annotated in the training data. Currently, it cannot discover any new opinion words and targets. This could be addressed by integrating a component which identifies new opinion targets by calculating the relevance of a word in the corpus based on statistical measures.

The AR introduces new sources of errors regarding the extraction of opinion targets: Errors in gender and number identification can lead to an incorrect selection of antecedent candidates. Even if the gender and number identification is correct, the algorithm might select an incorrect antecedent if there is more than one possible candidate. A non-robust algorithm as CogNIAC might leave a pronoun which is an actual opinion target unresolved, due to the ambiguity of its antecedent candidates.

The upper bound for the OM with perfect AR on top of the baseline would be recall: 0.649, precision: 0.562, f-measure: 0.602. Our best configuration reaches $\sim 50\%$ of the improvements which are theoretically possible with perfect AR.

6 Conclusions

We have shown that by extending an OM algorithm with AR for opinion target extraction significant improvements can be achieved. The rule based AR algorithm CogNIAC performs well regarding the extraction of opinion targets which are personal pronouns. The algorithm does not yield high precision when resolving impersonal and demonstrative pronouns. We present a set of extensions which address this challenge and in combination yield significant improvements over the off-the-shelf configuration. A robust AR algorithm does not yield any improvements regarding f-measure in the OM task. This type of algorithm creates many false positives, which are not filtered out by the dependency paths employed in the algorithm by Zhuang et al. (2006).

AR could also be employed in other OM algorithms which aim at identifying opinion targets by means of a statistical analysis. Vicedo and Ferrández (2000) successfully modified the relevance ranking of terms in their documents by replacing anaphora with their antecedents. The approach can be taken for OM algorithms which select the opinion target candidates with a relevance ranking (Hu and Liu, 2004; Yi et al., 2003).

Acknowledgments

The project was funded by means of the German Federal Ministry of Economy and Technology under the promotional reference "01MQ07012". The authors take the responsibility for the contents. This work has been supported by the Volkswagen Foundation as part of the Lichtenberg-Professorship Program under grant No. I/82806.

References

Breck Baldwin. 1997. Cogniac: High precision coreference with limited knowledge and linguistic resources. In *Proceedings of a Workshop on Operational Factors in Practical, Robust Anaphora Resolution for Unrestricted Texts*, pages 38–45, Madrid, Spain, July.

Eugene Charniak and Micha Elsner. 2009. EM works for pronoun anaphora resolution. In *Proceedings of the 12th Conference of the European Chapter of the ACL*, pages 148–156, Athens, Greece, March.

Jenny Rose Finkel, Trond Grenager, and Christopher Manning. 2005. Incorporating non-local information into information extraction systems by gibbs sampling. In *Proceedings of the 43rd Annual Meeting of the Association for Computational Linguistics*, pages 363–370, Michigan, USA, June.

Minqing Hu and Bing Liu. 2004. Mining and summarizing customer reviews. In *Proceedings of the 10th ACM SIGKDD International Conference on Knowledge Discovery and Data Mining*, pages 168–177, Seattle, WA, USA, August.

Jason Kessler and Nicolas Nicolov. 2009. Targeting sentiment expressions through supervised ranking of linguistic configurations. In *Proceedings of the Third International AAAI Conference on Weblogs and Social Media*, San Jose, CA, USA, May.

Soo-Min Kim and Eduard Hovy. 2006. Extracting opinions, opinion holders, and topics expressed in online news media text. In *Proceedings of the ACL Workshop on Sentiment and Subjectivity in Text*, pages 1–8, Sydney, Australia, July.

Ruslan Mitkov. 1998. Robust pronoun resolution with limited knowledge. In *Proceedings of the 36th Annual Meeting of the Association for Computational Linguistics and 17th International Conference on Computational Linguistics*, pages 869–875, Montreal, Canada, August.

Tetsuya Nasukawa and Jeonghee Yi. 2003. Sentiment analysis: Capturing favorability using natural language processing. In *Proceedings of the 2nd International Conference on Knowledge Capture*, pages 70–77, Sanibel Island, FL, USA, October.

Bo Pang and Lillian Lee. 2005. Seeing stars: Exploiting class relationships for sentiment categorization with respect to rating scales. In *Proceedings of the 43rd Annual Meeting of the Association for Computational Linguistics*, pages 115–124, Michigan, USA, June.

Massimo Poesio and Mijail A. Kabadjov. 2004. A general-purpose, off-the-shelf anaphora resolution module: Implementation and preliminary evaluation. In *Proceedings of the 4th International Conference on Language Resources and Evaluation*, pages 663–666, Lisboa, Portugal, May.

Ana-Maria Popescu and Oren Etzioni. 2005. Extracting product features and opinions from reviews. In *Proceedings of Human Language Technology Conference and Conference on Empirical Methods in Natural Language Processing*, pages 339–346, Vancouver, Canada, October.

Veselin Stoyanov and Claire Cardie. 2008. Topic identification for fine-grained opinion analysis. In *Proceedings of the 22nd International Conference on Computational Linguistics*, pages 817–824, Manchester, UK, August.

Peter Turney. 2002. Thumbs up or thumbs down? semantic orientation applied to unsupervised classification of reviews. In *Proceedings of the 40th Annual Meeting of the Association for Computational Linguistics*, pages 417–424, Philadelphia, Pennsylvania, USA, July.

José L. Vicedo and Antonio Ferrández. 2000. Applying anaphora resolution to question answering and information retrieval systems. In *Proceedings of the First International Conference on Web-Age Information Management*, volume 1846 of *Lecture Notes In Computer Science*, pages 344–355. Springer, Shanghai, China.

Jeonghee Yi, Tetsuya Nasukawa, Razvan Bunescu, and Wayne Niblack. 2003. Sentiment analyzer: Extracting sentiments about a given topic using natural language processing techniques. In *Proceedings of the 3rd IEEE International Conference on Data Mining*, pages 427–434, Melbourne, FL, USA, December.

Li Zhuang, Feng Jing, and Xiao-Yan Zhu. 2006. Movie review mining and summarization. In *Proceedings of the ACM 15th Conference on Information and Knowledge Management*, pages 43–50, Arlington, VA, USA, November.

Hierarchical Sequential Learning for Extracting Opinions and their Attributes

Yejin Choi and Claire Cardie
Department of Computer Science
Cornell University
Ithaca, NY 14853
{ychoi,cardie}@cs.cornell.edu

Abstract

Automatic opinion recognition involves a number of related tasks, such as identifying the boundaries of opinion expression, determining their polarity, and determining their intensity. Although much progress has been made in this area, existing research typically treats each of the above tasks in isolation. In this paper, we apply a hierarchical parameter sharing technique using Conditional Random Fields for fine-grained opinion analysis, jointly detecting the boundaries of opinion expressions as well as determining two of their key attributes — polarity and intensity. Our experimental results show that our proposed approach improves the performance over a baseline that does not exploit hierarchical structure among the classes. In addition, we find that the joint approach outperforms a baseline that is based on cascading two separate components.

1 Introduction

Automatic opinion recognition involves a number of related tasks, such as identifying expressions of opinion (e.g. Kim and Hovy (2005), Popescu and Etzioni (2005), Breck et al. (2007)), determining their polarity (e.g. Hu and Liu (2004), Kim and Hovy (2004), Wilson et al. (2005)), and determining their strength, or intensity (e.g. Popescu and Etzioni (2005), Wilson et al. (2006)). Most previous work treats each subtask in isolation: opinion expression extraction (i.e. detecting the boundaries of opinion expressions) and opinion attribute classification (e.g. determining values for polarity and intensity) are tackled as separate steps in opinion recognition systems. Unfortunately, errors from individual components will propagate in systems with cascaded component architectures, causing performance degradation in the end-to-end system (e.g. Finkel et al. (2006)) — in our case, in the end-to-end opinion recognition system.

In this paper, we apply a *hierarchical parameter sharing* technique (e.g., Cai and Hofmann (2004), Zhao et al. (2008)) using Conditional Random Fields (CRFs) (Lafferty et al., 2001) to fine-grained opinion analysis. In particular, we aim to jointly identify the boundaries of opinion expressions as well as to determine two of their key attributes — polarity and intensity.

Experimental results show that our proposed approach improves the performance over the baseline that does not exploit the hierarchical structure among the classes. In addition, we find that the joint approach outperforms a baseline that is based on cascading two separate systems.

2 Hierarchical Sequential Learning

We define the problem of joint extraction of opinion expressions and their attributes as a sequence tagging task as follows. Given a sequence of tokens, $x = x_1 \ldots x_n$, we predict a sequence of labels, $y = y_1 \ldots y_n$, where $y_i \in \{0, ..., 9\}$ are defined as conjunctive values of polarity labels and intensity labels, as shown in Table 1. Then the conditional probability $p(y|x)$ for linear-chain CRFs is given as (Lafferty et al., 2001)

$$P(y|x) = \frac{1}{Z_x} \exp \sum_i \Big(\lambda\, f(y_i, x, i) + \lambda'\, f'(y_{i-1}, y_i, x, i) \Big)$$

where Z_x is the normalization factor.

In order to apply a hierarchical parameter sharing technique (e.g., Cai and Hofmann (2004), Zhao et al. (2008)), we extend parameters as follows.

Proceedings of the ACL 2010 Conference Short Papers, pages 269–274,
Uppsala, Sweden, 11-16 July 2010. ©2010 Association for Computational Linguistics

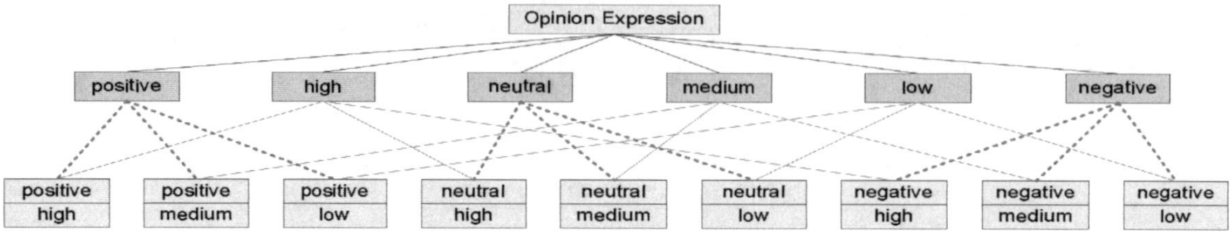

Figure 1: The hierarchical structure of classes for opinion expressions with polarity (positive, neutral, negative) and intensity (high, medium, low)

LABEL	0	1	2	3	4	5	6	7	8	9
POLARITY	none	positive	positive	positive	neutral	neutral	neutral	negative	negative	negative
INTENSITY	none	high	medium	low	high	medium	low	high	medium	low

Table 1: Labels for Opinion Extraction with Polarity and Intensity

$$\begin{aligned} \lambda\, f(y_i, x, i) &= \lambda_\alpha\, g_{\mathrm{O}}(\alpha, x, i) \\ &+ \lambda_\beta\, g_{\mathrm{P}}(\beta, x, i) \\ &+ \lambda_\gamma\, g_{\mathrm{S}}(\gamma, x, i) \end{aligned} \quad (1)$$

$$\begin{aligned} \lambda'\, f'(y_{i-1}, y_i, x, i) &= \lambda'_{\alpha,\hat{\alpha}}\, g'_{\mathrm{O}}(\alpha, \hat{\alpha}, x, i) \\ &+ \lambda'_{\beta,\hat{\beta}}\, g'_{\mathrm{P}}(\beta, \hat{\beta}, x, i) \\ &+ \lambda'_{\gamma,\hat{\gamma}}\, g'_{\mathrm{S}}(\gamma, \hat{\gamma}, x, i) \end{aligned}$$

where g_{O} and g'_{O} are feature vectors defined for **O**pinion extraction, g_{P} and g'_{P} are feature vectors defined for **P**olarity extraction, and g_{S} and g'_{S} are feature vectors defined for **S**trength extraction, and

$$\begin{aligned} \alpha, \hat{\alpha} &\in \{\text{OPINION, NO-OPINION}\} \\ \beta, \hat{\beta} &\in \{\text{POSITIVE, NEGATIVE, NEUTRAL, NO-POLARITY}\} \\ \gamma, \hat{\gamma} &\in \{\text{HIGH, MEDIUM, LOW, NO-INTENSITY}\} \end{aligned}$$

For instance, if $y_i = 1$, then

$$\begin{aligned} \lambda\, f(1, x, i) &= \lambda_{\text{OPINION}}\, g_{\mathrm{O}}(\text{OPINION}, x, i) \\ &+ \lambda_{\text{POSITIVE}}\, g_{\mathrm{P}}(\text{POSITVE}, x, i) \\ &+ \lambda_{\text{HIGH}}\, g_{\mathrm{S}}(\text{HIGH}, x, i) \end{aligned}$$

If $y_{i-1} = 0, y_i = 4$, then

$$\begin{aligned} &\lambda'\, f'(0, 4, x, i) \\ &= \lambda'_{\text{NO-OPINION,OPINION}}\, g'_{\mathrm{O}}(\text{NO-OPINION, OPINION}, x, i) \\ &+ \lambda'_{\text{NO-POLARITY, NEUTRAL}}\, g'_{\mathrm{P}}(\text{NO-POLARITY, NEUTRAL}, x, i) \\ &+ \lambda'_{\text{NO-INTENSITY, HIGH}}\, g'_{\mathrm{S}}(\text{NO-INTENSITY, HIGH}, x, i) \end{aligned}$$

This hierarchical construction of feature and weight vectors allows similar labels to share the same subcomponents of feature and weight vectors. For instance, all $\lambda\ f(y_i, x, i)$ such that $y_i \in \{1, 2, 3\}$ will share the same component $\lambda_{\text{POSITIVE}}\ g_{\mathrm{P}}(\text{POSITVE}, x, i)$. Note that there can be other variations of hierarchical construction. For instance, one can add $\lambda_\delta\ g_{\mathrm{I}}(\delta, x, i)$ and $\lambda'_{\delta,\hat{\delta}}\ g'_{\mathrm{I}}(\delta, \hat{\delta}, x, i)$ to Equation (1) for $\delta \in \{0, 1, ..., 9\}$, in order to allow more individualized learning for each label.

Notice also that the number of sets of parameters constructed by Equation (1) is significantly smaller than the number of sets of parameters that are needed without the hierarchy. The former requires $(2+4+4)+(2\times 2+4\times 4+4\times 4) = 46$ sets of parameters, but the latter requires $(10) + (10 \times 10) = 110$ sets of parameters. Because a combination of a polarity component and an intensity component can distinguish each label, it is not necessary to define a separate set of parameters for each label.

3 Features

We first introduce definitions of key terms that will be used to describe features.

- **PRIOR-POLARITY & PRIOR-INTENSITY:**
  We obtain these prior-attributes from the *polarity lexicon* populated by Wilson et al. (2005).
- **EXP-POLARITY, EXP-INTENSITY & EXP-SPAN:**
  Words in a given opinion expression often do not share the same prior-attributes. Such discontinuous distribution of features can make it harder to learn the desired opinion expression boundaries. Therefore, we try to obtain expression-level attributes (EXP-POLARITY and EXP-INTENSITY) using simple heuristics. In order to derive EXP-POLARITY, we perform simple

voting. If there is a word with a negation effect, such as "never", "not", "hardly", "against", then we flip the polarity. For EXP-INTENSITY, we use the highest PRIOR-INTENSITY in the span. The text span with the same expression-level attributes are referred to as EXP-SPAN.

3.1 Per-Token Features

Per-token features are defined in the form of $g_O(\alpha, x, i), g_P(\beta, x, i)$ and $g_S(\gamma, x, i)$. The domains of α, β, γ are as given in Section 3.

Common Per-Token Features

Following features are common for all class labels. The notation $\otimes$ indicates conjunctive operation of two values.

- PART-OF-SPEECH(x_i):
  based on GATE (Cunningham et al., 2002).
- WORD(x_i), WORD(x_{i-1}), WORD(x_{i+1})
- WORDNET-HYPERNYM(x_i):
  based on WordNet (Miller, 1995).
- OPINION-LEXICON(x_i):
  based on *opinion lexicon* (Wiebe et al., 2002).
- SHALLOW-PARSER(x_i):
  based on CASS partial parser (Abney, 1996).
- PRIOR-POLARITY(x_i) $\otimes$ PRIOR-INTENSITY(x_i)
- EXP-POLARITY(x_i) $\otimes$ EXP-INTENSITY(x_i)
- EXP-POLARITY(x_i) $\otimes$ EXP-INTENSITY(x_i) $\otimes$ STEM(x_i)
- EXP-SPAN(x_i):
  boolean to indicate whether x_i is in an EXP-SPAN.
- DISTANCE-TO-EXP-SPAN(x_i): $0, 1, 2, 3+$.
- EXP-POLARITY(x_i) $\otimes$ EXP-INTENSITY(x_i) $\otimes$ EXP-SPAN(x_i)

Polarity Per-Token Features

These features are included only for $g_O(\alpha, x, i)$ and $g_P(\beta, x, i)$, which are the feature functions corresponding to the polarity-based classes.

- PRIOR-POLARITY(x_i), EXP-POLARITY((x_i)
- STEM(x_i) $\otimes$ EXP-POLARITY(x_i)
- COUNT-OF-*Polarity*:
  where *Polarity* $\in$ {positive, neutral, negative}. This feature encodes the number of positive, neutral, and negative EXP-POLARITY words respectively, in the current sentence.
- STEM(x_i) $\otimes$ COUNT-OF-*Polarity*
- EXP-POLARITY(x_i) $\otimes$ COUNT-OF-*Polarity*
- EXP-SPAN(x_i) and EXP-POLARITY(x_i)
- DISTANCE-TO-EXP-SPAN(x_i) $\otimes$ EXP-POLARITY(x_p)

Intensity Per-Token Features

These features are included only for $g_O(\alpha, x, i)$ and $g_S(\gamma, x, i)$, which are the feature functions corresponding to the intensity-based classes.

- PRIOR-INTENSITY(x_i), EXP-INTENSITY(x_i)
- STEM(x_i) $\otimes$ EXP-INTENSITY(x_i)
- COUNT-OF-STRONG, COUNT-OF-WEAK:
  the number of strong and weak EXP-INTENSITY words in the current sentence.
- INTENSIFIER(x_i): whether x_i is an intensifier, such as "extremely", "highly", "really".
- STRONGMODAL(x_i): whether x_i is a strong modal verb, such as "must", "can", "will".
- WEAKMODAL(x_i): whether x_i is a weak modal verb, such as "may", "could", "would".
- DIMINISHER(x_i): whether x_i is a diminisher, such as "little", "somewhat", "less".
- PRECEDED-BY-τ(x_i),
  PRECEDED-BY-τ(x_i) $\otimes$ EXP-INTENSITY(x_i):
  where $\tau \in$ { INTENSIFIER, STRONGMODAL, WEAKMODAL, DIMINISHER}
- $\tau(x_i)$ $\otimes$ EXP-INTENSITY(x_i),
  $\tau(x_i)$ $\otimes$ EXP-INTENSITY(x_{i-1}),
  $\tau(x_{i-1})$ $\otimes$ EXP-INTENSITY(x_{i+1})
- EXP-SPAN(x_i) $\otimes$ EXP-INTENSITY(x_i)
- DISTANCE-TO-EXP-SPAN(x_i) $\otimes$ EXP-INTENSITY(x_p)

3.2 Transition Features

Transition features are employed to help with boundary extraction as follows:

Polarity Transition Features

Polarity transition features are features that are used only for $g'_O(\alpha, \hat{\alpha}, x, i)$ and $g'_P(\beta, \hat{\beta}, x, i)$.

- PART-OF-SPEECH(x_i) $\otimes$ PART-OF-SPEECH(x_{i+1}) $\otimes$ EXP-POLARITY(x_i)
- EXP-POLARITY(x_i) $\otimes$ EXP-POLARITY(x_{i+1})

Intensity Transition Features

Intensity transition features are features that are used only for $g'_O(\alpha, \hat{\alpha}, x, i)$ and $g'_S(\gamma, \hat{\gamma}, x, i)$.

- PART-OF-SPEECH(x_i) $\otimes$ PART-OF-SPEECH(x_{i+1}) $\otimes$ EXP-INTENSITY(x_i)
- EXP-INTENSITY(x_i) $\otimes$ EXP-INTENSITY(x_{i+1})

4 Evaluation

We evaluate our system using the Multi-Perspective Question Answering (MPQA) corpus[1]. Our gold standard opinion expressions cor-

[1]The MPQA corpus can be obtained at http://nrrc.mitre.org/NRRC/publications.htm.

Method Description	Positive			Neutral			Negative		
	r(%)	p(%)	f(%)	r(%)	p(%)	f(%)	r(%)	p(%)	f(%)
Polarity-Only ∩ Intensity-Only (BASELINE1)	29.6	65.7	40.8	26.5	69.1	38.3	35.5	77.0	48.6
Joint without Hierarchy (BASELINE2)	30.7	65.7	41.9	29.9	66.5	41.2	37.3	77.1	50.3
Joint with Hierarchy	31.8	67.1	**43.1**	31.9	66.6	**43.1**	40.4	76.2	**52.8**

Table 2: Performance of Opinion Extraction with Correct Polarity Attribute

Method Description	High			Medium			Low		
	r(%)	p(%)	f(%)	r(%)	p(%)	f(%)	r(%)	p(%)	f(%)
Polarity-Only ∩ Intensity-Only (BASELINE1)	26.4	58.3	36.3	29.7	59.0	39.6	15.4	60.3	24.5
Joint without Hierarchy (BASELINE2)	29.7	54.2	**38.4**	28.0	57.4	37.6	18.8	55.0	28.0
Joint with Hierarchy	27.1	55.2	36.3	32.0	56.5	**40.9**	21.1	56.3	**30.7**

Table 3: Performance of Opinion Extraction with Correct Intensity Attribute

Method Description	r(%)	p(%)	f(%)
Polar-Only ∩ Intensity-Only	43.3	92.0	58.9
Joint without Hierarchy	46.0	88.4	60.5
Joint with Hierarchy	48.0	87.8	**62.0**

Table 4: Performance of Opinion Extraction

respond to *direct subjective expression* and *expressive subjective element* (Wiebe et al., 2005).[2]

Our implementation of hierarchical sequential learning is based on the Mallet (McCallum, 2002) code for CRFs. In all experiments, we use a Gaussian prior of 1.0 for regularization. We use 135 documents for development, and test on a different set of 400 documents using 10-fold cross-validation. We investigate three options for jointly extracting opinion expressions with their attributes as follows:

[Baseline-1] Polarity-Only ∩ Intensity-Only: For this baseline, we train two separate sequence tagging CRFs: one that extracts opinion expressions only with the polarity attribute (using common features and polarity extraction features in Section 3), and another that extracts opinion expressions only with the intensity attribute (using common features and intensity extraction features in Section 3). We then combine the results from two separate CRFs by collecting all opinion entities extracted by both sequence taggers.[3] This baseline effectively represents a cascaded component approach.

[Baseline-2] Joint without Hierarchy: Here we use simple linear-chain CRFs without exploiting the class hierarchy for the opinion recognition task. We use the tags shown in Table 1.

Joint with Hierarchy: Finally, we test the hierarchical sequential learning approach elaborated in Section 3.

4.1 Evaluation Results

We evaluate all experiments at the opinion entity level, i.e. at the level of each opinion expression rather than at the token level. We use three evaluation metrics: recall, precision, and F-measure with equally weighted recall and precision.

Table 4 shows the performance of opinion extraction without matching any attribute. That is, an extracted opinion entity is counted as correct if it overlaps[4] with a gold standard opinion expression, without checking the correctness of its attributes. Table 2 and 3 show the performance of opinion extraction with the correct polarity and intensity respectively.

From all of these evaluation criteria, JOINT WITH

[2] Only 1.5% of the polarity annotations correspond to *both*; hence, we merge *both* into the *neutral*. Similarly, for gold standard intensity, we merge *extremely high* into *high*.

[3] We collect all entities whose portions of text spans are extracted by both models.

[4] Overlap matching is a reasonable choice as the annotator agreement study is also based on overlap matching (Wiebe et al., 2005). One might wonder whether the overlap matching scheme could allow a degenerative case where extracting the entire test dataset as one giant opinion expression would yield 100% recall and precision. Because each sentence corresponds to a different test instance in our model, and because some sentences do not contain any opinion expression in the dataset, such degenerative case is not possible in our experiments.

HIERARCHY performs the best, and the least effective one is BASELINE-1, which cascades two separately trained models. It is interesting that the simple sequential tagging approach even without exploiting the hierarchy (BASELINE-2) performs better than the cascaded approach (BASELINE-1).

When evaluating with respect to the polarity attribute, the performance of the negative class is substantially higher than the that of other classes. This is not surprising as there is approximately twice as much data for the negative class. When evaluating with respect to the intensity attribute, the performance of the LOW class is substantially lower than that of other classes. This result reflects the fact that it is inherently harder to distinguish an opinion expression with low intensity from no opinion. In general, we observe that determining correct intensity attributes is a much harder task than determining correct polarity attributes.

In order to have a sense of upper bound, we also report the individual performance of two separately trained models used for BASELINE-1: for the Polarity-Only model that extracts opinion boundaries only with polarity attribute, the F-scores with respect to the positive, neutral, negative classes are 46.7, 47.5, 57.0, respectively. For the Intensity-Only model, the F-scores with respect to the high, medium, low classes are 37.1, 40.8, 26.6, respectively. Remind that neither of these models alone fully solve the joint task of extracting boundaries as well as determining two attributions simultaneously. As a result, when conjoining the results from the two models (BASELINE-1), the final performance drops substantially.

We conclude from our experiments that the simple joint sequential tagging approach even without exploiting the hierarchy brings a better performance than combining two separately developed systems. In addition, our hierarchical joint sequential learning approach brings a further performance gain over the simple joint sequential tagging method.

5 Related Work

Although there have been much research for fine-grained opinion analysis (e.g., Hu and Liu (2004), Wilson et al. (2005), Wilson et al. (2006), Choi and Claire (2008), Wilson et al. (2009)),[5] none is directly comparable to our results; much of previous work studies only a subset of what we tackle in this paper. However, as shown in Section 4.1, when we train the learning models only for a subset of the tasks, we can achieve a better performance instantly by making the problem simpler. Our work differs from most of previous work in that we investigate how solving multiple related tasks affects performance on sub-tasks.

The hierarchical parameter sharing technique used in this paper has been previously used by Zhao et al. (2008) for opinion analysis. However, Zhao et al. (2008) employs this technique only to classify sentence-level attributes (polarity and intensity), without involving a much harder task of detecting boundaries of sub-sentential entities.

6 Conclusion

We applied a hierarchical parameter sharing technique using Conditional Random Fields for fine-grained opinion analysis. Our proposed approach jointly extract opinion expressions from unstructured text and determine their attributes — polarity and intensity. Empirical results indicate that the simple joint sequential tagging approach even without exploiting the hierarchy brings a better performance than combining two separately developed systems. In addition, we found that the hierarchical joint sequential learning approach improves the performance over the simple joint sequential tagging method.

Acknowledgments

This work was supported in part by National Science Foundation Grants BCS-0904822, BCS-0624277, IIS-0535099 and by the Department of Homeland Security under ONR Grant N0014-07-1-0152. We thank the reviewers and Ainur Yessenalina for many helpful comments.

References

S. Abney. 1996. Partial parsing via finite-state cascades. In *Journal of Natural Language Engineering*, 2(4).

E. Breck, Y. Choi and C. Cardie. 2007. Identifying Expressions of Opinion in Context. In *IJCAI*.

[5]For instance, the results of Wilson et al. (2005) is not comparable even for our Polarity-Only model used inside BASELINE-1, because Wilson et al. (2005) does not operate on the entire corpus as unstructured input. Instead, Wilson et al. (2005) evaluate only on known words that are in their opinion lexicon. Furthermore, Wilson et al. (2005) simplifies the problem by combining neutral opinions and no opinions into the same class, while our system distinguishes the two.

L. Cai and T. Hofmann. 2004. Hierarchical document categorization with support vector machines. In *CIKM*.

Y. Choi and C. Cardie. 2008. Learning with Compositional Semantics as Structural Inference for Subsentential Sentiment Analysis. In *EMNLP*.

H. Cunningham, D. Maynard, K. Bontcheva and V. Tablan. 2002. GATE: A Framework and Graphical Development Environment for Robust NLP Tools and Applications. In *ACL*.

J. R. Finkel, C. D. Manning and A. Y. Ng. 2006. Solving the Problem of Cascading Errors: Approximate Bayesian Inference for Linguistic Annotation Pipelines. In *EMNLP*.

M. Hu and B. Liu. 2004. Mining and Summarizing Customer Reviews. In *KDD*.

S. Kim and E. Hovy. 2004. Determining the sentiment of opinions. In *COLING*.

S. Kim and E. Hovy. 2005. Automatic Detection of Opinion Bearing Words and Sentences. In Companion Volume to the *Proceedings of the Second International Joint Conference on Natural Language Processing (IJCNLP-05)*.

J. Lafferty, A. McCallum and F. Pereira. 2001. Conditional Random Fields: Probabilistic Models for Segmenting and Labeling Sequence Data. In *ICML*.

A. McCallum. 2002. MALLET: A Machine Learning for Language Toolkit. http://mallet.cs.umass.edu.

G. A. Miller. 1995. WordNet: a lexical database for English. In *Communications of the ACM, 38(11)*.

Ana-Maria Popescu and O. Etzioni. 2005. Extracting Product Features and Opinions from Reviews. In *HLT-EMNLP*.

J. Wiebe, E. Breck, C. Buckley, C. Cardie, P. Davis, B. Fraser, D. Litman, D. Pierce, E. Riloff and T. Wilson. 2002. Summer Workshop on Multiple-Perspective Question Answering: Final Report. In *NRRC*.

J. Wiebe and T. Wilson and C. Cardie 2005. Annotating Expressions of Opinions and Emotions in Language. In *Language Resources and Evaluation, volume 39, issue 2-3*.

T. Wilson, J. Wiebe and P. Hoffmann. 2005. Recognizing Contextual Polarity in Phrase-Level Sentiment Analysis. In *HLT-EMNLP*.

T. Wilson, J. Wiebe and R. Hwa. 2006. Recognizing strong and weak opinion clauses. In *Computational Intelligence*. 22 (2): 73-99.

T. Wilson, J. Wiebe and P. Hoffmann. 2009. Recognizing Contextual Polarity: an exploration of features for phrase-level sentiment analysis. Computational Linguistics 35(3).

J. Zhao, K. Liu and G. Wang. 2008. Adding Redundant Features for CRFs-based Sentence Sentiment Classification. In *EMNLP*.

Jointly optimizing a two-step conditional random field model for machine transliteration and its fast decoding algorithm

Dong Yang, Paul Dixon and Sadaoki Furui
Department of Computer Science
Tokyo Institute of Technology
Tokyo 152-8552 Japan
{raymond, dixonp, furui}@furui.cs.titech.ac.jp

Abstract

This paper presents a joint optimization method of a two-step conditional random field (CRF) model for machine transliteration and a fast decoding algorithm for the proposed method. Our method lies in the category of direct orthographical mapping (DOM) between two languages without using any intermediate phonemic mapping. In the two-step CRF model, the first CRF segments an input word into chunks and the second one converts each chunk into one unit in the target language. In this paper, we propose a method to jointly optimize the two-step CRFs and also a fast algorithm to realize it. Our experiments show that the proposed method outperforms the well-known joint source channel model (JSCM) and our proposed fast algorithm decreases the decoding time significantly. Furthermore, combination of the proposed method and the JSCM gives further improvement, which outperforms state-of-the-art results in terms of top-1 accuracy.

1 Introduction

There are more than 6000 languages in the world and 10 languages of them have more than 100 million native speakers. With the information revolution and globalization, systems that support multiple language processing and spoken language translation become urgent demands. The translation of named entities from alphabetic to syllabary language is usually performed through transliteration, which tries to preserve the pronunciation in the original language.

For example, in Chinese, foreign words are written with Chinese characters; in Japanese, foreign words are usually written with special characters called Katakana; examples are given in Figure 1.

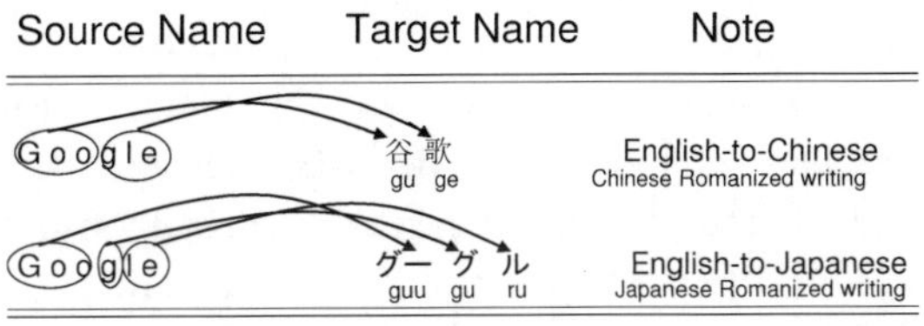

Figure 1: Transliteration examples

An intuitive transliteration method (Knight and Graehl, 1998; Oh et al., 2006) is to firstly convert a source word into phonemes, then find the corresponding phonemes in the target language, and finally convert them to the target language's written system. There are two reasons why this method does not work well: first, the named entities have diverse origins and this makes the grapheme-to-phoneme conversion very difficult; second, the transliteration is usually not only determined by the pronunciation, but also affected by how they are written in the original language.

Direct orthographical mapping (DOM), which performs the transliteration between two languages directly without using any intermediate phonemic mapping, is recently gaining more attention in the transliteration research community, and it is also the "Standard Run" of the "NEWS 2009 Machine Transliteration Shared Task" (Li et al., 2009). In this paper, we try to make our system satisfy the standard evaluation condition, which requires that the system uses the provided parallel corpus (without pronunciation) only, and cannot use any other bilingual or monolingual resources.

The source channel and joint source channel models (JSCMs) (Li et al., 2004) have been proposed for DOM, which try to model $P(T|S)$ and $P(T, S)$ respectively, where T and S denote the words in the target and source languages. Ekbal et al. (2006) modified the JSCM to incorporate different context information into the model for

Proceedings of the ACL 2010 Conference Short Papers, pages 275–280,
Uppsala, Sweden, 11-16 July 2010.

Indian languages. In the "NEWS 2009 Machine Transliteration Shared Task", a new two-step CRF model for transliteration task has been proposed (Yang et al., 2009), in which the first step is to segment a word in the source language into character chunks and the second step is to perform a context-dependent mapping from each chunk into one written unit in the target language.

In this paper, we propose to jointly optimize a two-step CRF model. We also propose a fast decoding algorithm to speed up the joint search. The rest of this paper is organized as follows: Section 2 explains the two-step CRF method, followed by Section 3 which describes our joint optimization method and its fast decoding algorithm; Section 4 introduces a rapid implementation of a JSCM system in the weighted finite state transducer (WFST) framework; and the last section reports the experimental results and conclusions. Although our method is language independent, we use an English-to-Chinese transliteration task in all the explanations and experiments.

2 Two-step CRF method

2.1 CRF introduction

A chain-CRF (Lafferty et al., 2001) is an undirected graphical model which assigns a probability to a label sequence $L = l_1 l_2 \ldots l_T$, given an input sequence $C = c_1 c_2 \ldots c_T$. CRF training is usually performed through the L-BFGS algorithm (Wallach, 2002) and decoding is performed by the Viterbi algorithm. We formalize machine transliteration as a CRF tagging problem, as shown in Figure 2.

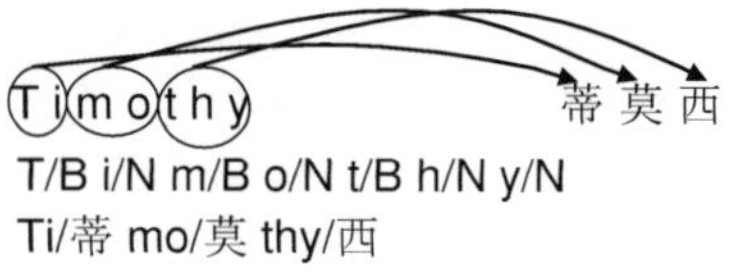

Figure 2: An pictorial description of a CRF segmenter and a CRF converter

2.2 CRF segmenter

In the CRF, a feature function describes a co-occurrence relation, and it is usually a binary function, taking the value 1 when both an observation and a label transition are observed. Yang et al. (2009) used the following features in the segmentation tool:

- Single unit features: $C_{-2}, C_{-1}, C_0, C_1, C_2$
- Combination features: $C_{-1}C_0, C_0C_1$

Here, C_0 is the current character, C_{-1} and C_1 denote the previous and next characters, and C_{-2} and C_2 are the characters located two positions to the left and right of C_0.

One limitation of their work is that only top-1 segmentation is output to the following CRF converter.

2.3 CRF converter

Similar to the CRF segmenter, the CRF converter has the format shown in Figure 2.

For this CRF, Yang et al. (2009) used the following features:

- Single unit features: CK_{-1}, CK_0, CK_1
- Combination features: $CK_{-1}CK_0$, CK_0CK_1

where CK represents the source language chunk, and the subscript notation is the same as the CRF segmenter.

3 Joint optimization and its fast decoding algorithm

3.1 Joint optimization

We denote a word in the source language by S, a segmentation of S by A, and a word in the target langauge by T. Our goal is to find the best word $\hat{T}$ in the target language which maximizes the probability $P(T|S)$.

Yang et al. (2009) used only the best segmentation in the first CRF and the best output in the second CRF, which is equivalent to

$$\hat{A} = \arg\max_{A} P(A|S)$$
$$\hat{T} = \arg\max_{T} P(T|S, \hat{A}), \quad (1)$$

where $P(A|S)$ and $P(T|S, A)$ represent two CRFs respectively. This method considers the segmentation and the conversion as two independent steps. A major limitation is that, if the segmentation from the first step is wrong, the error propagates to the second step, and the error is very difficult to recover.

In this paper, we propose a new method to jointly optimize the two-step CRF, which can be written as:

$$\begin{aligned}\hat{T} &= \arg\max_T P(T|S) \\ &= \arg\max_T \sum_A P(T,A|S) \\ &= \arg\max_T \sum_A P(A|S)P(T|S,A)\end{aligned} \tag{2}$$

The joint optimization considers all the segmentation possibilities and sums the probability over all the alternative segmentations which generate the same output. It considers the segmentation and conversion in a unified framework and is robust to segmentation errors.

3.2 N-best approximation

In the process of finding the best output using Equation 2, a dynamic programming algorithm for joint decoding of the segmentation and conversion is possible, but the implementation becomes very complicated. Another direction is to divide the decoding into two steps of segmentation and conversion, which is this paper's method. However, exact inference by listing all possible candidates explicitly and summing over all possible segmentations is intractable, because of the exponential computation complexity with the source word's increasing length.

In the segmentation step, the number of possible segmentations is 2^N, where N is the length of the source word and 2 is the size of the tagging set. In the conversion step, the number of possible candidates is $M^{N'}$, where N' is the number of chunks from the 1st step and M is the size of the tagging set. M is usually large, e.g., about 400 in Chinese and 50 in Japanese, and it is impossible to list all the candidates.

Our analysis shows that beyond the 10th candidate, almost all the probabilities of the candidates in both steps drop below 0.01. Therefore we decided to generate top-10 results for both steps to approximate the Equation 2.

3.3 Fast decoding algorithm

As introduced in the previous subsection, in the whole decoding process we have to perform n-best CRF decoding in the segmentation step and 10 n-best CRF decoding in the second CRF. Is it really necessary to perform the second CRF for all the segmentations? The answer is "No" for candidates with low probabilities. Here we propose a no-loss fast decoding algorithm for deciding when to stop performing the second CRF decoding.

Suppose we have a list of segmentation candidates which are generated by the 1st CRF, ranked by probabilities $P(A|S)$ in descending order A : $A_1, A_2, ..., A_N$ and we are performing the 2nd CRF decoding starting from A_1. Up to A_k, we get a list of candidates T : $T_1, T_2, ..., T_L$, ranked by probabilities in descending order. If we can guarantee that, even performing the 2nd CRF decoding for all the remaining segmentations $A_{k+1}, A_{k+2}, ..., A_N$, the top 1 candidate does not change, then we can stop decoding.

We can show that the following formula is the stop condition:

$$P_k(T_1|S) - P_k(T_2|S) > 1 - \sum_{j=1}^{k} P(A_j|S). \tag{3}$$

The meaning of this formula is that the probability of all the remaining candidates is smaller than the probability difference between the best and the second best candidates; on the other hand, even if all the remaining probabilities are added to the second best candidate, it still cannot overturn the top candidate. The mathematical proof is provided in Appendix A.

The stop condition here has no approximation nor pre-defined assumption, and it is a no-loss fast decoding algorithm.

4 Rapid development of a JSCM system

The JSCM represents how the source words and target names are generated simultaneously (Li et al., 2004):

$$\begin{aligned}& P(S,T) = P(s_1, s_2, ..., s_k, t_1, t_2, ..., t_k) \\ =\ & P(<s,t>_1, <s,t>_2, ..., <s,t>_k) \\ =\ & \prod_{k=1}^{K} P(<s,t>_k \mid <s,t>_1^{k-1})\end{aligned} \tag{4}$$

where $S = (s_1, s_2, ..., s_k)$ is a word in the source langauge and $T = (t_1, t_2, ..., t_k)$ is a word in the target language.

The training parallel data without alignment is first aligned by a Viterbi version EM algorithm (Li et al., 2004).

The decoding problem in JSCM can be written as:

$$\hat{T} = \arg\max_T P(S,T). \tag{5}$$

After the alignments are generated, we use the MITLM toolkit (Hsu and Glass, 2008) to build a trigram model with modified Kneser-Ney smoothing. We then convert the n-gram to a WFST M (Sproat et al., 2000; Caseiro et al., 2002). To allow transliteration from a sequence of characters, a second WFST T is constructed. The input word is converted to an acceptor I, and it is then combined with T and M according to $O = I \circ T \circ M$ where $\circ$ denotes the composition operator. The n–best paths are extracted by projecting the output, removing the epsilon labels and applying the n-shortest paths algorithm with determinization in the OpenFst Toolkit (Allauzen et al., 2007).

5 Experiments

We use several metrics from (Li et al., 2009) to measure the performance of our system.

1. Top-1 ACC: word accuracy of the top-1 candidate

2. Mean F-score: fuzziness in the top-1 candidate, how close the top-1 candidate is to the reference

3. MRR: mean reciprocal rank, 1/MRR tells approximately the average rank of the correct result

5.1 Comparison with the baseline and JSCM

We use the training, development and test sets of NEWS 2009 data for English-to-Chinese in our experiments as detailed in Table 1. This is a parallel corpus without alignment.

Training data	Development data	Test data
31961	2896	2896

Table 1: Corpus size (number of word pairs)

We compare the proposed decoding method with the baseline which uses only the best candidates in both CRF steps, and also with the well known JSCM. As we can see in Table 2, the proposed method improves the baseline top-1 ACC from 0.670 to 0.708, and it works as well as, or even better than the well known JSCM in all the three measurements.

Our experiments also show that the decoding time can be reduced significantly via using our fast decoding algorithm. As we have explained, without fast decoding, we need 11 CRF n-best decoding for each word; the number can be reduced to 3.53 (1 "the first CRF"+2.53 "the second CRF") via the fast decoding algorithm.

We should notice that the decoding time is significantly shorter than the training time. While testing takes minutes on a normal PC, the training of the CRF converter takes up to 13 hours on an 8-core (8*3G Hz) server.

Measure	Top-1 ACC	Mean F-score	MRR
Baseline	0.670	0.869	0.750
Joint optimization	**0.708**	**0.885**	**0.789**
JSCM	0.706	0.882	**0.789**

Table 2: Comparison of the proposed decoding method with the previous method and the JSCM

5.2 Further improvement

We tried to combine the two-step CRF model and the JSCM. From the two-step CRF model we get the conditional probability $P_{CRF}(T|S)$ and from the JSCM we get the joint probability $P(S, T)$. The conditional probability of $P_{JSCM}(T|S)$ can be calculuated as follows:

$$P_{JSCM}(T|S) = \frac{P(T,S)}{P(S)} = \frac{P(T,S)}{\sum_T P(T,S)}. \quad (6)$$

They are used in our combination method as:

$$P(T|S) = \lambda P_{CRF}(T|S) + (1 - \lambda) P_{JSCM}(T|S) \quad (7)$$

where λ denotes the interpolation weight (λ is set by development data in this paper).

As we can see in Table 3, the linear combination of two sytems further improves the top-1 ACC to 0.720, and it has outperformed the best reported "Standard Run" (Li et al., 2009) result 0.717. (The reported best "Standard Run" result 0.731 used target language phoneme information, which requires a monolingual dictionary; as a result it is not a standard run.)

Measure	Top-1 ACC	Mean F-score	MRR
Baseline+JSCM	0.713	0.883	0.794
Joint optimization + JSCM	**0.720**	0.888	**0.797**
state-of-the-art (Li et al., 2009)	0.717	**0.890**	0.785

Table 3: Model combination results

6 Conclusions and future work

In this paper we have presented our new joint optimization method for a two-step CRF model and its fast decoding algorithm. The proposed method improved the system significantly and outperformed the JSCM. Combining the proposed method with JSCM, the performance was further improved.

In future work we are planning to combine our system with multilingual systems. Also we want to make use of acoustic information in machine transliteration. We are currently investigating discriminative training as a method to further improve the JSCM. Another issue of our two-step CRF method is that the training complexity increases quadratically according to the size of the label set, and how to reduce the training time needs more research.

Appendix A. Proof of Equation 3

The CRF segmentation provides a list of segmentations: $A : A_1, A_2, ..., A_N$, with conditional probabilities $P(A_1|S), P(A_2|S), ..., P(A_N|S)$.

$$\sum_{j=1}^{N} P(A_j|S) = 1.$$

The CRF conversion, given a segmentation A_i, provides a list of transliteration output $T_1, T_2, ..., T_M$, with conditional probabilities $P(T_1|S, A_i), P(T_2|S, A_i), ..., P(T_M|S, A_i)$.

In our fast decoding algorithm, we start performing the CRF conversion from A_1, then A_2, and then A_3, etc. Up to A_k, we get a list of candidates $T : T_1, T_2, ..., T_L$, ranked by probabilities $P_k(T|S)$ in descending order. The probability $P_k(T_l|S)(l = 1, 2, ..., L)$ is accumulated probability of $P(T_l|S)$ over $A_1, A_2, ..., A_k$, calculated by:

$$P_k(T_l|S) = \sum_{j=1}^{k} P(A_j|S)P(T_l|S, A_j)$$

If we continue performing the CRF conversion to cover all N ($N \geq k$) segmentations, eventually we will get:

$$\begin{aligned} P(T_l|S) &= \sum_{j=1}^{N} P(A_j|S)P(T_l|S, A_j) \\ &\geq \sum_{j=1}^{k} P(A_j|S)P(T_l|S, A_j) \\ &= P_k(T_l|S) \end{aligned} \quad (8)$$

If Equation 3 holds, then for $\forall i \neq 1$,

$$\begin{aligned} P_k(T_1|S) &> P_k(T_2|S) + (1 - \sum_{j=1}^{k} P(A_j|S)) \\ &\geq P_k(T_i|S) + (1 - \sum_{j=1}^{k} P(A_j|S)) \\ &= P_k(T_i|S) + \sum_{j=k+1}^{N} P(A_j|S) \\ &\geq P_k(T_i|S) \\ &\quad + \sum_{j=k+1}^{N} P(A_j|S)P(T_i|S, A_j) \\ &= P(T_i|S) \end{aligned} \quad (9)$$

Therefore, $P(T_1|S) > P(T_i|S)(i \neq 1)$, and T_1 maximizes the probability $P(T|S)$.

References

Cyril Allauzen, Michael Riley, Johan Schalkwyk, Wojciech Skut and Mehryar Mohri 2007. *OpenFst: A General and Efficient Weighted Finite-State Transducer Library.* Proceedings of the Ninth International Conference on Implementation and Application of Automata, (CIAA), pages 11-23.

Diamantino Caseiro, Isabel Trancosoo, Luis Oliveira and Ceu Viana 2002. *Grapheme-to-phone using finite state transducers.* Proceedings IEEE Workshop on Speech Synthesis.

Asif Ekbal, Sudip Kumar Naskar and Sivaji Bandyopadhyay. 2006. *A modified joint source-channel model for transliteration*, Proceedings of the COLING/ACL, pages 191-198.

Bo-June Hsu and James Glass 2008. *Iterative Language Model Estimation: Efficient Data Structure & Algorithms.* Proceedings Interspeech, pages 841-844.

Kevin Knight and Jonathan Graehl. 1998. *Machine Transliteration*, Association for Computational Linguistics.

John Lafferty, Andrew McCallum, and Fernando Pereira 2001. *Conditional Random Fields: Probabilistic Models for Segmenting and Labeling Sequence Data.*, Proceedings of International Conference on Machine Learning, pages 282-289.

Haizhou Li, Min Zhang and Jian Su. 2004. *A joint source-channel model for machine transliteration*, Proceedings of the 42nd Annual Meeting on Association for Computational Linguistics.

Haizhou Li, A. Kumaran, Vladimir Pervouchine and Min Zhang 2009. *Report of NEWS 2009 Machine Transliteration Shared Task*, Proceedings of the 2009 Named Entities Workshop: Shared Task on Transliteration (NEWS 2009), pages 1-18

Jong-Hoon Oh, Key-Sun Choi and Hitoshi Isahara. 2006. *A comparison of different machine transliteration models* , Journal of Artificial Intelligence Research, 27, pages 119-151.

Richard Sproat 2000. *Corpus-Based Methods and Hand-Built Methods.* Proceedings of International Conference on Spoken Language Processing, pages 426-428.

Andrew J. Viterbi 1967. *Error Bounds for Convolutional Codes and an Asymptotically Optimum Decoding Algorithm.* IEEE Transactions on Information Theory, Volume IT-13, pages 260-269.

Hanna Wallach 2002. *Efficient Training of Conditional Random Fields.* M. Thesis, University of Edinburgh.

Dong Yang, Paul Dixon, Yi-Cheng Pan, Tasuku Oonishi, Masanobu Nakamura and Sadaoki Furui 2009. *Combining a Two-step Conditional Random Field Model and a Joint Source Channel Model for Machine Transliteration*, Proceedings of the 2009 Named Entities Workshop: Shared Task on Transliteration (NEWS 2009), pages 72-75

Arabic Named Entity Recognition: Using Features Extracted from Noisy Data

Yassine Benajiba[1] **Imed Zitouni**[2] **Mona Diab**[1] **Paolo Rosso**[3]
[1] Center for Computational Learning Systems, Columbia University
[2] IBM T.J. Watson Research Center, Yorktown Heights
[3] Natural Language Engineering Lab. - ELiRF, Universidad Politécnica de Valencia
{ybenajiba,mdiab}@ccls.columbia.edu, izitouni@us.ibm.com, prosso@dsic.upv.es

Abstract

Building an accurate Named Entity Recognition (NER) system for languages with complex morphology is a challenging task. In this paper, we present research that explores the feature space using both gold and bootstrapped noisy features to build an improved highly accurate Arabic NER system. We bootstrap noisy features by projection from an Arabic-English parallel corpus that is automatically tagged with a baseline NER system. The feature space covers lexical, morphological, and syntactic features. The proposed approach yields an improvement of up to 1.64 F-measure (absolute).

1 Introduction

Named Entity Recognition (NER) has earned an important place in Natural Language Processing (NLP) as an enabling process for other tasks. When explicitly taken into account, research shows that it helps such applications achieve better performance levels (Babych and Hartley, 2003; Thompson and Dozier, 1997). NER is defined as the computational identification and classification of Named Entities (NEs) in running text. For instance, consider the following text:

Barack Obama is visiting the Middle East.

A NER system should be able to identify *Barack Obama* and *Middle East* as NEs and classify them as *Person* (PER) and *Geo-Political Entity* (GPE), respectively. The class-set used to tag NEs may vary according to user needs. In this research, we adopt the Automatic Content Extraction (ACE) 2007 nomenclature[1].

According to (Nadeau and Sekine, 2007), optimization of the feature set is the key component in enhancing the performance of a global NER system. In this paper we investigate the possibility of building a high performance Arabic NER system by using a large space of available feature sets that go beyond the explored shallow feature sets used to date in the literature for Arabic NER. Given current state-of-the-art syntactic processing of Arabic text and the relative small size of manually annotated Arabic NER data, we set out to explore a main concrete research goal: to fully exploit the level of advancement in Arabic lexical and syntactic processing to explore deeper linguistic features for the NER task. Realizing that the gold data available for NER is quite limited in size especially given the diverse genres in the set, we devise a method to bootstrap additional instances for the new features of interest from noisily NER tagged Arabic data.

2 Our Approach

We use our state-of-the-art NER system described in (Benajiba et al., 2008) as our baseline system (BASE) since it yields, to our knowledge, the best performance for Arabic NER . BASE employs Support Vector Machines (SVMs) and Conditional Random Fields (CRFs) as Machine Learning (ML) approaches. BASE uses lexical, syntactic and morphological features extracted using highly accurate automatic Arabic POS-taggers. BASE employs a multi-classifier approach where each classifier is tagging a NE class separately. The feature selection is performed by using an incremental approach selecting the top n features (the features are ranked according to their individual impact) at each iteration and keeping the set that yields the best results. In case of conflict - a word is classified with more than one class/tag simultaneously - the global NER system selects the output of the classifier with the highest precision.

The following is the feature set used in (Benajiba et al., 2008) and accordingly in the BASE system. **1. Context:** a $-/+1$ token window; **2. Lexical:** character $n-grams$ where n ranges from $1-3$; **3. Gazetteers:** automatically harvested and manually cleaned Person NE class (PER), Geopolitical Entity NE class (GPE), and Organization NE class (ORG) lexica; **4. POS-tag and Base Phrase Chunk (BPC)**: automatically tagged using AMIRA (Diab et al., 2007) which yields F-measures for both tasks in the high 90's; **5. Morphological features:** automatically tagged using the Morphological Analysis and Disambiguation for Arabic (MADA) tool to extract information about gender, number, person, definiteness and as-

[1] http://www.nist.gov/speech/tests/ace/index.htm

Proceedings of the ACL 2010 Conference Short Papers, pages 281–285,
Uppsala, Sweden, 11-16 July 2010.

pect for each word (Habash and Rambow, 2005); **6. Capitalization:** derived as a side effect from running MADA. MADA chooses a specific morphological analysis given the context of a given word. As part of the morphological information available in the underlying lexicon that MADA exploits. As part of the information present, the underlying lexicon has an English gloss associated with each entry. More often than not, if the word is a NE in Arabic then the gloss will also be a NE in English and hence capitalized.
We devise an extended Arabic NER system (EXTENDED) that uses the same architecture as BASE but employs additional features to those in BASE. EXTENDED defines new additional syntagmatic features.

We specifically investigate the space of the surrounding context for the NEs. We explore generalizations over the kinds of words that occur with NEs and the syntactic relations NEs engage in. We use an off-the-shelf Arabic syntactic parser. State-of-the-art for Arabic syntactic parsing for the most common genre (with the most training data) of Arabic data, newswire, is in the low 80%s. Hence, we acknowledge that some of the derived syntactic features will be noisy.

Similar to all supervised ML problems, it is desirable to have sufficient training data for the relevant phenomena. The size of the manually annotated gold data typically used for training Arabic NER systems poses a significant challenge for robustly exploring deeper syntactic and lexical features. Accordingly, we bootstrap more NE tagged data via projection over Arabic-English parallel data. The role of this data is simply to give us more instances of the newly defined features (namely the syntagmatic features) in the EXTENDED system as well as more instances for the Gazetteers and Context features defined in BASE. It is worth noting that we do not use the bootstrapped NE tagged data directly as training data with the gold data.

2.1 Syntagmatic Features

For deriving our deeper linguistic features, we parse the Arabic sentences that contain an NE. For each of the NEs, we extract a number of features described as follows:

- Syntactic head-word (SHW): The idea here is to look for a broader **relevant** context. Whereas the feature lexical n-gram context feature used in BASE, and hence here for EXTENDED, considers the linearly adjacent neighboring words of a NE, SHW uses a parse tree to look at farther, yet related, words. For instance, in the Arabic phrase "SrH Ams An bArAk AwbAma ytrAs", which means "declared yesterday that Barack Obama governs ...", glossed "SrH/*declared* Ams/*yesterday* An/*that* bArAk/*Barack* AwbAmA/*Obama* ytrAs/*governs* ...", is parsed in Figure 1. According to the phrase structure parse, the first parent sub-tree headword of the NE "bArAk AwbAmA" is the verb 'ytrAs' (governs), the second one is 'An' (that) and the third one is the verb 'SrH' (declared). This example illustrates that the word "Ams" is ignored for this feature set since it is not a syntactic head. This is a lexicalized feature.

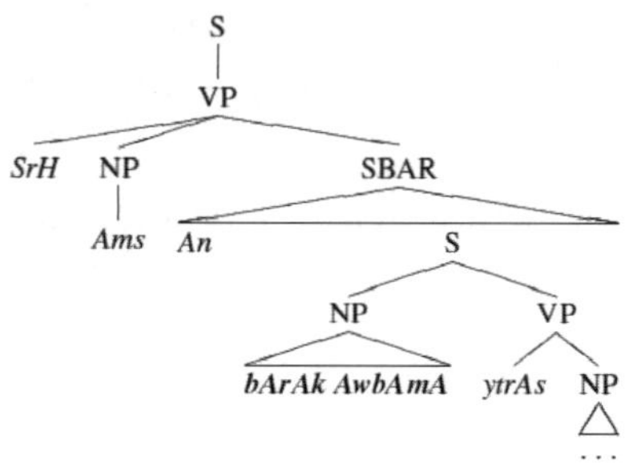

Figure 1: Example for the head word and syntactic environment feature

- Syntactic Environment (SE): This follows in the same *spirit* as SHW, but expands the idea in that it looks at the parent non-terminal instead of the parent head word, hence it is not a lexicalized feature. The goal being to use a more abstract representation level of the context in which a NE appears. For instance, for the same example presented in Figure 1, the first, second, and third non-terminal parents of the NE "bArAk AwbAmA" are 'S', 'SBAR' and 'VP', respectively.
In our experiments we use the Bikel implementation (Bikel, 2004) of the Collins parser (Collins, 1999) which is freely available on the web[2]. It is a head-driven CFG-style parser trained to parse English, Arabic, and Chinese.

2.2 Bootstrapping Noisy Arabic NER Data

Extracting the syntagmatic features from the training data yields relatively small number of instances. Hence the need for additional tagged data. The new Arabic NER tagged data is derived via projection exploiting parallel Arabic English data. The process depends on the availability of two key components: a large Arabic English parallel corpus that is sentence and word aligned, and a robust high performing English NER system. The process is as follows. We NE tag the

[2]http://www.cis.upenn.edu/∼dbikel/software.html#stat-parser

English side of the parallel corpus. We project the automatically tagged NER tags from the English side to the Arabic side of the parallel corpus. In our case, we have access to a large manually aligned parallel corpus, therefore the NER projection is direct. However, the English side of the parallel corpus is not NER tagged, hence we use an off-the-shelf competitive robust automatic English NER system which has a published performance of 92% (Zitouni and Florian, 2009). The result of these two processes is a large Arabic NER, albeit noisy, tagged data set. As mentioned earlier this data is used only for deriving additional instances for training for the syntagmatic features and for the context and gazetteer features.[3] Given this additional source of data, we changed the lexical features extracted from the BASE to the EXTENDED. We added two other lexical features: CBG and NGC, described as follows: - Class Based Gazetteers (CBG): This feature focuses on the surface form of the NEs. We group the NEs encountered on the Arabic side of the parallel corpus by class as they are found in different dictionaries. The difference between this feature and that in BASE is that the Gazetteers are not restricted to Wikipedia sources.

- N-gram context (NGC): Here we disregard the surface form of the NE, instead we focus on its lexical context. For each n, where n varies from 1 to 3, we compile a list of the $-n$, $+n$, and $-/+n$ words surrounding the NE. Similar to the CBG feature, these lists are also separated by NE class. It is worth highlighting that the NCG feature is different from the Context feature in BASE in that the window size is different $+/-1-3$ for EXTENDED versus $+/-1$ for BASE.

3 Experiments and Results

3.1 Gold Data for training and evaluation

We use the standard sets of ACE 2003, ACE 2004 and ACE 2005.[4] The ACE data is annotated for many tasks: Entity Detection and Tracking (EDT), Relation Detection and Recognition (RDR), Event Detection and Recognition (EDR). All the data sets comprise *Broadcast News* (BN) and *Newswire* (NW) genres. ACE 2004 includes an additional NW data set from the Arabic TreeBank (ATB). ACE 2005 includes a different genre of *Weblogs* (WL). The NE classes adopted in the annotation of the ACE 2003 data are: Person (PER), Geo Political Entity (GPE), Organization (ORG) and Facility (FAC). Additionally for the ACE 2004 and 2005 data, two NE classes are added to the ACE 2003 tag-set: Vehicles (e.g. Rotterdam Ship) and Weapons (e.g. Kalashnikof). We use the same split for train, development, and test used in (Benajiba et al., 2008).

3.2 Parallel Data

Most of the hand-aligned Arabic-English parallel data used in our experiments is from the Language Data Consortium (LDC).[5]. Another set of the parallel data is annotated in-house by professional annotators. The corpus has texts of five different genres, namely: newswire, news groups, broadcast news, broadcast conversation and weblogs corresponding to the data genres in the ACE gold data. The Arabic side of the parallel corpus contains 941,282 tokens. After projecting the NE tags from the English side to the Arabic side of the parallel corpus, we obtain a total of 57,290 Arabic NE instances. Table 1 shows the number of NEs for each class.

Class	Number of NEs	Class	Number of NEs
FAC	998	PER	17,964
LOC	27,651	VEH	85
ORG	10,572	WEA	20

Table 1: Number of NEs per class in the Arabic side of the parallel corpus

3.3 Individual Feature Impact

Across the board, all the features yield improved performance. The highest obtained result is observed where the first non-terminal parent is used as a feature, a Syntactic Environment (SE) feature, yielding an improvement of up to 4 points over the baseline. We experiment with different sizes for the SE, i.e. taking the first parent versus adding neighboring non-terminal parents. We note that even though we observe an overall increase in performance, considering both the {first, second} or the {first, second, and third} non-terminal parents decreases performance by 0.5 and 1.5 F-measure points, respectively, compared to considering the first parent information alone. The head word features, SHW, show a higher positive impact than the lexical context feature, NGC. Finally, the Gazetteer feature, CBG, impact is comparable to the obtained improvement of the lexical context feature.

3.4 Feature Combination Experiments

Table 2 illustrates the final results. It shows for each data set and each genre the F-measure obtained using the best feature set and ML approach. It shows results for both the dev and test data using the optimal number of features selected from

[3]Therefore, we did not do the full feature extraction for the other features described in BASE for this data.

[4]http://www.nist.gov/speech/tests/ace/

[5]All the LDC data are publicly available

		ACE 2003		ACE 2004			ACE 2005		
		BN	*NW*	*BN*	*NW*	*ATB*	*BN*	*NW*	*WL*
	FreqBaseline	*73.74*	*67.61*	*62.17*	*51.67*	*62.94*	*70.18*	*57.17*	*27.66*
dev	*All-Synt.*	83.41	79.11	76.90	**72.90**	74.82	81.42	**76.07**	54.49
	All	**83.93**	**79.72**	**78.54**	72.80	**74.97**	**81.82**	75.92	**55.65**
test	*All-Synt.*	83.50	78.90	76.70	**72.40**	73.50	81.31	75.30	57.30
	All	**84.32**	**79.4**	**78.12**	72.13	**74.54**	**81.73**	**75.67**	**58.11**

Table 2: Final Results obtained with selected features contrasted against all features combined

the all the features except the syntagmatic ones (`All-Synt.`) contrasted against the system including the semantic features, i.e. All the features, per class *All* . The baseline results, *FreqBaseline*, assigns a test token the most frequent tag observed for it in the gold training data, if a test token is not observed in the training data, it is assigned the most frequent tag which is the O tag.

4 Results Discussion

Individual feature impact results show that the syntagmatic features are helpful for most of the data sets. The highest improvements are obtained for the 2003 BN and 2005 WL data-sets. The improvement varies significantly from one data-set to another because it highly depends on the number of NEs which the model has not been able to capture using the contextual, lexical, syntactic and morphological features.

Impact of the features extracted from the parallel corpus per class: The syntagmatic features have varied in their influence on the different NE classes. Generally, the LOC and PER classes benefitted more from the head word features, SHW), than the other classes. On the other hand for the syntactic environment feature (SE), the PER class seemed not to benefit much from the presence of this feature. *Weblogs*: Our results show that the random contexts in which the NEs tend to appear in the WL documents stand against obtaining a significant improvement. Consequently, the features which use a more global context (syntactic environment, SE, and head word, SHW, features) have helped obtain better results than the ones which we have obtained using local context namely CBG and NGC.

5 Related Work

Projecting explicit linguistic tags from another language via parallel corpora has been widely used in the NLP tasks and has proved to contribute significantly to achieving better performance. Different research works report positive results when using this technique to enhance WSD (Diab and Resnik, 2002; Ng et al., 2003). In the latter two works, they augment training data from parallel data for training supervised systems. In (Diab, 2004), the author uses projections from English into Arabic to bootstrap a sense tagging system for Arabic as well as a seed Arabic WordNet through projection. In (Hwa et al., 2002), the authors report promising results of inducing Chinese dependency trees from English. The obtained model outperformed the baseline. More recently, in (Chen and Ji, 2009), the authors report their comparative study between monolingual and cross-lingual bootstrapping. Finally, in Mention Detection (MD), a task which includes NER and adds the identification and classification of nominal and pronominal mentions, (Zitouni and Florian, 2008) show the impact of using a MT system to enhance the performance of an Arabic MD model. The authors report an improvement of up to 1.6F when the baseline system uses lexical features only. Unlike the work we present here, their approach requires the availability of an accurate MT system which is a more expensive process.

6 Conclusion and Future Directions

In this paper we investigate the possibility of building a high performance Arabic NER system by using lexical, syntactic and morphological features and augmenting the model with deeper lexical features and more syntagmatic features. These extra features are extracted from noisy data obtained via projection from an Arabic-English parallel corpus. Our results show that we achieve a significantly high performance for almost all the data-sets. The greatest impact of the syntagmatic features (1.64 points of F-measure) is obtained for the ACE 2004, BN genre. Also, the WL genre yields an improvement of 1.16 F1 points absolute.

Acknowledgments

This work has been partially funded by DARPA GALE project. The research of the last author was funded by MICINN research project TEXT-ENTERPRISE 2.0 TIN2009-13391-C04-03 (Plan I+D+i).

References

B. Babych and A. Hartley. 2003. Improving Machine Translation Quality with Automatic Named Entity Recognition. In *Proc. of EACL-EAMT*.

Y. Benajiba, M. Diab, and P. Rosso. 2008. Arabic named entity recognition using optimized feature sets. In *Proceedings of EMNLP'08*, pages 284–293.

Daniel M. Bikel. 2004. *On the parameter space of generative lexicalized statistical parsing models*. University of Pennsylvania, Philadelphia, PA, USA. Supervisor-Marcus, Mitchell P.

Z. Chen and H. Ji. 2009. Can one language bootstrap the other: A case study of event extraction. In *Proceedings of NAACL'09*.

M. Collins. 1999. *Head-Driven Statistical Models for Nat- ural Language Parsing*. University of Pennsylvania, Philadelphia, PA, USA.

Mona Diab and Philip Resnik. 2002. An unsupervised method for word sense tagging using parallel corpora. In *Proceedings of 40th Annual Meeting of the Association for Computational Linguistics*, pages 255–262, Philadelphia, Pennsylvania, USA, July. Association for Computational Linguistics.

M. Diab, K. Hacioglu, and D. Jurafsky, 2007. *Arabic Computational Morphology: Knowledge-based and Empirical Methods*, chapter 9. Springer.

Mona Diab. 2004. Bootstrapping a wordnet taxonomy for arabic. In *Proceedings of First Arabic Language Technology Conference (NEMLAR), Cairo Egypt,*.

N. Habash and O. Rambow. 2005. Arabic Tokenization, Part-of-Speech Tagging and Morphological Disambiguation in One Fell Swoop. In *Proc. of the 43rd Annual Meeting of the Association for Computational Linguistics (ACL'05)*, pages 573–580, Ann Arbor, Michigan, June. Association for Computational Linguistics.

R. Hwa, P. Resnik, and A. Weinberg. 2002. Breaking the resource bottleneck for multilingual parsing. In *In Proceedings of the Workshop on Linguistic Knowledge Acquisition and Representation: Bootstrapping Annotated Language Data*.

D. Nadeau and S. Sekine. 2007. A Survey of Named Entity Recognition and Classification. *Linguisticae Investigationes*, 30(7).

H.-T. Ng, B. Wang, and Y.-S. Chan. 2003. Exploiting parallel texts for word sense disambiguation: An empirical study. In *ACL'03*, pages 455–462, Sapporo, Japan.

P. Thompson and C. Dozier. 1997. Name Searching and Information Retrieval. In *In Proc. of Second Conference on Empirical Methods in Natural Language Processing*, Providence, Rhode Island.

I. Zitouni and R. Florian. 2008. Mention detection crossing the language barrier. In *Proceedings of EMNLP'08*, Honolulu, Hawaii, October.

Imed Zitouni and Radu Florian. 2009. Cross language information propagation for arabic mention detection. *Journal of ACM Transactions on Asian Language Information Processing*, December.

Extracting Sequences from the Web

Anthony Fader, Stephen Soderland, and Oren Etzioni
University of Washington, Seattle
{afader,soderlan,etzioni}@cs.washington.edu

Abstract

Classical Information Extraction (IE) systems fill slots in domain-specific frames. This paper reports on SEQ, a novel open IE system that leverages a *domain-independent* frame to extract ordered sequences such as presidents of the United States or the most common causes of death in the U.S. SEQ leverages regularities about sequences to extract a coherent set of sequences from Web text. SEQ nearly doubles the area under the precision-recall curve compared to an extractor that does not exploit these regularities.

Most common cause of death in the United States: 1. heart disease, 2. cancer, 3. stroke, 4. COPD, 5. pneumonia, 6. cirrhosis, 7. AIDS, 8. chronic liver disease, 9. sepsis, 10. suicide, 11. septic shock.
Largest tobacco company in the world: 1. Philip Morris, 2. BAT, 3. Japan Tobacco, 4. Imperial Tobacco, 5. Altadis.
Largest rodent in the world: 1. Capybara, 2. Beaver, 3. Patagonian Cavies. 4. Maras.
Sign of the zodiac: 1. Aries, 2. Taurus, 3. Gemini, 4. Cancer, 5. Leo, 6. Virgo, 7. Libra, 8. Scorpio, 9. Sagittarius, 10. Capricorn, 11. Aquarius, 12. Pisces, 13. Ophiuchus.

Table 1: Examples of sequences extracted by SEQ from unstructured Web text.

1 Introduction

Classical IE systems fill slots in domain-specific frames such as the time and location slots in seminar announcements (Freitag, 2000) or the terrorist organization slot in news stories (Chieu et al., 2003). In contrast, open IE systems are domain-independent, but extract "flat" sets of assertions that are not organized into frames and slots (Sekine, 2006; Banko et al., 2007). This paper reports on SEQ—an open IE system that leverages a domain-independent frame to extract ordered sequences of objects from Web text. We show that the novel, domain-independent sequence frame in SEQ substantially boosts the precision and recall of the system and yields coherent sequences filtered from low-precision extractions (Table 1).

Sequence extraction is distinct from set expansion (Etzioni et al., 2004; Wang and Cohen, 2007) because sequences are *ordered* and because the extraction process does not require seeds or HTML lists as input.

The domain-independent *sequence frame* consists of a sequence name s (*e.g.*, presidents of the United States), and a set of ordered pairs (x, k) where x is a string naming a member of the sequence with name s, and k is an integer indicating its position (*e.g.*, (Washington, 1) and (JFK, 35)). The task of *sequence extraction* is to automatically instantiate sequence frames given a corpus of unstructured text.

By definition, sequences have two properties that we can leverage in creating a sequence extractor: *functionality* and *density*. Functionality means position k in a sequence is occupied by a single real-world entity x. Density means that if a value has been observed at position k then there must exist values for all $i < k$, and possibly more after it.

2 The SEQ System

Sequence extraction has two parts: identifying possible extractions (x, k, s) from text, and then classifying those extractions as either correct or incorrect. In the following section, we describe a way to identify candidate extractions from text using a set of lexico-syntactic patterns. We then show that classifying extractions based on sentence-level features and redundancy alone yields low precision, which is improved by leveraging the functionality and density properties of sequences as done in our SEQ system.

Proceedings of the ACL 2010 Conference Short Papers, pages 286–290,

Pattern	Example
the ORD	the fifth
the RB ORD	the very first
the JJS	the best
the RB JJS	the very best
the ORD JJS	the third biggest
the RBS JJ	the most popular
the ORD RBS JJ	the second least likely

Table 2: The patterns used by SEQ to detect ordinal phrases are noun phrases that begin with one of the part-of-speech patterns listed above.

2.1 Generating Sequence Extractions

To obtain candidate sequence extractions (x, k, s) from text, the SEQ system finds sentences in its input corpus that contain an ordinal phrase (OP). Table 2 lists the lexico-syntactic patterns SEQ uses to detect ordinal phrases. The value of k is set to the integer corresponding to the ordinal number in the OP.[1]

Next, SEQ takes each sentence that contains an ordinal phrase o, and finds candidate items of the form (x, k) for the sequence with name s. SEQ constrains x to be an NP that is disjoint from o, and s to be an NP (which may have post-modifying PPs or clauses) following the ordinal number in o.

For example, given the sentence "With help from his father, JFK was elected as the 35th President of the United States in 1960", SEQ finds the candidate sequences with names "President", "President of the United States", and "President of the United States in 1960", each of which has candidate extractions (JFK, 35), (his father, 35), and (help, 35). We use heuristics to filter out many of the candidate values (*e.g.*, no value should cross a sentence-like boundary, and x should be at most some distance from the OP).

This process of generating candidate extractions has high coverage, but low precision. The first step in identifying correct extractions is to compute a confidence measure $localConf(x, k, s|sentence)$, which measures how likely (x, k, s) is given the sentence it came from. We do this using domain-independent syntactic features based on POS tags and the pattern-based features "x {is,are,was,were} the kth s" and "the kth s {is,are,was,were} x". The features are then combined using a Naive Bayes classifier.

In addition to the local, sentence-based features, we define the measure *totalConf* that takes into account redundancy in an input corpus $\mathcal{C}$. As Downey *et al.* observed (2005), extractions that occur more frequently in multiple distinct sentences are more likely to be correct.

$$totalConf(x, k, s|\mathcal{C}) = \sum_{sentence \in \mathcal{C}} localConf(x, k, s|sentence) \quad (1)$$

2.2 Challenges

The scores *localConf* and *totalConf* are not sufficient to identify valid sequence extractions. They tend to give high scores to extractions where the sequence scope is too general or too specific. In our running example, the sequence name "President" is too general – many countries and organizations have a president. The sequence name "President of the United States in 1960" is too specific – there were not multiple U.S. presidents in 1960.

These errors can be explained as violations of functionality and density. The sequence with name "President" will have many distinct candidate extractions in its positions, which is a violation of functionality. The sequence with name "President of the United States in 1960" will not satisfy density, since it will have extractions for only one position.

In the next section, we present the details of how SEQ incorporates functionality and density into its assessment of a candidate extraction.

Given an extraction (x, k, s), SEQ must classify it as either correct or incorrect. SEQ breaks this problem down into two parts: (1) determining whether s is a correct sequence name, and (2) determining whether (x, k) is an item in s, assuming s is correct.

A joint probabilistic model of these two decisions would require a significant amount of labeled data. To get around this problem, we represent each (x, k, s) as a vector of features and train two Naive Bayes classifiers: one for classifying s and one for classifying (x, k). We then rank extractions by taking the product of the two classifiers' confidence scores.

We now describe the features used in the two classifiers and how the classifiers are trained.

Classifying Sequences To classify a sequence name s, SEQ uses features to measure the functionality and density of s. Functionality means

[1] Sequences often use a superlative for the first item ($k = 1$) such as "the deepest lake in Africa", "the second deepest lake in Africa" (or "the 2nd deepest ..."), etc.

that a correct sequence with name s has one correct value x at each position k, possibly with additional noise due to extraction errors and synonymous values of x. For a fixed sequence name s and position k, we can weight each of the candidate x values in that position by their normalized total confidence:

$$w(x|k, s, \mathcal{C}) = \frac{totalConf(x, k, s|\mathcal{C})}{\sum_{x'} totalConf(x', k, s|\mathcal{C})}$$

For overly general sequences, the distribution of weights for a position will tend to be more flat, since there are many equally-likely candidate x values. To measure this property, we use a function analogous to information entropy:

$$H(k, s|\mathcal{C}) = -\sum_x w(x|k, s, \mathcal{C}) \log_2 w(x|k, s, \mathcal{C})$$

Sequences s that are too general will tend to have high values of $H(k, s|\mathcal{C})$ for many values of k. We found that a good measure of the overall non-functionality of s is the average value of $H(k, s|\mathcal{C})$ for $k = 1, 2, 3, 4$.

For a sequence name s that is too specific, we would expect that there are only a few filled-in positions. We model the density of s with two metrics. The first is $numFilledPos(s|\mathcal{C})$, the number of distinct values of k such that there is some extraction (x, k) for s in the corpus. The second is $totalSeqConf(s|\mathcal{C})$, which is the sum of the scores of most confident x in each position:

$$totalSeqConf(s|\mathcal{C}) = \sum_k \max_x totalConf(x, k, s|\mathcal{C}) \quad (2)$$

The functionality and density features are combined using a Naive Bayes classifier. To train the classifier, we use a set of sequence names s labeled as either correct or incorrect, which we describe in Section 3.

Classifying Sequence Items To classify (x, k) given s, SEQ uses two features: the total confidence $totalConf(x, k, s|\mathcal{C})$ and the same total confidence normalized to sum to 1 over all x, holding k and s constant. To train the classifier, we use a set of extractions (x, k, s) where s is known to be a correct sequence name.

3 Experimental Results

This section reports on two experiments. First, we measured how the density and functionality features improve performance on the sequence name

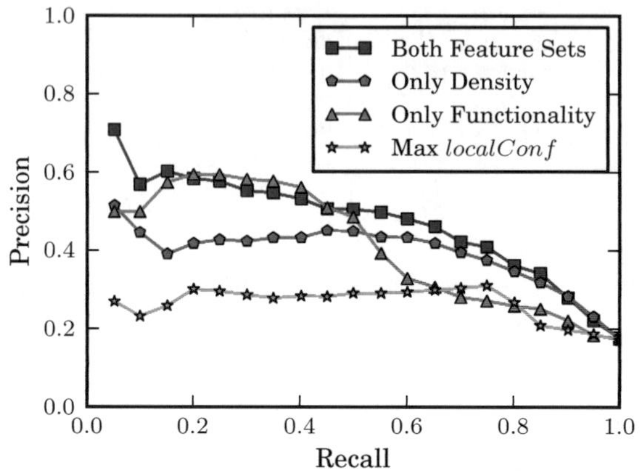

Figure 1: Using density or functionality features alone is effective in identifying correct sequence names. Combining both types of features outperforms either by a statistically significant margin (paired t-test, $p < 0.05$).

classification sub-task (Figure 1). Second, we report on SEQ's performance on the sequence-extraction task (Figure 2).

To create a test set, we selected all sentences containing ordinal phrases from Banko's 500M Web page corpus (2008). To enrich this set O, we obtained additional sentences from Bing.com as follows. For each sequence name s satisfying $localConf(x, k, s|sentence) \geq 0.5$ for some sentence in O, we queried Bing.com for "the kth s" for $k = 1, 2, \ldots$ until no more hits were returned.[2] For each query, we downloaded the search snippets and added them to our corpus. This procedure resulted in making $95,611$ search engine queries. The final corpus contained $3,716,745$ distinct sentences containing an OP.

Generating candidate extractions using the method from Section 2.1 resulted in a set of over 40 million distinct extractions, the vast majority of which are incorrect. To get a sample with a significant number of correct extractions, we filtered this set to include only extractions with $totalConf(x, k, s|\mathcal{C}) \geq 0.8$ for some sentence, resulting in a set of $2,409,211$ extractions.

We then randomly sampled and manually labeled $2,000$ of these extractions for evaluation. We did a Web search to verify the correctness of the sequence name s and that x is the kth item in the sequence. In some cases, the ordering relation of the sequence name was ambiguous (*e.g.*,

[2] We queried for both the numeric form of the ordinal and the number spelled out (e.g "the 2nd ..." and "the second ..."). We took up to 100 results per query.

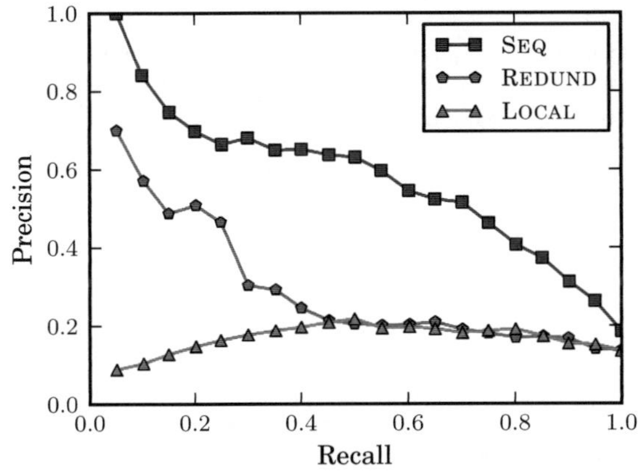

Figure 2: SEQ outperforms the baseline systems, increasing the area under the curve by 247% relative to LOCAL and by 90% relative to REDUND.

"largest state in the US" could refer to land area or population), which could lead to merging two distinct sequences. In practice, we found that most ordering relations were used in a consistent way (*e.g.*, "largest city in" always means largest by population) and only about 5% of the sequence names in our sample have an ambiguous ordering relation.

We compute precision-recall curves relative to this random sample by changing a confidence threshold. Precision is the percentage of correct extractions above a threshold, while recall is the percentage correct above a threshold divided by the total number of correct extractions. Because SEQ requires training data, we used 15-fold cross validation on the labeled sample.

The functionality and density features boost SEQ's ability to correctly identify sequence names. Figure 1 shows how well SEQ can identify correct sequence names using only functionality, only density, and using functionality and density in concert. The baseline used is the maximum value of $localConf(x, k, s)$ over all (x, k). Both the density features and the functionality features are effective at this task, but using both types of features resulted in a statistically significant improvement over using either type of feature individually (paired t-test of area under the curve, $p < 0.05$).

We measure SEQ's efficacy on the complete sequence-extraction task by contrasting it with two baseline systems. The first is LOCAL, which ranks extractions by $localConf$.[3] The second is REDUND, which ranks extractions by $totalConf$. Figure 2 shows the precision-recall curves for each system on the test data. The area under the curves for SEQ, REDUND, and LOCAL are 0.59, 0.31, and 0.17, respectively. The low precision and flat curve for LOCAL suggests that $localConf$ is not informative for classifying extractions on its own.

REDUND outperformed LOCAL, especially at the high-precision part of the curve. On the subset of extractions with correct s, REDUND can identify x as the kth item with precision of 0.85 at recall 0.80. This is consistent with previous work on redundancy-based extractors on the Web. However, REDUND still suffered from the problems of over-specification and over-generalization described in Section 2. SEQ reduces the negative effects of these problems by decreasing the scores of sequence names that appear too general or too specific.

4 Related Work

There has been extensive work in extracting lists or sets of entities from the Web. These extractors rely on either (1) HTML features (Cohen et al., 2002; Wang and Cohen, 2007) to extract from structured text or (2) lexico-syntactic patterns (Hearst, 1992; Etzioni et al., 2005) to extract from unstructured text. SEQ is most similar to this second type of extractor, but additionally leverages the sequence regularities of functionality and density. These regularities allow the system to overcome the poor performance of the purely syntactic extractor LOCAL and the redundancy-based extractor REDUND.

5 Conclusions

We have demonstrated that an extractor leveraging sequence regularities can greatly outperform extractors without this knowledge. Identifying likely sequence names and *then* filling in sequence items proved to be an effective approach to sequence extraction.

One line of future research is to investigate other types of domain-independent frames that exhibit useful regularities. Other examples include *events* (with regularities about actor, location, and time) and a generic *organization-role* frame (with regularities about person, organization, and role played).

[3] If an extraction arises from multiple sentences, we use the maximal $localConf$.

6 Acknowledgements

This research was supported in part by NSF grant IIS-0803481, ONR grant N00014-08-1-0431, DARPA contract FA8750-09-C-0179, and an NSF Graduate Research Fellowship, and was carried out at the University of Washington's Turing Center.

References

Michele Banko and Oren Etzioni. 2008. The tradeoffs between open and traditional relation extraction. In *Proceedings of ACL-08: HLT*, pages 28–36.

Michele Banko, Michael J. Cafarella, Stephen Soderland, Matthew Broadhead, and Oren Etzioni. 2007. Open information extraction from the web. In *IJCAI*, pages 2670–2676.

H. Chieu, H. Ng, and Y. Lee. 2003. Closing the gap: Learning-based information extraction rivaling knowledge-engineering methods. In *ACL*, pages 216–223.

William W. Cohen, Matthew Hurst, and Lee S. Jensen. 2002. A flexible learning system for wrapping tables and lists in html documents. In *In International World Wide Web Conference*, pages 232–241.

Doug Downey, Oren Etzioni, and Stephen Soderland. 2005. A probabilistic model of redundancy in information extraction. In *IJCAI*, pages 1034–1041.

O. Etzioni, M. Cafarella, D. Downey, A. Popescu, T. Shaked, S. Soderland, D. Weld, and A. Yates. 2004. Methods for domain-independent information extraction from the Web: An experimental comparison. In *Proceedings of the Nineteenth National Conference on Artificial Intelligence (AAAI-2004)*, pages 391–398.

Oren Etzioni, Michael Cafarella, Doug Downey, Ana maria Popescu, Tal Shaked, Stephen Soderl, Daniel S. Weld, and Er Yates. 2005. Unsupervised named-entity extraction from the web: An experimental study. *Artificial Intelligence*, 165:91–134.

D. Freitag. 2000. Machine learning for information extraction in informal domains. *Machine Learning*, 39(2-3):169–202.

Marti A. Hearst. 1992. Automatic acquisition of hyponyms from large text corpora. In *COLING*, pages 539–545.

Satoshi Sekine. 2006. On-demand information extraction. In *Proceedings of the COLING/ACL on Main conference poster sessions*, pages 731–738, Morristown, NJ, USA. Association for Computational Linguistics.

Richard C. Wang and William W. Cohen. 2007. Language-independent set expansion of named entities using the web. In *ICDM*, pages 342–350. IEEE Computer Society.

An Entity-Level Approach to Information Extraction

Aria Haghighi
UC Berkeley, CS Division
aria42@cs.berkeley.edu

Dan Klein
UC Berkeley, CS Division
klein@cs.berkeley.edu

Abstract

We present a generative model of template-filling in which coreference resolution and role assignment are jointly determined. Underlying template roles first generate abstract entities, which in turn generate concrete textual mentions. On the standard corporate acquisitions dataset, joint resolution in our entity-level model reduces error over a mention-level discriminative approach by up to 20%.

Template

(a)

SELLER	BUSINESS	ACQUIRED	PURCHASER
CSR Limited	Oil and Gas	Delhi Fund	Esso Inc.

Document

(b) [**S** CSR] has said that [**S** it] has sold [**S** its] [**B** oil interests] held in [**A** Delhi Fund]. [**P** Esso Inc.] did not disclose how much [**P** they] paid for [**A** Dehli].

Figure 1: Example of the corporate acquisitions role-filling task. In (a), an example template specifying the entities playing each domain role. In (b), an example document with coreferent mentions sharing the same role label. Note that pronoun mentions provide direct clues to entity roles.

1 Introduction

Template-filling information extraction (IE) systems must merge information across multiple sentences to identify all role fillers of interest. For instance, in the MUC4 terrorism event extraction task, the entity filling the *individual perpetrator* role often occurs multiple times, variously as proper, nominal, or pronominal mentions. However, most template-filling systems (Freitag and McCallum, 2000; Patwardhan and Riloff, 2007) assign roles to individual textual mentions using only local context as evidence, leaving aggregation for post-processing. While prior work has acknowledged that coreference resolution and discourse analysis are integral to accurate role identification, to our knowledge no model has been proposed which jointly models these phenomena.

In this work, we describe an entity-centered approach to template-filling IE problems. Our model jointly merges surface mentions into underlying entities (coreference resolution) and assigns roles to those discovered entities. In the generative process proposed here, document entities are generated for each template role, along with a set of non-template entities. These entities then generate mentions in a process sensitive to both lexical and structural properties of the mention. Our model outperforms a discriminative mention-level baseline. Moreover, since our model is generative, it can naturally incorporate unannotated data, which further increases accuracy.

2 Problem Setting

Figure 1(a) shows an example *template-filling* task from the corporate acquisitions domain (Freitag, 1998).[1] We have a template of K roles (PURCHASER, AMOUNT, etc.) and we must identify which entity (if any) fills each role (*CSR Limited*, etc.). Often such problems are modeled at the mention level, directly labeling individual mentions as in Figure 1(b). Indeed, in this data set, the mention-level perspective is evident in the gold annotations, which ignore pronominal references. However, roles in this domain appear in several locations throughout the document, with pronominal mentions often carrying the critical information for template filling. Therefore, Section 3 presents a model in which entities are explicitly modeled, naturally merging information across all mention types and explicitly representing latent structure very much like the entity-level template structure from Figure 1(a).

[1] In Freitag (1998), some of these fields are split in two to distinguish a full versus abbreviated name, but we ignore this distinction. Also we ignore the *status* field as it doesn't apply to entities and its meaning is not consistent.

Proceedings of the ACL 2010 Conference Short Papers, pages 291–295,
Uppsala, Sweden, 11-16 July 2010.

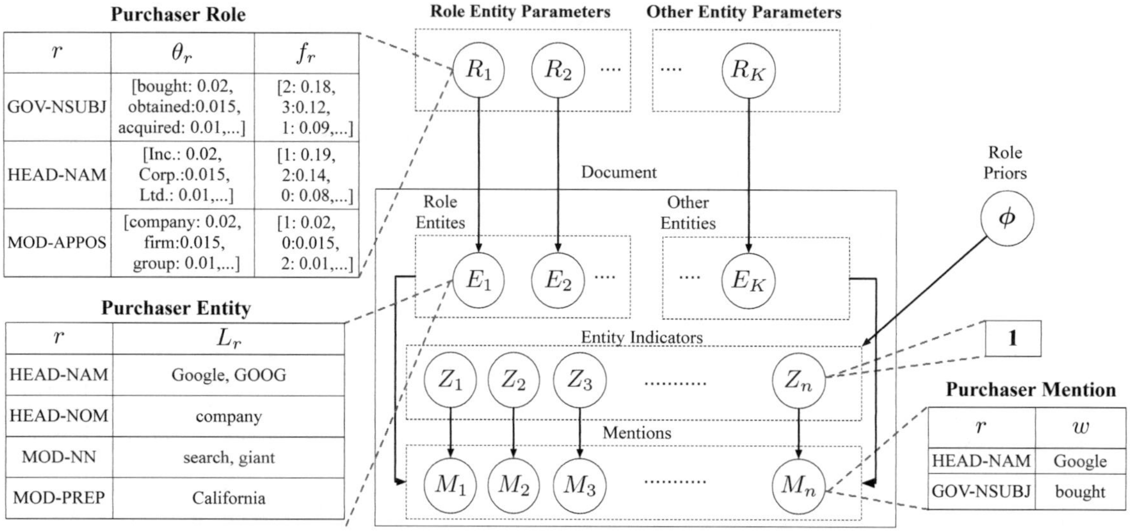

Figure 2: Graphical model depiction of our generative model described in Section 3. Sample values are illustrated for key parameters and latent variables.

3 Model

We describe our generative model for a document, which has many similarities to the coreference-only model of Haghighi and Klein (2010), but which integrally models template role-fillers. We briefly describe the key abstractions of our model.

Mentions: A mention is an observed textual reference to a latent real-world entity. Mentions are associated with nodes in a parse tree and are typically realized as NPs. There are three basic forms of mentions: proper (NAM), nominal (NOM), and pronominal (PRO). Each mention M is represented as collection of key-value pairs. The keys are called *properties* and the values are words. The set of properties utilized here, denoted $\mathcal{R}$, are the same as in Haghighi and Klein (2010) and consist of the mention head, its dependencies, and its governor. See Figure 2 for a concrete example. Mention types are trivially determined from mention head POS tag. All mention properties and their values are observed.

Entities: An entity is a specific individual or object in the world. Entities are always latent in text. Where a mention has a single word for each property, an entity has a *list* of signature words. Formally, entities are mappings from properties $r \in \mathcal{R}$ to lists L_r of "canonical" words which that entity uses for that property.

Roles: The elements we have described so far are standard in many coreference systems. Our model performs role-filling by assuming that each entity is drawn from an underlying role. These roles include the K template roles as well as 'junk' roles to represent entities which do not fill a template role (see Section 5.2). Each role R is represented as a mapping between properties r and pairs of multinomials (θ_r, f_r). θ_r is a unigram distribution of words for property r that are semantically licensed for the role (e.g., being the subject of "acquired" for the ACQUIRED role). f_r is a "fertility" distribution over the integers that characterizes entity list lengths. Together, these distributions control the lists L_r for entities which instantiate the role.

We first present a broad sketch of our model's components and then detail each in a subsequent section. We temporarily assume that all mentions belong to a template role-filling entity; we lift this restriction in Section 5.2. First, a semantic component generates a sequence of entities $\mathbf{E} = (E_1, \ldots, E_K)$, where each E_i is generated from a corresponding role R_i. We use $\mathbf{R} = (R_1, \ldots, R_K)$ to denote the vector of template role parameters. Note that this work assumes that there is a one-to-one mapping between entities and roles; in particular, at most one entity can fill each role. This assumption is appropriate for the domain considered here.

Once entities have been generated, a discourse component generates which entities will be evoked in each of the n mention positions. We represent these choices using *entity indicators* denoted by $\mathbf{Z} = (Z_1, \ldots, Z_n)$. This component utilizes a learned global prior ϕ over roles. The Z_i indicators take values in $1, \ldots, K$ indicating the entity number (and thereby the role) underlying the ith mention position. Finally, a mention generation component renders each mention conditioned on the underlying entity and role. Formally:

$$P(\mathbf{E}, \mathbf{Z}, \mathbf{M}|\mathbf{R}, \phi) =$$

$$\left(\prod_{i=1}^{K} P(E_i|R_i)\right) \quad \text{[Semantic, Sec. 3.1]}$$

$$\left(\prod_{j=1}^{n} P(Z_j|\mathbf{Z}_{<j}, \phi)\right) \quad \text{[Discourse, Sec. 3.2]}$$

$$\left(\prod_{j=1}^{n} P(M_j|E_{Z_j}, R_{Z_j})\right) \quad \text{[Mention, Sec. 3.3]}$$

3.1 Semantic Component

Each role R generates an entity E as follows: for each mention property r, a word list, L_r, is drawn by first generating a list length from the corresponding f_r distribution in R.[2] This list is then populated by an independent draw from R's unigram distribution θ_r. Formally, for each $r \in \mathcal{R}$, an entity word list is drawn according to,[3]

$$P(L_r|R) = P(\texttt{len}(L_r)|f_r) \prod_{w \in L_r} P(w|\theta_r)$$

3.2 Discourse Component

The discourse component draws the entity indicator Z_j for the jth mention according to,

$$P(Z_j|\mathbf{Z}_{<j}, \phi) = \begin{cases} P(Z_j|\phi), & \text{if non-pronominal} \\ \sum_{j'} \mathbf{1}[Z_j = Z_{j'}]P(j'|j), & \text{o.w.} \end{cases}$$

When the jth mention is non-pronominal, we draw Z_j from ϕ, a global prior over the K roles. When M_j is a pronoun, we first draw an antecedent mention position j', such that $j' < j$, and then we set $Z_j = Z_{j'}$. The antecedent position is selected according to the distribution,

$$P(j'|j) \propto \exp\{-\gamma \textsc{TreeDist}(j', j)\}$$

where $\textsc{TreeDist}(j',j)$ represents the tree distance between the parse nodes for M_j and $M_{j'}$.[4] Mass is restricted to antecedent mention positions j' which occur earlier in the same sentence or in the previous sentence.[5]

3.3 Mention Generation

Once the entity indicator has been drawn, we generate words associated with mention conditioned on the underlying entity E and role R. For each mention property r associated with the mention, a word w is drawn utilizing E's word list L_r as well as the multinomials (f_r, θ_r) from role R. The word w is drawn according to,

$$P(w|E, R) = (1 - \alpha_r)\frac{\mathbf{1}[w \in L_r]}{\texttt{len}(L_r)} + \alpha_r P(w|\theta_r)$$

For each property r, there is a hyper-parameter α_r which interpolates between selecting a word uniformly from the entity list L_r and drawing from the underlying role distribution θ_r. Intuitively, a small α_r indicates that an entity prefers to re-use a small number of words for property r. This is typically the case for proper and nominal heads as well as modifiers. At the other extreme, setting α_r to 1 indicates the property isn't particular to the entity itself, but rather always drawn from the underlying role distribution. We set α_r to 1 for pronoun heads as well as for the governor properties.

4 Learning and Inference

Since we will make use of unannotated data (see Section 5), we utilize a variational EM algorithm to learn parameters $\mathbf{R}$ and ϕ. The E-Step requires the posterior $P(\mathbf{E}, \mathbf{Z}|\mathbf{R}, \mathrm{M}, \phi)$, which is intractable to compute exactly. We approximate it using a surrogate variational distribution of the following factored form:

$$Q(\mathbf{E}, \mathbf{Z}) = \left(\prod_{i=1}^{K} q_i(E_i)\right)\left(\prod_{j=1}^{n} r_j(Z_j)\right)$$

Each $r_j(Z_j)$ is a distribution over the entity indicator for mention M_j, which approximates the true posterior of Z_j. Similarly, $q_i(E_i)$ approximates the posterior over entity E_i which is associated with role R_i. As is standard, we iteratively update each component distribution to minimize KL-divergence, fixing all other distributions:

$$q_i \leftarrow \operatorname*{argmin}_{q_i} KL(Q(\mathbf{E}, \mathbf{Z})|P(\mathbf{E}, \mathbf{Z}|\mathbf{M}, \mathbf{R}, \phi)$$
$$\propto \exp\{\mathbb{E}_{Q/q_i} \ln P(\mathbf{E}, \mathbf{Z}|\mathbf{M}, \mathbf{R}, \phi))\}$$

[2] There is one exception: the sizes of the proper and nominal head property lists are jointly generated, but their word lists are still independently populated.

[3] While, in principle, this process can yield word lists with duplicate words, we constrain the model during inference to not allow that to occur.

[4] Sentence parse trees are merged into a right-branching document parse tree. This allows us to extend tree distance to inter-sentence nodes.

[5] The sole parameter γ is fixed at 0.1.

	Ment Acc.	Ent. Acc.
INDEP	60.0	43.7
JOINT	64.6	54.2
JOINT+PRO	**68.2**	**57.8**

Table 1: Results on corporate acquisition tasks with given role mention boundaries. We report mention role accuracy and entity role accuracy (correctly labeling all entity mentions).

For example, the update for a non-pronominal entity indicator component $r_j(\cdot)$ is given by:[6]

$$\begin{aligned}\ln r_j(z) &\propto \mathbb{E}_{Q/r_j} \ln P(\mathbf{E}, \mathbf{Z}, \mathbf{M}|\mathbf{R}, \phi) \\ &\propto \mathbb{E}_{q_z} \ln \left(P(z|\phi)P(M_j|E_z, R_z)\right) \\ &= \ln P(z|\phi) + \mathbb{E}_{q_z} \ln P(M_j|E_z, R_z)\end{aligned}$$

A similar update is performed on pronominal entity indicator distributions, which we omit here for space. The update for variational entity distribution is given by:

$$\begin{aligned}\ln q_i(e_i) &\propto \mathbb{E}_{Q/q_i} \ln P(\mathbf{E}, \mathbf{Z}, \mathbf{M}|\mathbf{R}, \phi) \\ &\propto \mathbb{E}_{\{r_j\}} \ln \left(P(e_i|R_i) \prod_{j:Z_j=i} P(M_j|e_i, R_i) \right) \\ &= \ln P(e_i|R_i) + \sum_j r_j(i) \ln P(M_j|e_i, R_i)\end{aligned}$$

It is intractable to enumerate all possible entities e_i (each consisting of several sets of words). We instead limit the support of $q_i(e_i)$ to several sampled entities. We obtain entity samples by sampling mention entity indicators according to r_j. For a given sample, we assume that E_i consists of the non-pronominal head words and modifiers of mentions such that Z_j has sampled value i.

During the E-Step, we perform 5 iterations of updating each variational factor, which results in an approximate posterior distribution. Using expectations from this approximate posterior, our M-Step is relatively straightforward. The role parameters R_i are computed from the $q_i(e_i)$ and $r_j(z)$ distributions, and the global role prior ϕ from the non-pronominal components of $r_j(z)$.

5 Experiments

We present results on the corporate acquisitions task, which consists of 600 annotated documents split into a 300/300 train/test split. We use 50 training documents as a development set. In all documents, proper and (usually) nominal mentions are annotated with roles, while pronouns are not. We preprocess each document identically to Haghighi and Klein (2010): we sentence-segment using the OpenNLP toolkit, parse sentences with the Berkeley Parser (Petrov et al., 2006), and extract mention properties from parse trees and the Stanford Dependency Extractor (de Marneffe et al., 2006).

5.1 Gold Role Boundaries

We first consider the simplified task where role mention boundaries are given. We map each labeled token span in training and test data to a parse tree node that shares the same head. In this setting, the role-filling task is a collective classification problem, since we know each mention is filling some role.

As our baseline, INDEP, we built a maximum entropy model which independently classifies each mention's role. It uses features as similar as possible to the generative model (and more), including the head word, typed dependencies of the head, various tree features, governing word, and several conjunctions of these features as well as coarser versions of lexicalized features. This system yields 60.0 mention labeling accuracy (see Table 1). The primary difficulty in classification is the disambiguation amongst the acquired, seller, and purchaser roles, which have similar internal structure, and differ primarily in their semantic contexts. Our entity-centered model, JOINT in Table 1, has no latent variables at training time in this setting, since each role maps to a unique entity. This model yields 64.6, outperforming INDEP.[7]

During development, we noted that often the most direct evidence of the role of an entity was associated with pronoun usage (see the first "it" in Figure 1). Training our model with pronominal mentions, whose roles are latent variables at training time, improves accuracy to 68.2.[8]

5.2 Full Task

We now consider the more difficult setting where role mention boundaries are not provided at test time. In this setting, we automatically extract mentions from a parse tree using a heuristic ap-

[6]For simplicity of exposition, we omit terms where M_j is an antecedent to a pronoun.

[7]We use the mode of the variational posteriors $r_j(Z_j)$ to make predictions (see Section 4).

[8]While this approach incorrectly assumes that all pronouns have antecedents amongst our given mentions, this did not appear to degrade performance.

	Role ID			Overall		
	P	R	F_1	P	R	F_1
INDEP	79.0	65.5	71.6	48.6	40.3	44.0
JOINT+PRO	**80.3**	69.2	74.3	53.4	46.4	49.7
BEST	80.1	**70.1**	**74.8**	**57.3**	**49.2**	**52.9**

Table 2: Results on corporate acquisitions data where mention boundaries are not provided. Systems must determine which mentions are template role-fillers as well as label them. Role ID only evaluates the binary decision of whether a mention is a template role-filler or not. Overall includes correctly labeling mentions. Our BEST system, see Section 5, adds extra unannotated data to our JOINT+PRO system.

proach. Our mention extraction procedure yields 95% recall over annotated role mentions and 45% precision.[9] Using extracted mentions as input, our task is to label some subset of the mentions with template roles. Since systems can label mentions as non-role bearing, only recall is critical to mention extraction. To adapt INDEP to this setting, we first use a binary classifier trained to distinguish role-bearing mentions. The baseline then classifies mentions which pass this first phase as before. We add 'junk' roles to our model to flexibly model entities that do not correspond to annotated template roles. During training, extracted mentions which are not matched in the labeled data have posteriors which are constrained to be amongst the 'junk' roles.

We first evaluate role identification (Role ID in Table 2), the task of identifying mentions which play some role in the template. The binary classifier for INDEP yields 71.6 F_1. Our JOINT+PRO system yields 74.3. On the task of identifying and correctly labeling role mentions, our model outperforms INDEP as well (Overall in Table 2). As our model is generative, it is straightforward to utilize totally unannotated data. We added 700 fully unannotated documents from the mergers and acquisitions portion of the Reuters 21857 corpus. Training JOINT+PRO on this data as well as our original training data yields the best performance (BEST in Table 2).[10]

To our knowledge, the best previously published results on this dataset are from Siefkes (2008), who report 45.9 weighted F_1. Our BEST system evaluated in their slightly stricter way yields 51.1.

[9]Following Patwardhan and Riloff (2009), we match extracted mentions to labeled spans if the head of the mention matches the labeled span.

[10]We scaled expected counts from the unlabeled data so that they did not overwhelm those from our (partially) labeled data.

6 Conclusion

We have presented a joint generative model of coreference resolution and role-filling information extraction. This model makes role decisions at the entity, rather than at the mention level. This approach naturally aggregates information across multiple mentions, incorporates unannotated data, and yields strong performance.

Acknowledgements: This project is funded in part by the Office of Naval Research under MURI Grant No. N000140911081.

References

M. C. de Marneffe, B. Maccartney, and C. D. Manning. 2006. Generating typed dependency parses from phrase structure parses. In *LREC*.

Dayne Freitag and Andrew McCallum. 2000. Information extraction with hmm structures learned by stochastic optimization. In *Association for the Advancement of Artificial Intelligence (AAAI)*.

Dayne Freitag. 1998. Machine learning for information extraction in informal domains.

A. Haghighi and D. Klein. 2010. Coreference resolution in a modular, entity-centered model. In *North American Association of Computational Linguistics (NAACL)*.

P. Liang and D. Klein. 2007. Structured Bayesian nonparametric models with variational inference (tutorial). In *Association for Computational Linguistics (ACL)*.

S. Patwardhan and E. Riloff. 2007. Effective information extraction with semantic affinity patterns and relevant regions. In *Joint Conference on Empirical Methods in Natural Language Processing*.

S. Patwardhan and E Riloff. 2009. A unified model of phrasal and sentential evidence for information extraction. In *Empirical Methods in Natural Language Processing (EMNLP)*.

Slav Petrov, Leon Barrett, Romain Thibaux, and Dan Klein. 2006. Learning accurate, compact, and interpretable tree annotation. In *Proceedings of the 21st International Conference on Computational Linguistics and 44th Annual Meeting of the Association for Computational Linguistics*, pages 433–440, Sydney, Australia, July. Association for Computational Linguistics.

Christian Siefkes. 2008. *An Incrementally Trainable Statistical Approach to Information Extraction: Based on Token Classification and Rich Context Model*. VDM Verlag, Saarbrücken, Germany, Germany.

A Semi-Supervised Key Phrase Extraction Approach: Learning from Title Phrases through a Document Semantic Network

Decong Li[1], Sujian Li[1], Wenjie Li[2], Wei Wang[1], Weiguang Qu[3]
[1]Key Laboratory of Computational Linguistics, Peking University
[2]Department of Computing, The Hong Kong Polytechnic University
[3] School of Computer Science and Technology, Nanjing Normal University
{lidecong,lisujian, wwei }@pku.edu.cn cswjli@comp.polyu.edu.hk wgqu@njnu.edu.cn

Abstract

It is a fundamental and important task to extract key phrases from documents. Generally, phrases in a document are not independent in delivering the content of the document. In order to capture and make better use of their relationships in key phrase extraction, we suggest exploring the Wikipedia knowledge to model a document as a semantic network, where both *n*-ary and binary relationships among phrases are formulated. Based on a commonly accepted assumption that the title of a document is always elaborated to reflect the content of a document and consequently key phrases tend to have close semantics to the title, we propose a novel semi-supervised key phrase extraction approach in this paper by computing the phrase importance in the semantic network, through which the influence of title phrases is propagated to the other phrases iteratively. Experimental results demonstrate the remarkable performance of this approach.

1 Introduction

Key phrases are defined as the phrases that express the main content of a document. Guided by the given key phrases, people can easily understand what a document describes, saving a great amount of time reading the whole text. Consequently, automatic key phrase extraction is in high demand. Meanwhile, it is also fundamental to many other natural language processing applications, such as information retrieval, text clustering and so on.

Key phrase extraction can be normally cast as a ranking problem solved by either supervised or unsupervised methods. Supervised learning requires a large amount of expensive training data, whereas unsupervised learning totally ignores human knowledge. To overcome the deficiencies of these two kinds of methods, we propose a novel semi-supervised key phrase extraction approach in this paper, which explores title phrases as the source of knowledge.

It is well agreed that the title has a similar role to the key phrases. They are both elaborated to reflect the content of a document. Therefore, phrases in the titles are often appropriate to be key phrases. That is why position has been a quite effective feature in the feature-based key phrase extraction methods (Witten, 1999), i.e., if a phrase is located in the title, it is ranked higher.

However, one can only include a couple of most important phrases in the title prudently due to the limitation of the title length, even though many other key phrases are all pivotal to the understanding of the document. For example, when we read the title "China Tightens Grip on the Web", we can only have a glimpse of what the document says. On the other hand, the key phrases, such as "China", "Censorship", "Web", "Domain name", "Internet", and "CNNIC", etc. can tell more details about the main topics of the document. In this regard, title phrases are often good key phrases but they are far from enough.

If we review the above example again, we will find that the key phrase "Internet" can be inferred from the title phrase "Web". As a matter of fact, key phrases often have close semantics to title phrases. Then a question comes to our minds: can we make use of these title phrases to infer the other key phrases?

To provide a foundation of inference, a semantic network that captures the relationships among phrases is required. In the previous works (Turdakov and Velikhov, 2008), semantic networks are constructed based on the binary relations, and the semantic relatedness between a pair of phrases is formulated by the weighted edges that connects them. The deficiency of these approaches is the incapability to capture the *n*-ary relations among multiple phrases. For example, a group of

Proceedings of the ACL 2010 Conference Short Papers, pages 296–300,
Uppsala, Sweden, 11-16 July 2010.

phrases may collectively describe an entity or an event.

In this study, we propose to model a semantic network as a hyper-graph, where vertices represent phrases and weighted hyper-edges measure the semantic relatedness of both binary relations and n-ary relations among phrases. We explore a universal knowledge base – Wikipedia – to compute the semantic relatedness. Yet our major contribution is to develop a novel semi-supervised key phrase extraction approach by computing the phrase importance in the semantic network, through which the influence of title phrases is propagated to the other phrases iteratively.

The goal of the semi-supervised learning is to design a function that is sufficiently smooth with respect to the intrinsic structure revealed by title phrases and other phrases. Based on the assumption that semantically related phrases are likely to have similar scores, the function to be estimated is required to assign title phrases a higher score and meanwhile locally smooth on the constructed hyper-graph. Zhou et al.'s work (Zhou 2005) lays down a foundation for our semi-supervised phrase ranking algorithm introduced in Section 3. Experimental results presented in Section 4 demonstrate the effectiveness of this approach.

2 Wikipedia-based Semantic Network Construction

Wikipedia[1] is a free online encyclopedia, which has unarguably become the world's largest collection of encyclopedic knowledge. *Articles* are the basic entries in the Wikipedia, with each article explaining one Wikipedia term. Articles contain *link*s pointing from one article to another. Currently, there are over 3 million articles and 90 million links in English Wikipedia. In addition to providing a large vocabulary, Wikipedia articles also contain a rich body of lexical semantic information expressed via the extensive number of links. During recent years, Wikipedia has been used as a powerful tool to compute semantic relatedness between terms in a good few of works (Turdakov 2008).

We consider a document composed of the phrases that describe various aspects of entities or events with different semantic relationships. We then model a document as a semantic network formulated by a weighted hyper-graph $G=(V, E, W)$, where each vertex $v_i \in V$ $(1 \leq i \leq n)$ represents a phrase, each hyper-edge $e_j \in E$ $(1 \leq j \leq m)$ is a subset of V, representing binary relations or n-ary relations among phrases, and the weight $w(e_j)$ measures the semantic relatedness of e_j.

By applying the WSD technique proposed by (Turdakov and Velikhov, 2008), each phrase is assigned with a single Wikipedia article that describes its meaning. Intuitively, if the fraction of the links that the two articles have in common to the total number of the links in both articles is high, the two phrases corresponding to the two articles are more semantically related. Also, an article contains different types of links, which are relevant to the computation of semantic relatedness to different extent. Hence we adopt the weighted Dice metric proposed by (Turdakov 2008) to compute the semantic relatedness of each binary relation, resulting in the edge weight $w(e_{ij})$, where e_{ij} is an edge connecting the phrases v_i and v_j.

To define the n-ary relations in the semantic network, a proper graph clustering technique is needed. We adopt the weighted Girvan-Newman algorithm (Newman 2004) to cluster phrases (including title phrases) by computing their betweenness centrality. The advantage of this algorithm is that it need not specify a pre-defined number of clusters. Then the phrases, within each cluster, are connected by a n-ary relation. n-ary relations among the phrases in the same cluster are then measured based on binary relations. The weight of a hyper-edge e is defined as:

$$w(e) = \frac{\alpha}{|e|} \sum_{e_{ij} \subseteq e} w(e_{ij}) \quad (1)$$

where $|e|$ is the number of the vertices in e, e_{ij} is an edge with two vertices included in e and $\alpha \geq 0$ is a parameter balancing the relative importance of n-ary hyper-edges compared with binary ones.

3 Semi-supervised Learning from Title

Given the document semantic network represented as a phrase hyper-graph, one way to make better use of the semantic information is to rank phrases with a semi-supervised learning strategy, where the title phrases are regarded as labeled samples, while the other phrases as unlabeled ones. That is, the information we have at the beginning about how to rank phrases is that the title phrases are the most important phrases. Initially, the title phrases are assigned with a positive score of 1 indicating its importance and oth-

[1] www.wikipedia.org

er phrases are assigned zero. Then the importance scores of the phrases are learned iteratively from the title phrases through the hyper-graph. The key idea behind hyper-graph based semi-supervised ranking is that the vertices which usually belong to the same hyper-edges should be assigned with similar scores. Then, we have the following two constraints:

1. The phrases which have many incident hyper-edges in common should be assigned similar scores.

2. The given initial scores of the title phrases should be changed as little as possible.

Given a weighted hyper-graph *G*, assume a ranking function *f* over *V*, which assigns each vertex *v* an importance score *f*(*v*). *f* can be thought as a vector in Euclid space $R^{|V|}$. For the convenience of computation, we use an incidence matrix *H* to represent the hypergraph, defined as:

$$h(v,e)=\begin{cases}0, & \text{if } v\notin e\\ 1, & \text{if } v\in e\end{cases} \quad (2)$$

Based on the incidence matrix, we define the degrees of the vertex *v* and the hyper-edge *e* as

$$d(v)=\sum_{e\in E} w(e)h(v,e) \quad (3)$$

and

$$\delta(e)=\sum_{v\in V} h(v,e) \quad (4)$$

Then, to formulate the above-mentioned constraints, let y denote the initial score vector, then the importance scores of the phrases are learned iteratively by solving the following optimization problem:

$$\arg\min_{f\in R^{|V|}}\{\Omega(f)+\mu\|f-y\|^2\} \quad (5)$$

$$\Omega(f)=\frac{1}{2}\sum_{e\in E}\frac{1}{\delta(e)}\sum_{\{u,v\}\subseteq e} w(e)\left(\frac{f(u)}{\sqrt{d(u)}}-\frac{f(v)}{\sqrt{d(v)}}\right)^2 \quad (6)$$

where $\mu > 0$ is the parameter specifying the tradeoff between the two competitive items. Let D_v and D_e denote the diagonal matrices containing the vertex and the hyper-edge degrees respectively, *W* denote the diagonal matrix containing the hyper-edge weights, f^* denote the solution of (6). Zhou has given the solution (Zhou, 2005) as.

$$f^*=\beta\Theta f^*+(1-\beta)y \quad (7)$$

where $\Theta=D_v^{-1/2}HWD_e^{-1}H^TD_v^{-1/2}$ and $\beta=1/(\mu+1)$. Using an approximation algorithm (e.g. Algorithm 1), we can finally get a vector *f* representing the approximate phrase scores.

Algorithm 1: PhraseRank(*V*, *T*, *a*, *b*)

Input: Title phrase set = $\{v_1,v_2,\ldots,v_t\}$,the set of other phrases $=\{v_{t+1},v_{t+2},\ldots,v_n\}$, parameters α and β, convergence threshold ζ

Output: The approximate phrase scores *f*

Construct a document semantic network for all the phrases $\{v_1,v_2,\ldots,v_n\}$ using the method described in section 2.

Let $\Theta=D_v^{-1/2}HWD_e^{-1}H^TD_v^{-1/2}$;

Initialize the score vector *y* as $y_i=1, 1\le i\le t$, and $y_j=0, t<j\le n$;

Let $f^0=y$, $k=0$;

REPEAT

$f^{k+1}=\beta\Theta f^k+(1-\beta)y$;

$\nabla \leftarrow max|f_i^{k+1}-f_i^k|$, for $0\le i\le n$;

$k\leftarrow k+1$;

UNTIL $\nabla<\zeta$

END

Finally we rank phrases in descending order of the calculated importance scores and select those highest ranked phrases as key phrases. According to the number of all the candidate phrases, we choose an appropriate proportion, i.e. 10%, of all the phrases as key phrases.

4 Evaluation

4.1 Experiment Set-up

We first collect all the Wikipedia terms to compose of a dictionary. The word sequences that occur in the dictionary are identified as phrases. Here we use a finite-state automaton to accomplish this task to avoid the imprecision of preprocessing by POS tagging or chunking. Then, we adopt the WSD technique proposed by (Turdakov and Velikhov 2008) to find the corresponding Wikipedia article for each phrase. As mentioned in Section 2, a document semantic network in the form of a hyper-graph is constructed, on which Algorithm 1 is applied to rank the phrases.

To evaluate our proposed approach, we select 200 pieces of news from well-known English media. 5 to 10 key phrases are manually labeled in each news document and the average number of the key phrases is 7.2 per document. Due to the abbreviation and synonymy phenomena, we construct a thesaurus and convert all manual and automatic phrases into their canonical forms when evaluated. The traditional Recall, Precision and F1-measure metrics are adopted for evaluation. This section conducts two sets of experiment: (1) to examine the influence of two parameters: α and β, on the key phrase extraction performance; (2) to compare with other well known state-of-art key phrase extraction approaches.

4.2 Parameter tuning

The approach involves two parameters: α ($\alpha \geq 0$) is a relation factor balancing the influence of *n*-ary relations and binary relations; β ($0 \leq \beta \leq 1$) is a learning factor tuning the influence from the title phrases. It is hard to find a global optimized solution for the combination of these two factors. So we apply a gradient search strategy. At first, the learning factor is set to β=0.8. Different values of α ranging from 0 to 3 are examined. Then, given that α is set to the value with the best performance, we conduct experiments to find an appropriate value for β.

4.2.1 α: Relation Factor

First, we fix the learning factor β as 0.8 randomly and evaluate the performance by varying α value from 0 to 3. When α=0, it means that the weight of n-ary relations is zero and only binary relations are considered. As we can see from Figure 1, the performance is improved in most cases in terms of F1-measure and reaches a peak at α=1.8. This justifies the rational to incorporate *n*-ary relations with binary relations in the document semantic network.

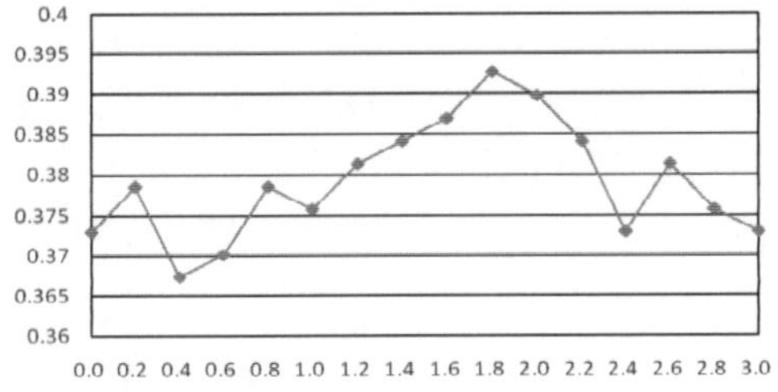

Figure 1. F1-measures with α in [0 3]

4.2.2 β: Learning factor

Next, we set the relation factor α=1.8, we inspect the performance with the learning factor β ranging from 0 to 1. β=1 means that the ranking scores learn from the semantic network without any consideration of title phrases. As shown in Figure 2, we find that the performance almost keep a smooth fluctuation as β increases from 0 to 0.9, and then a diving when β=1. This proves that title phrases indeed provide valuable information for learning.

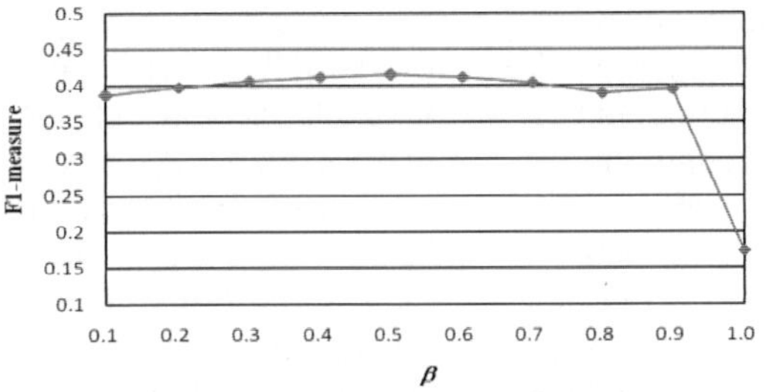

Figure 2. F1-measure with β in [0,1]

4.3 Comparison with Other Approaches

Our approach aims at inferring important key phrases from title phrases through a semantic network. Here we take a method of synonym expansion as the baseline, called WordNet expansion here. The WordNet[2] expansion approach selects all the synonyms of the title phrases in the document as key phrases. Afterwards, our approach is evaluated against two existing approaches, which rely on the conventional semantic network and are able to capture binary relations only. One approach combines the title information into the Grineva's community-based method (Grineva *et al.*, 2009), called title-community approach. The title-community approach uses the Girvan-Newman algorithm to cluster phrases into communities and selects those phrases in the communities containing the title phrases as key phrases. We do not limit the number of key phrases selected. The other one is based on topic-sensitive LexRank (Otterbacher *et al.*, 2005), called title-sensitive PageRank here. The title-sensitive PageRank approach makes use of title phrases to re-weight the transitions between vertices and picks up 10% top-ranked phrases as key phrases.

Approach	Precision	Recall	F1
Title-sensitive PageRank (*d*=0.15)	34.8%	39.5%	37.0%
Title-community	29.8%	**56.9%**	39.1%
Our approach (α=1.8, β=0.5)	**39.4%**	44.6%	**41.8%**
WordNet expansion (baseline)	7.9%	32.9%	12.5%

Table 1. Comparison with other approaches

Table 1 summarizes the performance on the test data. The results presented in the table show that our approach exhibits the best performance among all the four approaches. It follows that the key phrases inferred from a document semantic network are not limited to the synonyms of title phrases. As the title-sensitive PageRank ap-

[2] http://wordnet.princeton.edu

proach totally ignores the n-ary relations, its performance is the worst. Based on binary relations, the title-community approach clusters phrases into communities and each community can be considered as an n-ary relation. However, this approach lacks of an importance propagation process. Consequently, it has the highest recall value but the lowest precision. In contrast, our approach achieves the highest precision, due to its ability to infer many correct key phrases using importance propagation among n-ary relations.

5 Conclusion

This work is based on the belief that key phrases tend to have close semantics to the title phrases. In order to make better use of phrase relations in key phrase extraction, we explore the Wikipedia knowledge to model one document as a semantic network in the form of hyper-graph, through which the other phrases learned their importance scores from the title phrases iteratively. Experimental results demonstrate the effectiveness and robustness of our approach.

Acknowledgments

The work described in this paper was partially supported by NSFC programs (No: 60773173, 60875042 and 90920011), and Hong Kong RGC Projects (No: PolyU5217/07E). We thank the anonymous reviewers for their insightful comments.

References

David Milne, Ian H. Witten. 2008. *An Effective, Low-Cost Measure of Semantic Relatedness Obtained from Wikipedia Links.* In Wikipedia and AI workshop at the AAAI-08 Conference, Chicago, US.

Dengyong Zhou, Jiayuan Huang and Bernhard Schölkopf. 2005. *Beyond Pairwise Classification and Clustering Using Hypergraphs.* MPI Technical Report, Tübingen, Germany.

Denis Turdakov and Pavel Velikhov. 2008. *Semantic relatedness metric for wikipedia concepts based on link analysis and its application to word sense disambiguation.* In Colloquium on Databases and Information Systems (SYRCoDIS).

Ian H. Witten, Gordon W. Paynter, Eibe Frank , Carl Gutwin , Craig G. Nevill-Manning. 1999. *KEA: practical automatic keyphrase extraction*, In Proceedings of the fourth ACM conference on Digital libraries, pp.254-255, California, USA.

Jahna Otterbacher, Gunes Erkan and Dragomir R. Radev. 2005. *Using Random Walks for Question-focused Sentence Retrieval.* In Proceedings of HLT/EMNLP 2005, pp. 915-922, Vancouver, Canada.

Maria Grineva, Maxim Grinev and Dmitry Lizorkin. 2009. *Extracting key terms from noisy and multitheme documents*, In Proceedings of the 18th international conference on World wide web, pp. 661-670, Madrid, Spain.

Michael Strube and Simone Paolo Ponzetto. 2006.WikiRelate! *Computing Semantic Relatedness using Wikipedia.* In Proceedings of the 21st National Conference on Artificial Intelligence, pp. 1419–1424, Boston, MA.

M. E. J. Newman. 2004. *Analysis of Weighted Networks.* Physical Review E 70, 056131.

Domain Adaptation of Maximum Entropy Language Models

Tanel Alumäe*
Adaptive Informatics Research Centre
School of Science and Technology
Aalto University
Helsinki, Finland
tanel@cis.hut.fi

Mikko Kurimo
Adaptive Informatics Research Centre
School of Science and Technology
Aalto University
Helsinki, Finland
Mikko.Kurimo@tkk.fi

Abstract

We investigate a recently proposed Bayesian adaptation method for building style-adapted maximum entropy language models for speech recognition, given a large corpus of written language data and a small corpus of speech transcripts. Experiments show that the method consistently outperforms linear interpolation which is typically used in such cases.

1 Introduction

In large vocabulary speech recognition, a language model (LM) is typically estimated from large amounts of written text data. However, recognition is typically applied to speech that is stylistically different from written language. For example, in an often-tried setting, speech recognition is applied to broadcast news, that includes introductory segments, conversations and spontaneous interviews. To decrease the mismatch between training and test data, often a small amount of speech data is human-transcribed. A LM is then built by interpolating the models estimated from large corpus of written language and the small corpus of transcribed data. However, in practice, different models might be of different importance depending on the word context. Global interpolation doesn't take such variability into account and all predictions are weighted across models identically, regardless of the context.

In this paper we investigate a recently proposed Bayesian adaptation approach (Daume III, 2007; Finkel and Manning, 2009) for adapting a conditional maximum entropy (ME) LM (Rosenfeld, 1996) to a new domain, given a large corpus of out-of-domain training data and a small corpus of in-domain data. The main contribution of this paper is that we show how the suggested hierarchical adaptation can be used with suitable priors and combined with the class-based speedup technique (Goodman, 2001) to adapt ME LMs in large-vocabulary speech recognition when the amount of target data is small. The results outperform the conventional linear interpolation of background and target models in both N-grams and ME models. It seems that with the adapted ME models, the same recognition accuracy for the target evaluation data can be obtained with 50% less adaptation data than in interpolated ME models.

2 Review of Conditional Maximum Entropy Language Models

Maximum entropy (ME) modeling is a framework that has been used in a wide area of natural language processing (NLP) tasks. A conditional ME model has the following form:

$$P(x|h) = \frac{e^{\sum_i \lambda_i f_i(x,h)}}{\sum_{x'} e^{\sum_j \lambda_j f_j(x',h)}} \tag{1}$$

where x is an outcome (in case of a LM, a word), h is a context (the word history), and x' a set of all possible outcomes (words). The functions f_i are (typically binary) feature functions. During ME training, the optimal weights λ_i corresponding to features $f_i(x,h)$ are learned. More precisely, finding the ME model is equal to finding weights that maximize the log-likelihood $L(X;\Lambda)$ of the training data X. The weights are learned via improved iterative scaling algorithm or some of its modern fast counterparts (i.e., conjugate gradient descent).

Since LMs typically have a vocabulary of tens of thousands of words, the use of a normalization factor over all possible outcomes makes estimating a ME LM very memory and time consuming. Goodman (2001) proposed a class-based method that drastically reduces the resource requirements for training such models. The idea is to cluster

* Currently with Tallinn University of Technology, Estonia

Proceedings of the ACL 2010 Conference Short Papers, pages 301–306,
Uppsala, Sweden, 11-16 July 2010.

words in the vocabulary into classes (e.g., based on their distributional similarity). Then, we can decompose the prediction of a word given its history into prediction of its class given the history, and prediction of the word given the history and its class :

$$P(w|h) = P(C(w)|h) \cdot P(w|h, C(w)) \quad (2)$$

Using such decomposition, we can create two ME models: one corresponding to $P(C(w)|h)$ and the other corresponding to $P(w|h, C(w))$. It is easy to see that computing the normalization factor of the first component model now requires only looping over all classes. It turns out that normalizing the second model is also easier: for a context $h, C(w)$, we only need to normalize over words that belong to class $C(w)$, since other words cannot occur in this context. This decomposition can be further extended by using hierarchical classes.

To avoid overfitting, ME models are usually smoothed (regularized). The most widely used smoothing method for ME LMs is Gaussian priors (Chen and Rosenfeld, 2000): a zero-mean prior with a given variance is added to all feature weights, and the model optimization criteria becomes:

$$L'(X;\Lambda) = L(X;\Lambda) - \sum_{i=1}^{F} \frac{\lambda_i^2}{2\sigma_i^2} \quad (3)$$

where F is the number of feature functions. Typically, a fixed hyperparameter $\sigma_i = \sigma$ is used for all parameters. The optimal variance is usually estimated on a development set. Intuitively, this method encourages feature weights to be smaller, by penalizing weights with big absolute values.

3 Domain Adaptation of Maximum Entropy Models

Recently, a hierarchical Bayesian adaptation method was proposed that can be applied to a large family of discriminative learning tasks (such as ME models, SVMs) (Daume III, 2007; Finkel and Manning, 2009). In NLP problems, data often comes from different sources (e.g., newspapers, web, textbooks, speech transcriptions). There are three classic approaches for building models from multiple sources. We can pool all training data and estimate a single model, and apply it for all tasks. The second approach is to "unpool" the data, i.e, only use training data from the test domain. The third and often the best performing approach is to train separate models for each data source, apply them to test data and interpolate the results.

The hierarchical Bayesian adaptation method is a generalization of the three approaches described above. The hierarchical model jointly optimizes global and domain-specific parameters, using parameters built from pooled data as priors for domain-specific parameters. In other words, instead of using smoothing to encourage parameters to be closer to zero, it encourages domain-specific model parameters to be closer to the corresponding global parameters, while a zero mean Gaussian prior is still applied for global parameters. For processing test data during runtime, the domain-specific model is applied. Intuitively, this approach can be described as follows: the domain-specific parameters are largely determined by global data, unless there is good domain-specific evidence that they should be different. The key to this approach is that the global and domain-specific parameters are learned jointly, not hierarchically. This allows domain-specific parameters to influence the global parameters, and vice versa. Formally, the joint optimization criteria becomes:

$$L_{hier}(X;\Lambda) = \sum_d \left(L_{orig}(X_d, \Lambda_d) - \sum_{i=1}^{F} \frac{(\lambda_{d,i} - \lambda_{*,i})^2}{2\sigma_d^2} \right) - \sum_{i=1}^{F} \frac{\lambda_{*,i}^2}{2\sigma_*^2} \quad (4)$$

where X_d is data for domain d, $\lambda_{*,i}$ the global parameters, $\lambda_{d,i}$ the domain-specific parameters, σ_*^2 the global variance and σ_d^2 the domain-specific variances. The global and domain-specific variances are optimized on the heldout data. Usually, larger values are used for global parameters and for domains with more data, while for domains with less data, the variance is typically set to be smaller, encouraging the domain-specific parameters to be closer to global values.

This adaptation scheme is very similar to the approaches proposed by (Chelba and Acero, 2006) and (Chen, 2009b): both use a model estimated from background data as a prior when learning a model from in-domain data. The main difference is the fact that in this method, the models are estimated jointly while in the other works, background model has to be estimated before learning the in-domain model.

4 Experiments

In this section, we look at experimental results over two speech recognition tasks.

4.1 Tasks

Task 1: English Broadcast News. This recognition task consists of the English broadcast news section of the 2003 NIST Rich Transcription Evaluation Data. The data includes six news recordings from six different sources with a total length of 176 minutes.

As acoustic models, the CMU Sphinx open source triphone HUB4 models for wideband (16kHz) speech[1] were used. The models have been trained using 140 hours of speech.

For training the LMs, two sources were used: first 5M sentences from the Gigaword (2nd ed.) corpus (99.5M words), and broadcast news transcriptions from the TDT4 corpus (1.19M words). The latter was treated as in-domain data in the adaptation experiments. A vocabulary of 26K words was used. It is a subset of a bigger 60K vocabulary, and only includes words that occurred in the training data. The OOV rate against the test set was 2.4%.

The audio used for testing was segmented into parts of up to 20 seconds in length. Speaker diarization was applied using the LIUM_SpkDiarization toolkit (Deléglise et al., 2005). The CMU Sphinx 3.7 was used for decoding. A three-pass recognition strategy was applied: the first pass recognition hypotheses were used for calculating MLLR-adapted models for each speaker. In the second pass, the adapted acoustic models were used for generating a 5000-best list of hypotheses for each segment. In the third pass, the ME LM was used to re-rank the hypotheses and select the best one. During decoding, a trigram LM model was used. The trigram model was an interpolation of source-specific models which were estimated using Kneser-Ney discounting.

Task 2: Estonian Broadcast Conversations. The second recognition task consists of four recordings from different live talk programs from three Estonian radio stations. Their format consists of hosts and invited guests, spontaneously discussing current affairs. There are 40 minutes of transcriptions, with 11 different speakers.

The acoustic models were trained on various wideband Estonian speech corpora: the BABEL speech database (9h), transcriptions of Estonian broadcast news (7.5h) and transcriptions of radio live talk programs (10h). The models are triphone HMMs, using MFCC features.

For training the LMs, two sources were used: about 10M sentences from various Estonian newspapers, and manual transcriptions of 10 hours of live talk programs from three Estonian radio stations. The latter is identical in style to the test data, although it originates from a different time period and covers a wider variety of programs, and was treated as in-domain data.

As Estonian is a highly inflective language, morphemes are used as basic units in the LM. We use a morphological analyzer (Kaalep and Vaino, 2001) for splitting the words into morphemes. After such processing, the newspaper corpus includes of 185M tokens, and the transcribed data 104K tokens. A vocabulary of 30K tokens was used for this task, with an OOV rate of 1.7% against the test data. After recognition, morphemes were concatenated back to words.

As with English data, a three-pass recognition strategy involving MLLR adaptation was applied.

4.2 Results

For both tasks, we rescored the N-best lists in two different ways: (1) using linear interpolation of source-specific ME models and (2) using hierarchically domain-adapted ME model (as described in previous chapter). The English ME models had a three-level and Estonian models a four-level class hierarchy. The classes were derived using the word exchange algorithm (Kneser and Ney, 1993). The number of classes at each level was determined experimentally so as to optimize the resource requirements for training ME models (specifically, the number of classes was 150, 1000 and 5000 for the English models and 20, 150, 1000 and 6000 for the Estonian models). We used unigram, bigram and trigram features that occurred at least twice in the training data. The feature cut-off was applied in order to accommodate the memory requirements. The feature set was identical for interpolated and adapted models.

[1]`http://www.speech.cs.cmu.edu/sphinx/models/`

	Interp. models		Adapted models		
Adaptation data (No of words)	σ^2_{OD}	σ^2_{ID}	σ^2_*	σ^2_{OD}	σ^2_{ID}
English Broadcast News					
147K	$2e8$	$3e5$	$5e7$	$2e7$	$2e6$
292K	$2e8$	$5e5$	$5e7$	$2e7$	$2e6$
591K	$2e8$	$1e6$	$5e7$	$2e7$	$2e6$
1119K	$2e8$	$2e6$	$5e7$	$2e7$	$5e6$
Estonian Broadcast Conversations					
104K	$5e8$	$3e5$	$5e7$	$1e7$	$2e6$

Table 1: The unnormalized values of Gaussian prior variances for interpolated out-of-domain (OD) and in-domain (ID) ME models, and hierarchically adapted global (*), out-of-odomain (OD) and in-domain (ID) models that were used in the experiments.

For the English task, we also explored the efficiency of these two approaches with varying size of adaptation data: we repeated the experiments when using one eighth, one quarter, half and all of the TDT4 transcription data for interpolation/adaptation. The amount of used Gigaword data was not changed. In all cases, interpolation weights were re-optimized and new Gaussian variance values were heuristically determined.

The TADM toolkit[2] was used for estimating ME models, utilizing its implementation of the conjugate gradient algorithm.

The models were regularized using Gaussian priors. The variance parameters were chosen heuristically based on light tuning on development set perplexity. For the source-specific ME models, the variance was fixed on per-model basis. For the adapted model, that jointly models global and domain-specific data, the Gaussian priors were fixed for each hierarchy node (i.e., the variance was fixed across global, out-of-domain, and in-domain parameters). Table 1 lists values for the variances of Gaussian priors (as in equations 3 and 4) that we used in the experiments. In other publications, the variance values are often normalized to the size of the data. We chose not to normalize the values, since in the hierarchical adaptation scheme, also data from other domains have impact on the learned model parameters, thus it's not possible to simply normalize the variances.

The experimental results are presented in Table 2. Perplexity and word error rate (WER) results of the interpolated and adapted models are compared. For the Estonian task, letter error rate (LER) is also reported, since it tends to be a more indicative measure of speech recognition quality for highly inflected languages. In all experiments, using the adapted models resulted in lower perplexity and lower error rate. Improvements in the English experiment were less evident than in the Estonian system, with under 10% improvement in perplexity and 1-3% in WER, against 15% and 4% for the Estonian experiment. In most cases, there was a significant improvement in WER when using the adapted ME model (according to the Wilcoxon test), with and exception of the English experiments on the 292K and 591K data sets.

The comparison between N-gram models and ME models is not entirely fair since ME models are actually class-based. Such transformation introduces additional smoothing into the model and can improve model perplexity, as also noticed by Goodman (2001).

5 Discussion

In this paper we have tested a hierarchical adaptation method (Daume III, 2007; Finkel and Manning, 2009) on building style-adapted LMs for speech recognition. We showed that the method achieves consistently lower error rates than when using linear interpolation which is typically used in such scenarios.

The tested method is ideally suited for language modeling in speech recognition: we almost always have access to large amounts of data from written sources but commonly the speech to be recognized is stylistically noticeably different. The hierarchical adaptation method enables to use even a small amount of in-domain data to modify the parameters estimated from out-of-domain data, if there is enough evidence.

As Finkel and Manning (2009) point out, the hierarchical nature of the method makes it possible to estimate highly specific models: we could draw style-specific models from general high-level priors, and topic-and-style specific models from style-specific priors. Furthermore, the models don't have to be hierarchical: it is easy to generalize the method to general multilevel approach where a model is drawn from multiple priors. For

[2] `http://tadm.sourceforge.net/`

	Perplexity				WER			LER		
Adaptation data (No. of words)	Pooled N-gram	Interp. N-gram	Interp. ME	Adapted ME	Interp. N-gram	Interp. ME	Adapted ME	Interp. N-gram	Interp. ME	Adapted ME
English Broadcast News										
147K	290	255	243	230	27.2	26.3	25.9			
292K	286	250	236	223	26.7	25.8	25.6			
591K	280	243	228	215	26.6	25.9	25.6			
1119K	272	232	217	204	26.2	25.6	24.9			
Estonian Broadcast Conversations										
104K	237	197	200	169	40.5	38.9	37.4	17.7	17.3	16.6

Table 2: Perplexity, WER and LER results comparing pooled and interpolated N-gram models and interpolated and adapted ME models, with changing amount of available in-domain data.

instance, we could build a model for recognizing computer science lectures, given data from textbooks, including those about computer science, and transcripts of lectures on various topics (which don't even need to include lectures about computer science).

The method has some considerable shortcomings from the practical perspective. First, training ME LMs in general has much higher resource requirements than training N-gram models which are typically used in speech recognition. Moreover, training hierarchical ME models requires even more memory than training simple ME models, proportional to the number of nodes in the hierarchy. However, it should be possible to alleviate this problem by profiting from the hierarchical nature of n-gram features, as proposed in (Wu and Khudanpur, 2002). It is also difficult to determine good variance values σ_i^2 for the global and domain-specific priors. While good variance values for simple ME models can be chosen quite reliably based on the size of the training data (Chen, 2009a), we have found that it is more demanding to find good hyperparameters for hierarchical models since weights for the same feature in different nodes in the hierarchy are all related to each other. We plan to investigate this problem in the future since the choice of hyperparameters has a strong impact on the performance of the model.

Acknowledgments

This research was partly funded by the Academy of Finland in the project Adaptive Informatics, by the target-financed theme No. 0322709s06 of the Estonian Ministry of Education and Research and by the National Programme for Estonian Language Technology.

References

Ciprian Chelba and Alex Acero. 2006. Adaptation of maximum entropy capitalizer: Little data can help a lot. *Computer Speech & Language*, 20(4):382–399, October.

S. F. Chen and R. Rosenfeld. 2000. A survey of smoothing techniques for ME models. *IEEE Transactions on Speech and Audio Processing*, 8(1):37–50.

S. F. Chen. 2009a. Performance prediction for exponential language models. In *Proceedings of HLT-NAACL*, pages 450–458, Boulder, Colorado.

Stanley F. Chen. 2009b. Shrinking exponential language models. In *Proceedings of HLT-NAACL*, pages 468–476, Boulder, Colorado.

H. Daume III. 2007. Frustratingly easy domain adaptation. In *Proceedings of ACL*, pages 256–263.

P. Deléglise, Y. Estéve, S. Meignier, and T. Merlin. 2005. The LIUM speech transcription system: a CMU Sphinx III-based system for French broadcast news. In *Proceedings of Interspeech*, Lisboa, Portugal.

J. R. Finkel and Ch. Manning. 2009. Hierarchical Bayesian domain adaptation. In *Proceedings of HLT-NAACL*, pages 602–610, Boulder, Colorado.

J. Goodman. 2001. Classes for fast maximum entropy training. In *Proceedings of ICASSP*, Utah, USA.

H.-J. Kaalep and T. Vaino. 2001. Complete morphological analysis in the linguist's toolbox. In *Congressus Nonus Internationalis Fenno-Ugristarum Pars V*, pages 9–16, Tartu, Estonia.

R. Kneser and H. Ney. 1993. Improved clustering techniques for class-based statistical language modelling. In *Proceedings of the European Conference on Speech Communication and Technology*, pages 973–976.

R. Rosenfeld. 1996. A maximum entropy approach to adaptive statistical language modeling. *Computer, Speech and Language*, 10:187–228.

J. Wu and S. Khudanpur. 2002. Building a topic-dependent maximum entropy model for very large corpora. In *Proceedings of ICASSP*, Orlando, Florida, USA.

Decision detection using hierarchical graphical models

Trung H. Bui
CSLI
Stanford University
Stanford, CA 94305, USA
thbui@stanford.edu

Stanley Peters
CSLI
Stanford University
Stanford, CA 94305, USA
peters@csli.stanford.edu

Abstract

We investigate hierarchical graphical models (HGMs) for automatically detecting decisions in multi-party discussions. Several types of dialogue act (DA) are distinguished on the basis of their roles in formulating decisions. HGMs enable us to model dependencies between observed features of discussions, decision DAs, and subdialogues that result in a decision. For the task of detecting decision regions, an HGM classifier was found to outperform non-hierarchical graphical models and support vector machines, raising the F1-score to 0.80 from 0.55.

1 Introduction

In work environments, people share information and make decisions in multi-party conversations known as meetings. The demand for systems that can automatically process information contained in audio and video recordings of meetings is growing rapidly. Our own research, and that of other contemporary projects (Janin et al., 2004) aim at meeting this demand.

We are currently investigating the automatic detection of decision discussions. Our approach involves distinguishing between different dialogue act (DA) types based on their role in the decision-making process. These DA types are called Decision Dialogue Acts (DDAs). Groups of DDAs combine to form a decision region.

Recent work (Bui et al., 2009) showed that Directed Graphical Models (DGMs) outperform other machine learning techniques such as Support Vector Machines (SVMs) for detecting individual DDAs. However, the proposed models, which were non-hierarchical, did not significantly improve identification of decision regions. This paper tests whether giving DGMs hierarchical structure (making them HGMs) can improve their performance at this task compared with non-hierarchical DGMs.

We proceed as follows. Section 2 discusses related work, and section 3 our data set and annotation scheme for decision discussions. Section 4 summarizes previous decision detection experiments using DGMs. Section 5 presents the HGM approach, and section 6 describes our HGM experiments. Finally, section 7 draws conclusions and presents ideas for future work.

2 Related work

User studies (Banerjee et al., 2005) have confirmed that meeting participants consider decisions to be one of the most important meeting outputs, and Whittaker et al. (2006) found that the development of an automatic decision detection component is critical for re-using meeting archives. With the new availability of substantial meeting corpora such as the AMI corpus (McCowan et al., 2005), recent years have seen an increasing amount of research on decision-making dialogue. This research has tackled issues such as the automatic detection of agreement and disagreement (Galley et al., 2004), and of the level of involvement of conversational participants (Gatica-Perez et al., 2005). Recent work on automatic detection of decisions has been conducted by Hsueh and Moore (2007), Fernández et al. (2008), and Bui et al. (2009).

Fernández et al. (2008) proposed an approach to modeling the structure of decision-making dialogue. These authors designed an annotation scheme that takes account of the different roles that utterances can play in the decision-making process—for example it distinguishes between DDAs that initiate a decision discussion by raising an issue, those that propose a resolution of the issue, and those that express agreement to a proposed resolution. The authors annotated a portion of the AMI corpus, and then applied what

Proceedings of the ACL 2010 Conference Short Papers, pages 307–312,
Uppsala, Sweden, 11-16 July 2010.

they refer to as "hierarchical classification." Here, one *sub-classifier* per DDA class hypothesizes occurrences of that type of DDA and then, based on these hypotheses, a *super-classifier* determines which regions of dialogue are decision discussions. All of the classifiers, (sub and super), were linear kernel binary SVMs. Results were better than those obtained with (Hsueh and Moore, 2007)'s approach—the F1-score for detecting decision discussions in manual transcripts was 0.58 *vs.* 0.50. Purver et al. (2007) had earlier detected action items with the approach Fernández et al. (2008) extended to decisions.

Bui et al. (2009) built on the promising results of (Fernández et al., 2008), by employing DGMs in place of SVMs. DGMs are attractive because they provide a natural framework for modeling sequence and dependencies between variables, including the DDAs. Bui et al. (2009) were especially interested in whether DGMs better exploit non-lexical features. Fernández et al. (2008) obtained much more value from lexical than non-lexical features (and indeed no value at all from prosodic features), but lexical features have limitations. In particular, they can be domain specific, increase the size of the feature space dramatically, and deteriorate more in quality than other features when automatic speech recognition (ASR) is poor. More detail about decision detection using DGMs will be presented in section 4.

Beyond decision detection, DGMs are used for labeling and segmenting sequences of observations in many different fields—including bioinformatics, ASR, Natural Language Processing (NLP), and information extraction. In particular, Dynamic Bayesian Networks (DBNs) are a popular model for probabilistic sequence modeling because they exploit structure in the problem to compactly represent distributions over multi-state and observation variables. Hidden Markov Models (HMMs), a special case of DBNs, are a classical method for important NLP applications such as unsupervised part-of-speech tagging (Gael et al., 2009) and grammar induction (Johnson et al., 2007) as well as for ASR. More complex DBNs have been used for applications such as DA recognition (Crook et al., 2009) and activity recognition (Bui et al., 2002).

Undirected graphical models (UGMs) are also valuable for building probabilistic models for segmenting and labeling sequence data. Conditional Random Fields (CRFs), a simple UGM case, can avoid the label bias problem (Lafferty et al., 2001) and outperform maximum entropy Markov models and HMMs.

However, the graphical models used in these applications are mainly non-hierarchical, including those in Bui et al. (2009). Only Sutton et al. (2007) proposed a three-level HGM (in the form of a dynamic CRF) for the joint noun phrase chunking and part of speech labeling problem; they showed that this model performs better than a non-hierarchical counterpart.

3 Data

For the experiments reported in this study, we used 17 meetings from the AMI Meeting Corpus[1], a freely available corpus of multi-party meetings with both audio and video recordings, and a wide range of annotated information including DAs and topic segmentation. The meetings last around 30 minutes each, and are scenario-driven, wherein four participants play different roles in a company's design team: *project manager*, *marketing expert*, *interface designer* and *industrial designer*.

We use the same annotation scheme as Fernández et al. (2008) to model decision-making dialogue. As stated in section 2, this scheme distinguishes between a small number of DA types based on the role which they perform in the formulation of a decision. Besides improving the detection of decision discussions (Fernández et al., 2008), such a scheme also aids in summarization of them, because it indicates which utterances provide particular types of information.

The annotation scheme is based on the observation that a decision discussion typically contains the following main structural components: (a) A topic or issue requiring resolution is raised; (b) One or more possible resolutions are considered; (c) A particular resolution is agreed upon, and so adopted as the decision. Hence the scheme distinguishes between three main DDA classes: *issue* (*I*), *resolution* (*R*), and *agreement* (*A*). Class *R* is further subdivided into *resolution proposal* (*RP*) and *resolution restatement* (*RR*). *I* utterances introduce the topic of the decision discussion, examples being *"Are we going to have a backup?"* and *"But would a backup really be necessary?"* in Table 1. In comparison, *R* utterances specify the resolution which is ultimately adopted as the deci-

[1] http://corpus.amiproject.org/

(1) A: Are we going to have a backup? Or we do just–
B: But would a backup really be necessary?
A: I think maybe we could just go for the kinetic energy and be bold and innovative.
C: Yeah.
B: I think– yeah.
A: It could even be one of our selling points.
C: Yeah *–laugh–*.
D: Environmentally conscious or something.
A: Yeah.
B: Okay, fully kinetic energy.
D: Good.

Table 1: An excerpt from the AMI dialogue ES2015c. It has been modified slightly for presentation purposes.

sion. *RP* utterances propose this resolution (e.g. *"I think maybe we could just go for the kinetic energy ..."*), while *RR* utterances close the discussion by confirming/summarizing the decision (e.g. *"Okay, fully kinetic energy"*). Finally, *A* utterances agree with the proposed resolution, signaling that it is adopted as the decision, (e.g. *"Yeah"*, *"Good"* and *"Okay"*). Unsurprisingly, an utterance may be assigned to more than one DDA class; and within a decision discussion, more than one utterance can be assigned to the same DDA class.

We use manual transcripts in the experiments described here. Inter-annotator agreement was satisfactory, with kappa values ranging from .63 to .73 for the four DDA classes. The manual transcripts contain a total of 15,680 utterances, and on average 40 DDAs per meeting. DDAs are sparse in the transcripts: for all DDAs, 6.7% of the totality of utterances; for *I*,1.6%; for *RP*, 2%; for *RR*, 0.5%; and for *A*, 2.6%. In all, 3753 utterances (i.e., 23.9%) are tagged as decision-related utterances, and on average there are 221 decision-related utterances per meeting.

4 Prior Work on Decision Detection using Graphical Models

To detect each individual DDA class, Bui et al. (2009) examined the four simple DGMs shown in Fig. 1. The DDA node is binary valued, with value 1 indicating the presence of a DDA and 0 its absence. The evidence node (E) is a multi-dimensional vector of observed values of non-lexical features. These include utterance features (UTT) such as length in words[2], duration in milliseconds, position within the meeting (as percentage of elapsed time), manually annotated dialogue act (DA) features[3] such as *inform*, *assess*, *suggest*, and prosodic features (PROS) such as energy and pitch. These features are the same as the non-lexical features used by Fernández et al. (2008). The hidden component node (C) in the *-mix* models represents the distribution of observable evidence E as a mixture of Gaussian distributions. The number of Gaussian components was hand-tuned during the training phase.

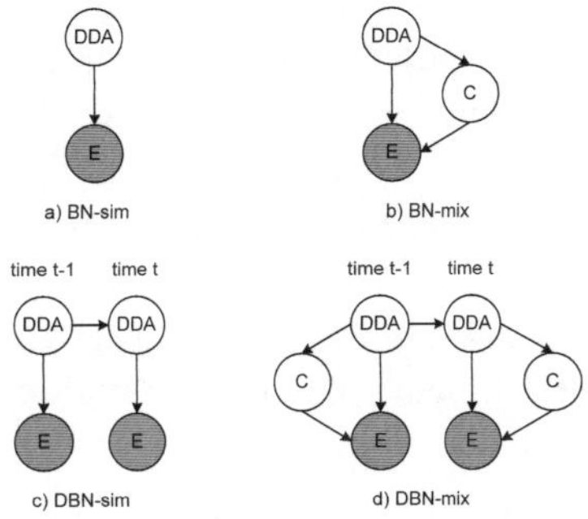

Figure 1: Simple DGMs for individual decision dialogue act detection. The clear nodes are hidden, and the shaded nodes are observable.

More complex models were constructed from the four simple models in Fig. 1 to allow for dependencies between different DDAs. For example, the model in Fig. 2 generalizes Fig. 1c with arcs connecting the DDA classes based on analysis of the annotated AMI data.

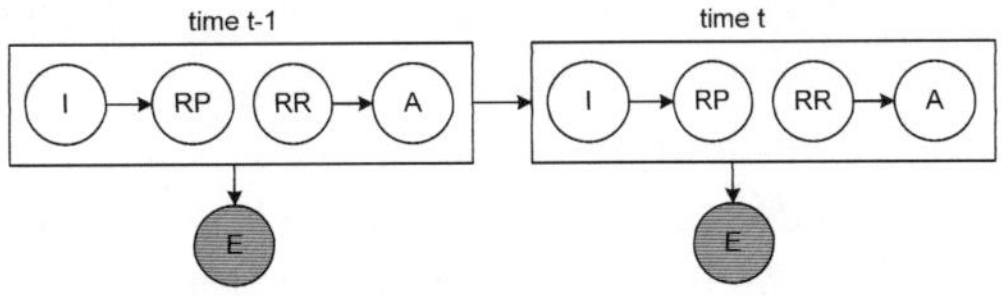

Figure 2: A DGM that takes the dependencies between decision dialogue acts into account.

Decision discussion regions were identified using the DGM output and the following two simple rules: (1) A decision discussion region begins with an *Issue* DDA; (2) A decision discussion region contains at least one *Issue* DDA and one *Resolution* DDA.

[2]This feature is a manual count of lexical tokens; but word count was extracted automatically from ASR output by Bui et al. (2009). We plan experiments to determine how much using ASR output degrades detection of decision regions.

[3]The authors used the AMI DA annotations.

The authors conducted experiments using the AMI corpus and found that when using non-lexical features, the DGMs outperform the hierarchical SVM classification method of (Fernández et al., 2008). The F1-score for the four DDA classes increased between 0.04 and 0.19 ($p < 0.005$), and for identifying decision discussion regions, by 0.05 ($p > 0.05$).

5 Hierarchical graphical models

Although the results just discussed showed graphical models are better than SVMs for detecting decision dialogue acts (Bui et al., 2009), two-level graphical models like those shown in Figs. 1 and 2 cannot exploit dependencies between high-level discourse items such as decision discussions and DDAs; and the "superclassifier" rule (Bui et al., 2009) used for detecting decision regions did not significantly improve the F1-score for decisions.

We thus investigate whether HGMs (structured as three or more levels) are superior for discovering the structure and learning the parameters of decision recognition. Our approach composes graphical models to increase hierarchy with an additional level above or below previous ones, or inserts a new level such as for discourse topics into the interior of a given model.

Fig. 3 shows a simple structure for three-level HGMs. The top level corresponds to high-level discourse regions such as decision discussions. The segmentation into these regions is represented in terms of a random variable (at each DR node) that takes on discrete values: {positive, negative} (the utterance belongs to a decision region or not) or {begin, middle, end, outside} (indicating the position of the utterance relative to a decision discussion region). The middle level corresponds to mid-level discourse items such as issues, resolution proposals, resolution restatements, and agreements. These classes ($C_1, C_2, ..., C_n$ nodes) are represented as a collection of random variables, each corresponding to an individual mid-level utterance class. For example, the middle level of the three-level HGM Fig. 3 could be the top-level of the two-level DGM in Fig. 2, each middle level node containing random variables for the DDA classes I, RP, RR, and A. The bottom level corresponds to vectors of observed features as before, e.g. lexical, utterance, and prosodic features.

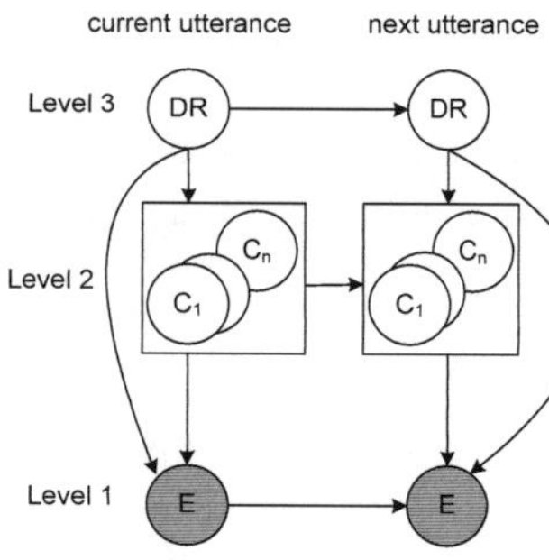

Figure 3: A simple structure of a three-level HGM: DRs are high-level discourse regions; $C_1, C_2, ..., C_n$ are mid-level utterance classes; and Es are vectors of observed features.

6 Experiments

The HGM classifier in Figure 3 was implemented in Matlab using the BNT software[4]. The classifier hypothesizes that an utterance belongs to a decision region if the marginal probability of the utterance's DR node is above a hand-tuned threshold. The threshold is selected using the ROC curve analysis[5] to obtain the highest F1-score. To evaluate the accuracy of hypothesized decision regions, we divided the dialogue into 30-second windows and evaluated on a per window basis.

The best model structure was selected by comparing the performance of various handcrafted structures. For example, the model in Fig. 4b outperforms the one in Fig. 4a. Fig. 4b explicitly models the dependency between the decision regions and the observed features.

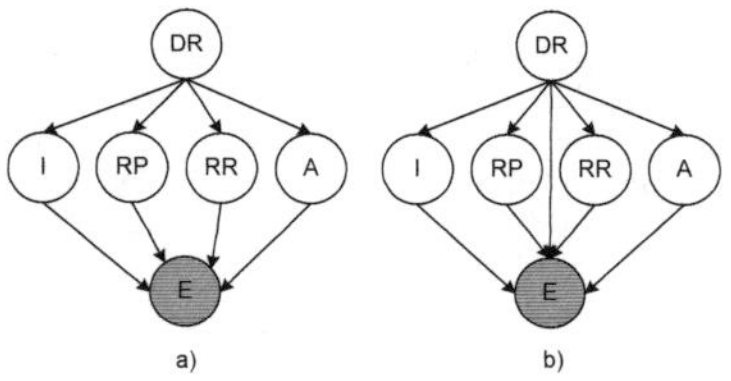

Figure 4: Three-level HGMs for recognition of decisions. This illustrates the choice of the structure for each time slice of the HGM sequence models.

Table 2 shows the results of 17-fold cross-validation for the hierarchical SVM classification (Fernández et al., 2008), rule-based classification with DGM output (Bui et al., 2009), and our HGM classification using the best combination of non-lexical features. All three methods

[4]http://www.cs.ubc.ca/~murphyk/Software/BNT/bnt.html

[5]http://en.wikipedia.org/wiki/Receiver_operating_characteristic

were implemented by us using exactly the same data and 17-fold cross-validation. The features were selected based on the best combination of non-lexical features for each method. The HGM classifier outperforms both its SVM and DGM counterparts ($p < 0.0001$)[6]. In fact, even when the SVM uses lexical as well as non-lexical features, its F1-score is still lower than the HGM classifier.

Classifier	Pr	Re	F1
SVM	0.35	0.88	0.50
DGM	0.39	0.93	0.55
HGM	0.69	0.96	0.80

Table 2: Results for detection of decision discussion regions by the SVM super-classifier, rule-based DGM classifier, and HGM classifier, each using its best combination of non-lexical features: SVM (UTT+DA), DGM (UTT+DA+PROS), HGM (UTT+DA).

In contrast with the hierarchical SVM and rule-based DGM methods, the HGM method identifies decision-related utterances by exploiting not just DDAs but also direct dependencies between decision regions and UTT, DA, and PROS features. As mentioned in the second paragraph of this section, explicitly modeling the dependency between decision regions and observable features helps to improve detection of decision regions. Furthermore, a three-level HGM can straightforwardly model the composition of each high-level decision region as a sequence of mid-level DDA utterances. While the hierarchical SVM method can also take dependency between successive utterances into account, it has no principled way to associate this dependency with more extended decision regions. In addition, this dependency is only meaningful for lexical features (Fernández et al., 2008).

The HGM result presented in Table 2 was computed using the three-level DBN model (see Fig. 4b) using the combination of UTT and DA features. Without DA features, the F1-score degrades from 0.8 to 0.78. However, this difference is not statistically significant (i.e., $p > 0.5$).

7 Conclusions and Future Work

To detect decision discussions in multi-party dialogue, we investigated HGMs as an extension of the DGMs studied in (Bui et al., 2009). When using non-lexical features, HGMs outperform the non-hierarchical DGMs of (Bui et al., 2009) and also the hierarchical SVM classification method of Fernández et al. (2008). The F1-score for identifying decision discussion regions increased to 0.80 from 0.55 and 0.50 respectively ($p < 0.0001$).

In future work, we plan to (a) investigate cascaded learning methods (Sutton et al., 2007) to improve the detection of DDAs further by using detected decision regions and (b) extend HGMs beyond three levels in order to integrate useful semantic information such as topic structure.

[6]We used the paired t test for computing statistical significance. http://www.graphpad.com/quickcalcs/ttest1.cfm

Acknowledgments

The research reported in this paper was sponsored by the Department of the Navy, Office of Naval Research, under grants number N00014-09-1-0106 and N00014-09-1-0122. Any opinions, findings, and conclusions or recommendations expressed in this material are those of the authors and do not necessarily reflect the views of the Office of Naval Research.

References

Satanjeev Banerjee, Carolyn Rosé, and Alex Rudnicky. 2005. The necessity of a meeting recording and playback system, and the benefit of topic-level annotations to meeting browsing. In *Proceedings of the 10th International Conference on Human-Computer Interaction*.

H. H. Bui, S. Venkatesh, and G. West. 2002. Policy recognition in the abstract hidden markov model. *Journal of Artificial Intelligence Research*, 17:451–499.

Trung Huu Bui, Matthew Frampton, John Dowding, and Stanley Peters. 2009. Extracting decisions from multi-party dialogue using directed graphical models and semantic similarity. In *Proceedings of the 10th Annual SIGDIAL Meeting on Discourse and Dialogue (SIGdial09)*.

Nigel Crook, Ramon Granell, and Stephen Pulman. 2009. Unsupervised classification of dialogue acts using a dirichlet process mixture model. In *Proceedings of SIGDIAL 2009: the 10th Annual Meeting of the Special Interest Group in Discourse and Dialogue*, pages 341–348.

Raquel Fernández, Matthew Frampton, Patrick Ehlen, Matthew Purver, and Stanley Peters. 2008. Modelling and detecting decisions in multi-party dialogue. In *Proceedings of the 9th SIGdial Workshop on Discourse and Dialogue*.

Jurgen Van Gael, Andreas Vlachos, and Zoubin Ghahramani. 2009. The infinite HMM for unsupervised PoS tagging. In *Proceedings of the 2009 Conference on Empirical Methods in Natural Language Processing*, pages 678–687.

Michel Galley, Kathleen McKeown, Julia Hirschberg, and Elizabeth Shriberg. 2004. Identifying agreement and disagreement in conversational speech: Use of Bayesian networks to model pragmatic dependencies. In *Proceedings of the 42nd Annual Meeting of the Association for Computational Linguistics (ACL)*.

Daniel Gatica-Perez, Ian McCowan, Dong Zhang, and Samy Bengio. 2005. Detecting group interest level in meetings. In *Proceedings of ICASSP*.

Pey-Yun Hsueh and Johanna Moore. 2007. Automatic decision detection in meeting speech. In *Proceedings of MLMI 2007*, Lecture Notes in Computer Science. Springer-Verlag.

Adam Janin, Jeremy Ang, Sonali Bhagat, Rajdip Dhillon, Jane Edwards, Javier Marcías-Guarasa, Nelson Morgan, Barbara Peskin, Elizabeth Shriberg, Andreas Stolcke, Chuck Wooters, and Britta Wrede. 2004. The ICSI meeting project: Resources and research. In *Proceedings of the 2004 ICASSP NIST Meeting Recognition Workshop*.

Mark Johnson, Thomas Griffiths, and Sharon Goldwater. 2007. Bayesian inference for PCFGs via Markov chain Monte Carlo. In *Proceedings of Human Language Technologies 2007: The Conference of the North American Chapter of the Association for Computational Linguistics*, pages 139–146, Rochester, New York, April. Association for Computational Linguistics.

John Lafferty, Andrew McCallum, and Fernando Pereira. 2001. Conditional random fields: Probabilistic models for segmenting and labeling sequence data. In *Proceedings of the 18th International Conference on Machine Learning*, pages 282–289. Morgan Kaufmann.

Iain McCowan, Jean Carletta, W. Kraaij, S. Ashby, S. Bourban, M. Flynn, M. Guillemot, T. Hain, J. Kadlec, V. Karaiskos, M. Kronenthal, G. Lathoud, M. Lincoln, A. Lisowska, W. Post, D. Reidsma, and P. Wellner. 2005. The AMI Meeting Corpus. In *Proceedings of Measuring Behavior, the 5th International Conference on Methods and Techniques in Behavioral Research*, Wageningen, Netherlands.

Matthew Purver, John Dowding, John Niekrasz, Patrick Ehlen, Sharareh Noorbaloochi, and Stanley Peters. 2007. Detecting and summarizing action items in multi-party dialogue. In *Proceedings of the 8th SIGdial Workshop on Discourse and Dialogue*, Antwerp, Belgium.

Charles Sutton, Andrew McCallum, and Khashayar Rohanimanesh. 2007. Dynamic conditional random fields: Factorized probabilistic models for labeling and segmenting sequence data. *Journal of Machine Learning Research*, 8:693–723.

Steve Whittaker, Rachel Laban, and Simon Tucker. 2006. Analysing meeting records: An ethnographic study and technological implications. In S. Renals and S. Bengio, editors, *Machine Learning for Multimodal Interaction: Second International Workshop, MLMI 2005, Revised Selected Papers*, volume 3869 of *Lecture Notes in Computer Science*, pages 101–113. Springer.

Using Speech to Reply to SMS Messages While Driving: An In-Car Simulator User Study

Yun-Cheng Ju, Tim Paek
Microsoft Research
Redmond, WA USA
{yuncj|timpaek}@microsoft.com

Abstract

Speech recognition affords automobile drivers a hands-free, eyes-free method of replying to Short Message Service (SMS) text messages. Although a voice search approach based on template matching has been shown to be more robust to the challenging acoustic environment of automobiles than using dictation, users may have difficulties verifying whether SMS response templates match their intended meaning, especially while driving. Using a high-fidelity driving simulator, we compared dictation for SMS replies versus voice search in increasingly difficult driving conditions. Although the two approaches did not differ in terms of driving performance measures, users made about six times more errors on average using dictation than voice search.

1 Introduction

Users love Short Message Service (SMS) text messaging; so much so that 3 trillion SMS messages are expected to have been sent in 2009 alone (Stross, 2008). Because research has shown that SMS messaging while driving results in 35% slower reaction time than being intoxicated (Reed & Robbins, 2008), campaigns have been launched by states, governments and even cell phone carriers to discourage and ban SMS messaging while driving (DOT, 2009). Yet, automobile manufacturers have started to offer infotainment systems, such as the Ford Sync, which feature the ability to listen to incoming SMS messages using text-to-speech (TTS). Automatic speech recognition (ASR) affords users a hands-free, eyes-free method of replying to SMS messages. However, to date, manufacturers have not established a safe and reliable method of leveraging ASR, though some researchers have begun to explore techniques. In previous research (Ju & Paek, 2009), we examined three ASR approaches to replying to SMS messages: dictation using a language model trained on SMS responses, canned responses using a probabilistic context-free grammar (PCFG), and a "voice search" approach based on template matching. Voice search proceeds in two steps (Natarajan et al., 2002): an utterance is first converted into text, which is then used as a search query to match the most similar items of an index using IR techniques (Yu et al., 2007). For SMS replies, we created an index of SMS response templates, with slots for semantic concepts such as time and place, from a large SMS corpus. After convolving recorded SMS replies so that the audio would exhibit the acoustic characteristics of in-car recognition, they compared how the three approaches handled the convolved audio with respect to the top n-best reply candidates. The voice search approach consistently outperformed dictation and canned responses, achieving as high as 89.7% task completion with respect to the top 5 reply candidates.

Even if the voice search approach may be more robust to in-car noise, this does not guarantee that it will be more usable. Indeed, because voice search can only match semantic concepts contained in the templates (which may or may not utilize the same wording as the reply), users must verify that a retrieved template matches the semantics of their intended reply. For example, suppose a user replies to the SMS message "*how about lunch*" with "*can't right now running errands*". Voice search may find "*nope, got errands to run*" as the closest template match, in which case, users will have to decide whether this response has the same meaning as their reply. This of course entails cognitive effort, which is very limited in the context of driving. On the other hand, a dictation approach to replying to SMS messages may be far worse due to misrecognitions. For example, dictation may interpret "*can't right now running errands*" as "*can right*

Proceedings of the ACL 2010 Conference Short Papers, pages 313–317,
Uppsala, Sweden, 11-16 July 2010. ©2010 Association for Computational Linguistics

now fun in errands". We posited that voice search has the advantage because it always generates intelligible SMS replies (since response templates are manually filtered), as opposed to dictation, which can sometimes result in unpredictable and nonsensical misrecognitions. However, this advantage has not been empirically demonstrated in a user study. This paper presents a user study investigating how the two approaches compare when users are actually driving – that is, when usability matters most.

2 Driving Simulator Study

Although ASR affords users hands-free, eyes-free interaction, the benefits of leveraging speech can be forfeit if users are expending cognitive effort judging whether the speech interface correctly interpreted their utterances. Indeed, research has shown that the cognitive demands of dialogue seem to play a more important role in distracting drivers than physically handling cell phones (Nunes & Recarte, 2002; Strayer & Johnston, 2001). Furthermore, Kun et al. (2007) have found that when in-car speech interfaces encounter recognition problems, users tend to drive more dangerously as they attempt to figure out why their utterances are failing. Hence, any approach to replying to SMS messages in automobiles must avoid distracting drivers with errors and be highly usable while users are engaged in their primary task, driving.

2.1 Method

To assess the usability and performance of both the voice search approach and dictation, we conducted a controlled experiment using the STISIM Drive™ simulator. Our simulation setup consisted of a central console with a steering wheel and two turn signals, surrounded by three 47" flat panels placed at a 45° angle to immerse the driver. Figure 1 displays the setup.

We recruited 16 participants (9 males, 7 females) through an email sent to employees of our organization. The mean age was 38.8. All participants had a driver's license and were compensated for their time.

We examined two independent variables: *SMS Reply Approach*, consisting of *voice search* and *dictation*, and *Driving Condition*, consisting of *no driving*, *easy driving* and *difficult driving*. We included *Driving Condition* as a way of increasing cognitive demand (see next section). Overall, we conducted a 2 (*SMS Reply Approach*) × 3 (*Driving Condition*) repeated measures, within-subjects design experiment in which the order of *SMS Reply* for each *Driving Condition* was counter-balanced. Because our primary variable of interest was *SMS Reply*, we had users experience both *voice search* and *dictation* with *no driving* first, then *easy driving*, followed by *difficult driving*. This gave users a chance to adjust themselves to increasingly difficult road conditions.

Figure 1. Driving simulator setup.

Driving Task: As the primary task, users were asked to drive two courses we developed with *easy driving* and *difficult driving* conditions while obeying all rules of the road, as they would in real driving and not in a videogame. With speed limits ranging from 25 mph to 55 mph, both courses contained five sequential sections which took about 15-20 minutes to complete: a residential area, a country highway, and a small city with a downtown area as well as a business/industrial park. Although both courses were almost identical in the number of turns, curves, stops, and traffic lights, the easy course consisted mostly of simple road segments with relatively no traffic, whereas the difficult course had four times as many vehicles, cyclists, and pedestrians. The difficult course also included a foggy road section, a few busy construction sites, and many unexpected events, such as a car in front suddenly breaking, a parked car merging into traffic, and a pedestrian jaywalking. In short, the difficult course was designed to fully engage the attention and cognitive resources of drivers.

SMS Reply Task: As the secondary task, we asked users to listen to an incoming SMS message together with a formulated reply, such as:

(1) *Message Received: "Are you lost?" Your Reply: "No, never with my GPS"*

The users were asked to repeat the reply back to the system. For Example (1) above, users would have to utter "*No, never with my GPS*". Users could also say "*Repeat*" if they had any difficulties understanding the TTS rendering or if they experienced lapses in attention. For each course, users engaged in 10 SMS reply tasks. SMS messages were cued every 3000 feet, roughly every 90 seconds, which provided enough time to complete each SMS dialogue. Once users uttered the formulated reply, they received a list of 4 possible reply candidates (each labeled as "*One*", "*Two*", etc.), from which they were asked to either pick the correct reply (by stating its number at any time) or reject them all (by stating "*All wrong*"). We did not provide any feedback about whether the replies they picked were correct or incorrect in order to avoid priming users to pay more or less attention in subsequent messages. Users did not have to finish listening to the entire list before making their selection.

Stimuli: Because we were interested in examining which was worse, verifying whether SMS response templates matched the meaning of an intended reply, or deciphering the sometimes nonsensical misrecognitions of dictation, we decided to experimentally control both the SMS reply uttered by the user as well as the 4-best list generated by the system. However, all SMS replies and 4-best lists were derived from the logs of an actual SMS Reply interface which implemented the dictation and the voice search approaches (see Ju & Paek, 2009). For each course, 5 of the SMS replies were short (with 3 or fewer words) and 5 were long (with 4 to 7 words). The mean length of the replies was 3.5 words (17.3 chars). The order of the short and long replies was randomized.

We selected 4-best lists where the correct answer was in each of four possible positions (1-4) or All Wrong; that is, there were as many 4-best lists with the first choice correct as there were with the second choice correct, and so forth. We then randomly ordered the presentation of different 4-best lists. Although one might argue that the four positions are not equally likely and that the top item of a 4-best list is most often the correct answer, we decided to experimentally control the position for two reasons: first, our previous research (Ju & Paek, 2009) had already demonstrated the superiority of the voice search approach with respect to the top position (i.e., 1-best), and second, our experimental design sought to identify whether the voice search approach was more usable than the dictation approach even when the ASR accuracy of the two approaches was the same.

In the *dictation* condition, the correct answer was not always an exact copy of the reply in 0-2 of the 10 SMS messages. For instance, a correct dictation answer for Example (1) above was "*no I'm never with my GPS*". On the other hand, the *voice search* condition had more cases (2-4 messages) in which the correct answer was not an exact copy (e.g., "*no I have GPS*") due to the nature of the template approach. To some degree, this could be seen as handicapping the *voice search* condition, though the results did not reflect the disadvantage, as we discuss later.

Measures: Performance for both the driving task and the SMS reply tasks were recorded. For the driving task, we measured the numbers of collisions, speeding (exceeding 10 mph above the limit), traffic light and stop sign violations, and missed or incorrect turns. For the SMS reply task, we measured duration (i.e., time elapsed between the beginning of the 4-best list and when users ultimately provided their answer) and the number of times users correctly identified which of the 4 reply candidates contained the correct answer.

Originally, we had an independent rater verify the position of the correct answer in all 4-best lists, however, we considered that some participants might be choosing replies that are semantically sufficient, even if they are not exactly correct. For example, a 4-best list generated by the dictation approach for Example (1) had: "*One: no I'm never want my GPS. Two: no I'm never with my GPS. Three: no I'm never when my GPS. Or Four: no no I'm in my GPS.*" Although the rater identified the second reply as being "correct", a participant might view the first or third replies as sufficient. In order to avoid ambiguity about correctness, after the study, we showed the same 16 participants the SMS messages and replies as well as the 4-best lists they received during the study and asked them to select, for each SMS reply, any 4-best list items they felt sufficiently conveyed the same meaning, even if the items were ungrammatical. Participants were explicitly told that they could select multiple items from the 4-best list. We did not indicate which item they selected during the experiment and because this selection task occurred months after the experiment, it was unlikely that they would remember anyway. Participants were compensated with a cafeteria voucher.

In computing the number of "correct" answers, for each SMS reply, we counted an answer to be correct if it was included among the participants' set of semantically sufficient 4-best list items. Hence, we calculated the number of correct items in a personalized fashion for every participant.

2.2 Results

We conducted a series of repeated measures ANOVAs on all driving task and SMS reply task measures. For the driving task, we did not find any statistically significant differences between the *voice search* and *dictation* conditions. In other words, we could not reject the null hypothesis that the two approaches were the same in terms of their influence on driving performance. However, for the SMS reply task, we did find a main effect for *SMS Reply Approach* ($F_{1,47} = 81.28$, $p < .001$, $\mu_{Dictation} = 2.13$ (.19), $\mu_{VoiceSearch} = .38$ (.10)). As shown in Figure 2, the average number of errors per driving course for *dictation* is roughly 6 times that for *voice search*. We also found a main effect for total duration ($F_{1,47} = 11.94$, $p < .01$, $\mu_{Dictation} = 113.75$ sec (3.54) or 11.4 sec/reply, $\mu_{VoiceSearch} = 125.32$ sec (3.37) or 12.5 sec/reply). We discuss our explanation for the shorter duration below. For both errors and duration, we did not find any interaction effects with *Driving Conditions*.

3 Discussion

We conducted a simulator study in order to examine which was worse while driving: verifying whether SMS response templates matched the meaning of an intended reply, or deciphering the sometimes nonsensical misrecognitions of dictation. Our results suggest that deciphering dictation results under the duress of driving leads to more errors. In conducting a post-hoc error analysis, we noticed that participants tended to err when the 4-best lists generated by the dictation approach contained phonetically similar candidate replies. Because it is not atypical for the dictation approach to have n-best list candidates differing from each other in this way, we recommend not utilizing this approach in speech-only user interfaces, unless the n-best list candidates can be made as distinct from each other as possible, phonetically, syntactically and most importantly, semantically. The voice search approach circumvents this problem in two ways: 1) templates were real responses and manually selected and cleaned up during the development phase so there were no grammatical mistakes, and 2) semantically redundant templates can be

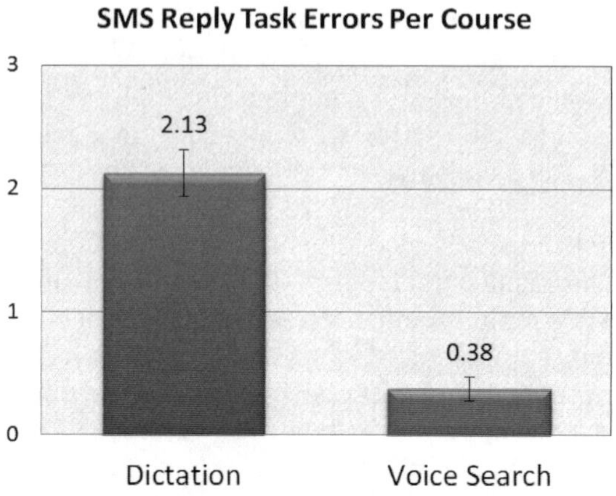

Figure 2. Mean number of errors for the dictation and voice search approaches. Error bars represent standard errors about the mean.

further discarded to only present the distinct concepts at the rendering time using the paraphrase detection algorithms reported in (Wu et al., 2010).

Given that users committed more errors in the *dictation* condition, we initially expected that *dictation* would exhibit higher duration than *voice search* since users might be spending more time figuring out the differences between the similar 4-best list candidates generated by the dictation approach. However, in our error analysis we observed that most likely users did not discover the misrecognitions, and prematurely selected a reply candidate, resulting in shorter durations. The slightly higher duration for the voice search approach does not constitute a problem if users are listening to all of their choices and correctly selecting their intended SMS reply. Note that the duration did not bring about any significant driving performance differences.

Although we did not find any significant driving performance differences, users experienced more difficulties confirming whether the dictation approach correctly interpreted their utterances than they did with the voice search approach. As such, if a user deems it absolutely necessary to respond to SMS messages while driving, our simulator study suggests that the most reliable (i.e., least error-prone) way to respond may just well be the voice search approach.

References

Distracted Driving Summit. 2009. Department of Transportation. Retrieved Dec. 1: http://www.rita.dot.gov/distracted_driving_summit

Y.C. Ju & T. Paek. 2009. A Voice Search Approach to Replying to SMS Messages in Automobiles. In *Proc. of Interspeech*.

A. Kun, T. Paek & Z. Medenica. 2007. The Effect of Speech Interface Accuracy on Driving Performance, In *Proc. of Interspeech*.

P. Natarajan, R. Prasad, R. Schwartz, & J. Makhoul. 2002. A Scalable Architecture for Directory Assistance Automation. In *Proc. of ICASSP*, pp. 21-24.

L. Nunes & M. Recarte. 2002. Cognitive Deamnds of Hands-Free-Phone Conversation While Driving. *Transportation Research Part F*, 5: 133-144.

N. Reed & R. Robbins. 2008. The Effect of Text Messaging on Driver Behaviour: A Simulator Study. Transport Research Lab Report, PPR 367.

D. Strayer & W. Johnston. 2001. Driven to Distraction: Dual-task Studies of Simulated Driving and Conversing on a Cellular Phone. *Psychological Science*, 12: 462-466.

R. Stross. 2008. "What carriers aren't eager to tell you about texting", New York Times, Dec. 26, 2008: http://www.nytimes.com/2008/12/28/business/28digi.html?_r=3

D. Yu, Y.C. Ju, Y.-Y. Wang, G. Zweig, & A. Acero. 2007. Automated Directory Assistance System: From Theory to Practice. In *Proc. of Interspeech*.

Wei Wu, Yun-Cheng Ju, Xiao Li, and Ye-Yi Wang, Paraphrase Detection on SMS Messages in Automobiles, in ICASSP, IEEE, March 2010

Classification of Feedback Expressions in Multimodal Data

Costanza Navarretta
University of Copenhagen
Centre for Language Technology (CST)
Njalsgade 140, 2300-DK Copenhagen
costanza@hum.ku.dk

Patrizia Paggio
University of Copenhagen
Centre for Language Technology (CST)
Njalsgade 140, 2300-DK Copenhagen
paggio@hum.ku.dk

Abstract

This paper addresses the issue of how linguistic feedback expressions, prosody and head gestures, i.e. head movements and face expressions, relate to one another in a collection of eight video-recorded Danish map-task dialogues. The study shows that in these data, prosodic features and head gestures significantly improve automatic classification of dialogue act labels for linguistic expressions of feedback.

1 Introduction

Several authors in communication studies have pointed out that head movements are relevant to feedback phenomena (see McClave (2000) for an overview). Others have looked at the application of machine learning algorithms to annotated multimodal corpora. For example, Jokinen and Ragni (2007) and Jokinen et al. (2008) find that machine learning algorithms can be trained to recognise some of the functions of head movements, while Reidsma et al. (2009) show that there is a dependence between focus of attention and assignment of dialogue act labels. Related are also the studies by Rieks op den Akker and Schulz (2008) and Murray and Renals (2008): both achieve promising results in the automatic segmentation of dialogue acts using the annotations in a large multimodal corpus.

Work has also been done on prosody and gestures in the specific domain of map-task dialogues, also targeted in this paper. Sridhar et al. (2009) obtain promising results in dialogue act tagging of the Switchboard-DAMSL corpus using lexical, syntactic and prosodic cues, while Gravano and Hirschberg (2009) examine the relation between particular acoustic and prosodic turn-yielding cues and turn taking in a large corpus of task-oriented dialogues. Louwerse et al. (2006) and Louwerse et al. (2007) study the relation between eye gaze, facial expression, pauses and dialogue structure in annotated English map-task dialogues (Anderson et al., 1991) and find correlations between the various modalities both within and across speakers. Finally, feedback expressions (head nods and shakes) are successfully predicted from speech, prosody and eye gaze in interaction with Embodied Communication Agents as well as human communication (Fujie et al., 2004; Morency et al., 2005; Morency et al., 2007; Morency et al., 2009).

Our work is in line with these studies, all of which focus on the relation between linguistic expressions, prosody, dialogue content and gestures. In this paper, we investigate how feedback expressions can be classified into different dialogue act categories based on prosodic and gesture features. Our data are made up by a collection of eight video-recorded map-task dialogues in Danish, which were annotated with phonetic and prosodic information. We find that prosodic features improve the classification of dialogue acts and that head gestures, where they occur, contribute to the semantic interpretation of feedback expressions. The results, which partly confirm those obtained on a smaller dataset in Paggio and Navarretta (2010), must be seen in light of the fact that our gesture annotation scheme comprises more fine-grained categories than most of the studies mentioned earlier for both head movements and face expressions. The classification results improve, however, if similar categories such as head nods and jerks are collapsed into a more general category.

In Section 2 we describe the multimodal Danish corpus. In Section 3, we describe how the prosody of feedback expressions is annotated, how their content is coded in terms of dialogue act, turn and agreement labels, and we provide inter-coder agreement measures. In Section 4 we account for the annotation of head gestures, including inter-

Proceedings of the ACL 2010 Conference Short Papers, pages 318–324,
Uppsala, Sweden, 11-16 July 2010.

coder agreements results. Section 5 contains a description of the resulting datasets and a discussion of the results obtained in the classification experiments. Section 6 is the conclusion.

2 The multimodal corpus

The Danish map-task dialogues from the DanPASS corpus (Grønnum, 2006) are a collection of dialogues in which 11 speaker pairs cooperate on a map task. The dialogue participants are seated in different rooms and cannot see each other. They talk through headsets, and one of them is recorded with a video camera. Each pair goes through four different sets of maps, and changes roles each time, with one subject giving instructions and the other following them. The material is transcribed orthographically with an indication of stress, articulatory hesitations and pauses. In addition to this, the acoustic signals are segmented into words, syllables and prosodic phrases, and annotated with POS-tags, phonological and phonetic transcriptions, pitch and intonation contours.

Phonetic and prosodic segmentation and annotation were performed independently and in parallel by two annotators and then an agreed upon version was produced with the supervision of an expert annotator, for more information see Grønnum (2006). The Praat tool was used (Boersma and Weenink, 2009).

The feedback expressions we analyse here are *Yes* and *No* expressions, i.e. in Danish words like *ja* (yes), *jo* (yes in a negative context), *jamen* (yes but, well), *nej* (no), *næh* (no). They can be single words or multi-word expressions.

Yes and *No* feedback expressions represent about 9% of the approximately 47,000 running words in the corpus. This is a rather high proportion compared to other corpora, both spoken and written, and a reason why we decided to use the DanPASS videos in spite of the fact that the gesture behaviour is relatively limited given the fact that the two dialogue participants cannot see each other. Furthermore, the restricted contexts in which feedback expressions occur in these dialogues allow for a very fine-grained analysis of the relation of these expressions with prosody and gestures. Feedback behaviour, both in speech and gestures, can be observed especially in the person who is receiving the instructions (the *follower*). Therefore, we decided to focus our analysis only on the follower's part of the interaction. Because of time restrictions, we limited the study to four different subject pairs and two interactions per pair, for a total of about an hour of video-recorded interaction.

3 Annotation of feedback expressions

As already mentioned, all words in DanPASS are phonetically and prosodically annotated. In the subset of the corpus considered here, 82% of the feedback expressions bear stress or tone information, and 12% are unstressed; 7% of them are marked with onset or offset hesitation, or both. For this study, we added semantic labels – including dialogue acts – and gesture annotation. Both kinds of annotation were carried out using ANVIL (Kipp, 2004). To distinguish among the various functions that feedback expressions have in the dialogues, we selected a subset of the categories defined in the emerging ISO 24617-2 standard for semantic annotation of language resources. This subset comprises the categories *Accept*, *Decline*, *RepeatRephrase* and *Answer*. Moreover, all feedback expressions were annotated with an agreement feature (*Agree*, *NonAgree*) where relevant. Finally, the two turn management categories *TurnTake* and *TurnElicit* were also coded.

It should be noted that the same expression may be annotated with a label for each of the three semantic dimensions. For example, a *yes* can be an *Answer* to a question, an *Agree* and a *TurnElicit* at the same time, thus making the semantic classification very fine-grained. Table 1 shows how the various types are distributed across the 466 feedback expressions in our data.

Dialogue Act		
Answer	70	15%
RepeatRephrase	57	12%
Accept	127	27%
None	212	46%
Agreement		
Agree	166	36%
NonAgree	14	3%
None	286	61%
Turn Management		
TurnTake	113	24%
TurnElicit	85	18%
None	268	58%

Table 1: Distribution of semantic categories

3.1 Inter-coder agreement on feedback expression annotation

In general, dialogue act, agreement and turn annotations were coded by an expert annotator and the annotations were subsequently checked by a second expert annotator. However, one dialogue was coded independently and in parallel by two expert annotators to measure inter-coder agreement. A measure was derived for each annotated feature using the agreement analysis facility provided in ANVIL. Agreement between two annotation sets is calculated here in terms of Cohen's *kappa* (Cohen, 1960)[1] and corrected *kappa* (Brennan and Prediger, 1981)[2]. Anvil divides the annotations in slices and compares each slice. We used slices of 0.04 seconds. The inter-coder agreement figures obtained for the three types of annotation are given in Table 2.

feature	**Cohen's *k***	**corrected *k***
agreement	73.59	98.74
dial act	84.53	98.87
turn	73.52	99.16

Table 2: Inter-coder agreement on feedback expression annotation

Although researchers do not totally agree on how to measure agreement in various types of annotated data and on how to interpret the resulting figures, see Artstein and Poesio (2008), it is usually assumed that Cohen's *kappa* figures over 60 are good while those over 75 are excellent (Fleiss, 1971). Looking at the cases of disagreement we could see that many of these are due to the fact that the annotators had forgotten to remove some of the features automatically proposed by ANVIL from the latest annotated element.

4 Gesture annotation

All communicative head gestures in the videos were found and annotated with ANVIL using a subset of the attributes defined in the MUMIN annotation scheme (Allwood et al., 2007). The MUMIN scheme is a general framework for the study of gestures in interpersonal communication. In this study, we do not deal with functional classification of the gestures in themselves, but rather with how gestures contribute to the semantic interpretations of linguistic expressions. Therefore, only a subset of the MUMIN attributes has been used, i.e. *Smile, Laughter, Scowl, FaceOther* for facial expressions, and *Nod, Jerk, Tilt, SideTurn, Shake, Waggle, Other* for head movements.

A link was also established in ANVIL between the gesture under consideration and the relevant speech sequence where appropriate. The link was then used to extract gesture information together with the relevant linguistic annotations on which to apply machine learning.

The total number of head gestures annotated is 264. Of these, 114 (43%) co-occur with feedback expressions, with *Nod* as by far the most frequent type (70 occurrences) followed by *FaceOther* as the second most frequent (16). The other tokens are distributed more or less evenly, with a few occurrences (2-8) per type. The remaining 150 gestures, linked to different linguistic expressions or to no expression at all, comprise many face expressions and a number of tilts. A rough preliminary analysis shows that their main functions are related to focusing or to different emotional attitudes. They will be ignored in what follows.

4.1 Measuring inter-coder agreement on gesture annotation

The head gestures in the DanPASS data have been coded by non expert annotators (one annotator per video) and subsequently controlled by a second annotator, with the exception of one video which was annotated independently and in parallel by two annotators. The annotations of this video were then used to measure inter-coder agreement in ANVIL as it was the case for the annotations on feedback expressions. In the case of gestures we also measured agreement on gesture segmentation. The figures obtained are given in Table 3.

feature	**Cohen's *k***	**corrected *k***
face segment	69.89	91.37
face annotate	71.53	94.25
head mov segment	71.21	91.75
head mov annotate	71.65	95.14

Table 3: Inter-coder agreement on head gesture annotation

These results are slightly worse than those obtained in previous studies using the same annotation scheme (Jokinen et al., 2008), but are still sat-

[1] $(Pa - Pe)/(1 - Pe)$.

[2] $(Po - 1/c)/(1 - 1/c)$ where c is the number of categories.

isfactory given the high number of categories provided by the scheme.

A distinction that seemed particularly difficult was that between nods and jerks: although the direction of the two movement types is different (down-up and up-down, respectively), the movement quality is very similar, and makes it difficult to see the direction clearly. We return to this point below, in connection with our data analysis.

5 Analysis of the data

The multimodal data we obtained by combining the linguistic annotations from DanPASS with the gesture annotation created in ANVIL, resulted into two different groups of data, one containing all *Yes* and *No* expressions, and the other the subset of those that are accompanied by a face expression or a head movement, as shown in Table 4.

Expression	Count	%
Yes	420	90
No	46	10
Total	466	100
Yes with gestures	102	90
No with gestures	12	10
Total with gestures	114	100

Table 4: *Yes* and *No* datasets

These two sets of data were used for automatic dialogue act classification, which was run in the Weka system (Witten and Frank, 2005). We experimented with various Weka classifiers, comprising Hidden Naive Bayes, SMO, ID3, LADTree and Decision Table. The best results on most of our data were obtained using Hidden Naive Bayes (HNB) (Zhang et al., 2005). Therefore, here we show the results of this classifier. Ten-folds cross-validation was applied throughout.

In the first group of experiments we took into consideration all the Yes and No expressions (420 *Yes* and 46 *No*) without, however, considering gesture information. The purpose was to see how prosodic information contributes to the classification of dialogue acts. We started by totally leaving out prosody, i.e. only the orthographic transcription (Yes and No expressions) was considered; then we included information about stress (stressed or unstressed); in the third run we added tone attributes, and in the fourth information on hesitation. Agreement and turn attributes were used in all experiments, while Dialogue act annotation was only used in the training phase. The baseline for the evaluation are the results provided by Weka's ZeroR classifier, which always selects the most frequent nominal class.

In Table 5 we provide results in terms of precision (P), recall (R) and F-measure (F). These are calculated in Weka as weighted averages of the results obtained for each class.

dataset	Algor	P	R	F
YesNo	ZeroR	27.8	52.8	36.5
	HNB	47.2	53	46.4
+stress	HNB	47.5	54.1	47.1
+stress+tone	HNB	47.8	54.3	47.4
+stress+tone+hes	HNB	47.7	54.5	47.3

Table 5: Classification results with prosodic features

The results indicate that prosodic information improves the classification of dialogue acts with respect to the baseline in all four experiments with improvements of 10, 10.6, 10.9 and 10.8%, respectively. The best results are obtained using information on stress and tone, although the decrease in accuracy when hesitations are introduced is not significant. The confusion matrices show that the classifier is best at identifying *Accept*, while it is very bad at identifying *RepeatRephrase*. This result if not surprising since the former type is much more frequent in the data than the latter, and since prosodic information does not correlate with *RepeatRephrase* in any systematic way.

The second group of experiments was conducted on the dataset where feedback expressions are accompanied by gestures (102 *Yes* and 12 *No*). The purpose this time was to see whether gesture information improves dialogue act classification. We believe it makes sense to perform the test based on this restricted dataset, rather than the entire material, because the portion of data where gestures do accompany feedback expressions is rather small (about 20%). In a different domain, where subjects are less constrained by the technical setting, we expect gestures would make for a stronger and more widespread effect.

The Precision, Recall and F-measure of the ZeroR classifier on these data are 31.5, 56.1 and 40.4, respectively. For these experiments, however, we used as a baseline the results obtained based on stress, tone and hesitation information, the combination that gave the best results on the larger dataset. Together with the prosodic information, Agreement and turn attributes were included just as earlier, while the dialogue act annotation was only used in the training phase. Face expression and head movement attributes were disregarded in the baseline. We then added face expression alone, head movement alone, and finally both gesture types together. The results are shown in Table 6.

dataset	Algor	P	R	F
YesNo	HNB	43.1	56.1	46.4
+face	HNB	43.7	56.1	46.9
+headm	HNB	44.7	55.3	48.2
+face+headm	HNB	49.9	57	50.3

Table 6: Classification results with head gesture features

These results indicate that adding head gesture information improves the classification of dialogue acts in this reduced dataset, although the improvement is not impressive. The best results are achieved when both face expressions and head movements are taken into consideration.

The confusion matrices show that although the recognition of both *Answer* and *None* improve, it is only the *None* class which is recognised quite reliably. We already explained that in our annotation a large number of feedback utterances have an agreement or turn label without necessarily having been assigned to one of our task-related dialogue act categories. This means that head gestures help distinguishing utterances with an agreement or turn function from other kinds. Looking closer at these utterances, we can see that nods and jerks often occur together with *TurnElicit*, while tilts, side turns and smiles tend to occur with *Agree*.

An issue that worries us is the granularity of the annotation categories. To investigate this, in a third group of experiments we collapsed *Nod* and *Jerk* into a more general category: the distinction had proven difficult for the annotators, and we don't have many jerks in the data. The results, displayed in Table 7, show as expected an improvement. The class which is recognised best is still *None*.

dataset	Algor	P	R	F
YesNo	HNB	43.1	56.1	46.4
+face	HNB	43.7	56.1	46.9
+headm	HNB	47	57.9	51
+face+headm	HNB	51.6	57.9	53.9

Table 7: Classification results with fewer head movements

6 Conclusion

In this study we have experimented with the automatic classification of feedback expressions into different dialogue acts in a multimodal corpus of Danish. We have conducted three sets of experiments, first looking at how prosodic features contribute to the classification, then testing whether the use of head gesture information improved the accuracy of the classifier, finally running the classification on a dataset in which the head movement types were slightly more general. The results indicate that prosodic features improve the classification, and that in those cases where feedback expressions are accompanied by head gestures, gesture information is also useful. The results also show that using a more coarse-grained distinction of head movements improves classification in these data.

Slightly more than half of the head gestures in our data co-occur with other linguistic utterances than those targeted in this study. Extending our investigation to those, as we plan to do, will provide us with a larger dataset and therefore presumably with even more interesting and reliable results.

The occurrence of gestures in the data studied here is undoubtedly limited by the technical setup, since the two speakers do not see each other. Therefore, we want to investigate the role played by head gestures in other types of video and larger materials. Extending the analysis to larger datasets will also shed more light on whether our gesture annotation categories are too fine-grained for automatic classification.

Acknowledgements

This research has been done under the project VKK (Verbal and Bodily Communication) funded by the Danish Council for Independent Research in the Humanities, and the NOMCO project, a collaborative Nordic project with participating research groups at the universities of Gothenburg, Copenhagen and Helsinki which is funded by the NOS-HS NORDCORP programme. We would also like to thank Nina Grønnum for allowing us to use the DanPASS corpus, and our gesture annotators Josephine Bødker Arrild and Sara Andersen.

References

Jens Allwood, Loredana Cerrato, Kristiina Jokinen, Costanza Navarretta, and Patrizia Paggio. 2007. The MUMIN Coding Scheme for the Annotation of Feedback, Turn Management and Sequencing. *Multimodal Corpora for Modelling Human Multimodal Behaviour. Special Issue of the International Journal of Language Resources and Evaluation*, 41(3–4):273–287.

Anne H. Anderson, Miles Bader, Ellen Gurman Bard, Elizabeth Boyle, Gwyneth Doherty, Simon Garrod, Stephen Isard, Jacqueline Kowtko, Jan McAllister, Jim Miller, Catherine Sotillo, Henry S. Thompson, and Regina Weinert. 1991. The HCRC Map Task Corpus. *Language and Speech*, 34:351–366.

Ron Artstein and Massimo Poesio. 2008. Inter-Coder Agreement for Computational Linguistics. *Computational Linguistics*, 34(4):555–596.

Paul Boersma and David Weenink, 2009. *Praat: doing phonetics by computer*. Retrieved May 1, 2009, from http://www.praat.org/.

Robert L. Brennan and Dale J. Prediger. 1981. Coefficient Kappa: Some uses, misuses, and alternatives. *Educational and Psychological Measurement*, 41:687–699.

Jacob Cohen. 1960. A coefficient of agreement for nominal scales. *Educational and Psychological Measurement*, 20(1):37–46.

Joseph L. Fleiss. 1971. Measuring nominal scale agreement among many raters. *Psychological Bullettin*, 76(5):378–382.

Shinya Fujie, Y. Ejiri, K. Nakajima, Y Matsusaka, and Tetsunor Kobayashi. 2004. A conversation robot using head gesture recognition as para-linguistic information. In *Proceedings of the 13th IEEE International Workshop on Robot and Human Interactive Communication*, pages 159 – 164, september.

Agustin Gravano and Julia Hirschberg. 2009. Turn-yielding cues in task-oriented dialogue. In *Proceedings of SIGDIAL 2009: the 10th Annual Meeting of the Special Interest Group in Discourse and Dialogue, September 2009*, pages 253–261, Queen Mary University of London.

Nina Grønnum. 2006. DanPASS - a Danish phonetically annotated spontaneous speech corpus. In N. Calzolari, K. Choukri, A. Gangemi, B. Maegaard, J. Mariani, J. Odijk, and D. Tapias, editors, *Proceedings of the 5th LREC*, pages 1578–1583, Genoa, May.

Kristiina Jokinen and Anton Ragni. 2007. Clustering experiments on the communicative prop- erties of gaze and gestures. In *Proceeding of the 3rd. Baltic Conference on Human Language Technologies*, Kaunas, Lithuania, October.

Kristiina Jokinen, Costanza Navarretta, and Patrizia Paggio. 2008. Distinguishing the communicative functions of gestures. In *Proceedings of the 5th MLMI*, LNCS 5237, pages 38–49, Utrecht, The Netherlands, September. Springer.

Michael Kipp. 2004. *Gesture Generation by Imitation - From Human Behavior to Computer Character Animation*. Ph.D. thesis, Saarland University, Saarbruecken, Germany, Boca Raton, Florida, dissertation.com.

Max M. Louwerse, Patrick Jeuniaux, Mohammed E. Hoque, Jie Wu, and Gwineth Lewis. 2006. Multimodal communication in computer-mediated map task scenarios. In R. Sun and N. Miyake, editors, *Proceedings of the 28th Annual Conference of the Cognitive Science Society*, pages 1717–1722, Mahwah, NJ: Erlbaum.

Max M. Louwerse, Nick Benesh, Mohammed E. Hoque, Patrick Jeuniaux, Gwineth Lewis, Jie Wu, and Megan Zirnstein. 2007. Multimodal communication in face-to-face conversations. In R. Sun and N. Miyake, editors, *Proceedings of the 29th Annual Conference of the Cognitive Science Society*, pages 1235–1240, Mahwah, NJ: Erlbaum.

Evelyn McClave. 2000. Linguistic functions of head movements in the context of speech. *Journal of Pragmatics*, 32:855–878.

Louis-Philippe Morency, Candace Sidner, Christopher Lee, and Trevor Darrell. 2005. Contextual Recognition of Head Gestures. In *Proceedings of the International Conference on Multi-modal Interfaces*.

Louis-Philippe Morency, Candace Sidner, Christopher Lee, and Trevor Darrell. 2007. Head gestures for perceptual interfaces: The role of context in improving recognition. *Artificial Intelligence*, 171(8–9):568–585.

Louis-Philippe Morency, Iwan de Kok, and Jonathan Gratch. 2009. A probabilistic multimodal approach for predicting listener backchannels. *Autonomous Agents and Multi-Agent Systems*, 20:70–84, Springer.

Gabriel Murray and Steve Renals. 2008. Detecting Action Meetings in Meetings. In *Proceedings of the 5th MLMI*, LNCS 5237, pages 208–213, Utrecht, The Netherlands, September. Springer.

Harm Rieks op den Akker and Christian Schulz. 2008. Exploring features and classifiers for dialogue act segmentation. In *Proceedings of the 5th MLMI*, pages 196–207.

Patrizia Paggio and Costanza Navarretta. 2010. Feedback in Head Gesture and Speech. To appear in *Proceedings of 7th Conference on Language Resources and Evaluation (LREC-2010)*, Malta, May.

Dennis Reidsma, Dirk Heylen, and Harm Rieks op den Akker. 2009. On the Contextual Analysis of Agreement Scores. In Michael Kipp, Jean-Claude Martin, Patrizia Paggio, and Dirk Heylen, editors, *Multimodal Corpora From Models of Natural Interaction to Systems and Applications*, number 5509 in Lecture Notes in Artificial Intelligence, pages 122–137. Springer.

Vivek Kumar Rangarajan Sridhar, Srinivas Bangaloreb, and Shrikanth Narayanan. 2009. Combining lexical, syntactic and prosodic cues for improved online dialog act tagging. *Computer Speech & Language*, 23(4):407–422.

Ian H. Witten and Eibe Frank. 2005. *Data Mining: Practical machine learning tools and techniques*. Morgan Kaufmann, San Francisco, second edition.

Harry Zhang, Liangxiao Jiang, and Jiang Su. 2005. Hidden Naive Bayes. In *Proceedings of the Twentieth National Conference on Artificial Intelligence*, pages 919–924.

Optimizing Informativeness and Readability for Sentiment Summarization

Hitoshi Nishikawa, Takaaki Hasegawa, Yoshihiro Matsuo and **Genichiro Kikui**
NTT Cyber Space Laboratories, NTT Corporation
1-1 Hikari-no-oka, Yokosuka, Kanagawa, 239-0847 Japan
{nishikawa.hitoshi, hasegawa.takaaki, matsuo.yoshihiro, kikui.genichiro}@lab.ntt.co.jp

Abstract

We propose a novel algorithm for sentiment summarization that takes account of informativeness and readability, simultaneously. Our algorithm generates a summary by selecting and ordering sentences taken from multiple review texts according to two scores that represent the informativeness and readability of the sentence order. The informativeness score is defined by the number of sentiment expressions and the readability score is learned from the target corpus. We evaluate our method by summarizing reviews on restaurants. Our method outperforms an existing algorithm as indicated by its ROUGE score and human readability experiments.

1 Introduction

The Web holds a massive number of reviews describing the sentiments of customers about products and services. These reviews can help the user reach purchasing decisions and guide companies' business activities such as product improvements. It is, however, almost impossible to read all reviews given their sheer number.

These reviews are best utilized by the development of automatic text summarization, particularly sentiment summarization. It enables us to efficiently grasp the key bits of information. Sentiment summarizers are divided into two categories in terms of output style. One outputs lists of sentences (Hu and Liu, 2004; Blair-Goldensohn et al., 2008; Titov and McDonald, 2008), the other outputs texts consisting of ordered sentences (Carenini et al., 2006; Carenini and Cheung, 2008; Lerman et al., 2009; Lerman and McDonald, 2009). Our work lies in the latter category, and a typical summary is shown in Figure 1. Although visual representations such as bar or rader charts are helpful, such representations necessitate some simplifications of information to presentation. In contrast, text can present complex information that can't readily be visualized, so in this paper we focus on producing textual summaries.

> This restaurant offers customers delicious foods and a relaxing atmosphere. The staff are very friendly but the price is a little high.

Figure 1: A typical summary.

One crucial weakness of existing text-oriented summarizers is the poor readability of their results. Good readability is essential because readability strongly affects text comprehension (Barzilay et al., 2002).

To achieve readable summaries, the extracted sentences must be appropriately ordered (Barzilay et al., 2002; Lapata, 2003; Barzilay and Lee, 2004; Barzilay and Lapata, 2005). Barzilay et al. (2002) proposed an algorithm for ordering sentences according to the dates of the publications from which the sentences were extracted. Lapata (2003) proposed an algorithm that computes the probability of two sentences being adjacent for ordering sentences. Both methods delink sentence extraction from sentence ordering, so a sentence can be extracted that cannot be ordered naturally with the other extracted sentences.

To solve this problem, we propose an algorithm that chooses sentences and orders them simultaneously in such a way that the ordered sentences maximize the scores of informativeness and readability. Our algorithm efficiently searches for the best sequence of sentences by using dynamic programming and beam search. We verify that our method generates summaries that are significantly better than the baseline results in terms of ROUGE score (Lin, 2004) and subjective readability measures. As far as we know, this is the first work to

Proceedings of the ACL 2010 Conference Short Papers, pages 325–330,
Uppsala, Sweden, 11-16 July 2010.

simultaneously achieve both informativeness and readability in the area of multi-document summarization.

This paper is organized as follows: Section 2 describes our summarization method. Section 3 reports our evaluation experiments. We conclude this paper in Section 4.

2 Optimizing Sentence Sequence

Formally, we define a summary $S^* = \langle s_0, s_1, \ldots, s_n, s_{n+1}\rangle$ as a sequence consisting of n sentences where s_0 and s_{n+1} are symbols indicating the beginning and ending of the sequence, respectively. Summary S^* is also defined as follows:

$$S^* = \underset{S \in T}{\mathrm{argmax}}[\mathrm{Info}(S) + \lambda \mathrm{Read}(S)] \quad (1)$$
$$\text{s.t. } \mathrm{length}(S) \leq K$$

where $\mathrm{Info}(S)$ indicates the informativeness score of S, $\mathrm{Read}(S)$ indicates the readability score of S, T indicates possible sequences composed of sentences in the target documents, λ is a weight parameter balancing informativeness against readability, $\mathrm{length}(S)$ is the length of S, and K is the maximum size of the summary.

We introduce the informativeness score and the readability score, then describe how to optimize a sequence.

2.1 Informativeness Score

Since we attempt to summarize reviews, we assume that a good summary must involve as many sentiments as possible. Therefore, we define the informativeness score as follows:

$$\mathrm{Info}(S) = \sum_{e \in E(S)} f(e) \quad (2)$$

where e indicates sentiment $e = \langle a, p\rangle$ as the tuple of *aspect* a and *polarity* $p = \{-1, 0, 1\}$, $E(S)$ is the set of sentiments contained S, and $f(e)$ is the score of sentiment e. Aspect a represents a standpoint for evaluating products and services. With regard to restaurants, aspects include *food*, *atmosphere* and *staff*. Polarity represents whether the sentiment is positive or negative. In this paper, we define $p = -1$ as negative, $p = 0$ as neutral and $p = 1$ as positive sentiment.

Notice that Equation 2 defines the informativeness score of a summary as the sum of the score of the sentiments contained in S. To avoid duplicative sentences, each sentiment is counted only once for scoring. In addition, the aspects are clustered and similar aspects (e.g. *air*, *ambience*) are treated as the same aspect (e.g. *atmosphere*). In this paper we define $f(e)$ as the frequency of e in the target documents.

Sentiments are extracted using a sentiment lexicon and pattern matched from dependency trees of sentences. The sentiment lexicon[1] consists of pairs of *sentiment expressions* and their polarities, for example, *delicious*, *friendly* and *good* are positive sentiment expressions, *bad* and *expensive* are negative sentiment expressions.

To extract sentiments from given sentences, first, we identify sentiment expressions among words consisting of parsed sentences. For example, in the case of the sentence "This restaurant offers customers delicious foods and a relaxing atmosphere." in Figure 1, *delicious* and *relaxing* are identified as sentiment expressions. If the sentiment expressions are identified, the expressions and its aspects are extracted as aspect-sentiment expression pairs from dependency tree using some rules. In the case of the example sentence, *foods* and *delicious*, *atmosphere* and *relaxing* are extracted as aspect-sentiment expression pairs. Finally extracted sentiment expressions are converted to polarities, we acquire the set of sentiments from sentences, for example, $\langle$ *foods*, 1$\rangle$ and $\langle$ *atmosphere*, 1$\rangle$.

Note that since our method relies on only sentiment lexicon, extractable aspects are unlimited.

2.2 Readability Score

Readability consists of various elements such as conciseness, coherence, and grammar. Since it is difficult to model all of them, we approximate readability as the natural order of sentences.

To order sentences, Barzilay et al. (2002) used the publication dates of documents to catch temporally-ordered events, but this approach is not really suitable for our goal because reviews focus on entities rather than events. Lapata (2003) employed the probability of two sentences being adjacent as determined from a corpus. If the corpus consists of reviews, it is expected that this approach would be effective for sentiment summarization. Therefore, we adopt and improve Lapata's approach to order sentences. We define the

[1] Since we aim to summarize Japanese reviews, we utilize Japanese sentiment lexicon (Asano et al., 2008). However, our method is, except for sentiment extraction, language independent.

readability score as follows:

$$\text{Read}(S) = \sum_{i=0}^{n} \mathbf{w}^\top \phi(s_i, s_{i+1}) \quad (3)$$

where, given two adjacent sentences s_i and s_{i+1}, $\mathbf{w}^\top \phi(s_i, s_{i+1})$, which measures the connectivity of the two sentences, is the inner product of $\mathbf{w}$ and $\phi(s_i, s_{i+1})$, $\mathbf{w}$ is a parameter vector and $\phi(s_i, s_{i+1})$ is a feature vector of the two sentences. That is, the readability score of sentence sequence S is the sum of the connectivity of all adjacent sentences in the sequence.

As the features, Lapata (2003) proposed the Cartesian product of content words in adjacent sentences. To this, we add named entity tags (e.g. LOC, ORG) and connectives. We observe that the first sentence of a review of a restaurant frequently contains named entities indicating location. We aim to reproduce this characteristic in the ordering.

We also define feature vector $\Phi(S)$ of the entire sequence $S = \langle s_0, s_1, \ldots, s_n, s_{n+1} \rangle$ as follows:

$$\Phi(S) = \sum_{i=0}^{n} \phi(s_i, s_{i+1}) \quad (4)$$

Therefore, the score of sequence S is $\mathbf{w}^\top \Phi(S)$. Given a training set, if a trained parameter $\mathbf{w}$ assigns a score $\mathbf{w}^\top \Phi(S^+)$ to an correct order S^+ that is higher than a score $\mathbf{w}^\top \Phi(S^-)$ to an incorrect order S^-, it is expected that the trained parameter will give higher score to naturally ordered sentences than to unnaturally ordered sentences.

We use Averaged Perceptron (Collins, 2002) to find $\mathbf{w}$. Averaged Perceptron requires an argmax operation for parameter estimation. Since we attempt to order a set of sentences, the operation is regarded as solving the Traveling Salesman Problem; that is, we locate the path that offers maximum score through all n sentences as s_0 and s_{n+1} are starting and ending points, respectively. Thus the operation is NP-hard and it is difficult to find the global optimal solution. To alleviate this, we find an approximate solution by adopting the dynamic programming technique of the Held and Karp Algorithm (Held and Karp, 1962) and beam search.

We show the search procedure in Figure 2. $\mathbf{S}$ indicates intended sentences and $\mathbf{M}$ is a distance matrix of the readability scores of adjacent sentence pairs. $\mathbf{H}^i(\mathbf{C}, j)$ indicates the score of the hypothesis that has covered the set of i sentences $\mathbf{C}$ and has the sentence j at the end of the path,

```
Sentences: S = {s_1, ..., s_n}
Distance matrix: M = [a_{i,j}]_{i=0...n+1, j=0...n+1}
1: H^0({s_0}, s_0) = 0
2: for i : 0 ... n − 1
3:   for j : 1 ... n
4:     foreach H^i(C\{j}, k) ∈ b
5:       H^{i+1}(C, j) = max_{H^i(C\{j},k)∈b} H^i(C\{j}, k)
6:                       +M_{k,j}
7: H* = max_{H_n(C,k)} H^n(C, k) + M_{k,n+1}
```

Figure 2: Held and Karp Algorithm.

i.e. the last sentence of the summary being generated. For example, $\mathbf{H}^2(\{s_0, s_2, s_5\}, s_2)$ indicates a hypothesis that covers s_0, s_2, s_5 and the last sentence is s_2. Initially, $\mathbf{H}^0(\{s_0\}, s_0)$ is assigned the score of 0, and new sentences are then added one by one. In the search procedure, our dynamic programming based algorithm retains just the hypothesis with maximum score among the hypotheses that have the same sentences and the same last sentence. Since this procedure is still computationally hard, only the top $\mathbf{b}$ hypotheses are expanded.

Note that our method learns $\mathbf{w}$ from texts automatically annotated by a POS tagger and a named entity tagger. Thus manual annotation isn't required.

2.3 Optimization

The argmax operation in Equation 1 also involves search, which is NP-hard as described in Section 2.2. Therefore, we adopt the Held and Karp Algorithm and beam search to find approximate solutions. The search algorithm is basically the same as parameter estimation, except for its calculation of the informativeness score and size limitation. Therefore, when a new sentence is added to a hypothesis, both the informativeness and the readability scores are calculated. The size of the hypothesis is also calculated and if the size exceeds the limit, the sentence can't be added. A hypothesis that can't accept any more sentences is removed from the search procedure and preserved in memory. After all hypotheses are removed, the best hypothesis is chosen from among the preserved hypotheses as the solution.

3 Experiments

This section evaluates our method in terms of ROUGE score and readability. We collected 2,940 reviews of 100 restaurants from a website. The

	R-2	R-SU4	R-SU9
Baseline	0.089	0.068	0.062
Method1	0.157	0.096	0.089
Method2	0.172	0.107	0.098
Method3	**0.180**	**0.110**	**0.101**
Human	0.258	0.143	0.131

Table 1: Automatic ROUGE evaluation.

	Numbers
Baseline	1.76
Method1	4.32
Method2	**10.41**
Method3	10.18
Human	4.75

Table 2: Unique sentiment numbers.

average size of each document set (corresponds to one restaurant) was 5,343 bytes. We attempted to generate 300 byte summaries, so the summarization rate was about 6%. We used CRFs-based Japanese dependency parser (Imamura et al., 2007) and named entity recognizer (Suzuki et al., 2006) for sentiment extraction and constructing feature vectors for readability score, respectively.

3.1 ROUGE

We used ROUGE (Lin, 2004) for evaluating the content of summaries. We chose ROUGE-2, ROUGE-SU4 and ROUGE-SU9. We prepared four reference summaries for each document set.

To evaluate the effects of the informativeness score, the readability score and the optimization, we compared the following five methods.

Baseline: employs MMR (Carbonell and Goldstein, 1998). We designed the score of a sentence as term frequencies of the content words in a document set.

Method1: uses optimization without the informativeness score or readability score. It also used term frequencies to score sentences.

Method2: uses the informativeness score and optimization without the readability score.

Method3: the proposed method. Following Equation 1, the summarizer searches for a sequence with high informativeness and readability score. The parameter vector $\mathbf{w}$ was trained on the same 2,940 reviews in 5-fold cross validation fashion. λ was set to 6,000 using a development set.

Human is the reference summaries. To compare our summarizer to human summarization, we calculated ROUGE scores between each reference and the other references, and averaged them.

The results of these experiments are shown in Table 1. ROUGE scores increase in the order of Method1, Method2 and Method3 but no method could match the performance of Human. The methods significantly outperformed Baseline according to the Wilcoxon signed-rank test.

We discuss the contribution of readability to ROUGE scores. Comparing Method2 to Method3, ROUGE scores of the latter were higher for all criteria. It is interesting that the readability criterion also improved ROUGE scores.

We also evaluated our method in terms of sentiments. We extracted sentiments from the summaries using the above sentiment extractor, and averaged the unique sentiment numbers. Table 2 shows the results.

The references (Human) have fewer sentiments than the summaries generated by our method. In other words, the references included almost as many other sentences (e.g. reasons for the sentiments) as those expressing sentiments. Carenini et al. (2006) pointed out that readers wanted "detailed information" in summaries, and the reasons are one of such piece of information. Including them in summaries would greatly improve summarizer appeal.

3.2 Readability

Readability was evaluated by human judges. Three different summarizers generated summaries for each document set. Ten judges evaluated the thirty summaries for each. Before the evaluation the judges read evaluation criteria and gave points to summaries using a five-point scale. The judges weren't informed of which method generated which summary.

We compared three methods; Ordering sentences according to publication dates and positions in which sentences appear after sentence extraction (**Method2**), Ordering sentences using the readability score after sentence extraction (**Method2+**) and searching a document set to discover the sequence with the highest score (**Method3**).

Table 3 shows the results of the experiment. Readability increased in the order of Method2, Method2+ and Method3. According to the

	Readability point
Method2	3.45
Method2+	3.54
Method3	**3.74**

Table 3: Readability evaluation.

Wilcoxon signed-rank test, there was no significance difference between Method2 and Method2+ but the difference between Method2 and Method3 was significant, $p < 0.10$.

One important factor behind the higher readability of Method3 is that it yields longer sentences on average (6.52). Method2 and Method2+ yielded averages of 7.23 sentences. The difference is significant as indicated by $p < 0.01$. That is, Method2 and Method2+ tended to select short sentences, which made their summaries less readable.

4 Conclusion

This paper proposed a novel algorithm for sentiment summarization that takes account of informativeness and readability, simultaneously. To summarize reviews, the informativeness score is based on sentiments and the readability score is learned from a corpus of reviews. The preferred sequence is determined by using dynamic programming and beam search. Experiments showed that our method generated better summaries than the baseline in terms of ROUGE score and readability.

One future work is to include important information other than sentiments in the summaries. We also plan to model the order of sentences globally. Although the ordering model in this paper is local since it looks at only adjacent sentences, a model that can evaluate global order is important for better summaries.

Acknowledgments

We would like to sincerely thank Tsutomu Hirao for his comments and discussions. We would also like to thank the reviewers for their comments.

References

Hisako Asano, Toru Hirano, Nozomi Kobayashi and Yoshihiro Matsuo. 2008. Subjective Information Indexing Technology Analyzing Word-of-mouth Content on the Web. *NTT Technical Review*, Vol.6, No.9.

Regina Barzilay, Noemie Elhadad and Kathleen McKeown. 2002. Inferring Strategies for Sentence Ordering in Multidocument Summarization. *Journal of Artificial Intelligence Research (JAIR)*, Vol.17, pp. 35–55.

Regina Barzilay and Lillian Lee. 2004. Catching the Drift: Probabilistic Content Models, with Applications to Generation and Summarization. In *Proceedings of the Human Language Technology Conference of the North American Chapter of the Association for Computational Linguistics (HLT-NAACL)*, pp. 113–120.

Regina Barzilay and Mirella Lapata. 2005. Modeling Local Coherence: An Entity-based Approach. In *Proceedings of the 43rd Annual Meeting of the Association for Computational Linguistics (ACL)*, pp. 141–148.

Sasha Blair-Goldensohn, Kerry Hannan, Ryan McDonald, Tyler Neylon, George A. Reis and Jeff Reynar. 2008. Building a Sentiment Summarizer for Local Service Reviews. WWW Workshop NLP Challenges in the Information Explosion Era (NLPIX).

Jaime Carbonell and Jade Goldstein. 1998. The use of MMR, diversity-based reranking for reordering documents and producing summaries. In *Proceedings of the 21st annual international ACM SIGIR conference on Research and development in information retrieval (SIGIR)*, pp. 335–356.

Giuseppe Carenini, Raymond Ng and Adam Pauls. 2006. Multi-Document Summarization of Evaluative Text. In *Proceedings of the 11th European Chapter of the Association for Computational Linguistics (EACL)*, pp. 305–312.

Giuseppe Carenini and Jackie Chi Kit Cheung. 2008. Extractive vs. NLG-based Abstractive Summarization of Evaluative Text: The Effect of Corpus Controversiality. In *Proceedings of the 5th International Natural Language Generation Conference (INLG)*, pp. 33–41.

Michael Collins. 2002. Discriminative Training Methods for Hidden Markov Models: Theory and Experiments with Perceptron Algorithms. In *Proceedings of the 2002 Conference on Empirical Methods on Natural Language Processing (EMNLP)*, pp. 1–8.

Michael Held and Richard M. Karp. 1962. A dynamic programming approach to sequencing problems. *Journal of the Society for Industrial and Applied Mathematics (SIAM)*, Vol.10, No.1, pp. 196–210.

Minqing Hu and Bing Liu. 2004. Mining and Summarizing Customer Reviews. In *Proceedings of the 10th ACM SIGKDD International Conference on Knowledge Discovery and Data Mining (KDD)*, pp. 168–177.

Kenji Imamura, Genichiro Kikui and Norihito Yasuda. 2007. Japanese Dependency Parsing Using Sequential Labeling for Semi-spoken Language. In *Proceedings of the 45th Annual Meeting of the Association for Computational Linguistics (ACL) Companion Volume Proceedings of the Demo and Poster Sessions*, pp. 225–228.

Mirella Lapata. 2003. Probabilistic Text Structuring: Experiments with Sentence Ordering. In *Proceedings of the 41st Annual Meeting of the Association for Computational Linguistics (ACL)*, pp. 545–552.

Kevin Lerman, Sasha Blair-Goldensohn and Ryan McDonald. 2009. Sentiment Summarization: Evaluating and Learning User Preferences. In *Proceedings of the 12th Conference of the European Chapter of the Association for Computational Linguistics (EACL)*, pp. 514–522.

Kevin Lerman and Ryan McDonald. 2009. Contrastive Summarization: An Experiment with Consumer Reviews. In *Proceedings of Human Language Technologies: the 2009 Annual Conference of the North American Chapter of the Association for Computational Linguistics (NAACL-HLT), Companion Volume: Short Papers*, pp. 113–116.

Chin-Yew Lin. 2004. ROUGE: A Package for Automatic Evaluation of Summaries. In *Proceedings of the Workshop on Text Summarization Branches Out*, pp. 74–81.

Jun Suzuki, Erik McDermott and Hideki Isozaki. 2006. Training Conditional Random Fields with Multivariate Evaluation Measures. In *Proceedings of the 21st International Conference on Computational Linguistics and 44th Annual Meeting of the ACL (COLING-ACL)*, pp. 217–224.

Ivan Titov and Ryan McDonald. 2008. A Joint Model of Text and Aspect Ratings for Sentiment Summarization. In *Proceedings of the 46th Annual Meeting of the Association for Computational Linguistics: Human Language Technologies (ACL-HLT)*, pp. 308–316.

Last but *Definitely* not Least:

On the Role of the Last Sentence in Automatic Polarity-Classification

Israela Becker and Vered Aharonson
AFEKA – Tel-Aviv Academic College of Engineering
218 Bney-Efraim Rd.
Tel-Aviv 69107, Israel
{IsraelaB,Vered}@afeka.ac.il

Abstract

Two psycholinguistic and psychophysical experiments show that in order to efficiently extract polarity of written texts such as customer-reviews on the Internet, one should concentrate computational efforts on messages in the final position of the text.

1 Introduction

The ever-growing field of polarity-classification of written texts may benefit greatly from linguistic insights and tools that will allow to efficiently (and thus economically) extract the polarity of written texts, in particular, online customer reviews.

Many researchers interpret "efficiently" as using better computational methods to resolve the polarity of written texts. We suggest that text units should be handled with tools of discourse linguistics too in order to reveal where, within texts, their polarity is best manifested. Specifically, we propose to focus on the last sentence of the given text in order to efficiently extract the polarity of the whole text. This will reduce computational costs, as well as improve the quality of polarity detection and classification when large databases of text units are involved.

This paper aims to provide psycholinguistic support to the hypothesis (which psycholinguistic literature lacks) that the last sentence of a customer review is a better predictor for the polarity of the whole review than other sentences in the review, in order to be later used for automatic polarity-classification. Therefore, we first briefly review the well-established structure of text units while comparing notions of topic-extraction vs. *our* notion of polarity-classification. We then report the psycholinguistic experiments that we ran in order to support our prediction as to the role of the last sentence in polarity manifestation. Finally, we discuss the experimental results.

2 Topic-extraction

One of the basic features required to perform automatic topic-extraction is sentence position. The importance of sentence position for computational purposes was first indicated by Baxendale in the late 1950s (Baxendale, 1958): Baxendale hypothesized that the first and the last sentence of a given text are the potential topic-containing sentences. He tested this hypothesis on a corpus of 200 paragraphs extracted out of 6 technical articles. He found that in 85% of the documents, the first sentence was the topic sentence, whereas in only 7% of the documents, it was the last sentence. A large scale study supporting Baxendale's hypothesis was conducted by Lin and Hovy (Lin and Hovy, 1997) who examined 13,000 documents of the Ziff-Davis newswire corpus of articles reviewing computer hardware and software. In this corpus, each document was accompanied by a set of topic keywords and a small abstract of six sentences. Lin and Hovy measured the yield of each sentence against the topic keywords and ranked the sentences by their average yield. They concluded that in ~2/3 of the documents, the topic keywords are indeed mentioned in the title and first five sentences of the document.

Baxendale's theory gained further psycholinguistic support by the experimental results of Kieras (Kieras, 1978, Kieras, 1980) who showed that subjects re-constructed the content

Proceedings of the ACL 2010 Conference Short Papers, pages 331–335,
Uppsala, Sweden, 11-16 July 2010. ©2010 Association for Computational Linguistics

of paragraphs they were asked to read by relying on sentences in initial positions. These finding subsequently gained extensive theoretical and experimental support by Giora (Giora, 1983, Giora, 1985) who correlated the position of a sentence within a text with its degree of informativeness.

Giora (Giora, 1985, Giora, 1988) defined a discourse topic (DT) as the least informative (*most uninformative)* yet *dominant* proposition of a text. The DT best represents the redundancy structure of the text. As such, this proposition functions as a reference point for processing the rest of the propositions. The text position which best benefits such processing is text initial; it facilitates processing of oncoming propositions (with respect to the DT) relative to when the DT is placed in text final position.

Furthermore, Giora and Lee showed (Giora and Lee, 1996) that when the DT appears *also* at the end of a text it is somewhat informationally redundant. However, functionally, it plays a role in wrapping the text up and marking its boundary. Authors often make reference to the DT at the end of a text in order to summarize and deliberately recapitulate what has been written up to that point while also signaling the end of discourse topic segment.

3 Polarity-classification *vs.* Topic-extraction

When dealing with polarity-classification (as with topic-extraction), one should again identify the *most uninformative* yet *dominant* proposition of the text. However, given the cognitive prominence of discourse final position in terms of memorability, known as "*recency effect*" (see below and see also (Giora, 1988)), we predict that when it comes to polarity-classification, the *last* proposition of a given text should be of greater importance than the *first* one (contrary to topic-extraction).

Based on preliminary investigations, we suggest that the DT of any customer review is the customer's evaluation, whether negative or positive, of a product that s/he has purchased or a service s/he has used, rather than the details of the specific product or service. The message that customer reviews try to get across is, therefore, of evaluative nature. To best communicate this affect, the DT should appear at the end of the review (instead of the beginning of the review) as a means of recapitulating the point of the message, thereby guaranteeing that it is fully understood by the readership.

Indeed, the cognitive prominence of information in final position - the *recency-effect* - has been well established in numerous psychological experiments (see, for example, (Murdock, 1962)). Thus, the most *frequent* evaluation of the product (which is the *most uninformative* one) also should surface at the end of the text due to the ease of its retrieval, which is presumably what product review readers would refer to as "the bottom line".

To the best of our knowledge, this psycholinguistic prediction has not been supported by psycholinguistic evidence to date. However, it has been somewhat supported by the computational results of Yang, Lin and Chen (Yang et al., 2007a, Yang et al., 2007b) who classified emotions of posts in blog corpora. Yang, Lin & Chen realized that bloggers tend to emphasize their feelings by using emoticons (such as: ☺,☹ and 👍) and that these emoticons frequently appear in final sentences. Thus, they first focused on the last sentence of posts as representing the polarity of the entire posts. Then, they divided the positive category into 2 sub-categories - happy and joy, and the negative category - into angry and sad. They showed that extracting polarity and consequently sentiments from last sentences outperforms all other computational strategies.

4 Method

We aim to show that the last sentence of a customer review is a better predictor for the polarity of the whole review than any other sentence (assuming that the first sentence is devoted to presenting the product or service). To test our prediction, we ran two experiments and compared their results. In the first experiment we examined the readers' rating of the polarity of reviews in their entirety, while in the second experiment we examined the readers' rating of the same reviews based on reading single sentences extracted from these reviews: the last sentence *or* the second one. The second sentence could have been replaced by any other sentence, *but* the first one, as our preliminary investigations clearly show that the first sentence is in many cases devoted to presenting the product or service discussed and does not contain any polarity content. For example: "I read Isaac's storm, by Erik Larson, around 1998. Recently I had occasion to thumb through it again which has prompted this review.....All in all a most interesting and rewarding book, one that I would recommend highly." (Gerald T. Westbrook, "GTW")

4.1 Materials

Sixteen customer-reviews were extracted from Blitzer, Dredze, and Pereira's sentiment database (Blitzer et al., 2007). This database contains product-reviews taken from Amazon [1] where each review is rated by its author on a 1-5 star scale. The database covers 4 product types (domains): Kitchen, Books, DVDs, and Electronics. Four reviews were selected from each domain. Of the 16 extracted reviews, 8 were positive (4-5 star rating) and the other 8 – negative (1-2 star rating).

Given that in this experiment we examine the polarity of the last sentence relative to that of the whole review or to a few other sentences, we focused on the first reviews (as listed in the aforementioned database) of at least 5 sentences or longer, rather than on too-short reviews. By "too-short" we refer to reviews in which such comparison would be meaningless; for example, ones that range between 1-3 sentences will not allow to compare the last sentence with any of the others.

4.2 Participants

Thirty-five subjects participated in the first experiment: 14 women and 21 men, ranging in age from 22 to 73. Thirty-six subjects participated in the second experiment: 23 women and 13 men ranging in age from 20 to 59. All participants were native speakers of English, had an academic education, and had normal or corrected-to-normal eye-vision.

4.3 Procedure

In the first experiment, subjects were asked to read 16 reviews; in the second experiment subjects were asked to read 32 single sentences extracted from the same 16 reviews: the last sentence and the second sentence of each review. The last and the second sentence of each review *were not* presented together but *individually*.

In both experiments subjects were asked to guess the ratings of the texts which were given by the authors on a 1-5 star scale, by clicking on a radio-button: "In each of the following screens you will be asked to read a customer review (or a sentence extracted out of a customer review). All the reviews were extracted from the www.amazon.com customer review section. Each review (or sentence) describes a different product. At the end of each review (or sentence) you will be asked to decide whether the reviewer who wrote the review recommended or did not recommend the reviewed product on a 1-5 scale: Number 5 indicates that the reviewer highly recommended the product, while number 1 indicates that the reviewer was unsatisfied with the product and did not recommend it."

In the second experiment, in addition to the psychological experiment, the latencies following reading of the texts up until the clicking of the mouse, as well as the biometric measurements of the mouse's trajectories, were recorded.

In both experiments each subject was run in an individual session and had an unlimited time to reflect and decide on the polarity of each text. Five seconds after a decision was made (as to whether the reviewer was in favor of the product or not), the subject was presented with the next text. The texts were presented in random order so as to prevent possible interactions between them.

In the initial design phase of the experiment we discussed the idea of adding an "irrelevant" option in addition to the 5-star scale of polarity. This option was meant to be used for sentences that carry no evaluation at all. Such an addition would have necessitated locating the extra-choice radio button at a separated remote place from the 5-star scale radio buttons, since conceptually it cannot be located on a nearby position. From the user interaction point of view, the mouse movement to that location would have been either considerably shorter or longer (depending on its distance from the initial location of the mouse curser at the beginning of each trial), and the mouse trajectory and click time would have been, thus, very different and difficult to analyze.

Although the reviews were randomly selected, 32 sentences extracted out of 16 reviews might seem like a small sample. However, the upper time limit for *reliable* psycholinguistic experiments is 20-25 minute. Although tempted to extend the experiments in order to acquire more data, longer times result in subject impatience, which shows on lower scoring rates. Therefore, we chose to trade sample size for accuracy. Experimental times in both experiments ranged between 15-35 minutes.

5 Results

Results of the distribution of differences between the authors' and the readers' ratings of the texts are presented in Figure 1: The distribution of differences for whole reviews is (unsurprisingly) the narrowest (Figure 1a). The dis-

[1] http://www.amazon.com

tribution of differences for last sentences (Figure 1b) is somewhat wider than (but still quite similar to) the distribution of differences for whole reviews. The distribution of differences for second sentences is the widest of the three (Figure 1c).

Pearson correlation coefficient calculations (Table 1) show that both the correlation between authors' ratings and readers' rating for whole reviews and the correlation between authors' rating and readers' rating upon reading the last sentence are similar, while the correlation between authors' rating and readers' rating when presented with the second sentence of each review is significantly lower. Moreover, when correlating readers' rating of whole reviews with readers' rating of single sentences, the correlation coefficient for last sentences is significantly higher than for second sentences.

As for the biometric measurements performed in the second experiment, since all subjects were computer-skilled, hesitation revealed through mouse-movements was assumed to be attributed to difficulty of decision-making rather than to problems in operating the mouse. As previously stated, we recorded mouse latency times following the reading of the texts up until clicking the mouse. Mouse latency times were not normalized for each subject due to the limited number of results. However, the average latency time is shorter for last sentences (19.61±12.23s) than for second sentences (22.06±14.39s). Indeed, the difference between latency times is not significant, as a paired t-test could not reject the null hypothesis that those distributions have equal means, but might show some tendency.

We also used the WizWhy software (Meidan, 2005) to perform combined analyses of readers' rating and response times. The analyses showed that when the difference between authors' and readers' ratings was $\leq |1|$ and the response time *much* shorter than average (<14.1 sec), then 96% of the sentences were *last* sentences. Due to the small sample size, we cautiously infer that last sentences express polarity better than second sentences, bearing in mind that the second sentence in our experiment represents any other sentence in the text except for the first one.

We also predicted that hesitation in making a decision would effect not only latency times but also mouse trajectories. Namely, hesitation will be accompanied by moving the mouse here and there, while decisiveness will show a firm movement. However, no such difference between the responses to last sentences or to second sentences appeared in our analysis; most subjects laid their hand still while reading the texts and while reflecting upon their answers. They moved the mouse only to rate the texts.

6 Conclusions and Future Work

In 2 psycholinguistic and psychophysical experiments, we showed that rating whole customer-reviews as compared to rating final sentences of these reviews showed an (expected) insignificant difference. In contrast, rating whole customer-reviews as compared to rating second sentences of these reviews, showed a considerable difference. Thus, instead of focusing on whole texts, computational linguists should focus on the last sentences for efficient and accurate automatic polarity-classification. Indeed, last but definitely not least!

We are currently running experiments that

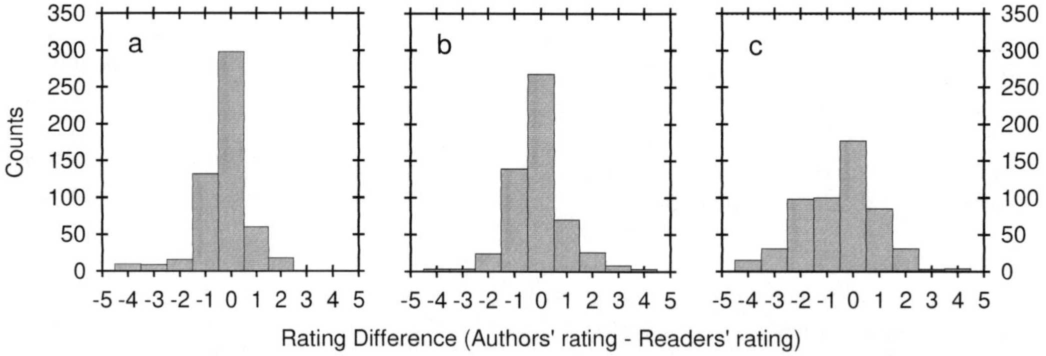

Figure 1. Histograms of the rating differences between the authors of reviews and their readers: for whole reviews (a), for last sentence only (b), and for second sentence only (c).

Readers' star rating of:	Correlated with:	Pearson Correlation Coefficient (P<0.0001)
Whole reviews	Authors' star rating of whole reviews	0.7891
Last sentences		0.7616
Second sentences		0.4705
Last sentences	Readers' star rating of whole reviews	0.8463
Second sentences		0.6563

Table 1. Pearson Correlation Coefficients

include hundreds of subjects in order to draw a profile of polarity evolvement throughout customer reviews. Specifically, we present our subjects with sentences in various locations in customer reviews asking them to rate them. As the expanded experiment is *not* psychophysical, we added an additional *remote* radio button named "irrelevant" where subjects can judge a given text as lacking any evident polarity. Based on the rating results we will draw polarity profiles in order to see where, within customer reviews, polarity is best manifested and whether there are other "candidates" sentences that would serve as useful polarity indicators. The profiles will be used as a feature in our computational analysis.

Acknowledgments

We thank Prof. Rachel Giora and Prof. Ido Dagan for most valuable discussions, the 2 anonymous reviewers – for their excellent suggestions, and Thea Pagelson and Jason S. Henry - for their help with programming and running the psychophysical experiment.

References

Baxendale, P. B. 1958. Machine-Made Index for Technical Literature - An Experiment. *IBM journal of research development* 2:263-311.

Blitzer, John, Dredze, Mark, and Pereira, Fernando. 2007. Biographies, Bollywood, Boom-boxes and Blenders: Domain Adaptation for Sentiment Classification. Paper presented at *Association of Computational Linguistics (ACL).*

Giora, Rachel. 1983. Segmentation and Segment Cohesion: On the Thematic Organization of the Text. *Text* 3:155-182.

Giora, Rachel. 1985. A Text-based Analysis of Nonnarrative Texts. *Theoretical Linguistics* 12:115-135.

Giora, Rachel. 1988. On the Informativeness Requirement. *Journal of Pragmatics* 12:547-565.

Giora, Rachel, and Lee, Cher-Leng. 1996. Written Discourse Segmentation: The Function of Unstressed Pronouns in Mandarin Chinese. In *Reference and Reference Accessibility* ed. J. Gundel and T. Fretheim, 113-140. Amsterdam: Benjamins.

Kieras, David E. 1978. Good and Bad Structure in Simple Paragraphs: Effects on Apparent Theme, Reading Time, and Recall. *Journal of Verbal Learning and Verbal Behavior* 17:13-28.

Kieras, David E. 1980. Initial Mention as a Cue to the Main Idea and the Main Item of a Technical Passage. *Memory and Cognition* 8:345-353.

Lin, Chen-Yew, and Hovy, Edward. 1997. Identifying Topic by Position. Paper presented at *Proceeding of the Fifth Conference on Applied Natural Language Processing*, San Francisco.

Meidan, Abraham. 2005. Wizsoft's WizWhy. In *The Data Mining and Knowledge Discovery Handbook*, eds. Oded Maimon and Lior Rokach, 1365-1369: Springer.

Murdock, B. B. Jr. 1962. The Serial Position Effect of Free Recall. *Journal of Experimental Psychology* 62:618-625.

Yang, Changua, Lin, Kevin Hsin-Yih, and Chen, Hsin-Hsi. 2007a. Emotion Classification Using Web Blog Corpora. In *IEEE/WIC/ACM/ International Conference on Web Intelligence.* Silicon Valley, San Francisco.

Yang, Changua, Lin, Kevin Hsin-Yih, and Chen, Hsin-Hsin. 2007b. Building Emotion Lexicon from Weblog Corpora. Paper presented at *Proceeding of the ACL 2007 Demo and Poster Session*, Prague.

Automatically generating annotator rationales to improve sentiment classification

Ainur Yessenalina **Yejin Choi** **Claire Cardie**
Department of Computer Science, Cornell University, Ithaca NY, 14853 USA
{ainur, ychoi, cardie}@cs.cornell.edu

Abstract

One of the central challenges in sentiment-based text categorization is that not every portion of a document is equally informative for inferring the overall sentiment of the document. Previous research has shown that enriching the sentiment labels with human annotators' "rationales" can produce substantial improvements in categorization performance (Zaidan et al., 2007). We explore methods to *automatically* generate annotator rationales for document-level sentiment classification. Rather unexpectedly, we find the automatically generated rationales just as helpful as human rationales.

1 Introduction

One of the central challenges in sentiment-based text categorization is that not every portion of a given document is equally informative for inferring its overall sentiment (e.g., Pang and Lee (2004)). Zaidan et al. (2007) address this problem by asking human annotators to mark (at least some of) the relevant text spans that *support each document-level sentiment decision*. The text spans of these "rationales" are then used to construct additional training examples that can guide the learning algorithm toward better categorization models.

But could we perhaps enjoy the performance gains of rationale-enhanced learning models without any additional human effort whatsoever (beyond the document-level sentiment label)? We hypothesize that in the area of sentiment analysis, where there has been a great deal of recent research attention given to various aspects of the task (Pang and Lee, 2008), this might be possible: using existing resources for sentiment analysis, we might be able to construct annotator rationales automatically.

In this paper, we explore a number of methods to automatically generate rationales for document-level sentiment classification. In particular, we investigate the use of off-the-shelf sentiment analysis components and lexicons for this purpose. Our approaches for generating annotator rationales can be viewed as *mostly unsupervised* in that we do not require manually annotated rationales for training.

Rather unexpectedly, our empirical results show that automatically generated rationales (91.78%) are just as good as human rationales (91.61%) for document-level sentiment classification of movie reviews. In addition, complementing the human annotator rationales with automatic rationales boosts the performance even further for this domain, achieving 92.5% accuracy. We further evaluate our rationale-generation approaches on product review data for which human rationales are not available: here we find that even randomly generated rationales can improve the classification accuracy although rationales generated from sentiment resources are not as effective as for movie reviews.

The rest of the paper is organized as follows. We first briefly summarize the SVM-based learning approach of Zaidan et al. (2007) that allows the incorporation of rationales (Section 2). We next introduce three methods for the automatic generation of rationales (Section 3). The experimental results are presented in Section 4, followed by related work (Section 5) and conclusions (Section 6).

2 Contrastive Learning with SVMs

Zaidan et al. (2007) first introduced the notion of *annotator rationales* — text spans highlighted by human annotators as support or evidence for each document-level sentiment decision. These rationales, of course, are only useful if the sentiment categorization algorithm can be extended to exploit the rationales effectively. With this in mind, Zaidan et al. (2007) propose the following *con-*

Proceedings of the ACL 2010 Conference Short Papers, pages 336–341,
Uppsala, Sweden, 11-16 July 2010.

trastive learning extension to the standard SVM learning algorithm.

Let $\vec{x}_i$ be movie review i, and let $\{\vec{r}_{ij}\}$ be the set of *annotator rationales* that support the positive or negative sentiment decision for $\vec{x}_i$. For each such rationale $\vec{r}_{ij}$ in the set, construct a *contrastive training example* $\vec{v}_{ij}$, by removing the text span associated with the rationale $\vec{r}_{ij}$ from the original review $\vec{x}_i$. Intuitively, the contrastive example $\vec{v}_{ij}$ should not be as informative to the learning algorithm as the original review $\vec{x}_i$, since one of the supporting regions identified by the human annotator has been deleted. That is, the *correct* learned model should be *less confident* of its classification of a contrastive example vs. the corresponding original example, and the classification boundary of the model should be modified accordingly.

Zaidan et al. (2007) formulate exactly this intuition as SVM constraints as follows:

$$(\forall i, j): \; y_i \left(\vec{w}\vec{x}_i - \vec{w}\vec{v}_{ij}\right) \geq \mu(1 - \xi_{ij})$$

where $y_i \in \{-1, +1\}$ is the negative/positive sentiment label of document i, $\vec{w}$ is the weight vector, $\mu \geq 0$ controls the size of the margin between the original examples and the contrastive examples, and ξ_{ij} are the associated slack variables. After some re-writing of the equations, the resulting objective function and constraints for the SVM are as follows:

$$\frac{1}{2}||\vec{w}||^2 + C\sum_i \xi_i + C_{contrast}\sum_{ij} \xi_{ij} \quad (1)$$

subject to constraints:

$$(\forall i): \quad y_i\, \vec{w} \cdot \vec{x}_i \geq 1 - \xi_i, \quad \xi_i \geq 0$$

$$(\forall i, j): \quad y_i\, \vec{w} \cdot \vec{x}_{ij} \geq 1 - \xi_{ij} \quad \xi_{ij} \geq 0$$

where ξ_i and ξ_{ij} are the slack variables for $\vec{x}_i$ (the original examples) and $\vec{x}_{ij}$ ($\vec{x}_{ij}$ are named as *pseudo examples* and defined as $\vec{x}_{ij} = \frac{\vec{x}_i - \vec{v}_{ij}}{\mu}$), respectively. Intuitively, the pseudo examples ($\vec{x}_{ij}$) represent the difference between the original examples ($\vec{x}_i$) and the contrastive examples ($\vec{v}_{ij}$), weighted by a parameter μ. C and $C_{contrast}$ are parameters to control the trade-offs between training errors and margins for the original examples $\vec{x}_i$ and pseudo examples $\vec{x}_{ij}$ respectively. As noted in Zaidan et al. (2007), $C_{contrast}$ values are generally smaller than C for noisy rationales.

In the work described below, we similarly employ Zaidan et al.'s (2007) contrastive learning method to incorporate rationales for document-level sentiment categorization.

3 Automatically Generating Rationales

Our goal in the current work, is to generate annotator rationales automatically. For this, we rely on the following two assumptions:

(1) Regions marked as annotator rationales are more subjective than unmarked regions.

(2) The sentiment of each annotator rationale coincides with the document-level sentiment.

Note that assumption 1 was not observed in the Zaidan et al. (2007) work: annotators were asked only to mark a few rationales, leaving other (also subjective) rationale sections unmarked.

And at first glance, assumption (2) might seem too obvious. But it is important to include as there can be subjective regions with seemingly conflicting sentiment in the same document (Pang et al., 2002). For instance, an author for a movie review might express a positive sentiment toward the movie, while also discussing a negative sentiment toward one of the fictional characters appearing in the movie. This implies that not all subjective regions will be relevant for the document-level sentiment classification — rather only those regions whose polarity matches that of the document should be considered.

In order to extract regions that satisfy the above assumptions, we first look for subjective regions in each document, then filter out those regions that exhibit a sentiment value (i.e., polarity) that conflicts with polarity of the document. Assumption 2 is important as there can be subjective regions with seemingly conflicting sentiment in the same document (Pang et al., 2002).

Because our ultimate goal is to reduce human annotation effort as much as possible, we do not employ supervised learning methods to directly learn to identify good rationales from human-annotated rationales. Instead, we opt for methods that make use of only the document-level sentiment and off-the-shelf utilities that were trained for slightly different sentiment classification tasks using a corpus from a different domain and of a different genre. Although such utilities might not be optimal for our task, we hoped that these basic resources from the research community would constitute an adequate source of sentiment information for our purposes.

We next describe three methods for the automatic acquisition of rationales.

3.1 Contextual Polarity Classification

The first approach employs OpinionFinder (Wilson et al., 2005a), an off-the-shelf opinion analysis utility.[1] In particular, OpinionFinder identifies phrases expressing positive or negative opinions. Because OpinionFinder models the task as a word-based classification problem rather than a sequence tagging task, most of the identified opinion phrases consist of a single word. In general, such short text spans cannot fully incorporate the contextual information relevant to the detection of subjective language (Wilson et al., 2005a). Therefore, we conjecture that good rationales should extend beyond short phrases.[2] For simplicity, we choose to extend OpinionFinder phrases to sentence boundaries.

In addition, to be consistent with our second operating assumption, we keep only those sentences whose polarity coincides with the document-level polarity. In sentences where OpinionFinder marks multiple opinion words with opposite polarities we perform a simple voting — if words with positive (or negative) polarity dominate, then we consider the entire sentence as positive (or negative). We ignore sentences with a tie. Each selected sentence is considered as a separate rationale.

3.2 Polarity Lexicons

Unfortunately, domain shift as well as task mismatch could be a problem with any opinion utility based on supervised learning.[3] Therefore, we next consider an approach that does not rely on supervised learning techniques but instead explores the use of a manually constructed polarity lexicon. In particular, we use the lexicon constructed for Wilson et al. (2005b), which contains about 8000 words. Each entry is assigned one of three polarity values: positive, negative, neutral. We construct rationales from the polarity lexicon for every instance of positive and negative words in the lexicon that appear in the training corpus.

As in the OpinionFinder rationales, we extend the words found by the PolarityLexicon approach to sentence boundaries to incorporate potentially relevant contextual information. We retain as rationales only those sentences whose polarity coincides with the document-level polarity as determined via the voting scheme of Section 3.1.

3.3 Random Selection

Finally, we generate annotator rationales randomly, selecting 25% of the sentences from each document[4] and treating each as a separate rationale.

3.4 Comparison of Automatic vs. Human-annotated Rationales

Before evaluating the performance of the automatically generated rationales, we summarize in Table 1 the differences between automatic vs. human-generated rationales. All computations were performed on the same movie review dataset of Pang and Lee (2004) used in Zaidan et al. (2007). Note, that the Zaidan et al. (2007) annotation guidelines did not insist that annotators mark **all** rationales, only that some were marked for each document. Nevertheless, we report precision, recall, and F-score based on overlap with the human-annotated rationales of Zaidan et al. (2007), so as to demonstrate the degree to which the proposed approaches align with human intuition. Overlap measures were also employed by Zaidan et al. (2007).

As shown in Table 1, the annotator rationales found by OpinionFinder (F-score 49.5%) and the PolarityLexicon approach (F-score 52.6%) match the human rationales much better than those found by random selection (F-score 27.3%).

As expected, OpinionFinder's positive rationales match the human rationales at a significantly lower level (F-score 31.9%) than negative rationales (59.5%). This is due to the fact that OpinionFinder is trained on a dataset biased toward negative sentiment (see Section 3.1 - 3.2). In contrast, all other approaches show a balanced performance for positive and negative rationales vs. human rationales.

4 Experiments

For our contrastive learning experiments we use SVM^{light} (Joachims, 1999). We evaluate the usefulness of automatically generated rationales on

[1] Available at www.cs.pitt.edu/mpqa/opinionfinderrelease/.

[2] This conjecture is indirectly confirmed by the fact that human-annotated rationales are rarely a single word.

[3] It is worthwhile to note that OpinionFinder is trained on a newswire corpus whose prevailing sentiment is known to be negative (Wiebe et al., 2005). Furthermore, OpinionFinder is trained for a task (word-level sentiment classification) that is different from marking annotator rationales (sequence tagging or text segmentation).

[4] We chose the value of 25% to match the percentage of sentences per document, on average, that contain human-annotated rationales in our dataset (24.7%).

Method	% of sentences selected	Precision			Recall			F-Score		
		ALL	POS	NEG	ALL	POS	NEG	ALL	POS	NEG
OPINIONFINDER	22.8%	54.9	56.1	54.6	45.1	22.3	65.3	49.5	31.9	59.5
POLARITYLEXICON	38.7%	45.2	42.7	48.5	63.0	71.8	55.0	52.6	53.5	51.6
RANDOM	25.0%	28.9	26.0	31.8	25.9	24.9	26.7	27.3	25.5	29.0

Table 1: Comparison of Automatic vs. Human-annotated Rationales.

five different datasets. The first is the movie review data of Pang and Lee (2004), which was manually annotated with rationales by Zaidan et al. (2007)[5]; the remaining are four product review datasets from Blitzer et al. (2007).[6] Only the movie review dataset contains human annotator rationales. We replicate the same feature set and experimental set-up as in Zaidan et al. (2007) to facilitate comparison with their work.[7]

The contrastive learning method introduced in Zaidan et al. (2007) requires three parameters: (C, μ, $C_{contrast}$). To set the parameters, we use a grid search with step 0.1 for the range of values of each parameter around the point (1,1,1). In total, we try around 3000 different parameter triplets for each type of rationales.

4.1 Experiments with the Movie Review Data

We follow Zaidan et al. (2007) for the training/test data splits. The top half of Table 2 shows the performance of a system trained with **no annotator rationales** vs. two variations of human annotator rationales. HUMANR treats each rationale in the same way as Zaidan et al. (2007). HUMANR@SENTENCE extends the human annotator rationales to sentence boundaries, and then treats each such sentence as a separate rationale. As shown in Table 2, we get almost the same performance from these two variations (91.33% and 91.61%).[8] This result demonstrates that locking rationales to sentence boundaries was a reasonable

Method	Accuracy
NORATIONALES	88.56
HUMANR	91.61$^{\bullet}$
HUMANR@SENTENCE	91.33$^{\bullet\,\dagger}$
OPINIONFINDER	91.78$^{\bullet\,\dagger}$
POLARITYLEXICON	91.39$^{\bullet\,\dagger}$
RANDOM	90.00*
OPINIONFINDER+HUMANR@SENTENCE	92.50$^{\bullet\,\triangle}$

Table 2: Experimental results for the movie review data.

– The numbers marked with $^{\bullet}$ (or *) are statistically significantly better than NORATIONALES according to a paired t-test with $p < 0.001$ (or $p < 0.01$).
– The numbers marked with $^{\triangle}$ are statistically significantly better than HUMANR according to a paired t-test with $p < 0.01$.
– The numbers marked with † are ***not*** statistically significantly worse than HUMANR according to a paired t-test with $p > 0.1$.

choice.

Among the approaches that make use of only automatic rationales (bottom half of Table 2), the best is OPINIONFINDER, reaching 91.78% accuracy. This result is slightly better than results exploiting human rationales (91.33-91.61%), although the difference is not statistically significant. This result demonstrates that automatically generated rationales are just as good as human rationales in improving document-level sentiment classification. Similarly strong results are obtained from the POLARITYLEXICON as well.

Rather unexpectedly, RANDOM also achieves statistically significant improvement over NORATIONALES (90.0% vs. 88.56%). However, notice that the performance of RANDOM is statistically significantly lower than those based on human rationales (91.33-91.61%).

In our experiments so far, we observed that some of the automatic rationales are just as good as human rationales in improving the document-level sentiment classification. Could we perhaps achieve an even better result if we combine the automatic rationales with human

[5]Available at http://www.cs.jhu.edu/~ozaidan/rationales/.

[6]http://www.cs.jhu.edu/~mdredze/datasets/sentiment/.

[7]We use binary unigram features corresponding to the unstemmed words or punctuation marks with count greater or equal to 4 in the full 2000 documents, then we normalize the examples to the unit length. When computing the pseudo examples $\vec{x}_{ij} = \frac{\vec{x}_i - \vec{v}_{ij}}{\mu}$ we first compute $(\vec{x}_i - \vec{v}_{ij})$ using the binary representation. As a result, features (unigrams) that appeared in both vectors will be zeroed out in the resulting vector. We then normalize the resulting vector to a unit vector.

[8]The performance of HUMANR reported by Zaidan et al. (2007) is 92.2% which lies between the performance we get (91.61%) and the oracle accuracy we get if we knew the best parameters for the test set (92.67%).

rationales? The answer is yes! The accuracy of OPINIONFINDER+HUMANR@SENTENCE reaches 92.50%, which is statistically significantly better than HUMANR (91.61%). In other words, not only can our automatically generated rationales replace human rationales, but they can also improve upon human rationales when they are available.

4.2 Experiments with the Product Reviews

We next evaluate our approaches on datasets for which human annotator rationales do not exist. For this, we use some of the product review data from Blitzer et al. (2007): reviews for Books, DVDs, Videos and Kitchen appliances. Each dataset contains 1000 positive and 1000 negative reviews. The reviews, however, are substantially shorter than those in the movie review dataset: the average number of sentences in each review is 9.20/9.13/8.12/6.37 respectively vs. 30.86 for the movie reviews. We perform 10-fold cross-validation, where 8 folds are used for training, 1 fold for tuning parameters, and 1 fold for testing.

Table 3 shows the results. Rationale-based methods perform statistically significantly better than NORATIONALES for all but the Kitchen dataset. An interesting trend in product review datasets is that RANDOM rationales are just as good as other more sophisticated rationales. We suspect that this is because product reviews are generally shorter and more focused than the movie reviews, thereby any randomly selected sentence is likely to be a good rationale. Quantitatively, subjective sentences in the product reviews amount to 78% (McDonald et al., 2007), while subjective sentences in the movie review dataset are only about 25% (Mao and Lebanon, 2006).

4.3 Examples of Annotator Rationales

In this section, we examine an example to compare the automatically generated rationales (using OPINIONFINDER) with human annotator rationales for the movie review data. In the following positive document snippet, automatic rationales are underlined, while **human-annotated rationales** are in bold face.

...But a little niceness goes a long way these days, and **there's no denying the entertainment value** of that thing you do! **It's just about impossible to hate**. **It's an inoffensive, enjoyable piece** of nostalgia that is **sure to leave audiences smiling and humming, if not singing**, "that thing you do!" –quite possibly for days...

Method	Books	DVDs	Videos	Kitchen
NORATIONALES	80.20	80.95	82.40	87.40
OPINIONFINDER	81.65^{*}	82.35^{*}	84.00^{*}	88.40
POLARITYLEXICON	$82.75^{\bullet}$	$82.85^{\bullet}$	$84.55^{\bullet}$	87.90
RANDOM	$82.05^{\bullet}$	$82.10^{\bullet}$	$84.15^{\bullet}$	88.00

Table 3: Experimental results for subset of Product Review data

– The numbers marked with $^{\bullet}$ (or *) are statistically significantly better than NORATIONALES according to a paired t-test with $p < 0.05$ (or $p < 0.08$).

Notice that, although OPINIONFINDER misses some human rationales, it avoids the inclusion of "impossible to hate", which contains only negative terms and is likely to be confusing for the contrastive learner.

5 Related Work

In broad terms, constructing annotator rationales automatically and using them to formulate contrastive examples can be viewed as learning with prior knowledge (e.g., Schapire et al. (2002), Wu and Srihari (2004)). In our task, the prior knowledge corresponds to our operating assumptions given in Section 3. Those assumptions can be loosely connected to recognizing and exploiting discourse structure (e.g., Pang and Lee (2004), Taboada et al. (2009)). Our automatically generated rationales can be potentially combined with other learning frameworks that can exploit annotator rationales, such as Zaidan and Eisner (2008).

6 Conclusions

In this paper, we explore methods to automatically generate annotator rationales for document-level sentiment classification. Our study is motivated by the desire to retain the performance gains of rationale-enhanced learning models while eliminating the need for additional human annotation effort. By employing existing resources for sentiment analysis, we can create automatic annotator rationales that are as good as human annotator rationales in improving document-level sentiment classification.

Acknowledgments

We thank anonymous reviewers for their comments. This work was supported in part by National Science Foundation Grants BCS-0904822, BCS-0624277, IIS-0535099 and by the Department of Homeland Security under ONR Grant N0014-07-1-0152.

References

John Blitzer, Mark Dredze, and Fernando Pereira. 2007. Biographies, bollywood, boom-boxes and blenders: Domain adaptation for sentiment classification. In *Proceedings of the 45th Annual Meeting of the Association of Computational Linguistics*, pages 440–447, Prague, Czech Republic, June. Association for Computational Linguistics.

Thorsten Joachims. 1999. Making large-scale support vector machine learning practical. pages 169–184.

Yi Mao and Guy Lebanon. 2006. Sequential models for sentiment prediction. In *Proceedings of the ICML Workshop: Learning in Structured Output Spaces Open Problems in Statistical Relational Learning Statistical Network Analysis: Models, Issues and New Directions*.

Ryan McDonald, Kerry Hannan, Tyler Neylon, Mike Wells, and Jeff Reynar. 2007. Structured models for fine-to-coarse sentiment analysis. In *Proceedings of the 45th Annual Meeting of the Association of Computational Linguistics*, pages 432–439, Prague, Czech Republic, June. Association for Computational Linguistics.

Bo Pang and Lillian Lee. 2004. A sentimental education: sentiment analysis using subjectivity summarization based on minimum cuts. In *ACL '04: Proceedings of the 42nd Annual Meeting on Association for Computational Linguistics*, page 271, Morristown, NJ, USA. Association for Computational Linguistics.

Bo Pang and Lillian Lee. 2008. Opinion mining and sentiment analysis. *Found. Trends Inf. Retr.*, 2(1-2):1–135.

Bo Pang, Lillian Lee, and Shivakumar Vaithyanathan. 2002. Thumbs up?: sentiment classification using machine learning techniques. In *EMNLP '02: Proceedings of the ACL-02 conference on Empirical methods in natural language processing*, pages 79–86, Morristown, NJ, USA. Association for Computational Linguistics.

Robert E. Schapire, Marie Rochery, Mazin G. Rahim, and Narendra Gupta. 2002. Incorporating prior knowledge into boosting. In *ICML '02: Proceedings of the Nineteenth International Conference on Machine Learning*, pages 538–545, San Francisco, CA, USA. Morgan Kaufmann Publishers Inc.

Maite Taboada, Julian Brooke, and Manfred Stede. 2009. Genre-based paragraph classification for sentiment analysis. In *Proceedings of the SIGDIAL 2009 Conference*, pages 62–70, London, UK, September. Association for Computational Linguistics.

Janyce Wiebe, Theresa Wilson, and Claire Cardie. 2005. Annotating expressions of opinions and emotions in language. *Language Resources and Evaluation*, 1(2):0.

Theresa Wilson, Paul Hoffmann, Swapna Somasundaran, Jason Kessler, Janyce Wiebe, Yejin Choi, Claire Cardie, Ellen Riloff, and Siddharth Patwardhan. 2005a. Opinionfinder: a system for subjectivity analysis. In *Proceedings of HLT/EMNLP on Interactive Demonstrations*, pages 34–35, Morristown, NJ, USA. Association for Computational Linguistics.

Theresa Wilson, Janyce Wiebe, and Paul Hoffmann. 2005b. Recognizing contextual polarity in phrase-level sentiment analysis. In *HLT-EMNLP '05: Proceedings of the conference on Human Language Technology and Empirical Methods in Natural Language Processing*, pages 347–354, Morristown, NJ, USA. Association for Computational Linguistics.

Xiaoyun Wu and Rohini Srihari. 2004. Incorporating prior knowledge with weighted margin support vector machines. In *KDD '04: Proceedings of the tenth ACM SIGKDD international conference on Knowledge discovery and data mining*, pages 326–333, New York, NY, USA. ACM.

Omar F. Zaidan and Jason Eisner. 2008. Modeling annotators: a generative approach to learning from annotator rationales. In *EMNLP '08: Proceedings of the Conference on Empirical Methods in Natural Language Processing*, pages 31–40, Morristown, NJ, USA. Association for Computational Linguistics.

Omar F. Zaidan, Jason Eisner, and Christine Piatko. 2007. Using "annotator rationales" to improve machine learning for text categorization. In *NAACL HLT 2007; Proceedings of the Main Conference*, pages 260–267, April.

Simultaneous Tokenization and Part-of-Speech Tagging for Arabic without a Morphological Analyzer

Seth Kulick
Linguistic Data Consortium
University of Pennsylvania
skulick@seas.upenn.edu

Abstract

We describe an approach to simultaneous tokenization and part-of-speech tagging that is based on separating the closed and open-class items, and focusing on the likelihood of the possible stems of the open-class words. By encoding some basic linguistic information, the machine learning task is simplified, while achieving state-of-the-art tokenization results and competitive POS results, although with a reduced tag set and some evaluation difficulties.

1 Introduction

Research on the problem of morphological disambiguation of Arabic has noted that techniques developed for lexical disambiguation in English do not easily transfer over, since the affixation present in Arabic creates a very different tag set than for English, in terms of the number and complexity of tags. In additional to inflectional morphology, the POS tags encode more complex tokenization sequences, such as *preposition* + *noun* or *noun* + *possessive pronoun*.

One approach taken to this problem is to use a morphological analyzer such as BAMA-v2.0 (Buckwalter, 2004) or SAMA-v3.1 (Maamouri et al., 2009c)[1], which generates a list of all possible morphological analyses for a given token. Machine learning approaches can model separate aspects of a solution (e.g., "has a pronominal clitic") and then combine them to select the most appropriate solution from among this list. A benefit of this approach is that by picking a single solution from the morphological analyzer, the part-of-speech and tokenization comes as a unit (Habash and Rambow, 2005; Roth et al., 2008).

In contrast, other approaches have used a pipelined approach, with separate models to first do tokenization and then part-of-speech tagging (Diab et al., 2007; Diab, 2009). While these approaches have somewhat lower performance than the joint approach, they have the advantage that they do not rely on the presence of a full-blown morphological analyzer, which may not always be available or appropriate as the data shifts to different genres or Arabic dialects.

In this work we present a novel approach to this problem that allows us to do simultaneous tokenization and core part-of-speech tagging with a simple classifier, without using a full-blown morphological analyzer. We distinguish between closed-class and open-class categories of words, and encode regular expressions that express the morphological patterns for the former, and simple regular expressions for the latter that provide only the generic templates for affixation. We find that a simple baseline for the closed-class words already works very well, and for the open-class words we classify only the possible stems for all such expressions. This is however sufficient for tokenization and core POS tagging, since the stem identifies the appropriate regular expression, which then in turn makes explicit, simultaneously, the tokenization and part-of-speech information.

2 Background

The Arabic Treebank (ATB) contains a full morphological analysis of each "source token", a whitespace/punctuation-delimited string from the source text. The SAMA analysis includes four fields, as shown in the first part of Table 1.[2] `TEXT` is the actual source token text, to be analyzed. `VOC` is the vocalized form, including diacritics. Each `VOC` segment has associated with it a `POS` tag and

[1] SAMA-v3.1 is an updated version of BAMA, with many significant differences in analysis.

[2] This is the analysis for one particular instance of *ktbh*. The same source token may receive another analysis elsewhere in the treebank.

Proceedings of the ACL 2010 Conference Short Papers, pages 342–347,
Uppsala, Sweden, 11-16 July 2010.

ATB analysis for one source token:

TEXT:	ktbh		
VOC:	kutub	u	hu
POS:	NOUN	CASE_NOM	POSS_PRON_3MS
GLOSS:	books	[def.nom.]	its/his

Results in two ATB tree tokens:

TEXT:	ktb	h
VOC:	kutub+u	hu
POS:	NOUN+CASE_NOM	POSS_PRON_3MS

Current work recovers:

TEXT:	ktb	h
POS:	NOA	POSS_PRON

Table 1: Example analysis of one source token

NOUN, ADJ, NOUN.VN, ADJ.VN, NOUN_NUM, ADJ_NUM, NOUN_QUANT, ADJ_COMP, ABBREV	NOA (Noun or Adjective)
IV, IV_PASS	IV
PV, PV_PASS	PV
IVSUFF_DO, PVSUFF_DO	OBJ_PRON

Table 2: Collapsing of ATB core tags into reduced core tags

NOA	173938	PART	288
PREP	49894	RESTRIC_PART	237
PUNC	41398	DET	215
NOUN_PROP	29423	RC_PART	192
CONJ	28257	FOCUS_PART	191
PV	16669	TYPO	188
IV	15361	INTERROG_PART	187
POSS_PRON	9830	INTERROG_ADV	169
SUB_CONJ	8200	INTERROG_PRON	112
PRON	6995	CV	106
REL_PRON	5647	VOC_PART	74
DEM	3673	VERB	62
OBJ_PRON	2812	JUS_PART	56
NEG_PART	2649	FOREIGN	46
PSEUDO_VERB	1505	DIALECT	41
FUT_PART	1099	INTERJ	37
ADV	1058	EMPHATIC_PART	19
VERB_PART	824	CVSUFF_DO	15
REL_ADV	414	GRAMMAR_PROB	4
CONNEC_PART	405	LATIN	1

Table 3: The 40 "reduced core tags", and their frequencies in ATB3-v3.2. The total count is 402291, which is the number of tree tokens in ATB3-v3.2.

GLOSS. While "tokenization" can be done in different ways on top of this analysis, the ATB splits the VOC/POS/GLOSS segments up based on the POS tags to form the "tree tokens" necessary for treebanking. As shown in the second part of Table 1, the first two segments remain together as one tree token, and the pronoun is separated as a separate tree token. In addition, the input TEXT is separated among the two tree tokens.[3]

Each tree token's POS tag therefore consists of what can be considered an "ATB core tag", together with inflectional material (case, gender, number). For example, in Table 1, the "core tag" of the first tree token is NOUN. In this work, we aim to recover the separation of a source token TEXT into the corresponding separate tree token TEXTs, together with a "reduced core tag" for each tree token. By "reduced core tag", we mean an ATB core tag that has been reduced in two ways:

(1) All inflectional material [infl] is stripped off six ATB core tags: PRON[infl], POSS_PRON[infl], DEM[infl], [IV|PV|CV]SUFF_DO[infl]

(2) Collapsing of some ATB core tags, as listed in Table 2.

These two steps result in a total of 40 reduced core tags, and each tree token has exactly one such reduced core tag. We work with the ATB3-v3.2 release of the ATB (Maamouri et al., 2009b), which has 339710 source tokens and 402291 tree tokens, where the latter are derived from the former as discussed above. Table 3 lists the 40 reduced tags we use, and their frequency among the ATB3-v3.2 tree tokens.

3 Description of Approach

Given a source token, we wish to recover (1) the tree tokens (which amounts to recovering the ATB tokenization), and (2) the reduced core POS tag for each tree token. For example, in Table 1, given the input source token TEXT *ktbh*, we wish to recover the tree tokens *ktb*/NOA and *h*/POSS_PRON.

As mentioned in the introduction, we use regular expressions that encode all the tokenization and POS tag possibilities. Each "group" (substring unit) in a regular expression (regex) is assigned an internal name, and a list is maintained of the possible reduced core POS tags that can occur with that regex group. It is possible, and indeed usually the case for groups representing affixes, that more than one such POS tag is possible. However, it is crucial for our approach that while some given source token TEXT may match many regular expressions (regexes), when the POS tag is also taken into account, there can be only one match among all the (open or closed-class) regexes. We say a source token "pos-matches" a regex if the TEXT matches and POS tags match, and "text-matches" if the TEXT matches the regex regardless of the POS. During training, the pos-matching

[3]See (Kulick et al., 2010) for a detailed discussion of how this splitting is done and how the tree token TEXT field (called INPUT STRING in the ATB releases) is created.

(REGEX #1) [w|f]lm
w: [PART, CONJ, SUB_CONJ, PREP]
f: [CONJ, SUB_CONJ, CONNEC_PART, RC_PART]
lm: [NEG_PART]
(REGEX #2) [w|f]lm
w: and f: same as above
lm: [REL_ADV,INTERROG_ADV]

Figure 1: Two sample closed-class regexes

regex for a source token TEXT is stored as the gold solution for closed-class patterns, or used to create the gold label for the open-class classifier.

We consider the open-class tags in Table 3 to be: NOUN_PROP, NOA, IV, CV, PV, VERB. A source token is considered to have an open-class solution if any of the tree tokens in that solution have an open-class tag. For example, *ktbh* in Table 1 has an open-class solution because one of the tree tokens has an open-class tag (NOA), even though the other is closed-class (POSS_PRON).

We encode the possible solutions for closed-class source tokens using the lists in the ATB morphological guidelines (Maamouri et al., 2009a). For example, Figure 1 shows two of the closed-class regexes. The text *wlm* can text-match either REGEX #1 or #2, but when the POS tag for *lm* is taken into account, only one can pos-match. We return to the closed-class regexes in Section 4.

We also encode regular expression for the open-class source tokens, but these are simply generic templates expressing the usual affix possibilities, such as:
`[wf] [blk] stem_NOA poss_pronoun`
where there is no list of possible strings for `stem_NOA`, but which instead can match anything. While all parts except for the stem are optional, we do not make such parts optional in a single expression. Instead, we multiple out the possibilities into different expressions with different parts (e.g., [wf]) being obligatory). The reason for this is that we give different names to the stem in each case, and this is the basis of the features for the classifier. As with the closed-class regexes, we associate a list of possible POS tags for each named group within a regular expression. Here the `stem_NOA` group can only have the tag NOA.

We create features for a classifier for the open-class words as follows. Each word is run through all of the open-class regular expressions. For each expression that text-matches, we make a feature which is the name of the stem part of the regular expression, along with the characters that match the stem. The stem name encodes whether there is a prefix or suffix, but does not include a POS tag. However, the source token pos-matches exactly one of the regular expressions, and the pos tag for the stem is appended to the named stem for that expression to form the gold label for training and the target for testing.

For example, Table 4 lists the matching regular expression for three words. The first, *yjry*, text-matches the generic regular expressions for *any string*/NOA, *any string*/IV, etc. These are summarized in one listing, *yjry*/all. The name of the stem for all these expressions is the same, just *stem*, and so they all give rise to the same feature, `stem=yjry`. It also matches the expression for a NOA with a possessive pronoun[4], and in this case the stem name in the regular expression is `stem_spp` (which stands for "stem with a possessive pronoun suffix"), and this gives rise to the feature `stem_spp=yjr`. Similarly, for *wAfAdt* the stem of the second expression has the name `p_stem`, for a prefix. The third example shows the different stem names that occur when there are both prefix and suffix possibilities. For each example, there is exactly one regex that not only text-matches, but also pos-matches. The combination of the stem name in these cases together with the gold tag forms the gold label, as indicated in column 3.

Therefore, for each source token TEXT, the features include the ones arising from the named stems of all the regexes that text-match that TEXT, as shown in column 4, and the gold label is the appropriate stem name together with the POS tag, as shown in column 3. We also include some typical features for each stem, such as first and last two letters of each stem, etc. For example, `wAfAdt` would also have the features `stem_fl=w`, `p_stem_fl=A`, indicating that the first letter of `stem` is `w` and the first letter of `p_stem` is `A`. We also extract a list of proper nouns from SAMA-v3.1 as a temporary proxy for a named entity list, and include a feature for a stem if that stem is in the list (`stem_in_list`, `p_stem_in_list`, etc.)

We do not model separate classifiers for prefix possibilities. There is a dependency between the

[4]The regex listed is slightly simplified. It actually contains a reference to the list of all possessive pronouns, not just *y*.

source TEXT	text-matching regular expressions	gold label	feature
yjry	yjry/all (*happens*)	stem:IV	stem=yjry
	yjr/NOA+y/POSS_PRON		stem_spp=yjr
wAfAdt	wAfAdt/all		stem=wAfAdt
	w + AfAdt/all (*and+reported*)	p_stem:PV	p_stem=AfAdt
lAstyDAHhm	lAstyDAHhm/all		stem=lAstyDAHhm
	l/PREP + AstyDAHhm/NOA		p_stem=AstyDAHhm
	l/PREP + AstyDAH/NOA + hm/POSS_PRON *for + request for clarification + their*	p_stem_spp:NOA	p_stem_spp=AstyDAH
	lAstyDAH/NOA + hm/POSS_PRON		stem_spp=lAstyDAH
	lAstyDAH/IV,PV,CV + hm/OBJ_PRON		stem_svop=lAstyDAH
	l/PREP,JUS_PART + AstyDAH/IV,PV,CV + hm/OBJ_PRON		p_stem_svop=AstyDAH

Table 4: Example features and gold labels for three words. Each text-matching regex gives rise to one feature shown in column 4, based on the stem of that regular expression. A `p_` before a stem means that it has a prefix, `_spp` after means that it has a possessive pronouns suffix, and `_svop` means that it has a (verbal) object pronoun suffix. "all" in the matching regular expression is shorthand for text-matching all the corresponding regular expressions with NOA, IV, etc. For each word, exactly one regex also pos-matches, which results in the gold label, shown in column 3.

possibility of a prefix and the likelihood of the remaining stem, and so we focus on the likelihood of the possible stems, where the open-class regexes enumerate the possible stems. A gold label together with the source token TEXT maps back to a single regex, and so for a given label, the TEXT is parsed by that regular expression, resulting in a tokenization along with list of possible POS tags for each affix group in the regex.[5]

During training and testing, we run each word through all the open and closed regexes. Text-matches for an open-class regex give rise to features as just described. Also, if the word matches any closed-class regex, it receives the feature `MATCHES_CLOSED`. During training, if the correct match for the word is one of the closed-class expressions, then the gold label is `CLOSED`. The classifier is used only to get solutions for the open-class words, although we wish to give the classifier all the words for the sentence. The cross-product of the stem name and (open-class) reduced core POS tags, plus the `CLOSED` tag, yields 24 labels for a CRF classifier in Mallet (McCallum, 2002).

4 Experiments and Evaluation

We worked with ATB3-v3.2, following the training/devtest split in (Roth et al., 2008) on a previous release of the same data. We keep a listing (List #1) of all (source token TEXT, solution) pairs seen during training. For an open-class solution, "solution" is the gold label as described in Section 3. For a closed-class solution, "solution" is the name of the single pos-matching regex. In addition, for every regex seen during training that pos-matches some source token TEXT, we keep a listing (List #2) of all ((regex-group-name, text), POS-tag) tuples. We use the information in List #1 to choose a solution for all words seen in training in the Baseline and Run 2 below, and in Run 3, for words text-matching a closed-class expression. We use List #2 to disambiguate all remaining cases of POS ambiguity, wherever a solution comes from.

For example, if *wlm* is seen during testing, List #1 will be consulted to find the most common solution (REGEX #1 or #2), and in either case, List #2 will be consulted to determine the most frequent tag for *w* as a prefix. While there is certainly room for improvement here, this works quite well since the tags for the affixes do not vary much.

We score the solution for a source token instance as correct for tokenization if it exactly matches the TEXT split for the tree tokens derived from that source token instance in the ATB. It is correct for POS if correct for tokenization and if each tree token has the same POS tag as the reduced core tag for that tree token in the ATB.

For a simple baseline, if a source token TEXT is in List #1 then we simply use the most frequent stored solution. Otherwise we run the TEXT through all the regexes. If it text-matches any closed-class expression, we pick a random choice from among those regexes and otherwise from the open-class regexes that it text-matches. Any POS ambiguities for a regex group are disambiguated

[5] In Section 4 we discuss how these are narrowed down to one POS tag.

Solution	Baseline			Run 2			Run 3		
Origin	# tokens	Tok	POS	# tokens	Tok	POS	# tokens	Tok	POS
All	51664	96.0%	87.4%	51664	**99.4%**	**95.1%**	51664	99.3%	95.1%
Stored	46072	99.8%	96.6%	46072	99.8%	96.6%	16145	99.6%	96.4%
Open	5565	64.6%	11.6%	10	10.0%	0.0%	11	54.5%	0.0%
Closed	27	81.5%	59.3%	27	81.5%	63.0%	27	81.5%	63.0%
Mallet	0			5555	96.0%	83.8%	35481	99.1%	94.5%

Table 5: Results for Baseline and two runs. Origin "stored" means that the appropriate regex came from the list stored during training. Origins "open" and "closed" are random choices from the open or closed regexes for the source token. "Mallet" means that it comes from the label output by the CRF classifier.

using List #2, as discussed above. The results are shown in Table 5. The score is very high for the words seen during training, but much lower for open-class words that were not. As expected, almost all (except 27) instances of closed-class words were seen during training.

For run 2, we continue to use the stored solution if the token was seen in training. If not, then if the TEXT matches one or more closed-class regexes, we randomly choose one. Otherwise, if the CRF classifier has produced an open-class match for that token, we use that (and otherwise, in only 10 cases, use a random open-class match). There is a significant improvement in the score for the open-class items, and therefore in the overall results.

For run 3, we put more of a burden on the classifier. If a word matches any closed-class expression, we either use the most frequent occurence during training (if it was seen), or use a random maching closed-class expression (if not). If the word doesn't match a closed-class expression, we use the mallet result. The mallet score goes up, almost certainly because the score is now including results on words that were seen during training. The overall POS result for run 3 is slightly less than run 2. (95.099% compared to 95.147%).

It is not a simple matter to compare results with previous work, due to differing evaluation techniques, data sets, and POS tag sets. With different data sets and training sizes, Habash and Rambow (2005) report 99.3% word accuracy on tokenization, and Diab et al. (2007) reports a score of 99.1%. Habash and Rambow (2005) reported 97.6% on the LDC-supplied reduced tag set, and Diab et al. (2007) reported 96.6%. The LDC-supplied tag set used is smaller than the one in this paper (24 tags), but does distinguish between NOUN and ADJ. However, both (Habash and Rambow, 2005; Diab et al., 2007) assume gold tokenization for evaluation of POS results, which we do not. The "MorphPOS" task in (Roth et al., 2008), 96.4%, is somewhat similar to ours in that it scores on a "core tag", but unlike for us there is only one such tag for a source token (easier) but it distinguishes between NOUN and ADJ (harder).

We would like to do a direct comparison by simply runing the above systems on the exact same data and evaluating them the same way. However, this unfortunately has to wait until new versions are released that work with the current version of the SAMA morphological analyzer and ATB.

5 Future Work

Obvious future work starts with the need to include determiner information in the POS tags and the important NOUN/ADJ distinction. There are various possibilities for recovering this information, such as (1) using a different module combining NOUN/ADJ disambiguation together with NP chunking, or (2) simply including NOUN/ADJ in the current classifier instead of NOA. We will be implementing and comparing these alternatives. We also will be using this system as a preprocessing step for a parser, as part of a complete Arabic NLP pipeline.

Acknowledgements

We thank Ann Bies, David Graff, Nizar Habash, Mohamed Maamouri, and Mitch Marcus for helpful discussions and comments. This work was supported by the Defense Advanced Research Projects Agency, GALE Program Grant No. HR0011-06-1-0003 and by the GALE program, DARPA/CMO Contract No. HR0011-06-C-0022. The content of this paper does not necessarily reflect the position or the policy of the Government, and no official endorsement should be inferred.

References

Tim Buckwalter. 2004. Buckwalter Arabic morphological analyzer version 2.0. Linguistic Data Consortium LDC2004L02.

Mona Diab, Kadri Hacioglu, and Daniel Jurafsky. 2007. Automatic processing of Modern Standard Arabic text. In Abdelhadi Soudi, Antal van den Bosch, and Gunter Neumann, editors, *Arabic Computational Morphology*, pages 159–179. Springer.

Mona Diab. 2009. Second generation tools (AMIRA 2.0): Fast and robust tokenization, pos tagging, and base phrase chunking. In *Proceedings of 2nd International Conference on Arabic Language Resources and Tools (MEDAR)*, Cairo, Egypt, April.

Nizar Habash and Owen Rambow. 2005. Arabic tokenization, part-of-speech tagging and morphological disambiguation in one fell swoop. In *Proceedings of the 43rd Annual Meeting of the Association for Computational Linguistics (ACL'05)*, pages 573–580, Ann Arbor, Michigan, June. Association for Computational Linguistics.

Seth Kulick, Ann Bies, and Mohamed Maamouri. 2010. Consistent and flexible integration of morphological annotation in the Arabic Treebank. In *Language Resources and Evaluation (LREC)*.

Mohamed Maamouri, Ann Bies, Sondos Krouna, Fatma Gaddeche, Basma Bouziri, Seth Kulick, Wigdane Mekki, and Tim Buckwalter. 2009a. Arabic Treebank Morphological and Syntactic guidelines, July. http://projects.ldc.upenn.edu/ArabicTreebank.

Mohamed Maamouri, Ann Bies, Seth Kulick, Sondos Krouna, Fatma Gaddeche, and Wajdi Zaghouani. 2009b. Arabic treebank part 3 - v3.2. Linguistic Data Consortium LDC2010T08, April.

Mohammed Maamouri, Basma Bouziri, Sondos Krouna, David Graff, Seth Kulick, and Tim Buckwalter. 2009c. Standard Arabic morphological analyzer (SAMA) version 3.1. Linguistic Data Consortium LDC2009E73.

Andrew McCallum. 2002. Mallet: A machine learning for language toolkit. http://mallet.cs.umass.edu.

Ryan Roth, Owen Rambow, Nizar Habash, Mona Diab, and Cynthia Rudin. 2008. Arabic morphological tagging, diacritization, and lemmatization using lexeme models and feature ranking. In *Proceedings of ACL-08: HLT, Short Papers*, pages 117–120, Columbus, Ohio, June. Association for Computational Linguistics.

Hierarchical A* Parsing with Bridge Outside Scores

Adam Pauls and **Dan Klein**
Computer Science Division
University of California at Berkeley
{adpauls,klein}@cs.berkeley.edu

Abstract

Hierarchical A* (HA*) uses of a hierarchy of coarse grammars to speed up parsing without sacrificing optimality. HA* prioritizes search in refined grammars using Viterbi outside costs computed in coarser grammars. We present Bridge Hierarchical A* (BHA*), a modified Hierarchial A* algorithm which computes a novel outside cost called a *bridge* outside cost. These bridge costs mix finer outside scores with coarser inside scores, and thus constitute tighter heuristics than entirely coarse scores. We show that BHA* substantially outperforms HA* when the hierarchy contains only very coarse grammars, while achieving comparable performance on more refined hierarchies.

1 Introduction

The Hierarchical A* (HA*) algorithm of Felzenszwalb and McAllester (2007) allows the use of a hierarchy of coarse grammars to speed up parsing without sacrificing optimality. Pauls and Klein (2009) showed that a hierarchy of coarse grammars outperforms standard A* parsing for a range of grammars. HA* operates by computing Viterbi inside and outside scores in an agenda-based way, using outside scores computed under coarse grammars as heuristics which guide the search in finer grammars. The outside scores computed by HA* are auxiliary quantities, useful only because they form admissible heuristics for search in finer grammars.

We show that a modification of the HA* algorithm can compute modified *bridge* outside scores which are tighter bounds on the true outside costs in finer grammars. These bridge outside scores mix inside and outside costs from finer grammars with inside costs from coarser grammars. Because the bridge costs represent tighter estimates of the true outside costs, we expect them to reduce the work of computing inside costs in finer grammars. At the same time, because bridge costs mix computation from coarser and finer levels of the hierarchy, they are more expensive to compute than purely coarse outside costs. Whether the work saved by using tighter estimates outweighs the extra computation needed to compute them is an empirical question.

In this paper, we show that the use of bridge outside costs substantially outperforms the HA* algorithm when the coarsest levels of the hierarchy are very loose approximations of the target grammar. For hierarchies with tighter estimates, we show that BHA* obtains comparable performance to HA*. In other words, BHA* is more robust to poorly constructed hierarchies.

2 Previous Work

In this section, we introduce notation and review HA*. Our presentation closely follows Pauls and Klein (2009), and we refer the reader to that work for a more detailed presentation.

2.1 Notation

Assume we have input sentence $s_0 \dots s_{n-1}$ of length n, and a hierarchy of m weighted context-free grammars $\mathcal{G}_1 \dots \mathcal{G}_m$. We call the most refined grammar $\mathcal{G}_m$ the *target* grammar, and all other (coarser) grammars *auxiliary* grammars. Each grammar $\mathcal{G}_t$ has a set of symbols denoted with capital letters and a subscript indicating the level in the hierarchy, including a distinguished goal (root) symbol G_t. Without loss of generality, we assume Chomsky normal form, so each non-terminal rule r in $\mathcal{G}_t$ has the form $r = A_t \rightarrow B_t\ C_t$ with weight w_r.

Edges are labeled spans $e = (A_t, i, j)$. The weight of a derivation is the sum of rule weights in the derivation. The weight of the best (minimum) inside derivation for an edge e is called the Viterbi inside score $\beta(e)$, and the weight of the

Proceedings of the ACL 2010 Conference Short Papers, pages 348–352,
Uppsala, Sweden, 11-16 July 2010.

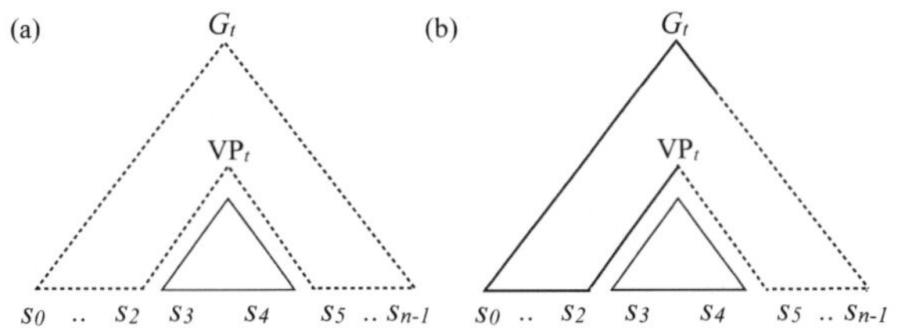

Figure 1: Representations of the different types of items used in parsing and how they depend on each other. (a) In HA*, the inside item $I(\text{VP}_t, 3, 5)$ relies on the coarse outside item $O(\pi_t(\text{VP}_t), 3, 5)$ for outside estimates. (b) In BHA*, the same inside item relies on the bridge outside item $\tilde{O}(\text{VP}_t, 3, 5)$, which mixes coarse and refined outside costs. The coarseness of an item is indicated with dotted lines.

best derivation of $G \rightarrow s_0 \ldots s_{i-1}\ A_t\ s_j \ldots s_{n-1}$ is called the Viterbi outside score $\alpha(e)$. The goal of a 1-best parsing algorithm is to compute the Viterbi inside score of the edge $(G_m, 0, n)$; the actual best parse can be reconstructed from backpointers in the standard way.

We assume that each auxiliary grammar $\mathcal{G}_{t-1}$ forms a *relaxed projection* of $\mathcal{G}_t$. A grammar $\mathcal{G}_{t-1}$ is a *projection* of $\mathcal{G}_t$ if there exists some many-to-one onto function π_t which maps each symbol in $\mathcal{G}_t$ to a symbol in $\mathcal{G}_{t-1}$; hereafter, we will use A'_t to represent $\pi_t(A_t)$. A projection is *relaxed* if, for every rule $r = A_t \rightarrow B_t\ C_t$ with weight w_r the projection $r' = A'_t \rightarrow B'_t\ C'_t$ has weight $w_{r'} \leq w_r$ in $\mathcal{G}_{t-1}$. In other words, the weight of r' is a lower bound on the weight of all rules r in $\mathcal{G}_t$ which project to r'.

2.2 Deduction Rules

HA* and our modification BHA* can be formulated in terms of prioritized weighted deduction rules (Shieber et al., 1995; Felzenszwalb and McAllester, 2007). A *prioritized weighted deduction rule* has the form

$$\phi_1 : w_1, \ldots, \phi_n : w_n \xrightarrow{p(w_1, \ldots, w_n)} \phi_0 : g(w_1, \ldots, w_n)$$

where $\phi_1, \ldots, \phi_n$ are the *antecedent items* of the deduction rule and ϕ_0 is the *conclusion item*. A deduction rule states that, given the antecedents $\phi_1, \ldots, \phi_n$ with weights $w_1, \ldots, w_n$, the conclusion ϕ_0 can be formed with weight $g(w_1, \ldots, w_n)$ and priority $p(w_1, \ldots, w_n)$.

These deduction rules are "executed" within a generic agenda-driven algorithm, which constructs items in a prioritized fashion. The algorithm maintains an *agenda* (a priority queue of items), as well as a *chart* of items already processed. The fundamental operation of the algorithm is to pop the highest priority item ϕ from the agenda, put it into the chart with its current weight, and form using deduction rules any items which can be built by combining ϕ with items already in the chart. If new or improved, resulting items are put on the agenda with priority given by $p(\cdot)$. Because all antecedents must be constructed before a deduction rule is executed, we sometimes refer to particular conclusion item as "waiting" on an other item(s) before it can be built.

2.3 HA*

HA* can be formulated in terms of two types of items. *Inside* items $I(A_t, i, j)$ represent possible derivations of the edge (A_t, i, j), while *outside* items $O(A_t, i, j)$ represent derivations of $G \rightarrow s_1 \ldots s_{i-1}\ A_t\ s_j \ldots s_n$ rooted at $(G_t, 0, n)$. See Figure 1(a) for a graphical depiction of these edges. Inside items are used to compute Viterbi inside scores under grammar $\mathcal{G}_t$, while outside items are used to compute Viterbi outside scores.

The deduction rules which construct inside and outside items are given in Table 1. The IN deduction rule combines two inside items over smaller spans with a grammar rule to form an inside item over larger spans. The weight of the resulting item is the sum of the weights of the smaller inside items and the grammar rule. However, the IN rule also requires that an outside score in the coarse grammar[1] be computed before an inside item is built. Once constructed, this coarse outside score is added to the weight of the conclusion item to form the priority of the resulting item. In other words, the coarse outside score computed by the algorithm plays the same role as a heuristic in standard A* parsing (Klein and Manning, 2003).

Outside scores are computed by the OUT-L and OUT-R deduction rules. These rules combine an outside item over a large span and inside items over smaller spans to form outside items over smaller spans. Unlike the IN deduction, the OUT deductions only involve items from the same level of the hierarchy. That is, whereas inside scores wait on coarse outside scores to be constructed, outside scores wait on inside scores at the same level in the hierarchy.

Conceptually, these deduction rules operate by

[1]For the coarsest grammar $\mathcal{G}_1$, the IN rule builds rules using 0 as an outside score.

HA*

IN:	$I(B_t, i, l) : w_1$	$I(C_t, l, j) : w_2$	$\underline{O(A'_t, i, j) : w_3}$	$\xrightarrow{w_1+w_2+w_r+\underline{w_3}}$	$I(A_t, i, j)$	:	$w_1 + w_2 + w_r$
OUT-L:	$O(A_t, i, j) : w_1$	$I(B_t, i, l) : w_2$	$I(C_t, l, j) : w_3$	$\xrightarrow{w_1+w_3+w_r+w_2}$	$O(B_t, i, l)$	:	$w_1 + w_3 + w_r$
OUT-R:	$O(A_t, i, j) : w_1$	$I(B_t, i, l) : w_2$	$I(C_t, l, j) : w_3$	$\xrightarrow{w_1+w_2+w_r+w_3}$	$O(C_t, l, j)$	:	$w_1 + w_2 + w_r$

Table 1: HA* deduction rules. Red underline indicates items constructed under the previous grammar in the hierarchy.

BHA*

B-IN:	$I(B_t, i, l) : w_1$	$I(C_t, l, j) : w_2$	$\tilde{O}(A_t, i, j) : w_3$	$\xrightarrow{w_1+w_2+w_r+w_3}$	$I(A_t, i, j)$	:	$w_1 + w_2 + w_r$
B-OUT-L:	$\tilde{O}(A_t, i, j) : w_1$	$\underline{I(B'_t, i, l) : w_2}$	$\underline{I(C'_t, l, j) : w_3}$	$\xrightarrow{w_1+w_r+\underline{w_2+w_3}}$	$\tilde{O}(B_t, i, l)$	:	$w_1 + w_r + \underline{w_3}$
B-OUT-R:	$\tilde{O}(A_t, i, j) : w_1$	$I(B_t, i, l) : w_2$	$\underline{I(C'_t, l, j) : w_3}$	$\xrightarrow{w_1+w_2+w_r+\underline{w_3}}$	$\tilde{O}(C_t, l, j)$	:	$w_1 + w_2 + w_r$

Table 2: BHA* deduction rules. Red underline indicates items constructed under the previous grammar in the hierarchy.

first computing inside scores bottom-up in the coarsest grammar, then outside scores top-down in the same grammar, then inside scores in the next finest grammar, and so on. However, the crucial aspect of HA* is that items from all levels of the hierarchy compete on the same queue, interleaving the computation of inside and outside scores at all levels. The HA* deduction rules come with three important guarantees. The first is a *monotonicity* guarantee: each item is popped off the agenda in order of its *intrinsic priority* $\hat{p}(\cdot)$. For inside items $I(e)$ over edge e, this priority $\hat{p}(I(e)) = \beta(e) + \alpha(e')$ where e' is the projection of e. For outside items $O(\cdot)$ over edge e, this priority is $\hat{p}(O(e)) = \beta(e) + \alpha(e)$.

The second is a *correctness* guarantee: when an inside/outside item is popped of the agenda, its weight is its true Viterbi inside/outside cost. Taken together, these two imply an *efficiency* guarantee, which states that only items x whose intrinsic priority $\hat{p}(x)$ is less than or equal to the Viterbi inside score of the goal are removed from the agenda.

2.4 HA* with Bridge Costs

The outside scores computed by HA* are useful for prioritizing computation in more refined grammars. The key property of these scores is that they form consistent and admissible heuristic costs for more refined grammars, but coarse outside costs are not the only quantity which satisfy this requirement. As an alternative, we propose a novel "bridge" outside cost $\tilde{\alpha}(e)$. Intuitively, this cost represents the cost of the best derivation where rules "above" and "left" of an edge e come from $\mathcal{G}_t$, and rules "below" and "right" of the e come from $\mathcal{G}_{t-1}$; see Figure 2 for a graphical depiction. More formally, let the *spine* of an edge $e = (A_t, i, j)$ for some derivation d be the sequence of rules between e and the root edge $(G_t, 0, n)$. A *bridge outside derivation* of e is a derivation d of $G \rightarrow s_1 \ldots s_i \; A_t \; s_{j+1} \ldots s_n$ such that every rule on or left of the spine comes from $\mathcal{G}_t$, and all other rules come from $\mathcal{G}_{t-1}$. The score of the best such derivation for e is the bridge outside cost $\tilde{\alpha}(e)$.

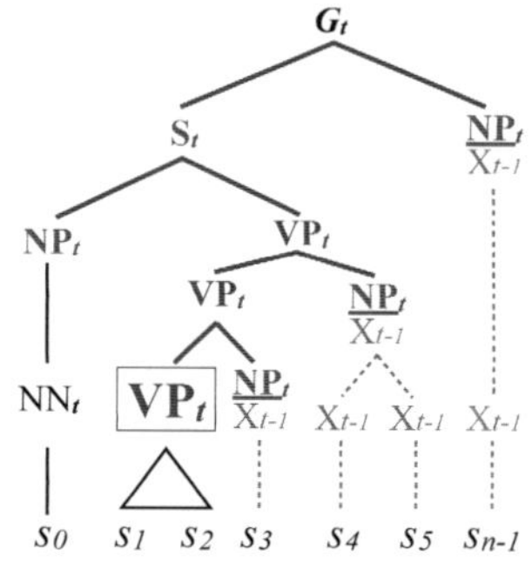

Figure 2: A concrete example of a possible bridge outside derivation for the bridge item $\tilde{O}(\text{VP}_t, 1, 4)$. This edge is boxed for emphasis. The spine of the derivation is shown in bold and colored in blue. Rules from a coarser grammar are shown with dotted lines, and colored in red. Here we have the simple projection $\pi_t(A) = X, \forall A$.

Like ordinary outside costs, bridge outside costs form consistent and admissible estimates of the true Viterbi outside score $\alpha(e)$ of an edge e. Because bridge costs mix rules from the finer and coarser grammar, bridge costs are at least as good an estimate of the true outside score as entirely coarse outside costs, and will in general be much tighter. That is, we have

$$\alpha(e') \leq \tilde{\alpha}(e) \leq \alpha(e)$$

In particular, note that the bridge costs become better approximations farther right in the sentence, and the bridge cost of the last word in the sentence is equal to the Viterbi outside cost of that word.

To compute bridge outside costs, we introduce

bridge outside items $\tilde{O}(A_t, i, j)$, shown graphically in Figure 1(b). The deduction rules which build both inside items and bridge outside items are shown in Table 2. The rules are very similar to those which define HA*, but there are two important differences. First, inside items wait for bridge outside items *at the same level*, while outside items wait for inside items from the previous level. Second, the left and right outside deductions are no longer symmetric – bridge outside items can extended to the left given two coarse inside items, but can only be extended to the right given an exact inside item on the left and coarse inside item on the right.

2.5 Guarantees

These deduction rules come with guarantees analogous to those of HA*. The monotonicity guarantee ensures that inside and (bridge) outside items are processed in order of:

$$\hat{p}(I(e)) = \beta(e) + \tilde{\alpha}(e)$$
$$\hat{p}(\tilde{O}(e)) = \tilde{\alpha}(e) + \beta(e')$$

The correctness guarantee ensures that when an item is removed from the agenda, its weight will be equal to $\beta(e)$ for inside items and $\tilde{\alpha}(e)$ for bridge items. The efficiency guarantee remains the same, though because the intrinsic priorities are different, the set of items processed will be different from those processed by HA*.

A proof of these guarantees is not possible due to space restrictions. The proof for BHA* follows the proof for HA* in Felzenszwalb and McAllester (2007) with minor modifications. The key property of HA* needed for these proofs is that coarse outside costs form consistent and admissible heuristics for inside items, and exact inside costs form consistent and admissible heuristics for outside items. BHA* also has this property, with bridge outside costs forming admissible and consistent heuristics for inside items, and coarse inside costs forming admissible and consistent heuristics for outside items.

3 Experiments

The performance of BHA* is determined by the efficiency guarantee given in the previous section. However, we cannot determine in advance whether BHA* will be faster than HA*. In fact, BHA* has the potential to be slower – BHA*

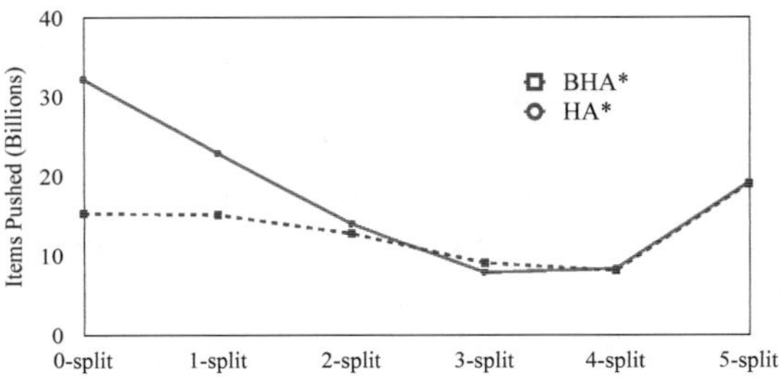

Figure 3: Performance of HA* and BHA* as a function of increasing refinement of the coarse grammar. Lower is faster.

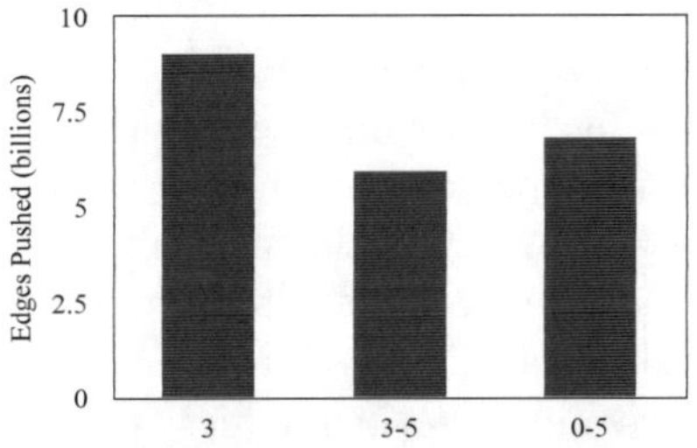

Figure 4: Performance of BHA* on hierarchies of varying size. Lower is faster. Along the x-axis, we show which coarse grammars were used in the hierarchy. For example, 3-5 indicates the 3-,4-, and 5-split grammars were used as coarse grammars.

builds both inside and bridge outside items under the target grammar, where HA* only builds inside items. It is an empirical, grammar- and hierarchy-dependent question whether the increased tightness of the outside estimates outweighs the additional cost needed to compute them. We demonstrate empirically in this section that for hierarchies with very loosely approximating coarse grammars, BHA* can outperform HA*, while for hierarchies with good approximations, performance of the two algorithms is comparable.

We performed experiments with the grammars of Petrov et al. (2006). The training procedure for these grammars produces a hierarchy of increasingly refined grammars through state-splitting, so a natural projection function π_t is given. We used the Berkeley Parser[2] to learn such grammars from Sections 2-21 of the Penn Treebank (Marcus et al., 1993). We trained with 6 split-merge cycles, producing 7 grammars. We tested these grammars on 300 sentences of length ≤ 25 of Section 23 of the Treebank. Our "target grammar" was in all cases the most split grammar.

[2]http://berkeleyparser.googlecode.com

In our first experiment, we construct 2-level hierarchies consisting of one coarse grammar and the target grammar. By varying the coarse grammar from the 0-split (X-bar) through 5-split grammars, we can investigate the performance of each algorithm as a function of the coarseness of the coarse grammar. We follow Pauls and Klein (2009) in using the number of items pushed as a machine- and implementation-independent measure of speed. In Figure 3, we show the performance of HA* and BHA* as a function of the total number of items pushed onto the agenda. We see that for very coarse approximating grammars, BHA* substantially outperforms HA*, but for more refined approximating grammars the performance is comparable, with HA* slightly outperforming BHA* on the 3-split grammar.

Finally, we verify that BHA* can benefit from multi-level hierarchies as HA* can. We constructed two multi-level hierarchies: a 4-level hierarchy consisting of the 3-,4-,5-, and 6- split grammars, and 7-level hierarchy consisting of all grammars. In Figure 4, we show the performance of BHA* on these multi-level hierarchies, as well as the best 2-level hierarchy from the previous experiment. Our results echo the results of Pauls and Klein (2009): although the addition of the reasonably refined 4- and 5-split grammars produces modest performance gains, the addition of coarser grammars can actually hurt overall performance.

Acknowledgements

This project is funded in part by the NSF under grant 0643742 and an NSERC Postgraduate Fellowship.

References

P. Felzenszwalb and D. McAllester. 2007. The generalized A* architecture. *Journal of Artificial Intelligence Research.*

Dan Klein and Christopher D. Manning. 2003. A* parsing: Fast exact Viterbi parse selection. In *Proceedings of the Human Language Technology Conference and the North American Association for Computational Linguistics (HLT-NAACL)*, pages 119–126.

M. Marcus, B. Santorini, and M. Marcinkiewicz. 1993. Building a large annotated corpus of English: The Penn Treebank. In *Computational Linguistics.*

Adam Pauls and Dan Klein. 2009. Hierarchical search for parsing. In *Proceedings of The Annual Conference of the North American Chapter of the Association for Computational Linguistics (NAACL).*

Slav Petrov, Leon Barrett, Romain Thibaux, and Dan Klein. 2006. Learning accurate, compact, and interpretable tree annotation. In *Proccedings of the Association for Computational Linguistics (ACL).*

Stuart M. Shieber, Yves Schabes, and Fernando C. N. Pereira. 1995. Principles and implementation of deductive parsing. *Journal of Logic Programming*, 24:3–36.

Using Parse Features for Preposition Selection and Error Detection

Joel Tetreault
Educational Testing Service
Princeton
NJ, USA
JTetreault@ets.org

Jennifer Foster
NCLT
Dublin City University
Ireland
jfoster@computing.dcu.ie

Martin Chodorow
Hunter College of CUNY
New York, NY, USA
martin.chodorow
@hunter.cuny.edu

Abstract

We evaluate the effect of adding parse features to a leading model of preposition usage. Results show a significant improvement in the preposition selection task on native speaker text and a modest increment in precision and recall in an ESL error detection task. Analysis of the parser output indicates that it is robust enough in the face of noisy non-native writing to extract useful information.

1 Introduction

The task of preposition error detection has received a considerable amount of attention in recent years because selecting an appropriate preposition poses a particularly difficult challenge to learners of English as a second language (ESL). It is not only ESL learners that struggle with English preposition usage — automatically detecting preposition errors made by ESL speakers is a challenging task for NLP systems. Recent state-of-the-art systems have precision ranging from 50% to 80% and recall as low as 10% to 20%.

To date, the conventional wisdom in the error detection community has been to avoid the use of statistical parsers under the belief that a WSJ-trained parser's performance would degrade too much on noisy learner texts and that the traditionally hard problem of prepositional phrase attachment would be even harder when parsing ESL writing. However, there has been little substantial research to support or challenge this view. In this paper, we investigate the following research question: *Are parser output features helpful in modeling preposition usage in well-formed text and learner text?*

We recreate a state-of-the-art preposition usage system (Tetreault and Chodorow (2008), henceforth T&C08) originally trained with lexical features and augment it with parser output features. We employ the Stanford parser in our experiments because it consists of a competitive phrase structure parser *and* a constituent-to-dependency conversion tool (Klein and Manning, 2003a; Klein and Manning, 2003b; de Marneffe et al., 2006; de Marneffe and Manning, 2008). We compare the original model with the parser-augmented model on the tasks of preposition selection in well-formed text (fluent writers) and preposition error detection in learner texts (ESL writers).

This paper makes the following contributions:

- We demonstrate that parse features have a significant impact on preposition selection in well-formed text. We also show which features have the greatest effect on performance.
- We show that, despite the noisiness of learner text, parse features can actually make small, albeit non-significant, improvements to the performance of a state-of-the-art preposition error detection system.
- We evaluate the accuracy of parsing and especially preposition attachment in learner texts.

2 Related Work

T&C08, De Felice and Pulman (2008) and Gamon *et al.* (2008) describe very similar preposition error detection systems in which a model of correct prepositional usage is trained from well-formed text and a writer's preposition is compared with the predictions of this model. It is difficult to directly compare these systems since they are trained and tested on different data sets

Proceedings of the ACL 2010 Conference Short Papers, pages 353–358,
Uppsala, Sweden, 11-16 July 2010.

but they achieve accuracy in a similar range. Of these systems, only the DAPPER system (De Felice and Pulman, 2008; De Felice and Pulman, 2009; De Felice, 2009) uses a parser, the C&C parser (Clark and Curran, 2007)), to determine the head and complement of the preposition. De Felice and Pulman (2009) remark that the parser tends to be misled more by spelling errors than by grammatical errors. The parser is fundamental to their system and they do not carry out a comparison of the use of a parser to determine the preposition's attachments versus the use of shallower techniques. T&C08, on the other hand, reject the use of a parser because of the difficulties they foresee in applying one to learner data. Hermet *et al.* (2008) make only limited use of the Xerox Incremental Parser in their preposition error detection system. They split the input sentence into the chunks before and after the preposition, and parse both chunks separately. Only very shallow analyses are extracted from the parser output because they do not trust the full analyses.

Lee and Knutsson (2008) show that knowledge of the PP attachment site helps in the task of preposition selection by comparing a classifier trained on lexical features (the verb before the preposition, the noun between the verb and the preposition, if any, and the noun after the preposition) to a classifier trained on attachment features which explicitly state whether the preposition is attached to the preceding noun or verb. They also argue that a parser which is capable of distinguishing between arguments and adjuncts is useful for generating the correct preposition.

3 Augmenting a Preposition Model with Parse Features

To test the effects of adding parse features to a model of preposition usage, we replicated the lexical and combination feature model used in T&C08, training on 2M events extracted from a corpus of news and high school level reading materials. Next, we added the parse features to this model to create a new model "+Parse". In 3.1 we describe the T&C08 system and features, and in 3.2 we describe the parser output features used to augment the model. We illustrate our features using the example phrase *many local groups around the country*. Fig. 1 shows the phrase structure tree and dependency triples returned by the Stanford parser for this phrase.

3.1 Baseline System

The work of Chodorow *et al.* (2007) and T&C08 treat the tasks of preposition selection and error detection as a classification problem. That is, given the context around a preposition and a model of correct usage, a classifier determines which of the 34 prepositions covered by the model is most appropriate for the context. A model of correct preposition usage is constructed by training a Maximum Entropy classifier (Ratnaparkhi, 1998) on millions of preposition contexts from well-formed text.

A context is represented by 25 lexical features and 4 combination features:

Lexical Token and POS n-grams in a 2 word window around the preposition, plus the head verb in the preceding verb phrase (PV), the head noun in the preceding noun phrase (PN) and the head noun in the following noun phrase (FN) when available (Chodorow et al., 2007). Note that these are determined not through full syntactic parsing but rather through the use of a heuristic chunker. So, for the phrase *many local groups around the country*, examples of lexical features for the preposition *around* include: *FN = country*, *PN = groups*, *left-2-word-sequence = local-groups*, and *left-2-POS-sequence = JJ-NNS*.

Combination T&C08 expand on the lexical feature set by combining the PV, PN and FN features, resulting in features such as PN-FN and PV-PN-FN. POS and token versions of these features are employed. The intuition behind creating combination features is that the Maximum Entropy classifier does not automatically model the interactions between individual features. An example of the *PN-FN* feature is *groups-country*.

3.2 Parse Features

To augment the above model we experimented with 14 features divided among five main classes. Table 1 shows the features and their values for our *around* example. The **Preposition Head and Complement** feature represents the two basic attachment relations of the preposition, i.e. its head (what it is attached to) and its complement (what is attached to it). **Relation** specifies the relation between the head and complement. The **Preposition Head and Complement Combined** features are similar to the T&C08 Combination features except that they are extracted from parser output.

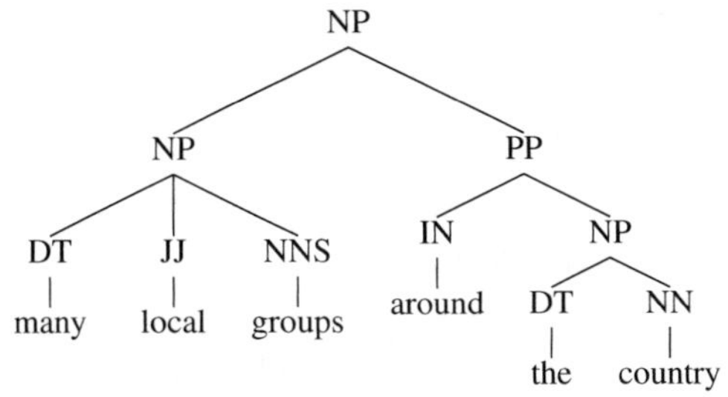


```
amod(groups-3, many-1)
amod(groups-3, local-2)
prep(groups-3, around-4)
det(country-6, the-5)
pobj(around-4, country-6)
```

Figure 1: Phrase structure tree and dependency triples produced by the Stanford parser for the phrase *many local groups around the country*

Prep. Head & Complement
1. head of the preposition: *groups*
2. POS of the head: `NNS`
3. complement of the preposition: *country*
4. POS of the complement: `NN`
Prep. Head & Complement Relation
5. Prep-Head relation name: `prep`
6. Prep-Comp relation name: `pobj`
Prep. Head & Complement Combined
7. Head-Complement tokens: *groups-country*
8. Head-Complement tags: `NNS-NN`
Prep. Head & Complement Mixed
9. Head Tag and Comp Token: `NNS`-*country*
10. Head Token and Comp Tag: *groups*-`NN`
Phrase Structure
11. Preposition Parent: `PP`
12. Preposition Grandparent: `NP`
13. Left context of preposition parent: `NP`
14. Right context of preposition parent: –

Table 1: Parse Features

Model	Accuracy
combination only	35.2
parse only	60.6
combination+parse	61.9
lexical only	64.4
combination+lexical (T&C08)	65.2
lexical+parse	68.1
all features (+Parse)	68.5

Table 2: Accuracy on preposition selection task for various feature combinations

The **Preposition Head and Complement Mixed** features are created by taking the first feature in the previous set and backing-off either the head or the complement to its POS tag. This mix of tags and tokens in a word-word dependency has proven to be an effective feature in sentiment analysis (Joshi and Penstein-Rosé, 2009). All the features described so far are extracted from the set of dependency triples output by the Stanford parser. The final set of features (**Phrase Structure**), however, is extracted directly from the phrase structure trees themselves.

4 Evaluation

In Section 4.1, we compare the T&C08 and +Parse models on the task of preposition selection on well-formed texts written by native speakers. For every preposition in the test set, we compare the system's top preposition for that context to the writer's preposition, and report accuracy rates. In Section 4.2, we evaluate the two models on ESL data. The task here is slightly different - if the most likely preposition according to the model differs from the likelihood of the writer's preposition by a certain threshold amount, a preposition error is flagged.

4.1 Native Speaker Test Data

Our test set consists of 259K preposition events from the same source as the original training data. The T&C08 model performs at **65.2%** and when the parse features are added, the +Parse model improves performance by more than 3% to **68.5%**.[1] The improvement is statistically significant.

[1]Prior research has shown preposition selection performance accuracy ranging from 65% to nearly 80%. The differences are largely due to different test sets and also training sizes. Given the time required to train large models, we report here experiments with a relatively small model.

Model	Accuracy
T&C08	65.2
+Phrase Structure Only	67.1
+Dependency Only	68.2
+Parse	68.5
+head-tag+comp-tag	66.9
+left	66.8
+grandparent	66.6
+head-token+comp-tag	66.6
+head-tag	66.5
+head-token	66.4
+head-tag+comp-token	66.1

Table 3: Which parse features are important? Feature Addition Experiment

Table 2 shows the effect of various feature class combinations on prediction accuracy. The results are clear: a significant performance improvement is obtained on the preposition selection task when features from parser output are added. The two best models in Table 2 contain parse features. The table also shows that the non-parser-based feature classes are not entirely subsumed by the parse features but rather provide, to varying degrees, complementary information.

Having established the effectiveness of parse features, we investigate which parse feature classes contribute the most. To test each contribution, we perform a feature addition experiment, separately adding features to the T&C08 model (see Table 3). We make three observations. First, while there is overlapping information between the dependency features and the phrase structure features, the phrase structure features *are* making a contribution. This is interesting because it suggests that a pure dependency parser might be less useful than a parser which explicitly produces both constituent and dependency information. Second, using a parser to identify the preposition head seems to be more useful than using it to identify the preposition complement.[2] Finally, as was the case for the T&C08 features, the combination parse features are also important (particularly the tag-tag or tag/token pairs).

4.2 ESL Test Data

Our test data consists of 5,183 preposition events extracted from a set of essays written by non-native speakers for the Test of English as a Foreign Language (TOEFL®). The prepositions were judged by two trained annotators and checked by the authors using the preposition annotation scheme described in Tetreault and Chodorow (2008b). 4,881 of the prepositions were judged to be correct and the remaining 302 were judged to be incorrect.

Method	Precision	Recall
T&C08	0.461	0.215
+Parse	0.486	0.225

Table 4: ESL Error Detection Results

The writer's preposition is flagged as an error by the system if its likelihood according to the model satisfied a set of criteria (e.g., the difference between the probability of the system's choice and the writer's preposition is 0.8 or higher). Unlike the selection task where we use accuracy as the metric, we use precision and recall with respect to error detection. To date, performance figures that have been reported in the literature have been quite low, reflecting the difficulty of the task. Table 4 shows the performance figures for the T&C08 and +Parse models. Both precision and recall are higher for the +Parse model, however, given the low number of errors in our annotated test set, the difference is not statistically significant.

5 Parser Accuracy on ESL Data

To evaluate parser performance on ESL data, we manually inspected the phrase structure trees and dependency graphs produced by the Stanford parser for 210 ESL sentences, split into 3 groups: the sentences in the first group are fluent and contain no obvious grammatical errors, those in the second contain at least one preposition error and the sentences in the third are clearly ungrammatical with a variety of error types. For each preposition we note whether the parser was successful in determining its head and complement. The results for the three groups are shown in Table 5. The figures in the first row are for correct prepositions and those in the second are for incorrect ones.

The parser tends to do a better job of determining the preposition's complement than its head which is not surprising given the well-known problem of PP attachment ambiguity. Given the preposition, the preceding noun, the preceding

[2]De Felice (2009) observes the same for the DAPPER system.

	OK	
	Head	Comp
Prep Correct Prep Incorrect	86.7% (104/120) -	95.0% (114/120) -
	Preposition Error	
	Head	Comp
Prep Correct Prep Incorrect	89.0% (65/73) 87.1% (54/62)	97.3% (71/73) 96.8% (60/62)
	Ungrammatical	
	Head	Comp
Prep Correct Prep Incorrect	87.8% (115/131) 70.8% (17/24)	89.3% (117/131) 87.5% (21/24)

Table 5: Parser Accuracy on Prepositions in a Sample of ESL Sentences

verb and the following noun, Collins (1999) reports an accuracy rate of 84.5% for a PP attachment classifier. When confronted with the same information, the accuracy of three trained annotators is 88.2%. Assuming 88.2% as an approximate PP-attachment upper bound, the Stanford parser appears to be doing a good job. Comparing the results over the three sentence groups, its ability to identify the preposition's head is quite robust to grammatical noise.

Preposition errors in isolation do not tend to mislead the parser: in the second group which contains sentences which are largely fluent apart from preposition errors, there is little difference between the parser's accuracy on the correctly used prepositions and the incorrectly used ones. Examples are

```
(S (NP I)
   (VP had
       (NP (NP a trip)
           (PP for (NP Italy))
       )
   )
)
```

in which the erroneous preposition *for* is correctly attached to the noun *trip*, and

```
(S (NP A scientist)
   (VP devotes
       (NP (NP his prime part)
           (PP of (NP his life))
       )
       (PP in (NP research))
   )
)
```

in which the erroneous preposition *in* is correctly attached to the verb *devotes*.

6 Conclusion

We have shown that the use of a parser can boost the accuracy of a preposition selection model tested on well-formed text. In the error detection task, the improvement is less marked. Nevertheless, examination of parser output shows the parse features can be extracted reliably from ESL data.

For our immediate future work, we plan to carry out the ESL evaluation on a larger test set to better gauge the usefulness of a parser in this context, to carry out a detailed error analysis to understand why certain parse features are effective and to explore a larger set of features.

In the longer term, we hope to compare different types of parsers in both the preposition selection and error detection tasks, i.e. a task-based parser evaluation in the spirit of that carried out by Miyao *et al.* (2008) on the task of protein pair interaction extraction. We would like to further investigate the role of parsing in error detection by looking at other error types and other text types, e.g. machine translation output.

Acknowledgments

We would like to thank Rachele De Felice and the reviewers for their very helpful comments.

References

Martin Chodorow, Joel Tetreault, and Na-Rae Han. 2007. Detection of grammatical errors involving prepositions. In *Proceedings of the 4th ACL-SIGSEM Workshop on Prepositions*, Prague, Czech Republic, June.

Stephen Clark and James R. Curran. 2007. Wide-coverage efficient statistical parsing with CCG and log-linear models. *Computational Linguistics*, 33(4):493–552.

Michael Collins. 1999. *Head-driven Statistical Models for Natural Language Parsing*. Ph.D. thesis, University of Pennsylvania.

Rachele De Felice and Stephen G. Pulman. 2008. A classifier-based approach to preposition and determiner error correction in L2 english. In *Proceedings of the 22nd COLING*, Manchester, United Kingdom.

Rachele De Felice and Stephen Pulman. 2009. Automatic detection of preposition errors in learning writing. *CALICO Journal*, 26(3):512–528.

Rachele De Felice. 2009. *Automatic Error Detection in Non-native English*. Ph.D. thesis, Oxford University.

Marie-Catherine de Marneffe and Christopher D. Manning. 2008. The stanford typed dependencies representation. In *Proceedings of the COLING08 Workshop on Cross-framework and Cross-domain Parser Evaluation*, Manchester, United Kingdom.

Marie-Catherine de Marneffe, Bill MacCartney, and Christopher D. Manning. 2006. Generating typed dependency parses from phrase structure parses. In *Proceedings of LREC*, Genoa, Italy.

Michael Gamon, Jianfeng Gao, Chris Brockett, Alexandre Klementiev, William B. Dolan, Dmitriy Belenko, and Lucy Vanderwende. 2008. Using contextual speller techniques and language modelling for ESL error correction. In *Proceedings of the International Joint Conference on Natural Language Processing*, Hyderabad, India.

Matthieu Hermet, Alain Désilets, and Stan Szpakowicz. 2008. Using the web as a linguistic resource to automatically correct lexico-syntactic errors. In *Proceedings of LREC*, Marrekech, Morocco.

Mahesh Joshi and Carolyn Penstein-Rosé. 2009. Generalizing dependency features for opinion mining. In *Proceedings of the ACL-IJCNLP 2009 Conference Short Papers*, pages 313–316, Singapore.

Dan Klein and Christopher D. Manning. 2003a. Accurate unlexicalized parsing. In *Proceedings of the 41st Annual Meeting of the ACL*, pages 423–430, Sapporo, Japan.

Dan Klein and Christopher D. Manning. 2003b. Fast exact inference with a factored model for exact parsing. In *Advances in Neural Information Processing Systems*, pages 3–10. MIT Press, Cambridge, MA.

John Lee and Ola Knutsson. 2008. The role of PP attachment in preposition generation. In *Proceedings of CICling*. Springer-Verlag Berlin Heidelberg.

Yusuke Miyao, Rune Saetre, Kenji Sagae, Takuya Matsuzaki, and Jun'ichi Tsujii. 2008. Task-oriented evaluation of syntactic parsers and their representations. In *Proceedings of the 46th Annual Meeting of the ACL*, pages 46–54, Columbus, Ohio.

Adwait Ratnaparkhi. 1998. *Maximum Entropy Models for natural language ambiguity resolution*. Ph.D. thesis, University of Pennsylvania.

Joel Tetreault and Martin Chodorow. 2008. The ups and downs of preposition error detection in ESL writing. In *Proceedings of the 22nd COLING*, Manchester, United Kingdom.

Joel Tetreault and Martin Chodorow. 2008b. Native Judgments of non-native usage: Experiments in preposition error detection. In *COLING Workshop on Human Judgments in Computational Linguistics*, Manchester, United Kingdom.

Distributional Similarity vs. PU Learning for Entity Set Expansion

Xiao-Li Li
Institute for Infocomm Research,
1 Fusionopolis Way #21-01 Connexis
Singapore 138632
xlli@i2r.a-star.edu.sg

Lei Zhang
University of Illinois at Chicago,
851 South Morgan Street, Chicago,
Chicago, IL 60607-7053, USA
zhang3@cs.uic.edu

Bing Liu
University of Illinois at Chicago,
851 South Morgan Street, Chicago,
Chicago, IL 60607-7053, USA
liub@cs.uic.edu

See-Kiong Ng
Institute for Infocomm Research,
1 Fusionopolis Way #21-01 Connexis
Singapore 138632
skng@i2r.a-star.edu.sg

Abstract

Distributional similarity is a classic technique for entity set expansion, where the system is given a set of seed entities of a particular class, and is asked to expand the set using a corpus to obtain more entities of the same class as represented by the seeds. This paper shows that a machine learning model called *positive and unlabeled learning* (PU learning) can model the set expansion problem better. Based on the test results of 10 corpora, we show that a PU learning technique outperformed distributional similarity significantly.

1 Introduction

The entity set expansion problem is defined as follows: Given a set *S* of seed entities of a particular class, and a set *D* of candidate entities (e.g., extracted from a text corpus), we wish to determine which of the entities in *D* belong to *S*. In other words, we "expand" the set *S* based on the given seeds. This is clearly a classification problem which requires arriving at a binary decision for each entity in *D* (belonging to *S* or not). However, in practice, the problem is often solved as a ranking problem, i.e., ranking the entities in *D* based on their likelihoods of belonging to *S*.

The classic method for solving this problem is based on *distributional similarity* (Pantel *et al.* 2009; Lee, 1998). The approach works by comparing the similarity of the surrounding word distributions of each candidate entity with the seed entities, and then ranking the candidate entities using their similarity scores.

In machine learning, there is a class of semi-supervised learning algorithms that learns from *positive* and *unlabeled* examples (PU learning for short). The key characteristic of PU learning is that there is no negative training example available for learning. This class of algorithms is less known to the natural language processing (NLP) community compared to some other semi-supervised learning models and algorithms.

PU learning is a two-class classification model. It is stated as follows (Liu *et al.* 2002): Given a set *P* of positive examples of a particular class and a set *U* of unlabeled examples (containing hidden positive and negative cases), a classifier is built using *P* and *U* for classifying the data in *U* or future test cases. The results can be either binary decisions (whether each test case belongs to the positive class or not), or a ranking based on how likely each test case belongs to the positive class represented by *P*. Clearly, the set expansion problem can be mapped into PU learning exactly, with *S* and *D* as *P* and *U* respectively.

This paper shows that a PU learning method called S-EM (Liu *et al.* 2002) outperforms distributional similarity considerably based on the results from 10 corpora. The experiments involved extracting named entities (e.g., product and organization names) of the same type or class as the given seeds. Additionally, we also compared S-EM with a recent method, called *Bayesian Sets* (Ghahramani and Heller, 2005), which was designed specifically for set expansion. It also does not perform as well as PU learning. We will explain why PU learning performs better than both methods in Section 5. We believe that this finding is of interest to the NLP community.

Proceedings of the ACL 2010 Conference Short Papers, pages 359–364,
Uppsala, Sweden, 11-16 July 2010. ©2010 Association for Computational Linguistics

There is another approach used in the Web environment for entity set expansion. It exploits Web page structures to identify lists of items using wrapper induction or other techniques. The idea is that items in the same list are often of the same type. This approach is used by Google Sets (Google, 2008) and Boo!Wa! (Wang and Cohen, 2008). However, as it relies on Web page structures, it is not applicable to general free texts.

2 Three Different Techniques

2.1 Distributional Similarity

Distributional similarity is a classic technique for the entity set expansion problem. It is based on the hypothesis that words with similar meanings tend to appear in similar contexts (Harris, 1985). As such, a method based on distributional similarity typically fetches the surrounding contexts for each term (i.e. both seeds and candidates) and represents them as vectors by using TF-IDF or PMI (*Pointwise Mutual Information*) values (Lin, 1998; Gorman and Curran, 2006; Paşca *et al.* 2006; Agirre *et al.* 2009; Pantel *et al.* 2009). Similarity measures such as *Cosine*, *Jaccard*, *Dice*, etc, can then be employed to compute the similarities between each candidate vector and the seeds centroid vector (one centroid vector for all seeds). Lee (1998) surveyed and discussed various distribution similarity measures.

2.2 PU Learning and S-EM

PU learning is a semi-supervised or partially supervised learning model. It learns from positive and unlabeled examples as opposed to the model of learning from a small set of labeled examples of every class and a large set of unlabeled examples, which we call LU learning (L and U stand for *labeled* and *unlabeled* respectively) (Blum and Mitchell, 1998; Nigam *et al.* 2000)

There are several PU learning algorithms (Liu *et al.* 2002; Yu *et al.* 2002; Lee and Liu, 2003; Li *et al.* 2003; Elkan and Noto, 2008). In this work, we used the S-EM algorithm given in (Liu *et al.* 2002). S-EM is efficient as it is based on naïve Bayesian (NB) classification and also performs well. The main idea of S-EM is to use a *spy* technique to identify some *reliable negatives* (*RN*) from the unlabeled set *U*, and then use an EM algorithm to learn from *P*, *RN* and *U–RN*.

The *spy* technique in S-EM works as follows (Figure 1): First, a small set of positive examples (denoted by *SP*) from *P* is randomly sampled (line 2). The default sampling ratio in S-EM is $s = 15\%$, which we also used in our experiments. The positive examples in *SP* are called "spies". Then, a NB classifier is built using the set $P - SP$ as positive and the set $U \cup SP$ as negative (line 3, 4, and 5). The NB classifier is applied to classify each $u \in U \cup SP$, i.e., to assign a probabilistic class label $p(+|u)$ (+ means positive). The probabilistic labels of the spies are then used to decide reliable negatives (*RN*). In particular, a probability threshold *t* is determined using the probabilistic labels of spies in *SP* and the input parameter *l* (noise level). Due to space constraints, we are unable to explain *l*. Details can be found in (Liu *et al.* 2002). *t* is then used to find *RN* from *U* (lines 8-10). The idea of the spy technique is clear. Since spy examples are from *P* and are put into *U* in building the NB classifier, they should behave similarly to the hidden positive cases in *U*. Thus, they can help us find the set *RN*.

Algorithm Spy(*P*, *U*, *s*, *l*)
1. $RN \leftarrow \varnothing$; // Reliable negative set
2. $SP \leftarrow Sample(P, s\%)$;
3. Assign each example in $P - SP$ the class label +1;
4. Assign each example in $U \cup SP$ the class label -1;
5. $C \leftarrow$NB($P - S$, $U \cup SP$); // Produce a NB classifier
6. Classify each $u \in U \cup SP$ using *C*;
7. Decide a probability threshold *t* using *SP* and *l*;
8. **for** each $u \in U$ **do**
9.   **if** its probability $p(+|u) < t$ **then**
10. $RN \leftarrow RN \cup \{u\}$;

Figure 1. Spy technique for extracting reliable negatives (*RN*) from *U*.

Given the positive set *P*, the reliable negative set *RN* and the remaining unlabeled set *U–RN*, an Expectation-Maximization (EM) algorithm is run. In S-EM, EM uses the naïve Bayesian classification as its base method. The detailed algorithm is given in (Liu *et al.* 2002).

2.3 Bayesian Sets

Bayesian Sets, as its name suggests, is based on Bayesian inference, and was designed specifically for the set expansion problem (Ghahramani and Heller, 2005). The algorithm learns from a seeds set (i.e., a positive set *P*) and an unlabeled candidate set *U*. Although it was not designed as a PU learning method, it has similar characteristics and produces similar results as PU learning. However, there is a major difference. PU learning is a classification model, while Bayesian Sets is a ranking method. This difference has a major implication on the results that they produce as we will discuss in Section 5.3.

In essence, Bayesian Sets learns a score function using P and U to generate a score for each unlabeled case $u \in U$. The function is as follows:

$$score(u) = \frac{p(u \mid P)}{p(u)} \quad (1)$$

where $p(u|P)$ represents how probable u belongs to the positive class represented by P. $p(u)$ is the prior probability of u. Using the Bayes' rule, equation (1) can be re-written as:

$$score(u) = \frac{p(u, P)}{p(u)p(P)} \quad (2)$$

Following the idea, Ghahramani and Heller (2005) proposed a computable score function. The scores can be used to rank the unlabeled candidates in U to reflect how likely each $u \in U$ belongs to P. The mathematics for computing the score is involved. Due to the limited space, we cannot discuss it here. See (Ghahramani and Heller, 2005) for details. In (Heller and Ghahramani, 2006), Bayesian Sets was also applied to an image retrieval application.

3 Data Generation for Distributional Similarity, Bayesian Sets and S-EM

Preparing the data for distributional similarity is fairly straightforward. Given the seeds set S, a seeds centroid vector is produced using the surrounding word contexts (see below) of all occurrences of all the seeds in the corpus (Pantel et al, 2009). In a similar way, a centroid is also produced for each candidate (or unlabeled) entity.

Candidate entities: Since we are interested in named entities, we select single words or phrases as candidate entities based on their corresponding part-of-speech (POS) tags. In particular, we choose the following POS tags as entity indicators — NNP (proper noun), NNPS (plural proper noun), and CD (cardinal number). We regard a phrase (could be one word) with a sequence of NNP, NNPS and CD POS tags as one candidate entity (CD cannot be the first word unless it starts with a letter), e.g., "Windows/NNP 7/CD" and "Nokia/NNP N97/CD" are regarded as two candidates "Windows 7" and "Nokia N97".

Context: For each seed or candidate occurrence, the *context* is its set of surrounding words within a window of size w, i.e. we use w words right before the seed or the candidate and w words right after it. Stop words are removed.

For S-EM and Bayesian Sets, both the positive set P (based on the seeds set S) and the unlabeled candidate set U are generated differently. They are not represented as centroids.

Positive and unlabeled sets: For each seed $s_i \in S$, each occurrence in the corpus forms a vector as a positive example in P. The vector is formed based on the surrounding words context (see above) of the seed mention. Similarly, for each candidate $d \in D$ (see above; D denotes the set of all candidates), each occurrence also forms a vector as an unlabeled example in U. Thus, each unique seed or candidate entity may produce multiple feature vectors, depending on the number of times that it appears in the corpus.

The components in the feature vectors are term frequencies for S-EM as S-EM uses naïve Bayesian classification as its base classifier. For Bayesian Sets, they are 1's and 0's as Bayesian Sets only takes binary vectors based on whether a term occurs in the context or not.

4 Candidate Ranking

For distributional similarity, ranking is done using the similarity value of each candidate's centroid and the seeds' centroid (one centroid vector for all seeds). Rankings for S-EM and Bayesian Sets are more involved. We discuss them below.

After it ends, S-EM produces a Bayesian classifier C, which is used to classify each vector $u \in U$ and to assign a probability $p(+|u)$ to indicate the likelihood that u belongs to the positive class. Similarly, Bayesian Sets produces a score $score(u)$ for each u (not a probability).

Recall that for both S-EM and Bayesian Sets, each unique candidate entity may generate multiple feature vectors, depending on the number of times that the candidate entity occurs in the corpus. As such, the rankings produced by S-EM and Bayesian Sets are not the rankings of the entities, but rather the rankings of the entities' occurrences. Since different vectors representing the same candidate entity can have very different probabilities (for S-EM) or scores (for Bayesian Sets), we need to combine them and compute a single score for each unique candidate entity for ranking.

To this end, we also take the entity frequency into consideration. Typically, it is highly desirable to rank those correct and frequent entities at the top because they are more important than the infrequent ones in applications. With this in mind, we define a ranking method.

Let the probabilities (or scores) of a candidate entity $d \in D$ be $V_d = \{v_1, v_2 \ldots, v_n\}$ for the n feature vectors of the candidate. Let M_d be the median of V_d. The final score (fs) for d is defined as:

$$fs(d) = M_d \times \log(1 + n) \quad (3)$$

The use of the median of V_d can be justified based on the statistical *skewness* (Neter *et al.* 1993). If the values in V_d are skewed towards the high side (negative skew), it means that the candidate entity is very likely to be a true entity, and we should take the median as it is also high (higher than the mean). However, if the skew is towards the low side (positive skew), it means that the candidate entity is unlikely to be a true entity and we should again use the median as it is low (lower than the mean) under this condition.

Note that here n is the frequency count of candidate entity d in the corpus. The constant 1 is added to smooth the value. The idea is to push the frequent candidate entities up by multiplying the logarithm of frequency. *log* is taken in order to reduce the effect of big frequency counts.

The final score $fs(d)$ indicates candidate d's overall likelihood to be a relevant entity. A high $fs(d)$ implies a high likelihood that d is in the expanded entity set. We can then rank all the candidates based on their $fs(d)$ values.

5 Experimental Evaluation

We empirically evaluate the three techniques in this section. We implemented *distribution similarity* and *Bayesian Sets*. S-EM was downloaded from http://www.cs.uic.edu/~liub/S-EM/S-EM-download.html. For both Bayesian Sets and S-EM, we used their default parameters. EM in S-EM ran only two iterations. For distributional similarity, we tested TF-IDF and PMI as feature values of vectors, and Cosine and Jaccard as similarity measures. Due to space limitations, we only show the results of the PMI and Cosine combination as it performed the best. This combination was also used in (Pantel *et al.*, 2009).

5.1 Corpora and Evaluation Metrics

We used 10 diverse corpora to evaluate the techniques. They were obtained from a commercial company. The data were crawled and extracted from multiple online message boards and blogs discussing different products and services. We split each message into sentences, and the sentences were POS-tagged using Brill's tagger (Brill, 1995). The tagged sentences were used to extract candidate entities and their contexts. Table 1 shows the domains and the number of sentences in each corpus, as well as the three seed entities used in our experiments for each corpus. The three seeds for each corpus were randomly selected from a set of common entities in the application domain.

Table 1. Descriptions of the 10 corpora

Domains	# Sentences	Seed Entities
Bank	17394	Citi, Chase, Wesabe
Blu-ray	7093	S300, Sony, Samsung
Car	2095	Honda, A3, Toyota
Drug	1504	Enbrel, Hurmia, Methotrexate
Insurance	12419	Cobra, Cigna, Kaiser
LCD	1733	PZ77U, Samsung, Sony
Mattress	13191	Simmons, Serta, Heavenly
Phone	14884	Motorola, Nokia, N95
Stove	25060	Kenmore, Frigidaire, GE
Vacuum	13491	Dc17, Hoover, Roomba

The regular evaluation metrics for named entity recognition such as precision and recall are not suitable for our purpose as we do not have the complete sets of gold standard entities to compare with. We adopt rank precision, which is commonly used for evaluation of entity set expansion techniques (Pantel *et al.*, 2009):

Precision @ N: The percentage of correct entities among the top N entities in the ranked list.

5.2 Experimental Results

The detailed experimental results for window size 3 (w=3) are shown in Table 2 for the 10 corpora. We present the precisions at the top 15-, 30- and 45-ranked positions (i.e., precisions @15, 30 and 45) for each corpus, with the average given in the last column. For distributional similarity, to save space Table 2 only shows the results of **Distr-Sim-freq**, which is the distributional similarity method with term frequency considered in the same way as for Bayesian Sets and S-EM, instead of the original distributional similarity, which is denoted by **Distr-Sim**. This is because on average, **Distr-Sim-freq** performs better than **Distr-Sim**. However, the summary results of both **Distr-Sim-freq** and **Distr-Sim** are given in Table 3.

From Table 2, we observe that on average **S-EM** outperforms **Distr-Sim-freq** by about 12 – 20% in terms of *Precision @ N*. **Bayesian-Sets** is also more accurate than **Distr-Sim-freq**, but **S-EM** outperforms **Bayesian-Sets** by 9 – 10%.

To test the sensitivity of window size w, we also experimented with w = 6 and w = 9. Due to space constraints, we present only their average results in Table 3. Again, we can see the same performance pattern as in Table 2 (w = 3): **S-EM** performs the best, **Bayesian-Sets** the second, and the two distributional similarity methods the third and the fourth, with **Distr-Sim-freq** slightly better than **Distr-Sim**.

Table 2. *Precision @ top N* (with 3 seeds, and window size $w = 3$)

	Bank	Blu-ray	Car	Drug	Insurance	LCD	Mattress	Phone	Stove	Vacuum	**Avg.**
	Top 15										
Distr-Sim-freq	0.466	0.333	0.800	0.666	0.666	0.400	0.666	0.533	0.666	0.733	**0.592**
Bayesian-Sets	0.533	0.266	0.600	0.666	0.600	0.733	0.666	0.533	0.800	0.800	**0.617**
S-EM	0.600	0.733	0.733	0.733	0.533	0.666	0.933	0.533	0.800	0.933	**0.720**
	Top 30										
Distr-Sim-freq	0.466	0.266	0.700	0.600	0.500	0.333	0.500	0.466	0.600	0.566	**0.499**
Bayesian-Sets	0.433	0.300	0.633	0.666	0.400	0.566	0.700	0.333	0.833	0.700	**0.556**
S-EM	0.500	0.700	0.666	0.666	0.566	0.566	0.733	0.600	0.600	0.833	**0.643**
	Top 45										
Distr-Sim-freq	0.377	0.288	0.555	0.500	0.377	0.355	0.444	0.400	0.533	0.400	**0.422**
Bayesian-Sets	0.377	0.333	0.666	0.555	0.377	0.511	0.644	0.355	0.733	0.600	**0.515**
S-EM	0.466	0.688	0.644	0.733	0.533	0.600	0.644	0.555	0.644	0.688	**0.620**

Table 3. Average precisions over the 10 corpora of different window size (3 seeds)

	Window-size $w = 3$			**Window-size $w = 6$**			**Window-size $w = 9$**		
Top Results	**Top 15**	**Top 30**	**Top 45**	**Top 15**	**Top 30**	**Top 45**	**Top 15**	**Top 30**	**Top 45**
Distr-Sim	0.579	0.466	0.410	0.553	0.483	0.439	0.519	0.473	0.412
Distr-Sim-freq	0.592	0.499	0.422	0.553	0.492	0.441	0.559	0.476	0.410
Bayesian-Sets	0.617	0.556	0.515	0.593	0.539	0.524	0.539	0.522	0.497
S-EM	**0.720**	**0.643**	**0.620**	**0.666**	**0.606**	**0.597**	**0.666**	**0.620**	**0.604**

5.3 Why does S-EM Perform Better?

From the tables, we can see that both S-EM and Bayesian Sets performed better than distributional similarity. S-EM is better than Bayesian Sets. We believe that the reason is as follows: Distributional similarity does not use any information in the candidate set (or the unlabeled set *U*). It tries to rank the candidates solely through similarity comparisons with the given seeds (or positive cases). Bayesian Sets is better because it considers *U*. Its learning method produces a weight vector for features based on their occurrence differences in the positive set *P* and the unlabeled set *U* (Ghahramani and Heller 2005). This weight vector is then used to compute the final scores used in ranking. In this way, Bayesian Sets is able to exploit the useful information in *U* that was ignored by distributional similarity. S-EM also considers these differences in its NB classification; in addition, it uses the reliable negative set (*RN*) to help distinguish negative and positive cases, which both Bayesian Sets and distributional similarity do not do. We believe this balanced attempt by S-EM to distinguish the positive and negative cases is the reason for the better performance of S-EM. This raises an interesting question. Since Bayesian Sets is a ranking method and S-EM is a classification method, can we say even for ranking (our evaluation is based on ranking) classification methods produce better results than ranking methods? Clearly, our single experiment cannot answer this question. But intuitively, classification, which separates positive and negative cases by pulling them towards two opposite directions, should perform better than ranking which only pulls the data in one direction. Further research on this issue is needed.

6 Conclusions and Future Work

Although distributional similarity is a classic technique for entity set expansion, this paper showed that PU learning performs considerably better on our diverse corpora. In addition, PU learning also outperforms Bayesian Sets (designed specifically for the task). In our future work, we plan to experiment with various other PU learning methods (Liu *et al.* 2003; Lee and Liu, 2003; Li *et al.* 2007; Elkan and Noto, 2008) on this entity set expansion task, as well as other tasks that were tackled using distributional similarity. In addition, we also plan to combine some syntactic patterns (Etzioni *et al.* 2005; Sarmento *et al.* 2007) to further improve the results.

Acknowledgements: Bing Liu and Lei Zhang acknowledge the support of HP Labs Innovation Research Grant 2009-1062-1-A, and would like to thank Suk Hwan Lim and Eamonn O'Brien-Strain for many helpful discussions.

References

Agirre, E., Alfonseca, E., Hall, K., Kravalova, J., Pasca, M., and Soroa, A. 2009. *A study on similarity and relatedness using distributional and WordNet-based approaches.* NAACL HLT.

Blum, A. and Mitchell, T. 1998. *Combining labeled and unlabeled data with co-training.* In Proc. of Computational Learning Theory, pp. 92–100, 1998.

Brill, E. 1995. *Transformation-Based error-Driven learning and natural language processing: a case study in part of speech tagging. Computational Linguistics.*

Bunescu, R. and Mooney, R. 2004. *Collective information extraction with relational Markov Networks.* ACL.

Cheng T., Yan X. and Chang C. K. 2007. *Entity-Rank: searching entities directly and holistically.* VLDB.

Chieu, H.L. and Ng, H. Tou. 2002. *Name entity recognition: a maximum entropy approach using global information.* In The 6th Workshop on Very Large Corpora.

Downey, D., Broadhead, M. and Etzioni, O. 2007. *Locating complex named entities in Web Text.* IJCAI.

Elkan, C. and Noto, K. 2008. *Learning classifiers from only positive and unlabeled data.* KDD, 213-220.

Etzioni, O., Cafarella, M., Downey. D., Popescu, A., Shaked, T., Soderland, S., Weld, D. Yates. 2005. A. *Unsupervised named-entity extraction from the Web: An Experimental Study. Artificial Intelligence,* 165(1):91-134.

Ghahramani, Z and Heller, K.A. 2005. *Bayesian sets.* NIPS.

Google Sets. 2008. *System and methods for automatically creating lists.* US Patent: US7350187, March 25.

Gorman, J. and Curran, J. R. 2006. *Scaling distributional similarity to large corpora.* ACL.

Harris, Z. Distributional Structure. 1985. In: Katz, J. J. (ed.), *The philosophy of linguistics.* Oxford University Press.

Heller, K. and Ghahramani, Z. 2006. *A simple Bayesian framework for content-based image retrieval.* CVPR.

Isozaki, H. and Kazawa, H. 2002. *Efficient support vector classifiers for named entity recognition.* COLING.

Jiang, J. and Zhai, C. 2006. *Exploiting domain structure for named entity recognition.* HLT-NAACL.

Lafferty J., McCallum A., and Pereira F. 2001. *Conditional random fields: probabilistic models for segmenting and labeling sequence data.* ICML.

Lee, L. 1999. *Measures of distributional similarity.* ACL.

Lee, W-S. and Liu, B. 2003. *Learning with Positive and Unlabeled Examples Using Weighted Logistic Regression.* ICML.

Li, X., Liu, B. 2003. *Learning to classify texts using positive and unlabeled data,* IJCAI.

Li, X., Liu, B., Ng, S. 2007. *Learning to identify unexpected instances in the test sSet.* IJCAI.

Lin, D. 1998. *Automatic retrieval and clustering of similar words.* COLING/ACL.

Liu, B, Lee, W-S, Yu, P. S, and Li, X. 2002. *Partially supervised text classification.* ICML, 387-394.

Liu, B, Dai, Y., Li, X., Lee, W-S., and Yu. P. 2003. *Building text classifiers using positive and unlabeled examples.* ICDM, 179-188.

Neter, J., Wasserman, W., and Whitmore, G. A. 1993. *Applied Statistics.* Allyn and Bacon.

Nigam, K., McCallum, A., Thrun, S. and Mitchell, T. 2000. *Text classification from labeled and unlabeled documents using EM.* Machine Learning, 39(2/3), 103–134.

Pantel, P., Eric Crestan, Arkady Borkovsky, Ana-Maria Popescu, Vishnu, Vyas. 2009. *Web-Scale Distributional similarity and entity set expansion,* EMNLP.

Paşca, M. Lin, D. Bigham, J. Lifchits, A. Jain, A. 2006. *Names and similarities on the web: fast extraction in the fast lane.* ACL.

Sarmento, L., Jijkuon, V. de Rijke, M. and Oliveira, E. 2007. *"More like these": growing entity classes from seeds.* CIKM.

Wang, R. C. and Cohen, W. W. 2008. *Iterative set expansion of named entities using the web.* ICDM.

Yu, H., Han, J., K. Chang. 2002. *PEBL: Positive example based learning for Web page classification using SVM.* KDD, 239-248.

Active Learning-Based Elicitation for Semi-Supervised Word Alignment

Vamshi Ambati, Stephan Vogel and Jaime Carbonell
{vamshi,vogel,jgc}@cs.cmu.edu
Language Technologies Institute, Carnegie Mellon University
5000 Forbes Avenue, Pittsburgh, PA 15213, USA

Abstract

Semi-supervised word alignment aims to improve the accuracy of automatic word alignment by incorporating full or partial manual alignments. Motivated by standard active learning query sampling frameworks like uncertainty-, margin- and query-by-committee sampling we propose multiple query strategies for the alignment link selection task. Our experiments show that by active selection of uncertain and informative links, we reduce the overall manual effort involved in elicitation of alignment link data for training a semi-supervised word aligner.

1 Introduction

Corpus-based approaches to machine translation have become predominant, with phrase-based statistical machine translation (PB-SMT) (Koehn et al., 2003) being the most actively progressing area. The success of statistical approaches to MT can be attributed to the IBM models (Brown et al., 1993) that characterize *word-level* alignments in parallel corpora. Parameters of these alignment models are learnt in an unsupervised manner using the EM algorithm over *sentence-level* aligned parallel corpora. While the ease of automatically aligning sentences at the word-level with tools like GIZA++ (Och and Ney, 2003) has enabled fast development of SMT systems for various language pairs, the quality of alignment is typically quite low for language pairs like Chinese-English, Arabic-English that diverge from the independence assumptions made by the generative models. Increased parallel data enables better estimation of the model parameters, but a large number of language pairs still lack such resources.

Two directions of research have been pursued for improving generative word alignment. The first is to relax or update the independence assumptions based on more information, usually syntactic, from the language pairs (Cherry and Lin, 2006; Fraser and Marcu, 2007a). The second is to use extra annotation, typically *word-level* human alignment for some sentence pairs, in conjunction with the parallel data to learn alignment in a semi-supervised manner. Our research is in the direction of the latter, and aims to reduce the effort involved in hand-generation of word alignments by using active learning strategies for careful selection of word pairs to seek alignment.

Active learning for MT has not yet been explored to its full potential. Much of the literature has explored one task – selecting sentences to translate and add to the training corpus (Haffari and Sarkar, 2009). In this paper we explore active learning for word alignment, where the input to the active learner is a sentence pair (S, T) and the annotation elicited from human is a set of links $\{a_{ij}, \forall s_i \in S, t_j \in T\}$. Unlike previous approaches, our work does not require elicitation of full alignment for the sentence pair, which could be effort-intensive. We propose active learning query strategies to selectively elicit partial alignment information. Experiments in Section 5 show that our selection strategies reduce alignment error rates significantly over baseline.

2 Related Work

Researchers have begun to explore models that use both labeled and unlabeled data to build word-alignment models for MT. Fraser and Marcu (2006) pose the problem of alignment as a search problem in log-linear space with features coming from the IBM alignment models. The log-

Proceedings of the ACL 2010 Conference Short Papers, pages 365–370,
Uppsala, Sweden, 11-16 July 2010.

linear model is trained on available labeled data to improve performance. They propose a semi-supervised training algorithm which alternates between discriminative error training on the labeled data to learn the weighting parameters and maximum-likelihood EM training on unlabeled data to estimate the parameters. Callison-Burch et al. (2004) also improve alignment by interpolating human alignments with automatic alignments. They observe that while working with such data sets, alignments of higher quality should be given a much higher weight than the lower-quality alignments. Wu et al. (2006) learn separate models from labeled and unlabeled data using the standard EM algorithm. The two models are then interpolated to use as a learner in the semi-supervised algorithm to improve word alignment. To our knowledge, there is no prior work that has looked at reducing human effort by selective elicitation of partial word alignment using active learning techniques.

3 Active Learning for Word Alignment

Active learning attempts to optimize performance by selecting the most informative instances to label where 'informativeness' is defined as maximal expected improvement in accuracy. The objective is to select optimal instance for an external expert to label and then run the learning method on the newly-labeled and previously-labeled instances to minimize prediction or translation error, repeating until either the maximal number of external queries is reached or a desired accuracy level is achieved. Several studies (Tong and Koller, 2002; Nguyen and Smeulders, 2004; Donmez and Carbonell, 2008) show that active learning greatly helps to reduce the labeling effort in various classification tasks.

3.1 Active Learning Setup

We discuss our active learning setup for word alignment in Algorithm 1. We start with an unlabeled dataset $U = \{(S_k, T_k)\}$, indexed by k, and a seed pool of partial alignment links $A_0 = \{a^k_{ij}, \forall s_i \in S_k, t_j \in T_k\}$. This is usually an empty set at iteration $t = 0$. We iterate for T iterations. We take a pool-based active learning strategy, where we have access to all the automatically aligned links and we can score the links based on our active learning query strategy. The query strategy uses the automatically trained alignment model M_t from current iteration t for scoring the links. Re-training and re-tuning an SMT system for each link at a time is computationally infeasible. We therefore perform batch learning by selecting a set of N links scored high by our query strategy. We seek manual corrections for the selected links and add the alignment data to the current labeled data set. The word-level aligned labeled data is provided to our semi-supervised word alignment algorithm for training an alignment model M_{t+1} over U.

Algorithm 1 AL FOR WORD ALIGNMENT

```
Unlabeled Data Set: U = {(S_k, T_k)}
Manual Alignment Set : A_0 = {a^k_ij, ∀s_i ∈ S_k, t_j ∈ T_k}
Train Semi-supervised Word Alignment using (U, A_0) → M_0
N: batch size
for t = 0 to T do
    L_t = LinkSelection(U, A_t, M_t, N)
    Request Human Alignment for L_t
    A_{t+1} = A_t + L_t
    Re-train Semi-Supervised Word Alignment on (U, A_{t+1}) → M_{t+1}
end for
```

We can iteratively perform the algorithm for a defined number of iterations T or until a certain desired performance is reached, which is measured by alignment error rate (AER) (Fraser and Marcu, 2007b) in the case of word alignment. In a more typical scenario, since reducing human effort or cost of elicitation is the objective, we iterate until the available budget is exhausted.

3.2 Semi-Supervised Word Alignment

We use an extended version of MGIZA++ (Gao and Vogel, 2008) to perform the constrained semi-supervised word alignment. Manual alignments are incorporated in the EM training phase of these models as constraints that restrict the summation over all possible alignment paths. Typically in the EM procedure for IBM models, the training procedure requires for each source sentence position, the summation over all positions in the target sentence. The manual alignments allow for one-to-many alignments and many-to-many alignments in both directions. For each position i in the source sentence, there can be more than one manually aligned target word. The restricted training will allow only those paths, which are consistent with the manual alignments. Therefore, the restriction of the alignment paths reduces to restricting the summation in EM.

4 Query Strategies for Link Selection

We propose multiple query selection strategies for our active learning setup. The scoring criteria is designed to select alignment links across sentence pairs that are highly uncertain under current automatic translation models. These links are difficult to align correctly by automatic alignment and will cause incorrect phrase pairs to be extracted in the translation model, in turn hurting the translation quality of the SMT system. Manual correction of such links produces the maximal benefit to the model. We would ideally like to elicit the least number of manual corrections possible in order to reduce the cost of data acquisition. In this section we discuss our link selection strategies based on the standard active learning paradigm of 'uncertainty sampling'(Lewis and Catlett, 1994). We use the automatically trained translation model θ_t for scoring each link for uncertainty, which consists of bidirectional translation lexicon tables computed from the bidirectional alignments.

4.1 Uncertainty Sampling: Bidirectional Alignment Scores

The automatic Viterbi alignment produced by the alignment models is used to obtain translation lexicons. These lexicons capture the conditional distributions of source-given-target $P(s/t)$ and target-given-source $P(t/s)$ probabilities at the word level where $s_i \in S$ and $t_j \in T$. We define certainty of a link as the harmonic mean of the bidirectional probabilities. The selection strategy selects the least scoring links according to the formula below which corresponds to links with maximum uncertainty:

$$Score(a_{ij}/s_1^I, t1^J) = \frac{2 * P(t_j/s_i) * P(s_i/t_j)}{P(t_j/s_i) + P(s_i/t_j)} \quad (1)$$

4.2 Confidence Sampling: Posterior Alignment probabilities

Confidence estimation for MT output is an interesting area with meaningful initial exploration (Blatz et al., 2004; Ueffing and Ney, 2007). Given a sentence pair (s_1^I, t_1^J) and its word alignment, we compute two confidence metrics at alignment link level – based on the posterior link probability as seen in Equation 5. We select the alignment links that the initial word aligner is least confident according to our metric and seek manual correction of the links. We use $t2s$ to denote computation using higher order (IBM4) target-given-source models and $s2t$ to denote source-given-target models. Targeting some of the uncertain parts of word alignment has already been shown to improve translation quality in SMT (Huang, 2009). We use confidence metrics as an active learning sampling strategy to obtain most informative links. We also experimented with other confidence metrics as discussed in (Ueffing and Ney, 2007), especially the IBM 1 model score metric, but it did not show significant improvement in this task.

$$P_{t2s}(a_{ij}, t_1^J/s_1^I) = \frac{p_{t2s}(t_j/s_i, a_{ij} \in A)}{\sum_i^M p_{t2s}(t_j/s_i)} \quad (2)$$

$$P_{s2t}(a_{ij}, s_1^I/t_1^J) = \frac{p_{s2t}(s_i/t_j, a_{ij} \in A)}{\sum_i^N p_{s2t}(s_i/t_j)} \quad (3)$$

$$Conf1(a_{ij}/S, T) = \frac{2 * P_{t2s} * P_{s2t}}{P_{t2s} + P_{s2t}} \quad (4)$$

$$(5)$$

4.3 Query by Committee

The generative alignments produced differ based on the choice of direction of the language pair. We use A_{s2t} to denote alignment in the source to target direction and A_{t2s} to denote the target to source direction. We consider these alignments to be two experts that have two different views of the alignment process. We formulate our query strategy to select links where the agreement differs across these two alignments. In general query by committee is a standard sampling strategy in active learning(Freund et al., 1997), where the committee consists of any number of experts, in this case alignments, with varying opinions. We formulate a query by committee sampling strategy for word alignment as shown in Equation 6. In order to break ties, we extend this approach to select the link with higher average frequency of occurrence of words involved in the link.

$$Score(a_{ij}) = \alpha \quad (6)$$

$$where \quad \alpha = \begin{cases} 2 & a_{ij} \in A_{s2t} \cap A_{t2s} \\ 1 & a_{ij} \in A_{s2t} \cup A_{t2s} \\ 0 & otherwise \end{cases}$$

4.4 Margin Sampling

The strategy for confidence based sampling only considers information about the best scoring link

$conf(a_{ij}/S,T)$. However we could benefit from information about the second best scoring link as well. In typical multi-class classification problems, earlier work shows success using such a 'margin based' approach (Scheffer et al., 2001), where the difference between the probabilities assigned by the underlying model to the first best and second best labels is used as a sampling criteria. We adapt such a margin-based approach to link-selection using the $Conf1$ scoring function discussed in the earlier sub-section. Our $margin$ technique is formulated below, where $\hat{a1}_{ij}$ and $\hat{a2}_{ij}$ are potential first best and second best scoring alignment links for a word at position i in the source sentence S with translation T. The word with minimum margin value is chosen for human alignment. Intuitively such a word is a possible candidate for mis-alignment due to the inherent confusion in its target translation.

$$Margin(i) = \\ Conf1(\hat{a1}_{ij}/S,T) \quad - Conf1(\hat{a2}_{ij}/S,T)$$

5 Experiments

5.1 Data Setup

Our aim in this paper is to show that active learning can help select the most informative alignment links that have high uncertainty according to a given automatically trained model. We also show that fixing such alignments leads to the maximum reduction of error in word alignment, as measured by AER. We compare this with a baseline where links are selected at random for manual correction. To run our experiments iteratively, we automate the setup by using a parallel corpus for which the gold-standard human alignment is already available. We select the Chinese-English language pair, where we have access to 21,863 sentence pairs along with complete manual alignment.

5.2 Results

We first automatically align the Cn-En corpus using GIZA++ (Och and Ney, 2003). We then use the learned model in running our link selection algorithm over the entire corpus to determine the most uncertain links according to each active learning strategy. The links are then looked up in the gold-standard human alignment database and corrected. In case a link is not present in the gold-standard data, we introduce a NULL alignment, else we propose the alignment as given in

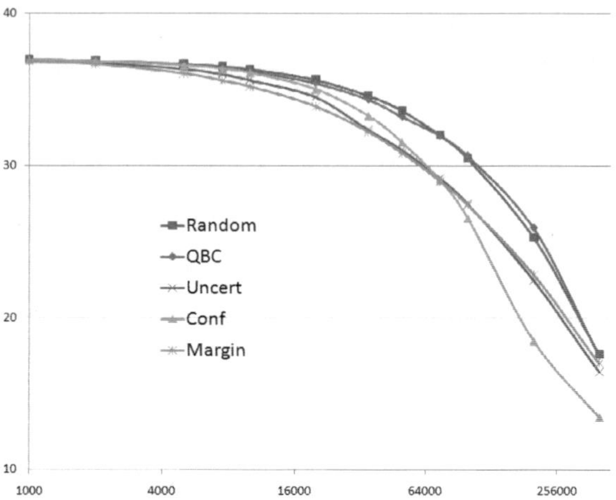

Figure 1: Performance of active sampling strategies for link selection

the gold standard. We select the partial alignment as a set of alignment links and provide it to our semi-supervised word aligner. We plot performance curves as number of links used in each iteration vs. the overall reduction of AER on the corpus.

Query by committee performs worse than random indicating that two alignments differing in direction are not sufficient in deciding for uncertainty. We will be exploring alternative formulations to this strategy. We observe that confidence based metrics perform significantly better than the baseline. From the scatter plots in Figure 1 [1] we can say that using our best selection strategy one achieves similar performance to the baseline, but at a much lower cost of elicitation assuming cost per link is uniform.

We also perform end-to-end machine translation experiments to show that our improvement of alignment quality leads to an improvement of translation scores. For this experiment, we train a standard phrase-based SMT system (Koehn et al., 2007) over the entire parallel corpus. We tune on the MT-Eval 2004 dataset and test on a subset of MT-Eval 2004 dataset consisting of 631 sentences. We first obtain the baseline score where no manual alignment was used. We also train a configuration using gold standard manual alignment data for the parallel corpus. This is the maximum translation accuracy that we can achieve by any link selection algorithm. We now take the best link selection criteria, which is the confidence

[1] X axis has number of links elicited on a log-scale

System	BLEU	METEOR
Baseline	18.82	42.70
Human Alignment	19.96	44.22
Active Selection 20%	19.34	43.25

Table 1: Alignment and Translation Quality

based method and train a system by only selecting 20% of all the links. We observe that at this point we have reduced the AER from 37.09 AER to 26.57 AER. The translation accuracy as measured by BLEU (Papineni et al., 2002) and METEOR (Lavie and Agarwal, 2007) also shows improvement over baseline and approaches gold standard quality. Therefore we achieve 45% of the possible improvement by only using 20% elicitation effort.

5.3 Batch Selection

Re-training the word alignment models after eliciting every individual alignment link is infeasible. In our data set of 21,863 sentences with 588,075 links, it would be computationally intensive to retrain after eliciting even 100 links in a batch. We therefore sample links as a discrete batch, and train alignment models to report performance at fixed points. Such a batch selection is only going to be sub-optimal as the underlying model changes with every alignment link and therefore becomes 'stale' for future selections. We observe that in some scenarios while fixing one alignment link could potentially fix all the mis-alignments in a sentence pair, our batch selection mechanism still samples from the rest of the links in the sentence pair. We experimented with an exponential decay function over the number of links previously selected, in order to discourage repeated sampling from the same sentence pair. We performed an experiment by selecting one of our best performing selection strategies ($conf$) and ran it in both configurations - one with the decay parameter ($batchdecay$) and one without it ($batch$). As seen in Figure 2, the decay function has an effect in the initial part of the curve where sampling is sparse but the effect gradually fades away as we observe more samples. In the reported results we do not use batch decay, but an optimal estimation of 'staleness' could lead to better gains in batch link selection using active learning.

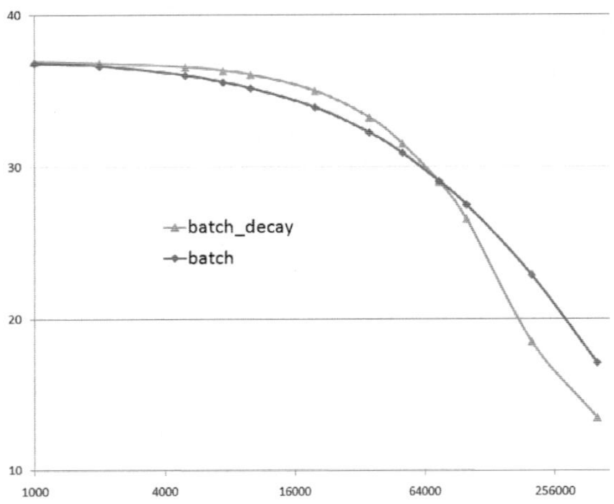

Figure 2: Batch decay effects on Conf-posterior sampling strategy

6 Conclusion and Future Work

Word-Alignment is a particularly challenging problem and has been addressed in a completely unsupervised manner thus far (Brown et al., 1993). While generative alignment models have been successful, lack of sufficient data, model assumptions and local optimum during training are well known problems. Semi-supervised techniques use partial manual alignment data to address some of these issues. We have shown that active learning strategies can reduce the effort involved in eliciting human alignment data. The reduction in effort is due to careful selection of maximally uncertain links that provide the most benefit to the alignment model when used in a semi-supervised training fashion. Experiments on Chinese-English have shown considerable improvements. In future we wish to work with word alignments for other language pairs like Arabic and English. We have tested out the feasibility of obtaining human word alignment data using Amazon Mechanical Turk and plan to obtain more data reduce the cost of annotation.

Acknowledgments

This research was partially supported by DARPA under grant NBCHC080097. Any opinions, findings, and conclusions expressed in this paper are those of the authors and do not necessarily reflect the views of the DARPA. The first author would like to thank Qin Gao for the semi-supervised word alignment software and help with running experiments.

References

John Blatz, Erin Fitzgerald, George Foster, Simona Gandrabur, Cyril Goutte, Alex Kulesza, Alberto Sanchis, and Nicola Ueffing. 2004. Confidence estimation for machine translation. In *Proceedings of Coling 2004*, pages 315–321, Geneva, Switzerland, Aug 23–Aug 27. COLING.

Peter F. Brown, Vincent J. Della Pietra, Stephen A. Della Pietra, and Robert L. Mercer. 1993. The mathematics of statistical machine translation: parameter estimation. *Computational Linguistics*, 19(2):263–311.

Chris Callison-Burch, David Talbot, and Miles Osborne. 2004. Statistical machine translation with word- and sentence-aligned parallel corpora. In *ACL 2004*, page 175, Morristown, NJ, USA. Association for Computational Linguistics.

Colin Cherry and Dekang Lin. 2006. Soft syntactic constraints for word alignment through discriminative training. In *Proceedings of the COLING/ACL on Main conference poster sessions*, pages 105–112, Morristown, NJ, USA.

Pinar Donmez and Jaime G. Carbonell. 2008. Optimizing estimated loss reduction for active sampling in rank learning. In *ICML '08: Proceedings of the 25th international conference on Machine learning*, pages 248–255, New York, NY, USA. ACM.

Alexander Fraser and Daniel Marcu. 2006. Semi-supervised training for statistical word alignment. In *ACL-44: Proceedings of the 21st International Conference on Computational Linguistics and the 44th annual meeting of the Association for Computational Linguistics*, pages 769–776, Morristown, NJ, USA. Association for Computational Linguistics.

Alexander Fraser and Daniel Marcu. 2007a. Getting the structure right for word alignment: LEAF. In *Proceedings of the 2007 Joint Conference on EMNLP-CoNLL*, pages 51–60.

Alexander Fraser and Daniel Marcu. 2007b. Measuring word alignment quality for statistical machine translation. *Comput. Linguist.*, 33(3):293–303.

Yoav Freund, Sebastian H. Seung, Eli Shamir, and Naftali Tishby. 1997. Selective sampling using the query by committee algorithm. *Machine. Learning.*, 28(2-3):133–168.

Qin Gao and Stephan Vogel. 2008. Parallel implementations of word alignment tool. In *Software Engineering, Testing, and Quality Assurance for Natural Language Processing*, pages 49–57, Columbus, Ohio, June. Association for Computational Linguistics.

Gholamreza Haffari and Anoop Sarkar. 2009. Active learning for multilingual statistical machine translation. In *Proceedings of the Joint Conference of the 47th Annual Meeting of the ACL and the 4th International Joint Conference on Natural Language Processing of the AFNLP*, pages 181–189, Suntec, Singapore, August. Association for Computational Linguistics.

Fei Huang. 2009. Confidence measure for word alignment. In *Proceedings of the Joint ACL and IJCNLP*, pages 932–940, Suntec, Singapore, August. Association for Computational Linguistics.

Philipp Koehn, Franz Josef Och, and Daniel Marcu. 2003. Statistical phrase-based translation. In *Proc. of the HLT/NAACL*, Edomonton, Canada.

Philipp Koehn, Hieu Hoang, Alexandra Birch Mayne, Christopher Callison-Burch, Marcello Federico, Nicola Bertoldi, Brooke Cowan, Wade Shen, Christine Moran, Richard Zens, Chris Dyer, Ondrej Bojar, Alexandra Constantin, and Evan Herbst. 2007. Moses: Open source toolkit for statistical machine translation. In *ACL Demonstration Session*.

Alon Lavie and Abhaya Agarwal. 2007. Meteor: an automatic metric for mt evaluation with high levels of correlation with human judgments. In *WMT 2007*, pages 228–231, Morristown, NJ, USA.

David D. Lewis and Jason Catlett. 1994. Heterogeneous uncertainty sampling for supervised learning. In *In Proceedings of the Eleventh International Conference on Machine Learning*, pages 148–156. Morgan Kaufmann.

Hieu T. Nguyen and Arnold Smeulders. 2004. Active learning using pre-clustering. In *ICML*.

Franz Josef Och and Hermann Ney. 2003. A systematic comparison of various statistical alignment models. *Computational Linguistics*, pages 19–51.

Kishore Papineni, Salim Roukos, Todd Ward, and Wei-Jing Zhu. 2002. Bleu: a method for automatic evaluation of machine translation. In *ACL 2002*, pages 311–318, Morristown, NJ, USA.

Tobias Scheffer, Christian Decomain, and Stefan Wrobel. 2001. Active hidden markov models for information extraction. In *IDA '01: Proceedings of the 4th International Conference on Advances in Intelligent Data Analysis*, pages 309–318, London, UK. Springer-Verlag.

Simon Tong and Daphne Koller. 2002. Support vector machine active learning with applications to text classification. *Journal of Machine Learning*, pages 45–66.

Nicola Ueffing and Hermann Ney. 2007. Word-level confidence estimation for machine translation. *Comput. Linguist.*, 33(1):9–40.

Hua Wu, Haifeng Wang, and Zhanyi Liu. 2006. Boosting statistical word alignment using labeled and unlabeled data. In *Proceedings of the COLING/ACL on Main conference poster sessions*, pages 913–920, Morristown, NJ, USA. Association for Computational Linguistics.

An Active Learning Approach to Finding Related Terms

David Vickrey
Stanford University
dvickrey@cs.stanford.edu

Oscar Kipersztok
Boeing Research & Technology
oscar.kipersztok@boeing.com

Daphne Koller
Stanford Univeristy
koller@cs.stanford.edu

Abstract

We present a novel system that helps non-experts find sets of similar words. The user begins by specifying one or more seed words. The system then iteratively suggests a series of candidate words, which the user can either accept or reject. Current techniques for this task typically bootstrap a classifier based on a fixed seed set. In contrast, our system involves the user throughout the labeling process, using active learning to intelligently explore the space of similar words. In particular, our system can take advantage of negative examples provided by the user. Our system combines multiple preexisting sources of similarity data (a standard thesaurus, WordNet, contextual similarity), enabling it to capture many types of similarity groups ("synonyms of crash," "types of car," etc.). We evaluate on a hand-labeled evaluation set; our system improves over a strong baseline by 36%.

1 Introduction

Set expansion is a well-studied NLP problem where a machine-learning algorithm is given a fixed set of *seed words* and asked to find additional members of the implied set. For example, given the seed set {"elephant," "horse," "bat"}, the algorithm is expected to return other mammals. Past work, e.g. (Roark & Charniak, 1998; Ghahramani & Heller, 2005; Wang & Cohen, 2007; Pantel et al., 2009), generally focuses on semi-automatic acquisition of the remaining members of the set by mining large amounts of unlabeled data.

State-of-the-art set expansion systems work well for well-defined sets of nouns, e.g. "US Presidents," particularly when given a large seed set. Set expansions is more difficult with fewer seed words and for other kinds of sets. The seed words may have multiple senses and the user may have in mind a variety of attributes that the answer must match. For example, suppose the seed word is "jaguar". First, there is sense ambiguity; we could be referring to either a "large cat" or a "car." Beyond this, we might have in mind various more (or less) specific groups: "Mexican animals," "predators," "luxury cars," "British cars," etc.

We propose a system which addresses several shortcomings of many set expansion systems. First, these systems can be difficult to use. As explored by Vyas et al. (2009), non-expert users produce seed sets that lead to poor quality expansions, for a variety of reasons including ambiguity and lack of coverage. Even for expert users, constructing seed sets can be a laborious and time-consuming process. Second, most set expansion systems do not use negative examples, which can be very useful for weeding out other bad answers. Third, many set expansion systems concentrate on noun classes such as "US Presidents" and are not effective or do not apply to other kinds of sets.

Our system works as follows. The user initially thinks of at least one seed word belonging to the desired set. One at a time, the system presents candidate words to the user and asks whether the candidate fits the concept. The user's answer is fed back into the system, which takes into account this new information and presents a new candidate to the user. This continues until the user is satisfied with the compiled list of "Yes" answers. Our system uses both positive and negative examples to guide the search, allowing it to recover from initially poor seed words. By using multiple sources of similarity data, our system captures a variety of kinds of similarity. Our system replaces the potentially difficult problem of thinking of many seed words with the easier task of answering yes/no questions. The downside is a possibly increased amount of user interaction (although standard set expansion requires a non-trivial amount of user interaction to build the seed set).

There are many practical uses for such a system. Building a better, more comprehensive thesaurus/gazetteer is one obvious application. Another application is in high-precision query expansion, where a human manually builds a list of ex-

Proceedings of the ACL 2010 Conference Short Papers, pages 371–376,
Uppsala, Sweden, 11-16 July 2010.

pansion terms. Suppose we are looking for pages discussing "public safety." Then synonyms (or near-synonyms) of "safety" would be useful (e.g. "security") but also non-synonyms such as "precautions" or "prevention" are also likely to return good results. In this case, the concept we are interested in is "Words which imply that safety is being discussed." Another interesting direction not pursued in this paper is using our system as part of a more-traditional set expansion system to build seed sets more quickly.

2 Set Expansion

As input, we are provided with a small set of seed words $\mathbf{s}$. The desired output is a target set of words G, consisting of all words that fit the desired concept. A particular seed set $\mathbf{s}$ can belong to many possible goal sets G, so additional information may be required to do well.

Previous work tries to do as much as possible using only $\mathbf{s}$. Typically $\mathbf{s}$ is assumed to contain at least 2 words and often many more. Pantel et al. (2009) discusses the issue of seed set size in detail, concluding that 5-20 seed words are often required for good performance.

There are several problems with the fixed seed set approach. It is not always easy to think of even a single additional seed word (e.g., the user is trying to find "German automakers" and can only think of "Volkswagen"). Even if the user can think of additional seed words, time and effort might be saved by using active learning to find good suggestions. Also, as Vyas et al. (2009) show, non-expert users often produce poor-quality seed sets.

3 Active Learning System

Any system for this task relies on information about similarity between words. Our system takes as input a rectangular matrix M. Each column corresponds to a particular word. Each row corresponds to a unique *dimension of similarity*; the jth entry in row i m_{ij} is a number between 0 and 1 indicating the degree to which w_j belongs to the ith similarity group. Possible similarity dimensions include "How similar is word w_j to the verb jump?" "Is w_j a type of cat?" and "Are the words which appear in the context of w_j similar to those that appear in the context of boat?" Each row r_i of M is labeled with a word l_i. This may follow intuitively from the similarity axis (e.g., "jump," "cat," and "boat", respectively), or it can be generated automatically (e.g. the word w_j with the highest membership m_{ij}).

Let θ be a vector of weights, one per row, which correspond to how well each row aligns with the goal set G. Thus, θ_i should be large and positive if row i has large entries for positive but not negative examples; and it should be large and negative if row i has large entries for negative but not positive examples. Suppose that we have already chosen an appropriate weight vector θ. We wish to rank all possible words (i.e., the columns of M) so that the most promising word gets the highest score. A natural way to generate a score z_j for column j is to take the dot product of θ with column j, $z_j = \sum_i \theta_i m_{ij}$. This rewards word w_j for having high membership in rows with positive θ, and low membership in rows with negative θ.

Our system uses a "batch" approach to active learning. At iteration i, it chooses a new θ based on all data labeled so far (for the 1st iteration, this data consists of the seed set $\mathbf{s}$). It then chooses the column (word) with the highest score (among words not yet labeled) as the candidate word w_i. The user answers "Yes" or "No," indicating whether or not w_i belongs to G. w_i is added to the positive set $\mathbf{p}$ or the negative set $\mathbf{n}$ based on the user's answer. Thus, we have a labeled data set that grows from iteration to iteration as the user labels each candidate word. Unlike set expansion, this procedure generates (and uses) both positive and negative examples.

We explore two options for choosing θ. Recall that each row i is associated with a label l_i. The first method is to set $\theta_i = 1$ if $l_i \in \mathbf{p}$ (that is, the set of positively labeled words includes label l_i), $\theta_i = -1$ if $l_i \in \mathbf{n}$, and $\theta_i = 0$ otherwise. We refer to this method as "Untrained", although it is still *adaptive* — it takes into account the labeled examples the user has provided so far.

The second method uses a standard machine learning algorithm, logistic regression. As before, the final ranking over words is based on the score z_j. However, z_j is passed through the logistic function to produce a score between 0 and 1, $z'_j = \frac{1}{1+e^{-z_j}}$. We can interpret this score as the probability that w_j is a positive example, $P_\theta(Y|w_j)$. This leads to the objective function

$$L(\theta) = log(\prod_{w_j \in \mathbf{p}} P_\theta(Y|w_j) \prod_{w_j \in \mathbf{n}} (1 - P_\theta(Y|w_j))).$$

This objective is convex and can be optimized using standard methods such as L-BFGS (Liu & Nocedal, 1989). Following standard practice we add an L_2 regularization term $-\frac{\theta^T \theta}{2\sigma^2}$ to the objective. This method does not use the row labels l_i.

Data	Word	Similar words
Moby	arrive	accomplish, achieve, achieve success, advance, appear, approach, arrive at, arrive in, attain,...
WordNet	factory	(plant,-1.9);(arsenal,-2.8);(mill,-2.9);(sweatshop,-4.1);(refinery,-4.2);(winery,-4.5);...
DistSim	watch	(jewerly,.137),(wristwatch,.115),(shoe,0.09),(appliance,0.09),(household appliance,0.089),...

Table 1: Examples of unprocessed similarity entries from each data source.

4 Data Sources

We consider three similarity data sources: the Moby thesaurus[1], WordNet (Fellbaum, 1998), and distributional similarity based on a large corpus of text (Lin, 1998). Table 1 shows similarity lists from each. These sources capture different kinds of similarity information, which increases the representational power of our system. For all sources, the similarity of a word with itself is set to 1.0.

It is worth noting that our system is not strictly limited to choosing from pre-existing groups. For example, if we have a list of luxury items, and another list of cars, our system can learn weights so that it prefers items in the intersection, luxury cars.

Moby thesaurus consists of a list of word-based thesaurus entries. Each word w_i has a list of similar words sim^i_j. Moby has a total of about 2.5 million related word pairs. Unlike some other thesauri (such as WordNet and thesaurus.com), entries are not broken down by word sense.

In the raw format, the similarity relation is not symmetric; for example, there are many words that occur only in similarity lists but do not have their own entries. We augmented the thesaurus to make it symmetric: if "dog" is in the similarity entry for "cat," we add "cat" to the similarity entry for "dog" (creating an entry for "dog" if it does not exist yet). We then have a row i for every similarity entry in the augmented thesaurus; m_{ij} is 1 if w_j appears in the similarity list of w_i, and 0 otherwise. The label l_i of row i is simply word w_i. Unlike some other thesauri (including WordNet and thesaurus.com), the entries are not broken down by word sense or part of speech. For polysemic words, there will be a mix of the words similar to each sense and part of speech.

WordNet is a well-known dictionary/thesaurus/ontology often used in NLP applications. It consists of a large number of synsets; a synset is a set of one or more similar word senses. The synsets are then connected with hypernym/hyponym links, which represent IS-A relationships. We focused on measuring similarity in WordNet using the hypernym hierarchy.[2]. There are many methods for converting this hierarchy into a similarity score; we chose to use the Jiang-Conrath distance (Jiang & Conrath, 1997) because it tends to be more robust to the exact structure of WordNet. The number of types of similarity in WordNet tends to be less than that captured by Moby, because synsets in WordNet are (usually) only allowed to have a single parent. For example, "murder" is classified as a type of killing, but not as a type of crime.

The Jiang-Conrath distance gives scores for pairs of word senses, not pairs of words. We handle this by adding one row for every word sense with the right part of speech (rather than for every word); each row measures the similarity of every word to a particular word sense. The label of each row is the (undisambiguated) word; multiple rows can have the same label. For the columns, we do need to collapse the word senses into words; for each word, we take a maximum across all of its senses. For example, to determine how similar (the only sense of) "factory" is to the word "plant," we compute the similarity of "factory" to the "industrial plant" sense of "plant" and to the "living thing" sense of "plant" and take the higher of the two (in this case, the former).

The Jiang-Conrath distance is a number between $-\infty$ and 0. By examination, we determined that scores below -12.0 indicate virtually no similarity. We cut off scores below this point and linearly mapped each score x to the range 0 to 1, yielding a final similarity of $\frac{min(0,x+12)}{12}$. This greatly sparsified the similarity matrix M.

Distributional similarity. We used Dekang Lin's dependency-based thesaurus, available at `www.cs.ualberta.ca/~lindek/downloads.htm`. This resource groups words based on the words they co-occur with in normal text. The words most similar to "cat" are "dog," "animal," and "monkey," presumably because they all "eat," "walk," etc. Like Moby, similarity entries are not divided by word sense; usually, only the dominant sense of each word is represented. This type of similarity is considerably different from the other two types, tending to focus less on minor details and more on broad patterns.

Each similarity entry corresponds to a single

[1]Available at `icon.shef.ac.uk/Moby/`.

[2]A useful similarity metric we did not explore in this paper is similarity between WordNet dictionary definitions

word w_i and is a list of *scored* similar words sim_j^i. The scores vary between 0 and 1, but usually the highest-scored word in a similarity list gets a score of no more than 0.3. To calibrate these scores with the previous two types, we divided all scores by the score of the highest-scored word in that list. Since each row is normalized individually, the similarity matrix M is not symmetric. Also, there are separate similarity lists for each of nouns, verbs, and modifiers; we only used the lists matching the seed word's part of speech.

5 Experimental Setup

Given a seed set s and a complete target set G, it is easy to evaluate our system; we say "Yes" to anything in G, "No" to everything else, and see how many of the candidate words are in G. However, building a complete gold-standard G is in practice prohibitively difficult; instead, we are only capable of saying whether or not a word belongs to G when presented with that word.

To evaluate a particular active learning algorithm, we can just run the algorithm manually, and see how many candidate words we say "Yes" to (note that this will not give us an accurate estimate of the recall of our algorithm). Evaluating several different algorithms for the same s and G is more difficult. We could run each algorithm separately, but there are several problems with this approach. First, we might unconsciously (or consciously) bias the results in favor of our preferred algorithms. Second, it would be fairly difficult to be consistent across multiple runs. Third, it would be inefficient, since we would label the same words multiple times for different algorithms.

We solved this problem by building a labeling system which runs all algorithms that we wish to test in parallel. At each step, we pick a random algorithm and either present its current candidate to the user or, if that candidate has already been labeled, we supply that algorithm with the given answer. We do NOT ever give an algorithm a labeled training example unless it actually asks for it – this guarantees that the combined system is equivalent to running each algorithm separately. This procedure has the property that the user cannot tell which algorithms presented which words.

To evaluate the relative contribution of active learning, we consider a version of our system where active learning is disabled. Instead of retraining the system every iteration, we train it once on the seed set s and keep the weight vector θ fixed from iteration to iteration.

We evaluated our algorithms along three axes. First, the method for choosing θ: Untrained and Logistic (U and L). Second, the data sources used: each source separately (M for Moby, W for WordNet, D for distributional similarity), and all three in combination (MWD). Third, whether active learning is used (+/-). Thus, logistic regression using Moby and no active learning is L(M,-). For logistic regression, we set the regularization penalty σ^2 to 1, based on qualitative analysis during development (before seeing the test data).

We also compared the performance of our algorithms to the popular online thesaurus `http://thesaurus.com`. The entries in this thesaurus are similar to Moby, except that each word may have multiple sense-disambiguated entries. For each seed word w, we downloaded the page for w and extracted a set of synonyms entries for that word. To compare fairly with our algorithms, we propose a word-by-word method for exploring the thesaurus, intended to model a user scanning the thesaurus. This method checks the first 3 words from each entry; if none of these are labeled "Yes," it moves on to the next entry. We omit details for lack of space.

6 Experimental Results

We designed a test set containing different types of similarity. Table 2 shows each category, with examples of specific similarity queries. For each type, we tested on five different queries. For each query, the first author built the seed set by writing down the first three words that came to mind. For most queries this was easy. However, for the similarity type Hard Synonyms, coming up with more than one seed word was considerably more difficult. To build seed sets for these queries, we ran our evaluation system using a single seed word and took the first two positive candidates; this ensured that we were not biasing our seed set in favor of a particular algorithm or data set.

For each query, we ran our evaluation system until each algorithm had suggested 25 candidate words, for a total of 625 labeled words per algorithm. We measured performance using mean average precision (MAP), which corresponds to area under the precision-recall curve. It gives an overall assessment across different stopping points.

Table 3 shows results for an informative subset of the tested algorithms. There are many conclusions we can draw. Thesaurus.Com performs poorly overall; our best system, L(MWD,+), outscores it by 164%. The next group of al-

Category Name	Example Similarity Queries
Simple Groups (SG)	car brands, countries, mammals, crimes
Complex Groups (CG)	luxury car brands, sub-Saharan countries
Synonyms (Syn)	syn of {scandal, helicopter, arrogant, slay}
Hard Synonyms (HS)	syn of {(stock-market) crash, (legal) maneuver}
Meronym/Material (M)	parts of a car, things made of wood

Table 2: Categories and examples

Algorithm	MAP
Thesaurus.Com	.122
U(M,-)	.176
U(W,-)	.182
U(D,-)	.211
L(D,-)	.236
L(D,+)	.288
U(MWD,-)	.233
U(MWD,+)	.271
L(MWD,-)	.286
L(MWD,+)	.322

Table 3: Comparison of algorithms

	SG	CG	Syn	HS	M
Thesaurus.Com	.041	.060	.275	.173	.060
L(D,+)	.377	.344	.211	.329	.177
L(M,-)	.102	.118	.393	.279	.119
U(W,+)	.097	.136	.296	.277	.165
U(MWD,+)	.194	.153	.438	.357	.213
L(MWD,-)	.344	.207	.360	.345	.173
L(MWD,+)	.366	.335	.379	.372	.158

Table 4: Results by category

gorithms, U(*,-), add together the similarity entries of the seed words for a particular similarity source. The best of these uses distributional similarity; L(MWD,+) outscores it by 53%. Combining all similarity types, U(MWD,-) improves by 10% over U(D,-). L(MWD,+) improves over the best single-source, L(D,+), by a similar margin.

Using logistic regression instead of the untrained weights significantly improves performance. For example, L(MWD,+) outscores U(MWD,+) by 19%. Using active learning also significantly improves performance: L(MWD,+) outscores L(MWD,-) by 13%. This shows that active learning is useful even when a reasonable amount of initial information is available (three seed words for each test case). The gains from logistic regression and active learning are cumulative; L(MWD,+) outscores U(MWD,-) by 38%.

Finally, our best system, L(MWD,+) improves over L(D,-), the best system using a single data source and no active learning, by 36%. We consider L(D,-) to be a strong baseline; this comparison demonstrates the usefulness of the main contributions of this paper, the use of multiple data sources and active learning. L(D,-) is still fairly sophisticated, since it combines information from the similarity entries for different words.

Table 4 shows the breakdown of results by category. For this chart, we chose the best setting for each similarity type. Broadly speaking, the thesauri work reasonably well for synonyms, but poorly for groups. Meronyms were difficult across the board. Neither logistic regression nor active learning always improved performance, but L(MWD,+) performs near the top for every category. The complex groups category is particularly interesting, because achieving high performance on this category required using both logistic regression and active learning. This makes sense since negative evidence is particularly important for this category.

7 Discussion and Related Work

The biggest difference between our system and previous work is the use of active learning, especially in allowing the use of negative examples. Most previous set expansion systems use bootstrapping from a small set of positive examples. Recently, the use of negative examples for set expansion was proposed by Vyas and Pantel (2009), although in a different way. First, set expansion is run as normal using a fixed seed set. Then, human annotators label a small number of negative examples from the returned results, which are used to weed out other bad answers. Our method incorporates negative examples at an earlier stage. Also, we use a logistic regression model to robustly incorporate negative information, rather than deterministically ruling out words and features.

Our system is limited by our data sources. Suppose we want actors who appeared in Star Wars. If we only know that Harrison Ford and Mark Hamill are actors, we have little to go on. There has been a large amount of work on other sources of word-similarity. Hughes and Ramage (2007) use random walks over WordNet, incorporating information such as meronymy and dictionary glosses. Snow et al. (2006) extract hypernyms from free text. Wang and Cohen (2007) exploit web-page structure, while Pasca and Durme (2008) examine query logs. We expect that adding these types of data would significantly improve our system.

References

Fellbaum, C. (Ed.). (1998). *Wordnet: An electronic lexical database*. MIT Press.

Ghahramani, Z., & Heller, K. (2005). Bayesian sets. *Advances in Neural Information Processing Systems (NIPS)*.

Hughes, T., & Ramage, D. (2007). Lexical semantic relatedness with random graph walks. *EMNLP-CoNLL*.

Jiang, J., & Conrath, D. (1997). Semantic similarity based on corpus statistics and lexical taxonomy. *Proceedings of International Conference on Research in Computational Linguistics*.

Lin, D. (1998). An information-theoretic definition of similarity. *Proceedings of ICML*.

Liu, D. C., & Nocedal, J. (1989). On the limited memory method for large scale optimization. *Mathematical Programming B*.

Pantel, P., Crestan, E., Borkovsky, A., Popescu, A., & Vyas, V. (2009). Web-scale distributional similarity and entity set expansion. *EMNLP*.

Pasca, M., & Durme, B. V. (2008). Weakly-supervised acquisition of open-domain classes and class attributes from web documents and query logs. *ACL*.

Roark, B., & Charniak, E. (1998). Noun-phrase co-occurrence statistics for semiautomatic semantic lexicon construction. *ACL-COLING*.

Snow, R., Jurafsky, D., & Ng, A. (2006). Semantic taxonomy induction from heterogenous evidence. *ACL*.

Vyas, V., & Pantel, P. (2009). Semi-automatic entity set refinement. *NAACL/HLT*.

Vyas, V., Pantel, P., & Crestan, E. (2009). Helping editors choose better seed sets for entity expansion. *CIKM*.

Wang, R., & Cohen, W. (2007). Language-independent set expansion of named entities using the web. *Seventh IEEE International Conference on Data Mining*.

Learning Better Data Representation using Inference-Driven Metric Learning

Paramveer S. Dhillon
CIS Deptt., Univ. of Penn.
Philadelphia, PA, U.S.A
dhillon@cis.upenn.edu

Partha Pratim Talukdar*
Search Labs, Microsoft Research
Mountain View, CA, USA
partha@talukdar.net

Koby Crammer
Deptt. of Electrical Engg.
The Technion, Haifa, Israel
koby@ee.technion.ac.il

Abstract

We initiate a study comparing effectiveness of the transformed spaces learned by recently proposed *supervised*, and *semi-supervised* metric learning algorithms to those generated by previously proposed *unsupervised* dimensionality reduction methods (e.g., PCA). Through a variety of experiments on different real-world datasets, we find IDML-IT, a *semi-supervised* metric learning algorithm to be the most effective.

1 Introduction

Because of the high-dimensional nature of NLP datasets, estimating a large number of parameters (a parameter for each dimension), often from a limited amount of labeled data, is a challenging task for statistical learners. Faced with this challenge, various *unsupervised* dimensionality reduction methods have been developed over the years, e.g., Principal Components Analysis (PCA).

Recently, several supervised metric learning algorithms have been proposed (Davis et al., 2007; Weinberger and Saul, 2009). IDML-IT (Dhillon et al., 2010) is another such method which exploits labeled as well as unlabeled data during metric learning. These methods learn a Mahalanobis distance metric to compute distance between a pair of data instances, which can also be interpreted as learning a transformation of the input data, as we shall see in Section 2.1.

In this paper, we make the following contributions:

Even though different supervised and semi-supervised metric learning algorithms have recently been proposed, effectiveness of the transformed spaces learned by them in NLP datasets has not been studied before. In this paper, we address that gap: we compare effectiveness of classifiers trained on the transformed spaces learned by metric learning methods to those generated by previously proposed *unsupervised* dimensionality reduction methods. We find IDML-IT, a *semi-supervised* metric learning algorithm to be the most effective.

* Research carried out while at the University of Pennsylvania, Philadelphia, PA, USA.

2 Metric Learning

2.1 Relationship between Metric Learning and Linear Projection

We first establish the well-known equivalence between learning a Mahalanobis distance measure and Euclidean distance in a linearly transformed space of the data (Weinberger and Saul, 2009). Let A be a $d \times d$ positive definite matrix which parameterizes the Mahalanobis distance, $d_A(x_i, x_j)$, between instances x_i and x_j, as shown in Equation 1. Since A is positive definite, we can decompose it as $A = P^\top P$, where P is another matrix of size $d \times d$.

$$\begin{aligned} d_A(x_i, x_j) &= (x_i - x_j)^\top A (x_i - x_j) \qquad (1) \\ &= (Px_i - Px_j)^\top (Px_i - Px_j) \\ &= d_{\text{Euclidean}}(Px_i, Px_j) \end{aligned}$$

Hence, computing Mahalanobis distance parameterized by A is equivalent to first projecting the instances into a new space using an appropriate transformation matrix P and then computing Euclidean distance in the linearly transformed space. In this paper, we are interested in learning a better representation of the data (i.e., projection matrix P), and we shall achieve that goal by learning the corresponding Mahalanobis distance parameter A.

We shall now review two recently proposed metric learning algorithms.

Proceedings of the ACL 2010 Conference Short Papers, pages 377–381,
Uppsala, Sweden, 11-16 July 2010.

2.2 Information-Theoretic Metric Learning (ITML): Supervised

Information-Theoretic Metric Learning (ITML) (Davis et al., 2007) assumes the availability of prior knowledge about inter-instance distances. In this scheme, two instances are considered similar if the Mahalanobis distance between them is upper bounded, i.e., $d_A(x_i, x_j) \leq u$, where u is a non-trivial upper bound. Similarly, two instances are considered dissimilar if the distance between them is larger than certain threshold l, i.e., $d_A(x_i, x_j) \geq l$. Similar instances are represented by set S, while dissimilar instances are represented by set D.

In addition to prior knowledge about inter-instance distances, sometimes prior information about the matrix A, denoted by A_0, itself may also be available. For example, Euclidean distance (i.e., $A_0 = I$) may work well in some domains. In such cases, we would like the learned matrix A to be as close as possible to the prior matrix A_0. ITML combines these two types of prior information, i.e., knowledge about inter-instance distances, and prior matrix A_0, in order to learn the matrix A by solving the optimization problem shown in (2).

$$\begin{aligned} \min_{A \succeq 0} \quad & D_{\mathrm{ld}}(A, A_0) \qquad (2) \\ \text{s.t.} \quad & \mathrm{tr}\{A(x_i - x_j)(x_i - x_j)^\top\} \leq u, \\ & \qquad \forall (i,j) \in S \\ & \mathrm{tr}\{A(x_i - x_j)(x_i - x_j)^\top\} \geq l, \\ & \qquad \forall (i,j) \in D \end{aligned}$$

where $D_{\mathrm{ld}}(A, A_0) = \mathrm{tr}(AA_0^{-1}) - \log\det(AA_0^{-1}) - n$, is the LogDet divergence.

To handle situations where exactly solving the problem in (2) is not possible, slack variables may be introduced to the ITML objective. To solve this optimization problem, an algorithm involving repeated Bregman projections is presented in (Davis et al., 2007), which we use for the experiments reported in this paper.

2.3 Inference-Driven Metric Learning (IDML): Semi-Supervised

Notations: We first define the necessary notations. Let X be the $d \times n$ matrix of n instances in a d-dimensional space. Out of the n instances, n_l instances are labeled, while the remaining n_u instances are unlabeled, with $n = n_l + n_u$. Let S be a $n \times n$ diagonal matrix with $S_{ii} = 1$ iff instance x_i is labeled. m is the total number of labels. Y is the $n \times m$ matrix storing training label information, if any. $\hat{Y}$ is the $n \times m$ matrix of estimated label information, i.e., output of any classifier, with $\hat{Y}_{il}$ denoting score of label l at node i. .

The ITML metric learning algorithm, which we reviewed in Section 2.2, is supervised in nature, and hence it does not exploit widely available unlabeled data. In this section, we review Inference Driven Metric Learning (IDML) (Algorithm 1) (Dhillon et al., 2010), a recently proposed metric learning framework which combines an existing *supervised* metric learning algorithm (such as ITML) along with *transductive* graph-based label inference to learn a new distance metric from labeled as well as unlabeled data combined. In self-training styled iterations, IDML alternates between metric learning and label inference; with output of label inference used during next round of metric learning, and so on.

IDML starts out with the assumption that existing supervised metric learning algorithms, such as ITML, can learn a better metric if the number of available labeled instances is increased. Since we are focusing on the semi-supervised learning (SSL) setting with n_l labeled and n_u unlabeled instances, the idea is to automatically label the unlabeled instances using a graph based SSL algorithm, and then include instances with low assigned label entropy (i.e., high confidence label assignments) in the next round of metric learning. The number of instances added in each iteration depends on the threshold β[1]. This process is continued until no new instances can be added to the set of labeled instances, which can happen when either all the instances are already exhausted, or when none of the remaining unlabeled instances can be assigned labels with high confidence.

The IDML framework is presented in Algorithm 1. In Line 3, any supervised metric learner, such as ITML, may be used as the METRICLEARNER. Using the distance metric learned in Line 3, a new k-NN graph is constructed in Line 4 , whose edge weight matrix is stored in W. In Line 5 , GRAPHLABELINF optimizes over the newly constructed graph, the GRF objective (Zhu et al., 2003) shown in (3).

$$\min_{\hat{Y}'} \ \mathrm{tr}\{\hat{Y}'^\top L \hat{Y}'\}, \ \text{s.t.} \ \hat{S}\hat{Y} = \hat{S}\hat{Y}' \qquad (3)$$

where $L = D - W$ is the (unnormalized) Lapla-

[1]During the experiments in Section 3, we set $\beta = 0.05$

Algorithm 1: Inference Driven Metric Learning (IDML)
Input: instances X, training labels Y, training instance indicator S, label entropy threshold β, neighborhood size k
Output: Mahalanobis distance parameter A

1: $\hat{Y} \leftarrow Y, \hat{S} \leftarrow S$
2: **repeat**
3: $A \leftarrow \text{METRICLEARNER}(X, \hat{S}, \hat{Y})$
4: $W \leftarrow \text{CONSTRUCTKNNGRAPH}(X, A, k)$
5: $\hat{Y}' \leftarrow \text{GRAPHLABELINF}(W, \hat{S}, \hat{Y})$
6: $U \leftarrow \text{SELECTLOWENTINST}(\hat{Y}', \hat{S}, \beta)$
7: $\hat{Y} \leftarrow \hat{Y} + U\hat{Y}'$
8: $\hat{S} \leftarrow \hat{S} + U$
9: **until** convergence (i.e., $U_{ii} = 0,\ \forall i$)
10: return A

cian, and D is a diagonal matrix with $D_{ii} = \sum_j W_{ij}$. The constraint, $\hat{S}\hat{Y} = \hat{S}\hat{Y}'$, in (3) makes sure that labels on training instances are not changed during inference. In Line 6, a currently unlabeled instance x_i (i.e., $\hat{S}_{ii} = 0$) is considered a new labeled training instance, i.e., $U_{ii} = 1$, for next round of metric learning if the instance has been assigned labels with high confidence in the current iteration, i.e., if its label distribution has low entropy (i.e., $\text{ENTROPY}(\hat{Y}'_{i:}) \leq \beta$). Finally in Line 7, training instance label information is updated. This iterative process is continued till no new labeled instance can be added, i.e., when $U_{ii} = 0\ \forall i$. IDML returns the learned matrix A which can be used to compute Mahalanobis distance using Equation 1.

3 Experiments

3.1 Setup

Dataset	Dimension	Balanced
Electronics	84816	Yes
Books	139535	Yes
Kitchen	73539	Yes
DVDs	155465	Yes
WebKB	44261	Yes

Table 1: Description of the datasets used in Section 3. All datasets are binary with 1500 total instances in each.

Description of the datasets used during experiments in Section 3 are presented in Table 1. The first four datasets – Electronics, Books, Kitchen, and DVDs – are from the sentiment domain and previously used in (Blitzer et al., 2007). WebKB is a text classification dataset derived from (Subramanya and Bilmes, 2008). For details regarding features and data pre-processing, we refer the reader to the origin of these datasets cited above. One extra preprocessing that we did was that we only considered features which occurred more 20 times in the entire dataset to make the problem more computationally tractable and also since the infrequently occurring features usually contribute noise. We use classification error (lower is better) as the evaluation metric. We experiment with the following ways of estimating transformation matrix P:

Original[2]: We set $P = I$, where I is the $d \times d$ identity matrix. Hence, the data is not transformed in this case.

RP: The data is first projected into a lower dimensional space using the Random Projection (RP) method (Bingham and Mannila, 2001). Dimensionality of the target space was set at $d' = \frac{\log n}{\epsilon^2 \log \frac{1}{\epsilon}}$, as prescribed in (Bingham and Mannila, 2001). We use the projection matrix constructed by RP as P. ϵ was set to 0.25 for the experiments in Section 3, which has the effect of projecting the data into a much lower dimensional space (84 for the experiments in this section). This presents an interesting evaluation setting as we already run evaluations in much higher dimensional space (e.g., Original).

PCA: Data instances are first projected into a lower dimensional space using Principal Components Analysis (PCA) (Jolliffe, 2002) . Following (Weinberger and Saul, 2009), dimensionality of the projected space was set at 250 for all experiments. In this case, we used the projection matrix generated by PCA as P.

ITML: A is learned by applying ITML (see Section 2.2) on the Original space (above), and then we decompose A as $A = P^\top P$ to obtain P.

[2]Note that "Original" in the results tables refers to original space with features occurring more than 20 times. We also ran experiments with original set of features (without any thresholding) and the results were worse or comparable to the ones reported in the tables.

Datasets	Original	RP	PCA	ITML	IDML-IT
	$\mu \pm \sigma$	$\mu \pm \sigma$	$\mu \pm \sigma$	$\mu \pm \sigma$	$\mu \pm \sigma$
Electronics	31.3 ± 0.9	42.5 ± 1.0	46.4 ± 2.0	33.0 ± 1.0	**30.7±0.7**
Books	37.5 ± 1.1	45.0 ± 1.1	34.8 ± 1.4	35.0 ± 1.1	**32.0±0.9**
Kitchen	33.7 ± 1.0	43.0 ± 1.1	34.0 ± 1.6	30.9 ± 0.7	**29.0±1.0**
DVDs	39.0 ± 1.2	47.7 ± 1.2	36.2 ± 1.6	37.0 ± 0.8	**33.9±1.0**
WebKB	31.4 ± 0.9	33.0 ± 1.0	27.9 ± 1.3	28.9 ± 1.0	**25.5±1.0**

Table 2: Comparison of SVM % classification errors (lower is better), with 50 labeled instances (Sec. 3.2). n_l=50. and $n_u = 1450$. All results are averaged over ten trials. All hyperparameters are tuned on a separate random split.

Datasets	Original	RP	PCA	ITML	IDML-IT
	$\mu \pm \sigma$	$\mu \pm \sigma$	$\mu \pm \sigma$	$\mu \pm \sigma$	$\mu \pm \sigma$
Electronics	27.0 ± 0.9	40.0 ± 1.0	41.2 ± 1.0	27.5 ± 0.8	**25.3±0.8**
Books	31.0 ± 0.7	42.9 ± 0.6	31.3 ± 0.7	29.9 ± 0.5	**27.7±0.7**
Kitchen	26.3 ± 0.5	41.9 ± 0.7	27.0 ± 0.9	26.1 ± 0.8	**24.8±0.9**
DVDs	34.7 ± 0.4	46.8 ± 0.6	32.9 ± 0.8	34.0 ± 0.8	**31.8±0.9**
WebKB	25.7 ± 0.5	31.1 ± 0.5	24.9 ± 0.6	25.6 ± 0.4	**23.9±0.4**

Table 3: Comparison of SVM % classification errors (lower is better), with 100 labeled instances (Sec. 3.2). n_l=100. and $n_u = 1400$. All results are averaged over ten trials. All hyperparameters are tuned on a separate random split.

IDML-IT: A is learned by applying IDML (Algorithm 1) (see Section 2.3) on the Original space (above); with ITML used as METRICLEARNER in IDML (Line 3 in Algorithm 1). In this case, we treat the set of test instances (without their gold labels) as the unlabeled data. In other words, we essentially work in the transductive setting (Vapnik, 2000). Once again, we decompose A as $A = P^\top P$ to obtain P.

We also experimented with the supervised large-margin metric learning algorithm (LMNN) presented in (Weinberger and Saul, 2009). We found ITML to be more effective in practice than LMNN, and hence we report results based on ITML only. Each input instance, x, is now projected into the transformed space as Px. We now train different classifiers on this transformed space. All results are averaged over ten random trials.

3.2 Supervised Classification

We train a SVM classifier, with an RBF kernel, on the transformed space generated by the projection matrix P. SVM hyperparameter, C and RBF kernel bandwidth, were tuned on a separate development split. Experimental results with 50 and 100 labeled instances are shown in Table 2, and Table 3, respectively. From these results, we observe that IDML-IT consistently achieves the best performance across all experimental settings. We also note that in Table 3, performance difference between ITML and IDML-IT in the Electronics and Kitchen domains are statistically significant.

3.3 Semi-Supervised Classification

In this section, we trained the GRF classifier (see Equation 3), a graph-based semi-supervised learning (SSL) algorithm (Zhu et al., 2003), using Gaussian kernel parameterized by $A = P^\top P$ to set edge weights. During graph construction, each node was connected to its k nearest neighbors, with k treated as a hyperparameter and tuned on a separate development set. Experimental results with 50 and 100 labeled instances are shown in Table 4, and Table 5, respectively. As before, we experimented with $n_l = 50$ and $n_l = 100$. Once again, we observe that IDML-IT is the most effective method, with the GRF classifier trained on the data representation learned by IDML-IT achieving best performance in all settings. Here also, we observe that IDML-IT achieves the best performance across all experimental settings.

Datasets	Original	RP	PCA	ITML	IDML-IT
	$\mu \pm \sigma$	$\mu \pm \sigma$	$\mu \pm \sigma$	$\mu \pm \sigma$	$\mu \pm \sigma$
Electronics	47.9 ± 1.1	49.0 ± 1.2	43.2 ± 0.9	34.9 ± 0.5	**34.0±0.5**
Books	50.0 ± 1.0	49.4 ± 1.0	47.9 ± 0.7	42.1 ± 0.7	**40.6±0.7**
Kitchen	49.8 ± 1.1	49.6 ± 0.9	48.6 ± 0.8	31.1 ± 0.5	**30.0±0.5**
DVDs	50.1 ± 0.5	49.9 ± 0.7	49.4 ± 0.6	42.1 ± 0.4	**41.2±0.5**
WebKB	33.1 ± 0.4	33.1 ± 0.3	33.1 ± 0.3	30.0 ± 0.4	**28.7±0.5**

Table 4: Comparison of transductive % classification errors (lower is better) over graphs constructed using different methods (see Section 3.3), with $n_l = 50$ and $n_u = 1450$. All results are averaged over ten trials. All hyperparameters are tuned on a separate random split.

Datasets	Original	RP	PCA	ITML	IDML-IT
	$\mu \pm \sigma$	$\mu \pm \sigma$	$\mu \pm \sigma$	$\mu \pm \sigma$	$\mu \pm \sigma$
Electronics	43.5 ± 0.7	47.2 ± 0.8	39.1 ± 0.7	31.3 ± 0.2	**30.8±0.3**
Books	48.3 ± 0.5	48.9 ± 0.3	43.3 ± 0.4	35.2 ± 0.5	**33.3±0.6**
Kitchen	45.3 ± 0.6	48.2 ± 0.5	41.0 ± 0.7	30.7 ± 0.6	**29.9±0.3**
DVDs	48.6 ± 0.3	49.3 ± 0.5	45.9 ± 0.5	42.6 ± 0.4	**41.7±0.3**
WebKB	33.4 ± 0.4	33.4 ± 0.4	33.4 ± 0.3	30.4 ± 0.5	**28.6±0.7**

Table 5: Comparison of transductive % classification errors (lower is better) over graphs constructed using different methods (see Section 3.3), with $n_l = 100$ and $n_u = 1400$. All results are averaged over ten trials. All hyperparameters are tuned on a separate random split.

4 Conclusion

In this paper, we compared the effectiveness of the transformed spaces learned by recently proposed *supervised*, and *semi-supervised* metric learning algorithms to those generated by previously proposed *unsupervised* dimensionality reduction methods (e.g., PCA). To the best of our knowledge, this is the first study of its kind involving NLP datasets. Through a variety of experiments on different real-world NLP datasets, we demonstrated that supervised as well as semi-supervised classifiers trained on the space learned by IDML-IT consistently result in the lowest classification errors. Encouraged by these early results, we plan to explore further the applicability of IDML-IT in other NLP tasks (e.g., entity classification, word sense disambiguation, polarity lexicon induction, etc.) where better representation of the data is a pre-requisite for effective learning.

Acknowledgments

Thanks to Kuzman Ganchev for providing detailed feedback on a draft of this paper. This work was supported in part by NSF IIS-0447972 and DARPA HRO1107-1-0029.

References

E. Bingham and H. Mannila. 2001. Random projection in dimensionality reduction: applications to image and text data. In *ACM SIGKDD*.

J. Blitzer, M. Dredze, and F. Pereira. 2007. Biographies, bollywood, boom-boxes and blenders: Domain adaptation for sentiment classification. In *ACL*.

J.V. Davis, B. Kulis, P. Jain, S. Sra, and I.S. Dhillon. 2007. Information-theoretic metric learning. In *ICML*.

P. S. Dhillon, P. P. Talukdar, and K. Crammer. 2010. Inference-driven metric learning for graph construction. Technical Report MS-CIS-10-18, CIS Department, University of Pennsylvania, May.

IT Jolliffe. 2002. *Principal component analysis*. Springer verlag.

A. Subramanya and J. Bilmes. 2008. Soft-Supervised Learning for Text Classification. In *EMNLP*.

V.N. Vapnik. 2000. *The nature of statistical learning theory*. Springer Verlag.

K.Q. Weinberger and L.K. Saul. 2009. Distance metric learning for large margin nearest neighbor classification. *The Journal of Machine Learning Research*.

X. Zhu, Z. Ghahramani, and J. Lafferty. 2003. Semi-supervised learning using Gaussian fields and harmonic functions. In *ICML*.

Wrapping up a Summary: from Representation to Generation

Josef Steinberger and **Marco Turchi** and **Mijail Kabadjov** and **Ralf Steinberger**
EC Joint Research Centre
21027, Ispra (VA), Italy
{Josef.Steinberger, Marco.Turchi, Mijail.Kabadjov, Ralf.Steinberger}@jrc.ec.europa.eu

Nello Cristianini
University of Bristol,
Bristol, BS8 1UB, UK
nello@support-vector.net

Abstract

The main focus of this work is to investigate robust ways for generating summaries from summary representations without recurring to simple sentence extraction and aiming at more human-like summaries. This is motivated by empirical evidence from TAC 2009 data showing that human summaries contain on average more and shorter sentences than the system summaries. We report encouraging preliminary results comparable to those attained by participating systems at TAC 2009.

1 Introduction

In this paper we adopt the general framework for summarization put forward by Spärck-Jones (1999) – which views summarization as a three-fold process: interpretation, transformation and generation – and attempt to provide a clean instantiation for each processing phase, with a particular emphasis on the last, summary-generation phase often omitted or over-simplified in the mainstream work on summarization.

The advantages of looking at the summarization problem in terms of distinct processing phases are numerous. It not only serves as a common ground for comparing different systems and understanding better the underlying logic and assumptions, but it also provides a neat framework for developing systems based on clean and extendable designs. For instance, Gong and Liu (2002) proposed a method based on Latent Semantic Analysis (LSA) and later J. Steinberger et al. (2007) showed that solely by enhancing the first source *interpretation* phase, one is already able to produce better summaries.

There has been limited work on the last summary generation phase due to the fact that it is unarguably a very challenging problem. The vast amount of approaches assume simple sentence selection, a type of extractive summarization, where often the summary representation and the end summary are, indeed, conflated.

The main focus of this work is, thus, to investigate robust ways for generating summaries from summary representations without recurring to simple sentence extraction and aiming at more human-like summaries. This decision is also motivated by empirical evidence from TAC 2009 data (see table 1) showing that human summaries contain on average more and shorter sentences than the system summaries. The intuition behind this is that, by containing more sentences, a summary is able to capture more of the important content from the source.

Our initial experimental results show that our approach is feasible, since it produces summaries, which when evaluated against the TAC 2009 data[1] yield ROUGE scores (Lin and Hovy, 2003) comparable to the participating systems in the Summarization task at TAC 2009. Taking into account that our approach is completely unsupervised and language-independent, we find our preliminary results encouraging.

The remainder of the paper is organised as follows: in the next section we briefly survey the related work, in §3 we describe our approach to summarization, in §4 we explain how we tackle the generation step, in §5 we present and discuss our experimental results and towards the end we conclude and give pointers to future work.

2 Related Work

There is a large body of literature on summarization (Hovy, 2005; Erkan and Radev, 2004; Kupiec et al., 1995). The most closely related work to the approach presented hereby is work on summarization attempting to go beyond simple sentence ex-

[1] http://www.nist.gov/tac/

Proceedings of the ACL 2010 Conference Short Papers, pages 382–386,
Uppsala, Sweden, 11-16 July 2010.

traction and to a lesser degree work on sentence compression. We survey below work along these lines.

Although our approach is related to sentence compression (Knight and Marcu, 2002; Clarke and Lapata, 2008), it is subtly different. Firstly, we reduce the number of terms to be used in the summary at a global level, not at a local per-sentence level. Secondly, we directly exploit the resulting structures from the SVD making the last generation step fully aware of previous processing stages, as opposed to tackling the problem of sentence compression in isolation.

A similar approach to our sentence reconstruction method has been developed by Quirk et al. (2004) for paraphrase generation. In their work, training and test sets contain sentence pairs that are composed of two different proper English sentences and a paraphrase of a source sentence is generated by finding the optimal path through a paraphrases lattice.

Finally, it is worth mentioning that we are aware of the 'capsule overview' summaries proposed by Boguraev and Kennedy (1997) which is similar to our TSR (see below), however, as opposed to their emphasis on a suitable browsing interface rather than producing a readable summary, we precisely attempt the latter.

3 Three-fold Summarization: Interpretation, Transformation and Generation

We chose the LSA paradigm for summarization, since it provides a clear and direct instantiation of Spärck-Jones' three-stage framework.

In LSA-based summarization the interpretation phase takes the form of building a term-by-sentence matrix $A = [A_1, A_2, \ldots, A_n]$, where each column $A_j = [a_{1j}, a_{2j}, \ldots, a_{nj}]^T$ represents the weighted term-frequency vector of sentence j in a given set of documents. We adopt the same weighting scheme as the one described in (Steinberger et al., 2007), as well as their more general definition of term entailing not only unigrams and bigrams, but also named entities.

The transformation phase is done by applying singular value decomposition (SVD) to the initial term-by-sentence matrix defined as $A = U\Sigma V^T$.

The generation phase is where our main contribution comes in. At this point we depart from standard LSA-based approaches and aim at producing a succinct summary representation comprised only of salient terms – Term Summary Representation (TSR). Then this TSR is passed on to another module which attempts to produce complete sentences. The module for sentence reconstruction is described in detail in section 4, in what follows we explain the method for producing a TSR.

3.1 Term Summary Representation

To explain how a term summary representation (TSR) is produced, we first need to define two concepts: *salience score* of a given term and *salience threshold*. Salience score for each term in matrix A is given by the magnitude of the corresponding vector in the matrix resulting from the dot product of the matrix of left singular vectors with the diagonal matrix of singular values. More formally, let $T = U \cdot \Sigma$ and then for each term i, the salience score is given by $|\vec{T_i}|$. Salience threshold is equal to the salience score of the top k^{th} term, when all terms are sorted in descending order on the basis of their salience scores and a cutoff is defined as a percentage (e.g., top 15%). In other words, if the total number of terms is n, then $100 * k/n$ must be equal to the percentage cutoff specified.

The generation of a TSR is performed in two steps. First, an initial pool of sentences is selected by using the same technique as in (Steinberger and Ježek, 2009) which exploits the dot product of the diagonal matrix of singular values with the right singular vectors: $\Sigma \cdot V^T$.[2] This initial pool of sentences is the output of standard LSA approaches.

Second, the terms from the source matrix A are identified in the initial pool of sentences and those terms whose *salience score* is above the *salience threshold* are copied across to the TSR. Thus, the TSR is formed by the most (globally) salient terms from each one of the sentences. For example:

- Extracted Sentence: "Irish Prime Minister Bertie Ahern admitted on Tuesday that he had held a series of private one-on-one meetings on the Northern Ireland peace process with Sinn Fein leader Gerry Adams, but denied they had been secret in any way."
- TSR Sentence at 10%: "Irish Prime Minister Bertie Ahern Tuesday had held one-on-one meetings Northern Ireland peace process Sinn Fein leader Gerry Adams"[3]

[2] Due to space constraints, full details on that step are omitted here, see (Steinberger and Ježek, 2009).

[3] The TSR sentence is stemmed just before feeding it to the reconstruction module discussed in the next section.

Average number of:	Human Summaries	System Summaries	At 100%	At 15%	At 10%	At 5%	At 1%
Sentences/summary	6.17	3.82	3.8	3.95	4.39	5.18	12.58
Words/sentence	15.96	25.01	26.24	25.1	22.61	19.08	7.55
Words/summary	98.46	95.59	99.59	99.25	99.18	98.86	94.96

Table 1: Summary statistics on TAC'09 data (initial summaries).

Metric	$\text{LSA}_{extract}$	At 100%	At 15%	At 10%	At 5%	At 1%
ROUGE-1	0.371	0.361	0.362	0.365	0.372	0.298
ROUGE-2	0.096	0.08	0.081	0.083	0.083	0.083
ROUGE-SU4	0.131	0.125	0.126	0.128	0.131	0.104

Table 2: Summarization results on TAC'09 data (initial summaries).

4 Noisy-channel model for sentence reconstruction

This section describes a probabilistic approach to the reconstruction problem. We adopt the noisy-channel framework that has been widely used in a number of other NLP applications. Our interpretation of the noisy channel consists of looking at a stemmed string without stopwords and imagining that it was originally a long string and that someone removed or stemmed some text from it. In our framework, reconstruction consists of identifying the original long string.

To model our interpretation of the noisy channel, we make use of one of the most popular classes of SMT systems: the Phrase Based Model (PBM) (Zens et al., 2002; Och and Ney, 2001; Koehn et al., 2003). It is an extension of the noisy-channel model and was introduced by Brown et al. (1994), using phrases rather than words. In PBM, a source sentence f is segmented into a sequence of I phrases $f^I = [f_1, f_2, \ldots f_I]$ and the same is done for the target sentence e, where the notion of phrase is not related to any grammatical assumption; a phrase is an n-gram. The best translation e_{best} of f is obtained by:

$$e_{best} = arg\max_e p(e|f) = arg\max_e \prod_{i=1}^{I} \phi(f_i|e_i)^{\lambda_\phi}$$
$$d(a_i - b_{i-1})^{\lambda_d} \prod_{i=1}^{|e|} p_{LM}(e_i|e_1 \ldots e_{i-1})^{\lambda_{LM}}$$

where $\phi(f_i|e_i)$ is the probability of translating a phrase e_i into a phrase f_i. $d(a_i - b_{i-1})$ is the distance-based reordering model that drives the system to penalize substantial reorderings of words during translation, while still allowing some flexibility. In the reordering model, a_i denotes the start position of the source phrase that was translated into the ith target phrase, and b_{i-1} denotes the end position of the source phrase translated into the $(i-1^{\text{th}})$ target phrase. $p_{LM}(e_i|e_1 \ldots e_{i-1})$ is the language model probability that is based on the Markov chain assumption. It assigns a higher probability to fluent/grammatical sentences. λ_ϕ, λ_{LM} and λ_d are used to give a different weight to each element (for more details see (Koehn et al., 2003)).

In our reconstruction problem, the difference between the source and target sentences is not in terms of languages, but in terms of forms. In fact, our source sentence f is a stemmed sentence without stopwords, while the target sentence e is a complete English sentence. "Translate" means to reconstruct the most probable sentence e given f inserting new words and reproducing the inflected surface forms of the source words.

4.1 Training of the model

In Statistical Machine Translation, a PBM system is trained using parallel sentences, where each sentence in a language is paired with another sentence in a different language and one is the translation of the other.

In the reconstruction problem, we use a set, S_1 of 2,487,414 English sentences extracted from the news. This set is duplicated, S_2, and for each sentence in S_2, stopwords are removed and the remaining words are stemmed using Porter's stemmer (Porter, 1980). Our stopword list contains 488 words. Verbs are not included in this list, because they are relevant for the reconstruction task. To optimize the lambda parameters, we select 2,000 pairs as development set.

An example of training sentence pair is:

- Source Sentence: "royal mail ha doubl profit 321 million huge fall number letter post"
- Target Sentence: "royal mail has doubled its profits to 321 million despite a huge fall in the number of letters being posted"

In this work we use Moses (Koehn et al., 2007), a complete phrase-based translation toolkit for academic purposes. It provides all the state-of-the-art components needed to create a phrase-based machine translation system. It contains different modules to preprocess data, train the Language Models and the Translation Models.

5 Experimental Results

For our experiments we made use of the TAC 2009 data which conveniently contains human-produced summaries against which we could evaluate the output of our system (NIST, 2009).

To begin our inquiry we carried out a phase of exploratory data analysis, in which we measured the average number of sentences per summary, words per sentence and words per summary in human vs. system summaries in the TAC 2009 data. Additionally, we also measured these statistics of summaries produced by our system at five different percentage cutoffs: 100%, 15%, 10%, 5% and 1%. [4] The results from this exploration are summarised in table 1. The most notable thing is that human summaries contain on average more and shorter sentences than the system summaries (see 2nd and 3rd column from left to right). Secondly, we note that as the percentage cutoff decreases (from 4th column rightwards) the characteristics of the summaries produced by our system are increasingly more similar to those of the human summaries. In other words, within the 100-word window imposed by the TAC guidelines, our system is able to fit more (and hence shorter) sentences as we decrease the percentage cutoff.

Summarization performance results are shown in table 2. We used the standard ROUGE evaluation (Lin and Hovy, 2003) which has been also used for TAC. We include the usual ROUGE metrics: R_1 is the maximum number of co-occurring unigrams, R_2 is the maximum number of co-occurring bigrams and R_{SU4} is the skip bigram measure with the addition of unigrams as counting unit. The last five columns of table 2 (from left to right) correspond to summaries produced by our system at various percentage cutoffs. The 2nd column, $LSA_{extract}$, corresponds to the performance of our system at producing summaries by sentence extraction only.[5]

In the light of the above, the decrease in performance from column $LSA_{extract}$ to column 'At 100%' can be regarded as reconstruction error.[6] Then, as we decrease the percentage cutoff (from 4th column rightwards) we are increasingly covering more of the content comprised by the human summaries (as far as the ROUGE metrics are able to gauge this, of course). In other words, the improvement of content coverage makes up for the reconstruction error, and at 5% cutoff we already obtain ROUGE scores comparable to $LSA_{extract}$. This suggests that if we improve the quality of our sentence reconstruction we would potentially end up with a better performing system than a typical LSA system based on sentence selection. Hence, we find these results very encouraging.

Finally, we admittedly note that by applying a percentage cutoff on the initial term set and further performing the sentence reconstruction we gain in content coverage, to a certain extent, on the expense of sentence readability.

6 Conclusion

In this paper we proposed a novel approach to summary generation from summary representation based on the LSA summarization framework and on a machine-translation-inspired technique for sentence reconstruction.

Our preliminary results show that our approach is feasible, since it produces summaries which resemble better human summaries in terms of the average number of sentences per summary and yield ROUGE scores comparable to the participating systems in the Summarization task at TAC 2009. Bearing in mind that our approach is completely unsupervised and language-independent, we find our results promising.

In future work we plan on working towards improving the quality of our sentence reconstruction step in order to produce better and more readable sentences.

[4] Recall from section §3 that the salience threshold is a function of the percentage cutoff.

[5] These are, effectively, what we called initial pool of sentences in section 3, before the TSR generation.

[6] The only difference between the two types of summaries is the reconstruction step, since we are including 100% of the terms.

References

B. Boguraev and C. Kennedy. 1997. Salience-based content characterisation of text documents. In I. Mani, editor, *Proceedings of the Workshop on Intelligent and Scalable Text Summarization at the Annual Joint Meeting of the ACL/EACL*, Madrid.

P. Brown, S. Della Pietra, V. Della Pietra, and R. Mercer. 1994. The mathematic of statistical machine translation: Parameter estimation. *Computational Linguistics*, 19(2):263–311.

J. Clarke and M. Lapata. 2008. Global inference for sentence compression: An integer linear programming approach. *Journal of Artificial Intelligence Research*, 31:273–318.

G. Erkan and D. Radev. 2004. LexRank: Graph-based centrality as salience in text summarization. *Journal of Artificial Intelligence Research (JAIR).*

Y. Gong and X. Liu. 2002. Generic text summarization using relevance measure and latent semantic analysis. In *Proceedings of ACM SIGIR*, New Orleans, US.

E. Hovy. 2005. Automated text summarization. In Ruslan Mitkov, editor, *The Oxford Handbook of Computational Linguistics*, pages 583–598. Oxford University Press, Oxford, UK.

K. Knight and D. Marcu. 2002. Summarization beyond sentence extraction: A probabilistic approach to sentence compression. *Artificial Intelligence*, 139(1):91–107.

P. Koehn, F. Och, and D. Marcu. 2003. Statistical phrase-based translation. In *Proceedings of NAACL '03*, pages 48–54, Morristown, NJ, USA.

P. Koehn, H. Hoang, A. Birch, C. Callison-Burch, M. Federico, N. Bertoldi, B. Cowan, W. Shen, C. Moran, R. Zens, C. Dyer, O. Bojar, A. Constantin, and E. Herbst. 2007. Moses: Open source toolkit for statistical machine translation. In *Proceedings of ACL '07, demonstration session.*

J. Kupiec, J. Pedersen, and F. Chen. 1995. A trainable document summarizer. In *Proceedings of the ACM SIGIR*, pages 68–73, Seattle, Washington.

C. Lin and E. Hovy. 2003. Automatic evaluation of summaries using n-gram co-occurrence statistics. In *Proceedings of HLT-NAACL*, Edmonton, Canada.

NIST, editor. 2009. *Proceeding of the Text Analysis Conference*, Gaithersburg, MD, November.

F. Och and H. Ney. 2001. Discriminative training and maximum entropy models for statistical machine translation. In *Proceedings of ACL '02*, pages 295–302, Morristown, NJ, USA.

M. Porter. 1980. An algorithm for suffix stripping. *Program*, 14(3):130–137.

C. Quirk, C. Brockett, and W. Dolan. 2004. Monolingual machine translation for paraphrase generation. In *Proceedings of EMNLP*, volume 149. Barcelona, Spain.

K. Spärck-Jones. 1999. Automatic summarising: Factors and directions. In I. Mani and M. Maybury, editors, *Advances in Automatic Text Summarization*. MIT Press.

J. Steinberger and K. Ježek. 2009. Update summarization based on novel topic distribution. In *Proceedings of the 9th ACM DocEng, Munich, Germany.*

J. Steinberger, M. Poesio, M. Kabadjov, and K. Ježek. 2007. Two uses of anaphora resolution in summarization. *Information Processing and Management*, 43(6):1663–1680. Special Issue on Text Summarisation (Donna Harman, ed.).

R. Zens, F. J. Och, and H. Ney. 2002. Phrase-based statistical machine translation. In *Proceedings of KI '02*, pages 18–32, London, UK. Springer-Verlag.

Author Index